ART IN THE WORLD

ART IN THE WORLD

Third Edition

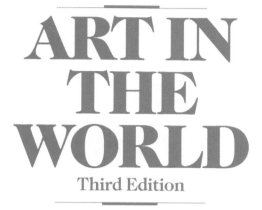

Stella Pandell Russell

Nassau Community College

Holt, Rinehart and Winston, Inc.

Fort Worth Chicago San Francisco Philadelphia
Montreal Toronto London Sydney Tokyo

For Janna, Jonathan, Loriann,
and their father, George

Publisher	Charlyce Jones Owen
Senior Acquisitions Editor	Karen Dubno
Picture Researcher	Elsa Peterson
Special Projects Editor	Jeanette Ninas Johnson
Design Supervisor	Gloria Gentile
Book and cover design	Art Ritter
Design layout	Connie Szewciuk
Composition and color	York Graphic Services
Printing and binding	Rand McNally

Printed in the United States of America
9 0 1 2   061   9 8 7 6 5 4 3 2 1

ISBN 0-03-016924-0

Library of Congress Cataloging-in-Publication Data

Russell, Stella Pandell.
    Art in the world / Stella Pandell Russell.—3rd ed.
        p.   cm.

    Bibliography: p. 446
    Includes index.
    1. Art appreciation.   I. Title.
N7477.R87   1989
701'.1—dc19   88-37642
                                                                    CIP

Holt, Rinehart and Winston, Inc.
The Dryden Press
Saunders College Publishing

Preface

Art in the World, third edition, is a basic art text for college and other interested students— offering a broad introduction to concepts, vocabulary, media, and history of art. Through examples from the past and the present, from many cultures, the universal qualities in human aesthetic responses, as well as the special differences that define societies, become clear.

Some of these goals have been addressed in many fine books, of course. But the aim of this book is to combine as much clarity as possible with broad coverage of these major areas—all in a relatively manageable size. I hope I have succeeded.

Besides fulfilling these needs, *Art in the World* focuses on areas often slighted in other texts.

1. **Contemporary art** For most students, the art of our own time is difficult to understand, let alone appreciate. For this reason, an entire section of *Art in the World* is devoted to 20th-century art and its roots in the art of the historical Age of Revolution. Wherever appropriate, modern works have been related in contrast or comparison with art of the past.
2. **Spectrum of the arts** A feature of this book is to treat all the arts with respect. Along with the so-called fine arts of painting, sculpture, and architecture, the graphic arts, for example, are presented with equal coverage, as is art found in objects designed to make daily living—where all of us have most contact with art, after all—more satisfying.
3. **Non-Western, minority, and Third World arts** The less familiar arts have all been chronologically integrated, and correlations between various cultures have been clarified. Our focus may remain on the Western world,

with which we have most experience, but our legacy from parallel civilizations and the diffusion of contributions from them have been noted with appreciation.

4. **"Exploring Art Through Technology"** Technology has arrived to assist the arts, to "multiply the hands" that produce the arts, and to facilitate research in the materials, techniques, and composition of traditional and contemporary art. A feature of each chapter provides a technological "assist" into the understanding of the process and the appreciation of art.
5. **"Focus on the Artist"** Brief yet insightful summaries of the life contributions of artists, past and present, help to make them "come alive." More men than women have had opportunities, apparently, to develop greater stature in the past, but, wherever possible, women have made significant contributions, and these are noted with equivalent coverage.

Art is inspired by living. In the years since *Art in the World* was first published, living artists with their unique ability to invent images that illuminate our world have continued to add to the body of art. Changes in the contemporary visual arts have therefore required a number of substantial adjustments to the text and illustrations of the second edition. Parts I and II have been revised and expanded to Parts I, II, and III to present a comprehensive survey of media, now organized into two- and three-dimensional processes. Chapter 2, "Exploring the Artist's Language," and Chapter 3, "Drawing, Painting, and Mixed Media," have been updated. Because of the modern focus on duplicate images, Chapter 4, "Printmaking," has been expanded so that printing processes may be analyzed and contrasted with the mass reproductions that surround us and so that the fresh interest of painters in the graphic arts may be acknowledged. In Chapter 5, "Arts of the Lens," the sections on television and film have been enriched by discussions of the roles of the director and the film critic. Occupying ever more of our interests and time, the photographic arts are examined particularly as an American phenomenon. The new Chapter 6, "Design in Print," presents two-dimensional forms of art not included in the earlier editions, forms of art that have become more and more relevant (examples are posters and wall coverings designed by fine artists of the past and the present). In response to our increasing concern about the depletion of energy sources, Chapter 9 includes a section, "Environmental Design," that discusses ecological balance and solar energy, contrasting age-old solutions with modern responses. The expanding role of the art museum and its increased contribution in the cultural context of day-to-day living have been appreciatively included. The sweeping changes of format in the first half of the book, an increasing focus on technology, and re-evaluation of world art throughout have produced a revision of more than one-third of the illustrations and analyses of art illustrated.

Though these changes make the third edition of *Art in the World* more relevant to the concerns of today, considerable effort has been made to retain a simple, entirely flexible organization, adaptable to many teaching styles and approaches. Part I introduces the visual arts and the nature of appreciation. New to this edition is a consideration of the roles of art and their function in society, past and present. The treatment of creativity has been expanded to focus not only on how art is perceived but also on how it is created. Part II, a more leisurely adventure in process, materials, and methods used to produce the various art forms, moves logically through two-dimensional media. Part III progresses through all three-dimensional media. Parts IV and V provide a chronological history of art beginning with the Stone Age and continuing to the most recent styles up to the late 1980s, with a glimpse of the 1990s. These main divisions may be taken up in any order.

Art in the World, third edition, has a new enlarged format that permits more than 500 illustrations, 125 of them in full color, reproduced in much larger sizes than in the earlier editions. The book also is printed on higher-quality paper to achieve greater clarity of detail and a fuller range of values. Each illustration, whether color or black and white, appears close to the textual discussion of it, usually on the same page or the facing page. To foster comprehension of complex subject matter, important terms are highlighted in boldface and defined the first time they appear in the text (and usually also defined in the glossary). Each chapter ends with several art activities and research exercises that can provide deeper learning opportunities to interested students. Concluding the book are a glossary of terms to clarify the specialized vocabulary of the visual arts and an annotated bibliography, arranged by chapters, to help students prepare papers or pursue topics of interest in greater depth. A significant addition is nine time lines, one at the beginning of each chapter in Parts IV and V. These, coupled with maps, provide the broader base of time and space correlations that are essential for true understanding and appreciation of the visual arts in their chronological and geographical contexts.

I hope that *Art in the World,* third edition, will prove to be a valuable guide to the world of art, that students will find in it stimulation to continue experiencing art in their own world, and that they will learn through it to understand and enjoy art in whatever form it appears.

Acknowledgments

The author wishes to thank the following teachers who read various drafts of the manuscript and made useful suggestions: Kenneth Burchett, University of Central Arkansas, Conway; Whitney Engeran, Jr., Indiana State University, Terre Haute; Ralph Jacobs, Mankato State University, Mankato, MN; Pauline Dove Lamal, Central Piedmont Community College, Charlotte, NC; John W. Linn, Henderson State University, Arkadelphia, AR; Helen Merritt, Northern Illinois University, DeKalb; Joseph Molinaro, Broward Community College; Donald A. Parks, Delaware State College, Dover; Ron Picco, College of Santa Fe, Santa Fe, NM; R.O. Sorenson, Furman University, Greenville, SC; Linda Summers, Palm Beach Junior College South, Boca Raton, FL; Ellen Todd, George Mason University, Fairfax VA; Marjorie Venit, University of Maryland, College Park.

Contents

Preface
v

Part Four
ART IN SOCIETY

10 Magic and Ritual: Prehistory and the Ancient World 216

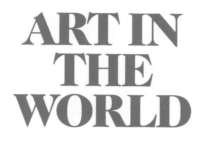

ART IN THE WORLD

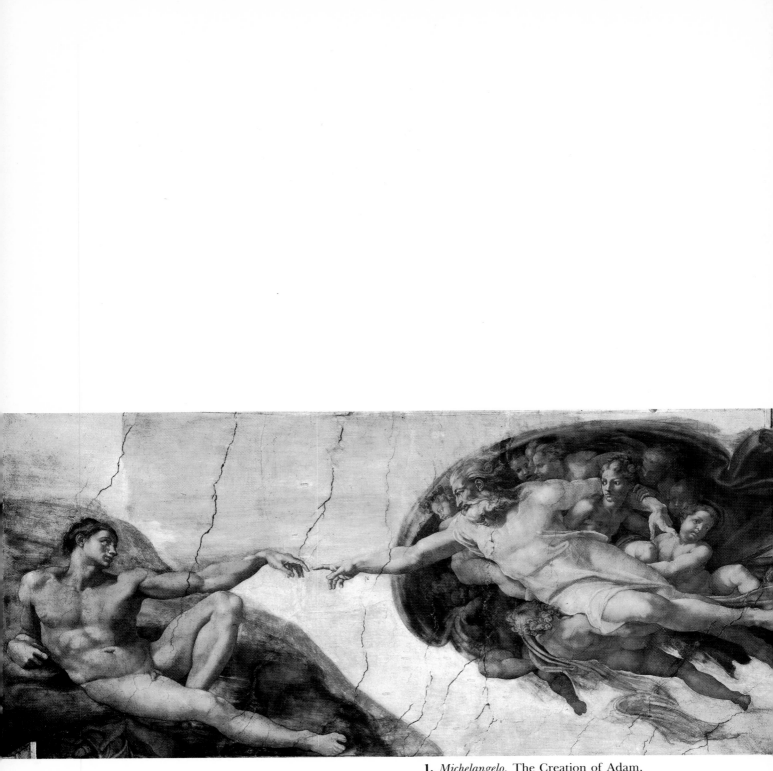

1. *Michelangelo.* The Creation of Adam,
detail of Sistine Chapel ceiling. 1511. Fresco,
45 × 130' (13.71 × 39 m). Vatican, Rome.

Part One
THE VISUAL ARTS

What is art? It is far easier to ask the question than to answer it simply. Defined as a creative act, activity, or product of a human being, **art** means different things to different people. President John F. Kennedy believed that "art establishes the basic human truths which must serve as the touchstone of our judgment." The great mime Charlie Chaplin went even further: "There are more valid facts and details in works of art than there are in history books." Perhaps the poet Robert Browning said it best: "Art remains the one way possible of speaking truth." Exploring what and how and why artists create can be a way to extend our own awareness beyond the ordinary and thus to enhance our lives.

We expect to find art when we visit great museums of painting and sculpture, but the term *art* is also applied to such varied fields as literature, theater, dance, and music. These areas are all considered branches of the humanities as distinguished from the sciences.

One element common to all these forms of art is the demonstration of skill. When we speak of the arts, however, we usually mean much more than skill in technique. We expect art to provide us with unique experiences that affect our senses in special ways. Art may convey a message that moves us deeply or awakens us to new insights. Art also reminds us of feelings all people share but few can express as profoundly as the artist. Great art stretches our awareness of how special we can be. For instance, while we all marvel at the creation of life, not many of us can represent the act of creation with the impact Michelangelo (1475–1564) achieved in his **fresco*** *The Creation of Adam* on the ceiling of the Sistine Chapel in Rome [1].

We cannot hope to discuss all the areas of art in this book. We will not be concerned with the art of literature, which depends on words, nor with the performing arts, which are fleeting experiences of music, dance, and drama designed to be heard or seen as sequential events. Although dance and drama have visual elements, their foundation is the human body; they leave nothing material behind them but costumes and stage props. We must confine ourselves to the visual arts, which consist of works created both to be seen and more or less to endure.

Works of art are not simple objects. A painting, a church, or a vase is a complex phenomenon, representative of the time and place in which it was produced, yet able to transcend its context when it is a very special painting, church, or vase: something we call a masterpiece. A work of art can be useful at the same time that it may represent beauty to us—that which gives pleasure as we view it. Many believe that beauty in art constitutes the best of all we know and may bring the viewer to psychological fulfillment, even, sometimes, to revelation. For many, art also represents cultural attainment,

*See the Glossary at the end of the book for the definitions of many terms, including most of the terms in bold type in the text.

social status, and often a form of investment. For all these reasons, society has supported the visual arts since the beginnings of recorded time.

In this book we will review the different areas of the visual arts and the history of the arts of various peoples. As a preliminary to our study, in Part I we will consider creativity and our responses to it. We will also explore the basic elements common to all the visual arts, like line and color, and the principles of composition, such as unity, balance, rhythm, and proportion. Throughout we will examine how current technology and the skill required to master it interact with works of art past and present.

1
Creation and Response

To draw lines and mix colors does not qualify one as an artist, but as a simple craftsman; it is a purely mechanical activity—whereas painting concerns the mind.

Félibien, artist, 1667

Cold exactitude is not art; ingenious artifice, when it pleases or when it expresses, is art itself.

Diderot, encyclopedist/critic, c. 1765

In painting . . . there are no longer any masters, since there are no longer any pupils. There are only artists without certitude who submit themselves to uncertain influences.

Apollinaire, philosopher/writer, c. 1910

Art has been with us since our beginnings in communal living. From the first stick figures hesitantly drawn in sand and the earliest animals painted and carved on stone [2] until today, people have reacted to their physical, psychological, and religious worlds by making images. The vitality of many of these images has far outlasted the societies in which they were created and first enjoyed.

The ancient Romans called these images *arti*, a word they defined as "skills." Artists were trained to be skilled in painting, carving, building, pottery-making, and other crafts. Today when we look at ancient works of art we are respectful of the skills involved in their creation, but we are moved most deeply by their beauty. Such works also show us how others once lived and the functions art served. With the legacy of art, which remains long after civilizations have flourished and disappeared, we can see what was important to the societies that preceded us. Art is our link with the past and our gift to the future.

Today art enters many aspects of our lives—in our homes, on the job, and at play. It speaks to the conscious and subconscious, to our intelligence and to our emotional being. Yet we tend to think of art as something so mysterious or complex that only an artist, scholar, or critic can fully understand it. The creative process, in fact, *is* complex, but as we observe it closely we find that we, too, can fully understand it.

Creativity

In the West we have a tradition of attributing creativity to something we call the imagination. The "imagining" of an idea—some call it visualization—may take place in one's mind long before any actual images are formed. Perhaps this is the route that most artists take, that is, creating art by following a mind's-eye view and realizing it in actual art materials. Of course, other ideas may feed into the creative process as the work of art evolves, but the seed of that initial

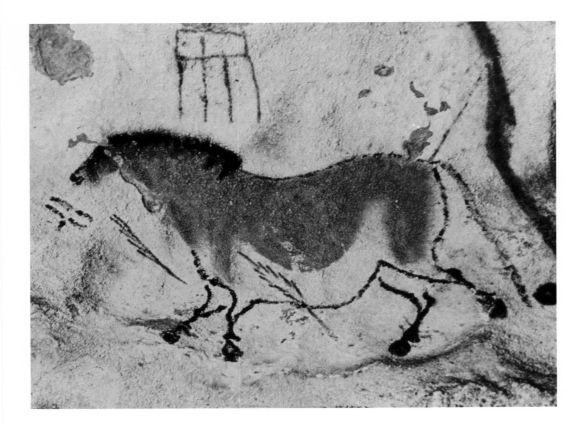

above: **2.** *Paleolithic cave painting.*
c. 15,000–10,000 B.C. *Approximately life size.*
Lascaux (Dordogne), France.

below: **3.** *M. C. Escher.* Drawing Hands. *1948.*
Lithograph, 11¼ × 13⅜″ (29 × 34 cm).
Collection Haags Gemeentemuseum, The Hague.

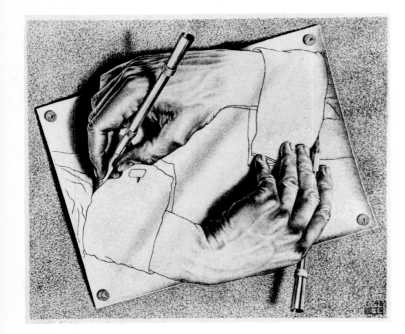

concept has determined for most the intensity of the work of art.

Universal Expressions of Art

We all share in the impulse to create, although not to the same degree. If you have ever held an audience spellbound with a story or grown a garden that draws admiring attention or drawn images you really cannot remember seeing, then you have been close to inspiration—and to the exhilaration that comes from creating something where nothing existed before. The Dutch artist M. C. Escher's (1898–1972) print *Drawing Hands* reflects creativity endlessly **[3]**.

Left vs. Right Brain

Scientific research has been helpful in mapping the human brain according to its areas of specialized functions and in so doing has helped us to better understand the mechanics of creativity. It is now widely accepted that the two halves of the brain, the right and left hemispheres, have specialized and complementary modes of functioning. In most people, the left hemisphere dominates, controlling verbal and logical as well as motor skills, while the right hemisphere seems superior at perceiving and remembering visual patterns, at processing emotional responses, and at monitoring one's actions. This left-brain domination coincides with right-handedness, which is by far more widespread than left-handedness. Surprisingly, the 10 percent of the population who are left-handed may have either a dominant left hemisphere or a dominant right one or even a shared function by both hemispheres. According to British psychologist Marian Annett, more than twice as many artists, musicians, mathematicians, and engineers are left-handed than would occur by chance. Both Michelangelo and Leonardo da Vinci were left-handed. The inclination of the right hemisphere toward superior perception in visual patterns and memory also suggests the importance of the right hemisphere in artistic creativity, a theory Dr. Betty Edwards has substantiated with exercises that call upon the right side of the brain. Basically, however, despite what split-brain research has discovered about their specialized functions, the two halves of the brain operate as one unit. It is likely that creativity in artists, as in all of us, fluctuates from left to right cortex, with the degree of dependency on either side at any time determining how we make our choices.

Children's Art

What we admire most in creative people—freshness of viewpoint, unique kinds of self-expression, and new approaches to everyday living—appears quite naturally in children. Certainly the child who dresses in her mother's clothes plays out a creative fantasy. This creative impulse is born in the child and is frequently stifled by demands from the adult world. By examining a child's art, springing as it does freely from that universal urge to share things felt or seen, we gain a notion of how an individual's power of expression grows. Such insights may tap our own wellsprings of creativity or, at the least, aid us in the appreciation of other creative expressions.

Probably most children are born with creative aptitude. Children reach out to their environment through the senses, continuing to investigate the world until or unless they are stopped or discouraged. In those early stages few are able to resist outside intervention. Psychological tests confirm that youngsters are very vulnerable to positive or negative reinforcement from those they respect the most—parents and teachers.

Born imitators of what they see, children learn to cope with an adult world by copying everything around them. The principle of imitation is expressed as much through art as through anything else. By two years of age, with some visual-motor control, children begin drawing swinging-arc scribbles. These circular shapes are not only the earliest but also the ones that some psychologists see as of the greatest significance, representing centeredness in the child. Children begin a slow departure from the circular form around three years of age, moving to rectilinear shapes at four and back to complex circles by five. These sun-like figures [4], noted authority Rhoda Kellog believes, perhaps represent the self to a child, for they are never identified as suns by the child; they gradually evolve into humanoids that psychologists call "tadpole" creatures.[1] While tadpole figures come in all shapes and sizes, most tend to have twin lines or appendages at the base that probably signify legs. Children's early drawings rarely show the same thing very long. Soon they become interested in differentiating the people they draw,

[1]Howard Gardner, *Artful Scribbles* (New York: Harper/Colophon, 1980), p. 56.

4. *Children's sun-like figures during three-year-old's* mandala *phase. Identified by Rhoda Kellog, specialist in children's drawings.*

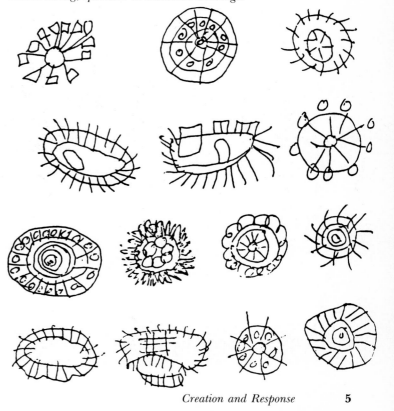

and as they get older, their repertoire increases. At this point, we may say that the child has entered the "golden age" of self-expression, when an innate sense of design prevails.

Perhaps mimicking her parents' use of art paints on canvas, Janna at age five created a credible likeness of her sister, using grains of sand and other seeds [5]. More important, perhaps, the expressive form, lively colors, and composition are pleasing to behold. The work suggests that artistic production plays an important role in the life of the child. Much of children's art at this stage is involved with story-telling, both from their own worlds and from the books they are learning to read. At seven years of age, Janna's figures are more controlled; though the choice of colors is limited by the palette she owned, the production of textures is inventive, with the resultant image full of life [6].

There is a universal quality in the artwork of children the world over that seems to follow the paths of expression we have traced at different stages of development. Inventiveness tends to persist if individual self-expression is encouraged. On the other hand, children soon lose the urge to produce unique images based on their own experiences when they are provided with coloring books and other "charted" art materials. How much the evolution of an artist is dependent on encouragement, imitation, or inherited abilities has yet to be determined.

The debate about nature (inherited skills) versus nurture (encouragement of the individual) is not the major issue here. The main point is that children's art affirms that creativity exists in all of us and may enrich our lives at any point if we permit it to happen.

Everyman as Artist

Working with the unhampered spirit of invention we have seen in children, an uneducated immigrant tile-setter, Simon Rodia, tried to express his gratitude to his adopted new land by meticulously building fantasy towers to God in his own tiny backyard in the Watts section of Los Angeles. Laboring for thirty-three years, using materials discarded from a lifetime's employment on small jobs [7], Rodia maintained a modesty in dramatic contrast to the fierce devotion many give to the "Watts Towers," as they are commonly known today, saying

I no have anybody help me out . . .
I never had a single helper.
Some of the people say
what was he doing . . .
some of the people

5. *Janna Russell.* Drawing of Her Sister. *1960. 13 × 9″ (33 × 22.9 cm).*

6. *Janna Russell.* The American Museum of Natural History. *1962. 13 × 17½″ (33 × 44.5 cm).*

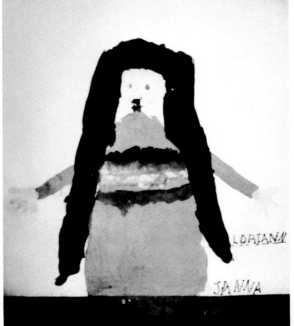

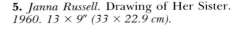

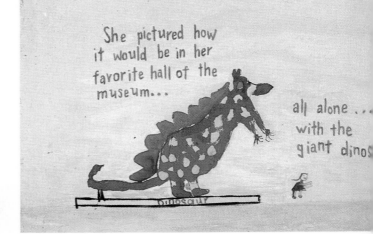

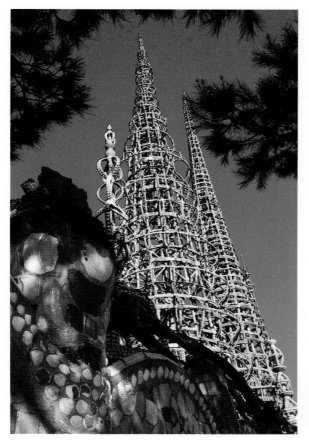

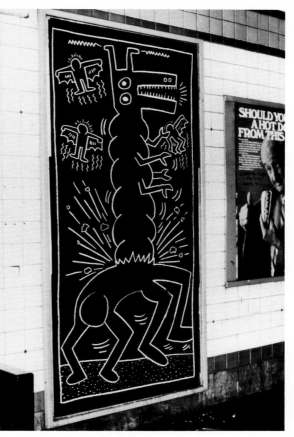

7. *Simon Rodia. Watts Towers, Los Angeles.*
c. 1921–1954. Now being restored and stabilized.

8. *Keith Haring. Subway drawing. 1983.*
Chalk on black paper. Destroyed.

think I was crazy
and some people said
I was going to do something.

I wanted to do something
for the United States
because I was raised here
you understand?
I wanted to do something
for the United States
because there are nice
people in this country.
                    Sabatino "Simon" Rodia

Embellishing an economically depressed area, Rodia's artwork enriches and distinguishes the life of the community, many of whose inhabitants have little other reason to feel "special."

Perhaps graffiti on subway cars and other public places indirectly derive from the same universal need for self-expression and recognition. The acceptance as works of art of these and the many wall paintings that spring up on abandoned buildings depends on the degree of skill demonstrated and the conformity of these works with the vocabulary and language of art that most of us are familiar with and respect. To many urbanites, these anonymous expressions brighten an otherwise dreary cityscape. In turn, the vitality and social criticism of graffiti have influenced such trained artists as Keith Haring (b. 1958), who uses unoccupied subway advertising sites for his work **[8]**.

Folk Art

The term *folk art* is applied by many to any art or craft by untrained artists, such as Simon Rodia. More precisely defined, however, folk art describes work produced outside the mainstream of academic teachings yet with long-standing traditions of its own. Craftwork by the Amish, also known as the Pennsylvania Dutch, is readily recognizable by decorative patterns that have been repeated for generations. The wonderful and delicate craft of Ukrainian egg-painting has been famous for hundreds of years [9]. Yugoslav glass painting is distinguished by the brightness of its colors and the constant vitality of its forms. In fact, almost all folk art has the same decorative goals—that is, making something wonderful of functional objects, sparing no amount of time to do so.

The Trained Artist

The role of the imagination in the complex activity of creation was mentioned earlier. There are also theories, such as those put forward by Freud, that artistic creativity is the result of neuroses and is therefore a form of therapy for the artist. The unhappy life story of the Dutch painter Vincent van Gogh (1853–1890) is cited to prove that art reflects high emotion or stress. It is true that some artists may produce their work under situations of severe personal demand, while others do best when the mood strikes them, but just as many work well at scheduled hours in the studio. For example, the contemporary New York artist Robert Longo says: "I want to be able to tell the world what it's like being an artist. It's not like cutting off your ear or hanging out in bars and drawing pictures of barmaids. It's a very sophisticated thing, very much like being a lawyer or a doctor."[2]

[2]Tony Godfrey, *The New Image: Painting in the 1980s* (New York: Abbeville Press, 1986), p. 119.

There is still another point of view, revealed by many creators of art who believe they work intuitively from observations made earlier, letting the work of art take its own direction. The artist Jackson Pollock (1912–1956) said: "Art has a life of its own. I let a painting live!" In our century, using this method of creation, a whole movement of art developed from such paintings as Pollock's *Number 1, 1948* [10]. However, trained artists like Pollock, or, indeed, most artists, create by drawing on all three techniques without even being aware of how much they owe to any one of the processes. Perhaps that is also the way all of us use some of our potential skill in creativity.

Innovation is often a characteristic of the creative temperament. For instance, in the 20th century many artists, searching for unique expression, have tried to free themselves creatively from the confines of traditional forms of art. Robert Smithson (1938–1973) rejected the long-held notion that sculpture is produced only in the artist's studio. Like the Japanese, whose carefully sculptured gardens are living, changing natural designs, he used the natural elements of earth and water in his startling earth sculpture *Spiral Jetty* [11]. An important feature of this large-scale public sculpture was change through erosion: the action of the water eventually left nothing of the work, and now we have only a photographic record of it. When we can be open to experiencing art without trying to establish its category or separate it from daily life

9. *Ukrainian eggs, painted for Easter.*

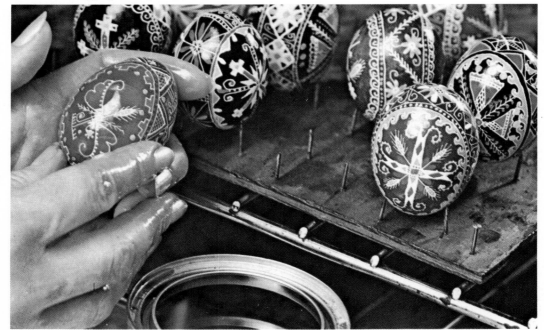

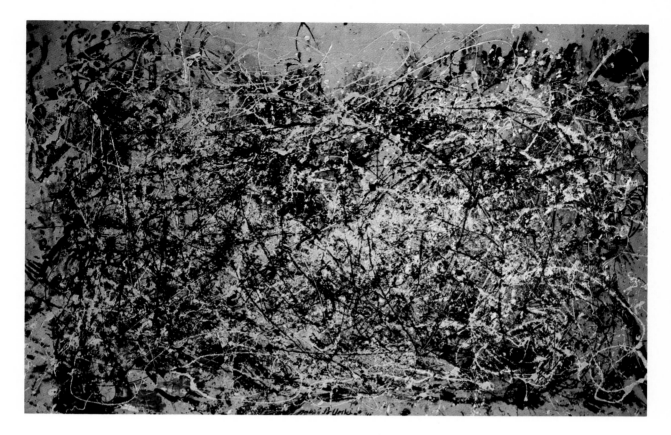

and nature, we are more likely to enjoy creativity in places we never expected it to be.

Functions of Art

Throughout the history of civilization works of art have served to enrich our lives in many different ways.

above: **10.** *Jackson Pollock.* Number 1, 1948. *1948. Oil on canvas, 5'8" × 8'8" (1.73 × 2.64 m). Collection, Museum of Modern Art, New York (purchase).*

below: **11.** *Robert Smithson.* Spiral Jetty. *1970. Black rock, salt crystals, earth, and red water (algae); coil 1500' (457.2 m) long, 15' (4.57 m) wide. Great Salt Lake, Utah.*

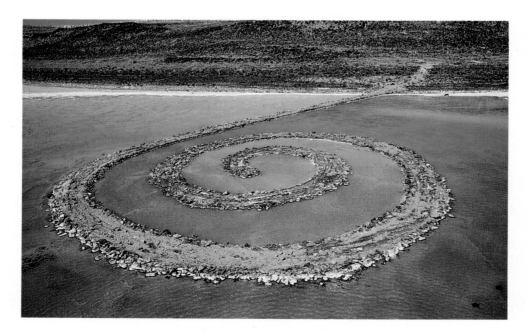

Art and Religion

From the beginning works of art seem to have been responses to universal human needs to address the mysteries of life or to propitiate powerful forces held in fear. The cave paintings [2], for instance, have been interpreted as an attempt to gain magic control over the animals on which the Stone Age culture depended, by painting animal images and, later, ritually "killing" the paintings. Works of art have also personified the deities of various religions. A transcendental state, beyond human stress, characterizes Western classical gods and goddesses and many medieval saints, as well as non-Western deities [12]; this state signifies the other-worldly concerns of the societies that produced the images. In addition to accommodating religious ritual, the structure and decoration of churches have surely attempted to create an atmosphere that would suggest mystery in order to encourage feelings of the sublime and of the unknown integral to the religious experience. Works of art often bring to life the verities of religion.

There is a tradition in the West, dating at least from the Renaissance, of artists identifying the inspiration leading to their successful artistic creations as a God-given gift. The spark of the divine believed to be present in artistic genius in turn seems to have been imparted to artistic creations. Fra Angelico (d. 1455) is said to have sunk to his knees in tearful adoration of the Madonna figure he had just finished painting on the walls of a monk's cell. In some oriental societies, the artist is seen as a medium between the here and now and the essence of God-given life. In the 20th century, in a more secular age, Wassily Kandinsky (1866–1944; [422]) continued this tradition in holding art to be a product of the human spirit rather than manual skill or external vision. In whatever other ways religion has depended on art, the church has been one of the greatest patrons of art, at least in Europe, until quite recently.

Art and Politics

Art has served to enhance the power of the ruling forces in societies. Perhaps evolving out of the magical properties that early peoples associated with art, the impact of works of art has been recognized by leaders in every era, who have sought to use art to their advantage. Like the church, government has provided support for artists who could glorify their patrons

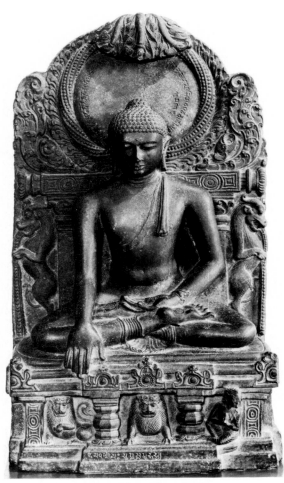

above: **12.** *Seated Buddha. Bihar, India; Pála period, 9th century* A.D. *Chlorite; height 33" (84 cm), width 17½" (44 cm). Asian Art Museum of San Francisco (Avery Brundage Collection).*

below: **13.** *Corita Kent.* Life Without War. *1984. Billboard on Highway 1, Moro Bay, California.*

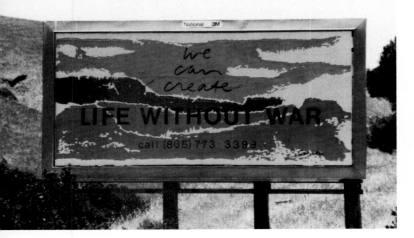

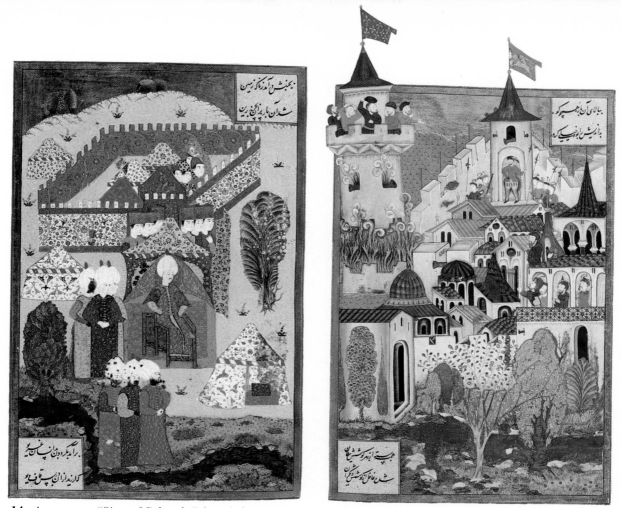

14. *Anonymous. "Siege of Belgrade," from* Süleymanname of Arifi, *fols. 108b–109a. Transcribed 1558. Miniature illumination. Topkapi Palace Museum, Istanbul.*

(whether individuals or a state) in idealized portraits. Today our television arts provide an arena for political candidates, as do other mass media, and the most successful politicians are those who understand and use these media to best effect.

Art has also served to register social protest, as in the work of Corita Kent (1918–1986; **[13]**), a former nun who chose mass-media formats—posters, and then the billboard—for all her work. The billboard became the perfect vehicle, in her hands, for protest. Artists have, of course, often stood outside the social order, either as critics or proponents of a new order. In turn, their work has sometimes provoked censorship, for governments understand only too well that ideas in visual form have a particular potency.

Art and Communication

All over the world, every age and civilization has recognized that by celebrating significant

events with art artists could provide records for the future, such as the *Süleymanname*, the illuminated manuscript biography of Sultan Süleyman the Magnificent, the 16th-century Ottoman ruler **[14]**. It must soon have become apparent that artists could also simulate experiences they had never viewed and create visual illusions of events that never happened! Artists, like historians, have thus served as society's chroniclers. The technology of today permits unprecedented accuracy in the ability to record external data; thus the artist has been freed to assume a role beyond mere recorder of events. In other words, artists perform the special role of interpreting world happenings for us and for posterity.

Art and Commerce

The appreciation of art for itself, for its collectibility, is hardly new. We have evidence that Attalus of Pergamum and his successors (3rd–

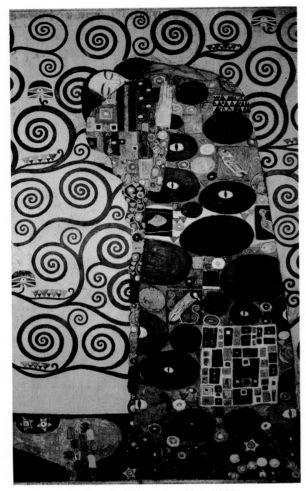

15. *Gustav Klimt. Fulfilment. 1905–1909. Mixed technique on paper. Österreisches Museum für Angewandte Kunst.*

sign areas. In a consumer culture the role of art either as a valuable commodity or means of promoting sales takes on increasing importance.

Art and Aesthetics

Not the least function of art may be its capacity to enrich the surfaces it adorns and the space it occupies while giving pleasure to the observer. Art is almost universally associated with beauty and an appeal to the senses. These characteristics, noted at least as early as the ancient Greeks, were formalized in 1820 by the German philosopher Hegel into a theory of **aesthetics** generally accepted today. The sensations and emotions inspired by art are for many its most important role and accommodate the artist's own need for self-expression and satisfaction in the successful execution of his or her visual goals. For example, Gustav Klimt's (1862–1918) brilliantly colored decorative paintings produce a sensuous richness hardly equaled in the history of modern art [15]. Arising from this point of view—that is, the aesthetic appeal of art—is the concept of "art for art's sake" to be enjoyed for itself rather than for any of the functions we have already described. No theory of art can be complete that does not encompass our deepest level of awareness, our feelings rather than our intellects. What we view as beautiful or sublime awakens senses that increase our faculty for the enjoyment of life itself.

Meaning

Before the 19th century, the basic goals of art were rarely satisfied with the achievement of beauty. More often, art conveyed meaning and expressed important ideas and feelings through arresting images. As Pablo Picasso (1881–1973) once said, "Art is not for interior decoration."

There are many kinds of meaning in art. They reflect the fact that art is an expression of thought or emotion and also a response to the world that nurtured the artist. One kind of meaning is the practical role art often plays in society, as discussed above. The purpose it serves and the form it takes reflect the values and concepts of beauty in different times and places.

Another kind of meaning, sometimes closely related to the practical purpose of art, is symbolism. If we are aware of the meaning of religious, political, or other symbols, we will better understand and enjoy a work of art. We may need to study Islamic art to know that Islamic artists

2nd centuries B.C.) sought out masterpieces from the great eras of Greek art. Greek pottery has been found in Ptolemaic Egyptian tombs, and Greek art and artists were imported to Rome and its provinces. Also, there is a collection of beautiful objects contributed to the Emperor Shomu by his countrymen as valuable gifts and later stored by Shomu's wife in the Shosoin at Nara, Japan, in A.D. 756. In the 16th century the Medici in Florence amassed large collections of classical and contemporary work. Works of art fetch huge prices at art auctions today as an outgrowth of these traditions of collecting. At the same time, art pervades the marketplace—it is used to sell products, services, and institutions by means of advertising art and illustration; it is used to create and enhance products by means of fashion design, industrial and architectural design, and other related de-

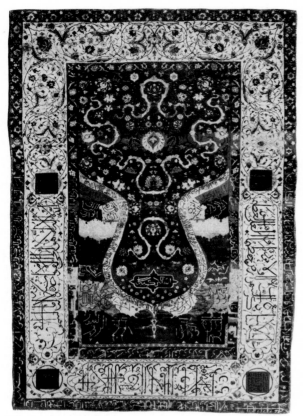

16. *Prayer rug. North Persian (probably Tabriz).*
19th century. Wool, 5'3½" × 3'6⅛"
(1.61 × 1.07 m). Metropolitan Museum of Art, New York
(bequest of Isaac D. Fletcher, 1917).

often incorporated Arabic sayings from the Koran into their designs, as in the border of this 19th-century Persian prayer rug **[16]**. Symbols used in much 20th-century art may be easier for us to follow because they derive chiefly from contemporary society, but some symbols are so personal to the artist that they remain baffling. Knowing what a car means to many Americans, we are able to decipher some of the messages conveyed in James Rosenquist's (b. 1933) *I Love You with My Ford* **[17]**. Through advertising we have been persuaded that success in love and possession of "wheels" are closely allied. In the Islamic rug, symbolism was used to strengthen the believer's faith. In the Rosenquist work, symbolism is a means of commenting on a society in which advertising shapes popular tastes, perhaps softening values, much as the overcooked canned spaghetti depicted is soft.

On a more personal level, meaning in art is to be found in the individual approach of the artist. Because everyone observes the world differently, each work of art is unique—a reflection of the artist's perceptions, insights, and experience. For instance, a favorite theme of artists, most of them men, has been women. An artist's approach to that theme reflects both the role of women in the period and the artist's feelings about women. Consider the art world's most familiar and perhaps endearing Renaissance portrait, Leonardo da Vinci's (1452–1519) *Mona*

17. *James Rosenquist.*
I Love You with My Ford.
1961. Oil on canvas,
7'1¼" × 7'11⅝"
(2.14 × 2.43 m).
Moderna Museet, Stockholm.

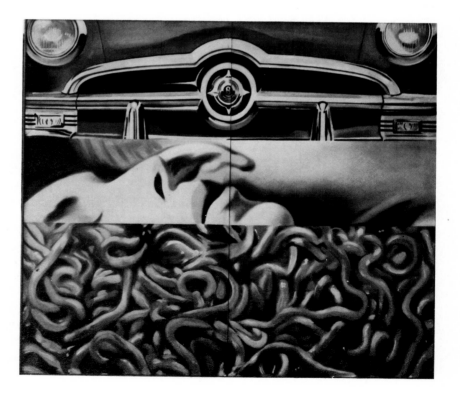

below: **18.** *Leonardo da Vinci.* La Gioconda (Mona Lisa). *c. 1503–1505. Oil on panel, 30¼ × 21" (77 × 53 cm). Louvre, Paris.*

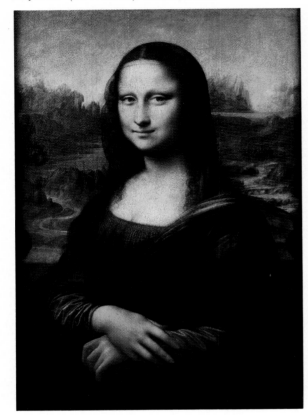

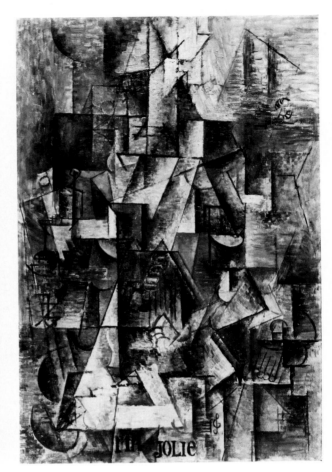

above: **19.** *Pablo Picasso.* Ma Jolie. *1911–1912. Oil on canvas, 39⅜ × 25¾" (100 × 65 cm). Collection, Museum of Modern Art, New York (acquired through the Lillie P. Bliss Bequest).*

left: **20.** *Marie Guillemine Benoist.* Portrait of a Negress. *1800. Oil on canvas, 31⅝ × 25¾" (81 × 65 cm). Louvre, Paris.*

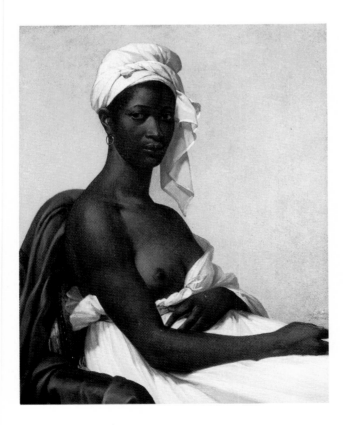

Lisa **[18]**, and Picasso's fractured cubistic portrait *Ma Jolie* **[19]**, rendered in the style he introduced to the 20th century. A quite different treatment of the theme of womanhood is Marie Guillemine Benoist's (1763–1826) *Portrait of a Negress* **[20]**. Although the artist sensitively records her subject's graceful form, long neck, and full breasts, she emphasizes not bodily features but her subject's quiet dignity and reserve. This artist was, perhaps, ahead of her time in her sympathetic portrayal of a black woman.

To express an individual approach, an artist consciously selects certain aspects of the world and eliminates others, adds some items and ex-

Exploring Art Through Technology

Methods of Art Detection

To aid in restoring art masterpieces or to analyze works whose origins may be in question, as well as to conserve existing art, historians are calling more and more on scientific procedures that involve new and specialized interpretative skills.

In brief, some techniques:

Cross-Section Analysis Under the microscope, a paint fragment may reveal a cross-section of several paint layers that can identify an artist by the characteristic manner in which the artist applied each layer.

Pigment Analysis Chemical, x-ray, and other analyses of paints may pinpoint the area and time of their use.

Infrared Reflectography Under infrared light, charcoal underdrawings on white ground show up clearly and demonstrate the artist's preliminary sketches in preparation for the final painting.

Raking Light Examination Side lighting reveals brush strokes, warping, cracks, and paint adherence to the surface.

Radiography The structure of a painting can be scrutinized by x-ray. Heavy paints like lead absorb more rays and yield lighter images than atomically light paints, revealing how and when each pigment was used in building up the work.

Computer Image Processing An art image can be encoded (similar to being photographed), can be enhanced (weak areas strengthened), and can be meticulously examined by other computer functions, like magnification, color changes, and reversal of details.

For example, Lillian Schwartz, computer expert from AT&T Bell Laboratories, links the *Mona Lisa* with Leonardo himself. She has computerized the only existing self-portrait of the artist **[21]**, mirrored it to face the same way as the *Mona Lisa,* scaled it to the same size, and discovered remarkable congruities. The nose, mouth, chin, forehead, and pupils

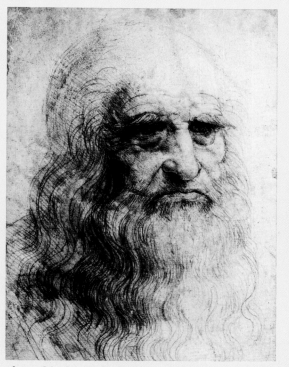

above: **21.** *Leonardo da Vinci.* Self-Portrait. *c. 1514. Red chalk 13⅛ × 8⅜" (33.3 × 21.3 cm). Biblioteca Reale, Turin.*

of the eyes precisely match. That the portrait began with La Gioconda, a recent widow from a prominent Italian family, there is little doubt, but that Leonardo may have used his own features as he looked into a mirror to complete the work is also possible. To back up her argument, Schwartz draws attention also to the design of the neckline knotting, called *vincire,* Leonardo's hometown name, in Italian. A similar knotting design appears in Leonardo's engraving signed *"Leonardus Vinci Academia."* For Leonardo, society was filled with paradox. Just think about his own reversed handwriting from right to left. It is tempting to consider that cryptic Mona Lisa smile that we all admire to be in fact Leonardo's own last laugh on the world of his day and, perhaps on our time as well.

aggerates others. In addition to choosing the subject, the artist also adopts materials, colors, and shapes to communicate a particular perception, shaping an image into a full artistic statement. Were it possible to clone nature without change, the result would not be art. It is the artist's creative translation of subject or materials that produces significant work.

The night sky, which all of us see and usually ignore, becomes a vehicle of emotional and aesthetic release for Van Gogh. His excited perception is communicated to us by his exaggerated swirling shapes, tense brush strokes, and brilliantly contrasting colors [22]. The tiny village sleeps beneath the turbulence of nature, unaware that both the sun and the moon have joined the stars to illuminate the heavens. As observers, we are filled with awe at the extraordinary event.

The Observer's Response

There is more than understanding meaning in appreciating a work of art. Responsiveness on the part of the observer is also necessary. Without it, the work of art might as well not exist. Responses can be of several different kinds.

Emotional Response

We can respond on an emotional level. Art can shock, disturb, or horrify us as well as soothe, delight, or excite us. For example, we may stand in a great cathedral and be overwhelmed with religious exaltation. Or we may be shocked, as we are by Artemesia Gentileschi's (c. 1597–c. 1651) depiction in pitiless detail of Judith's ferocious beheading of Holofernes [23]. The work is unique in the violence of the killing, the fury of the artist, and the horror we feel observing the scene.

All art, however, need not move us so intensely. We may open a magazine and enjoy the illustrations and the pleasing display lettering or type without being conscious of the graphic design. We may savor a fine dinner and be only subconsciously aware of the design and quality of the porcelain, silver, and crystal. We may take pleasure in the attractive groupings of furniture and subtle relationships of colors and textures in a palatial home. These reactions are also emotional responses to artistic expressions.

In developing an appreciation of art, such reactions are important for they lead to sensitiv-

---

Focus on the Artist

Leonardo da Vinci (1452–1519)

Born in 1452 in the small Tuscan town of Vinci near Florence, Leonardo was a love child—the product of a brief and illicit tryst between a young lawyer and a neighborhood girl. From this beginning came a man who is acknowledged to be an extraordinary figure in the history of civilization.

Although he was one of the world's greatest artists, few of his paintings have survived. He was neither a teacher nor a writer, and he published no consistent body of research. Instead he left behind thousands of pages of notes, teeming with observations that stretched from art, science, and philosophy to problems in engineering.

That he hoped one day to collect his notebooks into discourses for the general public is implicit in a passage dated March 22, 1508: "This is a collection without order, drawn from many papers that I have copied, hoping later to put them in their right order, according to the subjects which they treat." One senses a consistent thread through the pages of a teacher expounding his views to the reader. In any case, Leonardo never did arrange his notebooks, and they were lost and all but forgotten for many years after his death.

Leonardo spent his early childhood with his mother, and later with his father, never fully absorbed into a family circle. During much of his life, he was in some financial straits. Though known as a painter of supreme ability, associated with a succession of distinguished men of his time, something in his personality failed to make for leadership and success. At the age of twenty, Leonardo was enrolled as a member of the painters' guild, while still apprenticed to Verrocchio, the noted Renaissance sculptor. In later phases of his career Leonardo developed friendships with other great philosophers of his day, but his most fruitful association in his final years was with the gifted young anatomist Marc Antonio della Torre, a former student in medicine at the University of Padua. From Della Torre, Leonardo learned the practice of dissection, which, coupled with a natural ability to sketch anatomical detail, led to Leonardo's vivid anatomical drawings, many still accepted for their accuracy today.

Inheriting traditions of Renaissance humanism that encouraged human potential, Leonardo seems to have epitomized the hopes and achievements of his time. Intensive study of his recovered notebooks discloses the genius of his brilliant intellect, one of the select personalities in world history.

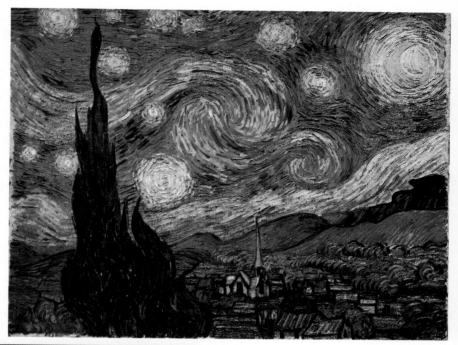

right: **22.** *Vincent van Gogh.*
The Starry Night. *1889. Oil on canvas,*
29 × 36¼" (74 × 92 cm). Collection,
Museum of Modern Art, New York (acquired
through the Lillie P. Bliss Bequest).

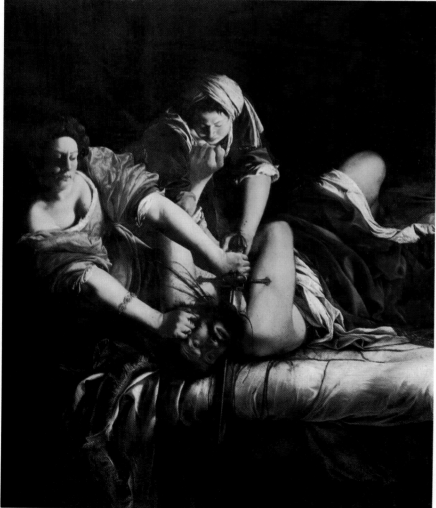

left: **23.** *Artemesia Gentileschi.*
Judith Beheading Holofernes. *c. 1620.*
Oil on canvas, 5'11" × 5'8"
(1.80 × 1.72 m). Uffizi, Florence.

ity. Whether you love or hate a work of art initially is really less important than that you try to understand it. It takes little effort to react pleasurably to paintings of colorful flowers or brilliant sunsets, yet many of us find difficulty in appreciating other works of art. Many viewers are confused by art that does not seem to record nature. Could it be that such works deal only with fractured aspects of today's complex society? For example, try to see and experience fully the interwoven web of colors and shapes created by Jackson Pollock [10]. His great paintings may serve like Japanese gardens designed not for a stroll but for visual delight. By mentally following the many-colored paths, we are distracted from worldly connections. Pollock's infatuation with color and his delight in the overlay of pulsations of paint can become our own vehicles of sensation.

Perceptual Awareness

Some understanding of the way the human eye and brain react to visual stimuli may help us achieve enriched responses. The 20th-century British author Aldous Huxley defined the art of seeing as three processes, occurring almost simultaneously: sensing, selecting, and perceiving.

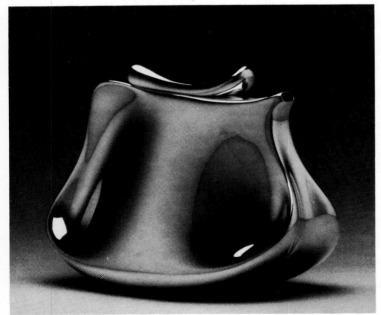

24. *Chungi Choo. Decanter. 1980.*
Silver plate on copper, 8 × 6¼ × 4½"
(20.3 × 15.9 × 11.4 cm).
Collection, Museum of Modern Art, New York.

Sensing is an instinctual response of the eyes and the nervous system. As the eye scans a crowd of people, it receives details of shape and color, light and dark. The physiological process takes care of sending these impulses to the brain.

Selecting is the process of focusing intensely on one part of the total visual field. From the huge number of stimuli the eye takes in, the brain chooses those that have meaning for the brain.

Perceiving gives meaning and significance to the whole act of seeing. Our perceptions are influenced by past experiences, knowledge, emotions, and expectations. What we finally say we "see" is the result of the combination of these influences.

Past experiences affect our perceptions to a greater extent than we realize. We may see what our observations have led us to expect rather than what is really there. Psychiatry informs us that we often project our inner emotions onto people and objects around us. *The Starry Night* depicts a wildly charged firmament, brilliant in color and steeped in emotion [22]. This fervent perception of nature appears to have been rendered by Van Gogh in a frenzy of excitement.

Aesthetic Response

The aesthetic satisfactions that our eyes, bodies, or hands receive from formal components of the art object itself also expand our appreciation. These responses may range from the beauty we perceive in the organization of colors in a painting to the exhilaration we experience passing through an impressive building or the tactile satisfaction we feel in handling a well-designed piece of silver [24]. In each of these situations, the aesthetic response comes from an interaction between the art object and the observer.

Surprisingly, what seems beautiful to us is determined not so much by what we instinctively feel as by what is commonly accepted by the culture in which we live. Thus, we must make an effort to put ourselves into the world in which the artist lived. If we know something about what people felt, thought, and experienced during a particular historical period, we can better understand their aesthetic aims.

Some experiences—particularly birth, love, and death—are universal. When art deals with these themes, we usually have less trouble responding to it. But even these emotions are experienced differently in certain cultures, so some knowledge of social and religious attitudes can heighten our aesthetic responses. For example, prehistoric peoples were deeply concerned with survival through perpetuation of the race. The *Venus of Willendorf* [25] may have been considered beautiful 22,000 years ago, but it is more likely that she was revered as a fertility symbol. Her enormous breasts and swollen belly reinforce her role as Earth Mother; her generous proportions outweigh her small size.

Concepts of beauty continue to fluctuate from culture to culture and throughout history. Not so long ago, an African woman from Zaire evoked an aesthetic response from her community not so much for her proportions as because it considered the intricate scarification decorating her back a mark of beauty [26]. If we did not know of her willingness to bear pain to be made "beautiful," we would have only a superficial appreciation of her scarification designs and those seen on many African sculptures as well [27].

Quite different is our concept of ideal beauty. The blonde film actress Marilyn Monroe has surely been a favorite symbol of femininity in the United States and possibly in much of the world for more than three decades. If a single

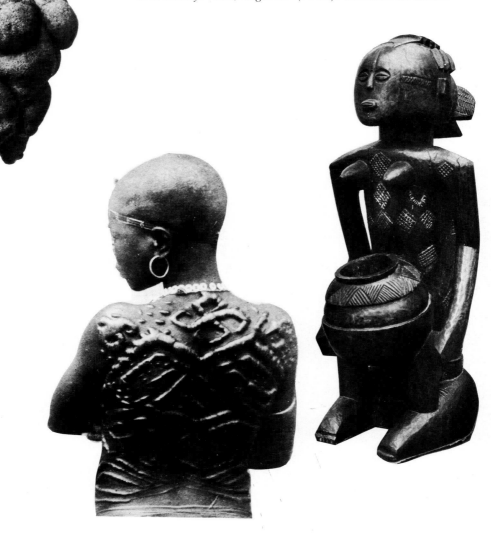

left: **25.** Venus of Willendorf. *Lower Austria. c. 30,000–25,000 B.C. Limestone, height 4⅜" (11 cm). Kunsthistorisches Museum, Vienna.*

below: **26.** *Maipimbe scarification. Boma, Zaire.*

below right: **27.** *Mendicant figure. Baluba, Zaire. 19th century. Wood, height 22" (56 cm). Collection the author.*

image of Marilyn Monroe was created to please, then consider the fifty identical pictures of her [28] presented in one work by Andy Warhol (1930–1987) in the year of Monroe's death. Warhol focused our attention on the mass media, which use multiple imagery and tantalizing packaging to promote a product, person, or point of view. By using the title *Diptych,* the word for a two-paneled work such as a medieval altarpiece, Warhol suggests that advertising values have replaced the religious orientation of other ages. We may contrast Marilyn Monroe with other portraits of women in this text to note further the changing concepts of feminine beauty in Western culture.

Intelligent appreciation of art, then, requires an understanding of its meaning, response to the artist's vision or emotion, and sensitivity to the work's aesthetic in its historical context.

Evaluation and Criticism

Historic Role of Criticism

Art criticism has a venerable history that goes back at least to Plato. It seems to be twofold, consisting of a sense of art history coexisting with a trust in intuitive judgment. There are no permanent and irrefutable critical viewpoints on art, but there is something like a consensus, which becomes evident over a period of time, about the value of individual works or a body of work. There is also a procedure for making critical judgments that has evolved out of Renaissance beginnings.

The medieval Italian poet Dante proclaimed that "art, as far as it is able, follows nature, as a pupil imitates his master; thus your art must be, as it will, God's grandchild." Leonardo da Vinci summed up the Renaissance move away from this God-centered world view in seeing paintings as products of the artist's mind. Giorgio Vasari in his pronouncements about individual artists in his *Lives of the Artists* (1550, 1568) began to grasp at the importance of understanding artistic personality in evaluating a body of work. The *Lives* was based on the thesis that there had been a steady progress in art since the 14th century, culminating, Vasari believed, in Michelangelo and Raphael in the 16th century.

It was an outgrowth of Renaissance thought that catapulted the artist above the craftsman, an attitude, however, that has come under siege in the 20th century. As an extension of the dis-

28. *Andy Warhol.* Marilyn, Diptych. *1962. Acrylic screen print on canvas, 6'9" × 9'6" (2.06 × 2.90 m); two panels, each 6'9" × 4'9" (2.06 × 1.45 m). Tate Gallery, London. Reproduced by courtesy of the Trustees.*

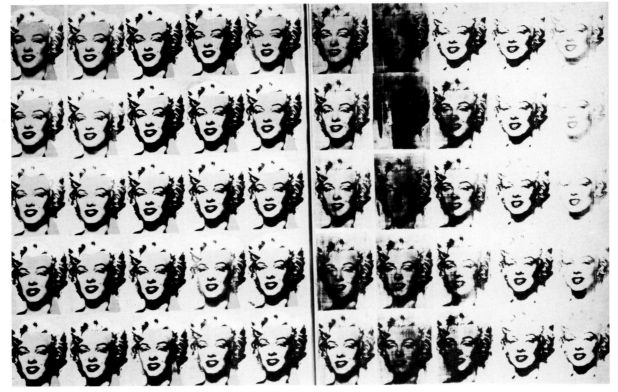

tinction between artist and craftsman, until this century the visual arts have been divided into two categories. The **fine arts,** or major arts, comprised drawing, painting, printmaking, sculpture, and architecture. The **decorative arts,** or minor arts, included ceramics, textiles, furniture, jewelry, metalwork, and the like.

In 1759 Denis Diderot, editor of the vast project known as the *Encyclopédie,* began to write the first critical reviews of exhibitions of the French Salon. By this time, Renaissance theory had hardened into academic formulas for judging art. Aside from distinguishing between fine and decorative arts, hierarchies within the arts were established. For instance, paintings were valued according to the subject matter they treated. Historical subjects were most important, **genre** (everyday life) subjects the least. But Diderot brought a belief in moral seriousness and an intuitive impulse to 18th-century criticism that modified the public's view of art.

The rigidity of academic, or official, art in 19th-century France threw into relief the revolutionary nature of serious work by such artists as Delacroix, Courbet, and Manet, for example. It was then that the tradition of the **avant-garde** began with the opening of a gulf between the public and the more innovative artists. The art critics who appreciated these artists used an understanding of individual artistic temperament as a departure point for their criticism.

Current Criticism

Modern art criticism has branched into several roles—the journalist who writes about art, the teacher who critically seeks to advance the level of his or her students' works, the scholar who comes closest to the critical methods of the past, and the majority of the public, which has minimal claims to expertise. Philosophical modes of art criticism include iconology, a system elaborated by Erwin Panofsky (1925) that "is a method of interpretation which arises from synthesis rather than analysis," a search for the intrinsic meaning of a work of art based on its content; phenomenology, a system concerned only with the characteristics of an art experience itself without extraneous reference or inference; and contextual criticism (evaluation based on the societal origins of art). For our purposes today, while the criteria for judging art change with time, formal criticism still plays a major role in the dynamics of cultural art life, with its main goal educational. Hilton Kramer, editor in chief

of *The New Criterion,* a monthly cultural journal he founded in 1982, and former art critic of the *New York Times,* described his job quite simply in the first issue of his journal:

The first task of the critic is to see the object for what it is, and to describe its qualities and attributes as clearly and concretely as possible. This is the task of elucidation. . . . Another important function of criticism is evaluation . . . best performed as frankly as possible with reasoned arguments and detailed examples and comparisons.

The key to the process, of course, is "to see the object."

Six Steps to Art Appraisal

While we may be helped in looking at art by drawing on the experience and insights of professionals, we have to remember that critics often come from specialized educational backgrounds, steeped in art history, philosophy, and often journalism, as well. Thus it is helpful to understand just how professionals approach critical assignments. Any observers confronting unfamiliar works can ask the same questions, of course.

1. How does this work fit into the history of art? In what way does it remind us of other works we have seen? Are there connections to be made between this piece and those that preceded it? For instance, does a 20th-century work imitate a masterpiece produced 100 years earlier? If so, its value as a unique contribution is questionable.
2. Is there anything known about this artist that might influence our responses to the work? For example, is this the work of an unknown or of a famous artist whose earlier works are all highly regarded? Most art by an established figure has instant market value.
3. When and where was this work created? What was the context that engendered the work? You might ask, for instance, "What induced Artemesia Gentileschi to create *Judith Beheading Holofernes*?" and learn it evolved from her life-long preoccupation with themes of heroic womanhood, primarily culled from biblical references [23].
4. Has the artist used the medium with an understanding of and sensitivity to its inherent physical properties? Does a watercolor, for instance, reveal freshness of hues

and, perhaps, transparent layers of colors and the crisp highlights of unpainted paper seen through the paint? Or does the wood grain of a block enrich a woodcut?

5. How has the artist's vocabulary—form, techniques, and organization—contributed to the total effect? Does the work evoke feelings and memories that you may associate with the artist's inspiration, like Van Gogh's *Starry Night* [22]?

6. Does the content and context of the work reveal the artist's goal in creating the piece? Corita Kent was involved with the peace movement from the 1960s until her death in 1986. In 1984, she chose the billboard format for her message [13]. Do you think she succeeded in her goal?

Armed with only these six steps to art appraisal— (1) art history, (2) the artist, (3) the art era, (4) the art medium, (5) the language of art, and (6) the content and context, if the theme is vital to the work—almost anyone should be able to look at art with an informed critical eye. Whether we view art on a neighbor's walls or in the greatest museums of the world, we will find our critical sensibilities growing with our exposure. One day, when we are experienced in the history of art, we may come across a work that we know is a special case—that moves us almost as must as it moves a critic or art historian. A seventh criterion in art criticism, in fact, might deal with uniqueness of art vision. Has the artist reported even a familiar fact of life with such remarkable insight that the old becomes as if new? Only a very few art works ever qualify to become historically significant, to affect the art that follows. These form pivotal links in the chain of art history—that record of arresting images from era to era and place to place.

The Role of the Critic   The question of value in art is a complex issue. We are accustomed to making judgments in every phase of life. We use our critical skills in making choices—size, color, style, or quantity; what to eat, what to wear, where to vacation. Aesthetic judgments originate from similar demands; they involve a process quite distinct from, yet linked to, art appreciation. They are not simply determining what we like. While there are no absolute standards for deciding if a work of art is beautiful or appraising its quality, every evaluation depends on the experience and education of the judge, not only his or her instincts. Actually, the influence of art criticism upon many of today's artists cannot be

underestimated. Trends in art can be affected and even created by art critics and galleries.

The livelihood of an artist is tenuous at best. Encouragement in competition, presentation in a gallery, recognition by a critic, and finally purchase by an art collector can make the difference between bare survival and success. The whole circle of activities that revolves around the actual creation of art is also affected by art criticism. Collectors, patrons, galleries and museums, art periodicals and newspapers, reproduction services, to name a few, depend on the professional critic for objective opinions.

Many artists quite naturally believe they are the people best qualified to evaluate works of art since their direct involvement with the process has expanded their awareness of the problems and the solutions. Professional art critics, however, argue that detachment is more important. Critics have usually studied art history in depth, are familiar with materials and processes, and have demonstrated informed skill in reviewing a wide range of art.

A critic's viewpoint is helpful when it provides a fresh interpretation of a work of art. Often a critic's knowledge of art methods and aesthetic tools will reveal new facets of the work. Some art is so startling that we are unable to accept the work as art without the critic's help. The critic clarifies the artist's message, helping us to look at unfamiliar images with more tolerant vision.

Critics, however, are not infallible. Some have been known to change their minds, while others are unwilling to accept new ideas. Today we are pleased by *Boulevard des Italiens* [29], painted by Camille Pissarro (1830–1903). Nothing about it disturbs or surprises us, for we have seen many similar views of city streets. But when it was created in 1897, most critics condemned Pissarro for his lack of sensitivity to what they termed real painterly concerns. They complained that *Boulevard des Italiens* was like a "slice of life" without redeeming creative contributions from the artist. Even the perspective, such as a bird might see from a lofty studio window, was considered a weakness by many critics.

Perhaps evaluation requires more professional knowledge than most of us have; however, all of us can develop appreciation, given time and a willingness to be involved.

We may conclude that while we can learn from a critic's comments, they should never serve as the only criteria for evaluation or for governing the degree of our appreciation. Our own unfolding exposure to art will lead us to value judgments like those of professionals. As

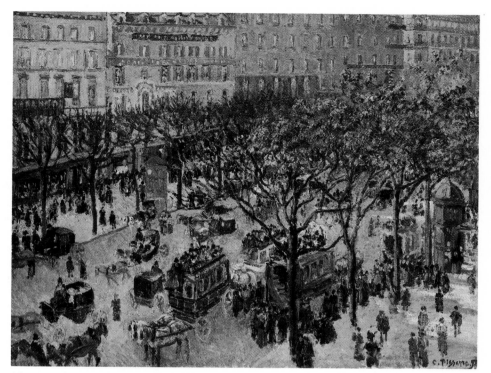

29. *Camille Pissarro.* Boulevard des Italiens, Morning, Sunlight. *1897. Oil on canvas, 28⅞ × 36¼" (73 × 92 cm). National Gallery of Art, Washington (Chester Dale Collection, 1962).*

with all skills, the trip that leads to informed judgments and deep appreciation must be taken alone by an individual who is sensitive to the work of art and the spirit that produced it. Ultimately, the most important effect of art is what the artist says directly to each individual observer.

Experiencing art can provide great joy and reveal discoveries about ourselves, our society, and, above all, our relationship to our world. Many people find contemporary art enjoyable and fascinating; yet others find it bewildering, unskillful, and even ugly. Its variety echoes the complexity of today's world and the differences in artists' reactions to it. We do not all like the same things. Nor do we all have the same tolerance for the new, the disturbing, or the disagreeable. In many situations what the artist is revealing about our society and ourselves may be welcome. But if we shut our eyes to everything that seems unpleasant or difficult to understand, if we refuse to expand our horizons or to look at art with a sense of adventure, we will surely lose the opportunity to profit from an artist's message. Certainly in such a situation a pioneering artist will suffer, but the greater loss is likely to be our own.

Our encounter with art can be made more satisfying if we learn how the artist creates by exploring the simple activities and materials that follow—noting basic elements like line or color and art principles, such as unity and balance.

Exercises and Activities

Research Exercises

1. Attend an art exhibit in a local gallery or museum. Write a one-page review, explaining why you do or do not like certain pieces of art. How has the artist individualized his or her personal art statement, that is, created a work that is memorable for you?

2. If possible, locate an art critic's review of the same exhibit. What appear to be the criteria the critic has used on which to base his or her comments? Write your own review.

3. What psychological, emotional, and aesthetic factors do you feel are involved in the appreciation of art? Can you explain, using the six

or seven criteria of art evaluation, why some masterpieces seem to have universal appeal?

4. Picasso's *Ma Jolie* and Leonardo's *Mona Lisa* are both portraits of women and masterworks. Discuss how they differ and cite some historical factors that may explain these differences.

5. Find five artworks in this book that have been inspired at least in part by the natural environment. Which appear to be duplications of nature? Which works reinterpret or abstract details from nature?

Studio Activities

1. Note the cage-like form painted near the leaping antelope in the first illustration of this chapter [2]. Since no one knows what it means, design another linear symbol that has meaning you can explain to take its place.

2. Find a piece of slate to use as a base for your version of a prehistoric painting. With colored chalks or paints, draw a "stone age" animal in action. Try to make use of any cracks, changes in surface levels of the slate, or color irregularities to enrich your design.

3. Form a **photo montage** (a composite image made by assembling parts of two or more photographs) dealing with materialism like Rosenquist's *I Love You with My Ford*.

4. Using clay instead of stone, shape your own version of the *Venus of Willendorf* celebrating fertility.

5. Observe a child's drawing. Express the same theme using the same medium and materials. Try to maintain the vigor of the child's concept. You may need heavier lines, brighter colors, or stronger textures to keep the same impact, because children's art often flows more freely than more repressed adults can imitate.

2
Exploring the Artist's Language

Art is human intelligence playing over the natural scene, ingeniously affecting it toward the fulfillment of human purposes.

Aristotle

It took me close to thirty years to comprehend why Cézanne was the father of modern art. . . . For hundreds of years, they had worked to capture the sheen and texture, the hairs, the dust, the flickering motes of light on the surface of a drape. . . . Did a painter work a canvas properly? Then one could cut out a square inch of canvas, show it to an unfamiliar eye, and the response would be that it was a piece of lace, or a square of velvet, for the canvas had been painted to look exactly like a lace or velvet.

Cézanne, however, had looked to destroy the surface. A tablecloth in any one of his still lifes, taken inch by square inch, resembled the snowfields of mountains. . . . He showed . . . a panorama of rises and depressions on every surface, the similarities between surfaces now more profound than the differences. As he succeeded, so the orders of magnitude vanished in his painting, and one could not know, looking at a detail, whether he was representing the inside of a flower or the inside of a tent.

Norman Mailer, *Of a Fire on the Moon*, 1957

Allow me to repeat what I was saying to you here; treat nature in terms of the cylinder, the sphere and the cone, all put in perspective, so that each side of an object, of a plane, moves towards a central point. Lines parallel to the horizon give the breadth. . . . Lines perpendicular to the horizon give the depth. . . .

Paul Cézanne, *Correspondence* (B. Grasset, Paris), 1937, extract from a letter to Emile Bernard

Our search for knowledge has pulled us high above the earth, far below its crust, and deep beneath the sea. From the dawn of human awareness on earth, we have reacted to this world in conscious and unconscious ways, some of which are termed art. Observations of the natural environment and of human experiences within it have been the inspiration for most art for thousands of years. Artists select, summarize, and then interpret what they have perceived. In reworking their responses, they transform ideas into art. Commenting on his work, Paul Klee (1879–1940) observed that the artist is like "the trunk of the tree, gathering vitality from the soil, from the depth (the unconscious), and transmitting it to the crown of the tree, which is beauty."

Inspiration

Most artists call the process of creativity simply inspiration. Scientists have defined four stages. Probably we all explore this process at one time or another.

Paul Klee (1879–1940)

Regarded today as one of the most important contributions to the art of the 20th century, the work of Paul Klee has achieved ever-increasing recognition since his death half a century ago. Klee's influence on modern art is perhaps best understood by examining his paintings and drawings. What he experienced within himself, especially in his later years, emerges in the work. One of the most prolific artists of the modern era, Paul Klee produced close to nine thousand works of art—most, if not all, of which give a sense of newness from work to work that is extraordinary [30].

Born of a Swiss mother and German father, a music teacher at a local school, Klee had the early advantage of a collegiate cultural atmosphere to which he was oriented all his life. He chose a career of art, eventually studying painting and drawing at the Art Academy in Munich. A year of travel in Italy, spent mostly in Rome, broadened his experiences further, while expanding his career. In 1920, he joined the faculty of the Bauhaus School of Design in Germany, a school whose reputation gradually extended worldwide. Its innovational philosophy of student and artist, designer, and teacher exploring professional projects together profoundly affected art education and inspired Klee's own *Pedagogical Sketchbook*, produced in his third year of Bauhaus teaching.

As a young man, Klee had developed a technique of continuous cobweb-thin lines that he drew upon all his life. After a trip to Tunisia, where he learned to paint in **watercolors,** he added the brilliance of pure color to his use of line, producing a style of fresh ingenuity that characterized all his work. He shared his creative credo with his students, but his artistic discoveries proved inspiring to many artists who never met him. "Whether they knew it or not," the art critic Clement Greenberg once commented, "everyone was learning from Paul Klee"—from his style and his philosophic base.

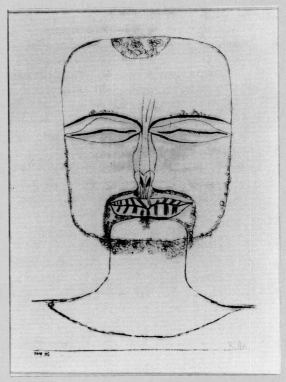

30. *Paul Klee.* Absorption (Self-Portrait). *1919. Lithograph, 9¼ × 6¼″ (23.5 × 15.9 cm). Paul Klee Foundation, Kunstmuseum, Bern.*

Klee's creative life derived from painting and music but was founded on nature in the observation of cyclic change and respect for cosmic forces. Yet, for all of Klee's symbolic ties to nature, his work reveals the mysterious course of civilization. Paul Klee did not experience a dramatic or adventurous life by almost any standard. His professional recognition was slow, though it accelerated with his appointment to the Bauhaus School. The refined subtleties of his imagination were such that *New York Times* art critic John Russell called Klee "as civilized a man as the history of art has to show."

1. Observation: intake of data, examination of tools and materials, unformed ideas, curiosity
2. Gestation: conscious and subconscious realignment of disorganized insights, time out
3. Inspiration: flashes of intuition and intimation of solutions, excitement
4. Verification: conscious, organized evolution and culmination of project

Artistic experiment for its own sake is simply not enough, and rarely is invention itself the goal of every artist. The process of creativity with inspiration often leads to significant contributions, but few can count on a masterpiece at the end of the road. Television and the film industry often portray artists as if they were driven by creative urges when, in fact, not many arise with the conviction that they will produce a work of art before the day is out. Most artists are committed to spending time in the studio, sometimes on a scheduled basis, where ideas, perhaps perceived at another time and place, can be reworked into art.

Picasso explained the process simply when he said, "I do not seek, I find." His *Bull's Head* [31] probably evolved from an idle observation of a discarded bicycle. With a flash of inspiration, Picasso quickly reconstituted the elements into a witty sculptural expression of a primal motif in Western art, the bull. We in turn are delighted by the unexpected origin of the new form.

Human beings seem to have a need for clarity, order, and, finally, full understanding. Artists in particular search for order and ultimate truth, often with the diligence we associate with the scientist. During the Renaissance, Leonardo da Vinci recorded thousands of exploratory details

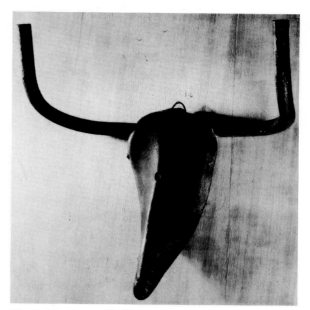

31. *Pablo Picasso.* Bull's Head. *1943. Bronze, height 16" (41 cm). Musée Picasso, Paris.*

of anatomy, botany, and mechanics. His notions of ballistics certainly predated modern projectiles. He also examined human physiology by studying such things as bone formations and the human head.

Usually, however, the artist's purpose is not so much to echo nature as to know nature well enough to feel free to comment in the language of art. Artistic inspiration transforms the world through skilled use of shape and mass, line, light and shade, values, color, and texture. The artist may abstract from nature and reinterpret it to give us heightened aesthetic experiences, just as Henri Matisse's (1869–1954) *Seated Woman* [32]

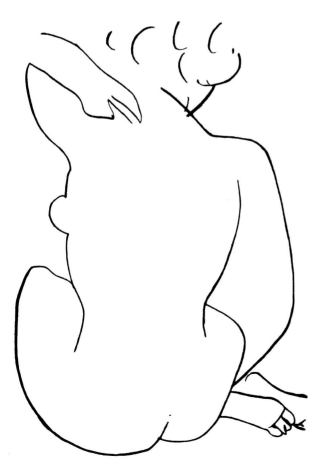

32. *Henri Matisse.* Seated Woman Seen from the Back. *1940. Pen drawing.*

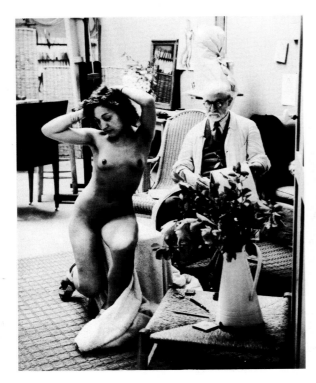

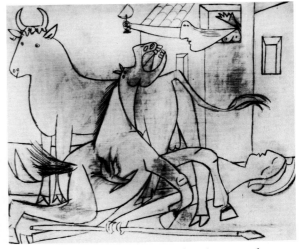

may have been derived from a similar, rather uninspired pose of this model [33].

Form and Content

We can tell the same story in many ways. When we retell an anecdote, we consciously select some details and omit others, depending on our audience. In a work of art the subject theme or story is the content and the structural way it is told is the form. When Picasso was preparing to paint his great mural *Guernica* to protest man's inhumanity to man shown by the bombing of a town during the Spanish Civil War, his preliminary drawings of the bull took many forms [34]; the content was somewhat altered in the final configuration [35].

The bull is probably the oldest subject of art in Western civilization. Appearing even earlier than images of human beings, the bull can be

35. *Pablo Picasso.* Guernica. *1937. Oil on canvas, $11'5\frac{1}{2}'' \times 25'5\frac{3}{4}''$ (3.49 × 7.77 m). Prado, Madrid.*

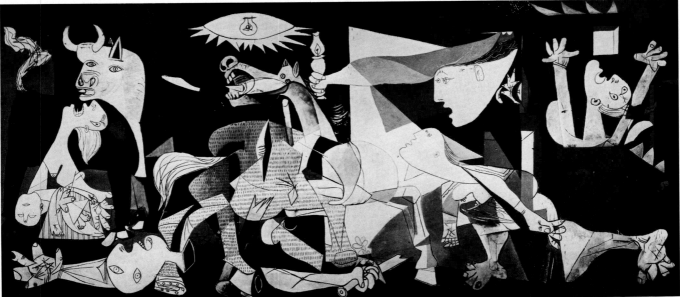

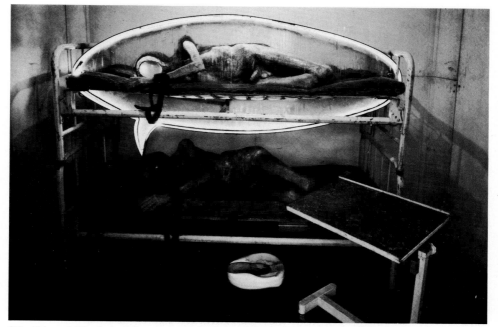

36. *Edward Kienholz*. The State Hospital, *detail. 1966. Mixed media, 8′ × 12′ × 10′ (2.44 × 3.66 × 3.05 m). Moderna Museet, Stockholm (© Edward Kienholz).*

traced from Paleolithic times in the Lascaux caves in France **[2]** to a dominant culmination in *Guernica*. The bull of the mural is perhaps a symbol of persecuted innocence or of unfeeling, brute force. The bull's form is balanced by the figure in the burning building on the right. Although Picasso seems to relate the bull and the victims of the destroyed town of Guernica to the misery of war-torn Spain, he never gave us an explanation of the painting, maintaining that art tells its own story. His studies for the bull, the only stable element of the composition, reveal many changes in form from a **Classical** image to the final bull, quietly dominating the composition, with enigmatic countenance. The horror of Guernica's story remained the same throughout the many changes in its presentation.

Sometimes an artist must be adventurous and creative to lead us into his or her vision. Sometimes artists present us with visual statements based on the familiar world presented in new, disturbing contexts. It takes courage to depart from tradition to upset visual conventions, but by tossing away preconceptions, the artist can often bring us a new reality with new symbols and a fresh point of view.

In *The State Hospital* **[36]**, Edward Kienholz (b. 1927) has assumed the mantle of social concern worn in the 18th century by William Hogarth (1697–1764). Both artists force us to confront an unpleasant scene behind the facade of a public institution. Hogarth's print of Bedlam, London's insane asylum **[37]**, clearly reveals the degeneration of a nobleman, strait-jacketed after debauchery, a fitting end, in Hogarth's

37. *William Hogarth*. In Bedlam, *from* The Rake's Progress. *c. 1734. Engraving, 24½ × 29½″ (62 × 75 cm). Metropolitan Museum of Art, New York (Harris Brisbane Dick Fund, 1932).*

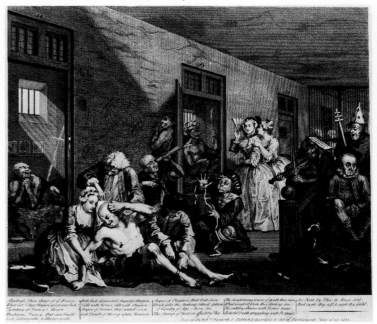

opinion, to the evils of excess in food, sex, and drink. Kienholz's representation of a cell block is more indirect. At first, we view the tableau with curiosity, until we realize the old man is chained to his cot. Details of horror appear in this victim of modern civilization, a living skeleton with mottled, leathery skin stretched over it. The duplicate upper figure, set off in cartoon style by neon tubing, may represent the old man's imagined self, lit up like a fish for all to see. The head of the lower figure has been replaced by a bowl in which a live fish darts fitfully. *The State Hospital* suggests to most of us loss of personal status. Have you ever felt stripped of identity by an institution that assigned you a bed and number for its convenience and kept extracting samples from you for endless record-keeping? Kienholz dramatizes the plight of the elderly and the infirm who struggle for self-worth within a public institution that deprives people of all individuality and pride. Contrast the different structural forms of these two works, both portraying weaknesses of society. Is today's artist more powerful because the language of art has changed to satisfy a new age? Surely, both works achieve the artists' intention of eliciting strong responses from their viewers.

Iconography

Closely allied with form and content is **iconography,** the images within a work of art that have symbolic meanings beyond the obvious that the audience is expected to understand. Images of the Buddha or Christ do not need to be labeled for identification by the devout. Many major works in Eastern and Western art history make religious, historical, or literary associations that are familiar to most.

During early periods of Christianity, to avoid persecution, religious themes were translated into symbols that were totally clear only to those initiated to the faith. We still use the wedding ring as a sign of eternity—there is no beginning and no end—just as the circle promised everlasting life to the first Christians. The vocabulary of these symbols became so elaborate during the next twelve hundred years that when the Master of Flémalle (probably Robert Campin, c. 1378–1444) meticulously painted the richly colored *Mérode Altarpiece* [**38**], practically every object in the picture bore some religious significance, represented by a method known as disguised symbolism. The central "Annunciation" scene depicts the Virgin as a middle-class Flemish

38. *Robert Campin.* Triptych of the Annunciation. *c. 1426.*
Central panel, the Annunciation; left wing, Kneeling Donors; right wing, Joseph in His Workshop.
Oil on wood; center panel, 25⅜ × 24⅞" (64.5 × 63.2 cm); wings, 25⅜ × 10" (64.5 × 25.4 cm).
Metropolitan Museum of Art, Cloisters Collection, New York.

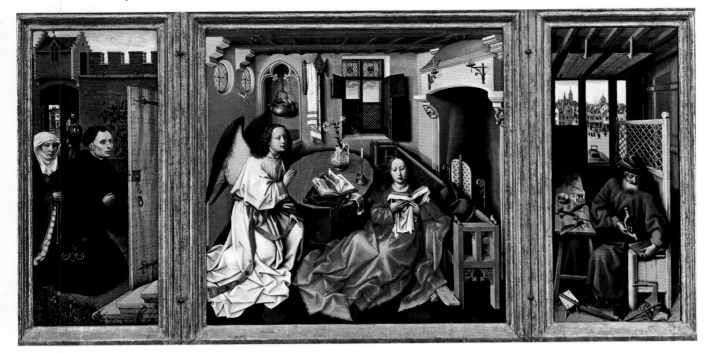

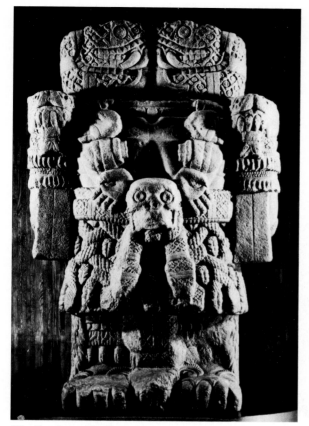

39. *Coatlicue (Goddess of Earth and Death).*
Aztec, 15th century. Basalt, height 8'3" (2.51 m).
National Museum of Anthropology, Mexico City.

(Aztec goddess of earth and death) with an iconography that we can partly understand despite its unfamiliarity [39]. Reflecting the warlike Aztec belief in the need for human sacrifice to satisfy the sun god, human skulls, a universal symbol for death, decorate the sculpture. Coatlicue's head consists of two serpents facing each other whose eyes, viewed frontally, dominate a formidable force! She wears a necklace of hands and hearts with a pendant skull and a skirt made of intertwined skulls and serpents. Since harmless snakes are so common in Middle America that snakes are considered to be benign, their appearance as deities may also represent forces for good, as shown by Quetzalcoatl, represented in any of three alternative images (bird = serpent = god effigy) [40], and considered a savior by the Toltec Indians. As we can see, no symbolism that is strange to us can be really understood or fully appreciated without knowledge of the iconography.

Important images in any culture are sometimes called **icons**; in such cases the image itself stands for what it represents. For example, in the Greek or Russian orthodox religion, a painted image of Christ is considered sacred and treated with veneration; similarly, the familiar

woman, virgin-pure as attested by the spotless room, the vase of lilies, and the immaculate bronze kettle hanging on the back wall. Seven rays of light stream through the window pane toward the Virgin's ear, through which she was believed to have conceived the infant Jesus. The wooden table and bench and partition isolate her from all other physical contacts. A small child bearing a cross, harbinger of future events, hovers in the "divine light" over the angel Gabriel's head. The gray-haired Joseph, the carpenter, fashions mousetraps, symbols of the trap for Satan, with the birth of Jesus expected to serve as the bait. Gabriel's counterpart, an earthly messenger, stands respectfully just outside the flower garden, another reference to Mary. There are many other symbols within the *Mérode Altarpiece;* they are less significant, perhaps, and in any case require further specialized knowledge of Renaissance iconography to understand.

From a different culture but the same millennium is a figure of the ferocious Coatlicue

40. *Temple of Quetzalcoatl,*
Teotihuacán, near Mexico City. 300–700 A.D.

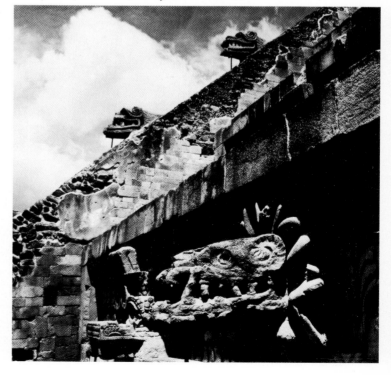

image of the American flag is seen by some to exemplify patriotism. Jasper Johns (b. 1930) devoted a whole series of works to the flag theme, questioning the role of the patriot. Many of those who viewed Johns' work thought it was radical and inflammatory. Yet these **Pop Art** paintings of the late 1950s and 1960s would have had no meaning to observers unfamiliar with the iconographic symbol of a modified American flag painted in unusual colors [41]. Therefore, understanding of the iconography and the culture that produced a work of art can greatly enhance our appreciation of it—or at least our ability to react to it.

Style and Subject

Closely related to form, content, and iconography are style and subject. Most people look at a work of art for the subject represented, such as a landscape or a portrait. Although the theme may be considered the most obvious element of the work, full appreciation demands much more than recognition of images. The viewer must go past the obvious subject to consider form and style. Style is the individual approach an artist takes in his or her art. Artists consciously and subconsciously choose to work in a certain way

according to what they wish to express and in doing so reveal different personal styles. Thus the work of well-known artists can often be identified as easily as the FBI distinguishes fingerprints. Art experts can quickly identify an artist's style in works they have never seen before.

As an example of personal style, consider Rosa Bonheur (1822–1899), whose forceful approach projected the artistic strength she needed to compete in the 19th-century art world dominated by men. She chose active subjects in energy-charged compositions, painting them carefully with the technical precision required for exhibition at the French Academy. *The Horse Fair* [42] typifies her style: vitality, skill in texture and color, and, above all, sure knowledge of complex composition, involving rhythmic interpenetration of space. Thirty-five years later, Vincent van Gogh's anti-Academic style can be noted in the way he applied thick paints in heavy strokes and strong outlines [22].

Romare Bearden (1914–1988), in contrast, developed his use of **photo montage** in a uniquely personal style. His work characteristically involved assembled pieces of photographs and paint arranged in **Cubist**-inspired compositions of urban blacks. The vitality of his art is based on the contrasting shapes and textures of

41. *Jasper Johns.* Flag. *1954. Encaustic, oil and collage on canvas; 3'6¼" × 5'⅝" (1.07 × 1.54 m). Collection, Museum of Modern Art, New York (gift of Philip Johnson in honor of Alfred Barr, Jr.).*

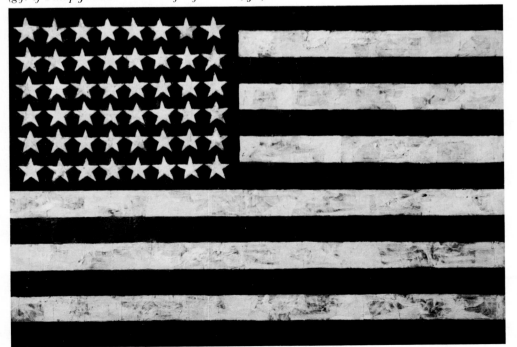

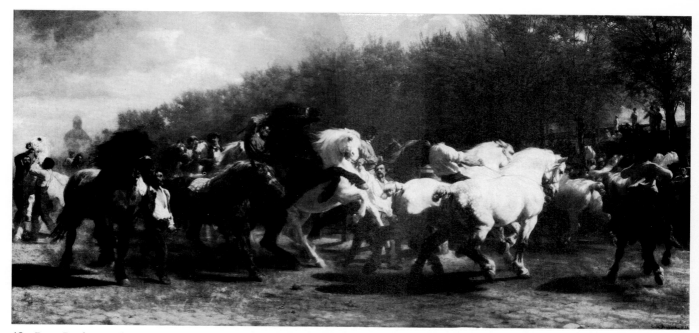

42. *Rosa Bonheur.* The Horse Fair. *1853–1855. Oil on canvas, 8'1¼" × 16'7½" (2.44 × 5.07 m).*
Metropolitan Museum of Art, New York (gift of Cornelius Vanderbilt, 1887).

his figures and their unexpected sizes, which are rarely faithful to reality **[43]**. An impossible seascape may be glimpsed through a bedroom window while utensils and other objects within violate gravity, floating in the orderly disorder of a room that cannot quite be believed.

Style is also, however, more than a personal approach. It is a way of treating a subject that may be shared by many artists who belong to a particular historical period or cultural region or who have a similar point of view. Thus subject matter may be representational, abstract, or nonobjective, depending on how faithful the artist is to the appearances of the real world.

Representational art reproduces the world we know with minimal change from the appearance of things in everyday experiences. Clearly, Piet Mondrian's (1877–1944) early landscape paint-

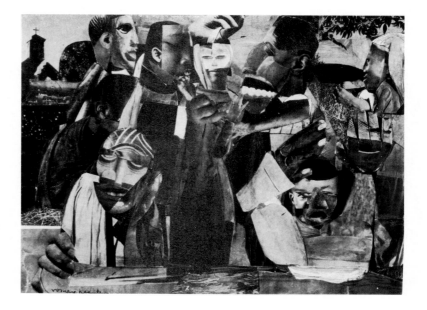

43. *Romare Bearden.*
The Prevalence of Ritual: Baptism.
1964. Synthetic polymer paint and pencil on paperboard; 9⅛ × 12"
(23.2 × 30.5 cm). Hirshhorn
Museum and Sculpture Garden,
Smithsonian Institution, Washington.

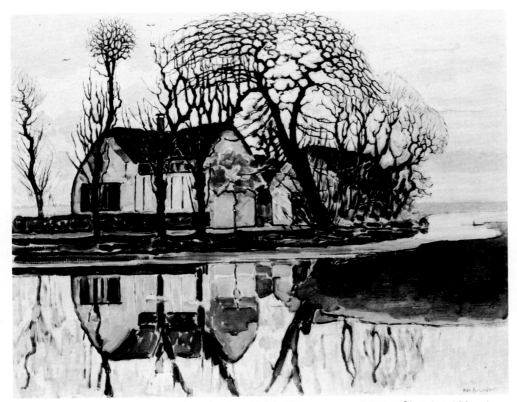

44. *Piet Mondrian.* Farm at Duivendrecht. *1906. Oil on canvas, 34 × 42¾″ (56 × 109 cm). Collection Dr. and Mrs. Isaac Schoenberg.*

ing of 1906 was dominated by a large tree hanging over an isolated farmhouse [44]. The style is representational and direct. Yet, as we examine

45. *Detail of Figure 44.*

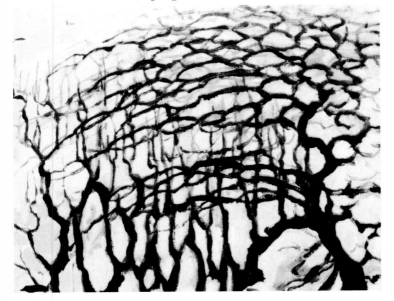

enlarged details, we note the artist's early concern with the pattern created by the tree's branches and his emphasis on the horizontal and vertical divisions of the shingles.

Abstract art alters the view of a real world, retaining only the essence of a thing or an idea, while freely changing qualities of the original. Mondrian's first interest in the tree he undertook to paint appears to have been gradually expanded to focus on the spaces trapped by the tree's branches, which primarily form a horizontal and vertical pattern [45]. The detail of branches appears to have been an early step that led to his eventual total concentration upon the whole tree and then on horizontal and vertical design.

Nonobjective art, also called nonrepresentational or nonfigurative art, depicts no recognizable object or clear reference to the real world. Had we not studied Mondrian's early work, tracing the evolution of his nonobjective compositions, we would be unaware that what became his lifelong preoccupation, the "essential plastic means of art"—line and color free from any particular subject—may have been originally inspired by a farmhouse, a tree, and its branches

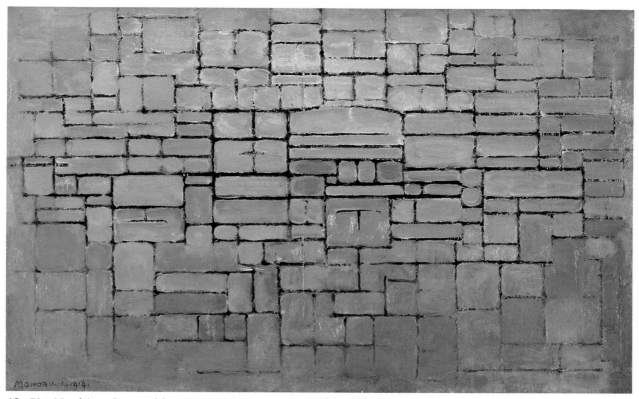

46. *Piet Mondrian. Composition V. 1914. Oil on canvas, 21⅝″ × 33⅝″ (55 × 85 cm). Collection, Museum of Modern Art, New York (Sidney and Harriet Janis Collection).*

[46]. Nonobjective art usually presents an aesthetically pleasing design, involving point, line, color, value, shape, and texture, some of the visual elements we will examine next.

The Visual Elements

Artists use certain basic artistic devices both consciously and unconsciously to develop a work fully. Though these elements are fundamental to all the visual arts and other arts as well, the manner in which each artist organizes them is unique.

An ancient Greek vase and a contemporary painting seem worlds apart in their inspiration, function, and material composition, yet they are somewhat related in that each uses some of the basic components of art. The Greek vase [47], an early grave marker from the Dipylon cemetery in Athens, has been decorated with an orderly composition of horizontal lines confining tiny figural and geometric motifs. The over-all design is flat, without reference to three-dimensional space. The small figures, rhythmically repeated, form a textural pattern of evenly balanced dark and light values. The decoration

47. *Dipylon vase, with funeral scenes. Attic, 8th century B.C. Terracotta, height 40½″ (103 cm). Metropolitan Museum of Art, New York (Rogers Fund, 1914).*

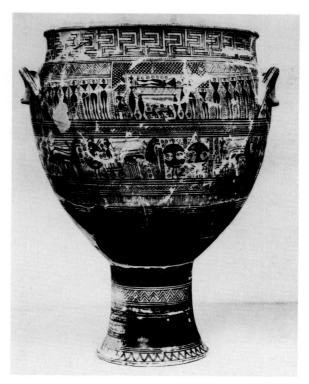

painted on the red clay is geometric and might be found in many other examples of early pottery. The key design at the lip of the vase, however, identifies the work as Greek.

In contrast, Pavel Tchelitchew's (1898–1957) **surrealistic** mid-20th-century painting *Hide-and-Seek* [48] is comprised of brilliant, highly imaginative figurative images, typical of the artist's style, with color the only additional element to those already noted. The vivid reds and yellows advance from the cold blues of the background. A multiplicity of lines in this work suggests a vast, pulsating circulatory system as the basic texture. The irregular foreground shapes, varying in size, are massed around the small child almost hidden in the dark shadows at the center. Amorphous human forms emerge mysteriously from the depths of the painting. In the game of "hide and seek," perhaps the child imagines her worst fears of the unknown. In both the vase and the painting, line, shape, value, texture (and color), the visual elements, have been organized to provide powerful aesthetic experiences.

Point

The tiniest element of design is a point, the smallest visible attention-getter. By its position in relation to the outside edges, a single dot on a surface may determine the configuration of a design. It may become the central focus or exist as a single point of emphasis in a total composition. Or it may be the design in itself.

For instance, every location on a computer screen can be precisely pinpointed, even when thousands of points may be involved in a total composition. With the magnification possibilities inherent in computer design, it becomes possible to view any of these points, called a picture element, on demand. Like a single sound in a quiet room, or the central element in a target, any point can be made to be the important focus of attention [49], as shown in the computerized detail of the *Mona Lisa*.

Line

We may begin to communicate what we see through **line,** the basis of most drawing and

48. *Pavel Tchelitchew.* Hide-and-Seek (Cache-cache). *1940–1942. Oil on canvas, 6'6½" × 7'3¾" (1.99 × 2.15 m). Collection, The Museum of Modern Art, New York (Mrs. Simon Guggenheim Fund).*

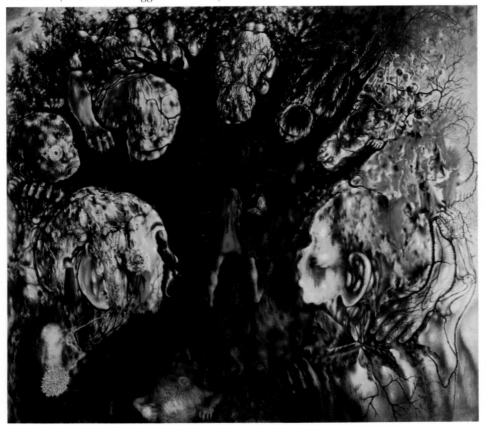

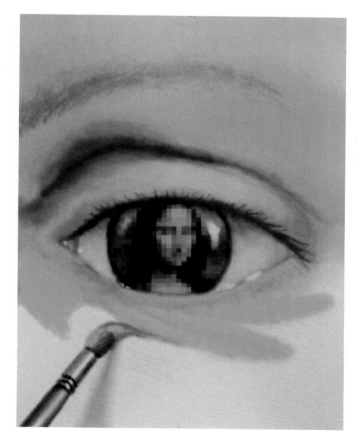

49. Digitized Mona Lisa. *1987.*
AT&T Truevision Image Processing System.
Courtesy Robert F. Tinney,
Robert Tinney Graphics,
Baton Rouge, Louisiana.

much painting. A moving point forms a line. A speeding arrow and the light of a moving flashlight demonstrate lines formed by connecting moving points in space. Line may consist of actual marks, drawn with pencil, pen, or brush, or it can refer to the outside of a shape. In paintings, lines often occur by contrast; lines may be drawn, but also the edges formed by contrasts of light and shadow or of different colors and shapes suggest lines. Whether it can actually be seen or is only implied, line undoubtedly is one of the artist's most eloquent tools, enclosing space, suggesting mass or volume, and creating a feeling of movement. Lines may vary from thick to thin to convey shape. Where light falls on the contours of an object, the outlines may be lightly drawn. Where the shadow is deepest, thicker lines can suggest and provide emphasis, while grouped lines create illusions of volume and shadow.

Quality of Line   Line also has the potential to convey emotion, and in this role it is one of the artist's most valuable tools. Line may be drawn forcefully (with strong, thick strokes) to focus a directional thrust, as to the apex of Elaine de Kooning's (b. 1920; **[50]**) composition, or nerv-

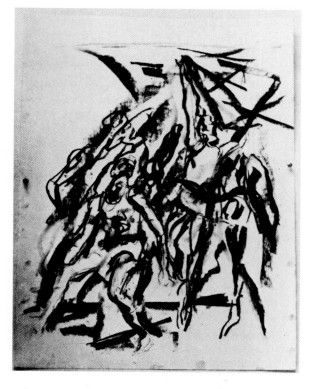

50. *Elaine de Kooning.* Basketball Players.
1979–1980. Charcoal, 28 × 22″ (71.1 × 55.9 cm).

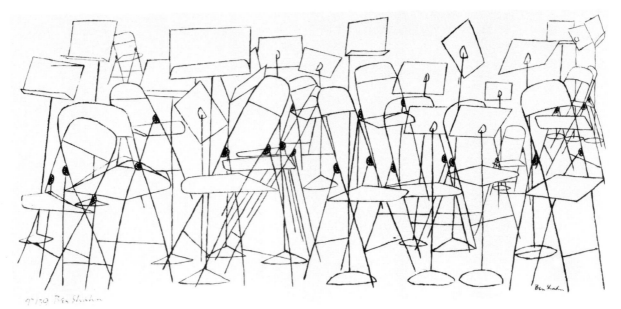

51. *Ben Shahn.* Silent Music. *1950. Serigraph printed in black; composition,*
17⅛ × 35⅛″ (44 × 89 cm). Collection, Museum of Modern Art, New York (purchase).

ously (with uneven, broken strokes), or smoothly (with stable, consistent strokes) to create a mood. In contrast, Ben Shahn (1898–1969) in *Silent Music* **[51]** uses a modified action line. This method is derived from the games children play in making a drawing while hardly lifting the tool from the paper to assure continuity of line and the communication of a sense of action.

The Machine Line We have depended on machines and provided systems for instructing them at least since the Industrial Revolution. Mechanical lines do not vary in thickness or value, but when machines such as computers are programmed to change their direction at random intervals, the design appears progressively more disorganized. The machine line has a special new character **[52]**, very different from the artist's variable line with its potential for thick and thin, dark and light, straight or free-form. That "machine" character, hardly yet explored, now serves as a fine counterpoint to the artist's line.

Calligraphy Line is basic not only to drawing and most painting but also to **calligraphy,** the art of decorative line, as in handwriting. Calligraphy has existed for centuries in the Orient and the Middle East, where calligraphy and painting are intimately related. The processes are produced with the same brushes and similar brush strokes and are frequently found in the same work of art. It we compare the charcoal work in

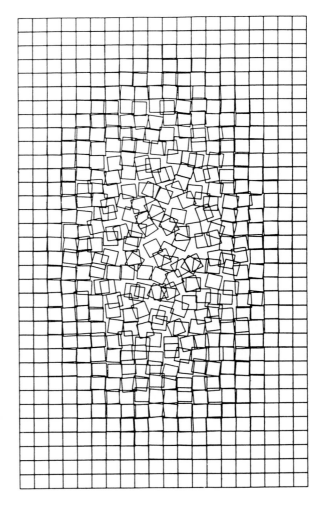

52. *William J. Kolomyjec.* Boxes I. *1980.*

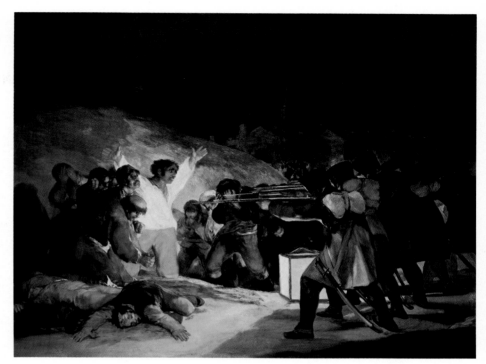

53. *Francisco Goya.* Execution of the Madrileños on May 3, 1808. *1814. Oil on canvas, 8'8¾" × 11'3¾" (2.66 × 3.45 m). Prado, Madrid.*

de Kooning's drawing of the basketball players **[50]** with the *Siege of Belgrade* by an unknown artist in 1558 **[14]**, we can see that both works, though quite different in style, are represented with clear strokes and emphatic lines, which produce an effect of vigor. Closer examination of the Turkish painting, however, also reveals very little difference in the quality of line between the calligraphic painted messages and the linear landscape details.

Line as Direction and Emphasis Another

kind of line is seen in the painting *Execution of the Madrileños on May 3, 1808* **[53]**, also known as *The Third of May, 1808,* by Francisco Goya (1746–1828). Here the contours of various shapes imply lines that serve to guide the viewer to the central theme: the brutal execution of hostages randomly chosen by the French troops of Napoleon occupying Madrid, in reprisal for the uprising of an unruly Spanish mob the day before. The directional lines are so strong that we can diagram them **[54]**. The contour of the hill leads us down through the body of the principal sol-

54. *Diagram of Figure 53.*

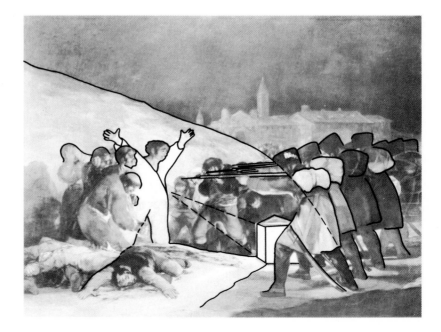

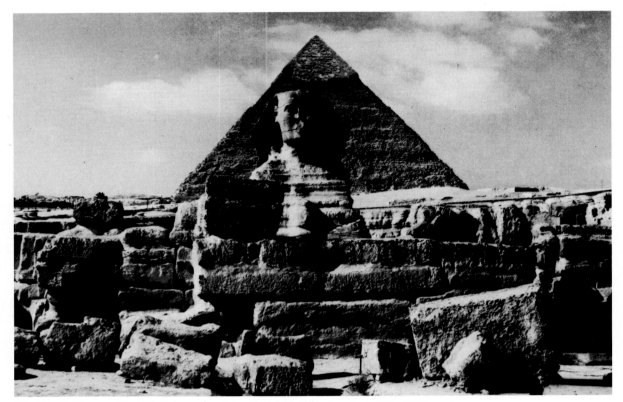

55. *The Sphinx (c. 2540–2514 B.C.) and the Pyramid of Chefren (c. 2590–2568 B.C.).*

dier, then up through the saber at his waist to the rifles pointing at the light-toned civilian whose arms are outstretched—as if on an invisible cross. You may find many other contour lines that reinforce this movement to focus our attention on the drama. Although the linear element is rarely so easy to see, it exists in most works of art.

Perception of Shape and Mass Line can be also followed in three-dimensional works of art, suggested by the silhouette of a figure, the upward thrust of a vault, or the long horizontal edge of a building. For example, the clear-cut shapes of the Great Pyramids [55] present a strong, simple geometry of linear planes, shapes that dominate the Egyptian desert and are visible for many miles. They perhaps represent the most familiar triangular silhouettes of all time.

In contrast, recent advances in our knowledge of optical laws have led to the complex new use of line in which images seem to shift as the viewer moves. In the hands of an artist such as Bridget Riley (b. 1931), repetitious lines of precisely equal weight, equally spaced, can create visual illusions that appear to advance and retreat as we observe the work [56].

Shape and Mass

In painting, in drawing, and sometimes in sculpture, any area enclosed by a line is usually perceived as a whole entity or **shape,** set apart from its surroundings. Shape can also be made to stand out through the use of strong contrasts in color, value, or texture. Shapes can be geometric or organic, symmetrical or asymmetrical, related to known objects or nonobjective. Artists may use shape, like line, to express different moods. The playful shapes in the whimsical **mobile [57]** by Alexander Calder (1898–1979) create a gay mood, reminiscent of a school of fish in formation. A truly original artist, Calder created highly intellectual and controlled works that delight us with the variety of movements of the abstract shapes as they interplay when the entire piece is set in motion. Many artists such as Calder evolve distinctive vocabularies of shapes they often repeat.

To the novice in art, shape is always easy to see. Few beginners, however, take the time really to look at the space around the shapes, which is generally ignored as mere background. Many times, however, these same areas, called **negative space,** are as important to the artwork as the positive shapes we usually see first. Artists

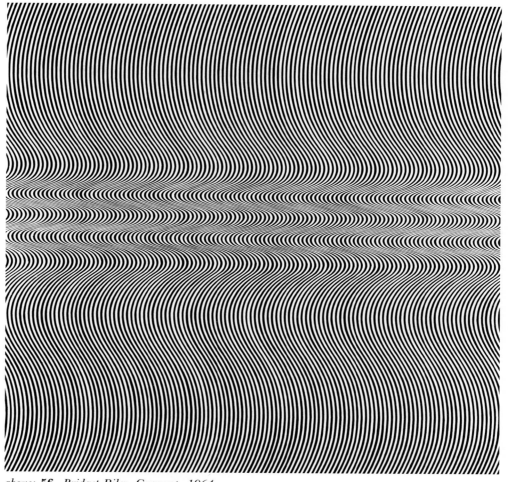

above: **56.** *Bridget Riley.* Current. *1964.*
Synthetic polymer paint on composition board, 4′10⅜″ × 4′10⅞″ (1.48 × 1.5 m).
Collection, Museum of Modern Art, New York (Philip Johnson Fund).

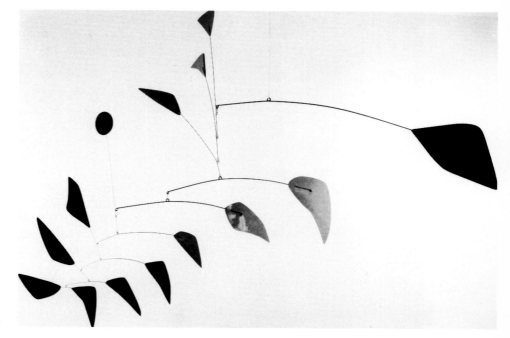

right: **57.** *Alexander Calder.*
Big Red. *1959. Painted*
sheet metal and steel wire,
6′2″ × 9′6″ (1.88 × 2.9 m).
Whitney Museum of American Art,
New York.

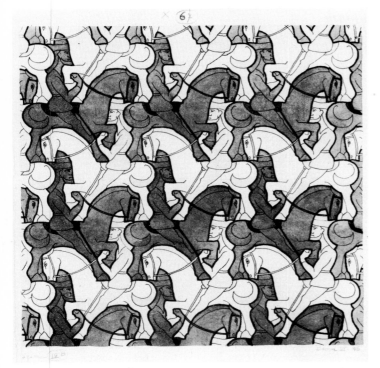

above: **58.** *M. C. Escher.* Study of Regular Division of the Plane with Horsemen. *1946.*
India ink and watercolor, 12 × 9″ (30 × 23 cm).
Collection Haags Gemeentemuseum, The Hague.

manipulate relationships of the figure to its ground to increase visual excitement and to take advantage of the different ways all of us perceive shapes in space. M. C. Escher is well known for his rather remarkable ability to manipulate negative-positive spaces into visually provocative new relationships **[58]**.

Converting Shape to Mass The term *shape* usually refers to defined areas in a painting or drawing, while **mass** is used more often in discussions of sculpture and architecture. However, the term *mass* may also occasionally be applied to paintings where the artist has concentrated upon the illusion of mass. During the Renaissance, many artists tested the newly discovered principles of geometry and linear perspective and produced more solid-looking forms on a two-dimensional surface than had been seen for a thousand years. In addition, many artists used heavy shadows in their paintings to exaggerate the appearance of three-dimensional weight. For example, the draperies massed in shadow on the left in the painting *The Artist in His Studio* by Jan Vermeer (1632–1675) form a strong contrast with the artist's model positioned in the bright central area **[59]**. The

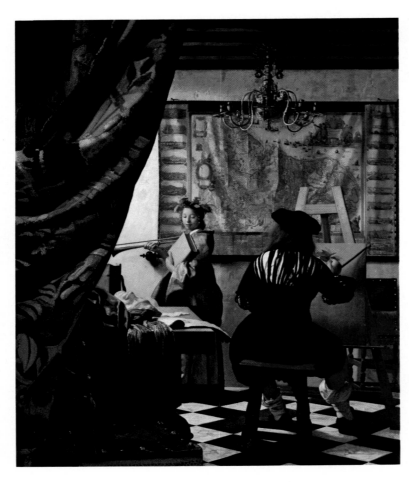

59. *Jan Vermeer.*
The Artist in His Studio.
c. 1665–1670. Oil on canvas,
47¼ × 39⅜″ (120 × 100 cm).
Kunsthistorisches Museum, Vienna.

above right: **60.** *Interior, Abbey Church of St.-Denis, Paris, 1144.*

below right: **61.** *Antoine Pevsner.*
Developable Column. *1942. Brass*
and oxidized bronze; height 20¾″
(53 cm), diameter of base 19⅜″ (49 cm).
Collection, Museum of Modern Art,
New York (purchase).

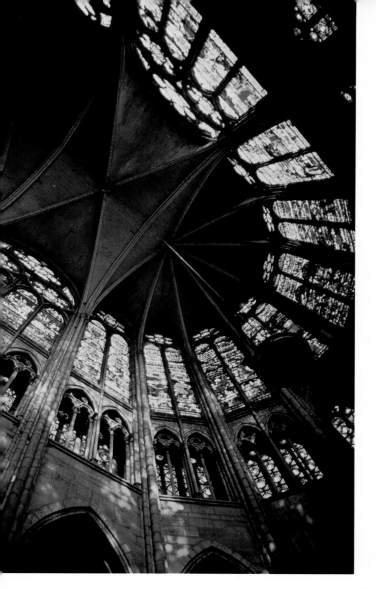

woman creates a focal point, which ties together the geometric shapes of the furniture and the room.

Mass can also be intentionally emphasized, as in the pyramids of Egypt, which were built to ensure a comfortable immortality for the pharaohs [55]. On the other hand, the sense of mass may be reduced or denied altogether by creating perforations, or openings, in a structure. A **Gothic** church like St.-Denis [60], an expression of spiritual aspirations toward heaven, appears light and fragile. Glass windows fill the spaces between structural supports, and the cathedral's strong vertical lines, just like those of the *Developable Column* [61] by Antoine Pevsner (1886–1962), imply a weight light enough to rise into the air. Pevsner's column was designed to simulate an upward twisting force. The emphatic silhouette of the sculpture plunges through space, while the heavy mass of the Sphinx appears stable, eternal, and static. Gaston Lachaise (1882–1935), whose wife served as his lifetime model [62], utilized the partial-figure concept in the creation of frankly erotic sculptures. Recalling the prehistoric Willendorf Venus [25], the exaggerated proportions of the reproductive female zones are focused in the fractioned figure.

below: **62.** *Gaston Lachaise.* Torso. *1932. Bronze, height 9½″ (24 cm). Lachaise Foundation. Courtesy Robert Schoelkopf Gallery, New York.*

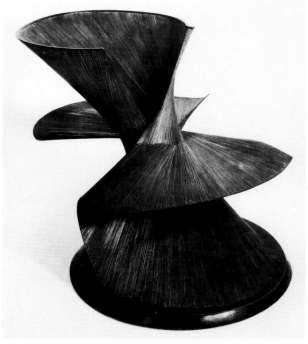

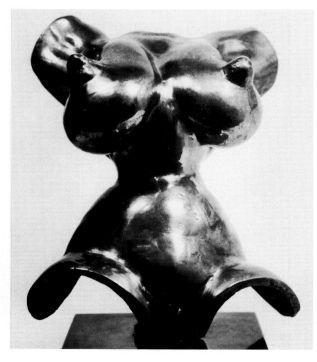

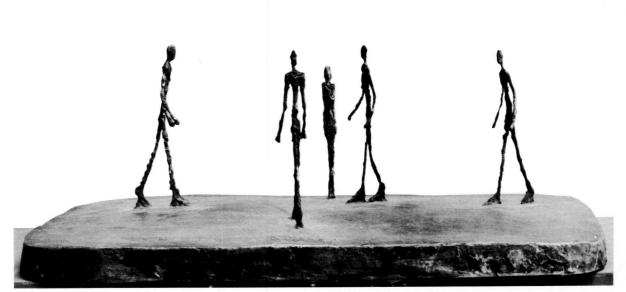

63. *Alberto Giacometti.* City Square. *1949. Bronze; base 25 × 17" (64 × 43 cm), height of tallest figure 8" (20 cm). Pierre Matisse Gallery, New York.*

Paradoxically, the long, open figures by Alberto Giacometti (1901–1966) in *City Square* **[63]** utilize so little solid material that we become more aware of the spaces the figures occupy than the small mass of matter that forms them. Such works investigate relationships of positive and negative space, as well as of mass. Giacometti is known for his attenuated figures—thin masses corroded by time. The indistinctness of the details and their apparent lack of weight suggest a spiritual isolation that projects loneliness.

Value

The degree of lightness or darkness of a surface is referred to as its **value.** In the visual arts

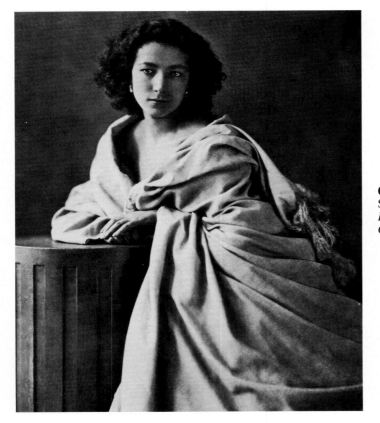

64. *Nadar (Gaspard Felix Tournachon).* Sarah Bernhardt. *1859. Photograph. International Museum of Photography, George Eastman House, Rochester, N.Y.*

value can range from the darkest to the very palest tones or from pure black through shades of gray to pure white. Variations and contrasts in values can be effective whether the artist is working with colors or black and white. For example, a photographic portrait of Sarah Bernhardt **[64]** shows a full range of values, from white through grays to black; the strongest contrasts of tone (the lightest and the darkest elements) are placed near the center of the photograph for dramatic emphasis. On the other hand, in the **conté** crayon drawing of *Interior with Stove* **[65]** by Charles Sheeler (1883–1965), we find a somewhat different treatment of tones. Although pure white and intense black values exist together in this work, the total effect is generally soft, because most of the picture is made up of delicate gradations of medium to dark tones.

However, Edouard Manet's (1832–1883) *The Execution of the Emperor Maximilian* **[66]** is strident and harsh. The contrasts in this work, concentrated black-and-white tones, have been reserved for the execution, while the mid-range values serve only as backdrop for the main event.

This pivotal painting by Manet may be compared with Goya's *The Third of May, 1808* **[53]**, a

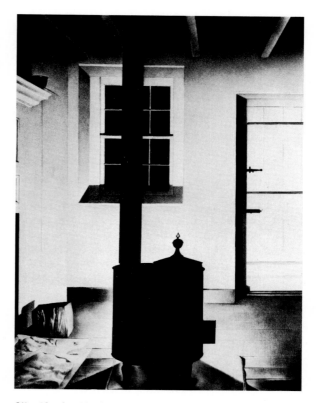

65. *Charles Sheeler.* Interior with Stove. *1932. Conté crayon, 25⅝ × 20¾″ (73 × 52 cm). Collection, Joanna T. Steichen, New York.*

66. *Edouard Manet.*
The Execution of the
Emperor Maximilian. *1867.*
Oil on canvas, 8′3″ × 10′
(2.52 × 3.05 m).
Kunsthalle, Mannheim.

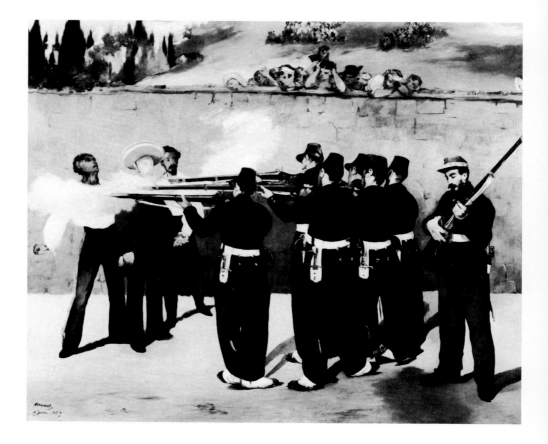

Exploring Art Through Technology

Radiography: Clues to the Past

In contrast to working methods in painting that had prevailed at least since the Renaissance, Edouard Manet rarely prepared preliminary drawings. His etchings sometimes served as sketches. Then he worked directly in oils on canvas. He said to his friend Antonin Proust: "There's just one real thing. To get down what one sees at the first shot. When it's there, it's there. When it's not there, one starts over. Everything else is nonsense." X-ray analysis of his paintings in combination with historical records shows us how difficult it was for Manet to get it right the first time and how he even on occasion reworked his canvases after they had gone on public view.

Anyone who experienced the frustration of sitting for a portrait by Manet saw one canvas after another discarded in the artist's attempt to capture what he envisioned. Manet would also scrape the pigment off the canvas when certain passages bothered him, as x-ray analysis shows us in several of his paintings. Sometimes he added strips of canvas to a painting to change the composition; conversely, at other times he cut one work into several, as was the case with his *Episode in a Bull Ring* shown in the 1864 Salon.

According to the press of the time, *Episode in a Bull Ring* showed several figures—one lying dead and others in the ring with tiers of spectators above. Manet seemed to demonstrate no understanding of perspective and the painting was therefore widely mocked. *Episode in a Bull Ring* disappeared afterward and does not exist today. One art historian has been able to prove through x-ray and laboratory analysis that two paintings, *The Dead Man* ([**67**] National Gallery of Art, Washington) and *The Bullfight* (Frick Collection, New York), which share the same border of the same canvas, were in fact segments of that original painting. Manet apparently cut and reworked the original painting into at least these two independent paintings. Further x-ray analysis shows that there originally was a bull in what is now *The Dead Man*, which, incidentally, was exhibited not long after the storm over *The Episode in a Bull Ring* and has since been hailed as one of Manet's masterpieces. We now know through study of the development of at least one of his masterpieces how hard Manet struggled to gain the appearance of spontaneity—a discovery we made through the benefits of technology.

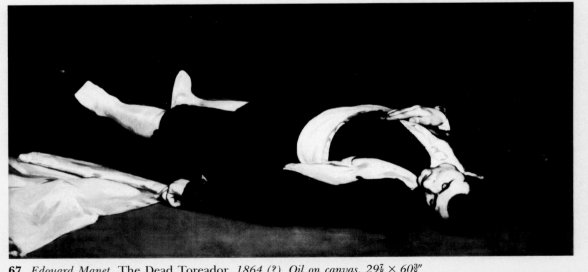

67. *Edouard Manet.* The Dead Toreador. *1864 (?). Oil on canvas, $29\frac{7}{8} \times 60\frac{3}{8}''$ (75.9 × 153.3 cm). National Gallery of Art, Washington (Widener Collection).*

work with a similar theme, and one that undoubtedly served as a reference for Manet; like Goya, he closely followed newspaper accounts and photographs. Both these works dealing with execution reinforce their message by portraying machine-like executioners set against strong contrasts in value.

Gradation Scale A value-gradation scale helps us to understand how we perceive tones

[68]. Even when tones are identical in value, they may appear quite different when the value of their surrounding tone is changed. The phenomenon is evident not only with black and white and gray tones, but also with color.

Variations in values can be used like line to guide the viewer's eye or to give a sense of movement. For example, an area of sharp contrast in a painting will attract our attention. Three or four such areas, if related in a composition, may cause our eye to travel from one to another, giving a sense of movement. Values are often used to create an emotional response. Sharply contrasting colors or blacks and whites can express dramatic tension or excitement. The portrait of the *Mona Lisa* by Leonardo [18] produces a dramatic emotional impact not only because the range of values is wide but also because the artist has effectively used lighting to focus on our center of interest. However, the areas of dark shadows in Leonardo's paintings are equally important. They are never voids of darkness but instead suggest details that our imaginations can enlarge upon. Light-toned values with few contrasts, on the other hand, can give a hazy or mystic feeling to a composition.

Only with illumination by natural or artificial light to create highlights and shadows is it possible to represent form. As light changes, the entire character of the subject may be revealed or concealed. Whether portraying the geometric shapes of cylinder, sphere, and cube or the human figure, the artist can emphasize shape and mass by manipulating tones of value.

The use of light and dark in a painting to represent the effect of light and shadow in nature is called **chiaroscuro,** an Italian word meaning "light and dark." This method of using light and shadow to reveal the modeling of three-dimensional forms was common to Western painting from the Renaissance to the 19th century. Leonardo developed a smokelike haze called **sfumato** to envelop his forms, resulting in transitions from light to dark so gradual as to be imperceptible [18]. In this technique, light seems to come from a source within the painting, creating soft contours.

Though Western painters have used value relationships for many effects, since the Renaissance they have been preoccupied with how contrasting values and light patterns play over solid objects to create the illusion of three-dimensional form on a flat surface. The patterns formed by light and dark shapes can evoke moods and emotions. Art works executed with limited gradations of tones, as in the flat, decorative style of Turkish paintings [14], are keyed to values that tend to heighten mood. Images limited to light shades are termed **high key**; they are associated with areas of intense light such as beach scenes or scrubbed-clean places like hospitals. **Low-key** locales shown in dark shades typically include night views of streets and intimate bars.

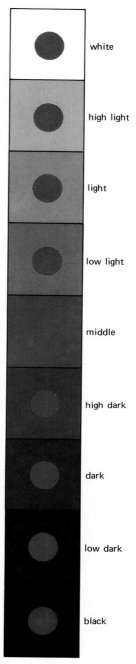

white

high light

light

low light

middle

high dark

dark

low dark

black

68. *The gray scale.*

Color

Perhaps the most effective of all available art elements is **color,** which is what we perceive when our eyes sense light reflected from an object. Artists have used color from prehistoric times, generally reproducing the natural, or local, color they saw. The science of color has developed more slowly. Although the Greeks as early as 400 B.C. realized that the apparent color of an object changes with the color of light that falls on it, it was not until the mid-17th century that the English mathematician Sir Isaac Newton discovered that white light passed through a prism is broken into a whole spectrum, or scale, of colors **[69]**.

Newton deduced from this discovery that white is actually a mixture of all colors. The prism fragments the light, breaking it into component color rays. When we see a rainbow with violet at one edge, moving step by step through the spectrum to red at the other, we are seeing an example of the same phenomenon. In this situation, however, instead of being fragmented by a prism, the sunlight is broken apart as it passes through the raindrops. Furthermore, Newton discovered that when various quantities of red, blue, and green light rays are projected onto a single area, they combine to form white light. These three colors of light—red, blue, and green—are therefore known as the **additive primary colors.** Conversely, when white light is projected through the **subtractive primary colors**—cyan (blue), magenta, and yellow—onto a single surface, all color is subtracted from the white light, resulting in black.

Hue, Value, Intensity　The colors, or **hues,** of the **spectrum** are produced by light rays, while artists' colors come from substances called **pigments.** Pigments absorb certain light rays and reflect others. Blue pigment, for example, absorbs almost all but the blue rays; blue paint therefore reflects the blue waves and we see blue. No pigment can produce as pure a color as the prism, so no paints have ever achieved the brilliance of light rays. Similar hues may reproduce differently. For example, one pure alizarin crimson (deep red) pigment may reflect more yellow rays than another red pigment, and colors look different under different kinds of illumination.

The **color wheel** is composed of the major colors in the spectrum plus other colors achieved by mixing the main colors. The twelve colors on

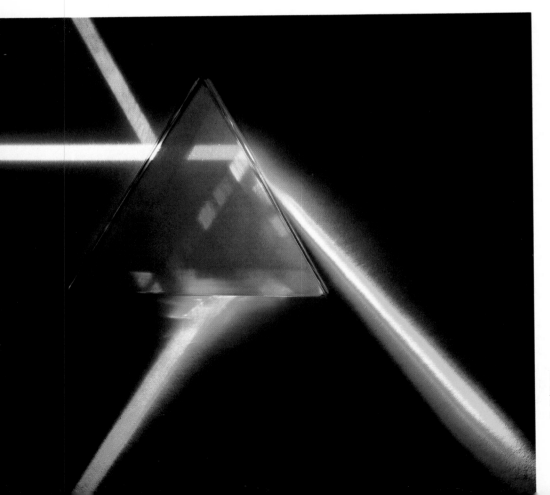

69. *A ray of white light projected through a prism separates into the hues of the rainbow.*

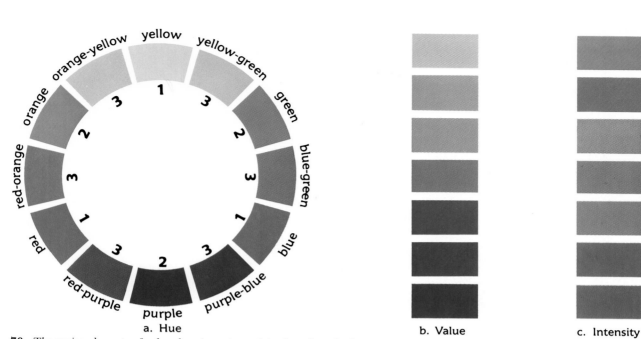

70. *The major elements of color: hue (as expressed in the color wheel), value and intensity.*

a. Hue   b. Value   c. Intensity

the wheel [70] can be divided into three groups: **primary**—blue, yellow, and red—those colors that cannot be produced by mixing other hues; **secondary,** combinations of primaries; and **tertiary,** or intermediaries. The artist can use mixtures of the three primary colors to create all other colors on the color wheel. When two primary hues are mixed, ideally, secondary hues are produced, although the proportions of each may vary with the pigments. The three secondary colors are created in this way: blue mixed with yellow yields green; blue mixed with red becomes purple; and red mixed with yellow makes orange. There are six tertiary colors, each a result of mixing a primary color with a nearby secondary color. Thus, red and orange make red-orange, orange and yellow produce orange-yellow, and purple and blue yield purple-blue, and so on.

Complementary colors are those that appear opposite each other on the color wheel. For example, blue and orange are complementary colors; so are red and green. Adjacent colors on the color wheel, such as blue and blue-green, are called **analogous** colors.

Each color varies in **value,** which ranges from light to dark, just as uncolored values may range from white through a series of grays to black [68]. A very light blue, for example, is high on the value scale and is called a **tint,** while a dark, low value of blue is called **shade** [70]. We may note that color values and hues may appear quite different depending on the local values and hues around them.

Intensity, or saturation, refers to the purity of a color. A pure blue, as it appears in the color wheel and as near the spectrum blue as possible, is said to have a full intensity, or saturation. Color complements neutralize the intensity of each other when they are combined in varied amounts; when mixed in equal amounts they create a neutral gray, but pigment impurities often make this gray difficult to achieve. The addition of shades of gray will also neutralize color intensity.

The three major elements of color may be summarized as follows:

1. *Hue:* an identifiable color on the color wheel and the spectrum; a specified wavelength of spectrum color
   a. primary hues: red, yellow, blue
   b. secondary hues: green, orange, purple
   c. tertiary hues: yellow-green, blue-purple, and so on
2. *Value:* the degree of lightness or darkness of a color
3. *Intensity or saturation:* the degree of purity of a hue; ideally, a pure hue reflects no other color rays

Artists achieve infinite color variations by mixing colored pigments with one another and with black and white. Even more vibrant colors than

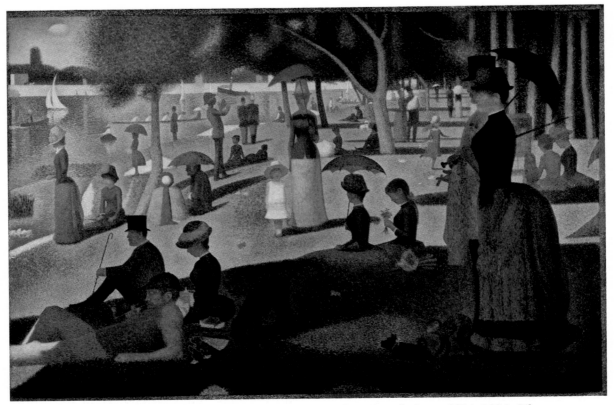

above: **71.** *Georges Seurat.* Sunday Afternoon on the Island of La Grande Jatte. *1884–1886. Oil on canvas,*
6'9¾" × 10'1¼" (2.08 × 3.08 m). Art Institute of Chicago (Helen Birch Bartlett Memorial Collection).

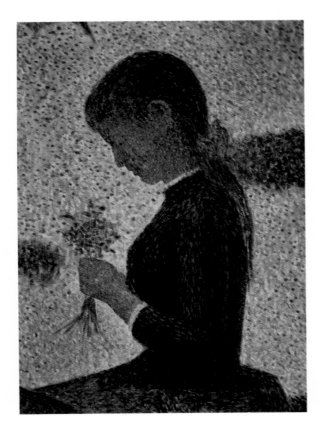

pigment mixtures seem to occur when dots of pure analogous color are placed next to one another, with the result that from some distance they appear to the viewer to be blended. This practice of optical color mixture was introduced by **Impressionists** in the 19th century. **Post-Impressionist** Georges Seurat (1851–1891) advanced these techniques further when he restricted his **palette**—the pigments he chose to use—mainly to the color primaries, applying tiny dots of color in a method he called **Pointillism.** Examination of a detail of *La Grande Jatte* [71] reveals a dot pattern very similar to the pattern shown in modern four-color printing—significant because it shows how artists often foreshadow technology. Even for shadows, Seurat used no black [72].

Artists make use of color schemes, or arrangements of certain colors, to produce special effects. In a color scheme where complementary

left: **72.** *Georges Seurat.* Sunday Afternoon on the Island of La Grande Jatte *(detail).*

colors are used next to each other, the effect will be one of strong contrast and emotional excitement. An analogous scheme made up of colors close to one another on the wheel has a subdued physical or emotional effect. Schemes with light colors, or tints, evoke different emotional responses from those with dark colors.

Such reactions appear to be almost universal— some colors depress us while others lighten our spirits. There is a sense of joy in *Vir Heroicus Sublimis* [73] by Barnett Newman (1905–1970), with its variations of reds. Psychologists believe that the satisfactions most of us associate with these hot colors ultimately go back to the pleasure given to us by the warmth of a fire on a wintry night or by the sun itself.

Color can be used symbolically as well as emotionally. The Virgin Mary, Queen of Heaven, is traditionally shown in a blue cloak because the color has come to symbolize heaven. Unlike emotional responses to color, however, symbolic color varies from culture to culture. For example, a particular color may symbolize mourning in one culture and joy in another. When complementary colors or colors of equal value are placed side by side, they seem to intensify one another's hue, a phenomenon known as **simultaneous contrast.** If, however, a neutral gray shape is placed on a yellow background, the gray appears violet, a phenomenon called **successive contrast.** There are many other optical effects like these that we have come to recognize, but none so familiar as rubbing our eyes and seeing

flashes of color. No one is entirely sure why these phenomena occur, only that our view of color is linked to the retina of the human eye as well as to the effects of the light.

Impressionist and Post-Impressionist painters often tried to duplicate the usual effect of sunlight on us by placing small brush strokes of contrasting colors next to each other [71]. Vibrations in the eye from these painted colors heightened the effect of dancing light. Artists today use light itself as a medium, trapped in neon sculptures, or in works to be viewed under changing light [222]. While colors are almost always dependent on existent light to create hues, under certain other conditions, special color effects can occur. For instance, after staring fixedly at the red shapes in *Vir Heroicus Sublimis* [73], when you shift your eyes quickly to a white surface, the complementary color to red, a definite green, will appear. This visual phenomenon is called **afterimage.**

Reducing color to its elemental characteristics [46], Mondrian generally simplified his paintings to the primary hues. Working in this way, he used colors at full intensity, and the apparent differences in their distance from the viewer come from the different sizes of the color areas and their relative warmth and coolness. The density and weight of his colors also affect the apparent balance. Large areas appear closer, small ones farther away. Warm colors—red and yellow, colors we associate with the sun—are dominant, tending to move forward toward the

73. *Barnett Newman.* Vir Heroicus Sublimus. *1950–1951. Oil on canvas, 7'11⅜" × 17'8¼" (2.4 × 5.4 m). Collection, Museum of Modern Art, New York (gift of Mr. and Mrs. Ben Heller).*

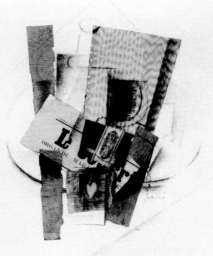

74. *Georges Braque.* Le Courrier. *1913.*
Collage, 20 × 22½" (51 × 57 cm).
Philadelphia Museum of Art
(A. E. Gallatin Collection).

eye. Cool colors—such as blue, like icy water—tend to recede from the viewer. It sometimes surprises a beginner studying art to realize that Mondrian often spent months determining slight differences in color areas. His works are so orchestrated that one cannot imagine any alteration to one area that would not have to be matched with corresponding changes in the others to balance the effect.

Because of the great number of visual effects that can be achieved through color and because of its effect on our emotions, and even well-being, color is an expressive device of endless excitement and visual variety. Although we think of color as the particular concern of the painter, it is also of vital concern to designers in other areas of art such as interiors, fashion, advertising, and theater.

Texture

The surface quality of an object, or its **texture,** appeals to our senses of both touch and sight. Nature is lavish with surfaces, which artists sometimes try to duplicate or even exaggerate in their work. Such textures, however, are not real—not tactile; they are only implied. An example of a real texture is an orange skin; a close look at one reveals true hills and valleys, which even compare with the surface of the moon. Paint may be applied to suggest the smoothness of human skin or of a river-polished rock. The sculptor grinds and polishes stone to simulate the sheen of satin. Rough, smooth and shining,

dull, hard, and soft texture are contrasted to increase the expressiveness of shapes and to avoid monotony. Infatuation with texture and with the tactile quality of oil paint has driven some artists to pile on pigment, creating frenzied surfaces, as in Van Gogh's *Starry Night* **[22]**. Often painters achieve a desired effect through the addition of actual textures like newspaper cutouts and pasted-on surfaces, that is, **collage,** a medium invented in the 20th century. See *Le Courrier* by Georges Braque (1882–1963; **[74]**).

Many artists have forsaken traditional use of brush and paint to create new tactile effects. **Abstract Expressionists** earlier in this century worked with heavy, irregular strokes as they became involved with the physical process of painting, following the lead of Pollock, who poured paint from the can directly onto prepared but unstretched canvas **[10]**. Such surfaces reveal unusual textures. Helen Frankenthaler (b. 1928), in contrast, has chosen to work on unstretched canvas surfaces that are not prepared—not coated with a **gesso** (thinned plaster-like composition) primer in the technique traditional since the Renaissance. Therefore, her paints sink into unprimed canvas, creating pools of deep color. The variations in dye surfaces of *Formation* **[75]** were achieved by sponging thinned acrylic dyes onto her large canvas areas.

Since the period of the Impressionists, sculptors also have been moving away from the traditional smooth surfaces of well-worked materials. August Rodin (1840–1917; *see* **194**) was said to have worked by flickering candlelight, slowly moved over his models, in order to simulate the effect of broken light sought by the Impressionists. In the 20th century, Giacometti's roughened sculptural surfaces intrigue us, perhaps because they suggest the corrosion of time **[63]**.

As much concerned with texture as are the other arts, architecture is also dependent on varieties of materials, such as glass, slate, marble, brick, and wood, to provide pleasing surfaces. The huge Gothic cathedral of Milan **[76]**, one of the largest in the world, was designed with setbacks and carved details that create pockets of shadows and highlights to add textural interest to what might otherwise have been a large, monotonous area. The various setbacks of structural parts and the open stonework on the façade of the cathedral are typical of the Gothic style, as are the sculpture in high niches and the carved decoration over the roof, which can be seen only by the birds or, perhaps, God.

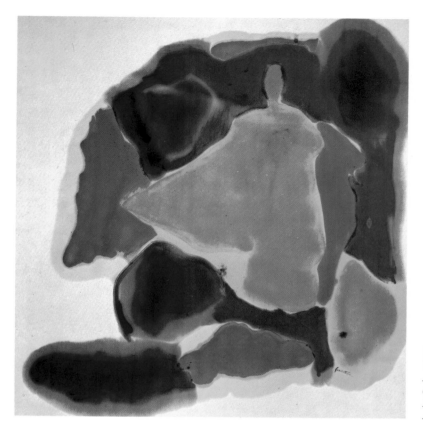

left: **75.** *Helen Frankenthaler.*
Formation. 1963 (4?).
Acrylic on canvas 6'4" × 5'5"
(1.93 × 1.65 m).
Private collection. Courtesy
André Emmerich Gallery, New York.

below: **76.** *Milan Cathedral. Begun 1368.*

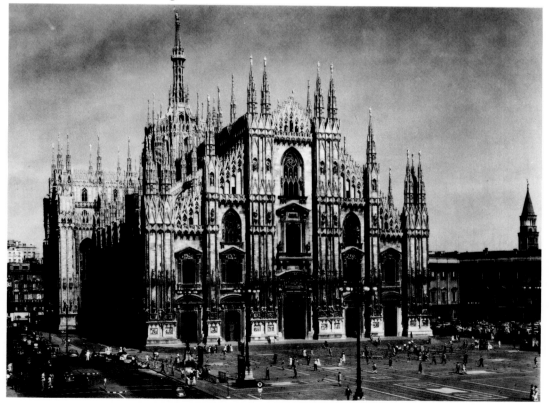

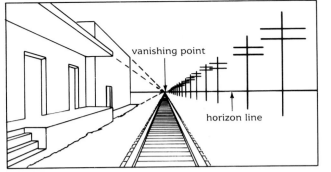

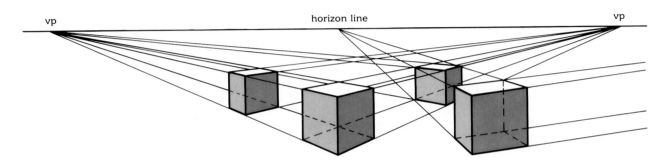

left: **77.** *One-point perspective.*

below: **78.** *Two-point perspective with multiple vanishing points.*

Space

A sense of space depends on what occupies it. The layperson sees space as emptiness. The artist regards space as a challenging arena in which to arrange forms and colors. The visual arts are often known as *spatial arts* because their elements are arranged in space. In contrast, the arts of theater, dance, music, and poetry are *temporal arts,* comprehended in sequences of time.

Perspective In two-dimensional art forms, such as drawing, painting, prints, and photography, the artist often wishes to create an illusion of three-dimensional space, or depth. Images are rendered on a two-dimensional surface, as in Vermeer's *The Artist in His Studio* **[59]**, through the device of **perspective,** to make them appear to vary in distance from the viewer. When we think of the term *perspective* we usually mean **linear perspective,** said to be a discovery of the Italian Renaissance architect Brunelleschi during his work on Florence Cathedral, influencing our way of creating and looking at art for centuries. In linear perspective the artist uses lines, either implied or actual, to give an illusion of great depth on a flat surface. The main rules of linear perspective follow:

1. All objects appear to grow smaller the farther away from the viewer they are.
2. Parallel lines receding into the distance

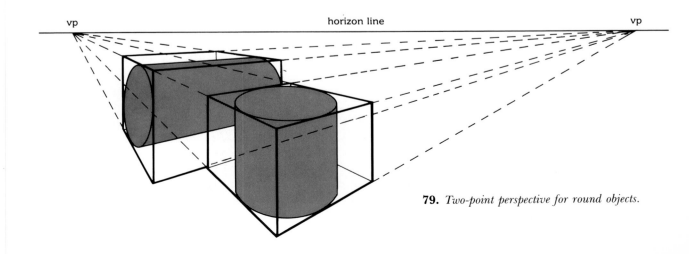

79. *Two-point perspective for round objects.*

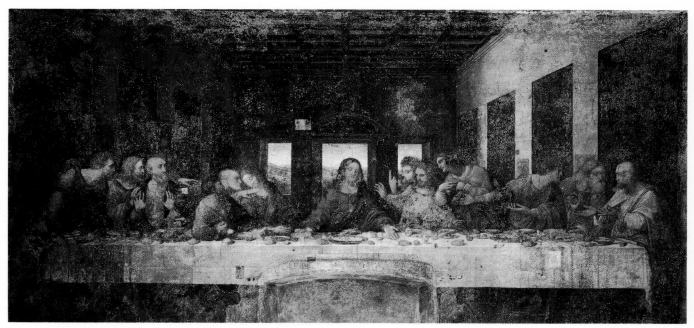

80. *Leonardo da Vinci.* The Last Supper. *1495–1498. Fresco, 14'5" × 28'¼" (4.39 × 8.61 m). Refectory, Sta. Maria delle Grazie, Milan.*

appear to converge. The point at which they seem to meet is called the **vanishing point.** Horizontal parallel lines cannot converge.

3. In **one-point perspective** the viewer appears to be looking at the object from directly in front of it, and all nonfrontal sets of parallel lines, if extended, meet at one vanishing point (VP) **[77]**.

4. In **two-point perspective** the viewer appears to be looking at the object from an angle so that no side is frontal; this must involve two vanishing points, one for each set of parallel lines receding in space. Objects viewed at different angles have their own vanishing points, which result in multiple vanishing points on the horizon line **[78]**.

5. Vanishing points are positioned along an imaginary line called the **horizon line**—generally, our eye level from level ground. Parallel lines above the horizon appear to converge down toward it. Parallel lines below the horizon appear to converge up toward it.

6. The horizon line may be arbitrarily raised or lowered by the artist to make the objects appear below (a bird's-eye view) or above (a worm's-eye view) the viewer's eye.

7. Round and irregularly shaped forms that do not have parallel sides are viewed in

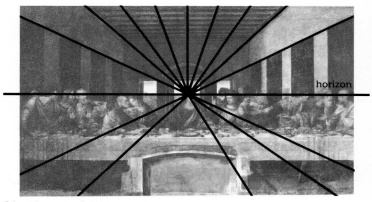

81. *Diagram of Figure 80, showing one-point perspective.*

perspective as if enclosed in regularly shaped blocks **[79]**.

Leonardo's *The Last Supper* **[80]** is often regarded as a **classic** example of one-point perspective **[81]**. The painting occupies the upper end wall of a long room. The lines of the walls, ceiling, and table in the painting continue the lines of the room and converge from above and below the imaginary horizon line toward a single point behind the frontal figure of Christ. His divine calm at the center of the painting thus becomes its focal point and is in dramatic contrast with the writhing, agitated forms of the disciples to his left and right.

The system of perspective at work in the photograph of Rockefeller Center [82] is a relatively recent extension of linear perspective brought to our consciousness by the camera and our ability to view tall structures from great heights or, as in this case, from the air. In this dense composition one vanishing point lies far below the base of the buildings; two others are outside the image on a horizon line far above the photograph, emphasizing the endlessness of urban centers [83]. This system is known as **three-point perspective.**

The Romans had only elementary knowledge of linear perspective. Then artists reported their surroundings from many **viewing positions,** or **vantage points,** which they combined into one single rendering with resultant inconsistencies in perspective [84]. After the Renaissance artists learned to confine their drawing to a single viewing position.

Many contemporary artists choose to ignore linear perspective or may combine it with other methods of producing spatial effects. The Cubists, for instance, rejected the rules of linear perspective altogether to create a different kind of space. In *Three Musicians* [85], Picasso used several vantage points and aspects of each figure, assembled with flat, overlapping shapes. He was not concerned with creating a three-dimensional illusion any more than were Egyptian painters, who combined front, top, and side views in order to show the clearest views of an

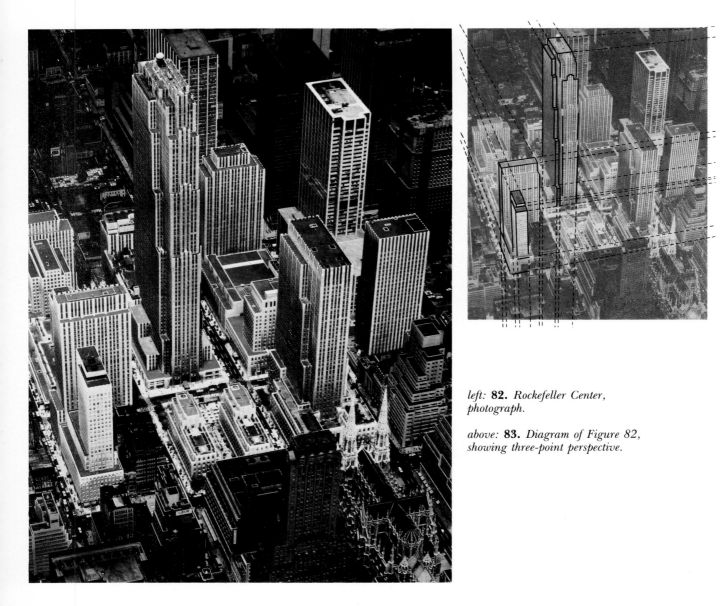

left: **82.** *Rockefeller Center, photograph.*

above: **83.** *Diagram of Figure 82, showing three-point perspective.*

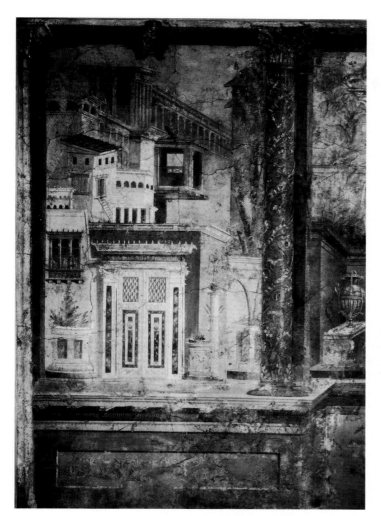

84. *Wall painting from the cubiculum of the villa at Boscoreale, Italy. 1st century* B.C. *Metropolitan Museum of Art, New York (Rogers Fund, 1903).*

85. *Pablo Picasso.*
Three Musicians.
1921 (summer).
Oil on canvas, 6'7" × 7'3¾"
(2.01 × 2.23 m). Collection,
Museum of Modern Art,
New York
(Mrs. Simon Guggenheim
Fund).

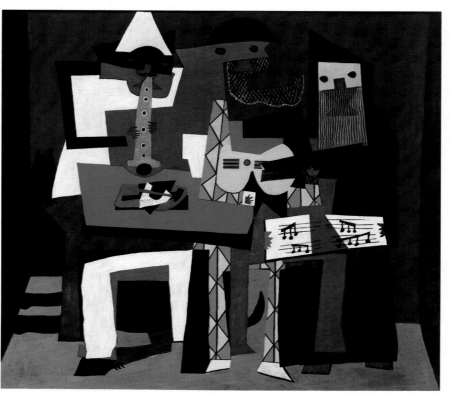

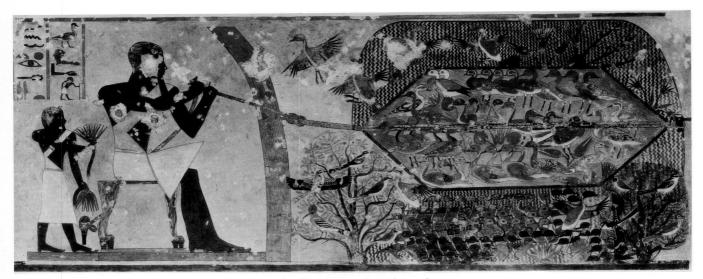

86. *Fowling scene, copy in tempera of wall paintings from the tomb of Khum-Hotep, Beni Hasan, XII Dynasty. c. 1900 B.C. Metropolitan Museum of Art, New York.*

object **[86]**. The most important figures were shown very large, while wives, servants, and children were much reduced. This tradition developed from the dominance of the pharoah in Egyptian society, not from any lack of artists' ability to place figures in space. Different experiences of space can be found in many other cultures where art is not concerned with three-dimensional representations of the real world. We may note the Middle Eastern approach to spatial representation **[14]**.

Atmospheric Perspective Another form of perspective is known as **atmospheric perspective,** or **aerial perspective.** It involves the use of cool colors and light values to make objects appear more distant. In a distant view individual parts merge, colors are less intense, and details seem diffused as a result of air and sunlight. Artists attempt to reproduce these effects to create a sense of deep space in painting **[18]**.

Dealing with Real Space Every civilization has dealt with real space differently. For example, in ancient Egypt great horizontal expanses of desert were blocked by huge temple complexes approached by vast walkways. In order to cover the immense areas of needed interior space, Egyptian architects used forests of mammoth columns to support flat stone roofs. Later in medieval Europe, the cathedral was at the heart of the medieval city and often positioned on high ground, where it dominated the living and working spaces clustered on three sides. Subsequent Gothic builders used fewer col-

umns, strengthened, as we shall see, by buttresses, to support vaulted roofs over huge interior spaces. Contrast the sense of the slivers of space between columns in the hypostyle hall of the Temple of Amun at Karnak **[87]** with the soaring interior space of St.-Denis **[60]**.

Compare these uses of space with the concentrated space of many major cities today, crowding boxlike skyscrapers together in a comparatively small area. Interior space is divided into numerous floors or stories, each further subdivided into tiny cubicles. The photograph of Rockefeller Center **[82]** softens the rigid geometry of the skyscrapers and, through its intricate pattern of light, offers limitless possibilities for visual exploration.

Like architecture, sculpture and other three-dimensional arts are designed in relationship to the space they occupy. Since ancient times, sculpture has been a solid form dominating space from a central position. Many contemporary sculptors, instead, emphasize space, which they enclose within the design of their work as, perhaps, a reflection of our preoccupation with the space age. Giacometti's *City Square* **[63]** appears to focus on the alienation of people in today's society by isolating the figures in a space that seems too large for their elongated bodies. As a result, they are lost in an urban environment that discourages human contacts.

Time and Motion

Artists have always recognized that paintings are illusionistic splinters of time. Some artists,

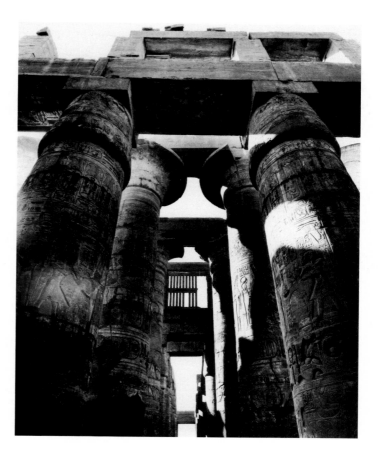

87. *Great Temple of Amun at Karnak. 1350–1205* B.C.

however, have been interested in implying the passage of time in a single work. When the Florentine painter Masaccio (1401–1428) told the story of *The Tribute Money* [88] he created an illusion of passing time by repeating the life-size figure of St. Peter three times to illustrate the three-part event that was painted at the viewer's eye level. First, we see St. Peter with the tax collector (right); then we observe him extracting a coin from a fish's mouth (left); finally we can see the payment of the tribute (center). Despite its sequential arrangement, *The Tribute Money* appears unified because of its clearly organized composition and its repeated colors and figures, standing out from their backgrounds of complementary colors.

88. *Masaccio.* The Tribute Money. *c. 1427. Fresco, 8'4" × 19'8" (2.54 × 5.9 m). Brancacci Chapel, Church of Sta. Maria del Carmine, Florence.*

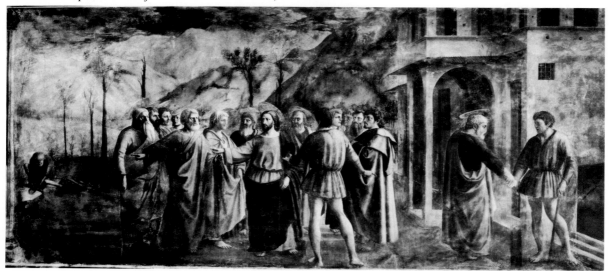

The photographic advances of Eadweard Muybridge (1830–1904), which inspired the invention of the motion picture camera, involved a series of twenty-four frames to be projected at speed, producing an illusion of time through motion [89]. In fact, we will learn how the marvel of the motion picture can manipulate time, contracting and expanding a timed experience. With the development of television, it has become possible to transmit images as they occur in the real world. The video synthesizer can mix past and present time in order to create the desired psychological and educational effect.

Motion has always fascinated people. Accordingly, there have been many allusions to motion in the static images of two-dimensional painting and drawing. Even the prehistoric representation of the leaping antelope on a wall in the Lascaux cave [2] shows the animal with front and rear legs spaced for the forward plunge into space. Later artists have attempted whole battle scenes, depicting men and animals in violent motion, as in the *Bayeux Tapestry* (c. 1080), which immortalized the Battle of Hastings [90]. In order to portray the correct sequence of events, the artists decorated a very long strip of linen with thousands of carefully embroidered soldiers, horses, and other figures. The features of the major characters are repeated to permit us to follow the action. In the 20th century, concurrent with the invention of cinematography, many artists combined multiple images to demonstrate the changes in position of a moving object.

Few illusionistic works, however, have ever created the furor of *Nude Descending a Staircase (No. 2)* [91] by Marcel Duchamp (1887–1968). In the vast 1913 Armory Show in New York comprising 1100 pieces of art, this painting of a technological Venus figure in motion is said to have moved former President Theodore Roosevelt to comment, "Explosion in a shingle factory!"

Recent styles in art have approached the illusion of movement by means of nonobjective designs. Some works, such as Bridget Riley's *Cur-*

89. *Eadweard Muybridge.* D———Walking, Hands Engaged in Knitting.
Photographed July 28, 1885, time interval 178 seconds. From Animal Locomotion,
Philadelphia, 1887. International Museum of Photography at George Eastman House, Rochester, N.Y.

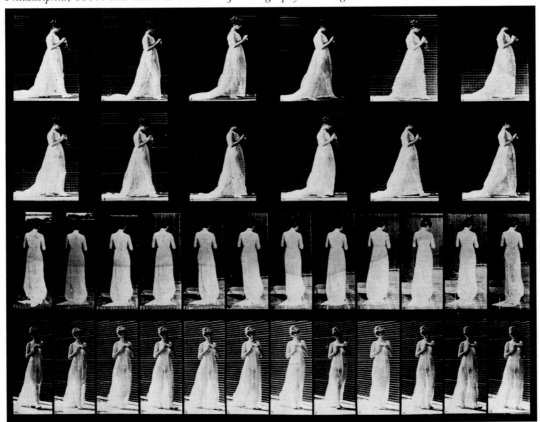

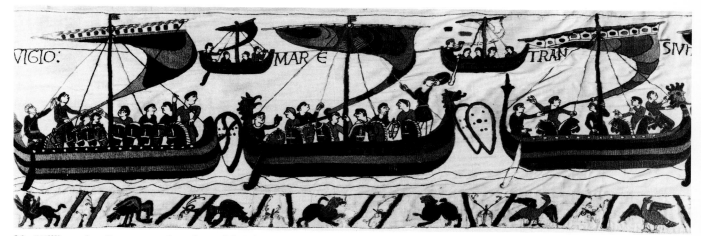

90. William the Conqueror Leaving with His Boats, *detail of* Bayeux Tapestry. *c. 1073–1088.*
Wool embroidery on linen; height, 1'8" (0.51 m), entire length 231' (70.41 m).
Town Hall, Bayeux, France.

rent [56], produce the effects of changing images as the position of the viewer is altered. Many optical paintings are simple, repetitive patterns of distinct, often geometric shapes, but after prolonged scrutiny, hard edges blur and colors vibrate, appearing to ripple before our eyes. Some works executed in fluorescent paints produce heightened visual experiences when viewed under black-light illumination.

Today, numbers of artists are exploring other time-motion dimensions of the visual arts. The hypnotic effect of moving bodies of water accounts for our delight in fountains. In some fountains, computers coordinate musically activated changes of light with changes in the flow of the water. The earth's rotation, the sway of branches in the wind, or the turbulence of waves breaking on a beach perhaps account for Alexander Calder's first notions of mobile art, an invention of the 20th century. Although the motions of the sun, fire, and steam-propelled machines have been noted since Leonardo's early preoccupation with motion in the 1400s, Calder's wind sculptures were revolutionary [57]. These kinetic works appear deceptively simple, but actually, many of the pieces rotate on separate axes, coordinating also with the larger movements of the whole sculpture. In es-

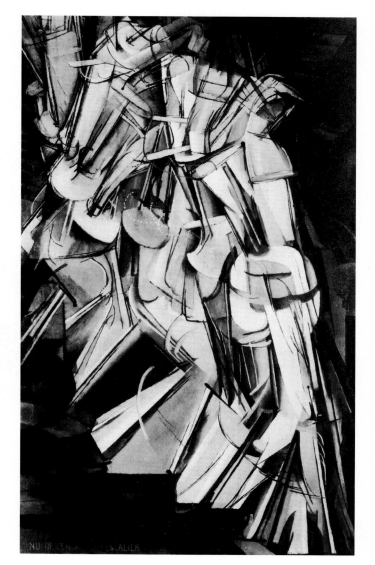

right: **91.** *Marcel Duchamp.*
Nude Descending a Staircase (No. 2). *1912.*
Oil on canvas, 4'10" × 2'11" (1.47 × 0.89 m).
Philadelphia Museum of Art
(Louise and Walter Arensberg Collection).

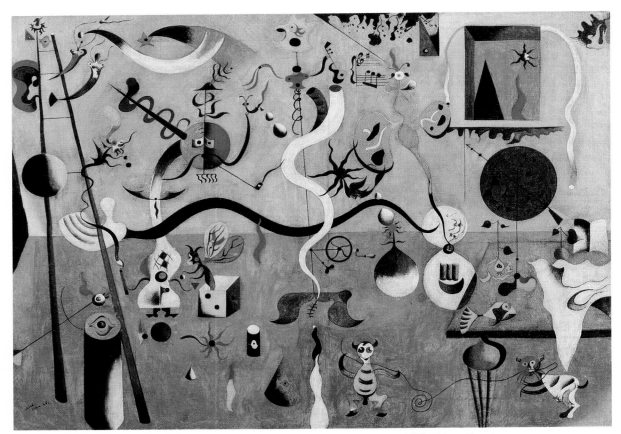

92. *Joan Miró.* Carnival of Harlequin. *1924–1925. Oil on canvas, 26 × 36⅝″ (66 × 93 cm). Albright-Knox Art Gallery, Buffalo (Room of Contemporary Art Fund, 1940).*

sence, motion in art is an evocation of motion in life and is a desirable part of human experience.

Principles of Design

Composition

The order of the universe has given us a basic appreciation of design and a need to create an orderly, harmonious existence. Natural designs inspire created designs. The visual arts are made up of elements organized into combinations. These arrangements, whether spontaneous or planned, are termed **composition.** Up to this point, we have been discussing the technical language of the artist dealing with those areas of concern unique to the visual arts. We are now ready to examine the language the artist uses in reference to composition, which is common to all the arts, visual and performing. That language includes words for principles basic not only to most of the arts but also to many other of life's experiences—unity and variety; rhythm;

balance; proportion and scale; and thrust, dominance, and subordination.

Unity and Variety

Visual **unity** (oneness) occurs through the interrelationship of all parts of an artwork so that they fit together in a recognizable order. This order may be simple or highly complex. A composition can be related and unified by repeating and echoing certain shapes, masses, colors, or lines, as, for example, the curved lines repeated in Riley's *Current* **[56]** and the processions of columns in the Temple of Amun at Karnak **[87]**. In these works the repetition and interrelationship of the parts give pleasure and satisfaction by creating unity.

Sometimes a work of art may appear to the inexperienced eye to have little unity, as in *Carnival of Harlequin* **[92]** by Joan Miró (1893–1983). The apparent disorganization adds to its sense of fantasy, yet the repetition of somewhat similar shapes, bright colors, and lines produces a unified composition that holds together. The differences between the elements themselves provides interesting variety within the basic unity.

Rhythm

A basic element of life is **rhythm.** It is created through the regular repetition of natural phenomena, such as waves pounding on a shore or a heart beating in a regular pattern that can be seen on a cardiogram. The natural rhythms of the tides, the phases of the moon, and the turning of the earth all suggest the rhythm of regular repetition. In the visual arts, rhythm is produced by the regular repetition of similar lines, shapes, colors, or textures. Our eyes quite naturally follow the pattern of repeats. Marcel Duchamp created a sense of flowing rhythm in *Nude Descending a Staircase (No. 2)* [91] by repeating shapes of the body as it moves down the stairs. The female form has been reduced to machined parts, reflecting the technological interest of many early-20th-century artists, but it has rarely been expressed more dramatically. Even the colors, muted grays and browns, remind us of the machine. Rhythm appears similarly in the repeated forms of the Temple of Amun at Karnak [87], and we are comfortable with their regularity. These are obvious examples of rhythm in art. A more subtle design appears in Michelangelo's *The Creation of Adam* [1], in which the lines of Adam's listless, still lifeless body are echoed but not exactly repeated in the vital, life-giving lines of God's figure.

Balance

There is a sense of **balance** in all of us; we are disturbed when our equilibrium is threatened. A teetering tightrope walker creates extremes of tension in the audience. In the same way, although the Leaning Tower of Pisa is famous for its imbalance, few of us are comfortable when actually climbing its ascending ramp. When we experience works of art, that same need for balance is involved.

Balance results from the unified relationship of two opposing forces. When almost equal shapes or masses are evenly distributed in a work of art, it is said to have formal balance. An example of informal balance may be seen in Miró's painting [92], while in some of Mondrian's work, geometric areas of color are balanced against white space.

Exhibiting yet another kind of balance, Calder's mobiles fascinate us with their ever-changing but totally balanced relationships. His subtle organic shapes move animatedly through space to create a vital rhythm [57].

Proportion and Scale

In art, as in mathematics, science, or even cooking, **proportion** refers to how parts relate to each other and to the whole. Human proportions affect architecture and furniture design. In contemporary design, the **module,** or core unit, is based on dimensions and ratios derived from the human body. Similarities in proportions within groups of people have permitted fashion designers to standardize clothing. Modern mass-produced plywood or plastic furnishings are also designed to suit average proportions. The scale of a building in relation to the size of the human figure has much to do with its emotional impact. For example, the immense size of many churches and public buildings dwarfs the individual's sense of importance. When the artist tampers with predictable proportions in order to create a desired **Surrealistic** effect, the viewer experiences a discomfort that often gives way to fascination.

Greek civilization was particularly concerned with proportion, both in life and in art—an attitude revealed in the subtle relationships incorporated in every work of Greek art; each small part was affected by every other part. One aspect of this refined sense of proportion was called the **Golden Section,** a principle that the Greeks applied to their temples and most other artworks [93], as can be seen in the spacing of parts of the Dipylon vase [47].

93. *The Golden Section.*

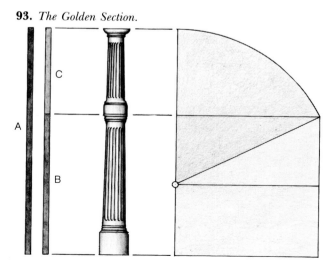

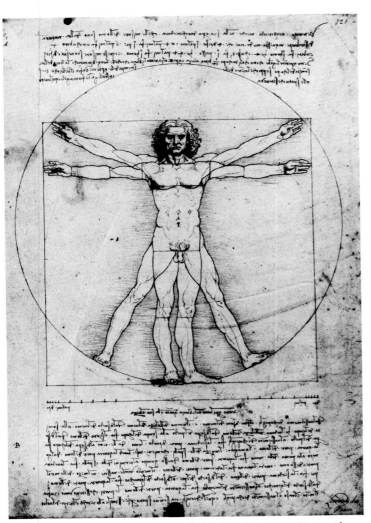

94. *Leonardo da Vinci.* Study of Human Proportions According to Vitruvius. *c. 1485–1490. Pen and ink, 13½" × 9¾" (34 × 25 cm). Aecademia, Venice.*

umental works, planned essentially to surround their viewers with painted environments. Consider that Jackson Pollock's *Number 1, 1948* [**10**] is about 5′8″ × 8′8″ (1.73 by 2.64 meters)—as large as a whole wall in many homes and a decidedly oversize scale for most.

People have often been concerned with the relationships of the parts of the body; the Greeks developed an idealized scale that served as a criterion of beauty for a thousand years. Classical Greek sculptures adhered to the scale set forth by Polykleitos in a set of standards—a canon. The Greek figure considered ideal measured seven and one-half head-lengths tall. Scale also intrigued Leonardo, who declared: "Man is the measure of all things." He placed the human figure as a unit of measurement in the center of the most perfect geometric shapes recognized by his day, the circle and the square [**94**].

Some rules can be set with considerable accuracy. A child's head is always larger in relation to the rest of the body than an adult's. However, sometimes artists disregard the rules for expressive purposes. In teaching figure drawing, an instructor may suggest that students measure a figure's length in relation to the head. The average adult is about seven to eight head-lengths tall, but the fashion artist may draw a figure whose height measures twelve heads, while a painter may elongate figures to suggest spirituality. Unlike the Greeks, contemporary artists feel free to alter conventional proportions, and to manipulate scale to create special effects.

Thrust, Dominance, and Subordination

Directional, linear forces are created in the basic structure of a work of art, as seen in de Kooning's drawing [**50**]. Vertical and horizontal lines suggest growth and repose, respectively, because they refer to natural states. Diagonal lines repeat the direction of driving snow or rain and consequently suggest lines of action to us. **Thrust** is created by the most dominant linear force within the work of art. Thrust is always directed (connected) to the focal point of the work, those aspects that are emphasized in the composition. Unless unimportant parts are subordinated, confusion results. For example, in order to direct attention to his model in *The Artist in His Studio* [**59**], Vermeer places the greatest contrasts in light and dark and the largest shapes near her figure. The thrust of the draperies echoes her pose and helps to frame her effectively. By subordinating all other forms through their reduced size and limited value contrasts,

According to this rule, a small part relates to a larger part as that larger part relates to the whole; that is, A:B = B:A + B. This ratio was likely derived unconsciously from natural laws we have only recently understood. Science has verified that this year's growth of a mollusk (or indeed of any living form) relates to last year's increase as that amount relates to the whole.

Scale, on the other hand, refers to size, that is, to the relative measurements of the viewer and the work. For instance, when we consider miniatures, which are small paintings or objects, we anticipate works that can be held in the hand. Most paintings and wall hangings are perhaps 2 to 5 feet (61 to 152 centimeters) wide, enough to serve as a focal point of decoration in the average building. Artists of the **New York School** of the 1950s overwhelmed their viewers with mon-

Vermeer assures the dominance of the model.

We have seen that sensitivity to design, inspired by the natural world, is as old as humanity. The veining of a leaf and the pattern of annual growth of a tree suggest designs of variety and complexity. Similar curved, spiral, wavelike, and animal designs based on nature are found everywhere in the world. Whether we view the decoration on a clay pot or analyze the complex plan of a building, we note a universal awareness of structure and order.

In our further studies of the visual arts, we will try to identify the devices used by all artists to achieve satisfying designs.

Exercises and Activities

Research Exercises

1. Select two artworks reproduced in this book to analyze on the basis of the artists' use of the following terms: line, shape, mass, value, color, texture. Find works that illustrate unity and variety; rhythm; and thrust, dominance, and subordination.
2. Study William Hogarth's two series dealing with 18th-century morals, i.e., *The Rake's Progress* and *The Harlot's Progress.* How many works were involved, which media, and what was Hogarth's purpose in these series? Contrast the similarities and differences between his works and those of Edward Kienholz.
3. The Precolumbian Aztec pantheon includes other deities as ferocious as Coatlicue and a few quite peaceable. Who were they and what powers did they represent?
4. Why is Francisco Goya's painting *The Execution of the Madrileños on May 3, 1808,* considered a milestone in modern art?
5. What moved Jasper Johns away from target paintings into flag icons? What was his goal with these works?

Studio Activities

1. Cover a sheet of paper with lines, using pencil, chalk, charcoal, pen and ink, and paint. Vary the thickness, length, direction, and spacing of the lines. Notice how the lines produce different effects.
2. Inside small squares draw groups of lines that express joy, sorrow, excitement, humor, confusion, tension, or other emotions. Analyze which kinds of lines express each emotion best.
3. Linear perspective has been used by painters to create the effect of three dimensions on a two-dimensional surface. To understand how artists use this method, place some solid objects, such as books, on a table. Try to see where the horizon line and vanishing points lie and make a simple drawing of the objects in perspective.
4. The traditional color wheel places the primary, secondary, and tertiary colors in a certain relationship. Using poster paints, mix the secondary and tertiary colors, painting all the colors on pieces of paper. Paste them in the order shown on the color wheel.
5. Take two complementary colors and mix them, producing a series of equal steps from one color to the other. Mix as neutral a gray in the middle as is possible.
6. Choose a simple landscape scene. Look at it to see how you might express a personal feeling by varying the colors. Choose two of the types of color schemes listed below and create two small color compositions to express your feelings:
   a. strongly contrasting values and hues
   b. analogous hues and values
   c. cool colors with warm accents
   d. warm colors with black-and-white accents
   e. opposite colors with black-and-white accents
   f. monochromatic color with a wide value range
7. The way in which varying types of shapes are combined produces different effects. To see how artists use shape as an expressive tool, draw groups of shapes inside small rectangles. Draw one arrangement that is balanced, another that suggests chaos.
8. Mass is used in the three-dimensional arts of sculpture and architecture. The illusion of mass is also often created in painting. Using clay, wood, or cardboard, make two compositions in which mass is used to create (a) a calm, quiet effect and (b) an exciting effect of tension. Or, paint two compositions creating the illusion of mass and producing these same effects.
9. Using chalk and sheets of newsprint, make rubbings of actual textures. Cut and paste these on a flat surface to create an interesting composition.

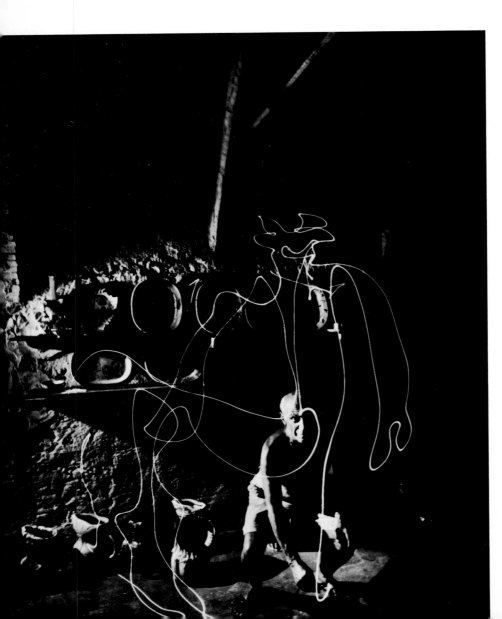

95. *Gjon Mili.*
A centaur drawn with
light. 1949. Pablo Picasso at
the Madoura Pottery,
Vallauris, France.

Part Two
TWO-DIMENSIONAL MEDIA AND TECHNIQUES

All the visual arts communicate some level of human experience that can be expressed through a wide range of media, materials, and techniques. In the next few chapters we will examine the many routes artists have pursued during the last several thousand years in their creation of art. For the most part, the original methods still work, but other techniques have been added through the centuries. The terms fine and applied arts, separating the beautiful from those arts concerned only with the functional, have gradually lost their distinctions. The crafts are no longer restricted to their utility, for the most part, and much fine art has often assigned a lesser role to beauty than, perhaps, to raising social consciousness in nontraditional ways. Therefore, we will proceed with study of all the two-dimensional arts, including graphics in advertising, such media as painting, drawing, and printmaking, as well as xerography and computer graphics. Part III will focus on the three-dimensional media, moving from sculpture through the arts for living: architecture and environmental design.

All these media depend on the same visual elements and principles of design we have explored in Chapter 2, but each has unique characteristics and potential depending on the materials used. These include traditional materials, such as stone, wood, clay, and paper and new materials developed in the 20th century, such as polyresins, gases, color film, and electric light. Some artists work in only one medium; others, like Picasso, try many. Painting, carving, etching, weaving, potting, even drawing with light, his final experiments with a new technique [95]—there is scarcely a medium he did not explore. The traditional distinctions among media, materials, and techniques are being eroded by many 20th-century artists, who use several (mixed) media in one work. By examining each medium in turn, we will be prepared to understand and enjoy art wherever we find it.

3
Drawing, Painting, and Mixed Media

It is not enough for a painter to be a clever craftsman; he must love to "caress" his canvas, too.

Pierre Auguste Renoir

I want to paint men and women with that something of the eternal which the halo used to symbolize, and which we seek to convey by the actual radiance and vibration of our coloring.

Vincent van Gogh

I have always tried to hide my own efforts and wished my works to have the lightness and joyousness of a springtime which never lets anyone suspect the labors it has cost. So I am afraid that the young, seeing in my work only the apparent facility and negligence in the drawing, will use this as an excuse for dispensing with certain efforts which I believe necessary. . . . I believe study by means of drawing is most essential. If drawing is of the Spirit and color of the Senses, you must draw first, to cultivate the spirit and to be able to lead color into spiritual paths.

Henri Matisse

Drawing, painting, and mixed media—each technique, basic to artists, has its particular characteristics, yet all share similarities. What related skills do they require?

Traditionally, the creation of an image on a flat surface through the application of some kind of coloring material has been the common element in all these art forms. Whether they are produced by drawing on parchment or on paper or by painting on plaster walls, wood, or canvas panels, these images have all appeared on flat surfaces. Artists have translated individual visions to a working surface by using brushes, pens, and assorted graphic tools. New techniques and materials, however, have changed the visual forms of these arts, for the changing world has led artists to search for new methods to express their ideas.

When we investigate the contemporary art world, we will discover that while many artists continue with familiar methods and materials, many are experimenting with industrially developed techniques and other new ways of creating images on two-dimensional surfaces.

Still others are rejecting the limitations of flat surfaces altogether. Such trends confirm that demarcations between the arts have broken down. Sculptured forms appear on paintings; paint is used on sculpture; and some graphic expressions are three-dimensional. Time and sound enter into many art experiences, and the viewer often becomes a participant in a staged

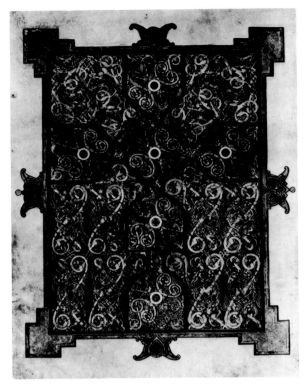

96. *Cross page from the* Lindisfarne Gospels.
Late 7th century. Manuscript illumination,
13 × 9½" (33 × 24 cm).
British Museum, London.

environment. We will examine these newer concepts of art in greater detail later.

Drawing

Of all the art skills, drawing is the foundation. As children we learned drawing was fun. We drew whatever caught our eye. Most of us began long before we learned to write. We drew in the sand at the beach and may have decorated the walls of our room before we began to doodle at the telephone or at the desk. However, when we learn to draw from observed form rather than from hazy recollection, we discover how to see more perceptively.

While a fine drawing may appear deceptively simple, basic drawing provides the underlying structure of many painted works. The lively images painted on the walls and ceilings of prehistoric caves also depend on the contour of drawn lines to express the action of the charging animals [2]. Earth pigments were used to fill the spaces between the lines with shaded color. Many scenes on the walls of Egyptian tombs were first drawn on with heavy outlines and then filled in with flat color [86]. Thousands of pottery jugs and drinking vessels throughout the Greek world were decorated with brush drawings outlining flat areas. The monks who decorated early medieval manuscripts usually outlined the complex, intertwined designs with a pen or brush before filling them in with color. A page from the *Lindisfarne Gospels* [96] is a complex linear delight, revealing fantastic monsters whose birdlike heads and clawed feet interlace with snake-like bodies.

Drawings also exist independently, falling into two groups: (1) drawings that serve as plans or studies for other works, and (2) drawings intended as completed artworks. The first (larger) category are notes or sketches for the artist's information and that may include studies for paintings, prints, sculptures, architecture, the decorative arts, and the industrial arts. Artists and designers make rough sketches for their final works much as writers jot down ideas and notes.

Drawings used as studies through which artists try out ideas in pencil, conté crayon, or pen can give us insight into how a final image evolved. They were probably intended only for personal use and were sometimes stored in artists' sketchbooks, such as the well-known folios by Leonardo. In them, he included his verbal observations, writing from right to left, perhaps in order to keep his discoveries somewhat secret. When Michelangelo was commissioned to paint the ceiling of the Sistine Chapel, he also doubtless prepared for that complicated project with considerable thought before he ever put chalk to paper. Actually, few of his drawings are still extant, but each is a record of search and discovery. Michelangelo's sketches for the *Libyan Sibyl* reveal careful observation and concern for accurate rendering of anatomy [97]. Those parts of the human form that presented problems to him, such as the big toe of the left foot, he drew three times, observing it from three different viewpoints. While he must have anticipated that the ceiling would receive considerable attention from Pope Julius II, who had commissioned it, and others, Michelangelo would have been much surprised at the affection the world has since given those very private, preliminary drawings.

Working from sketchbook notations, an artist, especially in the Renaissance, often created a preparatory full-scale drawing of the intended work called a **cartoon.** Once approved, the cartoon guided the artist in creating the **mural** or other work planned.

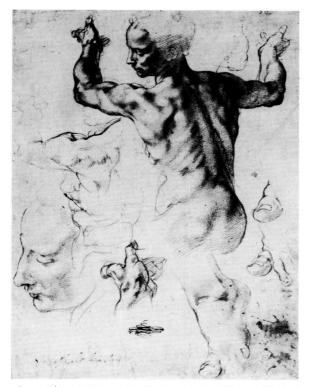

Architects and designers also use preliminary drawings to develop their ideas and communicate them to clients. Plans for buildings; sketches for furniture, utensils, or clothes; rough layouts for books and advertisements—all depend on drawing in one form or another.

Dry Media

Pencil Before the lead pencil was invented, artists used silver-tipped tools to draw delicate lines on paper coated with white or tinted pigment. Through oxidation, as the **silverpoint** slowly travels over the surface, the line tarnishes, darkening in time to a delicate gray-brown. Such lines cannot be erased. Modulated tones are developed from many individual parallel strokes. Silverpoint drawings are rare today, but such drawings as those by Leonda Finke (b. 1922) may result in works of refinement and sensitivity. In her study for a frieze, *Survivors* **[98]**, the line has a remarkable sensitivity to form and suggests light and dark in small areas. The small

above: **97.** *Michelangelo. Studies for the* Libyan Sibyl. *Red chalk on paper, 11⅜ × 8⅜″ (29 × 21 cm). Metropolitan Museum of Art, New York (purchase, 1924, Joseph Pulitzer Bequest).*

below: **98.** *Leonda Finke.* Survivors, *study for a frieze. 1980. Silverpoint, 36 × 24″ (91 × 61 cm). Collection Adrienne and Arthur Bloch.*

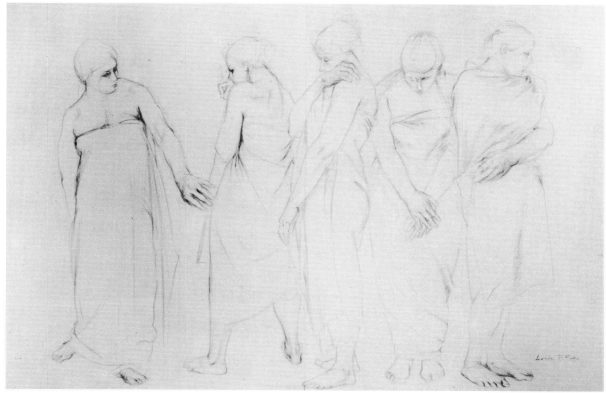

cross-hatchings lend some solidity to the figures while they define their contours.

The earliest pencils were lead points in a holder, but by the 18th century, the graphite pencil had widely replaced lead. Its wood-encased point creates lines that can be thin and hard or smudgy and soft. Today, pencils remain a prime medium. They range in grades from the soft 6B to the hard, fine 9H. Pencil does not smear as readily as chalk or charcoal. Though it is particularly suitable for small sketches and detailed drawings, it can serve for larger drawings, provided the artist has unlimited time and patience to work on that scale. Pencil is particularly effective in the hands of Robert Carter (b. 1938). His themes are generally concerned with black culture; lovingly handled, they are based on recollections or uniquely imagined forms [99]. The delicacy of the tones is applied and slowly built up with so long and fine a point that any excess pressure would instantly destroy it, yet huge areas of ground are effectively covered. His drawings are sometimes 6 feet (1.8 meters) high.

Chalk Chalk, suspended in a binding medium such as gum arabic and pressed into sticks,

became a popular drawing material in the Renaissance. It was available in black, white, and in shades of red and brown. Then, as now, it was a versatile material. It can be sharpened to a reasonably fine point, can be used bluntly, or can even be rubbed on its side across the paper to cover large areas. Chalk can be used strongly and vigorously or lightly and delicately. Many chalk drawings by the greatest artists of the Renaissance still exist. In them, we can see, for example, how Leonardo studied a series of heads or Michelangelo worked out the twist of a body or, as seen earlier, the detail of a foot [97]. Although this drawing was rendered on a sheet of paper small enough to fit into a modern typewriter, the study was large enough to lead Michelangelo to the life-size figure we know so well. We are brought very close to the creative inspiration of these great Renaissance masters when we view the studies they made for their major works.

Charcoal Charcoal has come a long way from the crumbled pieces our distant ancestors salvaged from the ashes of a fire to the present convenient prepared stick, made from hard,

99. *Robert Carter. "Mama She Loved Flowers." 1979. Pencil, 18 × 24" (46 × 61 cm). Present location unknown.*

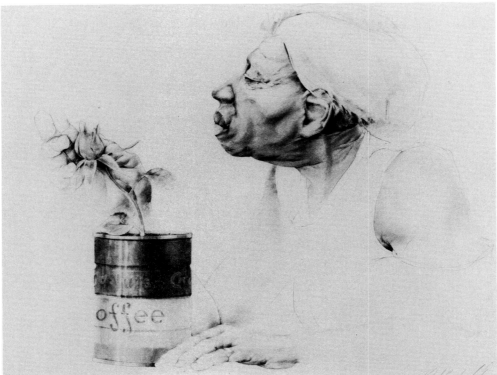

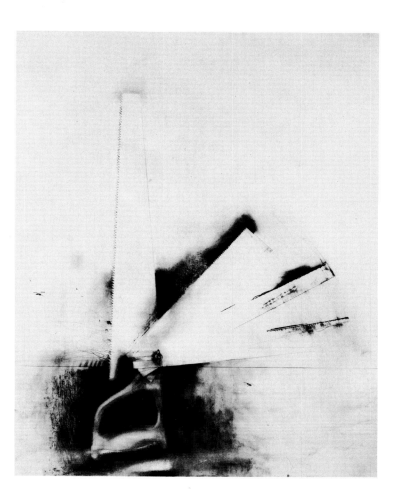

100. *Jim Dine.* Untitled
*(5-Bladed Saw), from a Series of
Seven Tool Drawings. 1973.
Charcoal and graphite, 25⅝ × 19⅞"
(65 × 51 cm). Collection,
Museum of Modern Art, New York
(purchase).*

close-grained wood. Artists find charcoal an easy material with which to work because they can quickly develop with it a wide range of different tones. It is especially useful in drawing large areas of light and shade or, if sharpened with sandpaper, charcoal may be used for linear drawings or, smudged and rubbed into the paper, can create soft, hazy effects. Traditionally, a popular way to use charcoal was to draw with it on gray-textured paper, adding white chalk highlights. Charcoal is limited because it smears easily. Consequently, charcoal drawings must be protected with a sprayed fixative to protect them from damage. Jim Dine (b. 1935), in an untitled series for a special exhibition of drawings for the Museum of Modern Art, rendered seven tools [100], using a combination of charcoal and graphite pencil to produce extraordinary drawings. The blurred, rubbed tones of the charcoal serve as a soft contrast for his impeccable pencil detail.

Crayon   Wax crayons have an advantage over charcoal in that they do not smear or rub off

paper so easily. Oil pastels known by the trade name *Craypas* are useful for drawing large colored areas of light and shade. With lithographic crayon, the artist can create rich, shining darks or, if handled lightly, soft mid-values as well. Conté crayon, perhaps more popular in the past than now, is a highly compressed pigment with binder that can be used like chalk, producing effects like lithographic crayon, in which velvety shadows contrast with brilliant whites. When conté is applied to a gesso surface, variations of tones are almost unlimited if the artist has patience to build up values slowly, with painstaking effort. Drawings by Charles Sheeler in conté [65] are starkly realistic and, as black-and-white studies, minutely render reflections of the artist's interests. The *Interiors* series demonstrates his concern with confined space.

Colored Pencils, Markers   In conclusion, colored pencils and markers designed to dry on contact, the latter most popular with illustrators especially since mid-century, provide a broad range of colors, and convenience for instant use.

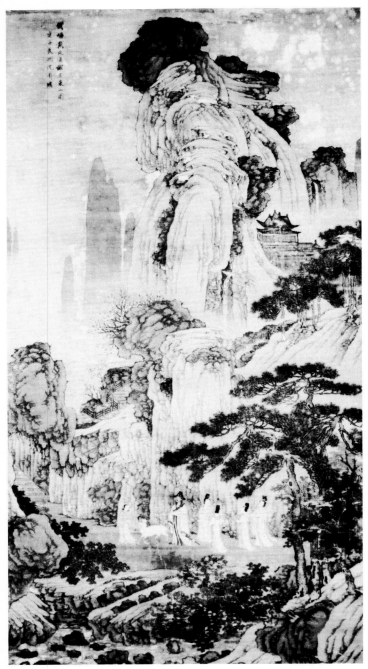

101. *Shen Zhou.* Xie An in the Dongshan Mountains. *1480. Hanging scroll, color painting on silk; $67\frac{1}{4} \times 35\frac{3}{8}''$ (170.8 × 90 cm). Collection of Wan-go H. C. Weng.*

Liquid Media

Ink; Wash The artist's basic fluid drawing medium, ink, has been in use for thousands of years. The Egyptians drew on papyrus with carbon ink, the ancient Chinese used ink on silk scrolls, and Western manuscript illuminators drew with ink on vellum made from animal skins. Paper is believed to have been developed in China around A.D. 100 and brought to Europe with the spread of Islamic culture. By the 15th century, paper was manufactured in Europe, offering a wider choice of drawing surfaces and techniques. Ink was brushed onto the paper with hair brushes or stroked on with a bamboo or quill pen. Depending on the materials and techniques used, artists could produce a wide variety of effects, ranging from broad brushstrokes to delicate pen lines.

Inks that are diluted to produce various tones are termed **washes.** The variety of tones possible with wash is well demonstrated in a Chinese landscape [101]. Also common to many Chinese and Japanese paintings is the vertical composition depicting an imagined idyllic landscape. While our eyes journey upward from the base of the work, delicate details of shrubs lead us to the mountain at the top. These tones are particularly characteristic of Oriental drawings, which are washed onto silk or paper with subtle value gradations. Here again, we find an instance where the distinction between drawing and painting disappears.

Pure (undiluted) ink is used when the artist wishes to make a strong statement that can be quickly understood. The classic pen drawing by Ben Shahn, *Silent Music* [51], was commissioned by CBS during a musicians' strike and commanded half a page in the *New York Times.* Shahn's brilliant use of line captivates our eyes, while we follow the path he has laid out for us, threading our way through the orchestra pit. CBS resolved its differences with the musicians almost immediately, but Shahn's drawing remains as a classic illustration of line.

Tones of gray can also be achieved by building up fine, parallel dark lines in pencil, ink, or chalk in a process known as **hatching.** By crossing the parallel lines in another direction, **cross-hatching** produces deeper and solid values, as in the powerful *Preacher* [102] by Charles White (1918–1979). The white highlight areas and light grays are almost devoid of inked lines. The enlarged left arm and foreshortened right arm emphasize the preacher's dramatic and dynamic arm positions while he exhorts his congregation.

Chinese White Though many of us are familiar with the detailed study, Albrecht Dürer's (1471–1528) *Praying Hands* [103], we are less aware that it is only a preliminary drawing for a much larger work, *The Assumption,* which few of us know. Artists, it seems, cannot always predict what will attract the public's fancy. The study of

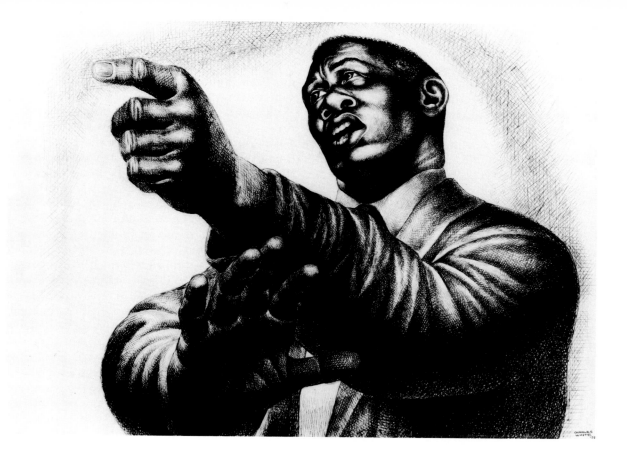

102. *Charles White.* Preacher. *1952. Ink on cardboard, 21⅜ × 29⅜″ (54 × 75 cm). Whitney Museum of American Art, New York.*

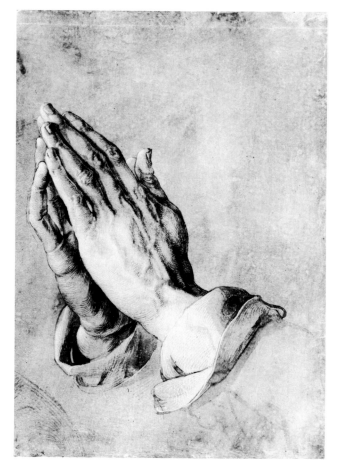

103. *Albrecht Dürer.* Praying Hands, *study for detail of* The Assumption. *1508. Wash drawing with opaque highlight, 11½ × 7¾″ (29 × 20 cm). Albertina, Vienna.*

reverent hands is meticulously rendered in a technique quite common in the Renaissance but rarely used today. Dürer used blue paper as the base for the drawing; then he slowly built up highlights with opaque Chinese white paint, while at the same time, he applied dilutions of ink (wash) for the shaded areas and pure ink for the deepest tones. The beauty of the drawing has commended it for study through the years both as inspiration for worship and as a model for imitations.

Combinations of Techniques

Today many drawing methods are used in untraditional ways to produce varied effects. Ink and chalk drawings may have bits of photographs or magazine reproductions pasted on them. Pencil drawings may be combined with commercial overlays of printed dot patterns just like the screen used to reproduce photographs and artwork for books, magazines, and newspapers. Some artists blow fine mists of paint and ink onto paper with **airbrushes**; many other draw with the same brushes with which they paint. It is difficult to say at which point drawing ceases and painting begins. These new methods have given artists freedom to express new ideas, so that drawing continues to serve as a base for all who work in the visual arts.

Painting

The most honored, perhaps, of all the art media, painting, by its very nature, offers the artist possibilities for visual images that cannot be accomplished in any other way. In painting, the first consideration is usually color, basic to most painted works. Drawings are sometimes colored, but paintings hardly exist without differentiation of color as the avenue for developing all the other elements. As we have learned, a painting need not be concerned with beauty to be aesthetically moving. The subject matter or emotional content may produce sensations of horror, while the composition and other elements of design are aesthetically organized.

Paint consists of **pigment** (dry coloring material) suspended in a **vehicle,** or mixing agent, which is a liquid made up of a **binder** (a sticky material) and a solvent (thinner). Various kinds of paint—oil, tempera, watercolor, and the paint used in fresco—differ in the vehicle, the surface to be covered, and the technique of application.

Pigments are made from both organic and inorganic substances. Traditional organic sources for pigments that occur naturally include charcoal (black), a kind of beetle (red), the urine of cows fed on mango leaves (yellow), and a vast variety of plants (indigo blue). In recent times, coal tars have become an important synthetic organic source. Among other organic pigment sources are natural earths, which produce yellow ocher and raw and burnt umber, and minerals such as zinc (white), cadmiums (yellow, orange, red), and cobalt (blue). In the Middle Ages ground lapis lazuli, a semiprecious stone, produced a beautiful blue, which was so costly that it was often reserved for images of sacred figures, such as the Virgin Mary's cloak. Today many inorganic pigments are artificially made.

In the past, artists ground their own pigments and mixed them with the appropriate vehicle. Paleolithic painters mixed charcoal and earth colors with animal fat to paint the walls of caves [2]. In the ancient and medieval world, artists mixed pigments with such binders as gum arabic, egg, beeswax, or lime and water to paint the walls of tombs and houses or the pages of books. The dryness of the Egyptian climate and the sealing of the tombs have combined to keep Egyptian painting fresh through thousands of years [86]. Most 20th-century artists use commercially prepared paints in which the pigment and vehicle are already mixed. Dry pigments are still available, however, for artists who wish to mix their own paints.

Fresco

The Italian term **fresco,** meaning "fresh," is the technique of painting on freshly plastered walls. The artist usually prepares a full-size drawing, or cartoon, and transfers the outline to the wet-plastered wall surface. Then he or she quickly brushes on pigments mixed with water. As the wall dries, the pigments form a permanent, strong, extremely durable surface, impervious to moisture. Indeed, the colors quite literally become part of the wall.

Because the pigment must be brushed on when the plaster is wet, only enough plaster is applied to cover an area that can be painted in one day. If you look closely at a frescoed wall, you can often see lines where one day's plastering stopped and the next began. Usually the artist tries to conceal these lines by planning them to fall along the edges of the shapes in the painting.

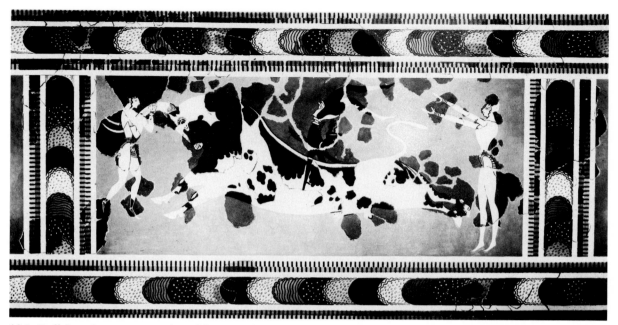

104. Bull Leaping, *reconstruction of fresco in the Palace of Minos, Knossos, Crete. c. 1500 B.C.*
34 × 63" (86 × 160 cm). University Museum, University of Pennsylvania, Philadelphia.

This technique on wet plaster is also called **buon fresco** ("true fresco") to distinguish it from **fresco secco,** in which pigments mixed with a binder are applied to plaster that has already dried. Fresco secco is less durable and brilliant than buon fresco.

Fresco secco was used by many early peoples to make murals. As far as we know, the earliest true frescoes were painted on the walls of the famous palace of King Minos in Knossos on the island of Crete. The representation of figures leaping over a bull for sport [104] formed the basis for the later Greek legend of the menacing bull-monster, the Minotaur. Crete's slender-waisted athletes dominate a fun-loving way of life, unique among frescoes in the ancient world, though the whole series inspired later murals on the Greek mainland.

Fresco was an important technique in Europe in the Greek, Roman, medieval, and Renaissance periods. However, early in the New World, concurrent with the early Middle Ages, Indians in Middle America also discovered buon fresco as early as the 7th century. Many later temples and palaces were decorated with colorful wall paintings. The fresco series from Bonampak in Yucatán about A.D. 700 are particularly fine examples [105]. Still later, at the height of the Renaissance, the Sistine Chapel ceiling by Michelangelo achieved the world renown that it has held ever since.

105. *Fresco from Bonampak. c. 700 A.D. Life size. Bonampak, Chiapas, Mexico. Watercolor reproduction by A. Tejeda. Peabody Museum, Harvard University. Copyright © President and Fellows of Harvard College 1972. All rights reserved.*

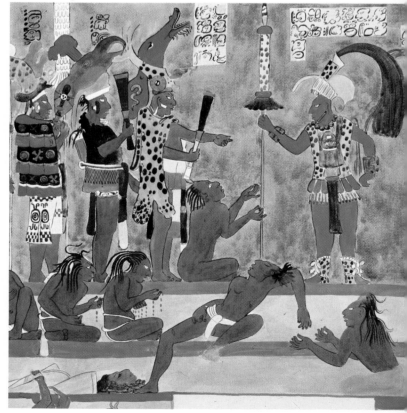

Drawing, Painting, and Mixed Media **77**

Restoration and Conservation of the Sistine Ceiling

A team of experts is well into a twelve-year project to restore Michelangelo's ceiling frescoes in the Sistine Chapel—a process that has provoked questions and controversy.

The vast panorama of hundreds of frescoes of biblical prophets, mythological figures, and Old Testament scenes was commissioned by Pope Julius II in 1508; through the centuries it has been viewed by hordes of visitors [106].

The scaffold designed by the master, erected some 60 feet (18 meters) above the floor, has been regarded with awe by engineers, especially since a modern scaffold had to be built. The original scaffold, strong enough to support Michelangelo and his helpers, plus plaster and other assorted items, was occupied for about four years without interruptions. The current cleaning program began when the new scaffold, built to repair water seepage, put Vatican conservators within reach of the frescoes.

In the nearly half millennium since the works were completed, the frescoes have accumulated some mold on the lunettes (semicircular areas) and dust and grime from the smoky stoves first used to heat the chapel and then from the airborne pollutants tracked in by tourists and worshippers. Though the need for some cleaning in a few areas seems apparent, there is by no means universal agreement as to how to go about it and when to stop. Since the paint thickness of the frescoes varies dramatically from $\frac{3}{8}$ to $\frac{3}{4}$ inches (1 to 2 centimeters), a uniform removal of the topmost layer is not practicable. Finally, questions arise as to how best to protect the frescoes during and after the cleaning process, when the usual 6000 to 18,000 daily visitors return to view them.

Chemical analyses from this Sistine project have confirmed what was suspected. Earlier water seepage had been repaired and cosmetic varnishing added. The procedures used in the restoration process are designed to prevent any loss of original paint. The protective patina covering the base (al fresco) layer is never touched. "A secco" areas (places where paints were applied "dry") are microscopically examined to determine if the pigments predate the 16th century and, if so, only the darkened varnishes are removed. Vatican officials are considering some form of climate control. All agree that a technological solution to the multiple concerns of temperature, humidity, and pollutants in the Sistine Chapel is needed now. Just what course that will take is less certain.

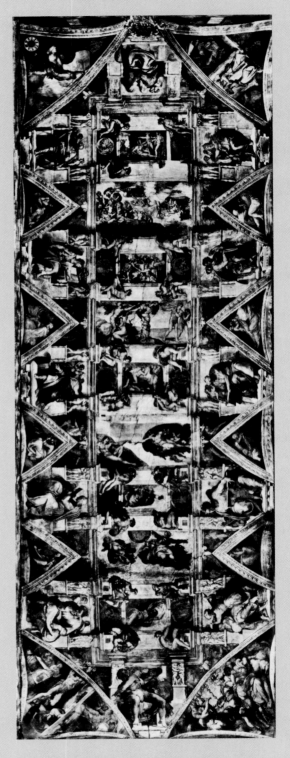

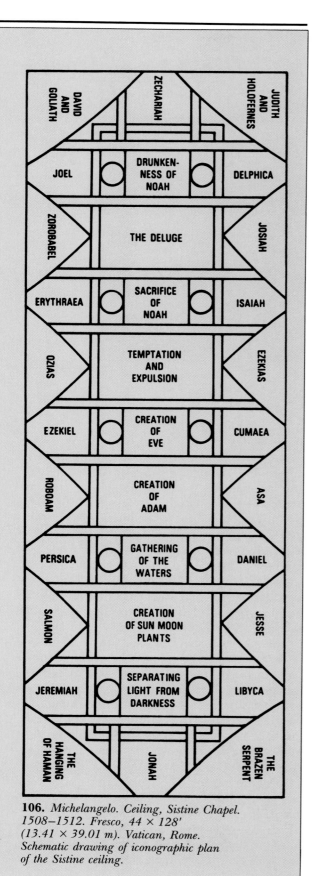

106. *Michelangelo. Ceiling, Sistine Chapel. 1508–1512. Fresco, 44 × 128' (13.41 × 39.01 m). Vatican, Rome. Schematic drawing of iconographic plan of the Sistine ceiling.*

Labels within the diagram:

DAVID AND GOLIATH · ZECHARIAH · JUDITH AND HOLOFERNES
JOEL · DRUNKENNESS OF NOAH · DELPHICA
ZOROBABEL · THE DELUGE · JOSIAH
ERYTHRAEA · SACRIFICE OF NOAH · ISAIAH
OZIAS · TEMPTATION AND EXPULSION · EZEKIAS
EZEKIEL · CREATION OF EVE · CUMAEA
ROBOAM · CREATION OF ADAM · ASA
PERSICA · GATHERING OF THE WATERS · DANIEL
SALMON · CREATION OF SUN MOON PLANTS · JESSE
JEREMIAH · SEPARATING LIGHT FROM DARKNESS · LIBYCA
THE HANGING OF HAMAN · JONAH · THE BRAZEN SERPENT

The artist's care in preparing and plastering the wall affects the durability of a fresco. Because Leonardo worked slowly, with great attention to detail, he experimented with new, slow-drying vehicles. Consequently, his famous fresco *Last Supper* [80] in the monastery refectory of Sta. Maria delle Grazie in Milan began flaking off the wall even during his lifetime.

Little used in succeeding centuries, fresco was revived in the early 20th century by Mexican painters responsive to their Indian heritage. Revolutionary figures in *The Modern Migration of the Spirit* by José Clemente Orozco (1883–1949) were painted in the same basic technique used by their forebears [471]. Fresco can still be found, chiefly for murals in public buildings, but it is an exacting technique far less commonly used than it once was.

Tempera

When you hear the term **tempera,** you probably think of the jars of poster paint you used in grade school. Probably these paints were gouache, or opaque watercolor paint bound with gum or glue, not true egg temperas, which depend on egg yolk or casein derived from milk as the binding material. Applied to a properly prepared surface called a **ground,** egg tempera is very durable. The most suitable surface is wood. A wood panel is first coated with a ground of **gesso,** a mixture of white pigment (chalk, plaster, or white clay) and animal glue. Perfect preparation of the gesso is important—an incorrect mix can cause cracks to develop all over the painting. After the ground is prepared, dry pigments are mixed with egg yolks and water and then applied to the absorbent gesso. Sometimes the egg yolks are mixed to create an emulsion with oil and varnishes. During the Middle Ages, this method of painting with egg tempera was widely used for household and church altar paintings on wood called **polyptychs** if many-paneled and **diptychs** if double-paneled. Later painters used tempera on canvas, which proved to be far less durable.

Tempera paintings can be built up by painting layer over layer. Early artists slowly built up dark and light values over an underpainting of umber pigment. Brilliance and crispness are characteristic of tempera paintings. Colors dry quickly with high gloss, and repainting over underpainted layers, when the artist wishes to alter the original concept, is simple. Although the technique fell into disuse when painting with oils was introduced, many contemporary illus-

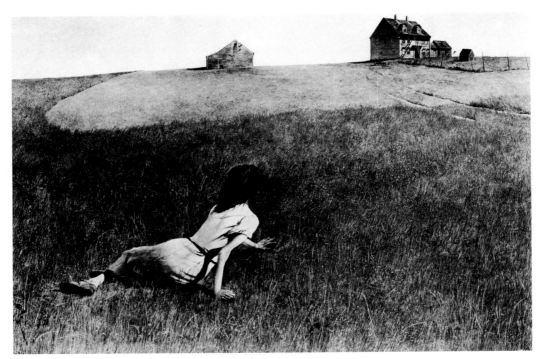

107. *Andrew Wyeth.* Christina's World. *1948.*
Tempera on gesso panel, 32¼ × 47¾″ (82 × 121 cm).
Collection, Museum of Modern Art, New York (purchase).

trators continue to use tempera. A few painters, such as Andrew Wyeth (b. 1917), choose tempera because of the opportunities it offers for precision. By overpainting several layers of varying tones, for instance, Wyeth retains our interest in the very broad foreground area of *Christina's World* [**107**]. By selectively etching with a knife blade various surface pigments he can achieve finely detailed blades of grass. The expanse of grass is particularly important in this work because it emphasizes Christina's physical limitations in reaching her distant house.

Watercolor; Gouache

Watercolor paints are made of pigments and binder such as glue, egg white, or gum arabic, which can be diluted with water. Washed over a white surface, which shows through the pigments, watercolors produce paintings of distinctive freshness, clarity, and transparency—qualities that can be easily lost if the painting becomes overworked. Watercolor has been used in the West since Classical times, and almost all medieval manuscripts were executed with watercolor or gouache. The *Lindisfarne Gospels* [**96**] demonstrate the delicacy and fine detail possible with watercolor.

Watercolor paintings using nonfading pigments on good-quality paper or silk are remarkably permanent, as can be judged from examination of many Oriental works, treasured for centuries. The Chinese landscape [**101**], showing the Oriental love of nature, demonstrates the endurance of watercolor despite a lifespan of five hundred years. The basic pigment used is lampblack mixed with glue, although Oriental artists also used some colored pigments. Years of training prepared the artist to use the brush skillfully and expressively. Unlike most Western painting, color was rarely used to give an illusion of reality. Eastern traditions generally required paintings to be quickly executed so that both the theme and calligraphic identification were not only handled with the same tools and materials but fulfilled the artist's original concept in minimal time. Suggestion, therefore, has always been more desirable than faithfully detailed representation.

In the West, for some time after oils became popular, watercolor was restricted primarily to sketches. It is a quick, spontaneous technique, which lends itself well to the notes an artist might make as the study for an oil painting. In the 18th century, watercolor was revived as an important art medium. Joseph Mallord William

Turner (1775–1851) created misty paintings in watercolor that were forerunners of later Impressionist works. His view of Venice [108] at sunrise is certainly very close to 19th-century Impressionism. Even though the variety of effects possible with watercolor does not measure up to the potential of oils, artists have used the medium in different ways to serve their purposes. Thinly diluted watercolor is also used in wash drawings to provide a wide range of tones. Wash works well with line drawing.

Gouache, watercolors bound with gum or glue, is opaque, and therefore light is not reflected from the white paper beneath the paint. Because of its opacity, gouache can be reworked more than watercolor. *Going Home* [109] by Jacob Lawrence (b. 1917) is a witty summary of day's end on a train. The highly stylized character of Lawrence's technique and themes, concentrating on his Afro-American heritage, works well with the gouache medium, which depends on strong accents of solid tone to carry the thrust of works. The rhythmic repetition of vertical seats and diagonally positioned passengers reinforces the message of returning home after a day's work, utterly exhausted.

Oil

Oil paints consist of a mixture of dry pigments with oil and sometimes varnishes diluted with turpentine. Developed in Flanders in the

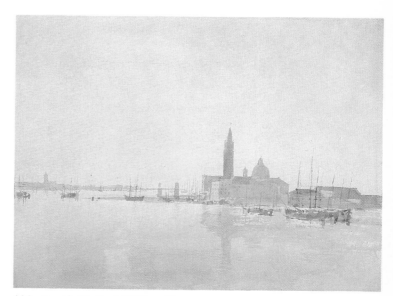

108. *Joseph Mallord William Turner.*
San Giorgio from the Dogana, Venice: Sunrise. *1819.*
Watercolor, $8\frac{13}{16} \times 11\frac{15}{16}''$ (22.6 × 30.4 cm).
Tate Gallery, London. Reproduced by courtesy of the Trustees.

15th century and gradually refined, oil painting was an outgrowth of the commercial developments of that period. Trade with many parts of the world brought new materials to Europe, including those from which oils and varnishes could be extracted. The transition from tempera to oil was slow. Oil paint was first used for trans-

109. *Jacob Lawrence.* Going Home. *1946. Gouache, $21\frac{1}{2} \times 29\frac{1}{2}''$ (55 × 75 cm). Collection IBM Corporation, Armonk, New York.*

Francesco Parmigianino (1503–1540)

In 1524 at the age of twenty-one, while preparing a small portfolio of his work with which to meet the great Renaissance master artists Raphael and Michelangelo in Rome, Francesco Mazzola, called Parmigianino, completed a small work destined perhaps to become the most startling portrait of his time. Fascinated by his own reflection in a barber's convex mirror, Parmigianino determined to reproduce it exactly. Sawing off a portion of a wooden sphere to use as the base, he painted himself as he was, looking outward and, as 16th century historian Vasari has stated, "so handsome, with the face of an angel rather than a man, his reflection in this ball appeared divine." His head was not distorted but the mirror from which he worked showed his hand and sleeve enormously enlarged. The sloping skylight of his studio as well as the opposite wall are curved to encircle the portrait, reflections, shadows, and lights. The finished work was greatly admired in Parma where the young Parmigianino was born, and as well received in Rome, even by Pope Clement, who was amazed by the youth of the artist.

As his professional skills expanded, he began to compete for commissions with the somewhat older, better known Correggio. In a brief twenty years or less, the two established new canons of European taste. Parmigianino's work was so highly regarded by many of his contemporaries that the noted poet and satirist of his day, Annibale Caro, declared that Parmigianino was the sum of all possible elegance and artifice and that "excess is an honest thing. Painters give to their things a measure beyond the natural," an outlook later associated with **Mannerism.**

Parmigianino's mature style culminated with his work in Parma, particularly in the *Madonna of the Long Neck* [355] demonstrating an other-worldly grandeur. In 1539, he fled to Casalmaggiore to avoid imprisonment for breach of contract, where he died at only thirty-seven years of age. He had promoted a new kind of beauty and a fresh way of seeing oneself and the world.

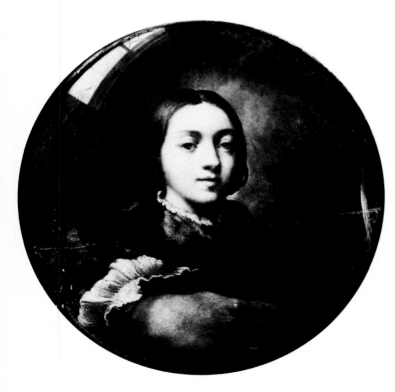

110. *Francesco Mazzola (Parmigianino).* Self-Portrait in a Convex Mirror. *c. 1523. Oil (?) on wood sphere, 15⅜" (29 cm) diameter. Kunsthistorisches Museum, Vienna.*

parent glazes over a tempera underpainting on gesso-covered wood panels; solid form was modeled with tempera, and the final painting was completed with thin oil glazes. The Renaissance practice of layering thin, semitransparent glazes of warm and cool colors on top of each other imparted a rich glow and depth to the painting. In his *Self-Portrait* Parmigianino (Francesco Mazzola) showed consummate skill in capturing human expression and great technical brilliance in rendering details of clothing and the textures of fabrics. These are painstakingly painted with oil glazes, which make the surfaces glow like enamel [110].

By the 16th century, in Italy, linen canvas had gradually replaced wooden panels as the preferred surface for oil paint, since fabric was light in weight, less costly, and easy to prime with gesso or with glue, white pigment, and oil. Although oil paint on canvas is not as durable as fresco or tempera on wood, other advantages led to oil becoming the major choice of artists in the Western world for centuries. Oil dries slowly and can be reworked for a long time. It can be applied in thin glazes over underpainting, or it can be put on in thick layers with a brush or palette knife. Oil allows a wide range of shades and easy blending of colors. Thin, transparent, dark shadows can be contrasted with thickly applied highlights, a combination that was unattainable with earlier methods of painting.

Rembrandt van Rijn (1606–1669) made full use of this quality of oil paint in his contrast of deep, mysterious shadows and concentrated brilliant light areas, particularly evident in *The Night Watch* [376]. Oil paint in the hands of a master like Frans Hals (1580–1666) can also be used to suggest spontaneity. Like all of Hals's work, the underdrawing of *The Bohemian Girl* [111] is precise and carefully painted; only in finishing it did Hals apply fluid fine strokes that make the portrait appear deceptively casual, much like the candid photographs of the 20th century.

Later painters, instead of using underpainting and glazes, applied the paint directly to canvas with free brushstrokes. For example, the Impressionists created an effect of vibrant light by placing small, thick strokes of complementary colors next to one another, a practice continued by Post-Impressionists Seurat [71] and Paul Cézanne (1839–1906). Cézanne's *Still Life* [112] is a careful attempt to direct the viewer's conscious attention to the changing volumes of the fruit and cloth by shifting tones, plane to plane, instead of portraying a literal photographic view. This deliberate counterbalancing of changing tones to suggest mass led directly to **Cubism** in the early 20th century.

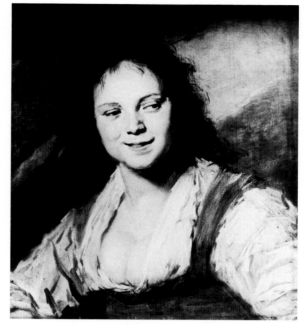

111. *Frans Hals.* The Bohemian Girl. *1628–1630. Oil on canvas, 22⅞ × 20½″ (58 × 54 cm). Louvre, Paris.*

Oil paint can also be applied heavily as **impasto,** a technique preferred by some painters, Van Gogh in particular, who used a palette knife to spread the thick paint. Observing a Van Gogh oil painting [22] becomes almost a tactile experience.

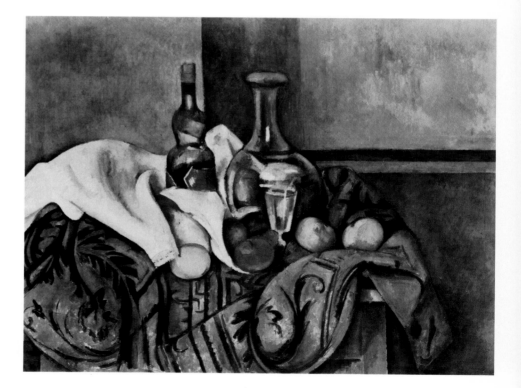

112. *Paul Cézanne.* Still Life with Peppermint Bottle. *c. 1894. Oil on canvas, 26 × 32⅜″ (66 × 82 cm). National Gallery of Art, Washington (Chester Dale Collection, 1962).*

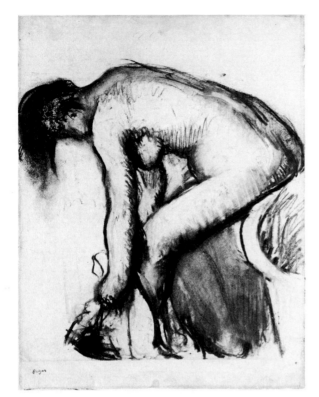

113. *Edgar Degas.*
After the Bath: Woman Drying Her Feet. *c. 1900.*
Pastel, charcoal, and black washed chalk
on buff paper; 22 × 15¾″ (55.8 × 40 cm).
The Art Institute of Chicago (gift of Mrs. Potter Palmer,
1945). © 1987 The Art Institute of Chicago.
All rights reserved.

With this change to direct techniques, painters generally became less concerned with the precise craft of painting than with the immediate effect produced. Thus many carelessly painted works from the 18th and 19th centuries are cracking. Very heavy paint is likely to crack when it is not properly applied, and some colors will darken and bleed into each other. Many artists, including Rembrandt, applied so many layers, resulting in such thick paint, that the solid, substantial-looking images become criss-crossed with countless fine cracks [376]. Despite these problems, oil makes possible such a variety of styles and techniques that it remains very popular.

Pastels

In their present form of pure pigment compressed into sticks with a minimum of gum binder, **pastels** date back about two hundred years. Sometimes classified as a drawing technique but more often as painting, pastels depend rather on broad areas of color for their effects than on drawn outlines. Because the colors are not mixed with egg or oil, they do not suffer from darkening or from other effects of age. When these nonfading colors are used on high-grade paper, the result is one of the most permanent types of painting. The colors do rub off, however, unless protected by glass or by a fixative spray. Because of its brilliant color and freshness of application, pastel appealed to Impressionist painters, who sought to capture momentary effects. During the latter part of his life, Edgar Degas (1834–1917) confined most of his painting to pastels, for the ease of achieving broad tones with them as well as for their effect of spontaneity. Many of his studies, such as *After the Bath* [113], are intimate glimpses of women at work or at ease.

Acrylics and Other New Materials

In their search for new ways to respond to inner emotions and the outer world and to achieve permanent color effects, many artists investigate new materials and techniques. Sometimes restricted access to traditional materials leads an artist to new materials with which he or she may develop an original approach to art. For example, Jackson Pollock [10] used oil-based house paints and metallic enamels for his canvases, he admitted, because he could not afford artists' oils. The fluidity of inexpensive paints from the hardware store, however, led him to experiment by pouring, dribbling, and flinging his paints onto canvas laid out on the floor. Such a process would have been impossible with oils from tubes brushed onto a canvas set on an easel.

New synthetic polymers probably have given artists the greatest shift in materials and techniques since the evolution of oils five hundred years ago. The most popular synthetic paints today are the **acrylic** and pyroxlin paints in which pigments are suspended in a polymer vehicle, producing opaque or transparent films. These paints have greater durability than oils and can be used on a wide range of surfaces. They are thinned with water, yet are resistant to water once they have dried. As synthetics, these paints are inert and will not change color or affect the surface on which they are applied. In addition, acrylics are brilliant, and they can be used as transparent glazes or built up in thick impasto surfaces. Thin-glazed areas can be contrasted with heavily painted textures. Since

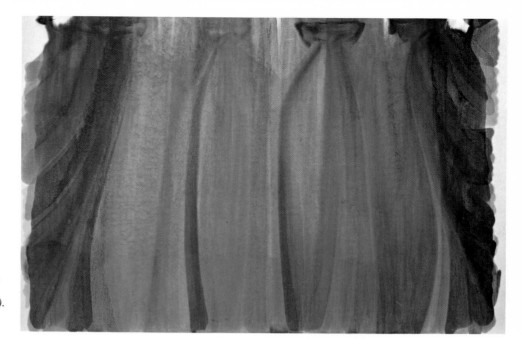

114. *Morris Louis. Saraband. 1959. Acrylic resin on canvas. 8'4½" × 12'5" (2.55 × 3.78 m). The Solomon R. Guggenheim Museum, New York.*

acrylic dries rapidly, it can be worked over in a matter of minutes, and many layers of paint can be built up. The viscosity of acrylics permits them to be laid directly on canvas that has not been primed, thereby permitting the paints to ink into the fibers of the cloth in highly personalized ways. While Morris Louis (1912–1962) never described his methods, it is apparent that he poured on his colors and then, setting the canvas on end, let gravity pull the paint down, as in *Saraband* [114]. Helen Frankenthaler has demonstrated the luminosity of acrylics when applied as dyes on the canvas. The huge areas involved surround the viewer with color [75].

The brilliance and vividness of synthetic paints account for their popularity in **Optical Art.** With further thinning, acrylics can be used in an airbrush. This small tool, barely larger than a ball-point pen, is a refined, small-scale paint sprayer, capable of producing effects ranging from fine lines to broad sprays. Intended for the commercial world of photo retouching and illustration, the airbrush has become a favorite of many artists who, influenced by **Pop Art,** rework images from advertising art. Many of the **Photo Realists** of the 1970s also took advantage of the airbrush to create detailed acrylic works, frequently derived in some way from original photographs. Don Eddy (b. 1944), youngest of the Photo Realists, sprays small dots of color, a technique particularly evident in the series depicting showcases of silverware. He prefers to paint from black-and-white photographs and to create his own color systems [115].

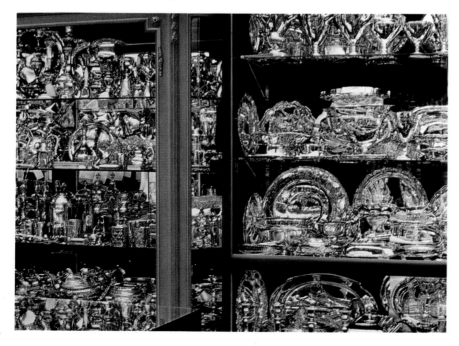

115. *Don Eddy. Gorevic Silver. 1975–1976. Acrylic on canvas, 4'2" × 5'10" (1.27 × 1.78 m). Private collection. Courtesy Nancy Hoffman Gallery, New York.*

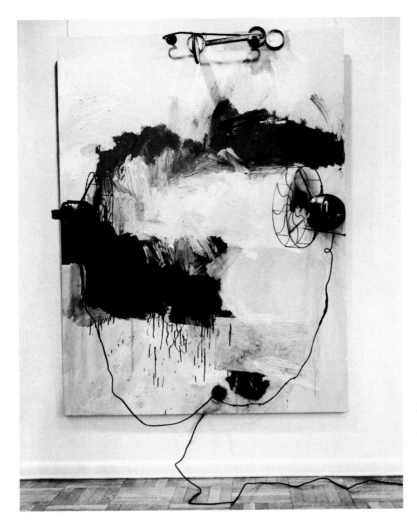

116. *Robert Rauschenberg.*
Pantomime. *1961. Combine painting, 7 × 5' (2.13 × 1.52 m). Courtesy Leo Castelli Gallery, New York.*

Mixed Media

In addition to experimenting with new paints and techniques, artists in the 20th century have also incorporated new kinds of materials into their paintings. Before 1920 Cubist painters in Paris such as Picasso and Braque **[74]** were pasting scraps of printed paper and fabric onto their painted canvases. They called these works **collages,** from the French word for "paste" or "glue." Many artists today combine a variety of materials—metal, fabric, wood, sand, string, and words or images photoprinted on paper, plastic, or canvas—with the painted surface to make **assemblages,** from the French word for "gathering together." The English term is **combine art.** These materials, along with three-dimensional, **ready-made** objects, are glued, stapled, nailed, or even welded onto paintings. Sometimes the shadows cast by the solid objects are painted onto the canvas to push further the **trompe l'oeil** ("trick the eye") effect. This technique, so

popular in the late 1600s, has become a favorite 20th-century device to point up the issue: what is real and what is illusion? Robert Rauschenberg's (b. 1925) *Pantomime* **[116]** is a combined work of canvas, dripping paint, and two real fans (trailing wires) to speed the drying of paint. The electric current reflects the current of life in a charade, the theme of the work.

Other artists use three-dimensional canvases. Lee Bontecou (b. 1931), for example, experiments with canvas stretched over three-dimensional armatures **[117]**. In her fascination with hollows and openings she brings actual space into the painting, instead of creating an illusion of space with paint. Frank Stella's (b. 1936) relief constructions, made of brightly painted aluminum, thrust boldly into space **[118]**. In their three-dimensionality, they also contribute to the breakdown of the demarcation lines separating painting and sculpture. However, their emphasis is strongly pictorial, and they are not meant to be seen from all sides. Stella says of his art that

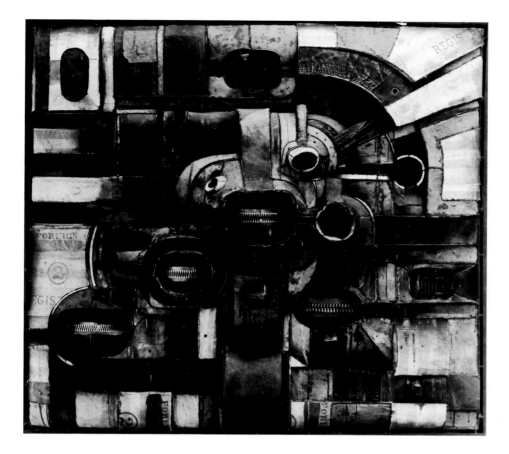

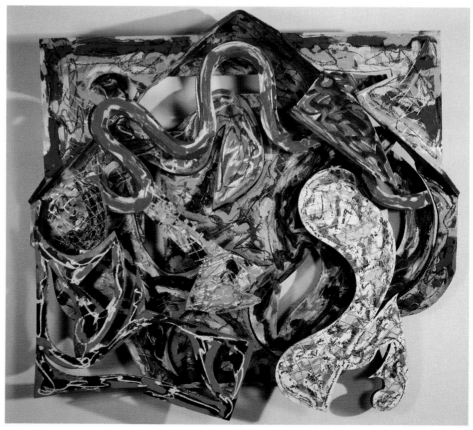

above: **117.** *Lee Bontecou.*
Untitled. *1964. Welded steel
and canvas, 6' × 6'10" × 1'6"
(1.83 × 2.03 × 0.46 m).
Honolulu Academy of Arts.*

right: **118.** *Frank Stella.*
Thruxton 3X. *1982.
Mixed media on etched aluminum,
6'3" × 7'1" × 1'3"
(1.90 × 2.16 × .38m).
The Shidler Collection, Honolulu.*

he is attempting to infuse new life into abstraction by sustaining its pictorial energy. Are these works sculptures or paintings? The frequently used term in today's art world is **mixed media,** a convenient way to get around the problem of how to classify much contemporary art.

Synthetic paints, new techniques, and mixed media have not replaced traditional materials and techniques; rather, they have enormously expanded the artist's possibilities for expression.

The great diversity that results is also a product of the changing concepts of subject matter, approach, and role of the artist that have characterized art since the late 19th century (see Chapter 16), freeing it from many traditional limitations. Yet does not this diversity also reflect an ambiguity in our society? Artists echo the boundless options of our world as much by their free choices of materials and media as by the themes they explore.

Exercises and Activities

Research Exercises

1. Powerful visual forces produced by drawing and/or painting techniques can evoke drama in a work of art. Using an example from this chapter, explain how such an effect was achieved.
2. Compare any three drawing techniques in regard to the medium and the expressive opportunities each offers. Use specific examples of artworks to clarify your statements.

3. In the same way, compare any three painting techniques.
4. Basing your conclusions on your understanding of the different approaches an artist may use from preliminary drawing to finished masterwork, trace the evolution of *Guernica* (Chapter 3).
5. Explain any difference you see from the initial concept of *Guernica* to the finished work.

Studio Activities

1. Since different drawing materials vary in flexibility, use several media, such as pencil, pen and ink, crayon, and poster paints, to create a full range of values from black to white. Arrange them in small squares in nine equal steps to determine the differences in effect and the difficulty of creating tone with some media.
2. Each drawing medium is capable of producing distinctive textures which may be expressively manipulated by the artist. Divide a large sheet of drawing paper into rectangles. Find a texture in your environment that pleases you and try to copy it in pencil, crayon, ink, or paint. Using the same media, create new textures.
3. Colors make a direct appeal to the emotions and have come to be associated with various feelings. Select a black-and-white photograph or reproduction that conveys a specific mood to you. Using any medium, make a simple composition based on the photograph, using a color scheme that expresses the mood.
4. The color of a subject may be modified by the artist in many different ways in order to express a personal feeling or emotion. Set up a still life and draw it in simple outline form. Fill in the outlines, using any three contrasting colors at full intensity, widely separated on the color wheel. Repeat the same grouping in an analogous color scheme and note the difference in effect.
5. Create a mixed-media composition using a combination of at least three techniques and materials.

4
Printmaking

One man may sketch something with his pen on half a sheet of paper in one day, or may cut it into a tiny piece of wood with his little iron, and it turns out to be better and more artistic than another's big work at which its author labors with the utmost diligence for a whole year. And this gift is miraculous.

Albrecht Dürer, 1523

It is not easy to retain the imagination's immediate, transitory intention and harmony of the first execution. . . . I have made observations for which ordinarily there is no place in commissioned works and in which imagination has been given full rein.

Francisco Goya, c. 1790

I make prints because in using the metal, the wood, and all other materials available, I can express things that I cannot express by any other means. In other words, I am interested in printmaking, not as a means of reproduction, but as an original, creative medium. Even if I could pull only one print from each of my plates, I would still make them.

Gabor Peterdi, 1960

[When making a print], you are performing on a stage. You can be heavy, you can be light—an accent here, an accent there. What you do alone today, thousands of people will see tomorrow.

Tatyana Grosman, 1980

In our multimedia world we are bombarded daily with thousands of images—printed, photographic, and electronic. From the moment we open the morning paper to the last page of a book we read before turning the lights out at bedtime, we have probably made our way past more printed images in a day than our ancestors faced in a lifetime. Messages, once written by hand before carbon copies, can today be duplicated almost endlessly by machine. Words and pictures are printed on countless packages, posters, cans, and magazines. Even works of art, once unique objects viewed by a handful or reproduced in a limited number of original prints, can today be duplicated millions of times through mechanized techniques. Andy Warhol's use of repeated images of bottles of Coca-Cola or the face of Marilyn Monroe reflects our involvement with multiple images [28]. It makes sense to try to understand and differentiate among the kinds of printed images we see.

Though the dependency of our society on the printed image is a recent phenomenon, the process of printing is ancient. **Printing** may be defined as transferring an inked image from a "master" surface to another surface, a method by which we can reproduce the same image many times. Printing has existed since ancient times in Egypt, China, and India. A process that was first developed to repeat textile designs, printing was much later applied also to paper.

Papermaking

Early surfaces for writing were papyrus scrolls in Egypt, clay tablets in Mesopotamia, and vellum scrolls and sheets in the West. All these were less convenient than scrolls and sheets of paper, made by the Chinese about A.D. 100. The Chinese adapted to papermaking the skills they had already developed in forming felt cloth. A hand-beaten mash of plant and rag fibers and water was put through a sieve, called a **mold.** As the water drained off, a sheet of vegetal felt was deposited in the mold. Such sheets, dried and sized with fish glue or soft rice paste to prevent fibers from absorbing ink, were translucent when held up to the light, like most modern book paper.

These sheets were of two kinds. **Wove paper,** possibly so called from the cloth that covered the first molds, revealed virtually no pattern when held to the light. **Laid paper** was thick and thin as a result of fibers lodging unevenly in the strips and spaces of the bamboo grid that formed later molds. Against the light it revealed a pattern of closely spaced horizontal lines and widely spaced verticals corresponding to the structure of the grid. The textural variations in laid papers enriched illustrations, but proved less satisfactory as a base for type wherein the clarity of a letter is essential to printed communication. These basic differences in paper have been continued in the wove and laid papers of today. The tough, smooth, cheap sheets of paper produced by the Chinese provided ideal printing surfaces.

When papermaking spread from China to Spain by about 1150, European printers of cloth extended their skills to papermaking. Italians used animal glue for sizing and substituted water-powered hammers for hand beating. About 1300 they made the first watermarks, simple crosses pressed into the damp paper to identify the kind or the paper mill. Increased stocks of paper stimulated the use of printing, which in turn created a market for more paper. Eventually papermaking became a large-scale mechanized industry.

In the 20th century, papermaking by hand, like other skills lost since preindustrial times, has been restored as a handcraft that can reach the level of art. The artist Douglass Morse Howell (b. 1906) has dedicated a lifetime to papermaking and achieved a reputation that spans continents. His papers are works of art in themselves, and his workshop is a showplace of inventive art with paper [119]. Howell's work with other pioneers has spawned a new generation of papermakers such as Coco Gordon (b. 1938) who enjoy the challenge of working with textural, handmade papers. Many find that beautiful papers themselves are their goal, without embellishment by printing.

Printing Techniques

The ancestor of printing was the early practice of stamping carved seals in the form of clay cylinders or rings into damp clay. Babylonians stamped the names of their kings on bricks, and Roman wine dealers stamped their names on wine jars. The Chinese cut pictures and characters in relief on wood blocks, which they inked and stamped, or printed, first on fabric and then also on paper in multiple copies. Anticipating modern commerce, they used copper plates to print bank notes, which were provided with inserts for changing the denomination.

In 15th-century Europe, **woodcuts,** made from wood blocks carved in relief, were used to print religious souvenirs and cheap playing cards. As paper became generally available and printing with movable metal type spread from Germany through Europe, handwritten, hand-painted books gave way to printed books, some of them illustrated with woodcuts. By the beginning of the 17th century illustrations were usually made by copperplate **engraving.** Playing cards for the wealthy were engraved, while princes commissioned painted and gilded one-of-a-kind masterpieces.

In succeeding centuries, as commercial printing techniques for mass production developed, artistic printmaking gradually evolved. Artists later adapted some artisans' techniques for their own use, often after these were discarded commercially as too costly and too slow. Many artists today, however, still use the traditional printing techniques; some artists continue to print their own work, but others prefer to have their designs reproduced by master printers.

In the past an artist might devote a whole lifetime to mastering a single technique, such as **aquatint.** Today there is much cross-fertilization of ideas and techniques between artists and between artists and printers' workshops. Since the 1960s major artists have freely shared their printing innovations developed alone or in conjunction with workshops. Run by highly skilled

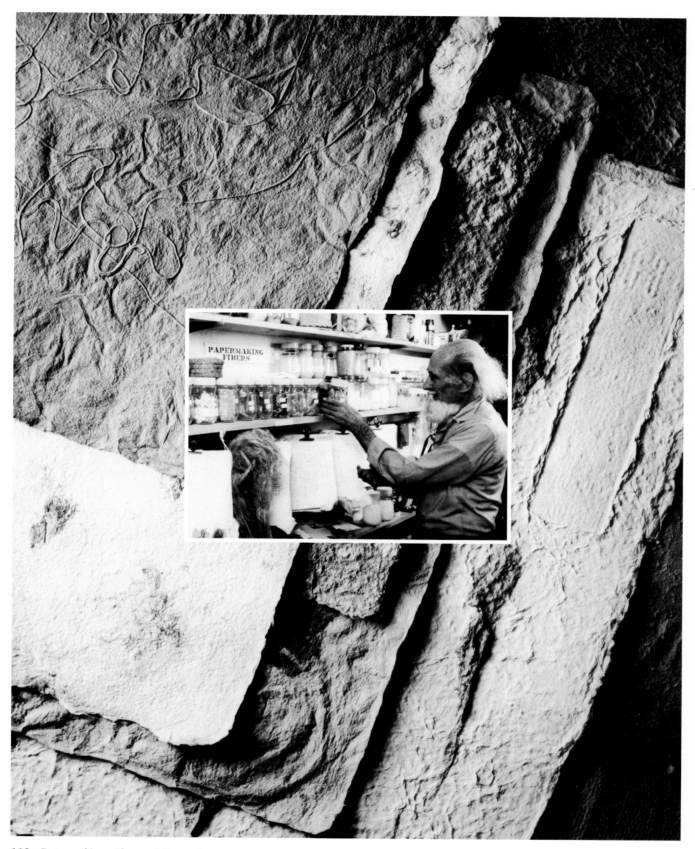

119. *Papermaking. Flax and linen sheets.*
Inset, Douglass Morse Howell in his Riverhead, New York, studio.

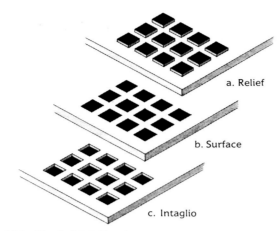

120. *Flat-bed printing processes.*

a. Relief

b. Surface

c. Intaglio

and trained master printers, workshops provide techniques that few artists in isolation could ever hope to learn.

The Edition

Since printmaking makes use of drawing skills, it is frequently difficult for the beginner to determine whether a particular work is a draw-

ing, a print, or a photographic reproduction. However, a familiarity with some of the most common printing techniques used by artists may be helpful in identifying prints. As part of the printmaking process, single proofs, which are sample prints, are **pulled** (printed) at various stages, or states, to determine how the image—on the broad surface (sometimes called **flat-bed**) of the block, plate, or screen—is progressing. When the image is finished to the artist's satisfaction, a series is run off called **artist's proofs.** A print labeled artist's proof is retained by the artist for personal record and comparison. After the inks are properly distributed on the printing surface to the artist's satisfaction, a **printer's proof** is pulled, labeled *bon à tirer* ("good to pull"), which becomes the standard by which the **edition** is judged. The entire edition is numbered. For example, the figure 20/100 at the lower left of the print indicates that it is the twentieth print pulled in an edition of one hundred. The artist's signature in pencil verifies its authenticity and his or her approval of its quality. After completing the edition, the artist may deliberately deface the block, plate, or screen and pull a print called a **cancellation proof** to guarantee that the edition is limited.

121. *Katsushika Hokusai.* Fuji Seen from the Bottom of a Wave *from* The Thirty-six Views of Mt. Fuji. *1823–1829. Color woodcut, 10 × 15" (25 × 38 cm). Metropolitan Museum of Art, New York (Rogers Fund, 1914).*

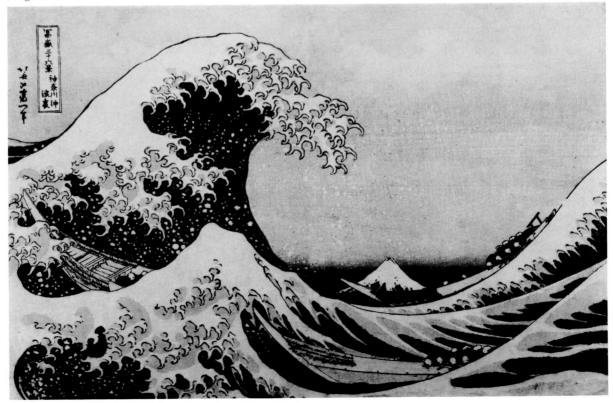

Printmaking was originally intended to provide thousands of copies for a mass market, but the modern trend has led to limited editions. Many painters also work in graphics to provide fine prints for those who cannot afford their paintings; they may limit their editions to fifty prints or less, each carefully signed and numbered.

Relief Printing

The oldest method of reproducing images is **relief** printing. The most common print types are **woodcuts,** wood **engravings,** and linoleum cuts. The artist first transfers a design to a block. Then, using sharp gouges, he or she cuts away all unwanted areas of wood or linoleum, leaving elevated only the design area that is to be printed **[120a]**. Ink is then spread over the block and paper is laid upon it. The ink is transferred from the relief surface to the paper by means of pressure, usually by a press, producing a "mirrored" printed image of the original design. The technique is characterized by bold lines and strong tonal contrasts between the inked images and the paper.

In the Orient, woodcuts have been a significant art form for centuries, fulfilling a need for inexpensive art for those who could not afford hand-painted scrolls. Many Oriental woodcuts were printed with black outlines and later colored by hand. Other woodcuts were produced by cutting a separate block for each color. Each block was carefully inked, registered over the image left by the preceding block, and printed.

The woodcut of Fuji **[121]**, also known as *The Great Wave,* is one of a series of different views of the mountain executed by Hokusai (Katsushika Hokusai, 1760–1849). In this engaging print we scarcely perceive the tiny fishermen's boats desperately trying to escape from the towering wave. The striking asymmetrical composition, in which the wave almost encircles the remote mountain peak, seems very different from the symmetrical work of Renaissance printmakers like Dürer.

Japanese woodcuts reached Europe after Japan was opened to world trade in the 19th century, when they inspired Western artists in new directions. Hokusai, Hiroshige (Utagawa Hiroshige, 1797–1858; **[122]**, and Utamaro (Kitagawa Utamaro, 1753–1806), somewhat later, were especially influential. As a result, many Western artists adapted Japanese asymmetry to their painting and some revived woodblock printing.

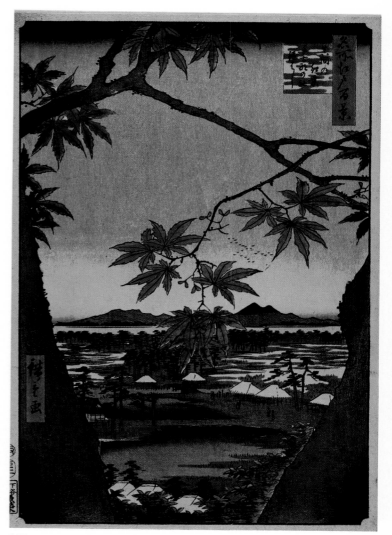

122. *Utagawa (Ando) Hiroshige.*
Maple Leaves at the Tekona Shrine, Mamma. *1857.*
Color woodcut, 13¾ × 9⅜" (35 × 24 cm).
Courtesy of the Trustees of the British Museum, London.

In Western Europe, woodcuts were important in the 15th and 16th centuries, when religious pictures were printed in editions of thousands and sold at popular prices. People believed that because of their holy subjects the woodcuts would protect the purchaser from sickness. Woodcut *taroc,* or *tarocci,* playing cards were also widely popular. These ancestors of today's playing cards and of Tarot cards, associated by some with fortune-telling and esoteric cults, came in standard packs of 62, 78, or 97. Venetian sets copied the four Islamic suits of cup, coin, sword, and polo stick. Twenty of Albrecht Dürer's pen-and-ink drawings of taroc cards, copied from a set in the Venetian style of 1462, still exist, as testament to the wide interest in these cards.

One of the most remarkable examples of Renaissance woodcuts is the mammoth *Triumphal Arch of Maximilian I* [123] by Dürer. Including the beautifully lettered explanation at the bottom, it measures about 11½ by 9¾ feet (3.5 by 2.97 meters) and is reputed to be the largest print ever commissioned before the 20th century. The work was printed from 192 separate blocks, required four separate printing shops and more than two years to complete, and was printed in five editions, three posthumously. The iconography, or meaning, of the images of this fantastic design involves many means of glorification, from the simple recording of historical events to cryptic emblematic allusions. The structure can be read like a book or decoded like a cryptogram. Yet, at the same time, it can be enjoyed like a collection of quaint and brilliant jewelry. The fine detail was possible because the design was probably cut on closely textured wood, such as cherry. The work is also remarkable in that the entire configuration is a product of Dürer's imagination. For the scenic representations he furnished slight sketches and supervised their

123. *Albrecht Dürer.* The Triumphal Arch of Maximilian I. *1515–1517. Woodcut (192 blocks), approximately 10' × 9'4" (3.05 × 2.85 m) without inscription. National Library of Austria, Vienna.*

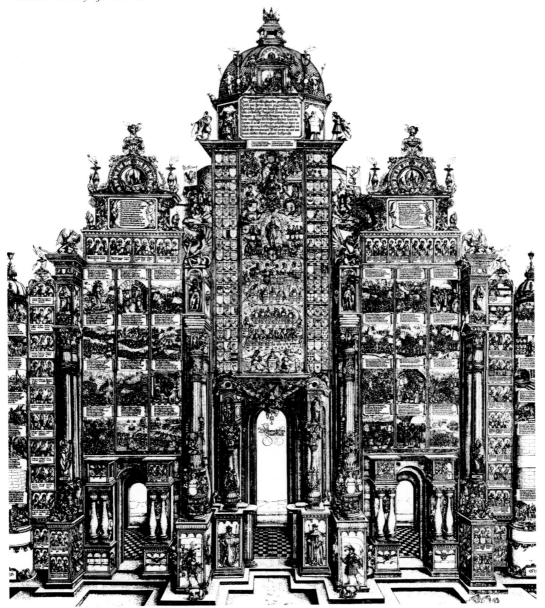

Focus on the Artist

Albrecht Dürer (1471–1528)

Perhaps the most prolific printmaker of all time, Albrecht Dürer was born in the south German city of Nuremberg, one of eighteen children of a not particularly prosperous goldsmith, also named Albrecht. As an early apprentice to his father, he acquired a thorough familiarity with the tools and materials of engraving, especially the jeweler's graver or **burin,** a tool unknown for printing before him. The young Dürer was brought up in the tradition of Jan van Eyck and Rogier van der Weyden, with whom his father had studied in the Netherlands. At fifteen, he was apprenticed to the foremost painter of the region, Michael Wolgemut, from whom he learned to handle the pen and brush, to copy and draw from life, and to work in other media— gouache, watercolor, and oils. The greatest publisher in Germany was his godfather, so Dürer became familiar early with the graphic processes that occupied him for the rest of his life. His prints set a new standard of perfection for more than a century and inspired countless other works in Italy, France, Russia, Spain, and even Persia. In 1494, Dürer visited Italy, enjoying a huge success, artistically, socially, and financially. In 1515, he was appointed court painter to Maximilian I, a position he retained even with the emperor's successor.

Dürer's most famous *Self-Portrait* of 1500 is the only one in which his figure is rigidly frontal in a vertical format [124]. This hieratic arrangement was traditionally reserved for images of Christ, with whom Dürer intended some resemblance. It seems certain that he also deliberately idealized his own features, softening his nose and cheekbones, while enlarging the size and shape of his eyes. The

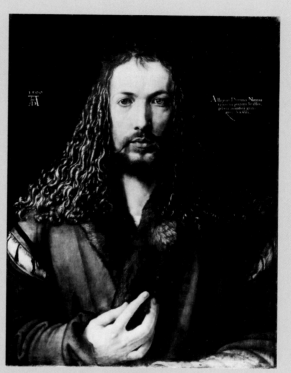

124. *Albrecht Dürer.* Self-Portrait. *1500. Panel, 25⅝ × 18⅞″ (64 × 48 cm). Alte Pinakothek, Munich.*

self-glorification of Dürer in the portrait implies a mystical relationship of the creative artist with God.

The last years of Dürer's life were devoted to his scholarship in books and treatises. As a Renaissance artist, he was attracted to perfection and an ideal beauty, believing in the genius of the artist whose hands and mind were in effect a gift of God.

---

execution by others. When the work of his assistants left too much to be desired, he supplied actual working drawings. When motifs had to be repeated symmetrically, he furnished only the designs for half of the woodcut, leaving it to his assistants to reverse them, change minor details, and, of course, the shadows, accordingly.

Woodcuts were commercially discarded in the West in favor of copper and steel engravings, but they continued to be used in cheap books and to illustrate political handbills, particularly during the French Revolution in the 18th cen-

tury and the Mexican Revolution in the 20th. Woodcuts were revived in the late 19th century as a result of Japanese influence and continue to be used by today's artists.

Intaglio Printing

The opposite of relief printing is **intaglio** printing, a term derived from the Italian word meaning "to cut in." In the intaglio processes of etching and engraving, the ink is forced into grooves in a metal plate with a felt-covered dauber [120b] so that it lies below the surface. When damp paper is pressed onto the plate by a press, it picks up ink from the grooves, in contrast to woodcut, where the ink lies on the wood that has been left raised.

The differences between etching and engraving lie in the different means used to cut the image into the metal plate. In **etching,** the plate is first coated with a waxy, acid-resistant substance, called a **ground.** The artist draws an image on the coated plate by scratching through the ground with a fine needle. When the plate is placed in an acid bath, the acid cannot reach the metal where it is covered, but along the lines where the ground has been removed it can bite, or etch, them into the bare metal. The remaining ground is then removed, the plate is inked and wiped off, leaving ink in the grooves, the paper is positioned, and then the print is pulled from the plate [125]. In **engraving,** the grooves in the plate are made by cutting directly into the metal with special tools. Lines are rarely as fine as those achieved by etching, but they are sharper and clearer.

In both etching and engraving, the artist builds up areas of darks by placing many lines close together. In both processes, the ink is lifted out of the grooves by the pressure of the press, forcing the ink to stand out on the surface of the paper. The ink can be felt as a raised edge when you run your finger over it. These processes yield sharply defined images. In other methods called **mezzotint** and **aquatint,** large areas of the plate can be roughened so that the ink adheres to a whole area and is printed as a flat tone. In

drypoint, a needle is used to scratch lines (furrows) into a plate surface. The ridge of metal at the furrows, called a "burr," catches and holds some ink, softening the lines of a drypoint etching. In the drypoint etching *The Caress* [126] by Mary Cassatt (1845–1926), both line and aquatint are combined to create dramatic images marked by intense light and shade. Compare this work with Hogarth's engraving from *The Rake's Progress* [37], which reveals infinite gradations and clarity in all details. Although both prints demonstrate careful draftsmanship and love of detail, the etching is far softer and is well suited to Cassatt's preoccupation with the intimate theme of mother and child.

Engraving on copper was first developed as a popular commercial process in the first half of the 15th century and was later used for illustration by artists such as Dürer, who designed many prints—more than one hundred engravings, etchings, and drypoints and more than three hundred woodcuts. Editions of thousands of his prints were not uncommon. Much finer detail is possible in the engraving process than in the woodcut, which may have accounted for its popularity.

Later, engravings were used for reproductions of artworks. Steel engravings of sentimental scenes were popular in Victorian homes. Few artists today, however, are as concerned with the sharp detail achieved by engraving; most, like Stanley Kaplan (b. 1925), prefer the versatility of etching [125]. Many artists, past and present, from Henri Matisse and Picasso to Kaplan, have illustrated books with etchings and have pro-

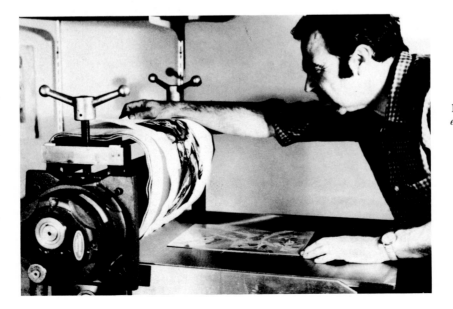

125. *Stanley Kaplan at etcher's press.*

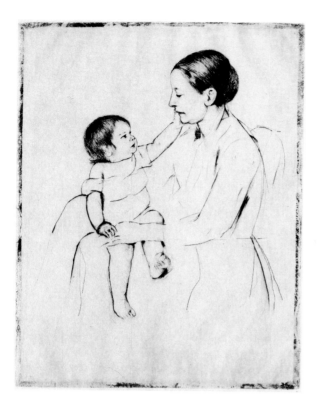

duced limited editions of individual etchings. An edition by Susan Rothenberg (b. 1945) rarely exceeds sixty, including one *bon à tirer* print that confirms the even distribution of inks, a printer's proof, and artist's proofs. Emblematic images of a single horse looming forward established her reputation. Their stark iconic quality suggest ghostly hallucinations. The tension between figure and ground that persists in her paintings is, if anything, intensified in the print by the expressionistic quality of her lines [127]. The equine silhouette projects the totemic look of a cave painting [2], and, perhaps, the isolation of a Munch figure [128].

Surface Printing

The third printing process is planographic, or surface, printing. **Lithography** is a planographic process that depends on the natural antipathy of

left: **126.** *Mary Cassatt. The Caress. 1891. Drypoint, $7\frac{11}{16} \times 5\frac{3}{4}''$ (20 × 15 cm). Metropolitan Museum of Art, New York (gift of Arthur Sachs, 1916).*

right: **127.** *Susan Rothenberg. Untitled (May #3). 1979. Etching: sugar lift, spit bite, soft ground, and burnishing from 2 steel-faced copper plates on Fabriano paper; $29\frac{5}{8} \times 22''$ (75.2 × 55.9 cm). Published by Parasol Press Ltd. Courtesy Barbara Krakow Gallery.*

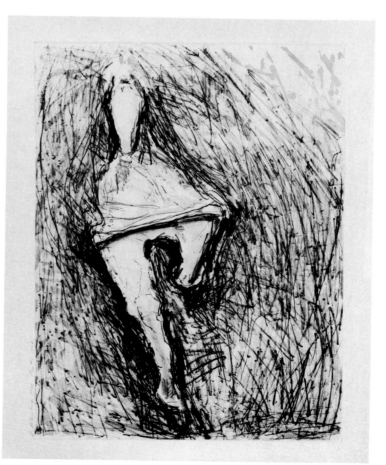

oil or grease to water for the transfer of ink to paper. Limestone slabs or sensitized metal plates are used as drawing surfaces [120c]. The artist draws with greasy lithographic crayon or with a special ink called **tusche.** Next a nitric-acid solution is applied to the stone or plate to make the sections that have not been drawn on resistant to the printing ink. The stone is kept wet with water during the entire printing process. The greasy printing ink adheres only to the crayon image and is repelled by the wet areas of the stone. When the stone and paper are run through a press, the paper picks up the ink from the drawn image, reproducing the artist's work. If the stone is not kept wet, the paper will be printed solid black, as any printmaker quickly learns.

The direct drawing methods in lithography allow the artist considerable spontaneity and variety. Drawing crayons are made in varying degrees of hardness and when stroked onto the grainy surface of the stone, they can create tones ranging from soft grays to rich, heavy darks. Crayons can be held on their edges to produce large areas of gray, while details can be drawn in

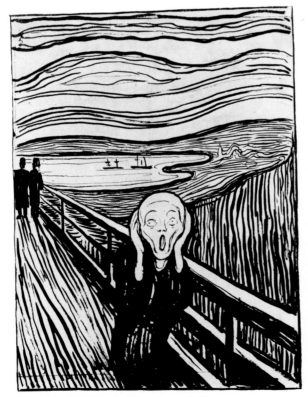

128. *Edvard Munch. The Cry. 1893. Lithograph on pink paper, 14½ × 9⅞″ (37 × 25 cm). Museum of Fine Arts, Boston (William Francis Warden Fund).*

with a pointed crayon or a pen dipped in tusche. In color lithography, as in color woodcuts, each color requires a separate drawing, which is printed in sequence on the one sheet faithfully following registration marks. In **offset** lithography, a more involved process, impressions are transferred via a rubber blanket, rather than directly from stone or plates [129] (see Chapter 6).

The lithograph by Edvard Munch (1863–1944) [128] is one of a series on a single theme, which occupied him on and off for much of his life. The anguish of the abandoned central figure is echoed by the land, sea, and sky, graphically demonstrated by the heavy, strident lines. The bridge on which the figures stand may represent the passage of time. Hands held to the ears, with the mouth open, the image is filled with anxiety and despair, while the torment reverberates even unto the land, the sky, and the sea. The face seems to exude death, while the distant passers-by suggest a world indifferent to private tragedy. Munch's lines are summary, yet express in their economical strokes the anguish of existence. Munch once said "I paint the scream in nature."

When lithography was invented in 1798, the technique quickly became popular for illustrations in newspapers and magazines because it is much easier to draw with crayons on a stone slab than to engrave lines into a metal plate. Honoré Daumier (1808–1879), for example, used the lithographic process on stone regularly for political and social comments. Many of Daumier's drawings and paintings [393] also carry on the social caricatures of Goya and presage political and social works by Käthe Kollwitz (1867–1945; [429]) and George Grosz (1893–1959), whose pen, brush, and ink drawing [430] reveals his skill at political satire. Moving away from these black-and-white expressions into strident color to depict insanity and murder, the theme of the opera *Wozzeck* by Alban Berg, Jan Lenica (b. 1928) makes use of strong color by contrasting a dominant red-orange with discordant bits of red-purple in the offset lithography medium [129]. The poster also suggests the composer's atonal untraditional musical harmony.

A legend even in his own time, Henri de Toulouse-Lautrec (1864–1901) evolved from an illustrator (of horses) to perhaps the most trenchant satirist of the café scene. His poster design for *Le Divan Japonais* [130] demonstrates graphic clarity, influenced by the late-19th-century exposure to the linear quality of Japanese prints, which avoid most illusions of depth provided by linear perspective. His forms are flattened, the

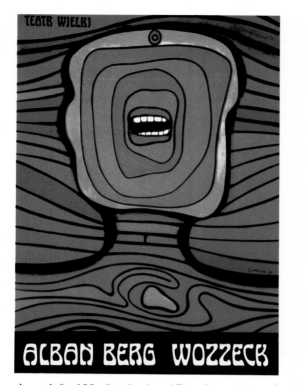

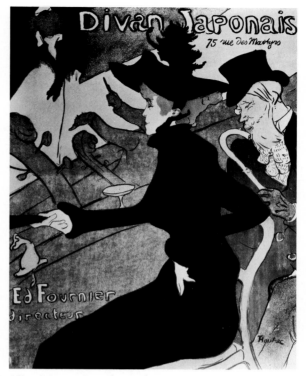

above left: **129.** *Jan Lenica.* Alban Berg Wozzeck. *1964. Offset lithograph, 38⅛ × 26½"*
(97 × 67 cm). Collection, Museum of Modern Art, New York (anonymous gift).

above right: **130.** *Henri de Toulouse-Lautrec.* Le Divan Japonais. *1892. Color lithograph,*
31⅝ × 23⅞" (80 × 61 cm). Collection, Museum of Modern Art, New York
(Abby Aldrich Rockefeller Purchase Fund).

viewpoint is unusual, and the memorable imagery is designed to be quickly seen and understood, for posters are rarely given long study. The lines are economically drawn, revealing the skill of an artist who successfully produced single paintings as well as multiple works for an unlimited audience.

A very different orientation to design can be seen in the lithographs of M. C. Escher. His highly imaginative works, which border on the surrealistic, also demonstrate a delight in detail and an eye for illusions of perspective. In *Drawing Hands* [3] we find a new dimension created through the physical and optical impossibilities which he has created.

Many artists print their own lithographs. Some alter the initial images as early proofs suggest, while others draw the image clearly at the start and maintain their original concept from beginning to end. As with other forms of printmaking, many artists entrust their works to master printers, whom they carefully supervise.

Serigraphy is a planographic process that uses a stencil placed on a screen of fine silk. The term is the fine-arts equivalent of the 20th-century commercial printing process called **silkscreen.** Many contemporary artists adopt serigraphy because it permits more variations in the material to be printed on than other printing processes. Used commercially, silkscreen can print images onto soft fabrics such as T-shirts or hard surfaces such as glasses, yielding almost unlimited possibilities. Used for fine art, silkscreen can produce prints (serigraphs) that incorporate complex images in multiple colors, which are particularly effective in large, flat areas on posters. Silkscreen, however, can also be used to achieve rich, subtle colors and varying textures.

The artist cuts a stencil from a special film, which is then fixed to the screen of silk stretched on a frame. Alternatively, the stencil may be painted directly onto the silk with glue, mascoid cement, or shellac. The stencil prevents the paint from seeping through the screen onto the paper beneath. Thus any area not covered by the stencil is printed. If the stencil is brushed on with glue, a loose, free-flowing image can result. With a firm stencil, the images are hard and sharp. The paint, which can be thick and opaque or thin and transparent, is dragged across the silk with a wide rubber squeegee and directly transmitted through to the paper. To produce multiple-color prints, the artist uses several stencils, printing each separately one over the other. The colors may be adjacent or built up in transparent layers, depending on the stencils.

Blue to Red Portal [131], a screened print by Richard Anuszkiewicz (b. 1930), shows a complex geometry of concentric rectangles and straight lines, yielding warm and subtle gradations of color and movement. This print, from the artist's series based only on straight lines, creates a visual excitement that demands perfect registration of the several superimposed stencils (and printings) involved.

131. *Richard Anuszkiewicz.* Blue to Red Portal. *1977. Screened on masonite, 7 × 4′ (2.1 × 1.2 m). Collection the artist.*

Monotype

It is perhaps fitting to round out our discussion of printmaking with media that may involve other processes as well. The "monotype" is defined as a single image—a unique work of art, produced from a drawing or painting applied to a non-absorbent plate surface of any material. Fine detail is achieved by scratching paint off the plate, using a sharp implement. If the image is transferred to paper by rolling it through a press, some printmakers identify the work as a monoprint. Others term all singular works of this kind, even those in which transfer of matrix to paper is accomplished by handrubbing, as monotypes. The edition is customarily numbered 1/1.

Expanded Techniques

Prints, like paintings, can make use of mixed media. Collages made of various materials glued onto metal or wooden panels can be inked and run through a press to produce unusual textures. This new and freer way of printing is called **collography.** The potential for this technique has barely been approached and is limited only by the inventiveness of the artist.

Collography can be combined with other printing methods. To achieve varied effects, prints can be given raised surfaces by printing damp papers under strong pressure onto carved wooden blocks to which textured materials such as metal scraps, screening, or heavy twine have been glued. Silkscreen and lithography have been used to print flat cutouts, many complete with slots and tabs, which can later be assembled into three-dimensional objects. Thus the artist, instead of trying to produce an illusion of solidity through the flat image of a print, may create a printed image that will become a three-dimensional object itself. Coco Gordon, a contemporary artist-poet who also produces her own paper, emphasizes wit as well as aesthetics in her work. Many of her pieces move through two- and three-dimensional space concurrently, while others are intellectual exercises, as signifi-

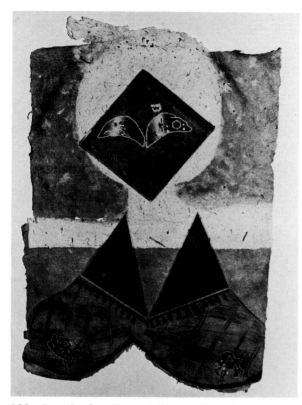

132. *Coco Gordon. Hum. 1979. Collograph, etching, and electric engraving on plexiglass (face), soft-ground and brushed aquatint (collar), on own method two-pulp linen handmade shaped paper; 12 × 18" (31 × 46 cm). Collection the author.*

cant for their creative concept as for the lasting work that is produced [132].

Photoprinting and other techniques have revolutionized printmaking in the second half of the 20th century. Artists are working in ways that make classification of their art impossible. For example, photographs printed on cloth may be cut out, stuffed, and sewn, becoming sculptural forms, while prints on styrofoam produce three-dimensional objects.

Printmaking, even more than the other visual arts, is characterized by almost unlimited experimentation. A host of new processes that artists have used with great success—photolithography, for example—creates an atmosphere of experiment and great vitality. Clearly, technology is the focus. The three-dimensional print *Gertrude* [133] was printed in six colors from two aluminum plates by the artist Red Grooms (b. 1937). The prints were die-cut, folded, and glued together in an amusing sculptural spoof of Gertrude Stein.

Photomechanical processes that developed from the 1850s to the 1880s have deeply affected printmaking in the 20th century, particularly with the advent and involvement of photography. Therefore, the arts of the lens are the basis of our next group of studies. Where the new vision will lead, no one knows, but, clearly, art will be changed radically.

133. *Red Grooms. Gertrude. 1975. Color lithograph on Arches cover; cut out, glued and mounted in plexiglass box; edition of 46; 19¼ × 22 × 10" (49 × 56 × 25 cm). Co-published by Brooke Alexander, Inc., and Marlborough Graphics, Inc.*

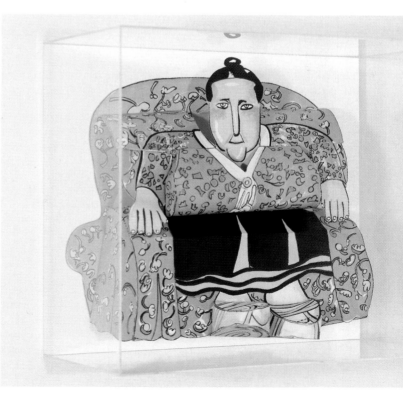

Exploring Art Through Technology

Technology as the Focus

The technical processes required in making prints have become for many printmakers the focus of much if not most of their attention in the latter half of the 20th century. This interest in process appeared first at the turn of the century when some artists began to turn away from traditional procedures in favor of experimenting with technique. Lithography is the graphic medium closest to drawing, where most artists begin, so it is not surprising that the lithograph has become the most popular arena for technological expression. As is apparent from *The Cry*, lithography provides a range of tones from the deepest, richest blacks to the pure white of the paper. The vigor of this drawing is exceptional, produced with thickened brush strokes using liquid tusche like black ink with a brush [128].

Toulouse-Lautrec's lithograph *Le Divan Japonais* [130] was achieved by departing even more from conventional lithographic procedures. Important in the history of printmaking, Lautrec enlarged the scope of a somewhat limited technique of drawing on stone to the rank of a flexible art form. For instance, after painting a few areas of the stone with tusche, he alternately covered other areas with pieces of paper, laid like stencils over the rest of the stone, then painted flat tones, echoing Japanese traditions.

In recent years, the medium of lithography has evolved still further, expanding from a ground base of stone to other surfaces like zinc plates, now used in the artist's studio and in commercial printing. Metal plates made by a photomechanical process are curved around rollers that can quickly transfer images from one roller to another and then to paper in the printing method called **offset.** Lithography has thus become with all its many variations the most popular print process today.

When Robert Rauschenberg was commissioned to produce a poster that would commemorate the hundredth anniversary of the Metropolitan Museum of Art [134], he made

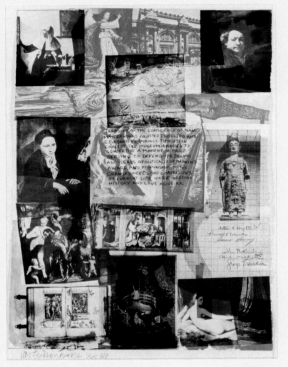

134. *Robert Rauschenberg.* Centennial Certificate, MMA. *1969. Color lithograph, 35⅞ × 25" (91.2 × 63.5 cm). Metropolitan Museum of Art (Florence and Joseph Singer Collection).*

use of these and other commercial innovations. Employing two stones and two aluminum plates in red, yellow, blue, and brown, he superimposed photographs on art reproductions transparently, adding signatures of museum officials and museum goals at the center. Rauschenberg has gone on to transfer selected newspaper and magazine impressions of advertisements and editorial comments onto a single lithograph, less concerned with the content of the rub-ons than to critique the media in our culture. The technology has surely become the artist's focus.

The Print Workshop

The atmosphere of today's print workshops with their invigorating smells of turpentine and ink is probably not much different from that in Renaissance shops like Dürer's. There is now an unprecedented interest in the print process in busy art centers all over the world. There has been a shift away from the traditional notion of a solitary individual plying his or her craft to a community where insights and skills are shared. The practice approaches the ideal of William Morris (1834–1896) a century ago (see Chapters 6 and 14); he and others so feared the loss of craftsmanship in the burgeoning industrial age that they encouraged artists to unite their skills in the common interest. Today print workshops are flourishing. Master printers' studios are visited by artists who are eager to experiment with new techniques and larger sizes not seen since Dürer's *Triumphal Arch*. In the United States major artists have taken to the printmaker's craft. The following list, though incomplete, suggests how good workshops have proliferated.

A pioneer in the workshop movement was Tatyana Grosman (1904–1982), a spiritual catalyst to many of the great artists of our time. The quotation that opens this chapter and the following remarks are based on the author's meeting with Mrs. Grosman in West Islip, New York, in the spring of 1980. Realizing that limestone slabs no longer used in construction on their property would be fine surfaces for lithography, she and her husband, Maurice, a painter and sculptor, set up a workshop for printing on stone in limited editions. With the registration of their **logo,** Universal Limited Art Editions, in 1956, the **atelier,** or workshop, was born. Younger artists were invited to share the facilities. The philosophy of the workshop went far beyond merely furnishing the necessary tools and presses. Work with stone was to be a revelation. Their first undertaking was with Robert Blackburn (b. 1920), an early apprentice chosen to print a work produced by a pioneering partnership **[135]** of a painter, Larry Rivers (b. 1923), and a poet, Frank O'Hara. As creative novices in printing on stone they even incorporated the outlined edge of the limestone slab into their design—a practice never approved by traditional printmakers, which made their work a unique blend of art, literature, and graphic experiment.

Everything was visual. Mrs. Grosman's personal philosophy of "glorifying existence" by inspiring artists "to do something extraordinary" brought to her door such well-known painters as Robert Rauschenberg **[134]**, Jasper Johns **[41]**, and Barnett Newman **[73]**, the sculptor Lee Bontecou **[117]**, and the painter Helen Frankenthaler **[75]**. She established a personal level of communication with each artist, involving them all in printmaking, encouraging them each time to surpass their previous work, yet allowing artists the private use of the premises and the master printers. Each print is made by hand and strives to capture the spirit of the artist's design drawn the day before. It is easy to see why some artists work best with particular printers in such a milieu.

The first master print shops on the West Coast were Gemini G.E.L. and the Tamarind Lithography workshop, founded by June Wayne (b. 1918). These and later master print shops provided facilities for famous artists of the 1960s. Wayne's skilled technicians created a whole new chemistry. The prints that emerged were often of a size, complexity, and degree of innovation that craftspeople with limited financial means could never otherwise have achieved. The impetus for these American workshops doubtless came from the English artist Stanley William Hayter (1901–1988), who in the 1930s established Atelier 17 in Paris as a center of experimental printmaking. In the 1940s, during World War II, Hayter brought his ideas to New York, providing inspiration to American artists.

As a result of such workshops there has been a resurgence of printmaking all over the United States—a renaissance brought about not, as might have been expected, through the efforts of printmakers or their students, but through the finished works, which have inspired broad public interest. Current achievements in the graphic arts, particularly in these print shops,

135. *Frank O'Hara and Larry Rivers working on* Stones, *Larry Rivers' studio. 1958.*

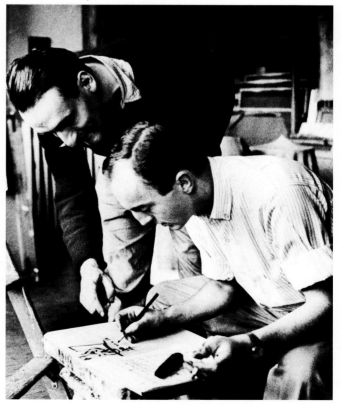

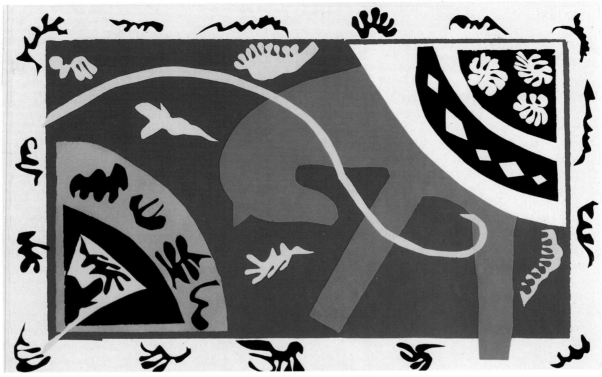

136. *Henri Matisse.* Horse, Rider and Clown, *plate 5 from* Jazz. *1947. Pochoir, printed in color, composition: $16\frac{1}{2} \times 25\frac{3}{4}''$ (41.9 × 65.4 cm). Collection, Museum of Modern Art, New York (Louis E. Stern Collection).*

which aim not for mass output but for creative production, are bound to be a major influence on art for many years to come.

The Artist's Book

The artist's book is based on the concept that the spaces enclosed within the covers of a book provide a legitimate area for artistic expression. Just as two-dimensional space is explored by the painter and graphic designer, three-dimensional space manipulated by the sculptor, and environmental space controlled by the architect, a growing number of artists are attracted to the artist's book. During his declining years, Henri Matisse created, with an assistant's help, such a book, called *Jazz.* Matisse supervised the cutouts of various brightly colored forms which were later displayed on the wall in an exhibition at the Museum of Modern Art in New York. Some of these designs were assembled (reduced) within the pages of *Jazz,* alternating with pages of text that incorporated ideas Matisse had expressed in his informal writings some years earlier. The original collated book is in a private collection, but *Jazz* was also offered by the Museum in soft and hard cover editions, printed by offset [136].

Variants of Matisse's procedures can be found today. There are at least three different kinds of books currently produced by artists.

1. A one-of-a-kind book may be created by drawing, painting, printing, and assembling elements through collage, with or without hand-lettered text.
2. The artist may design a book of limited edition, encompassing prints, type, or drawings reproduced by offset.
3. The printmaker may produce lithographs, etchings, and silkscreened prints, hand-stitch them together, and manually bind them into a book format as an original.

The existence of multiples, no matter how few, suggests that the special mystique of the original may be shared by many. When we look at a Hogarth engraving [37], we are viewing work intended to be seen by many. The artist's book, by the diverse nature of various examples, is the newest arena for the printmaker's creativity in the United States, though the ambiguities of terminology and valuation—original versus multiple printings—remain an open-ended issue, yet to be resolved.

Exercises and Activities

Research Exercises

1. Trace the origins of paper, distinguishing between "wove" and "laid."
2. Why is handmade paper important to many printmakers today?
3. Each category of printing—woodcut, etching, engraving, stencil, lithograph, or collograph—offers a different potential for creative expression. Explain the differences between these types of printing. How does engraving differ from etching both in method and final effect?
4. Select from the prints reproduced in this book three works that appeal to you and explain your reasons for choosing them.

Studio Activities

1. Transpose the black and white of Edvard Munch's *The Cry* into colors, using, perhaps, pastels. Does the work lose impact?
2. Eliminate linear perspective in *The Cry* to alter the spatial effect.
3. Design your own monogram and transfer it to a printing surface from which you can make a relief image. Use linoleum, styrofoam, or even a potato as a printing surface, being careful to cut a "mirrored" image so that the printed monogram can be read normally.
4. Design your own note cards, using a relief process. Do not concentrate on lines but focus instead on flat areas, which are easier to carve and then to print.

5
Arts of
the Lens

The camera, through its use in still photography, films, television, and the media, has shaped our lives in the 20th century perhaps more than any other single invention. Through the photographic image we have all been exposed to people, places, and ideas that we would never otherwise have witnessed. Much of our understanding of the world in which we live comes to us through the camera lens. In fact, we are so completely surrounded and seduced by photographic images that few will question the Canadian communicative specialist Marshall McLuhan's view that "the medium is the massage."

In this chapter, we shall explore how the camera lens records images on film, as well as how it transmits images to the television tube. The aesthetic considerations that relate to still photography and film apply as well to the electronic medium of television, much of which for many people has the potential to be the dominant visual art of our time.

Photography is both a complex science and a new art form. As a science it depends on laws of physics involving the passage of light through a lens and laws of chemistry involving sensitivity to light. Light transfers the image "seen" by the lens onto chemically sensitized film, and this image is then made visible and permanent by further chemical action.

The photographic image is a product of scientific laws, but it can also be a work of art whose impact is limited only by the creativity and imagination of the photographer. Though it is true that a camera more or less accurately records what it is focused on, the same subject can be interpreted in as many varied ways as the many visions of each photographer—or many photographers. Like all other artists, the photographer chooses what to portray, how to emphasize or eliminate various aspects, and what viewpoint would be most expressive.

An unusual vantage point permitted Margaret Bourke-White (1904–1971) to observe the face of nature given a new identity through indomitable human spirit [137]. The large shape that dominates *Contour Plowing* is made of striated furrow lines that course rhythmically throughout. Bourke-White's "message" may have been that, with determination, the human units of force (at the plow) can metamorphose the earth. Without a doubt, the photographer's creativity is able to transform the mechanical process of photography into fine art, separating the myriad snapshots and conventional photographs that surround us from the few truly expressive images.

Historical Roles of the Camera

Photography can be described as the most popular art form of this century—certainly the most widespread. The arts that depend on the lens dominate our visual environment, providing as many services to society as were once furnished by the more traditional medium of painting. Indeed the areas of photographic specialization we shall examine, in their historic sequence, evolved from roles formerly the exclusive domain of painters; that is, from photography as fine art with portraiture and nature studies its major preoccupation; then, the documenting of social problems, photojournalism and editorial photography; and on to fashion and advertising photography, relatively new fields that began in the 20th century. Within the broad range of camera arts that have developed since photography first became accessible to the public 140 or so years ago, its contribution to the fine arts has

been consistent, and perhaps still remains the focus of most photography today.

Documentation with the Still Camera

In still photography, the camera assures the photographer some success by assuming part of the process of recording the subject. The ease with which we can trip a camera shutter may make photography seem like a push-button art; with luck, we can expect some positive results almost from the start. To exploit the creative potentials of photography, however, a photographer must have considerable knowledge and expertise. But, as with any art form, even vast technical knowledge cannot guarantee masterpieces; a work of art in photography, as in all other art forms, is the result of a combination of its creator's personal vision, technical skill, and ability to express meaning in visual images. For most photographers, a double exposure means two wasted pictures of two events or scenes. Not

137. *Margaret Bourke-White.* Contour Plowing. *1954. Photograph.*

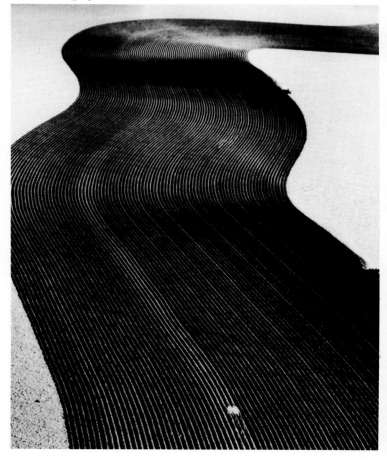

so for Ray Metzker (b. 1931) in his creative interpretation of a trolley stop [138]. His many stills, some recording movement and overlap of images, have produced a memorable configuration that few of us would have imagined was possible.

The principle of the camera dates at least as far back as Renaissance Italy, when artistic preoccupation with the creation of an illusion of depth on a flat surface led to the development of a device called **camera obscura,** literally, "dark room." By reproducing exactly the scenes they wished to portray, artists were helped in rendering three dimensions on a two-dimensional surface. As Leonardo da Vinci described the principle, "Light entering a tiny opening in one wall of a darkened room forms an inverted image of the outside scene on the opposite wall." This view could be traced to provide the correct representation for a painting. Later, artists found that if a lens replaced the pinhole opening, a clearer image could be produced.

It was not until the 19th century, however, that a way was found to capture an image on a sensitized surface. Though Thomas Wedgwood (1771–1805) in England had earlier been able to create impermanent solar pictures, the first fixed camera image was probably originated by Joseph Nicéphore Niépce (1765–1833) in France about 1826, and almost concurrently by Louis Jacques Mandé Daguerre (1787–1851) as well. Evolving from those early images that were little more than impressions, Daguerre's pioneering photograph of 1837 remains outstanding in its artful composition, which demonstrates depth along with a range of textures [139].

As the technique of photography improved and permanent images of people and places could be made more easily, many painters decided that in their primary role in society—as recorders of people, places, or events—they had been supplanted by the camera. Photographers began to use the new invention to duplicate art.

Portraits

Photography was officially accepted in the French Salon by 1859 and early creative photographers all over the world worked mostly on portraiture. People hastened to sit for their por-

138. *Ray K. Metzker. Trolley Stop (detail). 1966. Photograph; gelatin silver print; work in its entirety 40½ × 35" (103 × 89 cm). Collection, The Museum of Modern Art, New York (purchase).*

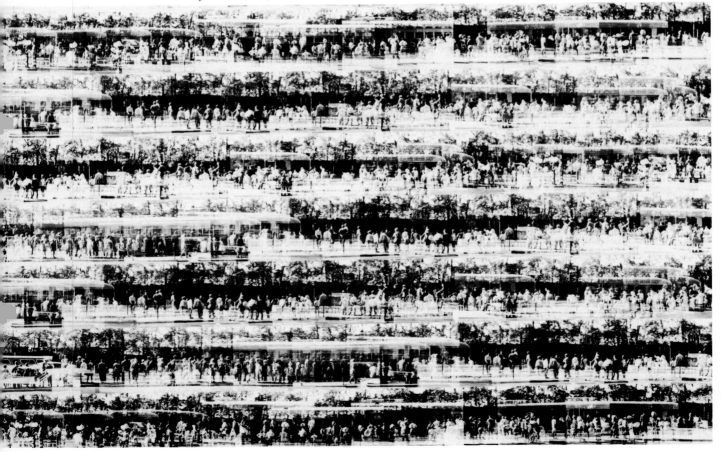

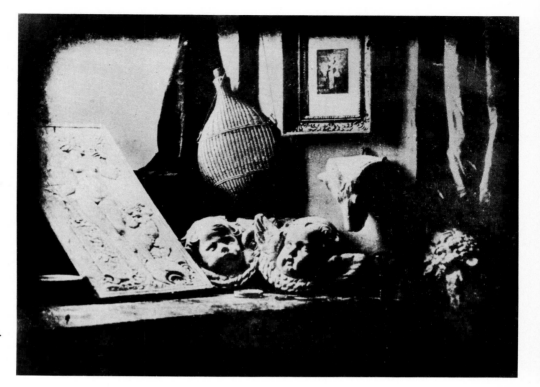

139. *Louis Jacques Mandé Daguerre.* The Artist's Studio. *1837. Daguerrotype. Société Française de Photographie, Paris.*

traits by these early photographers; despite the limitations imposed by the lengthy sittings required to register images on slow photographic emulsions and the constraints imposed by imitating painterly conventions, they produced some remarkable photographs through expressive use of pose, lighting, background, and point of view, as we have seen **[64]**.

The first major woman photographer, Julia Margaret Cameron (1815–1879), was almost fifty years old when she encountered the camera. Self-taught in the complexities of photographic processing, she began to exhibit her portraits first in England, then internationally, often preferring "soft-focus" instead of the pinpoint sharpness her critics admired. About her photograph of the great English historian, Thomas Carlyle **[140]**, Cameron explained: "[My goal was to reveal] Carlyle like a rough block of Michelangelo's sculpture." Cameron was the first to use the close-up vantage point to capture further intimacy with her subject. The dramatic contrasts in light and dark created by her lighting caused her subject's head to seem suspended in darkness and thereby much more than a likeness was captured. A broad range of values, from black through grays to white, engages our attention. However, we return with renewed interest to the intense personality revealed in the face.

140. *Julia Margaret Cameron.* Carlyle Like a Rough Block of Michelangelo's Sculpture. *1867. Albumen print, 13¼ × 11" (33.5 × 28 cm). Herschel Album, National Museum of Photography, Film, and Television, Bradford, Yorkshire, England.*

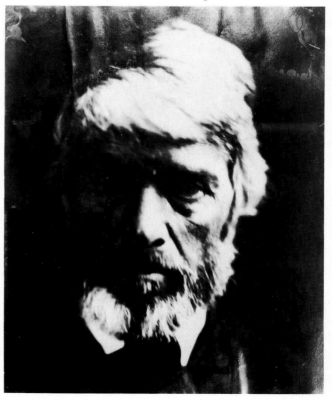

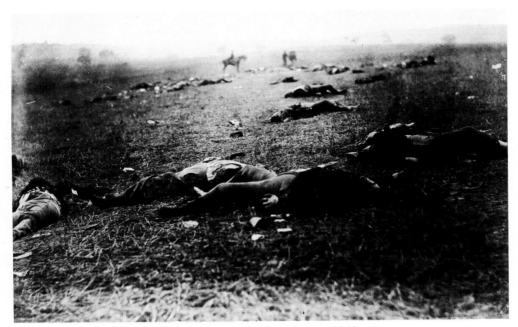

141. *Timothy O'Sullivan.* A Harvest of Death. Gettysburg. *1863.*
Photograph. New York Public Library Rare Books Collection.

Landscapes

Through the technical experiments made by photographers in the mid-19th century, the picture-taking process was shortened, making it

142. *Alfred Stieglitz.* The Terminal. *1893.*
Photograph. International Museum of Photography.
George Eastman House, Rochester, New York.

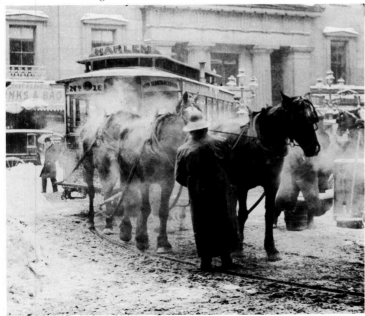

possible for photographers to record the horrors of war, which Mathew Brady (1823–1896) and Timothy O'Sullivan (1840–1882) **[141]** did with great expressive power. While photographers were learning how to create photographs that resembled paintings, painters were eagerly looking for ways to work that they were convinced cameras could never duplicate. By the 1860s, French artists were experimenting with changing light and atmosphere in a style the world was soon to label **Impressionism.** Not much later, however, the camera, in the hands of the American Alfred Stieglitz (1864–1945), was just as successful in capturing steam and smoke in a nostalgic view of a wintry New York horsecar scene called *The Terminal* **[142]**. By choosing a camera angle that leads the tracks in a diagonal path, Stieglitz produced an illusion of depth that focused attention on both the horsecar and the steam in the air.

By the end of the 19th century, photographers had become less concerned with imitating painting than with allowing photography to emerge as a new field of art. Many American photographers, rather than viewing photographs as duplications of realistic paintings, discovered that photography could present more expressive views of commonplace scenes. For example, Ansel Adams (1902–1984) brilliantly demonstrated the artistic potential of photography in his prints, which hint at infinity, deeply extending the range of black-and-white shades. His *Moon and Half Dome* [143] captures a mysterious feeling of vast, yet confined space, illuminated by the moon, hanging in an empty sky, while black, shadowy foreground masses effectively frame and complement the textured stone cliffs.

Adams found drama in nature by choosing a special station point from which he could observe nature's scale, her infinite variety in textures, the wonderful play of light against dark, and the true flowing sweep of her curves. By using shadowed mountains to frame the clarity of the moon suspended over the lighted expanse of the rock known as Half Dome, Adams captured an arresting image. The brilliant moon, despite its tiny scale in relation to the huge forms below, is a perfect balance and focus for the work. Not many of us might have been able

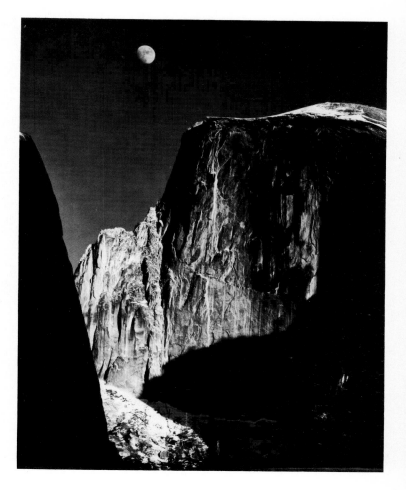

right: **143.** *Ansel Adams.* Moon and Half Dome, Yosemite National Park, California. *1960. Photograph.* © *Ansel Adams Publishing Rights Trust.*

below: **144.** *Dorothea Lange.* Migrant Mother, Nipomo, California. *1936. Photograph, gelatin silver print,* $12\frac{1}{2} \times 9\frac{7}{8}''$ *(31.7 × 25.1 cm). Collection, Museum of Modern Art, New York (purchase).*

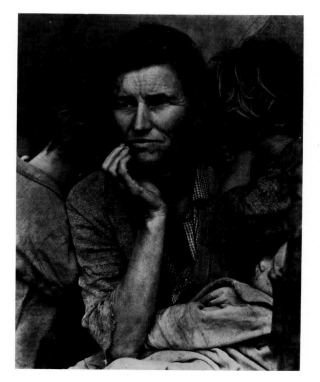

to achieve such a memorable image of a moonlit mountain scene.

Social Commentary

By applying such standards of creativity, photographers extended Brady's use of the camera to document moments in history in photojournalism. Dorothea Lange (1895–1965) recorded the desperate hopelessness of a migrant farm worker in the Depression of the 1930s in a portrait that has since become a classic [144]. Her field notes describe the migrant worker: "Camped on the edge of a pea field where the crop has failed in a freeze, the tires had just been sold from the car to buy food. She was 32 years old with seven children."

Later, Berenice Abbott (b. 1898) and others earned international reputations as documentary photographers who creatively interpreted the events, people, and places of the world around them. The news photo has now become an important part of our lives through its ability to capture a moment of history as well as to express visually what is often inexpressible in words.

Independent of photography, innovators have explored ways to capture images through noncamera techniques. Shadow pictures called **photograms** or **rayographs,** such as those made by **Bauhaus** instructor László Moholy-Nagy (1895–1946; [145]), are made by placing an object on a light-sensitive material and exposing it to light. Color photograms can be made in the same way, adding color-filter modulators. Other, more specialized noncamera techniques include **holography** and **solarization.**

Still Photography Technique

Still Cameras

The camera is surprisingly like the human eye, based on principles that are similar to those that enable the human eye to transmit images to the brain.

A simple box camera has a fixed **lens** and a nonadjustable **aperture,** or opening, which admits light rays. The rays are focused on light-sensitized film at the back of the camera. The

145. *László Moholy-Nagy. Photogram. 1926.*
© *William Larson.*

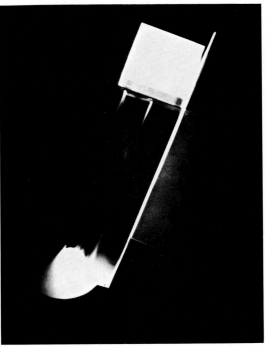

viewfinder allows the photographer to see what the final image will be. Early photographers used bulky cameras, composing their pictures in large viewfinders that showed images the same size as the intended photographic print. Later the development of more sophisticated portable cameras allowed pictures to be taken almost anywhere. The "candid" photography that resulted revolutionized the medium.

Many cameras today can be fitted with alternate lenses of different focal lengths for best use with near, far, or detailed subjects and can be operated by remote control. Many are equipped with photoelectric cells that can control the intake of light and change the shutter speed automatically. There are some cameras capable of processing the film and producing photographs in a matter of seconds. Some complex cameras are designed to probe unknown areas when used in conjunction with telescopes and microscopes.

The lens components are the most valuable part of a camera. Although even a pinhole will produce an image, a good lens concentrates the light, rapidly admitting more light in less time so that even dim moving objects can be photographed. Telephoto lenses permit detailed views of distant objects by magnifying them, while wide-angle lenses enable the photographer to focus on broad subjects at close range. Fish-eye lenses are an extreme form of wide-angle lenses; they distort subjects by magnifying only the central portion of the total image, just as fish tend to see their world. A photographer used a 7.5 mm fisheye lens positioned directly over the steering wheel of a boat in New York harbor. Linear perspective was somewhat sacrificed, since the horizon line follows the curvature of the earth as viewed through the windshield of the boat [146].

Other important parts of a camera are the shutter and diaphragm, which control the length of time light is admitted to the lens—speed—and the size of the opening—aperture size. Inexpensive nonadjustable cameras have only one shutter speed and one aperture size. The length of time the shutter is open and the size of the opening regulate the amount of light reflected from the subject onto the unexposed film. Different lenses, focal lengths, shutter speeds, and so on, provide flexibility. With the more refined cameras, shutter speeds can range from a 4000th of a second to unlimited time exposures. The size of the aperture opening is regulated by the f-stop control dial on the lens—the higher the f-stop number, the smaller the opening.

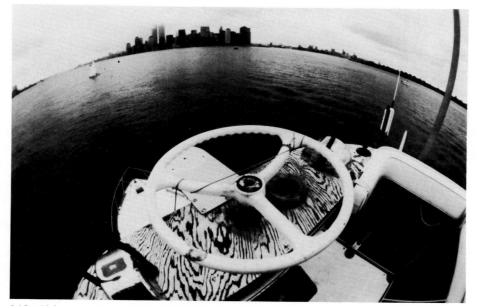

146. Fish-Eye View of New York Harbor. *Photograph.*

Film

Black-and-white film is formed from an **emulsion** of light-sensitized crystals (silver-halide particles) embedded in gelatin and laid on a transparent film backing. After exposure to light and processing, the light-sensitized crystals reverse to form the negative from which positive prints can be made.

Black-and-white films vary in their sensitivity to dark and light values; certain films will produce stronger contrasts than others—often an advantage in fashion photography. This unique art form, developed in the last fifty or so years along with advertising, must create the most effective presentation of the subject. A unique setting and effective lighting can evoke a sense of glamour that most of us could achieve only in dreams. The elegance suggested in the works of one of the leading fashion photographers of our time, Horst P. Horst (b. 1906), might have been seen in one Condé Nast publication or another ever since 1932, continuing to the present time. The drama of brilliant contrasts of dark and light has become Horst's hallmark, casting the face of his subject into shadow so that the garment might be better accented [147]. Picasso's daughter Paloma, herself a well-known artist, is here shown wearing a Karl Lagerfeld design.

Film speeds also vary, and the photographer must know which film to select for a particular subject and set of conditions. Moving objects must be recorded at rapid shutter speeds to stop the action and avoid blur; they require, therefore, films that are highly sensitive to light, "fast" films. To convey the essential quality of a dance, Barbara Morgan (b. 1900) chose the full

147. *Horst P. Horst.* Paloma Picasso. *1979. Photograph.*

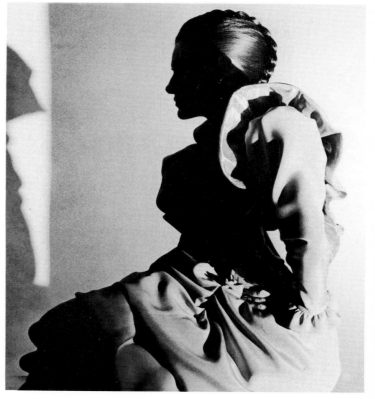

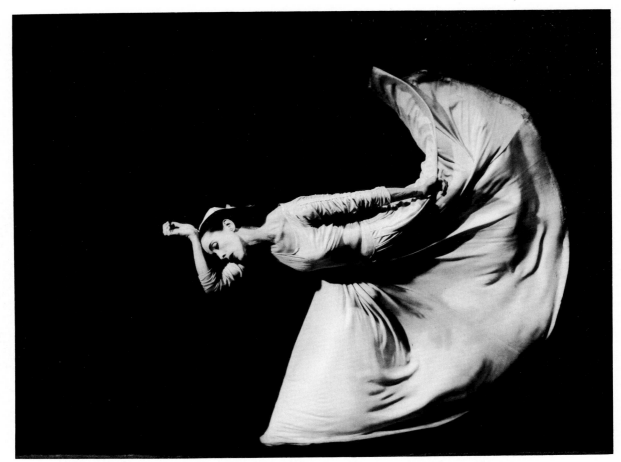

148. *Barbara Morgan.* Martha Graham: "Letter to the World" (Kick). *1940. Photograph.*

figure of Martha Graham. The merest suggestion of blur at the hemline and the arresting pose capture in a fraction of a second the emotional thrust of the entire dance sequence [148].

Color films vary. Some produce positive images that become color transparencies or slides; others produce negatives that are used to make color prints. Large photographic prints—whether black and white or color—are desirable for advertising or photojournalistic purposes where corrective photo retouching to clarify detail for reproduction is often necessary. Color films also vary according to their intended use in daylight or artificial light. As in black-and-white photography, the type of film selected is critical to the production of a high-quality final image.

Processing and Printing

Though the processing of black-and-white film is not nearly as complicated as color-film processing, it is not a simple procedure. Invisible chemical changes take place when light rays fall on the emulsion surface of black-and-white film.

These rays create visual images when the film is put into an alkaline developing solution. The processed negative that results is next rinsed in an acid stop bath, which prevents further development; then it is permanently fixed in a hypo-alum solution. The more complex procedure involved in developing color films requires highly controlled conditions for both color transparencies and prints. Because film is sensitive to light, heat, and chemicals, photographic developing processes must take place in the controlled conditions of the darkroom, utilizing appropriate color filters.

The printing process requires exposure of photosensitive paper to light that is passed through a negative under darkroom conditions. Contact prints are made the same size as the negative by placing negatives and contact paper together—emulsion side of negative in contact with emulsion side of paper—and exposing both to light. Enlargements of photographs are made by projecting light through the negative and the lens of an enlarger onto sensitized enlarging paper. The distance from the lens to the printing paper controls the size of the enlargement. As in film developing, the invisible images printed on the paper must then undergo the same three baths—developer, stop, and hypo-fixative—in order to be made permanently visible.

During the enlargement process the original image may be changed and refined. For instance, by using different kinds of papers the texture or value contrasts can be increased or diminished. The negative may also be masked in order to emphasize certain parts in the final print. The image may also be darkened or lightened, or parts may even be blocked out altogether. Portions of negatives may be combined into a **montage** by exposing various sections on the same enlargement. The print itself may be cropped or trimmed to change the composition.

As part of an advertising campaign for Safety-Klein, a company that deals in recycling vast numbers of industrial products, Brand Advertising Agency severely cropped a photograph taken by Dick Greene and Arnold Paley. The Statue of Liberty, depicted by a live model standing in a plastic-lined pool, appears to be sinking beneath a sludge-filled harbor. The

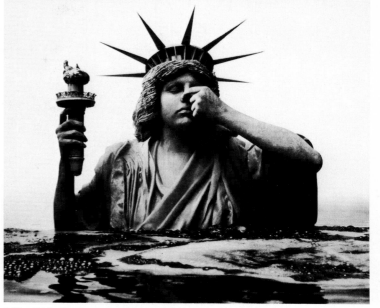

149. *Dick Green and Arnold Paley.* Clean up your act, America. *Photograph.*

150. *Imogen Cunningham.* Magnolia Blossom. *1925. Photograph. Imogen Cunningham Trust, Berkeley, California.*

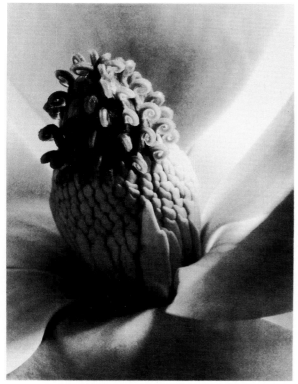

elimination of all but the upper portion of the body suggests the scale of the statue in a pose certain to attract attention to the anti-pollution campaign [149].

The variety of technical procedures available to the photographer through the camera and local controls in the darkroom allows experiment in a wide range of unusual possibilities, which may increase the expressiveness of the final print. When familiar subjects such as flowers and leaves are photographed in heroic terms, oversized and isolated from their botanical context, they can be explored for their design and structure. The magnolia [150] reveals a gently expressed sensuous quality. By cropping her image, focusing on the graceful curves of the petals, Imogen Cunningham (1883–1976) brings the viewer into her photograph. Light is diffused through the petals as well as on them so that they become luminous with delicate tones of gray. Such fine variations in tonality are usually rendered best with slower films. A few photographers still insist on "pure" prints made from their original unaltered negatives, but this kind of restraint is rare today.

There can be no question that still photography has fundamentally changed our concepts of the world around us. Certainly, photography

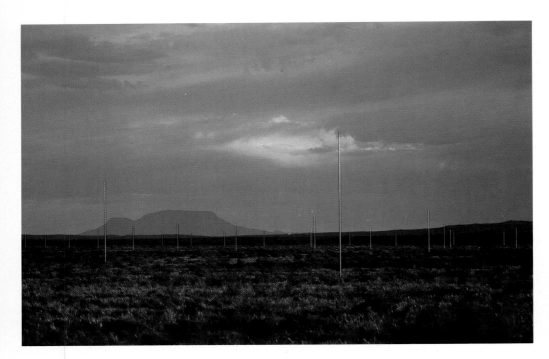

151. *Walter De Maria.*
The Lightning Field.
1971–1977. Earth Sculpture,
1 mile × 1 kilometer
Near Quenado, New Mexico.
Courtesy DIA Art Foundation.

has influenced other art forms, particularly painting. And, perhaps even more important, the exploitation of still photography led to the development of the motion picture, as we shall see.

Special Effects and Techniques

Occasionally the camera may be the only way of capturing a record of a special effect. For instance, few of us would have the courage, or desire, to observe 400 lightning rods during a lightning storm as would be necessary to judge the success or possible failure of Walter De Maria's (b. 1935) contemporary earthwork, *The Lightning Field,* designed to celebrate the awesome power of nature. But John Cliett's photograph documents the event for us [151]. In this case, the photograph enriches the work of art.

At times, the photographic image may serve only as a starting point in the hands of a creative artist. Artists like David Hockney (b. 1937) echo the fractured nature of communication with mass media in their works. The isolated "stills" from a full-length film, a brief selection from a videotape, clipped feature stories from a newspaper—these are the nature of modern mass communication with which we are all familiar. Hockney calls his configurations photo-mosaics, assembling his works in much the same way as we perceive our world in fragmented percep-

tions, each element a focus on a different aspect. The coherence of the finished artwork is achieved by repetition of similar colors, textures,

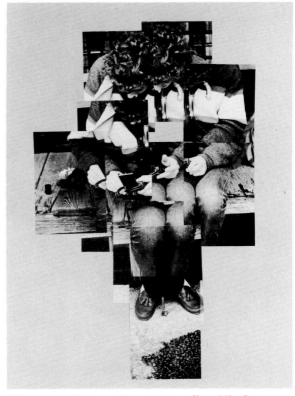

152. *David Hockney.* Gregory Loading His Camera, Kyoto, February, 1983. *1983. Photographic collage, 21 × 14" (53 × 36 cm).*

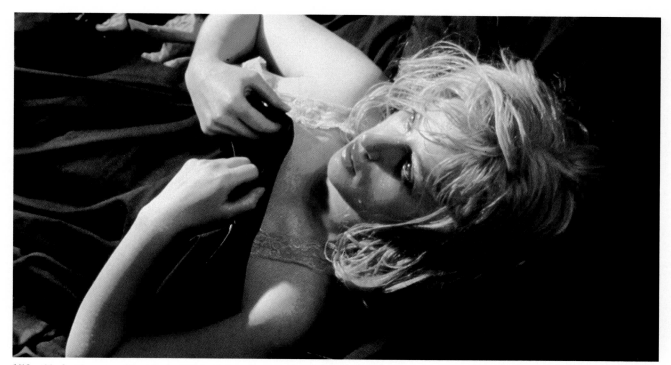

153. *Cindy Sherman.* Untitled. *1981. Color photograph, 2' × 4' (0.61 × 1.22 m).*
Courtesy of Metro Pictures, New York.

or themes [152]. Yet the use of multiple perspectives makes *Gregory Loading His Camera* disorienting to the viewer.

The influence of film-making indirectly has induced some artists to create fictional narratives in their work. Cindy Sherman (b. 1954), who combines traditional photographic techniques while calling attention to how the media portray women, produces large-scale (2 by 4 feet; .6 by 1.2 meters) color photographs that appear to be enlarged frames from films of the 1950s. Sherman eloquently personifies the stereotypical roles assigned to women in Hollywood by depicting passive figures that seem lifeless or, in this case, express mute, submissive eroticism [153]. Though Sherman serves as the model in

each case, with a variety of wigs and costumes, all of the images and none of them reveal the artist herself—photographer, designer, and actress.

Other photographers may combine images from different negatives to form a single-, double-, or triple-exposure print [154]. Many painters working in the Surrealist style, such as Man Ray (1890–1976), created special effects involving other experimental photographic techniques. It is now possible to photograph in outer space, under the seas, and inside the human body. The artist-photographer is an independent, self-sustaining creative force, unlimited by technology and often working outside the restraints of society.

154. *The Starn Twins.* Christ (Stretched). *1985–1986. Silverprint with scotch tape,*
2'4" × 11'10" × 3'9" (.71 × 3.61 × 1.14 m). Courtesy Stux Gallery, New York.

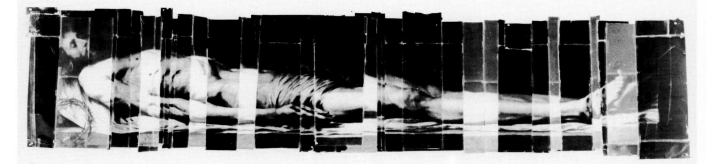

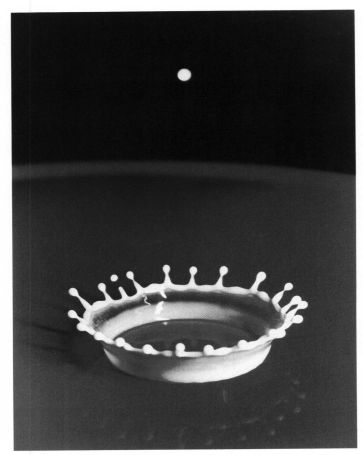

155. *Harold Edgerton*. Milk Drop Coronet, 1957. *1957. Dye transfer print.* © *Harold Edgerton. Courtesy Palm Press.*

Cinematography

Movement is inherent in all living organisms and has always fascinated people. It is not surprising, then, that the question of how to express motion has concerned artists from the Stone Age to Duchamp and from his *Nude Descending a Staircase* [91] early in the 20th century to the most advanced film-maker today. Our delight in the pattern formed by a drop of splashed milk reveals a continued preoccupation with simple movement [155]. The invention of the motion picture camera, which made possible the magic of cinema, has resulted in one of the most important and powerful forms of contemporary art.

A Brief History

The earliest noteworthy experiments in depicting motion through photography were those of Eadweard Muybridge in California [89]. Setting up twenty-four cameras to capture successive views of a horse in motion, Muybridge in 1878 confirmed the theory that in active movement all four hoofs of a horse leave the ground, as can be seen in [156]. (Those sequential photographs led to his invention of a piece of equipment capable of photographing a rapid succession of images.) Muybridge also invented a device he termed a **zoogyroscope,** through which these images could be projected onto a

156. *Eadweard Muybridge*. Galloping Horse. *1878. Photograph. International Museum of Photography at George Eastman House.*

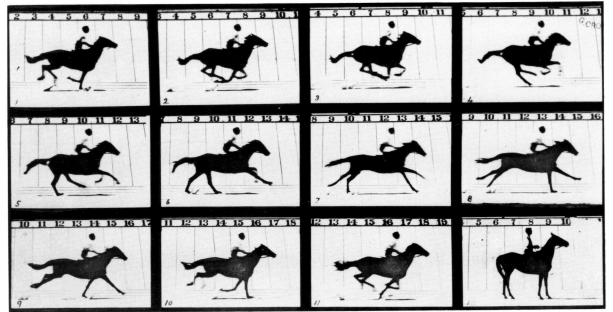

screen. In 1893, an amateur photographer named Alexander Black (1859–1940) had the idea of telling a story through sequential pictures, persuading the President of the United States to be photographed at the White House. The production, called *A Capitol Courtship,* shown with a projector perfected by the American inventor Thomas Edison, was the first practical motion film to win public acceptance as entertainment. With these inventions, film was born in England, France, Russia, Italy, and the United States, first in New York and then, beginning in the 1920s, in Hollywood. For eighty years the film industry has shifted back and forth from the West Coast for most of its studio work, back to the East for financial support, sites "on location," and some studio cinematography.

Motion pictures are actually made of thousands of photographic images, which produce an illusion of motion when the photographs, or frames, are projected in a succession of twenty-four frames per second. The human brain is unable to differentiate the individual images or even to see the blank screen flashed between them. This apparently single moving picture occurs because each frame differs only slightly from the one that preceded it, and each image projected lingers only briefly as an **afterimage** in the brain.

As soon as the camera was able to record motion believably, cinematographers began to experiment with a variety of space-time illusions. They soon learned that rapid movement over great distances of land or sea can appear to take place, while a brief event can be extended, because the camera is capable of accelerating, slowing down, reversing, or even holding action. A scene can be made to darken, or **fade out,** and a new sequence allowed to **fade in.** A scene can also be made to **dissolve** (merge) directly into another scene. When film scripts call for action that film codes will not permit an audience to view, such devices are invaluable. Film-makers are thus able to manipulate our perceptions of events and people. Such techniques were fully developed as early as 1915 by D. W. Griffith (1880–1948) in *Birth of a Nation* and continue to be used today.

Cinematographers discovered also that the motion picture camera can be made to imitate the human eye by scanning the overall scene or concentrating on significant details in the distant **long shot,** the closer **medium shot,** and the **close-up.** The close view creates an intense intimacy and can portray unusual views of form and texture, perhaps reminiscent of the vividness of childhood sensations when we first begin to see, feel, and touch the strange new world. Such extreme close-ups in films challenged the social conventions that have always existed regarding appropriate territorial distances between people. When such taboos were broken, the viewer became a participant in screened events, drawn into the film by the intimacy of the images, with a power akin to deities who can "see" everything. The shift in the late 1920s from silent films ("movies") to "talkies" was made possible by the addition of a magnetic sound strip to the film. By this revolutionary invention the gap between reality and illusion was further reduced, and another dimension was added to the cinema.

The moving picture also controls our perceptions of time. Other visual forms, such as architecture, painting, and sculpture, are restricted to the experience of the here and now. Like live theater, the cinema enjoys the benefits of extended visual experiences, but as an art form it has been most successful when it has rejected theatrical imitation and evolved its own kind of communication.

Visual narration has been a vital part of cinematography from early films through Sergei Eisenstein's (1898–1948) surrealistic shots in *Potemkin* (1925) **[157]** to the most recent films by avant-garde film-makers. Yet, unlike the theater

157. *Scene from* Potemkin, *directed by Sergei Eisenstein. 1925. The Museum of Modern Art, New York. Film Stills Archive.*

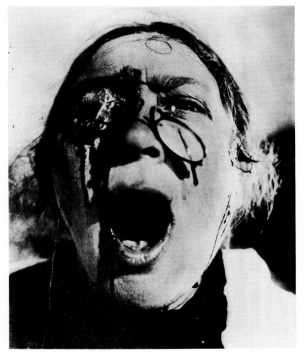

where the art form unfolds through live performance, in film-making, editing techniques make it possible for film-makers to use events in time creatively and to suggest rather than spell out an explicit narrative.

Concurrent with these developments in narrative cinema were experimental art films by painters such as Salvador Dalí (b. 1904) and Fernand Léger (1881–1955), who created surrealistic and abstract films for small audiences in the 1920s and 1930s. Today, the underground film continues to develop almost as an independent art form, produced by film-makers who are technically trained and alert to developments in cinema and other arts. Just as many actors such as Woody Allen have evolved their own unique film expressions drawing from other media and perspectives, the commercial film and the art film echo other art forms as well as each other.

A Critic's View of Film

From its beginnings, film—cinematography—was seen as art, enlightenment, and entertainment. The same is true of still photography and other forms of artistic expression. Thus many of the criteria used to evaluate art in general can be applied to film. Nevertheless, feature films—those intended to be shown in theaters—share so many special attributes that they must be reviewed in special ways.

A good starting point for considering a feature film might be the guidelines listed by Dwight Macdonald, former film critic for *Esquire* and *The New Republic*:

1. Are the characters consistent, and in fact are there characters at all?
2. Is it true to life?
3. Is the photography cliché, or is it adapted to the particular film and therefore original?
4. Do the parts go together; do they add up to something; is there a rhythm established so that there is form, shape, climax, building up tension and exploding it?
5. Is there a mind behind it; is there a feeling that a single intelligence has imposed his own view on the material?[1]

Let us consider Macdonald's points in their order of presentation:

1. Many viewers identify the characters of a film with the actors and actresses who play the parts; consistency of characters determines whether or not they become absorbed in the film.
2. For many of us a "slice of life" in the films we see may not be our major concern. Science-fiction buffs, for instance, look instead for "out of this world" special effects. Other movie-goers look for pure escape.
3. Probably the quality of the photography affects most of us, especially when it is particularly good or particularly bad.
4. To be successful, the film as determined by the script must build in form and shape until it reaches a climax that satisfies.
5. If a film is consistent and not disjointed, the director should receive primary credit, even though many of us tend to credit the actors and actresses.

The ultimate standards on which feature films may be judged have been well stated by Macdonald in his concluding words:

1. Did it change the way you look at things?
2. Did you find more (or less) in it the second, third, nth time? (Also, how did it stand up over the years, after one or more "periods" of cinematic history?)[2]

The Film Script

Few filmgoers are aware of the techniques required to rivet the attention of an audience for ninety minutes or more. The creation of a film is a complex communal venture, generally intended to reach vast numbers of viewers yearning to project themselves beyond the confines of their lives. The underlying structure of the film is provided by the script, the written form whose words are translated into an analogous but quite different symbolic representation—images that fill the screen. The film-maker's effectiveness grows from his or her ability to visualize these images and recreate them as art.

The script is not a fixed entity but a working outline that charts the long process of film-making. It incorporates both the initial conceptualization of the film and the sum total of insights discovered in the process of shooting scenes. For all great film-makers, a script that begins with one seemingly immutable sequence

[1]Dwight Macdonald, *Dwight Macdonald on Movies* (Englewood Cliffs, NJ: Prentice-Hall, 1969), p. ix.

[2]Macdonald, *Macdonald on Movies*, p. xi.

may evolve through the complex process of film-making, requiring thousands of decisions, into a film that begins in a quite different way. At a symposium at the 1966 Cannes Film Festival (the annual recognition of outstanding achievement in film-making), the master French short-story writer Henri Cluzot asked the film-maker Jean-Luc Godard (b. 1930), "You agree that films should have a beginning, a middle, and end?" Godard replied, "Yes, but not necessarily in that order."

Film-makers handle scripts differently. Ingmar Bergman (b. 1918) may be the foremost director to use the cinema as a medium for sustained philosophical and visionary meditation. In *Wild Strawberries* (1957) and others, he juxtaposes dreamlike sequences that never happened between scenes of past and present events. Federico Fellini (b. 1920), in the tradition of many Italian directors, develops his films with the skilled support of writers and other experts. His most successful films are said to be autobiographical; *8 1/2* (1963) and *La Dolce Vita* (1960) are replete with fantasy and sadistic sexual triumph. Eisenstein's *Potemkin* (1925) and *Ivan the Terrible* (1944) offer an inexhaustible source of inspiration for concept and form, including montage techniques; like most of his films, they were created while he filled workbooks with elaborate images and personal notations. Robert Altman's (b. 1925) films have often demonstrated his interest in "off-beat" subject matter and special effects: a sense of dream-like unreality. Certainly his popular *M*A*S*H* (1970) is considered an American classic by many. Documentaries evolve differently. Such classics as *Nanook of the North* (1921) through *Woodstock* (1970) may have been developed chronologically and rhythmically in successive sequences.

Current film imagery seems faster paced and often depends on space-time manipulation and complex technology for its impact. Many films are created in special-effects studios such as George Lucas's Industrial Light and Magic Company [158, 159]. Natural perspective and scale can be altered by unique technology designed especially for a particular film like *Star Wars* (1977).

Cameras, Films, and Techniques

The motion picture camera is based on many of the same principles as the still camera. The difference between the two lies in the obvious fact that the motion picture camera is capable of recording a rapid succession of images. The many different specialized needs of cinematography demand varied cameras, films, and modes

below: **158.** *Special effects set-up for* Star Wars *with the Rebel Cruiser model.* © 1983 Lucasfilm Ltd. *All rights reserved. Courtesy of Lucasfilm Ltd.*

right: **159.** *Millennium Falcon in Death Star tunnel* © 1983 Lucasfilm Ltd. All rights reserved. Courtesy of Lucasfilm Ltd.

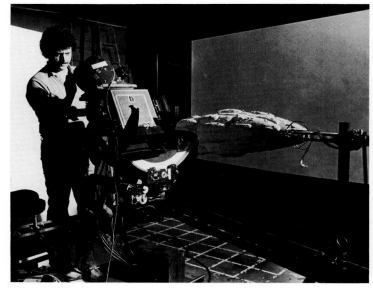

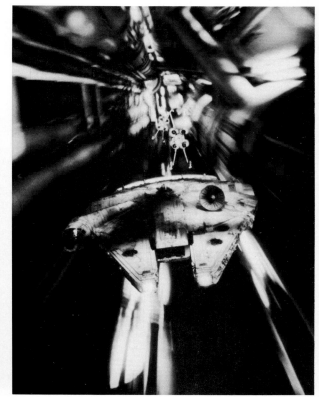

of operation. Camera sizes include 8 mm, 16 mm, 35 mm, and 70 mm. Generally, the smaller cameras and films are used by amateurs, while the larger, more expensive cameras are used by professionals because they accept large films that can be projected on wide screens for theater audiences.

Lenses control focal length, speed, and depth of field. For example, long-focal-length lenses bring the subject closer by magnifying only a portion of the scene. The zoom lens is generally used to change focal length in a range between the extremes of a wide-angle lens and a telephoto lens, bringing subjects closer, in focus, almost instantly. A smaller lens opening permits sharp focus over a greater depth of field or distance than is possible with a wide-open lens. Moving the camera horizontally **(panning)** or vertically **(tilting)** permits a panoramic view of an area, important when a moving subject must be photographed. By focusing on the subject, the photographer is able to center in while the remainder of the scene changes, imitating with the camera what we do with our eyes.

The process of editing the literally miles of exposed film (footage) into an artistically coherent work of manageable length is the last creative step in producing a film. The editing is determined by the vision of the film-maker, usually the director. A work print (positive film) of one or more scenes is run through an editing machine, or viewer, which consists of a lens, screen, and controls for moving the film forward and backward. When the editor decides what changes to make, frames are cut apart in the approximate places with scissors. A splicing machine glues cut frames together. Then the edited print is again run through the viewer. The process is repeated until the editor is satisfied. The sound track, which is recorded on a separate roll of tape, is finally synchronized with the film in the editing machine.

Other cinematographic influences appear in television and video—not surprising, since the newer media almost always begin by imitating their predecessors.

Television

Television, like cinema, has developed into a major medium for conveying information, artistic expression, and entertainment. It consists of visual images translated into electronic signals beamed through the air to a television receiver, which turns the signals back into images on the television screen. The sources of the images may be film, videotape (magnetic tape with electronic signals), or live action. Television's unique contribution is its instantaneous transmission of

---

Exploring Art Through Technology

New Film Environments Provided by Technology

A view of the world few could have imagined before the 20th century is now possible through advanced-technology projection. Perhaps inspired by increasing demand for special effects in all media and encouraged by the popular response to unusual visuals that are often offered on television, film technicians developed a new format that has recently appeared in museum auditoriums all over the country as well as in Disneyland, where the process originated.

Not yet found in conventional theaters, the new technology involves costly large-screen, multiscreen, and 3-D installations capable of accepting much larger than life-size projections of films especially prepared for such viewing. The impact of size, technical brilliance, and the creation of a total enveloping environment invites the audience to become part of the on-screen event. The eye and the mind are overwhelmed by sheer sensations and a multiplicity of details. In such films as *Nomads of the Deep* the viewer is seduced into an illusion of swimming, swooping, and soaring in the company of sharks and humpback whales off the coast of Hawaii.

Designed to correlate with the new projection techniques are electronic film-making processes that have been invented by George Lucas and developed with Francis Ford Coppola in such films as *Captain Eo,* a 3-D spectacle. Featuring Michael Jackson as a latter-day savior, the film must be viewed through polarized glasses in order to simulate actual space. Along with Jackson's music, a new total film environment can be experienced. Many will agree that in the dazzling combinations of electronic film-making, far larger than life-size screens and specially fitted auditoriums, a fresh means of visual communication has been created to bring film-making into the 21st century.

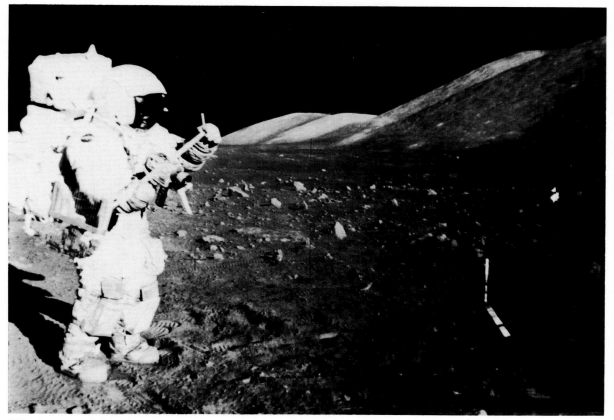

160. *Lunar Module Pilot Harrison H. Schmitt collects lunar samples during the Apollo 17 mission, December 1972.*

events as they happen to our homes. Such live coverage of news and sports events, which gives us a sense of participation in world and national affairs, provides some of television's most successful programming. For instance, the whole world watched with awe and excitement the exploration of the moon and witnessed at the same time one of television's proudest achievements [160].

The instant accessibility of television imagery helps relate events on the television screen personally to viewers. Extreme close-ups eliminate the psychological distance between the television image and our emotions, while the immediacy of television provides us with a way to enjoy and identify with dramatic presentations or events. Crowded into large cities, people tend to feel shut off from community living and isolated from others. Yet sometimes, as after the tragic assassination of President John F. Kennedy, television not only heightens the impact of an event but also helps draw millions of individual viewers together in a shared emotion that brings national unity.

Television programs range widely from feature-length drama to situation comedy to musi-cal programs, old motion pictures, interviews and panel discussions, game shows, animated cartoons, news analyses, soap operas, documentaries, and commercials. Some of these presentations are highly creative, others less so. Although panel discussions can rarely rise above the caliber of the guests, a skilled interviewer such as Dick Cavett or Barbara Walters offers the potential of memorable conversation.

Commercial television has been strongly criticized for its tendency to program for the lowest common denominator and its apparent reluctance to experiment with new ideas. Nevertheless, this is the result of the system: commercial TV is supported by businesses that buy advertising time and naturally want the largest possible viewing audience for their commercials; therefore, the programs must appeal to the broadest possible market. Television commercials, incidentally, have become a distinctive art form, frequently showing more creativity and sophistication than the programs they accompany. In any case, the public-supported television stations with no commercials are more free to show a wider range of programs, and they do, as we will see.

Special Features of Television and Video Art

In commercial television, the possibility of live transmission and the ability to produce instant magnetic videotapes offer several advantages over cinematography that, for viewers, make up for the small size of screens and the monotony of repeated commercials. These advantages are most obvious in the coverage of news events.

An application of videotape that is quite different from the commercial productions for television is video art, which many artists produce as contributions to fine art. Probably its greatest asset is the possibility of instant productions—no long processing delays. Video also offers the advantage over film of quick electronic procedures like interpolation (added frames), elimination, **splice**, and special effects. The video camera, instantly transportable, can accompany a teacher, for example, who demonstrates a particular studio art procedure (if the illumination is adequate).

Tape may be edited like film; there is no physical grafting of images, but rather an electronic "grabbing." Finally, the special effects that are rather easily accessible in video have made the medium particularly attractive to musical groups who tap the teen-aged and young twenties market. Video art for children has tremendous potential, as well. The evaluative criteria by which video art may be judged vary with the purpose of a tape. Though the medium is still in its formative stages, cinematographic standards seem to work generally for video, but future possibilities remain an uncharted course.

In a videotape distributed by Castelli-Sonnabend Tapes and Films called *Television Delivers People*, Richard Serra (b. 1939) and Carlota Schoolman (b. 1947) produced a six-minute program focusing on the political import of broadcasting as corporate monopoly and imperialism of the air. The subject of their videotape, notably video-filmed television material, is presented ironically, for their message criticizes commercial television but uses the medium itself to do it. As a parody on the seduction of advertising, Muzak plays while sentences Serra has excerpted from television conferences roll down a blue background in white lettering. For instance, "The product of television, commercial television, is the audience. . . . Television delivers people to an advertiser. . . . It is the consumer who is consumed."

Noncommercial television obviously is more free to experiment with new expressive forms and creative approaches. Some of these shows, having first won acceptance on public-supported television, have actually been filtered into commercial television. Public and educational television offer many creative possibilities in drama, news coverage, public-information programs, and children's programs. In order to survive, however, and to continue creative broadcasting, public television depends on grants from corporations and foundations and on the financial support of the viewing public—all of us.

Some experimental video art, like film, bases its appeal on the editing process itself. Nam

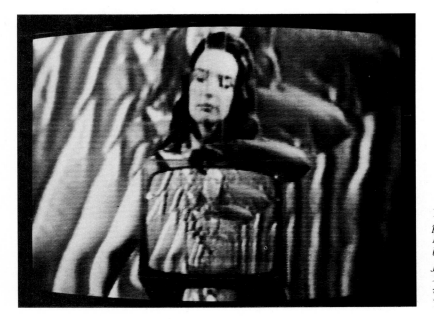

161. *Charlotte Moorman playing a TV cello by Nam June Paik in* Global Groove *by Nam June Paik and John Godfrey. 1973. 30-minute color/sound videotape. Produced by The TelevisionLab at WNET/Thirteen.*

Nam June Paik (b. 1932)

Regarded as a seminal force in the development of video art, Nam June Paik [162] is as well known for his experimental work in music. Born in Korea into a manufacturing family, he began his career as a composer and performer of **avant-garde** music, graduating from the University of Tokyo with a thesis on Arnold Schonberg and continuing his studies at the University of Munich. Paik's interest in performance art probably evolved from the time he spent at the Studio for Electronic Music in Cologne, where one of his 1960 presentations concluded, offstage in the audience, with a ceremonial cutting of the composer John Cage's tie and shirt. While the demand for his presentations took him all over northern Europe, not until 1963 did his first investment in television—thirteen second-hand TV sets—introduce him to the medium by which he is best known.

The first one-man exhibition of Paik's video art in March, 1963, occupied many rooms and included the thirteen altered television sets, three prepared pianos, and Joseph Beuys, an internationally known improvisational artist, who is said to have attacked one of the pianos with an axe. Since then, Paik's explorations, theories, ideas, and writings, his far-flung performances, and, in particular, his videotapes have shaped the contours of the development of television and video as an art form.

Paik's experiments have been supported by the Rockefeller Foundation's art program for video research, permitting him not only the opportunity to participate in numerous pro-

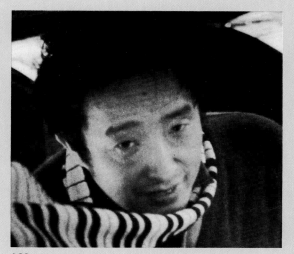

162. *Nam June Paik. Photograph.*

grams, but to "play" with the medium. In his "voyages" through television, his images are synthesized, distorted, chopped up, speeded and slowed down, split, combined and recombined. His satire and playfulness underscore his confidence in chance actions. His legacy has been absorbed by the rock-video movement, but his concern with the manipulation of events by the medium brings him much closer to another 20th-century philosopher, Marshall McLuhan. Both men forecast the power of media. And, indeed, the video camera has invaded the courtroom, the classroom, and the operating room. Nam June Paik's vision continues to inform us about ourselves through his videotapes.

June Paik uses the video synthesizer to alter the image on the monitor [161]. Through electronics, he may distort, blend, and combine images, entertaining us brilliantly with a thousand fluctuating views, including the commercial, even while he reminds us of the insidious pressures exerted by television, which often seduces, persuades, and numbs our sense of values.

It is interesting to speculate on the artistic potential of cable television, with its capacity for almost endless variety in programming. Another exciting innovation is the videotape cassette recorder, increasingly used in homes. Millions of VCRs are now in use; thus tapes of virtually any subject could be made available to

vast audiences. Nam June Paik forecasts a not-too-distant time when loss of fossil fuels will eliminate most travel. As he sees it, knowledge will be stored on videotapes, disc-computerized for rapid retrieval, and broadcast to the public.

We have only to look around us to see some of the technical and social results of the invention of the camera. The new art forms it has produced—photography, cinema, and television—are now a part of our everyday lives. Their very familiarity should make it easier for us to evaluate just how aesthetically successful and expressive they have become.

Video seems likely to expand its influence on society with every passing year, in aspects that

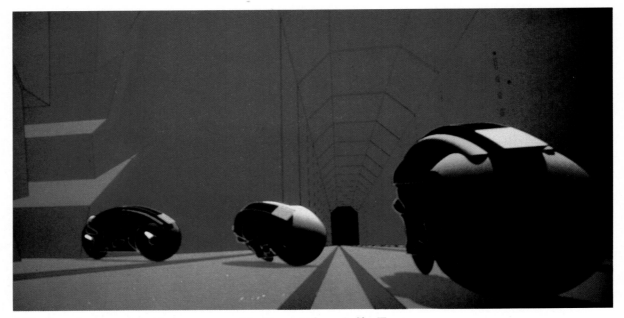

163. *Computer-generated video game segment in Steven Lisberger's film* Tron. © *1982 The Walt Disney Company.*

range from news clips to videotaped tutorials, from medical achievements to professional entertainment, such as the computer-generated video game segment **[163]** in Steven Lisberger's film *Tron*. More and more film-makers are incorporating computer-generated video sequences in their films; we will examine the total role of computer graphics in the next chapter.

Exercises and Activities

Research Exercises

1. The principle of the camera was first explored in the Renaissance device known as the *camera obscura*. What was the principle on which it was based? How was it applied to later cameras?
2. Photography is both an art and a science. Explain how it can be both.
3. The operation of a camera is related to the function of the human eye. Define or diagram the relationship between them.
4. Select several photographs from a magazine or from your own collection. Which do you believe qualify as works of art? Explain your reasons for your choices.
5. An illusion of life can be produced through the medium of the motion picture. How did motion picture photography develop out of Eadweard Muybridge's early experiments with multiple photographs? What are the advantages of cinematography and/or television over still photography? Explain the space-time concept involved in cinema and television.

Studio Activities

1. Cut out magazine photographs that you like. Select those that create different moods and assemble them into a photo montage. Or, if you have many photographs that you have taken, select some of them and assemble them into a photo montage. Perhaps you will find that you can create something that seems better than any of the individual photographs.
2. Select a theme such as the Student Government Association or the college newspaper and create a photo-essay on the subject.
3. Create a 15-frame sequence **(storyboard)** for a television commercial publicizing your college. You may sketch your ideas for each frame or photograph appropriate stills for successive images and carefully describe the audio and video changes from frame to frame.

6
Design in Print

Letters possess gracefulness, not when they have been written with listlessness and haste or with toil and diligence, but with heart and soul.

Giambattista Bodoni, 18th-century printer and type designer

You can do a good ad without good typography but you can't do a great ad without good typography.

Herb Lubalin, 20th-century type designer

The book is an extension of the eye . . . the extension of any one of our senses alters the way we think and act—the way we perceive the world. . . .

Marshall McLuhan, writer on media

The creation of paintings and the creation of computer programs are the creation of objects . . . constructed of ideas, concepts and craftsmanship . . . what kind of artist can get involved with the computer art medium? An artist interested in dealing with algebraic logic as well as . . . with aesthetics. . . .

Duane Palyka, computer artist, scientist

Before writing was invented, communication was bounded by open acoustic space—the distance speech traveled. With the advent of printing technology, most communication came to be perceived in terms of printing within confined vertical and horizontal spaces. The process of mechanically produced multiples created the portable book and a new reading public, hungry for printed visual imagery.

Millions of designs—books, magazines, newspapers, illustrations, corporate signs, symbols, and other printed materials—dominate the visual landscape of our century. Some are messages that inform; many change our lives; but all are intended to enrich day-to-day living in some way. The specialized artists who provide these printed products and services are known as graphic designers.

Graphic Design

Graphic design is generally considered to be the arrangement of words and/or images within a printed format. Arresting visual communications often determine the success of multimillion-dollar corporate ventures. From product trademarks to advertising design, professionals are indispensable to modern commerce. The range of their responsibilities is enormous. The larger field divisions include book and record production; advertising in newspapers, magazines, television, indoor and outdoor display; computer graphics (an open-ended art in itself); and wallpaper, fabric, and other planar surface arrangements. The common criteria for all these arts is their dependence on printing on a two-dimensional surface; also, they are generally

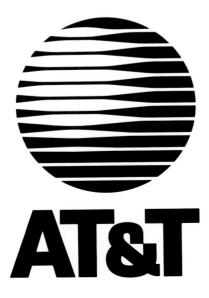

above: **164.** *Cuneiform tablet (detail). Sumerian, c. 2050 B.C. Baked clay, entire tablet 3⅛ × 5⅛″ (8 × 13 cm). Babylonian Collection, Yale University, New Haven, Connecticut.*

below: **165.** *Designer: Saul Bass, Bass/Yager & Assoc., AT&T trademark. © 1982 AT&T.*

considered to be designed for commercial purposes (and thus distinct from printmaking, as noted in Chapter 4).

Printing Industry

The printing industry, like cinema, television, and radio, serves mass communication. Printing communicates through graphic symbols—recognized images that stand for ideas. Since the earliest times societies have developed graphic symbols to communicate ideas. Some symbols are abstract, such as letters of the alphabet, Sumerian cuneiform characters representing sounds and ideas **[164]**, numbers, and musical notes. These are forms of written language. Other symbols are pictorial and almost universal, such as a drawing of a crown to symbolize royalty. Even in ancient times, symbols advertised what was for sale—for instance, a bakery in Pompeii was identified by a painting of bread. Many modern corporations have trademarks that are mainly pictorial symbols, and **logotypes,** which are usually the company's name or initials. Most Americans, for example, recognize AT&T. The letters stand for American Telephone and Telegraph, set with a revolving globe, embellished with thick and thin lines that connote paths of communication. The modern, squared-off computer-related style suggests the stability, accuracy, and forward-thinking image that the company wishes to convey **[165]**.

Sometimes communication is better served through a combination of abstract, written symbols and pictures, a practice that dates back hundreds of years. Compare the words inscribed in the unfurled banners of the illuminated medieval manuscript page of *Solomon as the Symbol of Wisdom* **[166]** with the message carried by the words in a "balloon" in any modern comic strip. In the medieval work, King Solomon is distributing bread to several beggars and unfurls a banner inscribed with a quotation from Proverbs 9:5 where Wisdom invites everyone to share her bread. In the corners above, the apostles Andrew and Paul unfurl banners inscribed with biblical quotations referring to the bread of the Eucharist. You can see that communication techniques have not changed substantially, although today's content and purpose are certainly different.

So accustomed are we to the printed page that we can easily forget that for thousands of years most words set down in permanent form were written by hand. Each book was in fact a manuscript (from the Latin words for "handwritten"), an original or a laboriously lettered copy. In China, Japan, and medieval Europe, handwriting developed into the highly decorative art of **calligraphy.** A study of the characters painted on a paper handscroll of the Kamakura period reveals the abstract nature of some Japanese calligraphy, which is very close to drawing and painting [167].

Printing began in ancient times as a way of repeating designs on fabric. There is evidence of printed textiles in India during the 4th century A.D. By the 9th century the Chinese and Japanese were printing on paper from wood blocks with characters and pictures cut into them. Movable type made of baked clay dates from A.D. 1041–1049 in China; by the 14th century the Chinese were using movable wooden type, many years before printers in the West devised movable type. Woodcut illustrations were common in Europe in the 15th century, as we saw in Chapter 4, although books were still lettered by hand. In the 1430s and 1440s Johann Gutenberg of Mainz coordinated into one process the

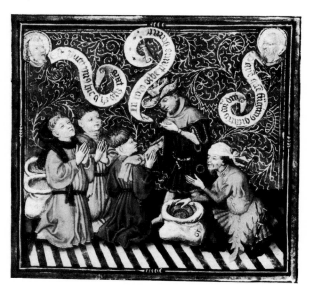

166. Solomon Distributing Bread
from the Hours of Catherine of Cleves. *c. 1440.*
Manuscript illumination, $2\frac{1}{2} \times 2\frac{5}{8}''$ (6 × 7 cm).
The Pierpont Morgan Library, New York
(M.945 f131, detail).

167. *Fujiwara Nobuzane (?).* Lady Kodai no Kimi, *fragment of* The Thirty-Six Immortal Poets Scroll (sanjūroku kasen emaki). *Early 13th century. Color on paper. Yamato Bunkakan Museum, Nara, Japan.*

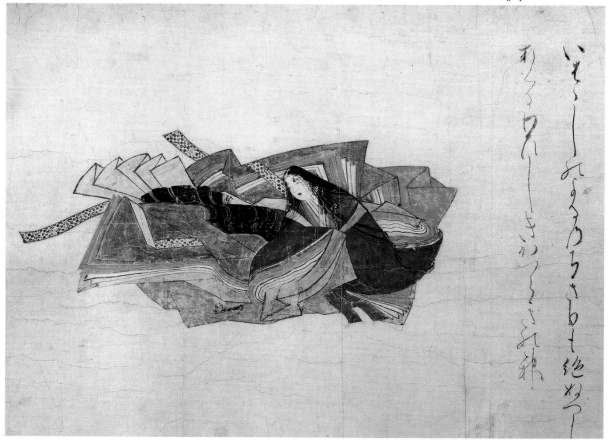

Old Style Roman

Modern Roman

Modern Italic

Script

𝔇𝔢𝔠𝔬𝔯𝔞𝔱𝔦𝔳𝔢

Sans Serif

168. *Sample typefaces.*

several elements needed to make the transition from single handwritten books to printed books in multiple copies—paper, ink, a printing press, and movable metal type. That type consisted of single cast letters that could be combined into words, locked into a form, and, after they had been used for printing, reused in other combinations.

Typography The common typefaces used today are derived from the square capital letters cut with hammer and chisel by ancient Roman stonecutters on monuments and written with chisel-ended pens on parchment by scribes. Such letters have thick and thin strokes ending in **serifs** (short lines set on angle to the stroke). Roman letters might well have been lost during the violence and unrest of the Dark Ages had not the Emperor Charlemagne in the 8th century encouraged a revival of ancient learning in the monasteries.

Over the centuries, Roman letters as copied by Carolingian scribes became modified into the angular, compressed style used in medieval manuscripts of the Gothic period. In the Renaissance Roman letters were revived by humanist scholars studying ancient manuscripts. Early designers of type were inspired by both styles. Today there are numerous typefaces to meet various requirements. They may be arranged into groups or families: Roman, black letter, script, and sans serif (often called Gothic). Italic is a sloping variant of roman and sans serif [168].

Roman type, with thick and thin elements and serifs, is traditionally used for books, newspapers, and other reading matter. It has two subgroups. Old Style roman letters have graceful, sloping serifs. Modern (18th-century) roman faces have straight serifs and a greater distinction between thick and thin elements. Typefaces were first—and still are—identified by the names of their designers, such as a **Bodoni** Roman typeface designed by the 18th-century Italian Giambattista Bodoni (1740–1813). The text of this book is set in Baskerville, a typeface named for the English printer and type designer John Baskerville (1706–1755).

The other type families are less common. **Black letter types,** also called **text** or **Old English,** are modeled on late medieval illuminated manuscripts. Gutenberg printed the Bible in black letter. This type family is decorative but often hard to read and is used today usually to suggest medieval times. **Script typefaces** imitate handwriting and are therefore slanted. Just as there are many styles of handwriting, so are there many script typefaces used almost entirely for announcements, invitations, and display heads.

Sans serif type is in wide use today. Unlike Roman, the letters are of almost uniform thickness, with no serifs. (Its name is French, meaning "without serifs.") Sans serif types, called Gothic by many typographers, are chosen to give a sense of modernity and efficiency.

It is surprising to note the variety within these type families. The differences from one typeface to another often seem small and take a practiced eye to recognize, but they greatly affect readability as well as the appearance of the page as a whole. For instance, a page of this book has a light gray tone, while pages of other books, set in heavier typefaces, appear darker. The head of Picasso, used as a promotion poster for The Word/Form Corporation, is composed of the words from an essay on Picasso. Yet this essay is less important than the textural effect created by varying the size of the typeface. The large white letters stand out sharply against the black background, while the smaller typefaces seem to recede as shadows [169]. Designers of printed matter, especially advertisements, must choose type carefully to give the material the desired appearance and mood. Pay special attention to advertisements, where you will often see unusual adaptations of the basic groups of type. Herb Lubalin (1918–1981), an internationally known type designer, created an elegant logo for *Avant Garde* magazine that has become a classic, although the magazine is now out of print [170]. He was one of the first American designers to position letters almost in contact with each other, a practice developed in the German Bauhaus school.

Typesetting In general, type design has not changed radically since the earliest days, but

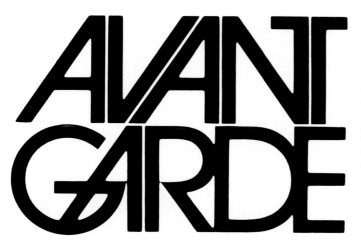

above: **169.** Paul Siemsen. *Picasso poster.*
1978. Four size/weight combinations
of type; 26 × 23" (66 × 58 cm).
© The Word/Form Corporation, 1978.

left: **170.** Avant Garde *logo, 1968.*
Designed by Herb Lubalin. Lettering
Tom Carnese. For the magazine
Avant Garde, *Ralph Ginzburg, publisher.*
Collection, Herb Lubalin Study Center
of Design and Typography, The Cooper Union,
New York.

typesetting has. For more than four hundred years, metal type was laboriously set by hand, as it still is for special headings. In the 19th century, numerous machines were invented to replace hand composition. Today two chief kinds of machines for composing (setting) metal type remain—linotype machines, which cast slugs, or lines of type, as one piece, and monotype machines, which cast individual characters. Both machines space the words to justify lines, or fill them out to the desired width.

Most type today is being set by special typewriters as cold type or by phototypesetters, which produce photographic images of characters on film or paper. In phototypesetting, varieties of type styles are stored on small discs, film strips, or grids. Computers usually run the systems that convert the type images to the specific type being set. Computers have revolutionized typesetting and are likely to induce further radical changes in the process and labor force.

Printing Processes Like typesetting, the method of impressing type on paper has changed enormously. Gutenberg and other early printers, using a hand-operated torsion screw to apply pressure on a flat wooden press, were able to turn out a few hundred sheets a day. Today's mechanized rotary presses are power-driven machines that can produce the same number of impressions in a few minutes or even seconds. The upper cylinders carry the paper—the lower ones are the printing plates, which transfer ink to paper at high speed.

There are three major printing processes, which correspond to the printmaking methods discussed in Chapter 4. Letterpress is printed from a raised, or relief, surface [**171a**]. Gravure is printed from an intaglio, or depressed, surface [**171b**]. Offset lithography is printed from a level, or plane, surface [**171c**].

Letterpress, evolving from the artist's woodcut, is the oldest and until recently the most common method of printing. Ink is applied to a raised surface and transferred directly to the paper through pressure. The ink rollers touch only the raised areas, not the lower, surrounding spaces. There are several different types of presses, but the basic principle is the same.

In **gravure,** derived from engraving, an image is etched below the surface of a copper plate or cylinder. The etched plate is inked and the excess ink is wiped off the surface. The ink remaining in the depressed areas is directly transferred to the paper by pressure. As with most such printing, the oily ink can be felt on the printed page. Gravure is considered to be the best method of reproducing illustrations, but since the plates are expensive to make, it is only used when a large number of impressions are to be printed. Art books and magazine sections of newspapers are mainly gravure.

Offset lithography, derived from direct lithography, is the most recent and now the most common of the three printing processes. The two main differences between it and other methods are the use of the lithographic principle that grease and water do not mix and the indirect way the images are transferred to the paper. The printing images, formed chemically on the same level of the plate with the nonprinting areas, are made receptive to greasy ink and water-repellent. After the plate has been dampened by water, the nonimage areas accept water but not ink. Thus when the plate is inked, only the image areas are transferred to a rubber roller called a blanket. The ·images are then transferred from the blanket to the paper (offset to the paper). One of the big advantages of offset printing is that the softer rubber blanket can produce a clearer impression on many kinds of surfaces.

Photomechanics The old ways of printing illustrations from handmade woodcuts, steel or copper engravings, or lithographic stones have

171. *Mechanized rotary press printing.*

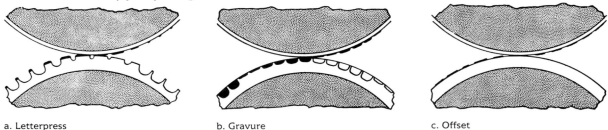

a. Letterpress   b. Gravure   c. Offset

been replaced by photomechanical processes, which transfer the image to be printed to a metal plate by photography. These processes vary somewhat for each of the major printing methods. The oldest, first used in the late 19th century, is photoengraving, which makes letterpress plates. The others are photogravure and photolithography. The cheapest and simplest kind of photoengraved plate is the **line plate,** or **line cut,** used to reproduce images made up of solid black-and-white lines or areas with no gray middle tones. Examples of line cuts are some diagrams in this book and pen-and-ink drawings. The artwork is photographed and the resulting image on the negative is transferred to the sensitized plate by a photographic process. The plate is then etched in acid to eat away the areas that are to remain white. An effect of intermediate tones can be produced by drawing the lines close together or by using prepared screens with dots or crosshatchings. Many artists from Rembrandt to Charles White have worked in cross-hatch [102].

Halftone plates are used to reproduce photographs, watercolor drawings, or paintings that require intermediate or continuous tones. When halftones are photographed, a screen, placed between the camera lens and the film, converts the image on the negative into dots. Like line cuts, the halftone plates are also etched in acid, and the dots remain in relief to pick up the ink. The tiny dots of fine reproductions can hardly be seen, but if you look at the pictures in a newspaper, you can see the dot patterns easily.

This complex process of printing with dots for black-and-white reproductions becomes even more critical when printing in color. The colored illustrations you see in books and magazines, like fine color prints, are made by printing several colors one on top of another. This is done by making a separate plate for each color to be printed. The plates are obtained by photographing a subject through special filters, which separate the colors of the original. Each color—yellow, magenta (red), cyan (blue), and black—is printed individually from separate plates. Alignment, or registration, is crucial for each printing; otherwise the dot patterns will not match up, and the illustration will appear fuzzy.

The many variations within the three major printing methods and different types of presses are numerous and complex. Specialized presses, inks, papers, and methods meet a variety of needs from printing metallic inks on drinking glasses to reproducing detailed colored paintings with every nuance of brushstroke. In addi-

172. *Pictographic images (icons): international themes. 1982.*

tion, there are many new technological developments, which may change printing completely. For example, electronic engraving machines, computers that decide on the exact degree of color correction needed, and new plastics, metals, and other products are all making for faster and more accurate printing.

Graphics

Most of us are comfortable with a combination of verbal and visual communications to convey varied messages and concepts effectively. Still, what Confucius said does sometimes seem to be very true—a picture is worth a thousand words. With the international marketing of goods and services, coupled with world tourism, in mind, the U.S. Department of Transportation called on The American Institute of Graphic Arts to modify international signs and symbols that might be refined for national use without any identification in words. The design association of Cook and Shanosky evolved what has become a universal language with simple imagery for travelers of any nationality [172]. The automobile and airline industries have developed comparable icons for use everywhere in the world.

Book and Record Jacket Design Perhaps the most prestigious assignments in the field of graphic arts are the jacket designs of books and record albums. Both are actually package designs of a sort, since they must attract attention while they protect the contents of the work while at the same time identifying the subject. Yet the designs are created as flat layouts and so are best analyzed within the two-dimensional framework now under consideration.

The book jacket for *Horst* [173], encompassing the work and world of a noted photographer of fashion [147] and society, is a case in point. Designed by Sara Eisenman for Alfred A. Knopf/ Random House Publishers, the jacket exemplifies high style. The open-spaced layout and hand-lettered title, a variant of the Roman typeface Carlton, convey the elegance of the world of the rich and famous that this book chronicles. The classic oxford gray of the background is a fine foil for the white lettered title. The 1939 fashion photograph encircled by the letter "O" shows a Mainbocher drawstring corset; Horst tells us that this was "the last photograph I took in Paris before the war . . . for me, it is the essence of that moment, and . . . all that I was leaving behind." The back jacket shows an irreverent peacock astride a sculpture in the garden of Maison-Lafitte near Paris.

Jackets for record albums are basic to the musical entertainment industry, serving both to attract the attention of potential consumers and to identify musical groups for the millions interested in record buying. For its very anonymity the Beatles' *White Album* jacket remains a classic, but more typical are surrealistic designs for rock music often combined with stunning lettering and typography, as in the front and back jacket designs for *Hear It Is-The Flaming Lips* [174].

Package Design The invention of the self-service supermarket indirectly revolutionized the packaging industry. No longer was product packaging designed primarily to identify and protect goods as they were transported from a warehouse to grocery store shelves. Competing for space and attention among the thousands of products in a supermarket, the manufacturers now aim to distinguish their products as well as to communicate the nature and quality of the contents within each package design. Today's busy consumer chooses a specific product quickly, sometimes in a fraction of a second.

In other words, in much the same way as record albums publicize a musical offering and musicians, package design must attract attention. Its design is configured in two dimensions, although the finished work will occupy space as well. The label on a can of soup, Andy Warhol reminds us, is one package from an assembly line of thousands [175]. This is indeed popular art planned for the public, the consumers who, with the purchase of every product, pay for the cost of the design, incorporated in the total price of every item. In virtually every exchange of goods, there is an expert who specializes in the particular aspect of packaging. The design for Sasaki crystal, for example, is carefully prepared to safeguard each crystal piece in its carton, but

173. Horst: His Life and Work *by Valentine Lawford. Jacket design by Sara Eisenman; photo by Horst. 1984. Courtesy Alfred A. Knopf.*

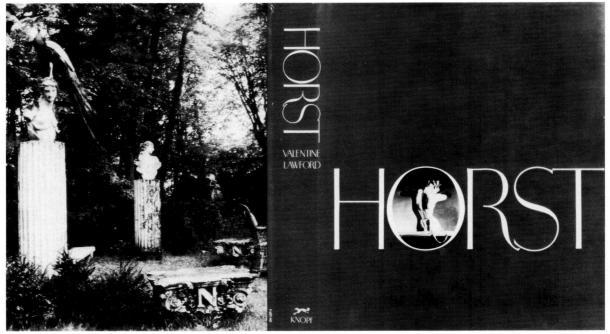

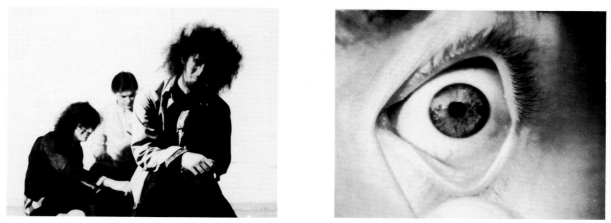

174. *The Flaming Lips. Front and back of album cover for* Hear It Is. *1986. © 1986 The Enigma Entertainment Corporation.*

175. *Andy Warhol. 200 Campbell's Soup Cans. 1962. Liquitex on canvas, 6' × 8'4" (1.83 × 2.54 m). Collection Kimiko and John Powers, Aspen, Colorado.*

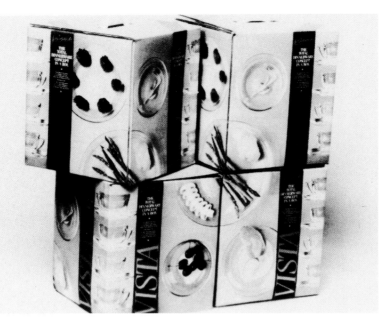

176. *Fabien Baron,*
Carl Lehman Haupt.
Package design for Sasaki
Crystal. 1983–1984.

further, each of the six faces of each box integrates with the other boxes on the shelf, as the pieces are stored [176]. Regardless of which face meets another face of another box, the designer has arranged an interesting and possibly memorable configuration.

New concepts in a package differentiate it from all others. Contrast with competing products is important in identifying the name of the product. The corporate image is generally coordinated to all items produced by the company, working as effectively on the side of the truck, which transports the items, as on the shelf in the market. Furthermore, packaging must identify products on at least front and back, or preferably on all six faces for freezer-stored products. Finally, both access and security are critical factors in the design of a package. Consumers are impatient with tricky openings, but in the case of medicines, assurance that containers are childproof and contents unmolested is vitally important—a fact no designer can ever dare to forget.

Advertising Campaigns

For our consumer-oriented society, advertising accounts for a major portion of the printed material in our visual environment. Before the Industrial Revolution, however, handbills and posters were the only visual means a tradesman could use to publicize his merchandise, except, perhaps, for the sign in front of his door, like the barber's striped pole of the past.

Today, advertising comprises a multimillion-dollar industry that measures its impact on commerce in part on the extent of its billings. The largest advertising agencies oversee ad art campaigns for internationally marketed products and services that may be advertised on radio, television, newspapers, magazines, etc. Large corporations allocate a significant portion of their total sales to cover the costs of hiring one or more agencies that will provide such complex services as research, art and layout production, media selection, and public relations. These and many more behind-the-scenes projects determine the success rate of any advertising art campaign that puts hundreds of thousands of dollars on the line.

A case study of the AMF sporting goods campaign, created by the Minneapolis-based Fallon McElligott Rice agency, shows a witty copy slant that makes use of headlines that can be read two ways. Marketing specialists have determined the best approach for the intended audience, directing the entire series of ads toward physical fitness and body-building, a focus of the growing group of young urban career people. The ad format appears deceptively simple; actually, the process of research, evaluation, and design necessary to produce this sophisticated approach was demanding, necessitating highly developed skills and many meetings between agency and sponsor. Without all this preparation, even the first-rate photographic images would fail to get our attention [177].

Most advertisements are prepared for a specific use, for a limited time and predetermined market, as we have noted. Once the theme of the ad is selected by the client, the artist makes rough "thumbnail" sketches of the layout. These eventually result in a final, carefully prepared pasted-up assembly of artwork and type called a **paste-up (mechanical),** which is photographed to make the printing plate.

Whether working in the field of magazines, books, package design, or advertising design, graphic artists must have a knowledge of lettering, typography, layout, reproduction methods, and printing techniques. Even more important, they must be skilled, creative, and imaginative in using the elements of design—balance, unity, line, color, and shape—that apply to all the visual arts. In the hands of a good designer, the graphic processes can be used creatively and expressively to produce visually exciting and satisfying designs.

Illustration The artwork for an advertisement consists of photographs or painted or drawn illustrations, which become vital elements in attracting our attention or setting the mood of a story. Many artists like Ronald Searle move easily into the commercial field with aesthetically pleasing results. This pen, ink, and **wash**

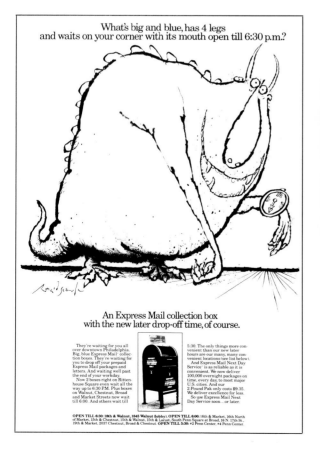

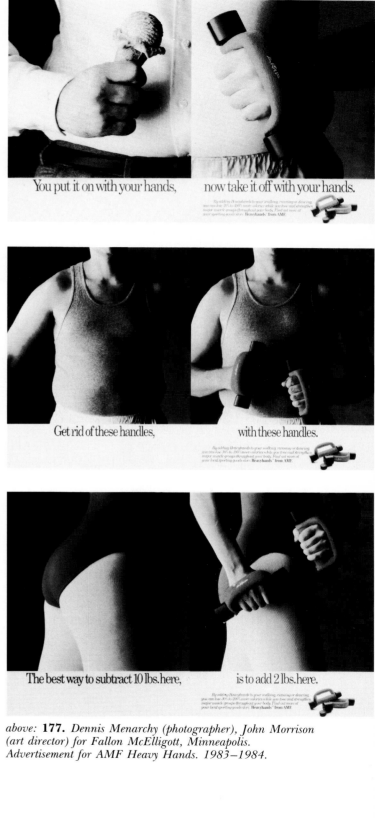

above: **177.** *Dennis Menarchy (photographer), John Morrison (art director) for Fallon McElligott, Minneapolis. Advertisement for AMF Heavy Hands. 1983–1984.*

left: **178.** *Ronald Searle. Express-Mail Animal. 1983–1984. Drawing. Courtesy Young and Rubicam, Inc. and the U.S. Postal Service.*

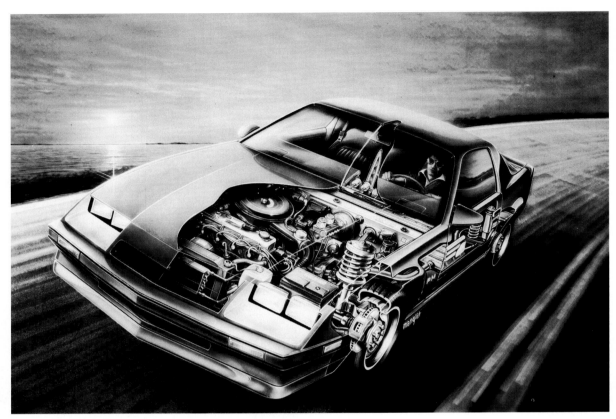

above: **179.** *Jeffrey Mangiat. Cut-away illustration of an automobile. 1984.*

below: **180.** *Shadow Riche advertisement for L'Oréal cosmetics.*
George D'Amato, art director; Herb Green, copywriter; Irving Penn, photographer.
Used with permission of Irving Penn and L'Oréal Corporation.

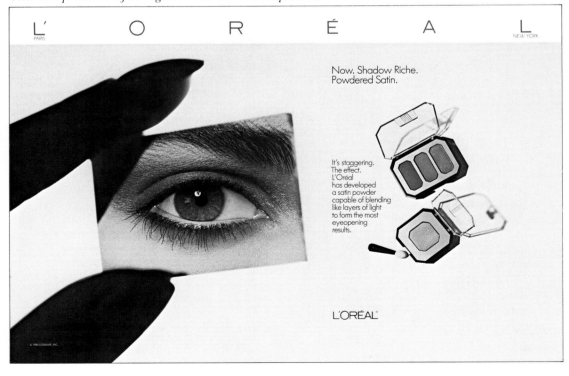

drawing by Searle, prepared for a Postal Service campaign to publicize Express Mail [178], is a particularly arresting image. The impact derives from its strong black and white linear quality, its line, and its humorous appeal.

Equally dramatic, but dependent on its mid-range of values and precision of details, is this **halftone** automobile illustration by Jeffrey Mangiat [179]. The interior workings of the car are revealed in a technical **cut-away** view, contrasting nicely with the highly refined exterior surface, rendered in **airbrush**-type smoothly graduated tones.

The popularity of **tempera** paints, **watercolors,** and pen and ink for advertisement illustrations has been matched somewhat in recent years by photography. The illusion of reality produced by many contemporary photographs perhaps has caused this shift from the more conventional techniques. A skilled photographer can create drama, elegance, mystery, and special visual effects that, when combined with the persuasiveness of literal camera transcription, make for notable imagery; see the photograph for L'Oréal cosmetics by Irving Penn (b. 1917; Fig. [180]). The assymmetrical balance first attracts, but it is the contrast of the stark, silhouetted fingers with the eye detail that is likely to sell the product.

The Poster Some of the early examples of public imagery, handpainted on rather broad sheets of paper for display on town walls, were first called broadsides in the 1500s; these were the forerunners of our modern posters. Layout design for this art form demands sparse simplicity of visual and verbal communication so that the message can be easily comprehended from a distance or in transit and, most important of all, may be easily remembered. Posters are used for many purposes: they inform us of forthcoming events (concerts, sports contests, museum exhibitions); they announce sales, usually, in this case, pasted on sidewalls of buildings or roof signs (residential properties, land, etc.); they sell products, usually in large billboard form (cigarettes, liquor, air travel, etc.).

Because of the clarity inherent in poster graphics, the poster format may be used to promote concepts as well as goods and services. The production of a poster for the Girl Scouts of America may serve as a typical case history. The organization is rich in traditions and service to millions of girls throughout the world. Originally called Girl Guides in England and re-named Girl Scouts in the United States, they chose a cloverleaf design, or trefoil, as their emblem in 1913. The basic outline has been retained through the years, but the interior has been changed from time to time, starting with an eagle in 1914. In 1978, Saul Bass was commissioned to update the design. The emblem that he evolved is made up of black shapes and a black face shape that seem to be at different distances from the viewer, while the two white face shapes also seem to be at different distances. The illusion that the open or negative spaces are white, while the black or positive shapes exist in different spaces is achieved by overlapping the forms. A unified total develops from the subshapes to illustrate the "one from many" concept inherent in the slogan "The new face of Girl Scouting"—a brilliant demonstration of effective poster design [181].

181. *"The new face of Girl Scouting." 1978. Saul Bass, art director; Saul Bass, Art Goodman, designers; Arnold Schwartzman, photographer.*

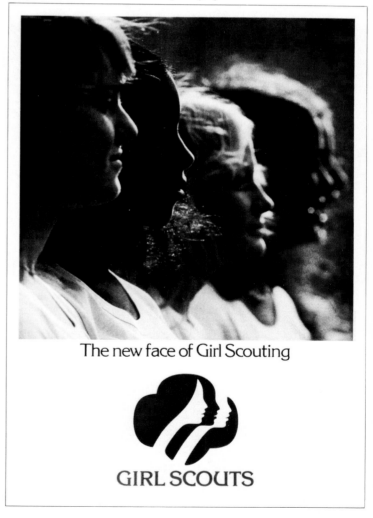

The new face of Girl Scouting

GIRL SCOUTS

Focus on the Artist

Saul Bass (b. 1920)

Little known outside graphic circles, Saul Bass [182], nonetheless, has shaped the face of much of what we see in the international world of print all around us. You run into his imagery wherever you turn. The designer and developer of numerous corporate identities in Europe, South America, the Far East, and the United States, Bass is in part responsible for the images we conjure up with the mention of AT&T Bell Laboratories, Celanese, Warner Communications, Minolta cameras, United Airlines, Alcoa aluminum, the Girl Scouts, United Way, Exxon-Esso gasoline, and Wesson Oil—to name only a few. Even a U.S. postage stamp—a 1983 stamp commemorating art and industry—bears his imprint. He is responsible for the introductory and concluding credit designs for some films that have become minor classics: *Man with a Golden Arm* (1955), the epilogue to *Around the World in Eighty Days* (1956), *Anatomy of a Murder* and *Psycho* (1960), *West Side Story* and *Exodus* (1961), *Spartacus* (1967), and *The Shining* (1980).

Bass' own short films are collector's pieces, flawless gems in design in a giant industry. He and his wife Elaine in part produce, direct, and supervise the production of art and animation involved in every film. Bass' latest work was developed from a Ray Bradbury story called *The Quest*. Using computer animation and other special effects, the film is

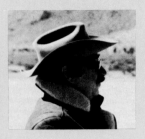

182. *Saul Bass.*

thought-provoking, emphasizing how precious life is [183].

Saul Bass was born in New York City; although he only attended Brooklyn College for a couple of years, he has received several honorary doctorates. His designs are represented in museums on both coasts. His design center, Saul Bass and Associates, Inc., in Los Angeles, undertakes total design concepts that may begin with corporate architectural considerations (such as Exxon-Esso gasoline stations), continue through trademark and logotype, and then appear in package and poster designs. But, undoubtedly, the average citizen has been most influenced by the Saul Bass film titles and symbols—his work that has made his name legendary with his peers in his own time. Bass has received the highest national and international awards for his graphics and for several of his films, produced with the full collaboration of his wife. The record of their achievements continues to grow.

183. *Saul Bass.* The Quest.

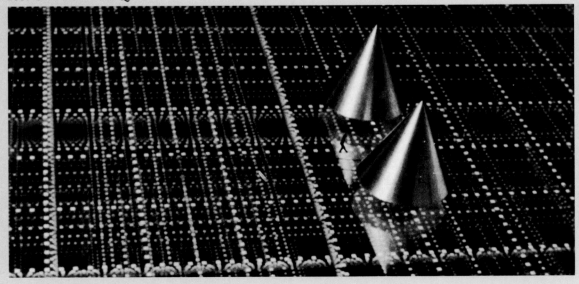

Exploring Art Through Technology

The Computer Connection

Computers are helping artists create more and more of the graphic images we see every day. These images produced on a computer screen are known as computer graphics, and they in turn pervade television, magazines, newspapers, books, and even museum exhibitions today. The special effects made possible by computers, commonplace in television news and sportscasts, involve innovative techniques—assembling pictures electronically, changing their colors instantly, enlarging and reducing images, and then adding on-screen color transformations that interact with the more traditional elements of form and shading that we find, for example, in painting and sculpture.

In its unparalleled range of possibilities, the computer has no precedent as a medium for images. Under computer control, television can freeze-frame an image on the basketball court and transform a monochromatic piece into a spectrum of colors. Computers help meet the demands of advertising in television commercials with instant photo montage and other combinations, such as the superposition of titles and backdrops or the simulation of cars flying through surreal space, for instance, or toothbrush bristles moving with impossible fluidity.

In the field of typography, typositors use computers to integrate type and artwork in layouts in a fraction of conventional typesetting time. Hundreds, even thousands, of experimental arrangements can be made, since the computer gives the artist the capacity to rapidly summon images that have been created and stored in computer memory by a layout artist.

In much the same way, a compositor can montage photographs stored in the computer's memory, extrapolating parts and assembling results with invisible seams. It now becomes possible to create a skyline that never existed. By using information on the on-screen display from two different photographs, a compositor can position the Statue of Liberty from one photograph into the middle of Manhattan Island in another. The "reality" of a photograph will increasingly become suspect [184].

With innovative handling, super-computers, the most powerful computers yet devised, can create images that look like photographs of landscapes and still lifes. Appropriate shadows and highlights convince the observer of their authenticity. When portions of the image are blurred to show speed or movement, few viewers can distinguish computer art from a direct photograph. The computer is at the heart of a revolution in image-making.

184. *Statue of Liberty in the middle of Manhattan Island.*

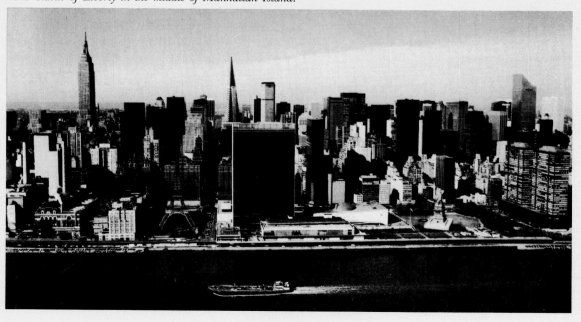

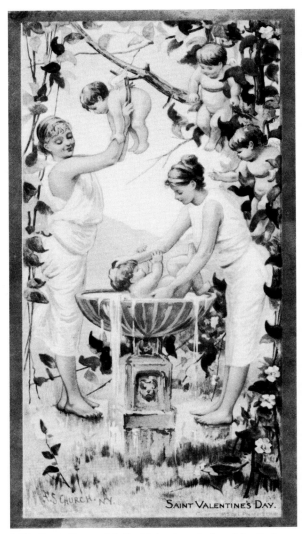

185. *Louis Prang & Co. Valentine, designed by F. S. Church. 1883. 9½ × 5" (24.1 × 12.7 cm) with ⅞" (2.03 cm) silk fringe. Hallmark Historical Collection, Hallmark Cards, Inc.*

Greeting Card Design

Greeting cards date back to the 15th and 16th centuries in Germany, when woodcut-printed sentiments were exchanged to celebrate New Year's Day. The idea of making personal Christmas cards became popular when the English artist John Caliott Horsley made some in the form of a self-caricature in 1843. The design of such cards soon expanded [185]. Louis Prang, a German immigrant, established his own company printing cards in Boston in 1856. His orthographic multicolor process used very fine mechanical projections—his cards were printed in no fewer than eight colors and occasionally twenty, to reproduce his popular florals and landscapes. The short printed sentiments were excerpted from Tennyson or Longfellow.

By the 1950s, most of the current card types had all been devised. Intricate card folds, lavish ornamentation, and complex cut-outs were competing for attention; some of the fanciest cards ever published had appeared by 1960. More recently, there has been a revised graphic look, spearheaded by the Hallmark card company, incorporating more space and more diversity in theme. The newer styles are no longer concerned with reproducing three-dimensional space on a flat surface, but feature designs in themselves. Local printers still supply cards of regional interest, but the greeting card industry is so firmly a part of our economy and customs that cards are sold almost everywhere—even all over the world.

Of the several "trendy" styles that are current, greeting cards executed in airbrush have held sway for several years and appear to be a continuing favorite. Expensive studio cards, often left blank for handwritten messages, seem to be more popular than ever. As for the future, few artists ever set the world on fresh paths without some help from the past. The graphic artist may be the deciding factor as to which direction new cards will take.

Calendars

The history of calendars dates back thousands of years. Virtually every culture developed a system of measuring time through the movements of the stars and recording the findings; the Hebrew, Chinese, and Egyptian cultures, among others, all evolved calendars. Many of us are familiar with Stonehenge, which is oriented to the solar solstice [281], but fewer are aware that New World Indians in Mexico kept calendar records that spanned hundreds of years. The Mixtec Indians were the most dedicated historians, creating books (codices) that consisted of long strips of leather, cotton cloth, or bark paper, folded in screen fashion and placed between wooden covers. The *Codex Vaticanus B* [186] is a calendar of the 260-day religious year. Each of the four pages shown depicts a different appearance of the rain god. Any glyphs (symbols) seen represent calendar days under the deity's protection. Scenes and ideographs were painted in flat colors, outlined in fine black or red lines.

Somewhat later, in Europe, calendar books that often included zodiacal signs were painted for the French aristocracy. Calendars are now an important field for graphic designers. The calendars, which vary widely, are planned several years ahead. Calendars with an illustration for

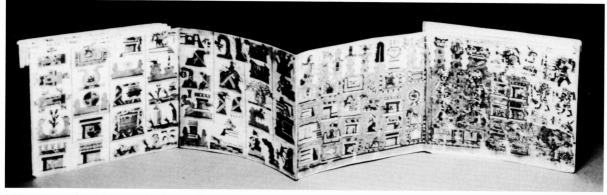

186. *Mixtec Calendar. pre-1063* A.D. *Vatican, Rome.*

each month may be reproductions of famous fine art sold at museums. Other fashionable trends are computer-generated images and fantasy visuals. Although the calendar market is active for less than half of each year, competition for its designs attracts some of the most successful graphic artists.

Wall Coverings

Paint-on Wall Coverings Walls affect the character of the rooms they enclose; often the pattern establishes a mood that influences everyday living. To produce interesting textures, paints can be stippled onto a wall with a stiff brush or can be applied with special rollers embellished with patterns. Easy and inexpensive to use, raised-design rollers effectively print a pattern on walls to create customized unique surfaces. A somewhat related procedure, which may be more in keeping with an irregular space and eclectic furnishings, is **stenciling.** By roller-painting, then repeating the painting of a design through an individualized stencil designed to fit the spatial requirements of a room, the wall surfaces may be enlivened in a particular way. This stencil process, resembling silkscreen printing, permits a much freer and more personal expression than standardized printed wallpaper could ever achieve.

Printed Wallpapers Used in the Orient for centuries and in Europe since the 17th century, wallpaper was introduced to the future United States late in the Colonial period. The earliest American wallpapers were imported from Europe; they were hand-painted with small oriental-type designs described as "chinoiserie" because of their Chinese inspiration. While wallpapers made in America soon became available in hand-painted designs and then in mechanically printed versions, they were known as "poor man's tapestry" because they imitated the expensive textiles preferred by the wealthy for wall coverings.

By the 1870s, English wallpapers were flooding the wealthy international market, primarily due to the popularity of William Morris' designs **[187].** His stylized motifs from nature were flat

187. *William Morris.* Pimpernel, *wallpaper design. 1876. Block-printed on machine-made paper; 22½" (57.1 cm) wide. Courtesy Cooper-Hewitt Museum, Smithsonian Institution, New York.*

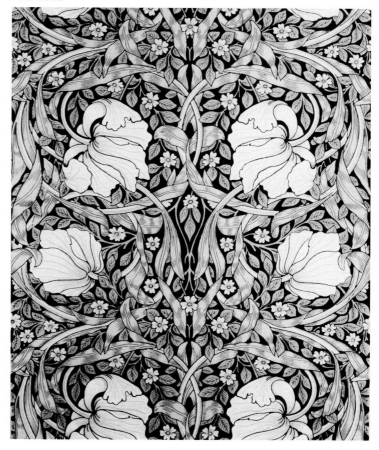

enough to suit English critics, while their naturalism pleased those who loved flowers on their walls. His first papers, printed in 1864, outshone even the French papers in the eyes of the fashionable; more important, they were executed in a style that led to **Art Nouveau.** The design is straight repeat or one that has been *mirrored* (design positions reversed).

William Morris' designs for wallpaper were planned to be repeated. In general, the same repeat procedures are used today. The original motif, called a *repeat,* varies in size from 4 to 16 inches (10 to 40.6 centimeters); the standard sizes ($9 \times 9''$, $9 \times 11''$, or $11 \times 11''$; 23×23, 23×30, 30×30 cms) are duplicated in straight repeats or locking repeats. While some designs are repeated only twice, most are duplicated eight or more times. A *straight repeat* involves an original design with straight edges, either square or rectangular; the pattern created by the repetition is integral to the design. *Locking repeats,* also called *lock-in repeats,* incorporate design elements that protrude outside the basic design and serve to conceal the duplications as much as possible.

Wallpapers are produced by roller printing, silkscreen printing, or even wood-block and lithographic printing; the colors, patterns, and designs are infinitely varied. A rotating cylinder, engraved with a design, prints the same design over and over again as the cylinder turns. Evolving from solid colors to textured effects, in patterns that range from small to large, from abstract to realistic scenes, wallpapers may create an illusion of depth or extended space. Strong printed designs set the character of a room, determining how other furnishings may be keyed to them. Wallpaper patterns are often coordinated to fabrics by fashion designers like Mary McFadden, who has made collections of wallcoverings and fabrics, as well as garment designs. Painter Roy Lichtenstein's (b. 1923) overscale pattern on silver Mylar dramatizes a stair wall in a house remodeled for his personal use by the architect Robert A. M. Stern **[188]**. Its bold pattern of diagonals and circular motifs emphasizes the existing wall paneling.

Computers contribute to wallpaper design, most obviously in the ease with which a computer can duplicate designs in the endless repeat patterns basic to wallpaper—full-drop, half-drop, etc. Images duplicated in vertical rows are termed **full-drop** repeats. In **half-drops,** horizontal repeats are spaced half-way between duplicate motifs. Less obvious, but potentially even more valuable a resource, is the capacity of a

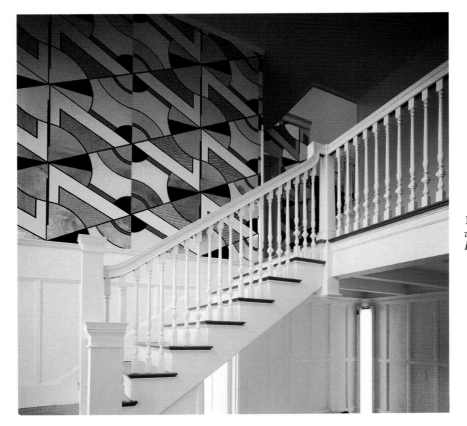

188. *Interior of house with wallpaper by Roy Lichtenstein.*

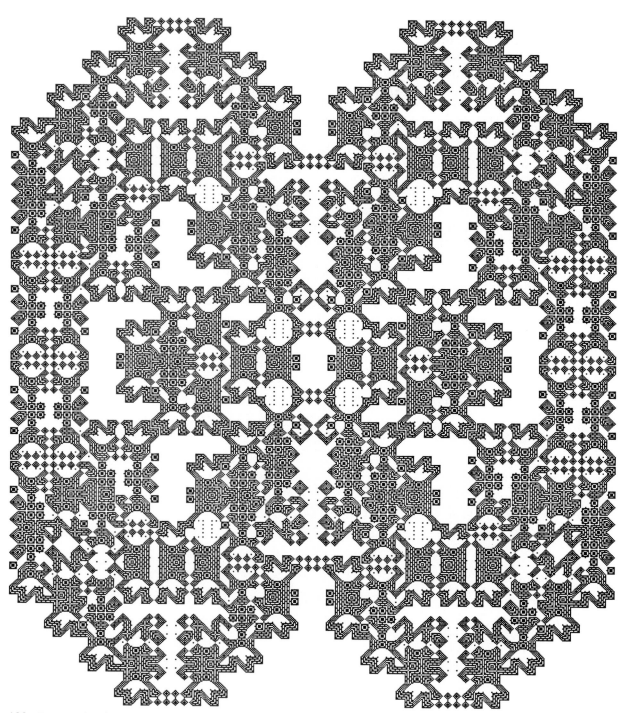

189. *Tony D. Smith. "Crossover" pattern. 1985. From Pattern Breeder program using Apple LaserWriter Plus printer, reduced to 96% using the FullPaint program; $8\frac{1}{4} \times 7\frac{1}{8}''$ (20.95 × 18.1 cm). Used by permission.*

computer, by means of a program that randomly generates designs (called Pattern Breeder), to reproduce patterns that can emulate rich embroidery, infinitely varied geometrics, or even curvilinear forms. Almost unlimited colors can be simulated to allow for further variation, with endless possibilities ahead **[189]**.

Fabric Design

Textiles are basic to contemporary living. They are rooted in fiber arts of the past whose evolution will be examined later with three-dimensional art forms. Natural fibers have been supplemented by rayon, fiberglass, and synthetics such as Orlon and nylon, which produce easy-to-care-for fabrics that resist dirt, wrinkles, and mildew. Similarly, hand-weaving and hand-decorating are almost replaced today by machines. Egyptian tomb paintings show cloth stamped with designs as early as 2100 B.C. African peoples have decorated their textiles for centuries, using many different processes. *Adinkera Cloth* from Ghana is produced by the Ashanti using various small patterns printed in repeated motifs in black dye with various small stampings cut from pieces of calabash [190].

In block printing, the oldest fabric printing process, a design is cut in wood and a colorant applied; the block is then pressed against the fabric, with the raised surface of the block printing the design. Each color requires a separate block and separate printing. Precise registration is important, so designs are usually simple and colors are limited.

Silkscreen printing is a stencil process, as described earlier. Originally a hand-printing tech-

nique, silkscreen is now electronically controlled and very fast, while continuing to provide richly pigmented printed fabric. When photographically coated, a silkscreen can include photographic imagery that reflects contemporary imagery in textile designs.

Computers are now often involved in textile design. Where precise repetition of pattern is essential, few artists can operate with the speed and efficiency of a machine. Color combinations can be unlimited when the operation is computerized. Textiles that are one of a kind, however, such as those made by batik or tie-dyeing, remain the special province of craftspeople.

Both batik and tie-dyeing are old methods of ornamenting fabric that have been revived in recent years and used to create wall hangings as well as fabrics for clothing. In batik, melted wax, which resists dye, is used to block out areas of the cloth that are to remain white or light colored. Each succeeding dye bath produces

190. *Adinkera cloth. Ashanti, Ghana. Printed in black dye with various stamps made from pieces of calabash. Reproduced by courtesy of the Trustees of the British Museum.*

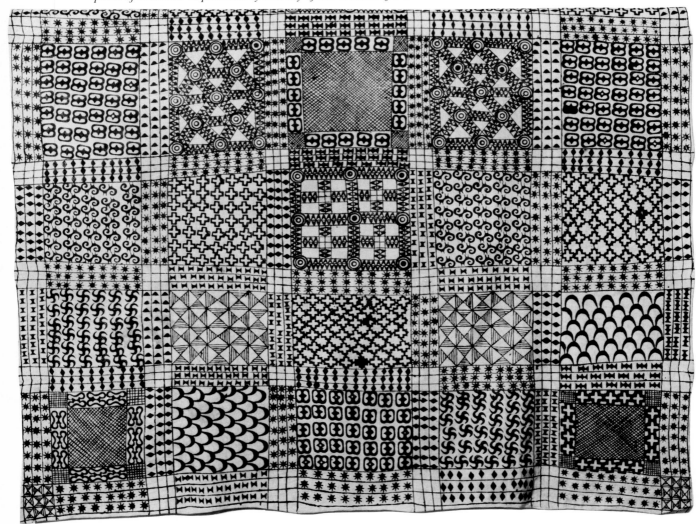

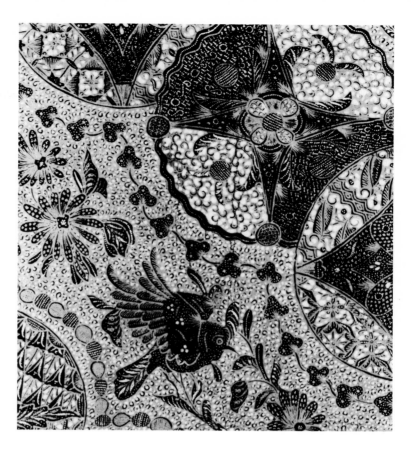

191. Kain panjang *(long cloth),*
Central Java, detail. Batik, entire work:
3′5¾″ × 8′6⅛″ (1.06 × 2.62 m). Textile
Museum, Washington, D.C.

deeper colors by dyeing over the lighter colors. Batik dye may also be used for painting directly over wax-blocked areas on fabric, as in the detail of a Javanese long cloth. The impact of the piece comes from the interesting shapes and the use of negative and positive space [191]. In tie-dyeing, the parts of the fabric that are to remain light are tied with string to prevent the dye bath from touching them.

We have observed the evolution of early visual printed communication into vast modern industries; yet treasured old hand processes have been retained and revitalized even while new forms of art have come into being. In the sculptural and other three-dimensional arts that follow, we will find the same regenerative spirit.

Exercises and Activities

Research Exercises

1. What is a logotype? List the major television and radio logotypes. What are the names represented by those logos?
2. How is it possible for early Chinese writing to be pictorial? Explain fully, or demonstrate by drawing Chinese characters.

Studio Activities

1. Design your own logotype. Determine for which kinds of business your design would be suitable.
2. Select an ad from your favorite magazine. Identify five different advertising elements in that ad. Rearrange the ad in a quick sketch, using all the same elements.
3. The instinct for decoration is basic. Redesign

3. What are the major printing processes? What is the advantage of rotary printing over its predecessor, flat-bed printing?
4. How are computers involved in fabric design?
5. Define computer graphics. How are graphics by computer useful in today's world?

a wallpaper design of one historical period and adapt it for use today.
4. Find examples of successful communication of ideas through visual means—in magazines, advertisements, and so on. Redesign those communications so that the ideas are very much clearer or produced with more arresting images.

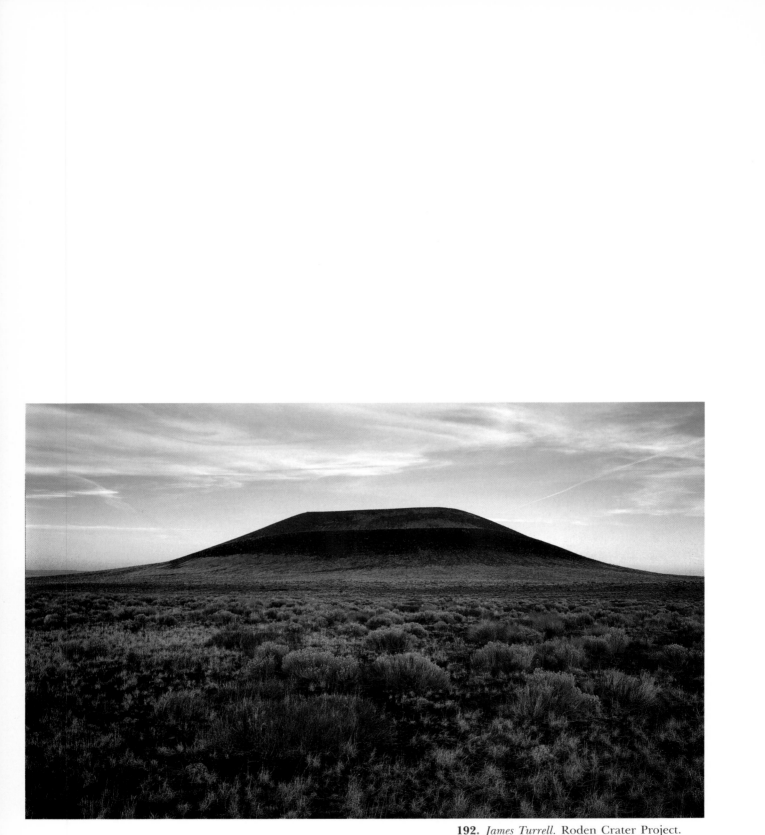

192. *James Turrell.* Roden Crater Project.
Currently in progress; volcanic crater near
Arizona Painted Desert, reworked in part by artist
for public viewing of astronomical events.

Part Three
THREE-DIMENSIONAL MEDIA AND TECHNIQUES

The media that occupy space in three dimensions also communicate to some deep level of human need and experience. These art forms perhaps have served human existence for the longest time, from the earliest art objects that remain from the past to our expressive needs for today and, no doubt, tomorrow.

Three-dimensional art visually provides more than the height and width that we see in two-dimensional art. The third dimension—depth—radically alters our perceptions. We experience two dimensions from only one single perspective. The multitude of aspects possible in viewing and dealing with works that occupy space often makes each view appear like a totally different configuration. Well-designed three-dimensional work should compel the viewer to move all around it, examining the artwork from many different angles.

Three-dimensional media make use of the same visual elements and principles of design with which we have already become familiar. Every age and society has made its contribution to these arts. In exploring how artists have used a wide range of materials we will consider the long evolution from hand-made works to today's industry, provoking such questions as: Can machines create art? Can art be produced by industry's machines if they are controlled by artists?

At the same time as technology's surge forward provides artists with new materials and processes to work with, some artists continue to try to address such issues as the human's relation to nature and the universe, using the environment as the forum for their discourse [192].

In the chapters to come, we will examine the sculptural arts, the arts for living, architecture and environmental design, and the effect of technology upon them.

7
The Sculptural Arts

When Michelangelo had finished the Moses, there was no other work to be seen, whether ancient or modern, which could rival it . . . one might almost believe that the chisel had become a brush. . . .

Giorgio Vasari, Renaissance historian

I say that the art of sculpture is eight times as great as any other art . . . because a statue has eight views and they must all be equally good. . . .

Benvenuto Cellini, sculptor, c. 1562

[Nature], the model, teaches us what we should do . . . to model shadow is to bring out the thought. . . . Sculpture is the art of the depression and the protuberance . . . Nature, by a divine law, tends constantly toward the best. . . .

Auguste Rodin, sculptor, c. 1890

Sculpture is such a physical thing that you must have manipulative ability—hit a nail with a hammer—cut metal and join metal. The better you know how to make things, the better you are as a sculptor.

Richard Stankiewicz, sculptor, 1973

Sculpture is a three-dimensional art form, probing space somewhat as architecture does. While architectural space, however, is large enough for us to walk through, most sculpture occupies more limited volume. We are used to looking at statues carved on a building's surface, set into niches, or standing free where we can walk around and enjoy them from every angle. Such forms of sculpture, whether seen only frontally or from all sides, change as the light and our angles of vision vary. The hollow spaces between sculptural masses can often become as important visually as the sculptural forms themselves. Our eyes follow the dominant lines of the work, and frequently our bodies respond as well. The human tactile response is so strong that our hands often long to touch the sculptural surfaces, to feel the smooth or rough textures.

When we cannot touch sculptures, we can usually imagine what it would feel like to run our hands over the surfaces. These are all immediate sensual responses, quite separate from any emotional feelings aroused by subject matter.

Some contemporary artists such as James Turrell (b. 1943) work on a vast scale. His *Roden Crater Project* involves partially reworking a volcanic crater for viewing astronomical events in an awe-inspiring setting. Such environmental sculptures seem to surround us, much like the original environments from which each sculpture was derived **[192]**.

Through the ages, sculpture has fulfilled many purposes: to teach religious beliefs, to create an emotional atmosphere of veneration, to depict the gods in visual form, to record historical events, to exalt rulers, and to honor the dead.

In contrast, today's sculpture is usually more concerned with communicating the individual artist's inner feelings or response to the outside world.

In addition, new ways of using traditional materials, new technical methods, and new ideas have transformed the nature of sculpture. In fact, the art has changed so radically over the last one hundred years that it is difficult to discuss much contemporary sculpture in conventional terms or to classify it in the usual way as carved wood, cast metal, or built-up clay. For example, in what category would you place these examples of present-day sculpture—a stuffed vinyl typewriter, or a laser-beam neon sculpture?

As we study the processes by which sculpture is made, we will see how the sculptor often uses complex techniques to create aesthetic sculptural experiences. Since a large part of the process of sculpture is problem-solving on a practical level, only after sculptors become technically proficient can they concentrate on expressive aspects of their works.

Traditional Materials and Processes

Stone, wood, clay, and metal have been used in sculpture for centuries in an infinite variety of ways, each reflecting different cultural concepts. **Relief** sculptures are close in appearance to two-dimensional works in that their three-dimensional mass is attached in some degree to a flat surface. In *bas-relief* (low relief), the forms project only slightly off the background. In *haut-relief* (high relief), at least half of the depth of the total form juts off the background. Sculpture in the round, as the name implies, consists of free-standing work. In the past, stone and wood have been carved in what are called direct processes; that is, the sculptor works with the actual material that forms the finished work. As a first step, a small sketch and/or model of the larger work is prepared to serve as a guide. This is then enlarged, either by eye or with a device that measures the original and notes the increased proportions on a block of wood or stone.

Once the material is marked, the sculptor chips away the excess until gradually by this subtractive process the image begins to emerge from the block. Michelangelo used to go to the quarry to pick out the stone he wanted for a particular piece of sculpture. He believed that he could visualize sculptural forms trapped inside the stone, waiting to be released by his carving. Through a similar sense of identification with

the source of their works, traditional African sculptors beseeched growing trees to give approval to the sculptures carved from their wood.

Stone

In the past, stone sculpture has varied from small fertility figures such as the *Venus of Willendorf* [25] to the enormous bulk of the *Sphinx*, which was made from huge blocks of stone added to the natural rock already there [55]. Granite, sandstone, marble, onyx, and many other dense stones have been carved by sculptors with tools that have changed little over the centuries. Chisels, heavy-headed mallets, rasps, and hand-finishing tools still in use by sculptors today are basically much the same as those Michelangelo used to carve his *Moses* [193]. But modern sculptors in stone usually also employ

193. *Michelangelo.* Moses. *1513–1515. Marble, height 8′4″ (2.54 m). San Pietro in Vincoli, Rome.*

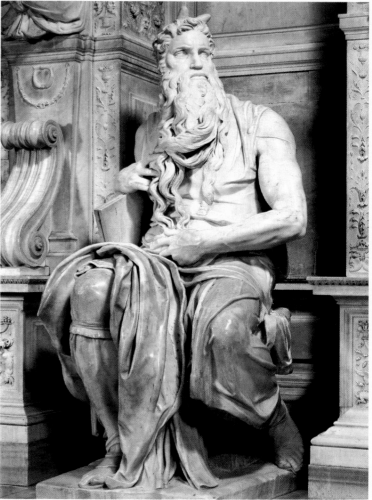

Auguste Rodin (1840–1917)

Whatever Rodin put his hand on exuded an overwhelming power, a force untamed.

Until the age of nine, the young Rodin attended a school run by monks in Paris, where he was born. He was a dull student, but so entranced with art that he was finally permitted to attend the Petite École du Dessin in 1857. "I had a violent longing at first to be a painter. Colour attracted me. I often went . . . to admire the Titians and Rembrandts. . . . But . . . such a passion for sculpture seized me that I could think of nothing else."

Rodin at eighteen was making a name as an artist of uncompromised boldness and originality. Plucked from obscurity and set into a show titled "New Currents," thirty-six of his sculptures joined seventy paintings by the Impressionist Monet. No less than the leading critic of his day, Octave Mirbeau, pronounced the show of "two wonderful" artists a colossal success.

As a consequence of a trip Rodin took to Italy, the influence on him of Michelangelo and ancient sculpture was enormous. Like Cézanne, he also came to believe "unfin-ished" art, that is, fragments of nature or of ancient art, projected extraordinary power—which often, when completed, lost considerable impact. These concepts of the fragment and the bittersweet poignancy of life itself followed Rodin and in fact dominated his art. He may also be credited with a fascination for incorporating free movement into his work, perhaps the first to do so [194].

Eroticism permeates much of Rodin's art. "People say I think too much about women," he once remarked. "Yet, after all, what is there more important to think about?" After he met Camille Claudel in 1883, she became his assistant and lover, serving also as inspiration for several of his sculptures. She also became a sculptor. In fact, Rodin's favorite portrait of himself was the bust she completed of him [195]. Meanwhile, his reputation spread. In 1900, a retrospective exhibition of his work, in Paris, launched with a banquet in his honor, was attended by the literary, musical, and artistic leaders at the turn of the century. Rodin's continued appeal to us today may lie with his own identification with the spirituality and the passions of humankind.

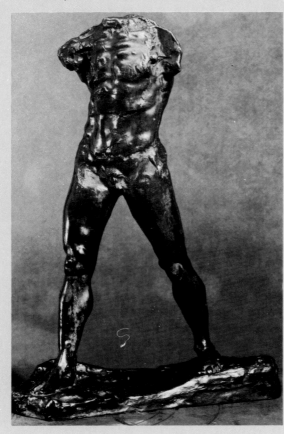

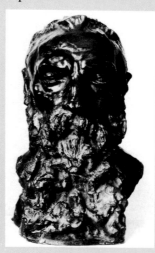

left: **194.** *Auguste Rodin.* The Walking Man. *1877–1878. Bronze, height 33⅛" (84 cm). National Gallery of Art, Washington (gift of Mrs. John W. Simpson, 1942).*

above: **195.** *Camille Claudel.* Auguste Rodin. *Bronze, 16 × 10 × 11" (40.7 × 25.7 × 28 cm). Rodin Museum, Paris.*

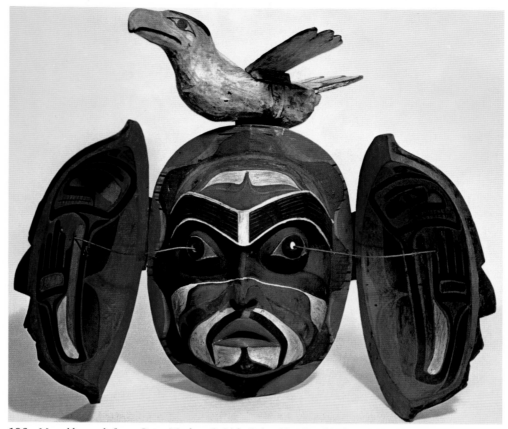

196. *Movable mask from Cape Mudge, British Columbia, Kwakiutl. 1850–1875. Painted Wood, height 21½" (55 cm). Courtesy Museum of the American Indian, Heye Foundation, New York.*

power tools to cut away the excess material fairly easily or to add a polish to the finished work. They may use hand tools only for the final carving and shaping, reducing to a fraction the time and effort once required for sculpture. If you were to try to chip off a few pieces of marble with a hand chisel, you would understand the difficulty of the task and the advantage electrically powered equipment has given the sculptor. The skills required, however, while somewhat different from those for hand tools, are just as demanding.

The character of the stone and the nature of the tools with which the sculptor chooses to work determine the appearance of the finished piece. For example, the texture of finished sculpture—highly polished or left rough—will vary depending on the type of surface worked as well as the tool with which unwanted material is eliminated. Many artists, such as Michelangelo and Rodin, have always left a small portion of their sculptures unworked to echo the original surfaces of the natural materials. If you carefully

examine Michelangelo's *Moses*, perhaps you can detect the virgin surfaces. In addition, the stone's special qualities, such as the marbled veining, must be respected and used expressively by the sculptor. Finally, because stone, for all its hardness, can break as it is being worked, care must be taken to choose blocks without flaws.

Wood

Wood has played an important role in every phase of human existence. The tombs of the ancient Egyptians were full of wooden utensils and furniture put there to make the dead comfortable in the afterlife. The peoples of Africa, Oceania, and pre-Columbian America used wood for boat decorations, sculpture, furniture, and masks [196]. Along the Pacific Northwest Coast whole tree trunks, set near large wooden plank houses, were carved into totemic animal images that identified the crests of the several families who shared the house. Such totem poles served somewhat like house directories [197].

Like sculpting in stone, wood carving is a direct technique that involves removing unwanted material until the desired form emerges from the piece of wood. As with stone, the hardness and graining of woods vary. Each kind presents a different technical problem of possible breakage or splitting. Today we value the grain of the wood both from a technical and an aesthetic point of view, since the character of the material chosen by the artist affects the appearance of the final piece of sculpture. In early cultures, however, after a wood sculpture was completed, it was frequently painted or coated with fine sheets of bronze or gold, so that the texture or grain of the wood was masked by the overlying layers. For example, the mummy of the Egyptian pharaoh Tutankhamen was found in a nest of wood-and-gold coffins, each inner container slightly smaller than the outer. The innermost one, just fitting his body, was solid gold, but was enclosed within an oak coffin almost totally covered by layers of precious gold and inlays of semiprecious stones [198].

Medieval cathedrals are treasure houses of carved wooden choir screens, choir stalls, and altars. Inheriting these religious traditions, the Renaissance sculptor Donatello created sculptures that embodied the piety of the earlier age.

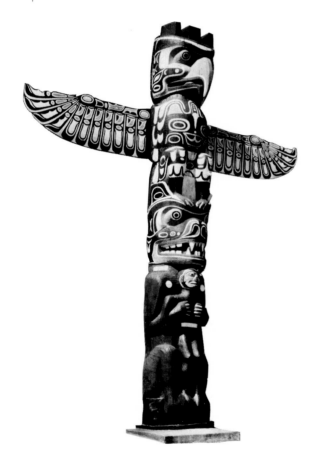

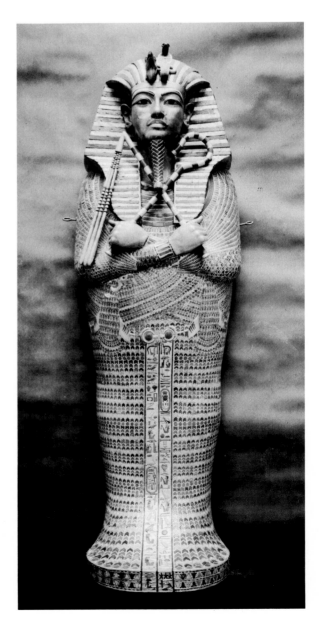

above: **197.** *Totem pole, Stanley Park, Vancouver, British Columbia.*

right: **198.** *Tomb of King Tutankhamen, second coffin: lid. Egyptian, XVIII Dynasty. c. 1365 B.C. $6'8\frac{3}{8}'' \times 2'2\frac{3}{4}'' \times 2'6\frac{7}{8}''$ (2 × .68 × .78 m). Treasure of Tutankhamen, Egyptian Museum, Cairo.*

Restoration Sheds Light on Two Works by Donatello

As disastrous as a storm in November, 1966, was for Northern Italy—its inhabitants as well as its art treasures—there were some consequent benefits. In particular, our knowledge was enlarged of one of the greatest sculptors of all time, the 15th-century Italian, Donatello (1386–1466). Two of his statues art historians had attributed to the 1450s, or later, the *St. John the Baptist* in the church of the Frari in Venice and the *Penitent Mary Magdalen* [199] in the Baptistry in Florence, had been dated on stylistic grounds because documentation did not provide sure-fire evidence of when they were made. Both statues, made of wood, came in contact with the flood waters resulting from the 1966 storm, necessitating drying and restoration. In the process of restoring both, it was discovered that a thick layer of brown paint covered the polychrome (colored paints) and gilt that was originally intended to be seen. Further, on the *St. John the Baptist* an authentic signature came to light and the statue's date was uncovered: 1438.

Both sculptures show an intense spirituality and fierce expressiveness that some art historians believe arose out of a mature artist coming to terms with the dissolution of the flesh that accompanies age and the preparation of a religious man for death. Uncovering the date on the *St. John* not only gave a new slant to traditional notions of Donatello's development, but also caused the conventional dating of the *Penitent Magdalen* in the 1450s to be rethought. The latter statue is now also believed to date from the late 1430s or the 1440s.

Just as modern viewers of classical Greek statuary see it devoid of the coloring that marked it when it was new, so we have come to accept Medieval and Renaissance sculpture without its decorative coloring. We now see the tan of the Magdalen's face, arms, and legs setting off the intense blue of her eyes and, even more, the flickering highlights of gold in her hair, which she wears as a garment, contributing to the other-worldly quality which her gaunt, emaciated form expresses. We also know more about Donatello's working methods after the restoration of these two famous wood sculptures. To help overcome some of the restrictions of the subtractive method of carving, Donatello added **gesso** in some portions of the *Magdalen* to build up areas, unlike

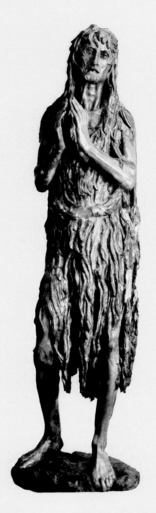

199. *Donatello.* St. Mary Magdalene. *1435–1450. Polychromed wood, height 6'2" (1.88 m). Museo dell'Opera del Duomo, Florence.*

earlier sculptors, who used gesso mainly as a ground preparation for polychromy. Thanks to contemporary expertise in and attitudes toward restoration, which favor returning to the object's original appearance when feasible, we can now see and appreciate these two important statues of Donatello's as the sculptor originally intended them.

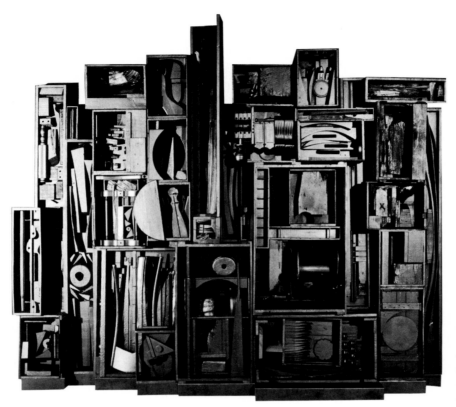

200. *Louise Nevelson. Sky Cathedral— Moon Garden + One. 1957–1960. Black painted wood, 9'1" × 10'10" × 1'7" (2.77 × 3.3 × 0.48 m). Collection Arnold and Milly Glimcher, New York.*

Contemporary sculptors often use wood in the traditional manner, carving from solid blocks. But they also use it in new ways, such as the additive process called **assemblage.** Louise Nevelson (1899–1988) collected ready-made pieces of wood and combined them into compositions that suggest walls or niches taken from architectural settings. Her works are concerned with the play of light and shade over forms and can be looked at as symbolic spaces for retreat and protection from our plastic, streamlined world. She started by picking up scraps of wood in furniture and pattern shops. After nailing and gluing them together, she painted them all flat black, white, or gold, thus unifying the hundreds of separate pieces. The entire work shown here is large, but each of the small boxes is a self-contained rectangular relief composition, recalling the intricacy of Gothic carving—a cathedral of modern times, touched with poetry and magic [200].

Newly developed processes have further increased the flexibility and versatility of wood as a material for sculpture. For example, plywood can be bent and shaped when heated and built up into almost any form; it can then be painted or left with the natural grain and color intact. Nevelson herself is the subject of an assemblage by Marisol (Marisol Escobar, b. 1930), a work formed of plywood, wood block, hair, some plastic, some paint, and other materials [201]. Like many of her works, it is a witty spoof of the mighty figures of our time.

201. *Marisol (Escobar). Portrait of Louise Nevelson. 1981. Pencil and oil on wood and plaster, 54 × 72¼ × 78" (137.16 × 183.51 × 198.12 cm); backboard 96 × 108" (243.84 × 274.32 cm). Courtesy Sidney Janis Gallery, New York.*

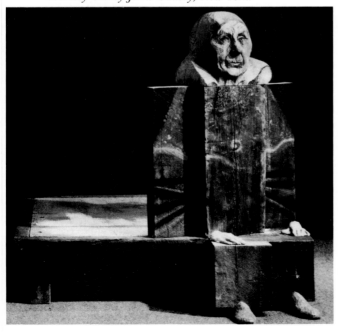

Clay

Clay has been shaped into sculpture ever since human beings first discovered this material that covers much of the earth. It is a very motile substance, easy to model, which permits a great deal of spontaneity, especially in small sculptures. Pre-Columbian Indians from the Valley of Mexico, from an ancient settlement at Tlatilco, for example, modeled lively clay figures of humans and animals for religious purposes [202]. This little figurine has a simple charm and human quality often lacking in the larger complex clay or stone figures that we normally associate with Middle American cultures. Clay can also be built up into very large forms by coil and slab methods, provided that care is taken to prevent the shaped clay from collapsing before hardening. Such clay sculptures are generally hollow and may be built to a height of several feet.

A particular piece of sculpture may be copied one or more times by means of a plaster mold made in sections from the original. Clay is diluted with water until it has a creamy consistency (slip) and is then poured into the mold. When the liquid has hardened, the sectioned molds are removed from the sculpture. The molds can be used over and over again to produce many replicas of the original.

Clay can be baked in **kilns** heated to high temperatures to make it more durable. This firing process, discussed in the section on **pottery,** causes physical changes to take place in the clay, hardening it and making it nonporous. Fired clay, whether shaped by hand or cast in molds, can be decorated with paint or **glazes,** minerals that, when fired, fuse into a glassy coating. Most Renaissance sculptors glazed their ceramic sculptures, and there is a revival of interest in the technique today. Contemporary artists are producing sculptural pieces using hand-building, casting, or combined techniques. Well-known West Coast ceramic sculptor Robert Arneson (b. 1930) has evolved a career that offers humor as the height of art. In an earthenware work he sets the cultural hero of our century Pablo Ruiz Picasso on a Greek column that recalls sculptures in the Roman Forum which celebrate victorious generals. In this case, he has rendered the artist in an all-too-human pose, stretching to scratch an elusive itch. [203].

below: **202.** *Figurine from Tlatilco, Mexico*
Middle Formative Period 800–300 B.C.
Clay, height 3¾" (9.5 cm). Dumbarton Oaks
Research Library and Collections, Washington
(Robert Woods Bliss Collection of Pre-Columbian Art).

right: **203.** *Robert Arneson.* Pablo Ruiz with Itch.
1980. Glazed earthenware, height 7'3½" (2.2 m).
The Nelson-Atkins Museum of Art, Kansas City
(gift of The Friends of Art).

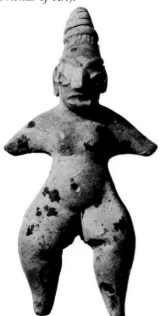

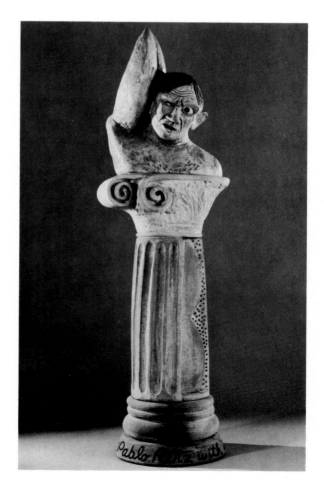

The making of **ceramic** wares, shaped out of damp clay and fired (baked) in a kiln, was one of the earliest crafts to develop. Clay vessels were used in most settled societies for cooking and storage. They became a form of high art in many civilizations.

There are three kinds of ceramics, depending on the kind of clay and the firing temperature. **Earthenware,** made from coarse, impure clays and fired at low temperatures (about 800°C, or 1470°F), has a soft, porous body suitable for rough pottery vessels and bricks. **Stoneware** is made from finer, purer clays and fired at higher temperatures (about 1300°C, or 2370°F), which fuse the clays into a harder, vitreous (glasslike) body. It is used for sturdy vessels. Responding perhaps to the shapes and design of ancient Greek pots [47], Peter Voulkos (b. 1924) makes a bold new statement in his stoneware pot, assembled with clay layers [204]. **Porcelain** is made from the finest white kaolin and other clays and fired at the highest temperatures (from about 1400°C, or 2250°F, to 1613.4°C, or 3000°F). When struck with a hard instrument, its vitreous body produces a clear, resonant sound, and when thin enough it is translucent. Porcelain makes some of the finest-quality vases and tableware, with harder surfaces than stoneware. All three kinds of ceramics are used for sculpture.

Potters can pat and pinch clay into shape or form it into coils or slabs to build the walls of a vessel, which are then smoothed by hand or with

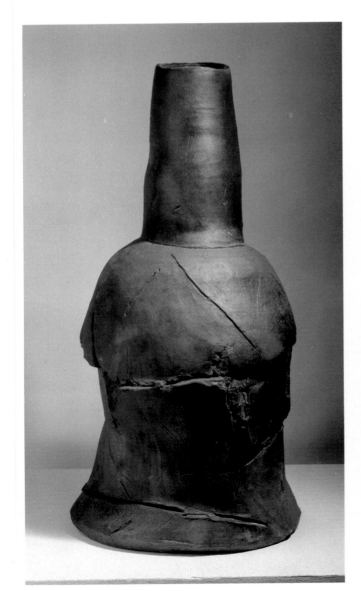

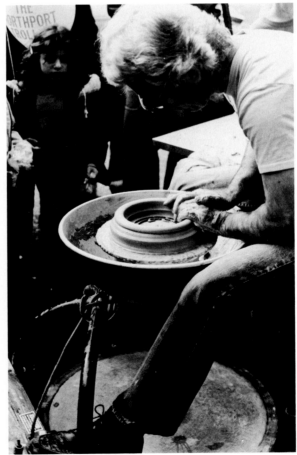

left: **204.** *Peter Voulkos.* Untitled (Stack). *1981. Woodfired stoneware bottle. Height 40" (101.6 cm). Modesto Lanzone, San Francisco.*

below: **205.** *Potter John C. Fink at his wheel.*

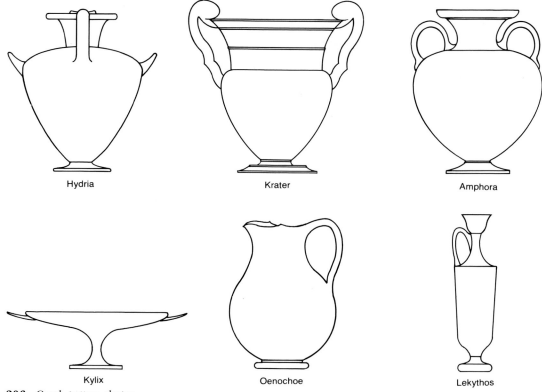

Hydria

Krater

Amphora

Kylix

Oenochoe

Lekythos

206. *Greek pottery shapes.*

a stone or shell. American Indians of the Southwest still make pots by these techniques. Using more sophisticated methods, potters like John Fink shape clay on a rotating potter's wheel [205], pulling the clay up from the base with the hands, or pour slip (a cream-like mixture of clay and water) into a mold. The wheel and mold enable them to produce more pots of greater uniformity and smoothness and more ambitious design.

The clay pot must then be dried in the air. If such **greenware,** as it is called, is to be made hard and watertight, it must then be fired to remove all moisture from the clay. Early peoples baked their earthenware pots in the coals of a fire or in covered pits. Since then pottery has been fired in special furnaces, or kilns, such as the multichambered dragon kilns with firing chambers usually stairstepped up the hillsides of southern China, or in modern electric kilns.

The pot after the first firing is called **bisque.** It may then be decorated with colored stains, or it may be painted with or dipped in **glaze,** a coating of ground chemicals and water. A glazed pot is then fired a second time at a higher temperature, which fuses the glaze to the surface of the

pot, making it more durable. Glazes range in color from muted earth tones to brilliant primary hues, and they can produce a variety of rough, mat, and shiny textures. Additional glaze decorations can be added in subsequent firings. Each step in firing requires great technical knowledge and skill, whether it is done by an individual or a large factory. Errors can produce drastic changes in glazes or ruin pots completely.

The early Greeks and the Chinese, Koreans, and Japanese produced some of the world's great ceramics, pieces of exceptional beauty in shape, glaze, and ornamentation. Greek potters designed graceful shapes for specific purposes. They made narrow-necked jars and bottles to hold costly wine, oil, and perfume safely and wide-mouthed bowls and cups for mixing and drinking water and wine [206]. Heavy jars had three handles to make them easier to move, dip into, or pour from. These vessels were often painted with figural scenes.

Chinese potters developed subtle shapes and a variety of glazes that depended on precise control of the heat and oxygen supply in the kiln. Ding ware is a delicate, creamy white porcelain

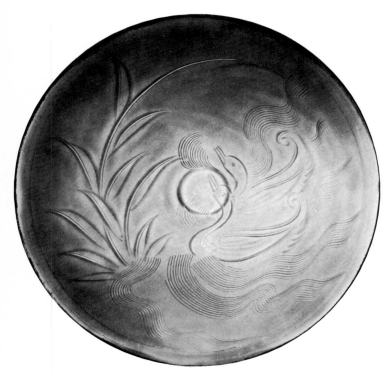

207. *Chinese Ding ware bowl. Sung Dynasty. Porcelain. Museum of Fine Arts, Boston (purchased from the Helen and Alice Coburn Fund).*

from northern China **[207]**; covered with a transparent, almost colorless glaze. Ding ware consists chiefly of bowls, whose rims, left raw in the firing process, are usually hidden with a copper band. Heavier kinds of porcelain, incised or

smooth, are covered with celadon (sea-green porcelain) glazes in an attempt to give the effect of jade. Chinese porcelains were widely imitated in the West in the 17th and 18th centuries.

Japanese potters were inspired by sophisticated Chinese and Korean porcelains, but they also developed **raku,** a simpler, coarser earthenware and stoneware, one of several kinds of ware appropriate for use in the tea ceremony, which stressed simplicity and love of nature. Raku, from the Japanese word *raku,* "enjoyment," is modeled by hand, usually in straight-sided bowls and often covered with runny glazes in colors suggesting nature—brown, light orange, dull green, and straw. The calligrapher and painter Koetsu (Hon-Ami Koetsu, 1558–1637) made raku tea bowls that are highly prized by connoisseurs **[208]**. Today hand potters make use of traditional methods, some of which were ignored for years because of the Western emphasis on industrialization. Many contemporary potters have been much influenced in particular by Oriental styles.

Finally, in addition to the goal of forming finished sculpture, clay has been used for centuries to make small models of large projected sculptures or to build up full-size sculptures from which metal statues are cast, as we shall see.

Metal

Until the 20th century, metal sculpture, usually bronze, was cast. The same lengthy process with few changes has been used for hundreds of

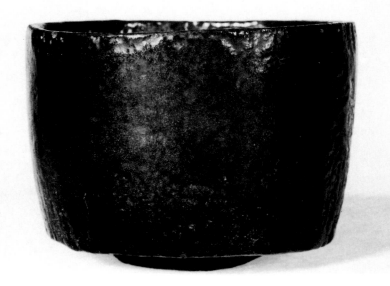

208. *Hon-Ami Koetsu. Tea bowl. Japanese, Edo Period, 1558–1637. Raku stoneware, $3\frac{7}{16} \times 14\frac{15}{16}''$ (8.7 × 12.5 cm). Freer Gallery of Art, Smithsonian Institution, Washington.*

years. Metal sculpture cannot be spontaneously produced. It takes careful planning and considerable engineering skill to foresee the problems of casting and to prepare for them.

First the sculptor creates a full-size original sculpture. This is the creative part. Most of the rest of the process is technical. The sculpture is usually made of clay or of **plasticene,** a plastic clay, surrounding a wooden or metal framework called an **armature.** The armature, like a skeleton, keeps the clay from collapsing as it is built up, allowing the sculptor to produce slender forms and extended arms and legs, otherwise impossible with soft clay. After the sculpture is completed, a sectioned plaster or flexible gelatin mold is made from it. Since the sculptor usually wants a hollow metal casting, which is obviously cheaper and lighter than solid metal, he makes a wax model as a hollow shell, usually by brushing melted wax onto the mold until a thin shell is built up and then filling the middle of the mold with a solid core of heat-resistant material. When the mold is removed, the wax appears as a replica of the original sculpture. Wax rods are attached to the replica to create vents and channels called **gates**; then the replica is placed upside down in a container. A mixture of plaster, silica, and clay is poured around it. This hardens into a fireproof mold that is called an **investiture.**

The investiture is heated in a kiln and the melted wax runs out. For this reason the process is called **lost wax,** or *cire perdue.* What is now left is a hollow space, in the shape of the original clay sculpture. Molten bronze is poured into the hot investiture and allowed to harden **[209]**. When the investiture and core are removed, the emerging bronze looks odd with the vents and gates sticking out from it. These must be removed and the surface cleaned and finished according to the sculptor's wishes. A finish, or **patina,** is usually applied to the bronze. Depending on the chemicals used, surfaces range in color from greens to dark brown.

Renaissance sculptors usually cast their own pieces or, like Benvenuto Cellini (1500–1571), directed assistants who did the work.[1] Today most metal sculpture is cast in foundries by trained technicians. Sculptors who produce large cast sculptures may have assistants to help them to build the armatures, enlarge the models, and prepare the sculptures for casting. Henry Moore (1898–1986), a contemporary

[1]In his autobiography, Cellini included a charming and humorous account of the casting of his great bronze statue, *Perseus* (18 feet, or 5.5 meters, high).

sculptor whose works were often cast in bronze, made small models of his large figures, turning them over to assistants, who built them up to their final size in plaster shaped over armatures. Moore supervised their work throughout the process, refining the final plaster sculpture himself. He also completed the finishing of the bronze when it came back from the foundry.

Some sculptors today carve the original sculpture from styrofoam, a material that, like wax, melts when the investiture is baked in the kiln. Metal sculpture can also be cast with the industrial sand-mold technique. In this method the sculptor's original model is placed in a sectional metal container, and a special fine damp sand is packed tightly around it. This sand holds the impression of the original even when the metal sections are removed from the model. These sections are reassembled and clamped firmly together around a sand core suspended inside. Then liquid metal is poured into the hollow space formed between the sand mold and the core. Relief sculpture can also be cast by pouring metal into an impression made in a flat bed of sand.

Through the technique of casting, several metal sculptures can be made from original clay or wax sculpture, each reproducing the original model. Sometimes the sculptor works on the

209. *Bronze casting.*

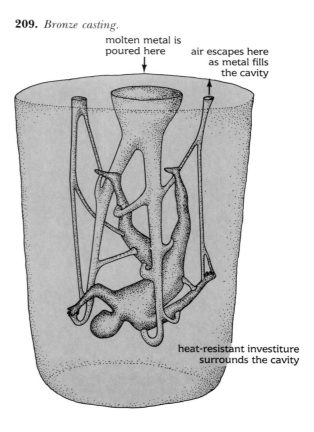

molten metal is poured here

air escapes here as metal fills the cavity

heat-resistant investiture surrounds the cavity

final finishing of all so that each piece can be considered an "original" work. However, molds can also be made from any existing sculpture, so that frequently the duplicates you see are actually reproductions, not finished by the artist. Whether the artist casts his or her own work or turns it over to a foundry, the final shape in metal exactly reproduces the handwork of the sculptor. This is particularly evident in the work of Rodin, who intentionally left parts of his works rough or with only suggestions of details. The marks of his fingers or tools in the clay can be seen exactly reproduced in some of his bronze figures [194]. Bronze casts are still made, but today most metal sculptors build up their sculpture, using soldering and welding techniques to join and shape the pieces of metal.

Enamels and Jewelry-Making

In the ancient art of **enameling,** fine particles of colored glass are applied to a metal, glass, or ceramic ground and fused to it by firing. There are many techniques of applying enamel. In **cloisonné** the design is outlined by cloisons (thin metal strips) that form partitions separating the various colors. Byzantine enamel **reliquaries** were cloisonné on gold. In **champlevé** (raised field) the ground is dug away to leave ridges forming the outlines of the design. Romanesque enamels in medieval France and Germany were usually champlevé on copper. Enamel may also be painted on metal or other grounds to achieve effects as varied as those produced by oil painting. In the 16th century particularly fine enamel was made in Limoges, France.

The desire to enhance the human form with jewelry is universal. Men and women of the Old Stone Age decorated themselves with necklaces and bracelets of stones, shells, feathers, and bones. The jewelry of ancient civilizations involved metalwork, enameling, and cutting and polishing gemstones. Modern tastes in jewelry range from precious gold and diamonds, often regarded as an investment, to costume jewelry in artificial materials and plastic. Jewelry by Bebe Dushey (b. 1927) reflects her obvious love for the materials she uses. Each of Dushey's designs, which balance positive and negative shapes, has also been exhibited as small sculpture [210]. Many artists work in enamel today, producing colorful jewelry, plaques, and ritual vessels.

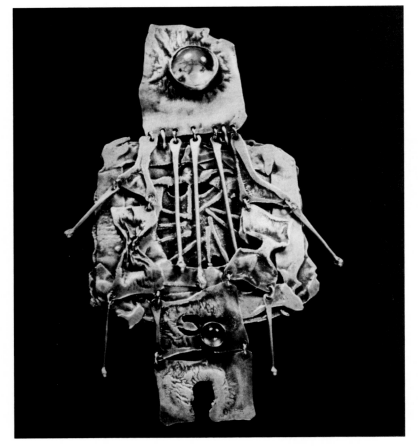

210. *Bebe Dushey. Wearable jewelry, pendant pin. 1978. Fused, soldered, and oxidized sterling silver with large moss agate and smaller moonstone; $4\frac{1}{2} \times 2\frac{1}{2}''$ (11 × 6 cm). Collection the artist.*

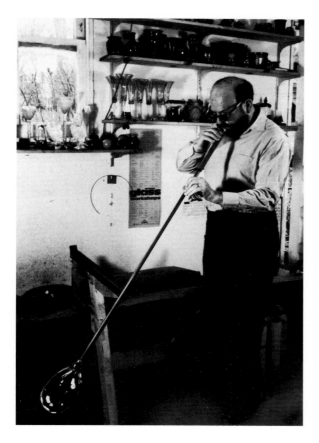

211. *Julian Wolff in his glass-blowing studio.*

Glass

The making of glass, a mixture of silica (sand) and other chemicals, heated and shaped, was well developed by 1500 B.C. Depending on the ingredients, glass can be thick or thin, transparent or opaque, dull or brilliant. Color is produced by adding to the mixture various minerals such as copper, cobalt, or cadmium. When the glass is heated in a furnace to a molten state, it can be blown, poured, pressed into molds, or drawn into threads. It can also be free-blown. In that technique the glassworker dips a globule of glass from the molten mixture with the end of a blowpipe. As air is blown through the pipe, the molten glass forms a bubble [211], which is then shaped with a wooden tool, calipers, and shears, the glass being reheated as necessary to keep it pliable. Modern commercial glassware is mostly molded glass made by machine.

Glassware need not be decorated, relying solely on its attractive shape, texture, and brilliance or color. But it can be ornamented by cutting and faceting; engraving, etching, or sandblasting; or painting, gilding, or enameling. Medieval stained-glass windows relied on color and transparency for their rich, luminous glow [60]. In the 20th century many artists are exploring the possibilities of creating new forms in glass, such as Dale Patrick Chihuly (b. 1941), Seattle-based glass artist and educator [212].

212. *Dale Chihuly.* Sea Form Series, 1984. *Blown glass, 44″ (111.76 cm) wide. Courtesy the artist.*

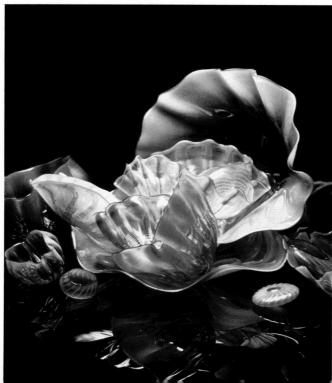

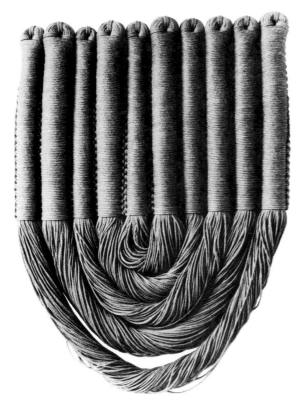

Fibers

Today artists often combine embroidery of various kinds with printing techniques, hand-weaving, and macramé. **Macramé** is the art of knotting strands of fiber together to produce a variety of openwork patterns. Originally used to make fishing nets, it is used today also to create belts, handbags, clothing, plant hangers, and wall hangings. Using macramé and weaving techniques, artists have created three-dimensional wrapped wall hangings [213], free-standing sculpture, and environments large enough to walk into [214].

left: **213.** *David H. Kaye.* Bound Linen and Loops. *1972. Linen blocking cord, knotted, wrapped, and sewn; 22 × 16" (56 × 40.05 cm). Collection Mr. and Mrs. Lee Howard, Willowdale, Ontario.*

below: **214.** *Magdalena Abakanowicz. Black-Brown Composition in Space. 1971–1972. Woven fibers, 19'8" × 26'2" × 11'4" (6 × 8 × 3.5 m). Courtesy Stockholm County Council, Sweden.*

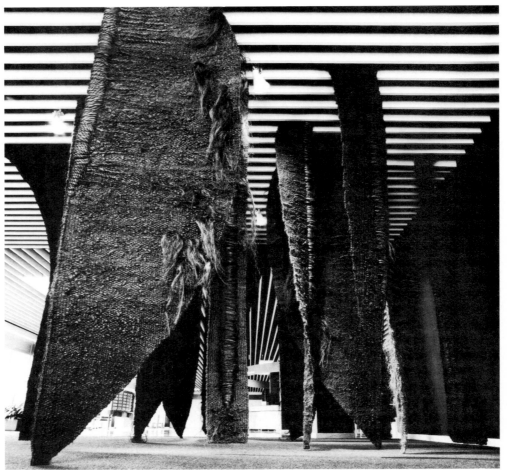

Other old textile techniques have been revived and are used with great inventiveness. Quilted fabric, in which ornamental stitching holds stuffing in place, looped and knotted textiles, and the incorporation of grasses and twigs with woven fibers are some of the techniques contemporary artists use to produce interesting textures. Walter Nottingham (b. 1930) reflects the current interest in soft sculpture in his primeval figure, which uses a variety of fibers to produce a macabre effect that somehow both intrigues and disturbs us [215].

New Materials, New Methods, New Forms

Many of today's sculptors reject traditional materials in favor of new ones, but even when they do use stone, metal, wood, and clay, they frequently use them in new ways. Industrial techniques, such as metal welding, lamination of wood, and the casting and vacuum-forming of plastic, are explored by contemporary artists as rapidly as they are invented.

To increase their knowledge of industrial techniques, some contemporary sculptors have spent time in the laboratories and plants of large corporations studying new methods used by engineers and technicians and collaborating with them to apply these techniques to art. Out of this joint experimentation come aesthetic uses of industrial techniques that not only produce works of art but may in turn influence industrial and commercial products.

Sculptors in metal today may weld steel directly or hand-hammer iron, while wood sculptors build up their pieces using techniques taken from modern furniture production and carpentry. Much sculpture is constructed, built, assembled, or arranged, rather than cast or carved, such as Marisol's *Louise Nevelson* [201] or Jacqueline Winsor's (b. 1941) *Bound Square* [216], which is wrapped with hemp, embracing simple shapes, extolling the virtues of natural materials expressed with a new emphasis upon confined space.

below left: **215.** *Walter Nottingham.* Skins of Us, *detail. 1972.*
Sculpture in fiber: crocheted wool, rayon, and horsehair mounted on velvet platform with plexiglass,
1'4" × 5'6" × 2'6" (0.41 × 1.68 × 0.76 m).
American Craft Museum of the American Crafts Council, New York.

below right: **216.** *Jacqueline Winsor.* Bound Square. *1972.*
Wood and twine, 6'3½" × 6'4" × 14½" (191 × 198 × 36.8 cm). Collection,
Museum of Modern Art, New York (Joseph G. and Grace Mayer Fund in honor of
Alfred H. Barr, Jr., and James Thrall Soby).

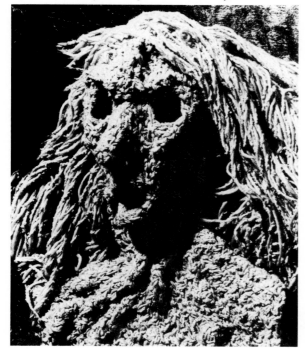

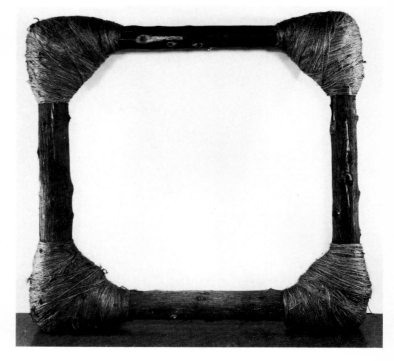

Constructed Sculpture

Picasso was the first artist to fit objects he found around him—handlebars, bones, a feather duster—into sculptural assemblages [31]. Today, many sculptors incorporate bits and pieces found in junkyards or auto graveyards into their work. Constructions of sheet metal, wire, or translucent plastic often replace the traditional sculptural masses with lighter shapes in which space becomes an important element, as with Magdalena Abakanowicz's (b. 1930) work [214]. With this new use of materials the sculptor expresses his or her concern with shaping and dividing space rather than filling it.

Alexander Calder used sheet metal to produce flat-painted shapes, some of which were welded or riveted together into metallic sculp-

217. *Claes Oldenburg.* Giant Soft Fan. *1966–1967. Vinyl filled with foam rubber, wood, metal and plastic tubing; fan 10' × 10'4" × 6'4" (3.05 × 3.15 × 1.93 m), variable; plus cord and plug 24'3¼" (7.41 m). Museum of Modern Art, New York (Sidney and Harriet Janis Collection, gift).*

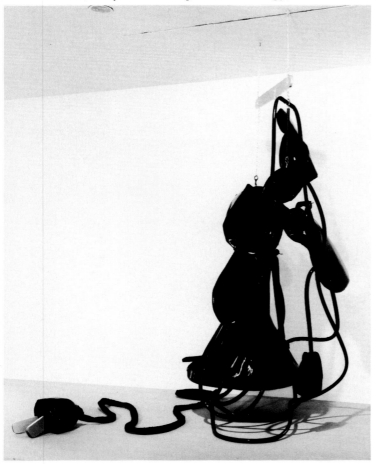

tures attached to the ground. Whenever it was possible, he placed these **stabiles** in natural settings so that the clouds and sky seen through the openings become active elements of his compositions. A dynamic and inventive artist, Calder created both stable and moving sculptures. Using electrical motors to create movement in some of his works, Calder early became fascinated with the changing relationships between sections of his sculptures. Some of his later **mobiles,** which depended on air currents to propel them in complex, ever-changing patterns, were even arranged to clank or ring as they moved [57].

Clearly, 20th-century sculptors have been fascinated by the machine. Many, such as Marcel Duchamp, Naum Gabo (1890–1977), and Calder, made **kinetic sculpture,** propelled by mechanical means. They programmed the parts of the sculpture to move at varying speeds and through changing patterns so that the sculptured object was enriched by a new element of time.

Mixed Media

The new technique of assembling sculpture out of found objects and different materials led to what are called mixed-media combinations or **assemblages,** such as Kienholz's *The State Hospital* [36]. In these works, sculptors use materials that have never been considered sculptural or even aesthetic. Sometimes objects are combined with painted canvases, so that the line between sculpture and painting is at times difficult to define. For example, what kind of art is produced when Rauschenberg attaches an operating (moving) electric fan to a canvas (*Pantomime* [116])—sculpture or painting? What is it when Picasso draws with light in space [95]?

Three-dimensional canvases, constructed on frames and painted in the artist's individual style, are also difficult to classify. Are they dimensional paintings or painted sculptures? Canvases by Lee Bontecou seem to have a resemblance to primitive masks. Her technique, which involves stretching and gluing fabric over a wireframe skeleton, is similar to early aircraft construction. Using this method, Bontecou has created openings that can be interpreted as eyes, mouths, entrances to caves, or sexual cavities [117].

The term **soft sculpture** may seem to be a contradiction, but it describes work created by some contemporary sculptors. For example, many artists make stuffed fabric forms of one kind or another, and some weavers make free-standing or hanging shapes that are sculptural or environmental in form. Claes Oldenburg (b. 1929), a **Pop** artist, uses vinyl, canvas, and other materials to create his soft, larger-than-life-size sculptures of electric fans [217], typewriters, and other everyday objects. He often uses vinyls to emphasize contemporary materialism and the frequent choice of cheap plastic over natural materials.

Issey Miyake, contemporary fashion designer, created this black rattan cross-over bodice as part of her 1982 *Spring-Summer* collection [218]. The design is considered "wearable art"— a term recently evolved. Is this work craft or costume? In a similar, somewhat playful, vein, Scott Burton (b. 1939) has sculpted two ruggedly massive stone hulks that surely make a solid statement about chairs [219]. Again, is this work sculpture or furniture?

Plastics

Among the many industrial materials now also popular with sculptors is plastic, which they use in a variety of ways. Cast in solid pieces, formed into sheets, or built up of fiberglass and resin, plastic can achieve seemingly endless effects. Lightweight and colorful, it can be made into tiny forms through which light may filter or it can be built up over wire-mesh supports or cast in solid, brilliantly colored, jewel-like forms.

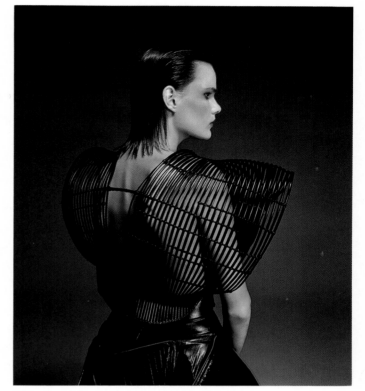

218. *Issey Miyake, designer. Black rattan cross-over bodice. 1982.*

219. *Scott Burton.* Pair of Rock Chairs. *1980–1981. Gneiss, left 49⅜ × 36 × 47" (125.1 × 91.4 × 119.5 cm); right 44 × 46 × 74" (111.8 × 116.8 × 188 cm). Collection, Museum of Modern Art, New York (acquired through the Philip Johnson, Mr. and Mrs. Joseph Pulitzer, Jr., and Robert Rosenblum Funds).*

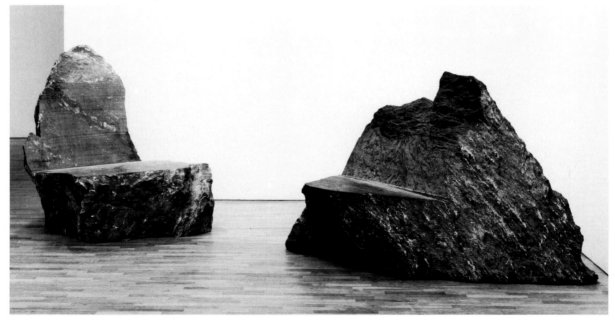

Sculptors have found fascinating possibilities for expression in plastic materials and in the industrial techniques used to form them. Duane Hanson (b. 1925), for example, has discovered that plastics can simulate the real thing so well that art and reality are indistinguishable. In *Man on a Bench,* Hanson celebrates (as always) a non-heroic figure—the ordinary in most of us [220]. In *Adhesive Products* [221] by Linda Benglis (b. 1941), plastic polyurethane has been effectively pushed and pulled into nine imaginative configurations that conjure up fantastic projections resembling hands. The creations which have resulted are so varied that there is no single visual trait common to all.

Light

While all sculpture involves light—natural or artificial—playing over its forms and through its spaces, new lighting techniques have been adapted by sculptors to create spatial environments. Tubing with neon gas inside can be bent and formed into any shape. When lit, such a sculpture makes a visual statement in neon lights. Sculptors familiar with these materials could surely design signs that would be more aesthetically satisfying than most of those we see around us. Plastic rods can also be used to carry light from a light source at one end of the rod; translucent colored resins can be lighted from within to create sculptural objects. In Larry Bell's *The Iceberg and Its Shadow,* ever-changing movement and light seem to dematerialize the surrounding world [222]. In other sculptures, changing waves of colored light are programmed to play over and through the sculpture. It is apparent that light can be utilized by sculptors in new ways, which represent their individual approaches to sculpture. Some works are highly organic; others, geometric; still others, mechanical.

In further explorations of contemporary technology, many artists have experimented with communications media, building rooms in which we can watch video or film images projected around us, accompanied by electronically synthesized sound. Some artists have directed bulldozers to shape huge earthworks, while still

220. *Duane Hanson.* Man on a Bench. *1977. Polyester and fiberglass, life-size. Larry Gutsch, New York. Courtesy O. K. Harris Works of Art.*

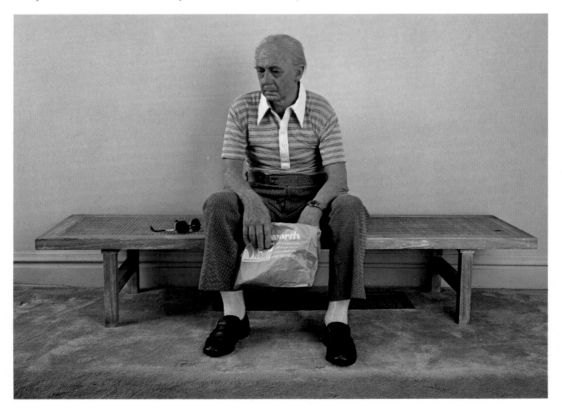

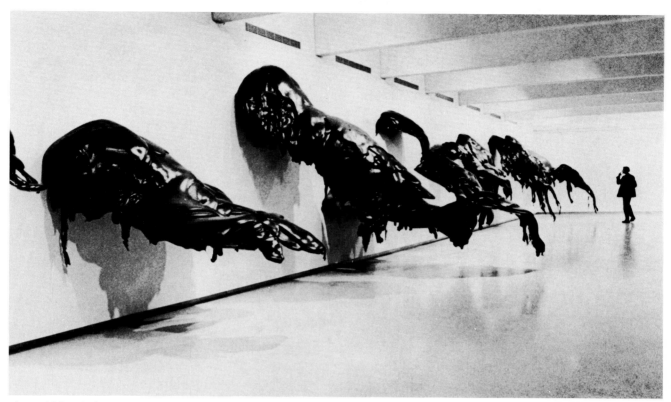

above: **221.** *Linda Benglis.* Adhesive Products. *1971. Nine individual configurations of iron oxide and black pigmented polyurethane, 13'6" × 80' × 15' (4.11 × 24.38 × 4.6 m). Installation* Works for New Spaces, *Walker Art Center, Minneapolis, May 15–July 25, 1971.*

below: **222.** *Larry Bell.* The Iceberg and Its Shadow. *1975. Plate glass coated with quartz and metallic inconel, 56 sections, various heights. Permanent collection Massachusetts Institute of Technology, Cambridge, Massachusetts (gift of Albert and Vera List Family Collection).*

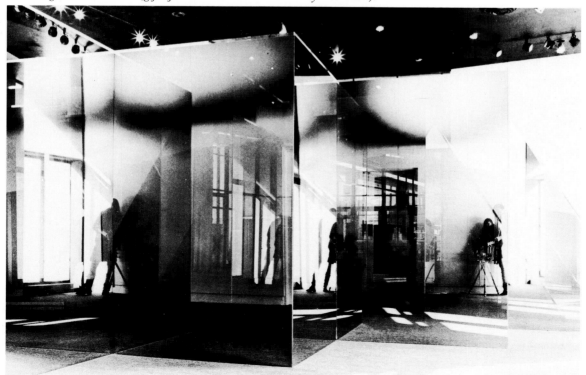

others have created environments intended to surround us with art [214]. All of these are new sculptural responses to space, form, and light.

So we find the artist again often inspired by his or her era, making use of whatever timely techniques are available. Current forms evolve from the methods and materials of today, just as an ancient Greek marble carving grew out of the materials and methods available then. Sculpture, like architecture, has accepted the challenge of new methods to create new concepts within an ancient art.

Exercises and Activities

Research Exercises

1. Select five sculptural works from this book that appeal to you and explain why they do.
2. Although sculpture, unlike architecture, usually has no functional purpose, it serves society in other ways. List some of them.
3. Many consider sculpture to have been the earliest medium of art developed by humankind. Explain why this theory may, in fact, be valid.

4. Distinguish between additive and subtractive sculpture.
5. The materials for creating sculpture can be found in any environment. What are the traditional sculptural materials? What materials and processes are unique to 20th-century sculpture? Discuss how contemporary and ancient sculpture differ in regard to materials.

Studio Activities

1. Using clay, papier-mâché, soft wool, or soap, create a sculptural form that re-creates a recognizable natural object. Using any of these same materials and the same subject, create an abstract sculptural form.
2. Using 20th-century materials, create a three-dimensional form that relates to contemporary technology and also makes a personal artistic statement that expresses your own feelings.

3. Build a direct sculpture, using wood, burlap, and plaster of Paris.
4. Create a soft sculpture, perhaps using a plastic sack and filling it with some loose materials.
5. Manipulate a piece of paper and then use it as a mold into which plaster of Paris may be poured. When the material has hardened, cut away any unwanted plaster, refining edges as may be required to form a sculpture that pleases you.

8
Design for Living

Form follows function.

Louis Sullivan, architect

The roadside strips, the consumer products, the billboards, the fantasy cars, the monster junk piles are all portraits of us, not someone else. There is no "they."

George Nelson, designer

. . . the small, obscure, but vital bits of seemingly unrelated information which accumulate in any tradition . . . in the end [will be] these details that give the product its life.

Charles Eames, designer

From earliest times, men and women have fashioned objects to meet their daily needs, such as serving food and drink. People have never been content, however, with merely useful objects. Even when living conditions were difficult they have always found time and energy to refine the shape of useful objects or give them pleasing texture, finish, or decoration. In the hands of skilled artists, even simple artifacts for telling time or serving food become more pleasing to see or touch. The ceremonial wine vessel is a case in point. It was designed to fill a function, to please the taste of an emperor [223], and to pay homage to the ancestors and the gods. Any object that both serves a useful purpose and pleases us aesthetically may be called **functional art** (sometimes called **decorative art**). The category of functional art includes handcrafts, mass-produced industrial arts, textiles, costume, furniture, and interior design.

Functional art addresses human needs through its structure or form. As we look about us, we see that physical structure, order, or design is basic to life. In a living thing the arrangement of cells is related to the environment and

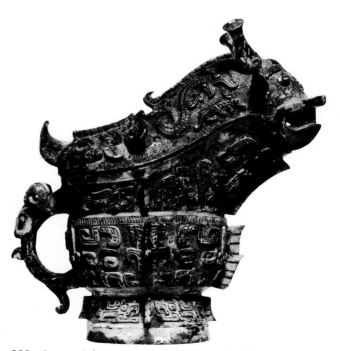

223. *Ceremonial wine vessel. Late Shang Period, 12th–11th century B.C. Bronze, height 9" (23 cm). Asian Art Museum of San Francisco (Avery Brundage Collection).*

to an organism's functional needs. The structure of an organism, however, can also be aesthetically inspiring to human beings. For example, the snail shell has fascinated scientists for centuries because as it grows to accommodate the growing animal it reveals a constant logarithmic spiral. This rate of growth, which also exists in other forms of life, appears to have been the basis for the Golden Section [93]. The rule for achieving pleasing proportion was established long ago in Greece and revived by many Renaissance artists, convinced that it corresponded with the laws of the universe and should therefore apply to artistic creation as well. Whether or not we agree that art should be tied to nature's laws, we often seem drawn to artworks that embody the Golden Section.

The incredibly complex designs created by animals provide unlimited suggestions to human beings. The structures of honeycombs, beavers' dams, and bird's nests all express the materials used in them and the purposes they serve. Today many designers and craftspeople believe that any article designed for use—a steel chair, a piece of power machinery, a silver pitcher—must also honestly express its materials and purposes as well as be appropriate for the time and place it is used. In addition, the elements of design, already discussed in earlier chapters, are as important in the functional arts as they are in the fine arts. Rhythm, balance, and proportion are basic to all well-designed objects; line, mass, color, and texture are critical concerns if a functional object is also to be aesthetically satisfying.

In the Old Stone Age, men and women shaped weapons and tools from available resources to fit a specific purpose. Even the earliest flintstones were differentiated in size and shape to please the eye as well as to fit a specific purpose. Missiles aimed at birds and small animals were small and finely shaped. Harpoons and hand axes intended for heavy animals might weigh as much as 6 pounds (2.72 kilograms).

With the advent of the Industrial Revolution, the fascination for machine-made objects often superseded concern for their aesthetic appeal. By the turn of the century, objects were so elaborately burdened with machined decorations that they were almost unusable. People began to direct their attention to **industrial design** and a return to more natural materials.

Crafts offer a practical way for people to explore new materials and ideas. The unprecedented interest in handcrafts today amidst the abundance of machine-made products ranges from simple sewing to complicated furniture-making. Schools and colleges provide studios with elaborate facilities, but many private homes also have space allocated for workshops and hobbies. Public libraries and bookshops are well stocked with all kinds of do-it-yourself craft books. Surely the satisfaction of making something entirely with our own hands may be matched by a corresponding rise in our levels of aesthetic appreciation and productivity.

Throughout history the needs of society have been met from available resources. Ancient flint and ivory tools, baskets, pottery, and weavings fulfilled the same kinds of functions served by the 20th-century synthetic and natural materials found in our pottery, steel tools, and polyester fabrics. Early in most societies the crafts of pottery and weaving developed to provide containers and clothing. As societies became more complex and sophisticated, the crafts of woodworking and metalworking evolved.

Although hand-made and machine-made objects involve the same principles of design, hand-made objects fulfill human needs in a more personal way. The most obvious difference lies in the touch of the creator, which is usually visible in handcrafted objects. For example, in an oversized horn ladle [224] we can sense the handwork of the American Indian of the Northwest Coast who carved it for a feast.

Also characteristic of handcrafts is the close relationship between the material and the form of the object. A glass vase blown from molten material looks quite different from a clay vase shaped on a wheel from wet clay. In addition, there is close contact between the artisan and the material. He or she uses tools with great care and a personal concern for the object's appearance and durability, its aesthetic and utilitarian qualities.

Traditionally, a hand-made object was both designed and executed by the same person and so could justifiably be called one of a kind. There was also a close tie between designer and consumer. It demanded a two-way responsibility, for the artisan respected the consumer's needs, while the consumer valued the product and knew and trusted the person who made it. Modern industry does not always reveal this concern for the purchaser of its goods.

Textile Arts

One of the most ancient and widespread arts is the process of interlacing horizontal and vertical threads, called **weaving.** In the process of weaving cloth, whether by hand or machine, a loom holds taut lengthwise threads, called the **warp,** and a shuttle carries crosswise threads, called the **weft, woof,** or **filling,** in and out between them. Fabrics were traditionally made from natural fibers such as animal hair, cotton, linen, or silk. Today artificial fibers, including rayon, fiberglass, nylon, and polyester, are used alone or in combination with natural fibers.

The fibers used and the types of weaves determine the weight and texture of the cloth produced. There are three basic types of cloth weaves. In **plain weave,** the simplest and strongest, the filling yarn passes over one warp thread and under the next, as in broadcloth, burlap, muslin, or taffeta. In **satin weave,** or **floating-yarn weave,** the filling yarn floats over several warp threads at a time, producing a lustrous surface. In **twill weave,** which is also strong, warp and filling yarns are interlaced in broken diago-

nal patterns, as in gabardine and denim. Other types of weave include **tapestry weave,** a plain weave in which the weft makes little irregular patches of color, and **pile weave,** in which the weft forms loops, which are cut so as to make a soft, even surface, as in velvet.

By using different kinds of threads, threading the loom in different ways, and varying the way the weft is interwoven, weavers can create an almost infinite variety of fabrics, ranging from rough, sturdy wool cloth for workers' jackets to very delicate cotton muslins and rich figured silks for the most expensive evening dresses. For generations, Indians, such as the Mixtec of Monte Albán, Mexico, have woven fabrics on hand looms, perpetuating the ancient geometrical motifs, which seem to accentuate the horizontal and vertical structure of the weaving [225]. Renaissance Europe was infatuated with brilliantly colored rich silks and velvets of com-

below: **224.** *Ladle. British Columbia. c. 1850–1870. Horn length 17¼" (44 cm). Metropolitan Museum of Art, New York (Michael C. Rockefeller Memorial Collection; bequest of Nelson A. Rockefeller, 1979).*

right: **225.** *Fabric on hand loom. Oaxaca, Mexico. 1971. Wool, 19 × 34" (48 × 86 cm). Collection the author.*

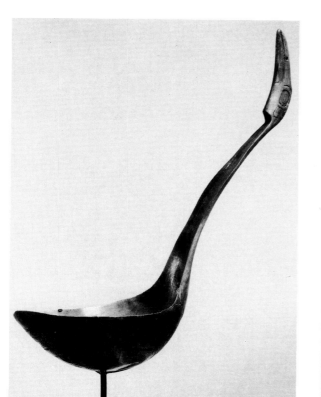

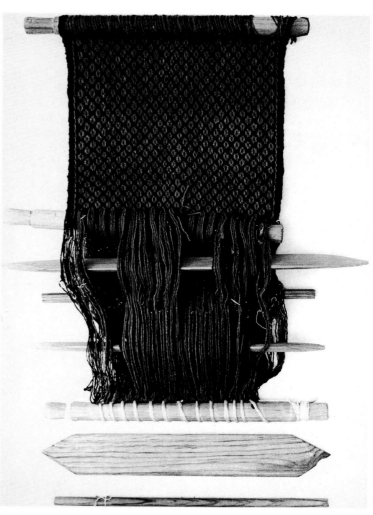

plex design. In paintings of the period, such as *The Journey of the Magi* [226] by Benozzo Gozzoli (1420–1497), worshippers' garments reveal finely detailed figural weaves that contrast with heavy velvets and edgings of gold or silver thread.

Weavers today combine some of the earliest techniques with others that have been developed over the centuries. They may use traditional fibers, new synthetic fibers, or a combination of both. Although some of the effects achieved by hand weavers can be attempted on high-speed mechanical looms, machine-made textiles are usually more aesthetically satisfying when the designer has used the machine to produce its own effects rather than trying to duplicate hand-woven material.

Textile designers, familiar with the properties of various fibers and weaves and the history and technique of designing patterned fabrics, may design textiles for furnishing or for clothing, a major field. Clothing design includes two important divisions: fashion and the theater.

Clothing

We usually assume that one of the basic reasons for wearing clothing is protection from the elements, but throughout history, people have also felt a strong impulse to decorate themselves and to be distinguished from (or else made to resemble) everyone else. In the past only the upper classes were privileged to wear clothes for decorative or ceremonial reasons. Today mass production has made it possible for millions to indulge their desire to be fashionable.

The earliest wardrobes included not only protective animal skins but also body paint, tattoos, headdresses, masks, and jewelry to enhance the wearer's appearance or, hopefully, to produce magical or religious effects. Later, body scarification, bloodstains, and hunting scars probably had as much social significance for the African tribal hunter as makeup had for an Egyptian noblewoman or a laurel wreath for a victorious Greek athlete. Clothing, then, was frequently linked to the wearer's status.

One of the oldest and most constant marks of status has been headgear; even if he wore little else, the early king was distinguished by his crown or headdress; religious leaders in all societies have been set apart by their headdresses and vestments. Other examples of status-giving clothing are the long robes and hoods worn by academics and the wigs worn by British judges. Uniforms provide instant identification for sol-

226. *Benozzo Gozzoli.* Journey of the Magi, *detail. c. 1459–1461. Fresco, length 12'4¼" (3.77 m). Chapel, Medici-Riccardi Palace, Florence.*

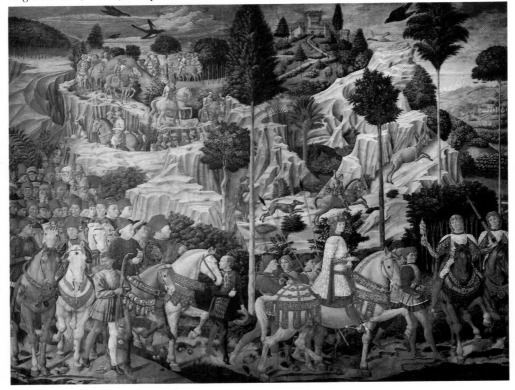

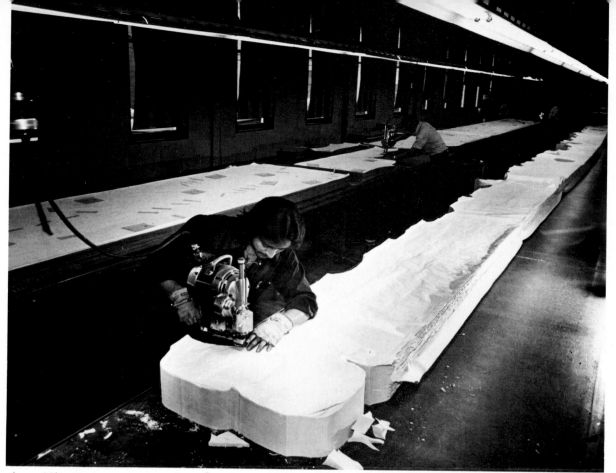

above: **227.** *Cutting 400 pairs of Levis©.*

right: **228.** *Hyacinthe Rigaud.* Louis XIV. *1701. Oil on canvas, 9'1½" × 6'3¾" (2.75 × 1.84 m). Louvre, Paris.*

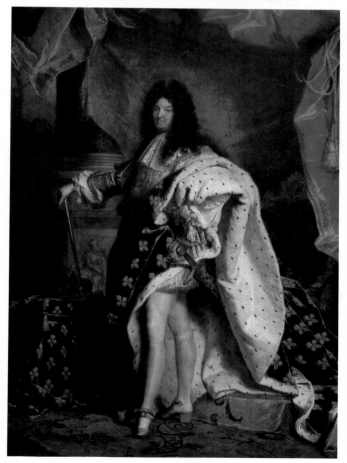

diers, nurses, mail carriers, police officers, and Scouts. Modern athletes wear numbers and team uniforms on the field. For many young people, blue jeans have become at the same time a means of conformity and a status symbol, especially if a designer's label is affixed to a pocket. Foreign designers now also make jeans, once solely an American product, but American jeans still dominate most others on the international market [**227**].

Since the purpose of clothing is largely social, fashion in dress has been subject to as many changes as society itself, and clothing styles seem to express the social concerns of each period. Trends usually develop from the tastes of a social elite, whether an 18th-century French king, as depicted in an elegant portrait [**228**] by Hyacinthe Rigaud (1659–1743) or the popular figures in today's entertainment world. Paris has traditionally been the center of high fashion, or **haute couture,** since the time of Louis XIV, and the semiannual showing of the latest Parisian

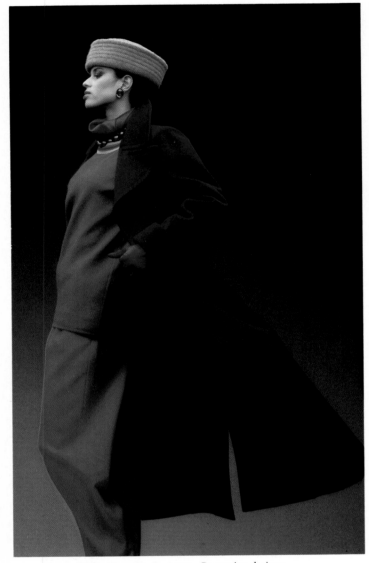

229. *Yves St. Laurent. Couturier design: Geranium red pants with fuscia tunic, raspberry hat, lime green and grape accessories at neckline; coat of midnight blue.*

other well-designed article. Clothing, like sculpture, is to be seen from all sides, a fact that the designer must always keep in mind. But, in addition, since clothing is seen in action, gathers of cloth should be designed to emphasize the rhythmic flow of the figure.

It is interesting that there is no form of clothing worn today (with the possible exception of underwear and the jumpsuit) that did not exist a thousand years ago. For example, cloaks, tunics, and sandals date from earliest times; trousers were worn by ancient Persians, as well as by the barbarians of northern Europe; gloves and long (trunk) hose were medieval creations. Knowledge of the evolution of costume is essential to every fashion designer, therefore, partly because it often provides inspiration for contemporary dress.

In the 20th century, fashion has been adapted to mass production. The latest creations of top designers, hand-sewn in their workrooms [229], are usually modified by less exclusive fashion houses and then finally produced in quantity from cheaper materials according to standardized patterns in factories. The ready-to-wear fashion industry is a multimillion-dollar business in the United States, depending on constant changes to provide a constantly renewed market for its products.

Like the fashion designer, the designer of costumes for the theater must also have a basic knowledge of the history of dress. The theatrical designer creates garments that should not only establish the mood and character of the individual players but also fit the nature of the total production.

Theatrical costume designs must be stylized and slightly exaggerated to carry across the footlights to the last row in the house. Often the designer has to find ways to produce historical costumes with present-day fabrics and accessories that may be quite different from the originals. Within budget restrictions the designer must create costumes that satisfy the director, meet the physical needs of the actors, contribute to the mood of the play, and interact successfully with the lighting.

Tapestries

The tapestry-weaving technique, which dates from ancient times, has been used by some civilizations to make tightly woven, figured hangings (**tapestries**) that are considered a major art form. The silk tapestry of China and the wool tapestry made in Europe after the Middle Ages

designs continues to stimulate the fashion world [229]. European influence, however, is not so dominant an element in American fashion today as it was thirty years ago. Now outstanding American designers have done much to replace our dependence on elegant imports with new appreciation for American styles.

A common characteristic of contemporary clothing design is that it generally conforms to the shape of the body that wears it. The awkward hoop skirts of the Victorian era find few counterparts in today's comfortable, active clothing. The same considerations of color, balance, line, and texture apply to dress as to any

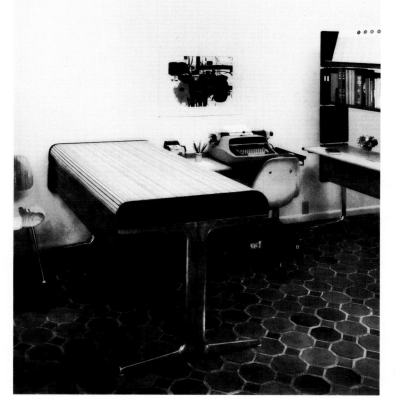

234. *George Nelson and Robert Propst.*
Executive Office System. 1964.
Wood with aluminum, laminated
plastic and vinyl, 2.7 × 5.5 × 2.7'
(0.8 × 1.7 × 0.8 m). Herman Miller, Inc.,
Zeeland, Michigan.

20th-century style of severe simplicity called **De Stijl,** exemplified in a chair by the Dutch industrial designer and architect Gerrit Rietvelt (1888–1964). An experimental design of elementary colors and cubic forms, the chair shows a pioneering use of rectilinear plywood planes, brightly painted in red, blue, and black; the simply joined structure of the chair is totally revealed **[233]**.

The simplification of wooden shapes in a system of **modules** (units) of standardized dimensions that can be produced in a factory has allowed the mass manufacturer to produce a maximum number of coordinated variations in furnishings with minimal effort. Purchasers can rearrange modules in varied space-saving combinations to suit their individual needs **[234]**. Other new industrial versions of wood that have been applied to mass-produced furniture are laminated plywood and wood bent under heat and pressure. Plywoods use thin layers of wood and thus help conserve wood—important as natural materials become scarce while the demand for wood products grows. Pioneers in bent plywood furnishings, Ray and Charles Eames are best known for their molded plywood chair **[235]** now considered a classic.

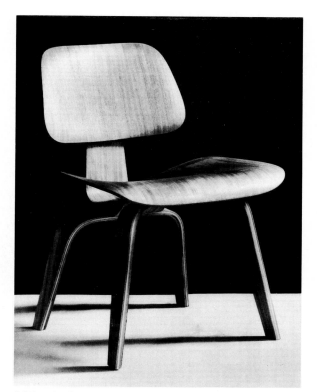

235. *Charles and Ray Eames. Dining chair. 1946.*
Molded plywood, 30 × 16 × 20" (76.2 × 40.6 × 50.8 cm);
seat height 18" (45.7 cm). Herman Miller, Inc., Zeeland, Michigan.

Focus on the Artists

Charles Eames (1907–1978)
Ray Eames (1915–1988)

Internationally famous furniture designer Charles Eames, born in St. Louis in 1907, demonstrated early in his life a fascination for architecture and design that would occupy him ever after. Influenced by architects Walter Gropius and Ludwig Mies van der Rohe on a trip to Europe, Eames opened his architectural office in St. Louis. At the same time, in 1936, he accepted a fellowship at Cranbrook Academy in Michigan, where he helped develop an experimental design department that became by mid-century a national center for furniture design. His collaboration with Eero Saarinen (1910–1961), the son of Eliel, director of Cranbrook, produced for the first time ever a molded plywood chair that echoed the human body and soon became an early prototype for molded chair design.

In 1941, Eames married Ray Kaiser, moving their now joint business to California, where she was born. While designing equipment for the United States Navy during World War II, Charles Eames developed one of the great chair designs of the century—a separate molded plywood back joined to a seat with plywood or metal frames on rubber shock mounts that give the chair resiliency and comfort [235]. The design also used new materials in a new way that could be mass-produced. The fine design and the sculptural quality of the chair led the Eameses to expand the line with plastic variations that still retain an organic shape. In the same year, Eames designed storage cabinets with interchangeable parts—a concept that, along with fiberglass, had never before been used in domestic furniture. The success of these designs, and many others, led to thousands of "look-alikes" that serve as testaments to the Eameses' facile creativity. In 1949, the Eameses built their now-famous prefabricated home in Santa Monica. Constructed in just two days, the enclosure provided maximum space at minimal cost.

Charles' collaboration with Ray was so intensive in all their design undertakings that each one's contribution cannot be isolated. As a student of the abstract painter Hans Hofmann for many years and founding member of the American Abstract Artists, Ray's particular forte was surface design with brilliant colors—projects she continued after Charles' death in 1978. Co-recipient of many awards, the Eameses demonstrate the love of simple form and color that they shared [236].

236. *Ray and Charles Eames, photograph.*

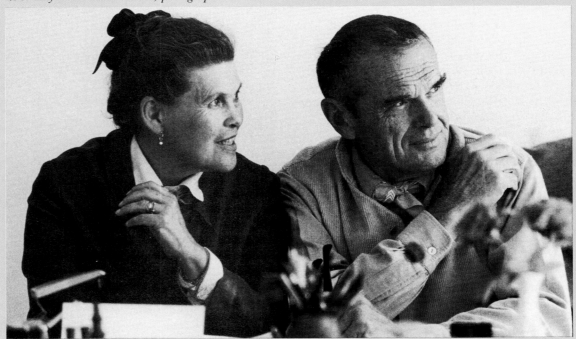

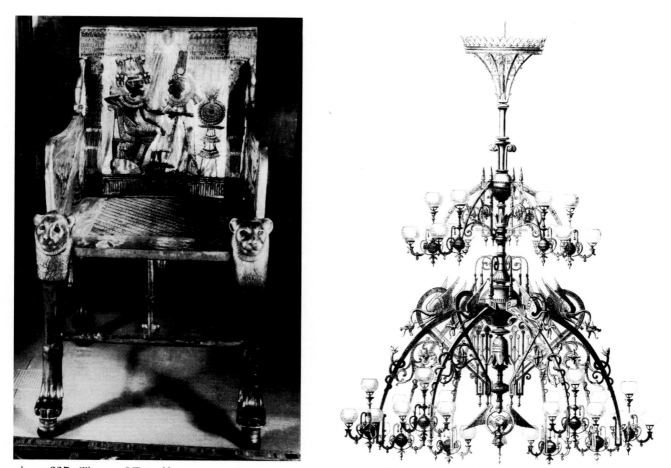

above: **237.** *Throne of Tutankhamen. c. 1365 B.C. Wood covered with gold leaf and colored inlays of faience, glass, and stone, 41 × 25⅜ × 20⅞" (104 × 64.5 × 53 cm). Treasure of Tutankhamen, Egyptian Museum, Cairo.*

right: **238.** *Chandelier from* Household Taste, *by Walter Smith, published 1876.*

Metal

Metal has been used for jewelry, weapons, ritual objects, and household goods since ancient times, but because metalworking requires more complex technology, it developed later than ceramics and weaving. Each metal, ranging from rare gold and silver to common copper, tin, their alloy bronze, and iron, has different qualities that requires different handling, but all are worked by the same techniques—**hammering**, **raising** (hammering a flat shape into a hollow vessel), and **casting** (see Chapter 7 on sculpture). Decorative techniques include **embossing**, or **repoussé** (raised work); **chasing** (depressed work); **engraving;** and **inlay** with other metals, gemstones, or enamel. Metal can also be used to cover less expensive materials such as wood. For example, gold hammered into thin sheets was used to plate Tutankhamen's wooden throne [**237**]. Gold and gilded silver inlaid with jewels or

enamels were used in the Middle Ages and Renaissance for everything from book covers to chalices (cups used for the celebration of Mass) and vessels for wine. Steel armor was often engraved and inlaid with gold. Iron was—and still is—hammered into hinges or elaborate grilles and gates.

The Industrial Revolution ushered in machine production of metal household objects in large numbers. Throughout the 19th century industrial production seemed to be completely separated from questions of aesthetics and good design. Cheap production was a primary goal of most 19th-century manufacturers; as a result, manufactured articles were often inferior in quality to handcrafted items. Excessive ornamentation, which actually became almost an obsession, took the place of quality. For instance, this chandelier, fabricated around 1876 [**238**] reflects the elaboration of form that a ma-

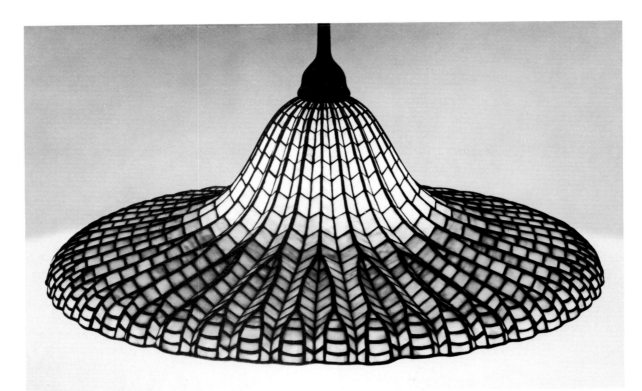

239. *Louis Comfort Tiffany. Hanging "Lotus" lamp. c. 1905. Favrile glass and metal, diameter of shade 31½" (80 cm). Collection, Museum of Modern Art, New York (Joseph H. Heil Fund).*

240. *Ludwig Mies van der Rohe. "Barcelona" chair. 1929. Chrome-plated flat steel bars with pigskin cushions, 29⅞ × 29½" (75.9 × 74.9 cm). Collection, Museum of Modern Art, New York (gift of Knoll International).*

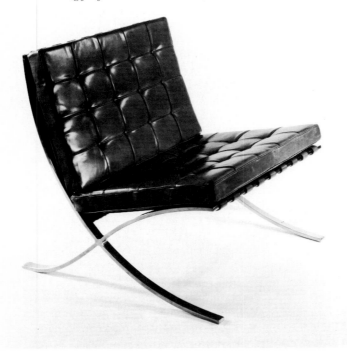

chine could achieve in seconds but that might have taken an artisan weeks to execute by hand. In reaction, William Morris and other designers in England launched the Arts and Crafts movement, hoping to lead society back to fine hand-craftsmanship, such as demonstrated in this later **Art Nouveau**-style lamp by Louis Comfort Tiffany (1848–1933) **[239]**.

Due in large part to the **Bauhaus** curriculum, designers for industry were trained to use the machine to create objects that are both aesthetically pleasing and useful and appeal to a broad spectrum of consumers. To the traditional metals of iron and bronze 20th-century designers have added aluminum and stainless steel for furniture and utensils; these metals, which can be worked by hand or machine, are particularly adaptable to mass production. An example of modern industrial craftsmanship in metal is the "Barcelona" chair **[240]** by the architect Ludwig Mies van der Rohe (1886–1969). Considered a classic for its fine design and honest use of materials, it proves again that industrially produced objects can be as aesthetically pleasing as hand-crafted ones.

Today's typical house uses more than four tons of metal, much of it invisible as structural supports; other uses of metal in the home include such furnishings as refrigerators, lighting fixtures, stoves, and, of course, many more. Metal's high tensile strength and ability to conduct heat, cold, and electricity have made it invaluable in the domestic realm. Whatever metal is chosen, metalworkers must consider its special properties, such as its degree of malleability, color and surface, ability to support weight, and susceptibility to corrosion. They must explore all the possibilities of shaping the metal and finishing the surface in order to create an object that serves its function as well as achieving an aesthetic effect.

Synthetics

The invention of synthetic materials has opened new avenues of exploration and challenge to the designer. Probably the most important synthetic products are the plastic resins. Acrylic (plastic) resins make up the various types of lucites and plexiglass used for furniture and other objects. Another group, vinyl resins, are particularly adapted to tools and toys as well as to working surfaces and floors in homes and offices. All of these synthetic materials are used by designers to replace older natural materials. Using these versatile plastics, the industrial designer can quickly and economically create handsome designs for mass production, such as furniture with a unipod base [241] by the architect Eero Saarinen.

On the other hand, no way has yet been discovered to recycle plastic, and as a result we are rapidly running out of places to put our discarded products. With the population pressures the world faces, artists and designers must consider potential use of products by vast numbers of people, as well as means of disposal, possible depletion of natural resources, and the power sources needed for production. If we are to continue to survive on this earth, we must reevaluate our goals in design and product development. What, indeed, will we leave to future generations if the industrial products we create today destroy the balance and resources of nature tomorrow?

241. *Eero Saarinen. Table and chairs. 1956. Molded plastics. Courtesy Knoll International U.S.A.*

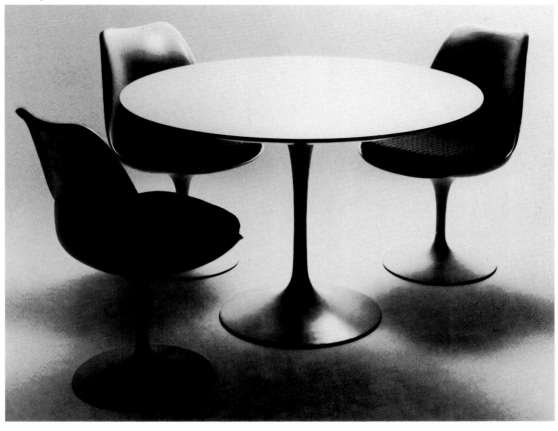

Interior Design

Interiors need to be as carefully designed as the architectural structures that enclose them. Just as Frank Lloyd Wright believed **Organic Architecture** evolves from the character of the site selected [260] and the occupants' needs for living, so are organic interiors designed for the needs of those who occupy them. Major 20th-century architects are frequently involved in both exterior and interior design. The German Pavilion at the Barcelona World's Fair in 1929 by Mies van der Rohe [242] had a profound effect on many later architects, including Philip Johnson (b. 1906). The original source of inspiration for both men was the traditional Japanese house, which, with its sliding screens and walls, continuously modifies interior space in relation to its occupants' needs and the outside world. Incidentally, note the Barcelona chair, which made its first appearance at the fair [240].

The main living area of Philip Johnson's house that he designed for his own use in New Canaan, Connecticut, is a glass box. The glass shields the interior from the weather but also makes the structure seem part of the landscape. The colors of the softly polished brick floor and leather furnishings inside harmonize with the grass and trees outside. The house exhibits clarity of structure, beauty of proportion, and carefully refined details [243]. While not designed for ecological balance in severe temperature fluctuations, nonetheless the glass walls permit unity of the house with its surroundings and provide an effect of great serenity.

In inevitable reaction to the austerity of such modernism, post-modern architects have for some years tried to reincorporate ornament with historical associations into their building exteriors and interiors. For example, the architect Charles Moore (b. 1925) rescued a 19th-century pediment from a condemned building and gave it a prominent place in the library of his own home [244], reinterpreting a classical form in a more intimate setting.

242. *Ludwig Mies van der Rohe. German Pavilion, International Exposition, Barcelona, Spain. 1929. Photograph courtesy Mies van der Rohe Archive, Museum of Modern Art, New York.*

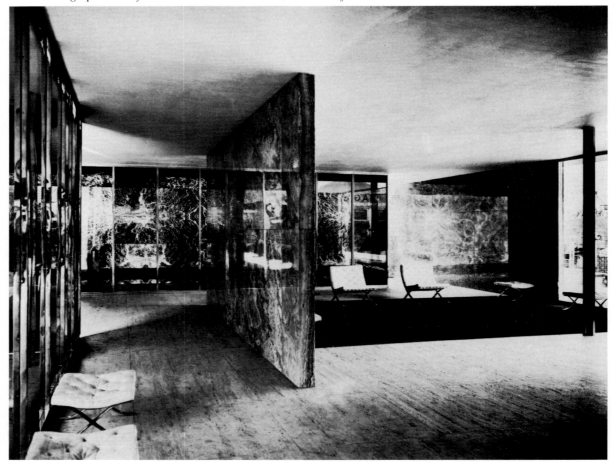

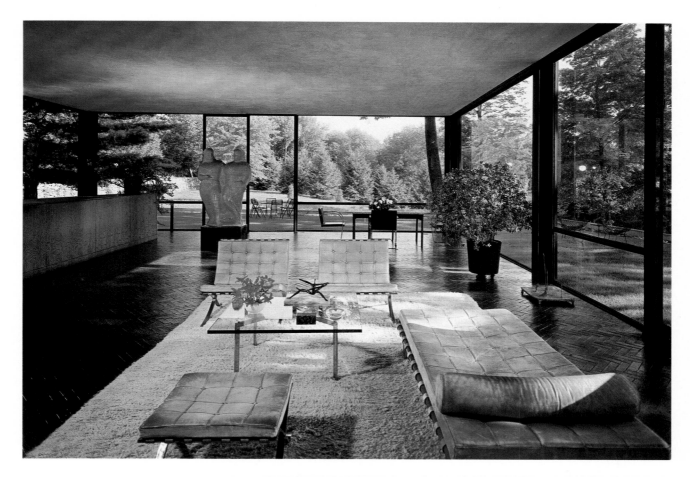

above: **243.** *Philip Johnson.*
Glass House, interior. 1949.
New Canaan, Connecticut.

right: **244.** *Library of*
Charles Moore's house.

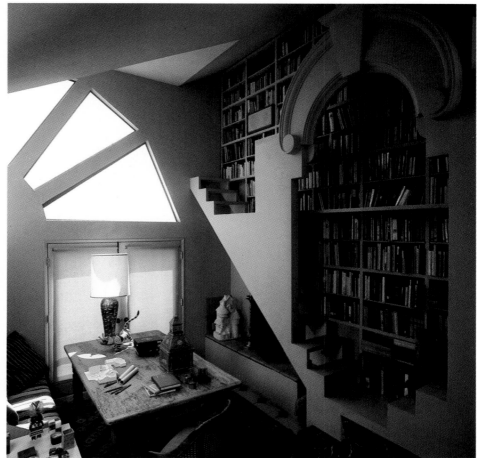

Ergometrics

At least since Vitruvius in the 1st century B.C. wrote the only architectural treatise that survives from antiquity, thinkers about the man-made environment have been fascinated with the human body as a source for measurement. It was observed long ago that Euclid's **Golden Section**—the ideal proportion, to which Renaissance theorists attached almost mystical properties—involves the human body as well as other forms of life. The overall height of a human figure relates to the distance from the floor to the navel in the ratio of 1.618, or fairly close to the Golden Section. Today, the discipline of human-factors engineering, or **ergometrics,** attempts to apply anthropometrics, or the study of human body measurement, to our environment, from the design of consumer products and transportation vehicles to interior spaces, whether the home, office, health facility, or school. Anthropometrics is actually one aspect of the complex discipline of ergometrics, which combines psychology, anthropology, physiology, and medicine with engineering, according to one definition.

Human factors engineering received impetus during World War II when it became very important to design sophisticated military equipment to be operated at maximum efficiency with the least possible human error. A more recent application has involved the interiors of vehicles traveling to outer space. It has become a question of devising design standards to use for constant reference to ensure a good fit between the individual and the interior environment in which people live, work, or play. Ergometrics can be called upon to meet single individual needs or the needs of people from differing races, cultures, and ethnic backgrounds. Some of the specific applications can be to determine work-surface heights in a kitchen, office, or home workshop; allowances for seating around a dining or conference table; heights for shelves in an apartment or library; corridor widths in a home or public building—all of which should reflect the human factor of body size. If we found ourselves squeezed into Tutankhamen's throne [237] or when we discovered that we had to crouch to enter early American Colonial rooms displayed in a museum, we might have noted that these designs did not consider possibly changing human dimensions. Ergometrics might have foreseen those problems.

Le Corbusier, the noted 20th-century Swiss-French architect, developed a scale system for modern architecture of the floor-to-ceiling distance based on human proportions that he called the Modulor [245]. Acceptance of his system has been slow in coming, since people resist change, even if it may be potentially beneficial.

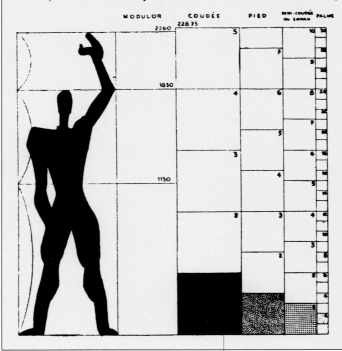

245. *Diagram from Le Corbusier's book,* Modulor 2, 1955. *Reprinted by permission of Harvard University Press.*

Exercises and Activities

Research Exercises

1. Many of the principles of design found in hand-crafted products are based on the natural environment. Find examples in this book and elsewhere. Discuss the way these basic principles are applied to one specific piece of functional art.
2. Explain the place of proportion in the design of useful objects. What was the Greek Golden Section? Can you find an object that seems to reflect this principle?
3. Select from two to five crafts to trace from their earliest beginnings to the present. What differences, if any, do you note in those crafts as practiced today?
4. On what basis are materials and processes usually selected for industry? Locate an example of an industrially produced object that seems honestly to express the material from which it is made. Find one that attempts to copy another material.
5. How may our man-made environment be affected by industrial design? What effects may industrial design have on the ecology of our natural environment? What changes do you think could be made in our attitude toward the functional arts that might improve our environment?

Studio Activities

1. Experiment with a craft you have always admired, perhaps macramé or pottery. Use a reference text on the subject, chosen from the recommended bibliography, as a guide.
2. In a spirit of adventure, investigate a craft that is less familiar to you, such as origami. Attempt some of the earlier projects listed in a book on the subject. You may be surprised at how satisfying it is to work with your hands in a new medium.
3. Using plasticene clay and a rolling pin, roll out two slabs, each about $\frac{3}{8}''$ thick and $8''$ square. Fold over the sides of one slab to form an open box. Smooth the corners. Shape a lid with the second slab.
4. Take a fistful of clay (almost any kind will do) and, using your thumb as you hold the clay lump, shape the piece into a small pinch pot.
5. Roll out five or six tubes (coils) of clay, each about $\frac{3}{8}''$ thick and $6''$ long. Coil the clay lengths into a coil pot, smoothing the inside of the pot with your fingers.

9
Architecture and Environmental Design

Architects, painters, and sculptors must rediscover and understand the many-sided aspects of building both as a whole and in all its parts; only then will their work be informed with an architectonic spirit which was lost in salon art.

Walter Gropius, The Bauhaus Manifesto

Architecture is the first manifestation of man creating his own universe. . . .

Le Corbusier, *Towards a New Architecture*

Less is more.

Ludwig Mies van der Rohe, architect

A sense of the organic is indispensable to an architect.

Frank Lloyd Wright, *An American Architecture*

The modern vernacular can only take you so far . . . the role of the architect as civic leader . . . has been my contribution.

I. M. Pei, architect

Of all the visual arts, architecture probably has the greatest impact on us. Most of us spend the largest portions of our lives within walls. On the way to work or school we pass buildings, for all around us space has been enclosed and walled in. Architecture, the art of building, could as well be called the art of enclosing space in a useful and pleasing way.

What impels us to build? Obviously, the most basic reason is to provide shelter or protection from the weather or from animals or unfriendly human beings. Imagine living on earth before there were buildings. What would you do for shelter? You could crawl under the branches of a tree, or—if you were lucky—you could find a cave to serve as refuge. Eventually, however, you would probably wish to create a more comfortable home.

After solving the problem of personal shelter, early people everywhere worked in communities to build permanent ceremonial temples to gods, fortresses for protection, and palaces and tombs for rulers. The appearance of these structures, then as now, was directly influenced by the climate, the available materials, the building site, and the needs of the people who used them.

Architectural Considerations and Plans

Architectural design involves certain basic concerns. These include (1) convenient arrangement and flow of space; (2) illumination from outside and within; (3) protection from the weather and interior climate control at all times; (4) efficient use of fuel, with possible solar alternatives. Roofs, walls, floors, doors, and windows must all be designed in the light of these requirements as well as to suit the owner and the location.

In the process of designing a building the architect makes many drawings, and if the design is complex, a three-dimensional model. An architect's plans may include:

floor plan: structural layout in scale, viewed from above

elevations: front, side, and rear views, in scale, showing all walls and openings

cross sections with details of electrical, heating, cooling, plumbing, and other special installations

perspective renderings: three-dimensional views, including landscaping and locations for sculpture

Architects' designs utilize a variety of materials and types of construction. Some date back thousands of years. Others are totally new materials and techniques developed during the Industrial Revolution and in the 20th century. Some architects have tried to maintain the familiar appearance of buildings while using new materials and methods, while others have designed structures that courageously reflect the new advances in construction [246].

Construction Methods and Building Techniques

Over the centuries, builders have developed a number of methods of construction supporting both the weight of the building materials and the structures. The simplest method is the **bearing wall,** in which the whole length of the wall supports the roof. Its use is limited because the higher the roof, the heavier the wall must be. The second method is **frame construction,** including **post-and-lintel** and other kinds. The third is the **arch** and **vault.** The fourth is **cantilever.**

Frame Construction

Post and Lintel   More efficient than a bearing wall is a series of upright posts supporting a hor-

246. *Renzo Piano and Richard Rogers.*
Georges Pompidou National Center for Art and Culture (Beaubourg), Paris. 1977.

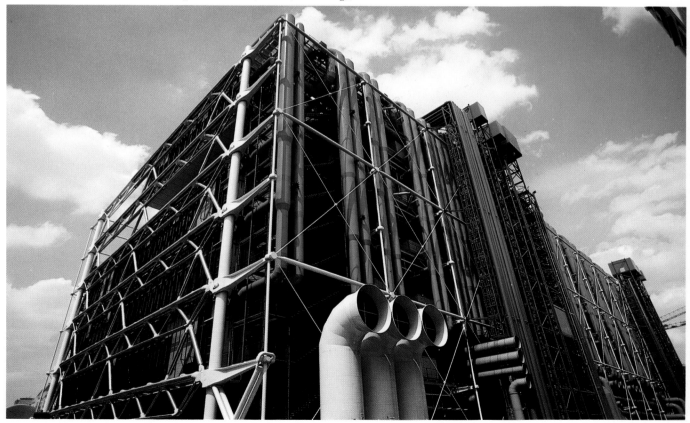

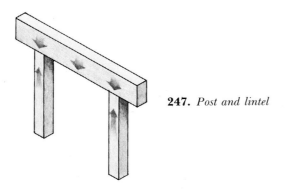

247. *Post and lintel*

izontal beam, or **lintel,** to form a strong rectangular frame **[247]**. Some lintels are placed in walls to span openings for doors and windows. The size of the opening depends on the length and strength of the lintel. Other lintels span interior space and support the roof, which may be flat in hot, dry regions or pitched (gabled) in cold, wet regions to allow snow and rain to run off. There is no limit to the size of the interior space so long as there is no objection to its being interrupted by many posts.

The earliest post-and-lintel buildings were made of heavy tree trunks cut and fitted together, often with wooden pegs. In many ancient civilizations, temples and palaces were of post-and-lintel construction in stone. There are only a few stones large enough to be lintels, however, and no stone can be very long without breaking of its own weight.

Truss Frame construction can span a large space without many interior posts if it uses **trusses,** or cross braces, whose members act together in tension and compression **[248]**. The most common type of truss is triangular. Essentially it consists of two sloping bars fastened at the top and connected at the bottom by a third bar to create a rigid triangle strong enough to support a heavy weight. Triangular trusses of

248. *Triangular trusses*

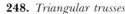
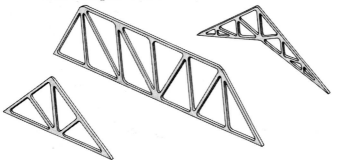

wood were used under the wooden roofs of stone churches in the early Middle Ages. Later, more elaborate forms of wooden trusses developed. In the 19th and 20th centuries trusses have been made of iron and steel. Truss construction is the basis of modern A-frame buildings and of prefabricated modular systems that provide an ingenious, efficient, and economical way to span space.

Skeleton Frame A more complex form of frame construction is the **skeleton frame.** The parts are lighter than posts and lintels and support one another to make a standing cage. In wooden construction the parts are made of light pieces of lumber nailed together, and the outside wall is nailed to the frame to increase its strength. A particularly light type called **balloon framing** developed in the 19th century when factories made iron nails in quantity and sawmills cut lumber in standard sizes. Most wooden houses today are built with balloon framing **[249]**. The outside walls, which used to be made of board siding, are now often sheets of plywood.

Skeleton frames are also used in iron and steel construction **[250]**. The parts are bolted or riveted together to make a **cage** that is lighter and stronger than wood and able to span large interiors with many fewer posts. The walls are attached to the cage but carry no weight and can therefore be glass or have many large windows. Such **curtain walls,** or **screen walls,** are only thin panels to keep out the weather and enclose the space. Iron- and steel-frame construction developed in the late 19th and early 20th centuries, making use of factory-made parts shipped by rail and assembled at the building site. Today steel-frame construction is all around us, as is very apparent when you observe office and apartment buildings and factories under construction. The Georges Pompidou National Center for Art and Culture in Paris **[246]** is essentially a glass box, supported by structural steel. Visible on the exterior are brightly colored heating and air-conditioning ducts, escalators, and elevators, all usually concealed within the lower basements and inner core of a building.

Geodesic Dome A modification of frame construction that uses the principle of the triangular truss is the **geodesic dome** invented by R. Buckminster Fuller (1895–1983) in the 1940s. It is a spherical shape consisting of a spidery framework of short struts forming a three-way grid composed of various arrangements of tetrahe-

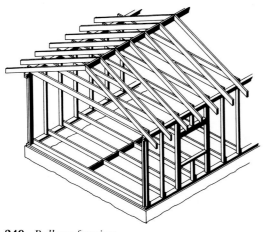

249. *Balloon framing*

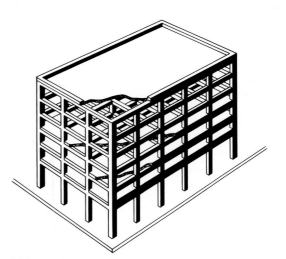

250. *Steel cage construction*

drons (solids with four triangular faces). Drawing on late-19th-century discoveries that tetrahedrons are the basic structure of organic material, Fuller insisted that the tetrahedronal structure was naturally stronger than that of cubes or squares, which tend to collapse if they are not braced. The frame, usually of aluminum or other light material, can withstand pressure because it distributes stress equally among all its parts. It is covered with a skin of plastic or other light substance. Geodesic domes are made in prefabricated modular units and can be easily assembled on the site.

Fuller's golden-hued geodesic dome for the United States Pavilion at Montreal's Expo '67 covered an area 250 feet (76 meters) in diameter **[251]**. Considered revolutionary at that time, such domes today come in all sizes and are accepted by most as a strong, efficient, and inexpensive way to enclose large areas quickly.

251. *R. Buckminster Fuller. United States Pavilion, Expo '67, Montreal. 1967. Steel and plexiglass; three-quarter sphere: height 137' (41.97 m), diameter 250' (76.25 m).*

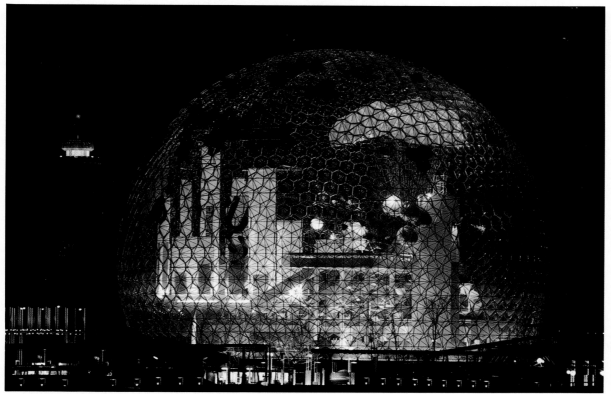

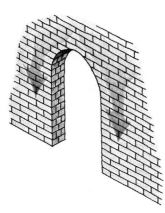

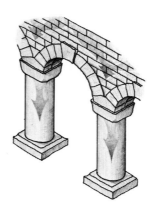

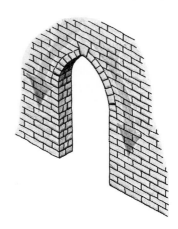

252a. *Corbelled arch*

252b. *Round arch*

252c. *Pointed arch*

Arch, Vault, Dome

Still another way to span a wide opening or other large space without posts is with the **arch,** a curved line of bricks or stones. This method, which developed later than the post-and-lintel system, made possible the evolution of architecture from structures made of massed materials to structures with vast, open interior spaces.

The simplest form of arch is the **corbelled arch [252a]**, in which bricks or stones are built up from two sides, each projecting a little beyond the one below it, until they meet in the middle. These carefully balanced masonry units are held in place by gravity. Corbelled arches were developed in ancient Mesopotamia, where clay for brick was plentiful but there was little wood or stone.

The true arch, developed in ancient Mesopotamia and refined by the Etruscans and Romans, is an improvement over the corbelled arch because its wedge-shaped masonry units support each other through mutual pressure. In a round (semicircular) arch, such as used by the Romans, stones or bricks, shaped into wedges to fit snugly into the curve of the arch, are built up from the two sides, shoulders, or **imposts** framing the opening to meet at the **keystone,** the final wedge in the center [252b]. During construction they are held in place by wooden scaffolding called **centering,** which is removed when the keystone is in place. The wedges are squeezed together, and the weight of the wall or roof they support is sent through the arch outward and down to the ground. The sides are braced by massive **buttresses** to contain the outward pressure. Arches may also be horseshoe-shaped, as in Islamic architecture, or pointed, as in Gothic architecture [252c], or may take other shapes.

253. *Pont du Gard, Nîmes, France. Late 1st century* B.C.

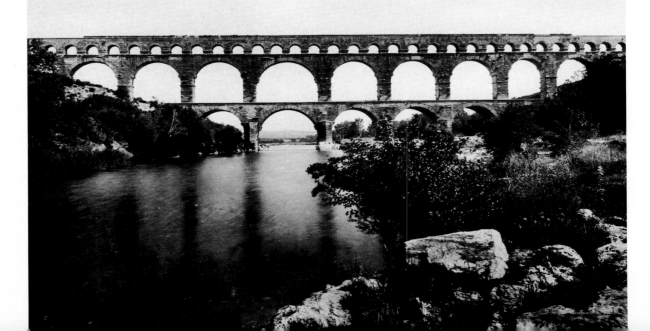

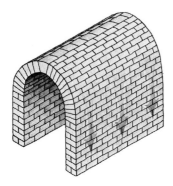

254a. *Barrel vault*

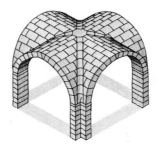

254b. *Early ribbed vault with round arches covering square*

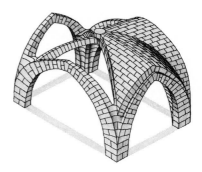

254c. *Gothic ribbed vault with pointed arches covering rectangle*

A row of arches, side by side, forms an **arcade,** used as a wall or to hold an aqueduct, such as the ones that brought water to Roman cities **[253]**. A series of round arches placed one behind the other and connected by a roof produces an arch in depth called a **barrel vault [254a]**. A vault is more efficient than a wood lintel, which could burn, or a stone one, which could break. Because it is heavy, however, it must be supported by solid, buttressed walls, which can only have a few small windows.

Two barrel vaults intersecting at right angles make a **cross vault,** or **groin vault,** such as those used in Roman buildings and over the side aisles of Romanesque churches. Because the two vaults support each other, they need buttressing only at the corners; the walls can be lighter and permit larger windows.

A **rib vault** is a groin vault made of thin stone panels supported by a framework of stone ribs that follow the lines of the arches and joints **[254b]**. In Gothic architecture the ribs form pointed arches **[254c]**. The weight of the vaulting is concentrated along the lines of the ribs, which transmit it to the **piers** (supports) at the corners of the **bay** (the area covered by the vault). The piers in turn transfer the lateral pressure from the vaulting to buttresses against the outside walls **[255]**. Because the weight rests on the stone skeleton formed by the ribs and on the buttressed piers, the bays can be rectilinear, and the wall spaces between the piers can be higher and filled with lighter stone panels or large windows of stained glass. Rib vaulting, pointed arches, piers, and buttressing made possible the lofty, light-filled Gothic cathedrals.

Another form of vaulting is the hemispherical **dome.** A dome, formed by stones or bricks built up in circles of diminishing size, may cover a

roof with wood trusses

central vault

vertical buttress

flying buttresses

ribs on piers

side aisle vault

255. *The Gothic system; cross section of a cathedral*

circular or square space. Various devices such as the **pendentive** (a concave triangle) **[256]** are used to make the transition between the circular dome and the square space below it.

A triumph of Roman engineering is the Pantheon, shown in Panini's painting of the interior **[257]**, a round brick and concrete temple built in Rome in the 2nd century A.D., which has one of the largest domes ever constructed. The dome of Hagia Sophia **[258]**, built as a church in Constantinople (Istanbul) in the 6th century, rests on pendentives. Your city hall or state capitol may have a dome inspired by Roman or Renaissance models.

In the 20th century, arches, vaults, and domes are often made of reinforced concrete. Examples are bridges and the concrete shells in such buildings as Eero Saarinen's TWA terminal at New York's Kennedy Airport **[272]**, designed to echo the wings of a bird in flight. Shells can also be made of metal or plywood shaped under stress.

Cantilever

A building technique common in modern architecture is the **cantilever,** a beam or floor slab that juts out from the wall that supports it **[259]**. The wall acts as a fulcrum. The weight of the projecting end of the cantilever needs no posts to support it because it is balanced by the weight of the building on the interior end, much as your weight on one end of a seesaw can be balanced by that of another person on the other end. Cantilevers can also support walls, which may be hung from a cantilevered floor. Cantilevers may be wood beams, steel girders, or slabs of reinforced concrete.

Frank Lloyd Wright achieved a breathtaking effect by dramatically cantilevering the Kaufman House over a waterfall in Bear Run, Pennsylvania **[260]**. By making it appear to float over the water, he tied it visually to the natural environment of which it seemed to be an organic

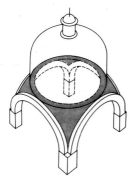

above: **256.** *Pendentives (shaded area) supporting a dome*

right: **257.** *Giovanni Paolo Pannini. Interior of the Pantheon, Rome. c. 1750. Oil on canvas, 4'2½" × 3'3" (1.28 × .99 m). National Gallery of Art, Washington (Samuel H. Kress Collection, 1939).*

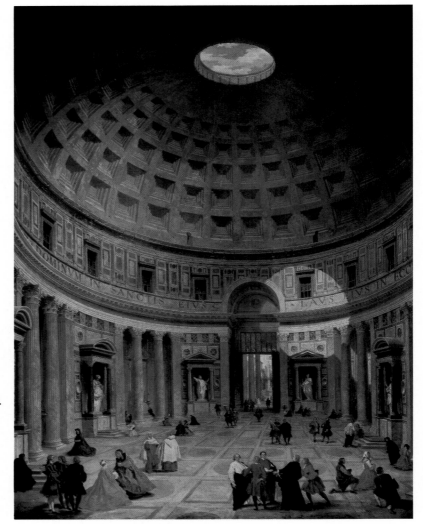

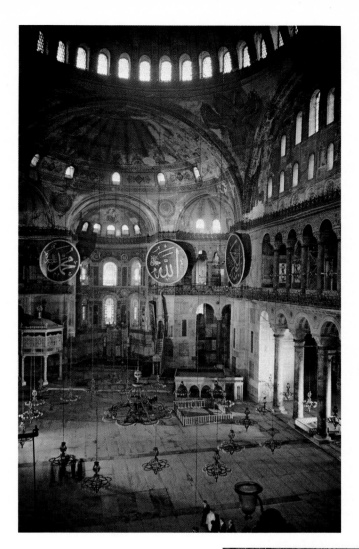

258. *Anthemius of Tralles and Isidore of Miletus.* Hagia Sophia, Constantinople *(Istanbul). 532–537, 553–563.*

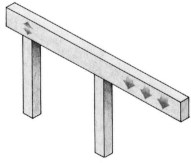

above: **259.** *Cantilever construction*

right: **260.** *Frank Lloyd Wright. "Falling Water" (Kaufman House), Bear Run, Pennsylvania. 1936–1937.*

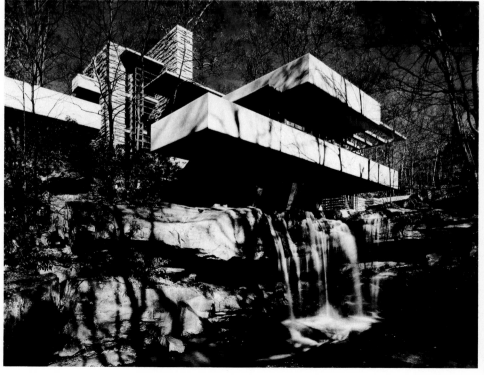

part. The tower of Wright's Johnson Wax Building in Racine, Wisconsin, is built around an elevator shaft supporting cantilevered slab floors from which the glass outside walls are hung.

Construction Materials

For centuries, architects built out of wood, stone, and brick, depending on the availability and cost of the material. The Industrial Revolution introduced new kinds of factory-made building materials, such as iron, steel, and reinforced concrete, which have largely replaced the earlier materials.

Wood

In the forested regions of the world the most commonly used building material has been wood, which is cheap and easy to work. We know little about early wood structures because wood burns or rots, leaving us nothing to examine. We can, however, guess at their forms by studying the wooden structures built in many rural communities in more recent times. Villagers on lush, tropical Polynesian islands, for example, still use houses made from boards, posts, palm leaves, and other vegetable matter, much like those of their ancestors. In chilly, pine-covered Scandinavia, old farm buildings made of logs with mud and grasses stuffed between them, roofed with bark or sod, may still be seen. Such buildings and the log cabins built by American colonists and pioneers are probably much like the wood dwellings of early northern Europe.

These simple wooden buildings used post-and-lintel construction, which was developed into complex forms in 7th-century Japan. The Japanese built elaborate palaces and temples on stone bases, spanning spaces with wooden posts and beams fitted together in beautifully crafted joints. An outstanding example is the temple at Nara, dating from the 7th century, which is the oldest wood temple in the world. A five-storied pagoda with up-curving roofs from the Nara temple complex demonstrates how complicated wooden post-and-lintel construction combined with elaborate bracketing can be [261].

In medieval Europe, builders experimented with wooden trusses for the roofs of stone churches, as we noted. These were developed into complex arrangements of triangles by such Renaissance architects as Andrea Palladio. The half-timbered houses of 16th-century England, using beams and plaster, and the clapboard houses of colonial New England, both still copied by 20th-century builders, are further examples of wooden architecture. In the late 20th century, laminated plywood shaped under stress into curved forms is used to make shells that serve as both structure and enclosure.

261. *Five-storied pagoda. Horyuji Temple, Nara, Japan. 607* A.D.

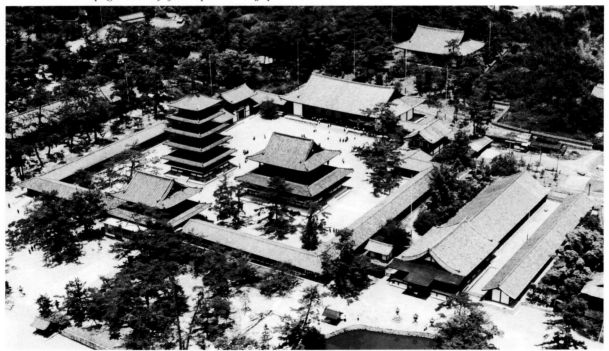

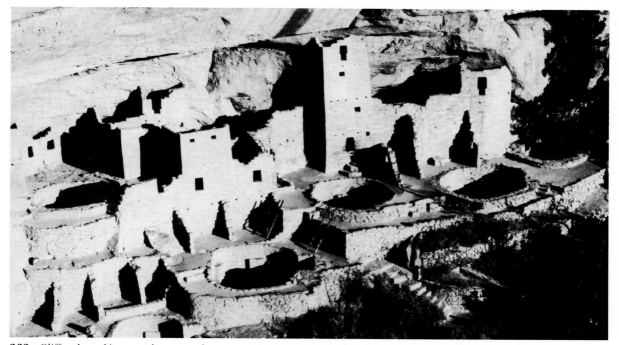

262. *Cliff palace, kivas, and rectangular towers, Mesa Verde National Park, Colorado. 12th century.*

Stone

Stone is one of the most widely used building materials for permanent structures. The many ancient stone buildings still standing today, such as Egyptian and Roman temples, are evidence of its durability.

Stone can support a great deal of weight, but stonework must be carefully designed or the weight will make it collapse. You may recall that as a child when you tried to build a tower out of blocks you were successful only when you placed them carefully, one on top of the other, and did not pile them too high. The earliest stone buildings were made by placing unshaped stones one above another. The downward thrust of their weight gave the structure stability. Later buildings were made of shaped, or dressed, stone. In the 12th century, Pueblo Indians built the cliff dwellings in Mesa Verde, Colorado, using the cliff as one wall and adding walls of shaped stones set in clay mortar. These multiple dwellings consisted of levels of units, each level set back from the one below to form a terrace reached by wooden ladders, an early example of apartment housing [262]. The Incas of Peru built the city of Machu Picchu of stones so skillfully fitted together that a knife cannot be pushed between them, and they do not need mortar to hold them together.

Most early stone building used post-and-lintel construction [247]. One of the earliest examples is Stonehenge, a mysterious Neolithic (New Stone Age) monument in southern England. It consists of three concentric circles of enormous vertical stones with horizontal stones as lintels [263]. How the massive stones were transported

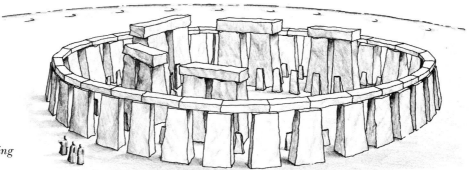

263. *Reconstruction drawing of Stonehenge.*

miles from the nearest quarry and raised into position is still discussed by archaeologists. The stones may have been dragged over log rollers by hundreds of workers. The stones seem to have been precisely arranged for sighting astronomical configurations [281].

The Egyptians, who had an abundant supply of stone, which they transported down the Nile River on rafts from the quarries to the building sites, built massive stone temples using posts and lintels. In the Temple of Amun at Karnak the tops of the posts (capitals) are shaped like lotus plants, probably derived from the shape of carved wooden posts in earlier structures. The immense interior space of the entry hall is filled with a forest of columns, which are necessary to hold up the heavy stone lintels.

The Greeks also built post-and-lintel temples of stone. We can detect evidence of earlier wood architecture in the decorative elements of their stonework. Despite the simplicity of post-and-lintel construction [247], the refinements of proportions, workmanship, and detail rank Greek marble temples among the finest of architectural achievements.

The Romans built early works of stone, using posts and lintels or arches [254*b*] and vaults [254*a*], but later used stone chiefly as a veneer over structures of brick or poured concrete.

Most of the great churches and cathedrals of the Middle Ages were built of stone. Massive Romanesque churches had round arches and often barrel vaulting, as we have seen. Gothic churches rose to great heights supported by a cage of ribbed vaulting, piers, and buttresses [254*c*]. The religious exaltation of the period was expressed in the cathedral of Amiens, France, one of the tallest in the world. The vaulted nave reaches up toward heaven and is bathed in twilight pierced at intervals by light from brilliant stained-glass windows. You can sense the dynamic quality of the structure of a Gothic cathedral in which each part depends on the counterbalancing weight of every other part. The thrust moves from towers and vaults through ribs and piers out to buttresses and **flying buttresses** (half arches between buttresses and a wall) and so to the ground [255].

Many of these cathedrals took hundreds of years to build, and it is easy to imagine the failures the builders must have experienced while trying to solve the dual problems of weight and thrust. A few cathedrals did, in fact, reach too high. The one in Beauvais, France, collapsed and was never completed. Most Gothic cathedrals, however, still stand as examples of the creativity and daring of medieval builders.

Many important Renaissance churches and palaces were built of stone, usually adapting the styles of classical Rome. One of the most outstanding structures is St. Peter's Basilica in Rome [264]. Succeeding a series of earlier archi-

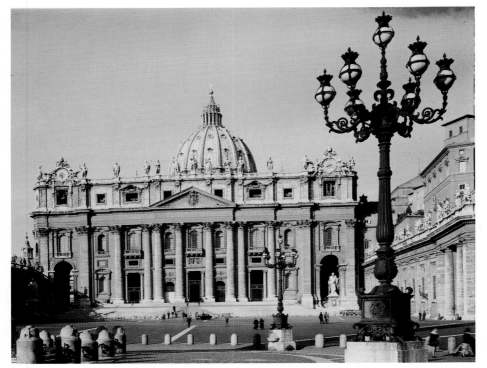

264. *Façade, St. Peter's Basilica, Rome. 1601–1626.*

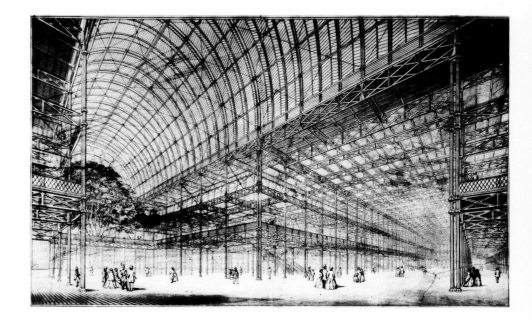

265. *Joseph Paxton.*
Crystal Palace, London.
1851. Cast iron and glass,
width 1851' (564.18 m).
Engraving by R. P. Cluff.

tects, Michelangelo drew plans for an enormous structure that was not finished until after his death. His floor plan of a Greek cross was later modified, but his ribbed stone dome, in a slightly more elongated version, soars above the city. The upward lines of the **pilasters** (flat columnar forms) on the walls of the massive arches that support the dome and the curving ribs reach toward the center in a restless climax. The interior of the church is so large that it is impossible to experience the whole interior from any one point within the church.

Brick

In regions where wood and stone are scarce, the common building material is brick shaped out of local clay. Early bricks were dried in the heat of the sun but crumbled when exposed to rain or flood waters, as often happened in ancient Mesopotamia. Bricks fired in a kiln are hard enough to prevent such dissolution and are a tremendous advance over sun-dried ones. Bricks can be built into thick-walled houses, roofed with wooden beams, and into huge towers. The adobe brick houses built by some Indians in the American Southwest and Mexico are examples of brick architecture.

The Romans built extensively in brick and concrete, using arches, vaults, and domes to cover large areas and distances. Their basilicas (law courts), theaters, sports arenas, baths, aqueducts, and triumphal arches appeared all over the Roman world. The comfort and well-being of the Romans depended on their engineering feats. Stone or brick-faced concrete aqueducts, for instance, such as the Pont du Gard in Nîmes, France [253], brought water from distant mountains to supply Roman city fountains and luxurious baths and villas. Apartments up to five stories high crowded the streets of Rome and Ostia. Structural remains, including stairways, colonnades, light wells, and room layouts, can still be seen today.

Brick was commonly used in northern Europe after the forests were cleared; in particular, many German churches and Dutch houses were built of brick. Brick was also popular for Georgian houses in 18th-century England.

Iron

Before the Industrial Revolution, iron was worked by craftsmen and used primarily for nails, dowels, tie rods, and hinges to fasten together parts of wood or stone structures. As a result of mechanized mass production and the development of railroads, it became an important building material, lighter, stronger, and more fire-resistant than wood and easier to work than stone. Iron was especially useful for the large, open, well-lit spaces required by factories. Expanding rail networks created the need for railway stations and bridges, which led to further experimentation with iron frames and trusses.

One of the most dramatic early examples of iron-frame construction was the Crystal Palace, built for the Great Exhibition in London in 1851 [265]. Covering 17 acres (7 hectares), it was the first completely prefabricated building; all its parts were made in factories and shipped to the site, where they were assembled in just six months. The weight-bearing iron frame held the largest panels of plate glass that had ever been produced. They supported no weight but only enclosed space. The enormous open interior with its high, curved glass roof impressed viewers with its unusual approach to building.

The designer, Joseph Paxton (1801–1865), had been a gardener experienced in building greenhouses. He regarded the structural frame as an organic skeleton, commenting: "Nature was the engineer. Nature has provided the leaf with longitudinal and transverse girders and supports that I, borrowing from it, have adopted in this building." Paxton's creative vision and innovative use of materials produced completely new architectural forms, which critics of the day correctly predicted would revolutionize architecture.

A later triumph of iron construction was the 990-foot (300-meter) Eiffel Tower, built in Paris for the exhibition of 1889. Consisting of a cross-braced lattice girder, it too was made of prefabricated parts.

Steel

The lessons builders learned in constructing iron bridges, factories, and other buildings provided the basis for construction in steel. Steel is stronger, lighter, more fire-resistant, and more workable than iron and holds up well under tension, where iron tends to snap. Steel-frame buildings faced in stone or brick were erected in the cities of Europe and North America, especially in New York and Chicago, where, in both cities the need to use all the space between rivers led to ever higher structures. Further refinements in steel frames and the invention of the

---

Focus on the Artist

Louis Sullivan (1856–1924)

Born in Boston and educated at Massachusetts Institute of Technology, Sullivan began his architectural career in Chicago in the office of William Le Baron Jenney, a later pioneer in metal skeletal construction, which was a forerunner of the first true skyscrapers. After four years in Jenney's office, in 1879 Sullivan joined forces with Dankmar Adler. Their friendship strengthened with their business association and in 1881 the two set up a firm, Sullivan and Adler, which made its name designing the celebrated Auditorium Building and the great Stock Exchange in Chicago (destroyed by 1976).

Sullivan's tall buildings, like the Wainwright in St. Louis and the Guaranty in Buffalo, were the beginnings of the mature American skyscraper. His philosophy saw ornament as a means to heighten perception of a building's fundamental structure, but his passionate quest was to evolve a fundamental American architecture, not based on any elements of historical European style. In all, the partners designed 120 buildings. One of their outstanding designs was the Transportation Building at the World's Columbian Exposition in 1893. Very different from the Victorian and classic styles that dominated the fair, this building was plain and bright with color, winning international recognition.

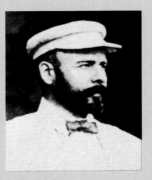

266. *Louis Sullivan.*

To Louis Sullivan, ornament could heighten recognition of a building's fundamental structure, and most of the motifs he created presage the Art Nouveau movement that appeared at the turn of the century.

Sullivan was soon eclipsed by his later famous student, Frank Lloyd Wright, his chief assistant from 1887 to 1893. Nevertheless, he is remembered for his own form of genius— the ability to fuse ornament with a new architectural modernity.

Sullivan's declining years were spent alone; his wife abandoned him because of his alcoholism; he received few commissions. In the end he wrote the poetic *Autobiography of an Idea,* published before his death, a fitting legacy for one of the greatest architects America ever produced [266].

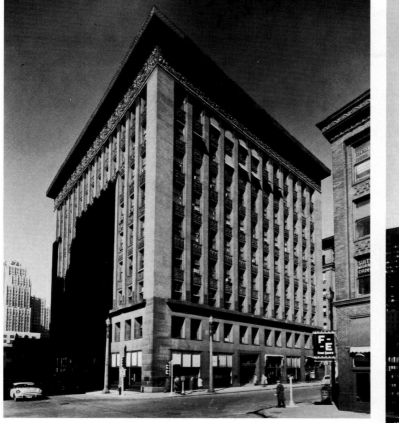

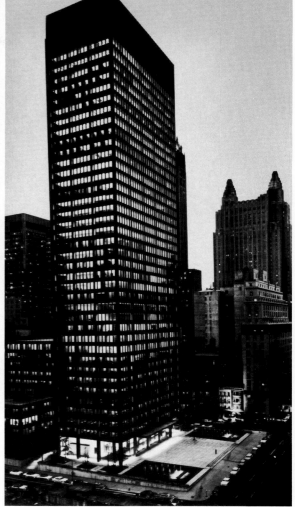

above: **267.** *Louis Sullivan. Wainwright Building, St. Louis. 1891.*

right: **268.** *Ludwig Mies van der Rohe with Philip Johnson. Seagram Building, New York. 1956–1958.*

elevator made such high-rise buildings possible.

In the Wainwright Building, built in St. Louis in 1891, Louis Sullivan openly used new methods and materials and designed surface ornament to emphasize the vertical [267]. Sullivan's buildings are the forerunners of modern skyscrapers.

Certainly the steel cage [250] can produce overwhelming skyscrapers that dehumanize the urban environment. Frank Lloyd Wright, a student of Sullivan, was aware of that potential problem. In his *Autobiography* (1932) he said:

The tall steel frame may have its aspects of beneficence; but as long as many may say, "I shall do as I please with my own," it presents opposite aspects of social menace and danger. . . . The tall office building loses its validity when the surroundings are uncongenial to its nature; and when such buildings are crowded together upon narrow streets or lanes they become mutually destructive.[1]

In the hands of a skilled architect such as Mies van der Rohe, steel can be used to make even a large building light and elegant. Sometimes the steel frame may be exposed to view and made to emphasize the vertical thrust of the building, as in Mies' Seagram Building in New York, designed with Philip Johnson [268]. The ground level was left with no walls or windows to permit pedestrian access to the continuation of exterior space. The exposed metal has taken on a mellow patina in the more than thirty years since the building was finished, just as planned.

[1] Wright's prophecy has come true in midtown Manhattan in New York, where megastructures like the IBM and AT&T buildings crowded on narrow streets have become "mutually destructive."

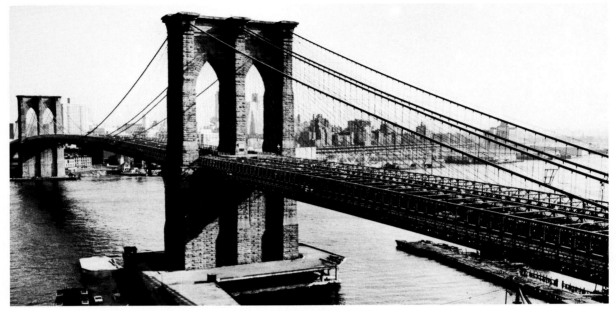

269. *John Augustus Roebling. Brooklyn Bridge, New York. 1869–1883.*

Steel is also used to make cables from which bridges may be suspended, as in the Brooklyn Bridge in New York [269], designed by the engineer John Augustus Roebling (1806–1869). Roebling invented the steel cable, which is made up of many parallel wires, and the machine to attach the cables to the two towers that hold up the bridge. Twentieth-century suspension bridges are still built by his methods. Some of them contain spans almost a mile (1.6 kilometers) long. Not only do the cables support the weight of the spans but they also permit fluctuations of several feet—caused by wind or load stresses—between the span and the water. Steel cables are also used for buildings. For example, pavilions for fairs and sports events often have their roofs and walls hanging on steel cables attached to central posts.

Reinforced Concrete

Concrete, a mixture of sand, gravel, cement, and water, was used in Roman times for aqueducts and other large structures. Not until the 20th century, when it was reinforced with metal rods or mesh, was its full potential achieved. Reinforced concrete is a versatile, fire-resistant, durable material that can be molded into columns, beams, slabs, and vaults that can be self-supporting with few or no interior posts.

Builders first used reinforced concrete for factories, silos, and other utilitarian structures. As early as 1905, bridge designers in Europe used curved slabs supported on thin vertical members to create graceful arches. Since then, as technical understanding of concrete has increased, engineers have been able to calculate exactly what stresses and loads a structure can support and have experimented more audaciously. At the same time, architects have recognized the aesthetic possibilities of reinforced concrete. In 1903, the French architect Auguste Perret (1874–1954) built an apartment house in Paris as a rectangular cage of reinforced concrete with walls of glass or thin panels of cast concrete. Perret made no attempt to cover the concrete, believing that decoration frequently hides errors in construction. Inside, the only immovable parts are slim columns and stairs; the rest of the space is left open for flexible arrangement of rooms. In the late 20th century, the Whitney Museum in New York and the Pompidou Center (Beaubourg) in Paris [246] both reveal their structure while permitting infinite modification of interior space for changing art exhibitions.

Architects have used reinforced concrete for sweeping arches and vaults that are thin shells and for sculptural forms such as those in Le Corbusier's (1887–1965) chapel at Ronchamp, France [270]. The Italian architect Pier Luigi Nervi (1891–1979) developed a more efficient kind of reinforced concrete consisting of layers of fine steel mesh sprayed with cement mortar. This material is well suited to making prefabricated modular sections of shell vaults with curved rib framing. Nervi designed elegant, airy

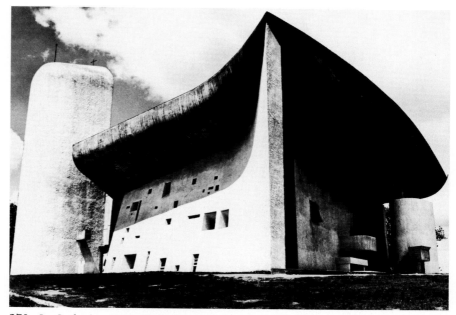

270. *Le Corbusier. Notre Dame du Haut, Ronchamp, France. 1950–1955.*

shell vaults based on complex geometry to roof vast spaces in many different types of structures, including the Palazzetto dello Sport for the 1960 Olympics in Rome [271].

Reinforced concrete seems able to solve almost any architectural problem. Eero Saarinen's TWA terminal at Kennedy Airport, New York, as we noted, uses winglike sculptural shapes cast in concrete that are stimulating but not overwhelming. They create a large open area broken only by curving staircases, ramps, and balconies. The building, reminiscent of a bird in flight, can accommodate moving groups of people but also allows space for others to sit and watch the

271. *Pier Luigi Nervi. Palazzetto dello Sport, Rome. 1960.*

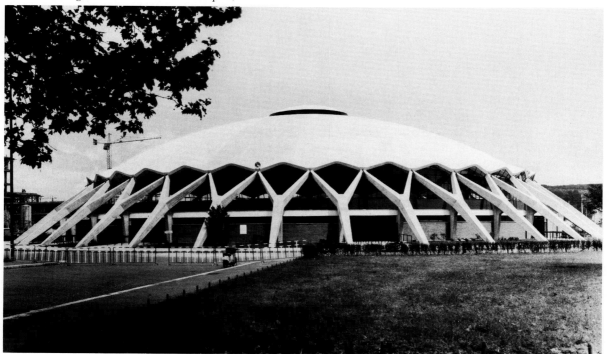

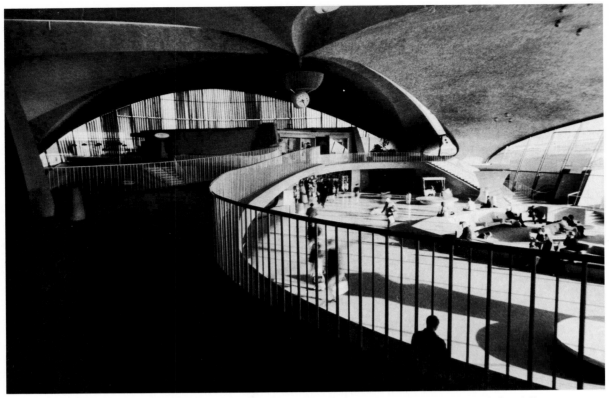

272. *Eero Saarinen. Trans World Airlines Flight Center. Kennedy International Airport, New York. 1962.*

crowds while waiting for arrivals and departures. The movement of people increases the visual excitement provided by the architectural forms and the spaces they define, an appropriate quality in an air terminal [272]. The building was constructed in a few months with the same number of workers, at any given time, that were involved in building a Gothic cathedral over several centuries!

As you review the history of architecture in the following chapters, try to remember its structural methods and materials. Look at the buildings around you today to see whether they remain from earlier periods or whether they are recent structures. If you find some that use new materials and techniques to copy traditional appearances and methods, how do they look compared with other new and exciting buildings, many of which openly reveal their materials and construction?

Environmental Design

Harmony with our environment is based on an awareness of the interdependence of all life. We have discovered that from a single cell to the billions of cells in a single human being to the multitudes of people in our sprawling cities, all are living organisms whose satisfying existence depends on how each element is related. Even the smallest alteration to the ecological balance of our world makes changes we rarely predict.

People have altered the landscape through the millennia by building farms and cities. Such incursions on the land were all influenced by the natural environment that existed before them. Today, however, that environment, to which our biological rhythms are still keyed, has all but disappeared. The vast forest broken by streams and meadows that once covered the eastern United States is gone, and the environment we have put in its place bears little resemblance to it. What has happened to the natural beauty of our country, and how have our communities changed from the human scale of early colonial towns to the overpowering roadscapes and skyscrapers of our time?

In our current concern about the environment, perhaps we can adapt age-old solutions to our universal needs for comfort and efficiency in the home, the neighborhood, and the city.

The Environmentally Designed House

Fundamental to any community design is the plan of each house in relation to its setting. In many eras, people believed that a building should stand apart from its background as a visual reflection of the architect or the client. But today's viewpoint seems to be turning toward traditions in which a structure is a natural outgrowth of its surroundings.

Wright's term "Organic Architecture" is a rephrasing of this time-honored concept. It is reflected in the work of Luis Barragán (b. 1902), Mexican recipient of the 1980 first international Pritzker prize for architectural achievement. He describes his designs as providing "shelter against the aggressions of the modern world." His major project has been El Pedregal, Mexico, a residential area on a stretch of lava left 2500 years ago. Sensitive to the lava's unearthly shapes and lush vegetation, Barragán transmuted 865 acres (350 hectares) of what was regarded as unusable land into houses and gardens [273]. Using the simplest architectural elements—abstract geometric forms and carefully arranged planes—he achieved a modern

design that profoundly respects his country's indigenous ways of building and living. Lava walls give privacy and create interior gardens, many imaginatively embellished by regenerative ponds and streams.

The Pueblo Indians of the arid Southwest crowded their dwellings together, side by side and one atop another. This compact mass both reduced the area exposed to the sun and provided defense. The few small windows placed high in the walls allowed only late afternoon sun to enter, to be absorbed by the adobe brick walls. This "heat sink" slowly reradiated heat into the dwelling at night. A similar solar design appears in the five-story cliff dwellings called Montezuma Castle, built by the Sinaqua and Anasez Indians of Arizona in 1100 and now a national monument. The mud, stone, and other indigenous materials served as heat capacitors to absorb solar radiation for later release. In addition, the overhanging mountainside blocked high summer sun, thus cooling the dwellings natu-

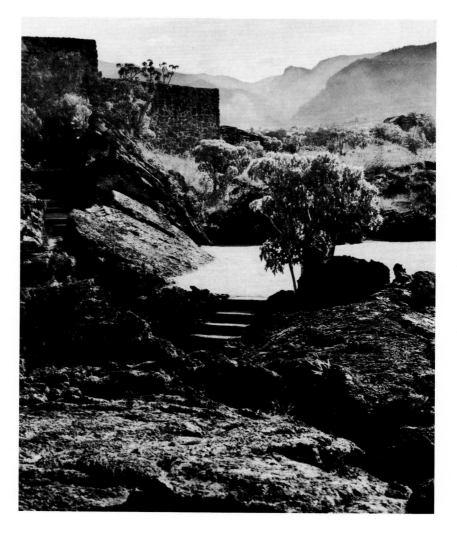

273. *Luis Barragán.*
Garden in El Pedregal,
Mexico City. 1945–1950.

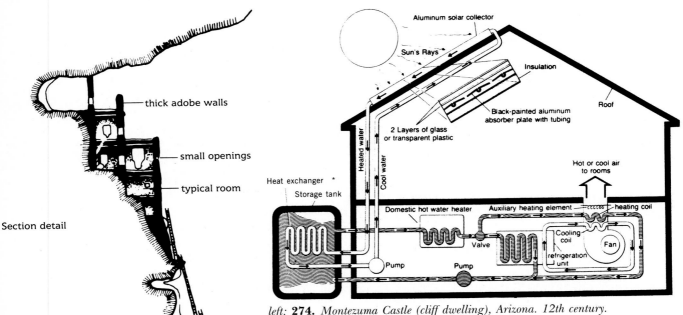

Section detail

thick adobe walls

small openings

typical room

Aluminum solar collector

Sun's Rays

Insulation

Roof

Black-painted aluminum absorber plate with tubing

2 Layers of glass or transparent plastic

Heated water

Cool water

Hot or cool air to rooms

Heat exchanger *

Storage tank

Domestic hot water heater

Auxiliary heating element

heating coil

Valve

Cooling coil

Fan

refrigeration unit

Pump

Pump

left: **274.** *Montezuma Castle (cliff dwelling), Arizona. 12th century.*

above: **275.** *Diagram of solar heating system.*

rally. Heat collection, heat storage, and insulation are basic components of such environmentally directed Indian design [**274**].

Pueblo and colonial houses, using solar radiation, were perhaps intuitive responses to local climatic conditions. Japan, Israel, and Australia have long relied on sun, water, and wind with windmills and water pumps to heat domestic hot water. India, France, and the Soviet Union apply solar heating and cooling technology to both commercial and residential units. Only within the last few years has the United States directed any efforts toward energy-efficient methods of heating and cooling. Drawing on early models by native peoples, modern systems vary widely in design [**275**].

Regardless of the region, four elements of climate are critical for energy-efficient heating and cooling systems—solar radiation, air temperature, humidity, and air movement. In addition, a system requires a large collector and storage area of energy that is different from any associated with conventional heating and cooling systems. Although many houses today tap solar and wind resources (and some even incorporate greenhouses for heating and cooling as well as growing food), few are able to be totally self-sufficient. Furthermore, designs must be adaptable to all conditions because every climate variation requires a different system to maintain an ecological balance. Despite these limitations,

many houses like the author's will undoubtedly be designed that are responsive to sun and wind, in natural harmony with their surroundings.

Neighborhoods

Within a city, satellite town, or suburb, a neighborhood of 5000 to 10,000 people is generally considered to be ideal for community life. Such a community should contain the services needed to support everyday life—shops, schools, a health clinic, and a library. A neighborhood must also be integrated into a larger community, which can provide schools for higher education, fully equipped hospitals, and larger and more extensive commercial and manufacturing facilities. Neighborhoods developed naturally in the past. In newer cities, however, built on a grid pattern and characterized by large apartment houses, widely spaced shopping centers, and streets full of traffic, it is almost impossible for a comfortably sized neighborhood to develop spontaneously. Also inhibiting the growth of organic neighborhoods is the segregation of people into areas once based, if no longer, on religion, on age, ethnic origin, or economic level.

Le Corbusier's master plan for Chandigarh, the new capital of the Punjab in India, divides the city into sections that are about the size of a village and that respect the centuries-old living patterns of the inhabitants. Each section has a market, a park, blocks of housing, paths for pedestrians, and roads for slow traffic. Because of the high cost of land, such a plan would not be suitable in more crowded areas. For this reason, apartments are often clustered in tall buildings, like the one Le Corbusier designed for Marseilles [505], which allow for more open space between them.

Can a sense of neighborhood be created without building a whole new city? Some designers have suggested placing a kiosk at the intersection of several streets to provide a place where residents could pick up newspapers, cigarettes, and perhaps some groceries. Such a device would cut door-to-door deliveries and short trips by car. A tree or two and benches combined with a bus stop and a car-pool stop could make these intersections into meeting places where people might come to know one another. In New York, the residents of one block of old brownstone houses combined their backyards to create a large, shared green space. With a pleasant place to sit or play, residents developed a sense of community, something rare in the anonymous city. Since many American cities did not develop as organic communities, they have to be planned along such lines to approach the quality of urban life that exists naturally in older European cities.

The Art Museum as Community Cultural Center
For many, the museum has become a center of culture for the community. There are poetry readings and concerts in the garden; there is dining within a few feet of the museum's art treasures; and, for scholars, there is access to special collections of books. In some respects, the museum has assumed the role filled in medieval times by the church in its indirect focus—a place for learning and a retreat when the day's labor was past. For these reasons, the 1980s have been growth years for museums throughout the world.

The Pompidou National Center of Art and Culture [see 246] was planned to satisfy many needs; it is described by its director as offering "a creative, changing, multi-media, kinetic, cross-cultural presentation of the arts of our time." Also, the lively plaza flanking it attracts street artists, folk singers, and magicians. In this sense, the magnetism of the museum perhaps echoes the distant past when the church plaza served as the site for miracle plays and other community events.

The National Gallery's East Wing in Washington reflects this dual nature of many modern museums in its structural divisions that separate the art collection from the newly established Center for Advanced Study in the Visual Arts, which provides space for a library and reading room, as well.

Frank Lloyd Wright designed the Solomon R. Guggenheim Museum in New York with flowing curves and human proportions [276]. The interior arrangement of the building, in which elevators carry viewers to the top so that they can walk down a sloping circular ramp to see the paintings, is frankly expressed. The top-heavy

276. *Frank Lloyd Wright.*
Ramp and reflecting pool, Solomon R. Guggenheim Museum, New York. 1957–1959.

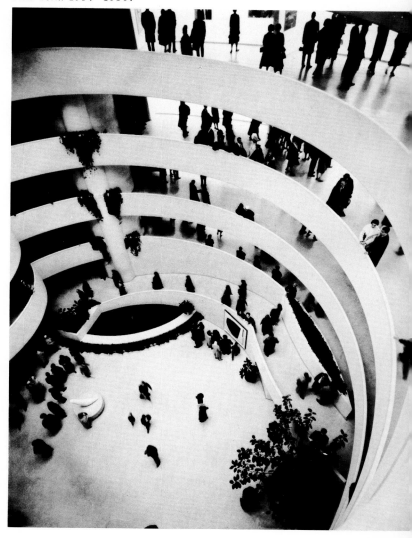

shape of the building itself would be disturbing if it were not balanced and tied to the ground by the mass of offices and library at one side.

The Museum of Modern Art, New York's major museum of international contemporary art, is a handsome building with a pleasant courtyard and garden where people can wander or sit surrounded by sculpture. It is a haven in the middle of the city, even though the building itself, which invites us inside as we look through the glass front, had to be wedged between existing buildings. Individual projects like this can give some relief from the otherwise deadening effect of the city.

However, architects for today's museums, whether they plan for wholly new structures or add to existing structures, are bound to respect the local conditions, without sacrificing the aesthetic integrity of the museum as an active participant in the community. Among the many museums built since World War II, some are major architectural achievements, but only a minority of these—Louis Kahn's 1972 Kimbell Art Museum in Fort Worth, perhaps—boast exhibition space appropriate to the art. Critics of the most breathtaking museum designs, such as Wright's 1959 Guggenheim and Mies van der Rohe's 1968 New National Gallery in Berlin, question exhibition spaces that tend to overpower the paintings and sculptures within them. Additional problems challenge architects engaged in expansion projects for major museums who own vast storerooms of art that warrant exhibition. Such new designs must not only satisfy museum officials, but also Landmark Preservation Committees, determined to protect cherished structures, as well as their surroundings. Public interest in traveling exhibitions requires broad spaces, while high attendance demands provision for circulation of large numbers of people. Finally, the need for income-producing facilities, including shops, restaurants, or rental space such as that in the pioneering residential tower of the Museum of Modern Art, forces unprecedented demands on the limited space of an urban museum and of its designers.

Cities

The pueblo of the American Southwest and an unspoiled New England village share certain qualities—human scale, an ordered relationship of parts to the whole, and above all a sense of identity with a settled place. Some old European cities also have these advantages. They are generally lost in the huge, crowded cities of modern America. When did this change take place?

Growth of Cities The cities and towns of medieval and Renaissance Europe were relatively small by today's standards and were built to human scale. Many city houses had gardens with trees and flowers, while open fields and forest lay just beyond the city walls. These advantages perhaps offset the dirt, odors, and crowding in the poorer sections.

Venice, for example, is still organized in much the same way that was possible hundreds of years ago. Each neighborhood has its own piazza, or square, which offers all the vitality and stimulus that local inhabitants need. The trees, fountain, shops, and cafés of the square are reached by streets only for pedestrians. The main arteries of traffic are the canals, where boats transport people and goods without as much noise and exhaust as cars and trucks produce.

City Planning Although most cities grew haphazardly as a result of private enterprise, in a few there was planned development. Inspired by belief in the power of reason and science to solve all problems and by desires for personal glorification, several European rulers ordered vast plans involving public buildings on large squares and the layout of streets on a grid pattern or, as in 19th-century Paris, a star pattern of radiating boulevards. Such plans provided for impressive displays of power and the rapid movement of marching troops, but the wide, tree-lined Parisian boulevards do not encourage neighborhood life any more than 20th-century freeways do.

In the United States, many towns and cities since colonial times have been laid out on the grid system or, in the case of Washington, on the star pattern. One reason was the settlers' European-derived confidence in the power of reason. Another was their natural desire to impose human design on the frightening vastness and wilderness of a new land.

Modern city planning began in the 1890s in Britain, where Ebenezer Howard (1850–1928) and Raymond Unwin (1863–1940) rejected the assumption that individual lives were unimportant. They planned garden cities outside industrial areas, where people could live near their work and find the necessary services for daily life, but still be surrounded by greenbelts with

Exploring Art Through Technology

Sinking Venice

Venice was built on a series of islands in a shallow, marshy lagoon separating the mainland of Italy from the northern shore of the Adriatic. Despite awareness that the city was sinking—in some areas as much as 7 inches (18 centimeters) between 1908 and 1961—the disastrous ramifications of the settling only became dramatically apparent after November 3, 1966, when during a windstorm the high tide rose to an all-time peak that did not subside until some 24 hours later. The flooding that occurred caused some 6 billion dollars' worth of damage and galvanized efforts on an international scale, including such organizations as UNESCO, to clean, repair, and conserve the buildings and monuments that had been damaged.

Located as it is at the basin of the Po River, separated from the Adriatic by a narrow spit of peninsula, Venice—only a few inches above sea level in some areas and at sea level now for about 15 percent of the population—has depended for its survival on a natural balance being preserved in the lagoon. That natural balance has been disturbed, especially since World War II, by the industrial development on the mainland near Venice, requiring the extraction of fresh water from the subsoil under Venice, accelerating the process of sinking that had been naturally occurring as the Adriatic rises. Land reclamation has also contributed to upsetting the natural balance, as has pollution resulting from the industrial development. The problem of salt water entering the porous brick out of which most of Venice's buildings are constructed is compounded by the chemicals that industry contributes to that water. The result has been permanent damage and decay.

Individuals from around the world responded to Venice's plight. These individuals brought expertise in fields as varied as art history, engineering, and conservation, among others. As the lagoon is the key to preserving Venice, an oceanographer was brought in to study it. Among his important tools was a computer with which he constructed a mathematical model of the lagoon and the surrounding area. The water in the lagoon behaves according to known hydraulic laws. If certain modifications are entered into the mathematical model, how they will affect the lagoon can be ascertained thanks to the computer. With this, it became possible to predict within six hours any flooding that might occur.

Sea walls that had helped protect Venice had fallen into disrepair, and the oceanographer sought ways—unsuccessfully, because politics came to bear on the matter—to close off the entrances to the lagoon when flood threatened. This problem remains.

One of the largest continuous cores was extracted from the earth under Venice—4 inches in diameter by 3250 feet long (10 centimeters by 990 meters). Study of it showed that not only was Venice sinking, but, as it did so, its buildings were slipping sideways into the canals. Borrowed from methods used in the U.S., mud-jacking was proposed to raise some buildings. This technique involves injecting mud under pressure into the ground around the building to be lifted. (Incidentally, engineers in the U.S. believed mud-jacking would also straighten the leaning tower of Pisa.) It has been found that silicone injected into brickwork helps consolidate it and make it waterproof.

An engineer from New Zealand whose firm had been engaged in damp-proofing and restoring the Temple of the Dawn in Bangkok put forward methods used there to raise and dry the floor of the church of San Nicole dei Mendiceli. This consisted of taking up the floor, excavating to 15 inches (38 centimeters) below, then laying gravel to be covered with concrete, then the original floor. This procedure had been used somewhat ineffectively before. What the engineer proposed improved on this method by pouring concrete in small sections joined to each other by a watertight but slightly flexible sealing compound, which would make the floor more flexible and the concrete less likely to crack. The concrete in turn was covered with a waterproof membrane of resin, followed by as many of the original tiles as would work.

Venice is still in peril. Its settling is more seriously threatening than in other cities that do not consist of islands at sea level. Technological resources continue to be needed. The city's plight is well described by the notice put up at Santa Marie delle Salute in the early days of restoration: "Beware falling angels."

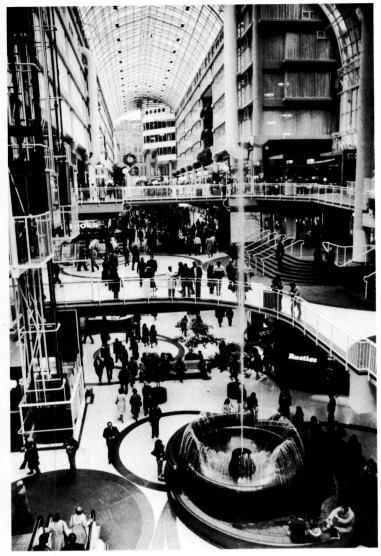

277. *Eaton Centre, Toronto.*

for recreation and employment, provide these circumstances, but they also pose special problems for planners. Architects of such buildings must meet the physical needs of crowds, such as traffic flow, and also minimize occasions for confusion, inconvenience, and danger.

An example of a large-scale cultural complex is Lincoln Center in New York [278]. It consists of Avery Fisher Hall, the Metropolitan Opera House, and the New York State Theater surrounding three sides of a huge plaza with a round fountain in the center. The austere, grandiose buildings create for some people an anonymous and, perhaps, overwhelming grouping that has little reference to human scale or familiar natural details to which people can relate. The impressive architectural scale is carried also to the interior.

Looking Toward the Future

The appearance of cities could change if some of the new, less costly building techniques suggested by creative architects were widely adopted. Buckminster Fuller's geodesic dome [251] is one such technique. Modules, or interchangeable sections, such as those used by Paxton in the Crystal Palace [265] in the 19th century and by Nervi in his Palazzetto dello Sport [271] in the 20th, are already used in prefabricated buildings, which can be fitted together quickly and easily at the building site.

The Israeli architect Moishe Safdie (b. 1938) has designed complete housing complexes consisting of modular systems that fit together in a variety of ways, providing different floor plans for individual units. Safdie's Habitat was a prototype of modular housing built for Expo '67 in Montreal [279]. Its precast reinforced concrete boxes, which were fitted with wiring, plumbing, doors, windows, and kitchens, were swung into place by a crane and attached to one another with rods and cables. Along with the obvious advantages of easily assembled units like these, Safdie's design takes other urban needs into account. These Habitat units are human in scale, allow for privacy and roof-gardens, and avoid monotony—important features for urban dwellers. Safdie also planned pedestrian malls to join the units and provided covered parking underneath. He believes that groups of Habitats could be clustered around city parks, and residents could walk on pedestrian overpasses or on paths through open spaces to reach shopping and community facilities. He has applied this principle to housing developments in Israel and other

gardens. In the United States in 1928 Clarence Stein (1882–1975) and Henry Wright (b. 1904) built Sunnyside Gardens, a nonsegregated, economically mixed community on Long Island. These ventures formed models for the many "new towns" built in Britain after World War II.

In addition to providing for small-scale local communities, modern city planners must also be concerned with large-scale design for cities. Cities can be exhilarating but also frustrating and depressing. The individual, lost in a vast area and often monotonous routine, needs to be publicly reminded of people's capacity to experience emotion in large-scale, collective circumstances. Theaters, concert halls, opera houses, sports stadiums, and pedestrian malls, such as Toronto's Eaton Centre [277], which draw people together

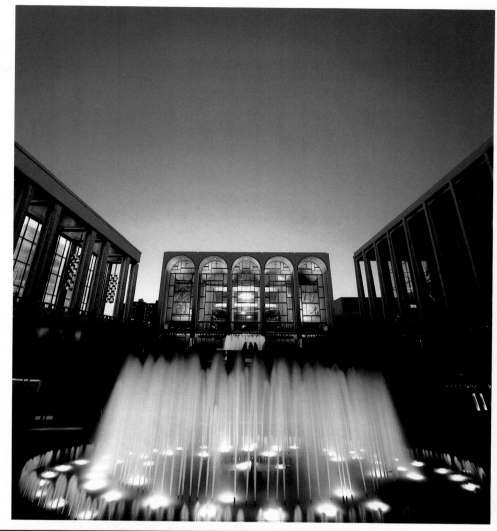

right: **278.** Harrison and Abramowitz.
Lincoln Center, New York.
1959–1966.
Metropolitan Opera House
(center), 1962–1966;
Avery Fisher Hall (right),
1959–1962. Philip Johnson.
New York State Theater (left),
1964.

below: **279.** Moishe Safdie.
Habitat, Montreal. 1967.

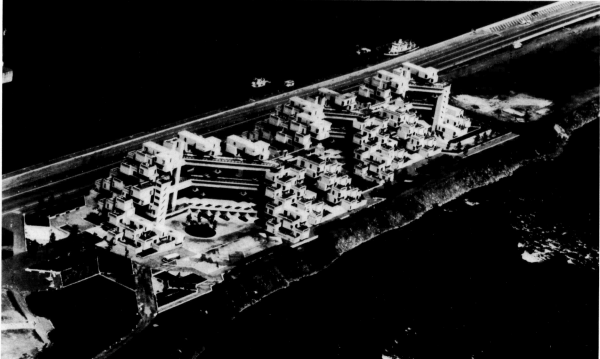

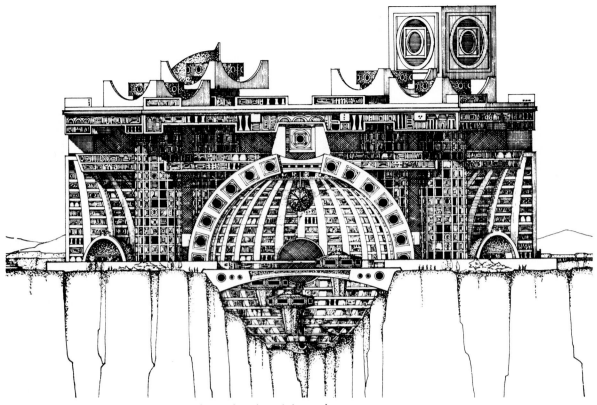

280. *Paolo Soleri. Arcosanti, east-southeast elevation. Arizona desert. Construction begun 1969.*

countries as well as Canada, where the original Habitat is not only in use but still in considerable demand.

Although some people fear that technological progress can result in spiritual impoverishment, Nervi is hopeful about the possibilities that it opens for us. He plans a city of tomorrow in which residential buildings, of clean and honest construction, will be made lively and cheerful through their relationship to streets, plazas, and gardens. Such a city would have a few large public buildings to serve "the highest and most significant expression of the new architecture." Indeed, we may note that the Crystal Palace in London [**265**], the German Pavilion at the Barcelona World's Fair [**242**], the Palazzetto dello Sport in Rome [**271**], and Habitat in Montreal were all public buildings planned for international events, which provided the opportunity for unprecedented public exposure to avant-garde design.

Still in the future are a number of visionary architectural schemes; but as space flight has passed from futuristic fantasy to reality, so perhaps some of these schemes may be worth exploring. Architects have designed cities that burrow underground, hang from poles, or seem to float in the air. Designs by the Italian-born architect Paolo Soleri (b. 1919) suggest a radical organic architectural system called **Arcology,** often made of enormous vertical elements tied together by automatic transportation systems. His forms are unusual, often cylindrical or hemispherical, and totally alien to our traditional concept of cities. While other architects have suggested self-contained houses, which could be plugged into central utility masts and taken along when the family moved, few designers have aroused the devotion accorded to Soleri. At a site far out in the desert in the United States Southwest, a cult of young architects and other followers daily contribute to an *Arcosanti* in the making [**280**].

Since we know that much of our environment—cities, towns, and highways—is unattractive and may actually cause us bodily and spiritual harm, we should be able to use our advanced techniques to rebuild and reshape our surroundings to make them more uplifting. To change our surroundings radically, the architects and city planners of the future, and the corporations they serve, must respond to people's psychological needs as much as to the needs of commerce, industry, and transportation.

Such changes are possible. The old attitude that you cannot fight city hall is out of date, for even small improvements help. To bring about alteration requires hours of effort—attending community planning meetings, telephoning, and writing letters. Changes occur only when ordinary people decide that the environment matters and that aesthetic pleasure in surroundings is necessary to personal well-being. In the final analysis, the basic materials of environmental design are not only stone, glass, and steel, or even trees, air, and fountains. The essence of such design is concern for human lives as they are enriched by the natural and human-made surroundings of our world.

Exercises and Activities

Research Exercises

1. List several ancient and modern structural methods or building devices. You may also draw simple diagrams of each.
2. What qualities of 20th-century construction distinguish it from past methods? List examples.
3. Locate several buildings in your community that copy historical styles of architecture, such as Gothic or Renaissance. Can you tell if old methods of building were used or if the historical detail is merely applied to the surface?
4. Locate and, if you like, sketch other buildings that appear to use more contemporary structural methods. How do these methods and materials vary from the older methods you have studied?
5. Referring to a text on house construction, learn to read an architectural plan and to understand the symbols for windows, doors, solid walls, closets, steps, etc. Determine how scale is used in a plan.

Studio Activities

1. Look at house plans in magazines. Pick out one you would like to live in and compare it with one you dislike. What features do you like about it? Are the rooms conveniently placed? What would the traffic flow be like? Change the plan to meet your needs.
2. Draw a plan of an existing school or other public building. Pick out the features you would change to make it more convenient and draw a revised plan showing these changes.
3. Choose a natural setting in your community. Design a structure that could be incorporated into that setting without damage to the natural environment.
4. Sketch the exterior and interior plan of a home to demonstrate the circulation pattern of the occupants and the functions that home must serve.
5. Alter the exterior design of that home to reflect fidelity to a different architectural period. For instance, if you have designed a contemporary home, translate the facade into a neoclassic exterior. How would interior flow or house functions be altered?

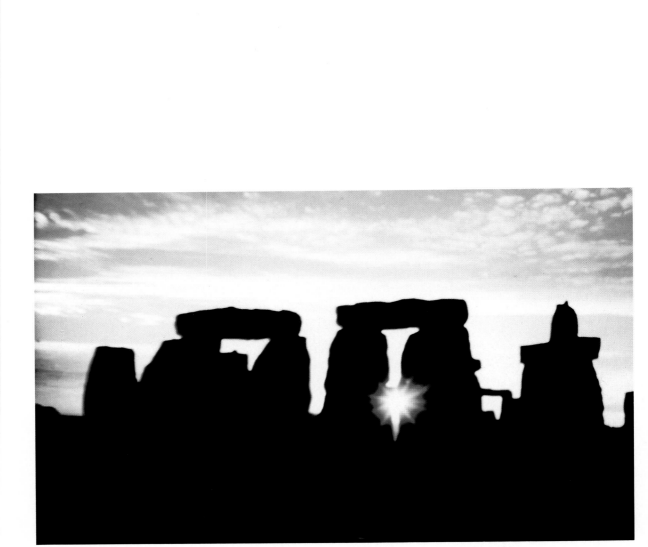

281. *Stonehenge. c. 1800–1400* B.C.
Diameter of circle 97' (29.57 m),
height of stones above ground 13'6" (4.11 m).
Salisbury Plain, Wiltshire, England.

Part Four
ART IN SOCIETY

Art began when people first created images to express their responses to the world around them **[281]**. Our ancestors must have known fear and awe at the forces of nature, joy in the warmth of fire and the taste of food, and pleasure in sexual union. Certainly survival occupied most of their time and energy for thousands of years. These primal drives—survival, food, fertility—run as a constant thread in the art of early peoples; the need to express these themes in various ways was apparently common to all.

In the Old Stone Age, artists reflected concern with the capricious forces of nature. The art of later peoples expressed other universals—the crises of birth, puberty, marriage, death. In various civilizations, artists have been dedicated to preparing for life after death and glorifying gods and rulers. Later artists turned to depicitng the growing middle class, and in the 19th century art also began to reflect an awareness of the machine age and its disharmony with nature. The art of our own time echoes a preoccupation with technology and the environment as well.

Although we may never know exactly what went on in the minds of artists of the past, as we try to reconstruct their societies we can better understand some of their reasons for creating art. At the same time, by examining examples of their artistic expression, we come closer to understanding the life of a people or an age, their ways of dealing with the needs and experiences that are universal.

The following chapters emphasize Western art—that is, European and American art—because it most directly affects us in the late 20th century. But we also note the abundant artistic expressions of other civilizations beyond the influence of the West. We will find some points in common in the arts of all peoples—enrichment in the interchange of cultures.

10
Magic and Ritual: Prehistory and the Ancient World

[Imhotep], master-builder who causes people to live . . .
Papyrus of the Kings, Ramesside period (1340–1167 B.C.)

[Mycerinus], King of Upper and Lower Egypt . . . is a god by whose dealings one lives, the father and mother of all men, alone by himself without an equal.
Rekmire, Egyptian Minister of State

Cheops succeeded to the throne, and plunged into all manner of wickedness. . . . A hundred thousand men laboured constantly, and were relieved every three months by a fresh lot. . . . The pyramid itself was twenty years in building . . . no stone is less than thirty feet in length.

Herodotus, Greek historian

To understand our early ancestors who first carved or painted images, we assume that most lived in an uneasy and baffling world, with little comprehension of the natural forces that affected them. Floods and fires, the migrations of the animals and birds on which they depended for food, and hurricanes and tornadoes were all inexplicable events to them. These natural phenomena must have seemed an expression of frightening forces over which they had no control. Their dwellings may have sheltered them from the wind or rain, but what could they do about other events that so intimately affected their lives? For example, how could they ensure that they would always have food or guarantee that life would go on?

Europe

The Old Stone Age

Prehistoric human beings of the Paleolithic period, or Old Stone Age (see the chronology), apparently saw no division between objects of utility and beauty, for their world was not as specialized as ours is today. The tools and utensils they made—some lasting, others expendable—to help them hunt, cook, sew, carve, and later build were all a part of their struggle with the powers of nature and were not separated from their everyday lives.

Most of their energies were needed to survive, but, even then, they took the time to create art—**prehistoric art.** The oldest hand-fashioned objects were simple tools and arrowheads, which were made by flaking stones or by carving bones. Certainly most tools were created for use, but the animals and symbols carved into some of them indicate that the need to create an image was also strong. Although the animals were probably depicted in an attempt to control the outcome of the hunt through symbolic power over the prey, we can surmise that the carver also was expressing a basic artistic need in shaping the forms with such vitality. The later, more complex weapons had barbed tips, which lodged in the body of an animal, becoming more deeply embedded when the creature struggled for free-

THE VISUAL ARTS		HISTORICAL NOTES
	B.C.	
	Paleolithic	
	(Old Stone Age)	
Flaked-stone tools	c. 40,000	Interglacial Period
		Emergence of homo sapiens
30,000–25,000 *Venus of Willendorf* **[25]**	c. 18,000	Final Glacial Period
c. 15,000 *Venus of Lespugue* **[282]**	15,000	Evolution of bow and arrow
c. 15,000–10,000 Cave paintings:		The Great World Floods
Lascaux, Altamira **[2]**		Migration from Asia to America
	Mesolithic	
	c. 8000–6000	Domestication of animals
		Crops and settlements
		4000–2300 Sumerian Period: Sumer
		Wheeled vehicles: Sumeria, China
	Neolithic	
	(New Stone Age)	
	3000	**c. 3000–2500** Cuneiform script
		2800 Old Kingdom: Egypt
2600–2500 Great Pyramids; Sphinx **[55]**		
2100 Ziggurat of Ur **[294]**		
c. 2000–1500 Stonehenge **[281]**	2000	**2000** Middle Kingdom: Egypt
		1760 Code of Hammurabi
		1600 New Kingdom: Egypt
1480 Temple of Hatshepsut **[291]**		**1400–600** Assyrian Period: Ashur
c. 1344–1365 Tomb of Tutankhamen **[237]**		**1370** Monotheism introduced by Akhenaton
c. 1355 *Queen Nefertiti* **[292]**		
1350–1205 Temple of Amun at		
Karnak **[87]**		
c. 1150 Ceremonial vessel: Shang **[223]**		
		c. 1100–1000 Phoenician script
c. 1000 The White Lady of Brandberg	1000	**776** Olympic Games founded in Greece
[288]		**753** Rome founded
		c. 700–c. 1000 A.D. Great Wall of China
c. 600 Tower of Babel **[295]**		
c. 575 Ishtar Gate **[296]**		
		551 Confucius born
		523–465 Empire of Cyrus, Darius, Xerxes
504–496 Double-bull capital;		**457–429** Golden Age of Pericles, Athens
Persepolis **[300]**		**332–323** Alexander conquers Persia, Egypt
		306–30 Ptolemaic dynasty: Egypt
210 Burial of Qin Shihunagdi's		**51–30** Cleopatra queen of Egypt
clay army **[287]**		**30** Rome conquers Egypt

dom. Technical knowledge and artistic creativity slowly advanced as the Ice Age, or Glacial Period, disappeared. Humans still roamed as hunters, but their arts extended to sculptures and paintings.

Fertility Sculpture Sculptured stone figures, found on the floors of painted caves, apparently date from about the same time as early tools. Although most of the sculptures were female, like the *Venus of Willendorf* **[25]**, a few were male, and a very few were bisexual, like an ivory her-maphroditic image **[282]** that looks quite different when seen from the front, side, and rear. Repetitions of bulbous shapes, which link the arms, are surely sexual references. Generally considered to be fertility symbols, these images were likely used with rituals in early attempts to influence the human life cycle.

The New Stone Age

Gradually, over several thousand years, prehistoric peoples ceased to depend solely on hunting for food and turned instead to agricul-

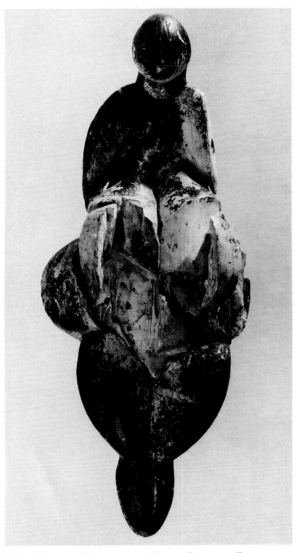

282. Venus of Lespugue, *Haute Garonne, France.*
Late Paleolithic. Mammoth tusk.
Musée de l'Homme, Paris.

ture and herding animals during the Neolithic period, or New Stone Age. They also acquired the skills of making pottery, weaving, and building. As society became more complex, the caves of the Paleolithc era were apparently abandoned. It is now believed that the paintings and tools of the Old Stone Age were not seen again for millennia, until they were rediscovered in the 19th century.

Cave Paintings The huge boulders overlooking the caves in Lascaux, France, must have seemed overwhelming to prehistoric peoples, emphasizing their helplessness in a frightening world. Trying desperately to come to terms with the unknown, they may have believed that magi-

cal painted and carved images would help them provide for their most basic needs—food and fertility.

For instance, the paintings of animals that cover the walls of caves in Spain, France, and North Africa are probably a part of magico-religious rituals [2]. Images of pregnant animals cross-cut with spears suggest a belief in the ritual killing of a painted image to ensure a food supply. When these paintings were first discovered in the late 19th century, most of the art world believed that they had been recently painted, rather than being vivid and accurate impressions of bison, mammoth, and deer made by Paleolithic artists working more than twenty thousand years ago. But carbon 14 tests that gauge the status of this element have proven the antiquity of the images and it is now generally agreed that these works were created by early hunters who had an intimate knowledge of the animals they stalked and who used that knowledge to record their essential features with great sensitivity. Working by torchlight, deep in recessed caves, and perhaps depending on their recollection of living models seen only during the hunt, prehistoric artists must have experienced many difficulties. A visit to these caves, now lit with electricity or powerful flashlights, is an awe-inspiring experience (currently restricted to scholars).

Many game species that the hunters wished to kill were painted on those walls in realistic action scenes—the animals were occasionally depicted pierced with arrows or spears. In the same way, aboriginal tribes in Australia today still make drawings of prey struck by arrows because they believe that symbolic killings will assure their success in hunting. Probably the same kind of ritual took place inside the caves of the Old Stone Age. Scholars still debate the purpose of some of the images. Do they represent prehistoric scorecards used after the hunt to record success, or were they actually painted and pierced with arrows earlier? We may never know the answer.

Parts of the caves are more fully covered with paintings than others. Possibly this is because new generations felt that the pictures painted by people who preceded them were sacred, and if more paintings were added to these areas, it might assure success for their own rituals. Perhaps that is why in the Lascaux caves images of horses were painted next to a 40-foot (12-meter) painting of a cow that was already eight thousand years old. But can you guess what the geometric symbol near the animal that many scholars regard as a pregnant mare in [2] represents? Some scholars suggest these markings may be symbolic representations of male and female, but we remain unsure about many such enigmatic works.

Monuments in Northern Europe Little remains of the perishable dwellings of the New Stone Age farmers of northern Europe, but many of their impressive monuments still stand. Some of these megalithic structures, made of huge stones (**megaliths**) dragged from distant places, are set in careful arrangements and combinations, which must have served in unknown rituals. Brittany, in northern France, has thousands of **dolmens** (upright boulders with a slab for a roof, sometimes serving as tombs) and **menhirs** (single stones) set in rows. In southern England there are circles of stones such as Stonehenge, discussed in Chapter 9, built around 1800 B.C.

The people living in Britain at that time were less sophisticated than their contemporaries in the Middle East and the Far East and, somewhat later, in the New World [186], who had developed distinctive civilizations. Nevertheless, Stonehenge is evidence that its builders had precise knowledge of the movements of the sun and the stars; the exact placement of the stones in three concentric circles ensured that at dawn on June 21, the first rays of the sun would pass through the rings of stones to strike the altar in their center. Computer analysis reveals only a tenth of a degree of misjudgment. This impressive event at the summer solstice, the longest day of the year, is enhanced by the height of the stones, more than 12 feet (4 meters), which dwarf human observers. A modern photograph of Stonehenge [281] recreates the religious mood that probably surrounded it when it was in use.

The Middle East

Long before civilization began in Europe, Neolithic farming villages along two river valleys developed into two great civilizations in the Middle East. The Fertile Ribbon of Egypt hugs both sides of the Nile River [283]. Though it is generally only 16 miles (25.75 kilometers) across, it is

283. *The ancient Near East.*

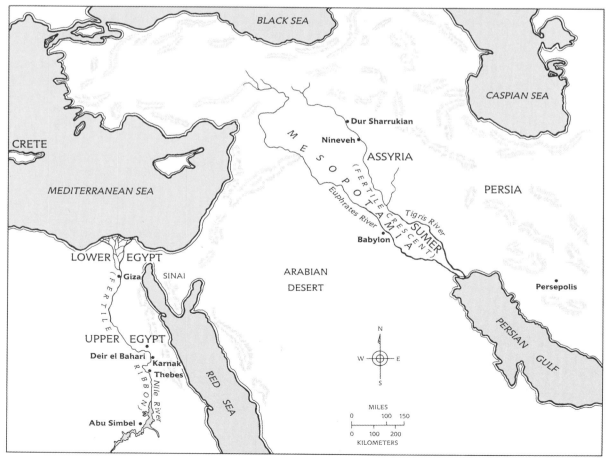

nearly 500 miles (804.67 kilometers) long, from ancient Nubia in the south to the wide delta in the north where the river joins the Mediterranean Sea. Quite different in shape is the valley between the Tigris and Euphrates rivers in Mesopotamia, called the Fertile Crescent.

Archaeological evidence indicates that both areas had active societies around 4000 B.C. By 3000 B.C. the peoples of these valleys had begun to form larger communities and keep written records. Precise dates are difficult to establish. The details of the many dynasties that ruled Egypt and the many different peoples that controlled Mesopotamia cannot concern us here, but the main outlines of their history are clear.

Asia

The diversity of Asian art began with the emergence of human beings in Java and China, perhaps a half million years ago. These peoples gradually evolved from stone choppers to the makers of the honed and polished tools (and beads) of the New Stone Age; their great transition from the nomadic life to art-producing urban settlements occurred earliest, as far as we know, in the Indus Valley of Northwest India.

India

Civilization flourished in Mohenjo Daro on the Indus River in the Indian subcontinent as early as 3000 B.C. Indo-Aryans from the northwest invaded the area about 1800 B.C. They brought with them the Vedic religion that is at the root of later Brahmanism and Hinduism. Common to all three religions is the view that men and women are part of nature, which leads to the Brahmanist belief that everyone must go through cycles of rebirth but that all beings are ultimately one. Such an outlook permits enjoyment of the senses, a view that is reflected in the art of Hindu India.

Buddhist Art In the 6th century B.C. Prince Siddhartha gave up wealth and family to seek the enlightenment that would release him from endless reincarnation and human suffering. Having become known as the Enlightened One, or Buddha, he preached that only through renouncing worldly attachments could a person escape rebirth and win salvation, or Nirvana. His saintly teaching inspired an order of monks who wandered with him through India begging in symbolic identification with the Buddha until his death.

Early Buddhists built stupas, domed monuments holding relics, such as Stupa No. 1 at Sanchī [284]. Stupas stood on platforms surrounded by walls or railings and large gateways. On top of the domes were finials, like small umbrellas, signifying royalty. The rails and gates were often carved with reliefs of scenes from the

284. *Stupa No. 1, Sanchī, India. 70–25 B.C. Diameter 120' (36.58 m).*

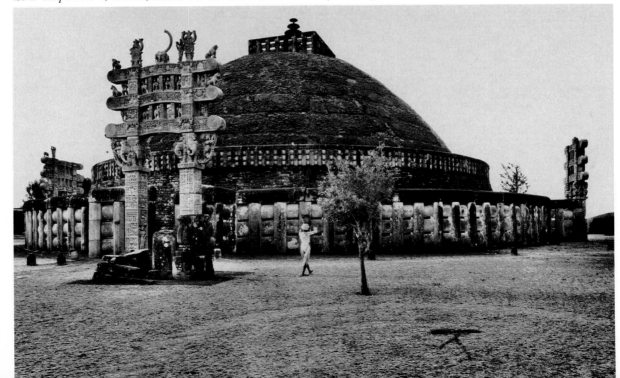

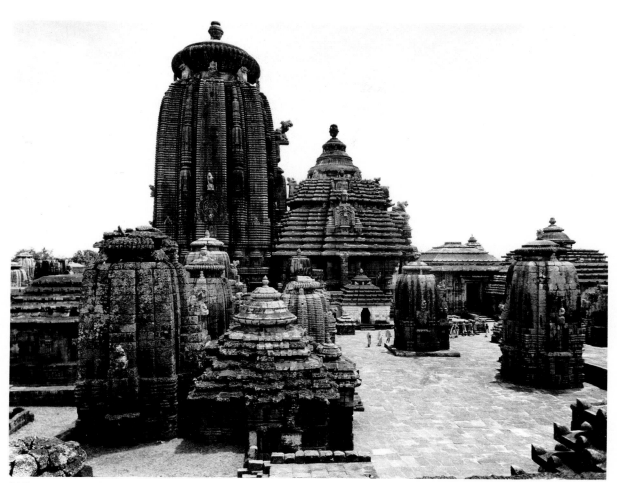

285. *Hindu temple compound. 8th–13th centuries* A.D.

Buddha's life. They never portrayed the Buddha himself but used symbols such as his footprint or the Wheel of Existence, escape from which, he preached, was possible only through nonworldliness.

Over the centuries many Buddhists came to believe that Buddha was divine. They built cave temples in his honor and carved free-standing statues, showing him teaching or in meditation [12]. His gentle smile and halo suggest saintliness. His long ear lobes show how attentively he listens to the secrets of the cosmos and are a symbolic reflection of his pre-Nirvana existence, when he wore the heavy jewelry of a prince. The *ūrnā* in the middle of the forehead of a Buddha image is a tuft of hair, and the *ushnisha* a protuberance of wisdom. The figure is serene, far beyond sensual pleasure and other attachments. As Buddhism spread to Southeast Asia and north to Tibet, China, and Japan, painters and sculptors adapted this Indian concept of the

Buddha with their own modifications in local imagery.

Hindu Art Although Buddhism became a major world religion, it did not persist in India. Hinduism, which fused with Brahmanism and incorporated some features of Buddhism, had much greater appeal, perhaps because of its delight in the physical world, which dominates Hindu imagery.

The Hindus built large temple complexes, which included a cella, or chamber, for the god surmounted by a tower, assembly halls, ritual baths, and loggias [285]. These structures were often completely covered with miles of relief sculpture of intertwining human, animal, and floral motifs expressing the rhythm of life. Leaving no surface undecorated, the sculptors carved a lavish testament to their belief in the unity of all living forms. Because sexual desire was a re-

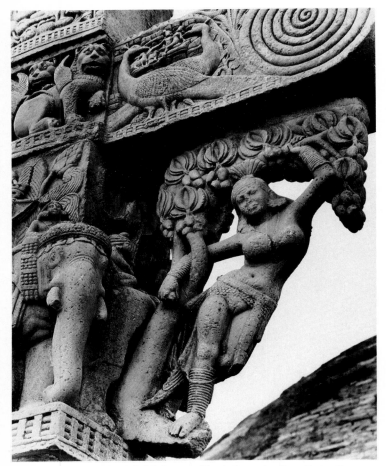

286. Yakshi *(tree goddess), from the East Gate of the Great Stupa, Sanchī, India. Early Andhra period, 1st century B.C.*

vered part of life and physical union was believed to be one way to attain unity with the gods and the universe, erotic subjects were frequent. The exaggerated curves of a Hindu tree or earth goddess also express the rhythm that pulses through creation **[286]**.

China

Only one civilization, namely, that of China, was able to hold a pattern of characteristic forms for almost four thousand years, yet within those stable traditions was also able to absorb and transform new and foreign ideas into native culture. The neolithic societies of China developed fine painted pottery as early as 2000 B.C., modeling slab-worked clay and firing vessels of complex form. The oriental love of jade appeared also at that time, evolving into fine cut and carved jade disks; these later, perhaps, serving as symbols of the sky.

Rule by dynasties, we believe, first began with the Xia Dynasty and then the Shang Dynasty in the valley of the Yellow River. By the second millennium B.C., more than a hundred Bronze Age (when bronze was evolved) sites had flourished under successive rulers who claimed divine mandate. Well-furnished royal Shang tombs were accompanied by pit burials of numerous men, women, dogs, and horses. The most highly developed pre-industrial bronze techniques appeared in Shang ritual vessels made for ancestor worship, some by hammering, most by casting in two-piece molds and, much later, by using the **lost-wax** (*cire perdue*) process (Chapter 7). Shang designs depend for their considerable effect on the linear decoration, often planned to be "read" as two sides of a single form or as the symmetry of two profiles. This distinctive concept of form can also be found in Northwest Coast Indian art, two thousand years later—and nowhere else before then or to this day **[196]**. Shang bronze vessels remain unsurpassed technically anywhere in the world **[223]**.

The Shang people were defeated by vigorous stock from Chou (Zhou) in the west, and a new empire endured almost a thousand years (1027–256 B.C.). The late Zhou Period (c. 600–222 B.C.) witnessed a great expansion of Chinese techniques and knowledge of raw materials— glazing of pottery, lacquer-refinement of wood, and the likely beginning of painting that was to become so highly developed in China.

As empires were expanding in the West, larger numbers of Chinese became familiar with higher culture and writing. This was the period when the great philosophers Lao-Xi and Confucius and many philosopher-statesmen were born; their writings furthered the rise of the totalitarian Qin Dynasty (221–206 B.C.) in that period of artistic ferment and great intellect. Ch'in Shih Huang Ti (also known as Qin Shi Huang Di), from whom the name China was derived, became the first emperor who consolidated the Great Wall of China, as impressive a structure today as it must have been more than two thousand years ago. Buried nearby in 210 B.C. under a mound close to 150 feet (49 meters) high, was the emperor's guardian army of six thousand life-size battle-ready pottery men and horses **[287]**—symbolic substitutes for the ancient practice of live burials that had been discontinued a few hundred years earlier. Ssu-ma Ch'ien, China's great early historian, tells us that 700,000 conscripts worked for thirty-six

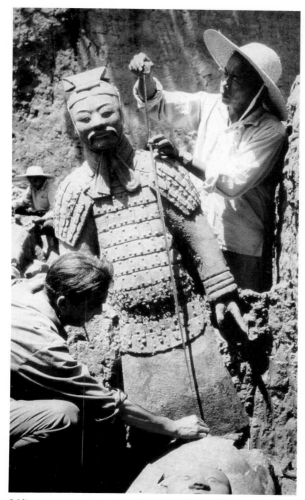

287. *Unknown warrior. 210 B.C. Clay, life-size.*

years on the project, which began the moment Qin (Ch'in) assumed leadership at the age of thirteen.

Africa

Many paleontologists believe that human life began in Africa, where the oldest human skeletal remains were found in southern Rhodesia. The huge continent, three times as large as the United States, with close to a thousand different languages, has produced almost as many distinctive art styles, some with traditions that persisted for a thousand years.

As African culture developed, the peoples of northern Africa, bordering on the Mediterranean, were influenced by travelers who periodically came by sea. Their racial stock and their art are in many ways more closely related to those of the Middle East than to those of the rest of Africa, south of the Sahara. The art of the sub-Saharan regions, however, is considered to be indigenous to Africa, coming from traditions that were generally independent of outside influences for many millennia, until the 1500s.

Before 3000 B.C. Africans of the Old Stone Age painted animated scenes on rocks in the Tassili region of the Sahara and in the south, often of hunters pursuing their game [288]. They also depicted their religious beliefs; one scene of a creation myth shows the first man mating with the morning and evening stars to produce all the creatures of the earth.

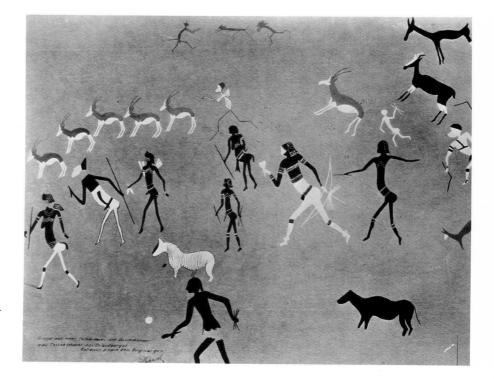

288. The White Lady of Brandberg. *Bushman cave painting. c. 1000 B.C. Namibia, South-West Africa.*

Egypt

Ninety-seven percent of Egypt is arid desert, while the remaining three percent is fertile only because of water supplied by the Nile River. Life was, therefore, restricted to the areas bordering the river that could easily be nourished by the annual flooding of its waters. For this reason the Greek historian Herodotus called Egypt's civilization "the gift of the Nile." In addition to providing water for agriculture, the Nile also was a means of transportation, communication, and sanitation for the peoples living along its banks. Finally, the wide deserts on both sides of the Nile insulated and protected the Egyptians from foreign intruders, for few invaders could survive the rigors of long desert travel.

In such a favorable environment, Egyptian civilization developed a characteristic continuity over a period of nearly three thousand years. Egyptian history is customarily divided into three main periods:

Old Kingdom, c. 2800–2000 B.C. (Dynasties III–VI)

Middle Kingdom, c. 2000–1600 B.C. (Dynasties XI–XIII)

New Kingdom and later periods, c. 1600–350 B.C. (Dynasties XVIII–XX)

Dynasty followed dynasty with little alteration in the customs of the Egyptians or the art forms that reflected them. We, who live in a changing era, find it difficult to imagine so static a society, but to the Egyptians it seemed natural and desirable.

To cultivate the soil along the Nile, the Egyptians had to develop an irrigation system, which meant that many individuals and whole villages had to work together. From such communal efforts the complex Egyptian civilization arose. Cooperation also made possible the earliest monumental architecture: tombs for the important dead.

Pyramids and Other Tombs The first architectural structure used for burial was the **mastaba,** a low, flat-topped mound with **battered** (sloping) sides. Several mastaba shapes of diminishing size, set one on top of another, form a stepped pyramid, such as that of the ruler Zoser [289]. Stepped pyramids were solid masses of rubble smoothly faced with brick or stone.

The design for stepped pyramids was gradually refined into smooth-sided pyramids, the most famous of which were created for three pharaohs, a father, son, and grandson of the Old Kingdom at Giza about 2600 to 2500 B.C. [55]. The power structure of Egypt centered on the pharaoh, or king, supported by the priests,

289. *Stepped pyramid, funerary district of King Zoser, Saqqara. c. 2610 B.C.*

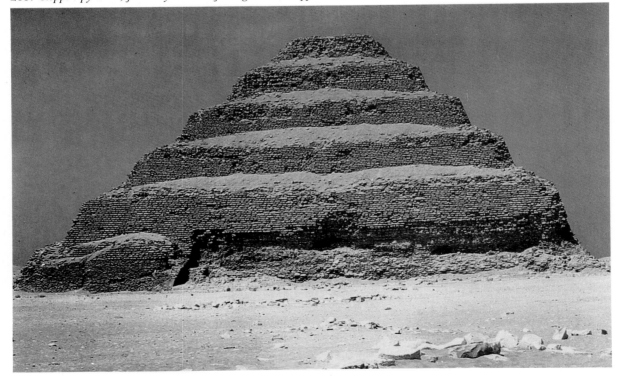

who could command thousands of men to construct the huge pyramids and the temples that accompanied them. They believed that these structures would safeguard the pharaoh's immortality.

The earliest, largest, and most famous pyramid is that of Pharaoh Khufu (Cheops). Nearby is that of Khafre (Chefren), which has a few limestone blocks at the top, all that remains of the limestone that once covered all three pyramids. The pyramid of Khafre, like the others, was connected by a causeway to a valley temple. Beside the causeway stands the gigantic sculpture of the Sphinx, representing a pharaoh in a royal linen headdress and (before weathering and vandalism) displaying the features of Khafre. A small portrait statue of Khafre from his valley temple is made of diorite, a kind of stone so hard that it would quickly dull a modern steel carving tool [290]. We can only assume that the Egyptians carved with tools of a still harder stone, which would be a very slow process indeed.

Inside the pyramids, which were almost solid mounds of limestone, earth, and rubble, were small rooms full of the rich belongings of the pharaoh, left to provide him with what his subjects believed he would need in his life after

290. Khafre. *Giza, c. 2530 B.C. Dark green diorite, height 5'6" (1.68 m). Egyptian Museum, Cairo.*

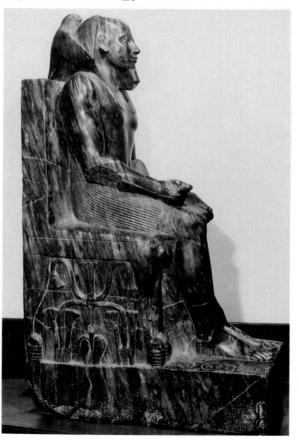

death. Another replica of the pharaoh was set up in front of the burial chamber to hold his *Ka,* or spirit, when his body could no longer contain it. The brilliantly colored wall paintings in the burial chambers give us a vivid view of Egyptian life and customs [86], as do the many objects found in the tombs. Jewelry, cosmetics, toys, furniture, models of houses, pieces of clothing, figurines depicting such daily events as slaves baking bread—thousands of these have survived to tell us what life was like for a well-to-do Egyptian.

Since the images in the royal tombs were meant to last the pharaoh through eternity, they were carved and painted as clearly as possible, according to strict guidelines. People, scenery, animals, and furnishings were always depicted from an angle or point of view that gave the most characteristic contour. For example, a pond or a lake was painted as if seen from above or from the side. Fish swimming underwater through the reeds and birds and trees were all drawn in profile. A table was shown from one side or from the top.

Human figures usually seem to stand in poses that even the most supple of us could never achieve. The reason for this convention was the Egyptian concept of representing details of the human body as a composite of its most typical shapes. They believed that since the head was most easily seen in profile, it should be painted that way. For the same reason the eyes were shown from the front, as were both shoulders; but arms, legs, and feet were presented in profile. Egyptian art is not based on what the artists saw but on what they knew about their subjects. In somewhat the same way a 20th-century Cubist painter showed many simultaneous views of a human figure in a composite [19].

Paintings in these tombs were detailed because pious Egyptians believed that the pharaoh could enjoy in the afterlife only what was provided for him in reality or in replica in his tomb. For example, they thought that the pharaoh would starve if foods were not depicted. Originally, the relatives brought real meals, but it was quickly found that piety is short-lived, while paintings of food are durable. Similarly, birds were reproduced so accurately in tomb paintings that they can be identified now as varieties still living in Egypt.

The architects of the pyramids tried to hide their entrances to prevent the valuables inside from being stolen, but the simplicity of the exterior surface of the pyramid made concealment difficult. No matter what pains the architects took, robbers located the entrances, broke in, and stole the pharaoh's belongings. Apparently, even for those who believed that the pharaoh was descended from the sun god, the lust for worldly treasure was stronger than the fear of the divine.

New burial places had to be devised to protect the royal dead. During the Middle Kingdom, hidden tombs were constructed out of living rock, such as those at Beni Hasan. New Kingdom tombs, at the Valley of the Kings, for instance, were hewn out of the cliffs west of the Nile, near Thebes. Tomb entrances were concealed, with no monuments to mark the burial spot. Despite these precautions, most tombs were broken into by robbers. This meant more than the loss of the pharaoh's treasures; it also meant that he was deprived of the belongings he needed to exist in his afterlife.

Archaeologists have to date uncovered only one richly furnished royal tomb, that of the New Kingdom pharaoh Tutankhamen, who flourished around 1350 B.C. When his tomb was discovered almost intact in the 1920s, the archaeologists found among other treasures a throne [237] and a great deal of jewelry inlaid with glass and semiprecious stones. This included golden amulets of the gods, rings, bracelets, necklaces, and even golden guards to protect the mummy's toes. Small sculptures, pottery glazed deep blue, clothing, alabaster boxes and vases, and many ritual objects found in the tomb attested to the delicate and advanced craftsmanship of the ancient Egyptians. The royal mummy was found in a nest of four wood [198] and gold coffins, each one smaller than the last, with the innermost one, solid gold, just fitting his body. The delicate throne fashioned for the young king is made of wood, inlaid with gold and enamels. In a scene on the back of the throne, Tutankhamen's fifteen-year-old bride adjusts the lavish jewelry covering his chest by the light of the symbolic sun above. The portraits of the king and queen combine naturalism with the sensitive modeling found in fine portrait sculpture.

Temples The pharaohs of the New Kingdom built magnificent stone temples, using **post-and-lintel** construction, as noted in Chapter 9. Their immense columns were often shaped like bundles of papyrus stems, which are believed to have been used in place of scarce wood in early Egyptian buildings. Other columns were topped with capitals inspired by the lotus flowers of the Nile [87].

The exquisite marble funerary temple at Deir

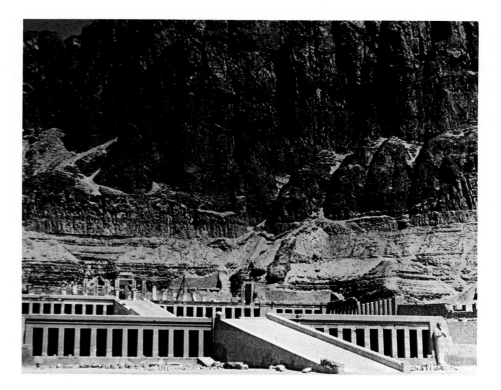

291. *Mortuary temple of Hatshepsut, Deir el Bahari. c. 1485 B.C.*

el Bahari that gleams across the Nile at the entrance to the Valley of the Kings was built about 1485 B.C. by Hatshepsut, the only woman to interrupt the male succession of pharaohs and the only one to build a temple **[291]**. The building, dedicated to the sun god Amun, is carved from the living rock of the cliffs and is fronted impressively by three tiers of colonnades connected by ramps. After an unparalleled reign of peace and trade with kingdoms as distant as legendary Punt in the Middle East, Hatshepsut was killed, probably by her stepson and successor Thutmose III. She never occupied any of the three graves she had carefully prepared in the Valley of the Kings, and Thutmose obliterated her inscriptions wherever he could. Her story is told only in wall paintings and hieroglyphs in her temple and on her **obelisks,** tall four-sided monuments, which still stand proudly in the Temple of Karnak. Though Thutmose III once walled in these obelisks to conceal Hatshepsut's monuments, their gold tops shone above the wall.

A little more than one hundred years later the remarkable pharaoh Akhenaton tried to reduce the complex Egyptian polytheism to the simple worship of one god, the sun god Aton. He built a new temple to Aton at Amarna, which was destroyed by his successors and their priests, anxious to restore the old religion. The chief remains from his reign are some reliefs and murals in a realistic style full of movement and

individuality. The portrait bust of his queen, Nefertiti, a partner in his reforms, presents her as a specific person rather than an abstract symbol **[292]**, yet the artist has depicted a commanding presence.

292. Queen Nefertiti. *c. 1355 B.C. Painted limestone, height 20" (51 cm). State Museums, West Berlin.*

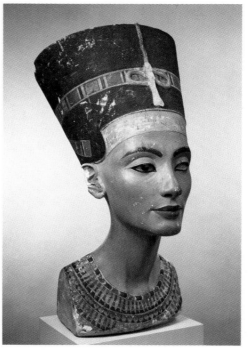

Magnetometry in the Valley of the Kings

With magnetometers as aids, archaeologists in Egypt are uncovering new passageways, unexpected chambers, and, in some cases, even new tombs that could yield now unknown treasures and new insights into vanished peoples.

Early in 1987, remote sensing technology, including sonar, radar, and magnetometry, was used to locate what may be viewed as the most spectacular finds since 1922, when the almost untouched tomb of the young Tutankhamen was discovered by Howard Carter. A recently discovered 3300-year-old tomb was probably the burial place of several of the many sons of Ramses II, who ruled from 1290 to 1224 B.C. A huge central room, supported by sixteen large pillars and filled almost to the ceiling with rubble, was found; measuring 100 feet (30 meters) on all sides, it is one of the largest in any of the known burial sites in the Valley of the Kings.

In a site only 50 feet from the known tomb of Ramses II, the magnetometer data recorded a change, significant enough for a team of archaeologists, guided by Dr. Kent R. Weeks of the University of California at Berkeley, to start digging. Within ten days they found the entrance to the hidden tomb—a door 5 feet (1.5 meters) high and wide. A rush of hot, moist air bridging centuries greeted the explorers as they crawled through the passageway into the central chamber. Though the tomb has suffered water damage, possibly from the modern irrigation practiced since completion of the Aswan Dam further south, evidence such as may remain from any of the more than eighty children of Ramses II increases our understanding of the Egyptian empire at its height.

Remote-sensing apparatus, responding to the particles of iron in limestone bedrock, generates a signal that measures the intensity of the magnetic field. A dip in intensity of the signal indicates a break in the rock, such as may be caused by a tomb. While the technology is expensive, it is so accurate that it eliminates wasted digging and speeds discoveries. French, Japanese, and Egyptian authorities are now busily exploring anew the Pyramid of Cheops and the hollows beneath the Sphinx with magnetometry in hopes of locating further treasure.

293. *Temple of Ramses II, Abu Simbel. c. 1250 B.C. Height of large statues approximately 60' (18.3 m).*

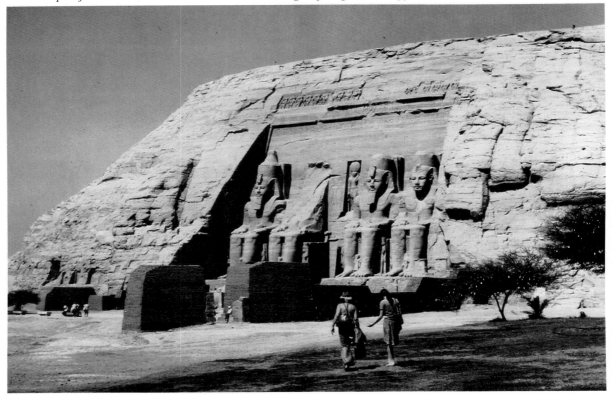

While the Great Temple of Amun at Karnak with its hypostyle halls, discussed in Chapter 9, is characteristic of Egyptian temples, the one built by Ramses II in the cliffs at Abu Simbel on the upper Nile [293] is unique. Four colossal statues, intended to inspire awe by their sheer size, guarded the entrance. The building was so designed that twice a year, at the equinoxes, a ray of sunlight would pierce the entrance at dawn, cross the main hall, and penetrate far back to reach the tiny inner shrine containing four statues of the sun god, other gods, and Ramses. The scientific skill of these ancient Egyptian builders, shown in the temple at Abu Simbel, is staggering even when measured against today's engineering skills. When construction of the Aswan Dam was to raise the level of the Nile, the entire temple was moved to the top of the cliffs in 1968 to save it from being flooded. As a result of faulty calculations, however, the sun rays at the equinox now light the inner sanctum one day later on February 23rd.

The complex arts preserved in the tombs and architectural remains combine to give us a picture of ancient Egypt as an aesthetically sophisticated civilization. Egyptian art, however, required a wealthy ruling class as patrons. When internal power struggles within the structured society led to the collapse of the government, Egyptian art slowly declined as well.

Mesopotamia

Like the Fertile Ribbon along Egypt's Nile roughly 600 miles (1000 kilometers) away, the Fertile Crescent, between the Tigris and the Euphrates, was flooded when the rivers overflowed in spring but in summer was parched by the sun. Here, also, irrigation was necessary to maintain agriculture. Unlike Egypt, however, Mesopotamia had no natural desert barriers to repel invaders and foreign influences. Therefore, over a period of thousands of years, the whole area became the home of many peoples, and its history was in constant flux. The story is confusing, with many shifts of power, especially between the empires of Babylonia and Assyria. We can, however, touch briefly on the four main societies that dominated this land:

Sumer, c. 4000–2300 B.C.

Neo-Sumerian, c. 2100–2000 B.C.

Babylonia, c. 2000–550 B.C.

Assyria, c. 1400–600 B.C.

Persia, c. 550–325 B.C.

Persisting throughout Mesopotamian civilization were the basic achievements of the Sumerians, which later peoples developed or modified.

Sumerian Art The Sumerians were great builders. Living in a land that lacked stone and wood but had plenty of clay, they built large cities, palaces, and temples out of brick. Eventually they learned to fire the bricks and glaze them to make them more weatherproof. In trying to span openings with bricks they developed the arch (see Chapter 9), a principle known but little used by the Egyptians or the later Greeks.

The characteristic form of Sumerian architecture was the **ziggurat,** an artificial mountain of packed earth surfaced with bricks, crowned by a temple to a god of an aspect of nature such as water, sky, or storm. The temple was believed to be the god's home. All that is left of the ziggurats today are eroded, truncated mounds of sun-dried clay brick, but an artist's drawing [294]

294. *Reconstruction drawing of the Ziggurat at Ur. Neo-Sumerian, c. 2100–2000 B.C.*

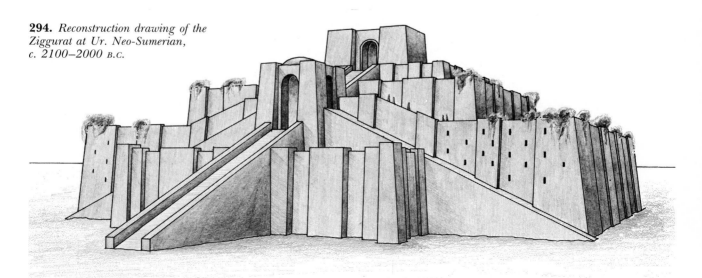

shows us how the Ziggurat in Ur may have looked, with Sumerian-style ramps leading up from terraces on all sides through archways, past gardens and trees. The structure called the hanging gardens of Babylon seems likely to have been a ziggurat with trees and flowers planted on its terraces. From a distance the brick ziggurat blended with the dry, surrounding countryside, but the lush greenery seemed suspended in air. Mesopotamia without irrigation was dry and poor. When the inhabitants tried to imagine a more desirable existence, or Paradise, they thought of it as a garden, such as the garden of Eden described in the Bible.

The Sumerians were among the first people to have developed a written language, the cuneiform [164]. They also divided the hour into 60 minutes and the circle into 360 degrees, divisions we still use today.

Babylonian Art The Babylonians built cities and ziggurats like the Sumerians. Hammurabi, king of Babylon from about 1727 to 1686 B.C., established an empire and created the first written code of laws.

The Old Babylonian Empire founded by Hammurabi was succeeded by the Assyrian Empire, which in turn was replaced by the New Babylonian, or Chaldean, Empire, described in the Bible, which emerged about 625 B.C. The palace of Nebuchadnezzar II and the ziggurat of the great god Marduk, called the Tower of Babel, are both gone. Artists throughout history have tried to imagine how the Tower of Babel looked, but without drawings or plans of it no one can be sure. Certainly the painting by Pieter Brueghel the Elder (c. 1525–1569), set in a 16th-century Flemish landscape peopled with workers in Renaissance dress [295], must be far

295. *Pieter Brueghel the Elder.* The Tower of Babel. *1563. Oil on canvas, $3'8\frac{7}{8}'' \times 5'1''$ (1.24 × 1.55 m). Kunsthistorisches Museum, Vienna.*

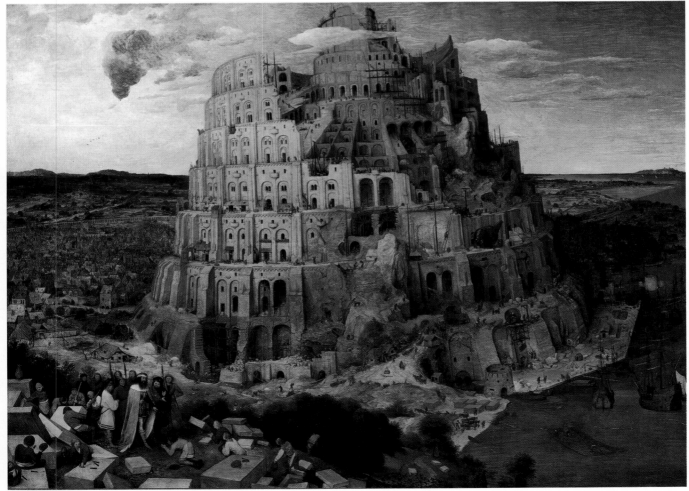

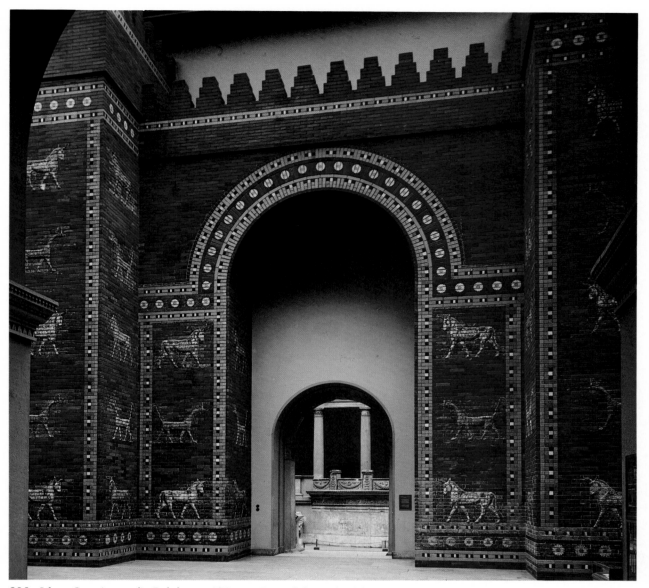

296. *Ishtar Gate (restored), Babylon. c. 575 B.C. Enameled sun-dried brick, height 48'9" (15 m). Near Eastern Museum, State Museums, East Berlin.*

removed from the original palace, but the Mesopotamian ramp shown in the painting remains an authentic feature.

Scholars have, however, restored the Ishtar Gate of Babylon dedicated to the goddess Ishtar **[296]**. It is faced with glazed brick and decorated with reliefs of animals, some two-headed and some 20 feet (6 meters) long. Similar glazed brick reliefs in brilliant colors lined the Processional Route to Marduk, which led to the Ishtar Gate, the only major monument remaining from this period, now located in the East Berlin museum.

Assyrian Art The Assyrians, from the upper Tigris River, established an empire between the 9th and 7th centuries B.C. At its height it stretched from modern western Iran in the east through Mesopotamia to Asia Minor and the Mediterranean in the west. The Assyrians built their palaces at Dur Sharrukin (modern Khorsabad) and Nineveh (modern Kuyunik), retaining Babylon in its original importance in the South. The Assyrians adopted much of Babylonian civilization, to which they gave their own distinctive character.

The Assyrians introduced no new construction methods. They built highly elaborate palaces decorated with great stone slabs carved in relief. The 200-room palace-temple complex of Sargon II at Khorsabad **[297]**, is known to have enclosed 25 acres (10.11 hectares), and included

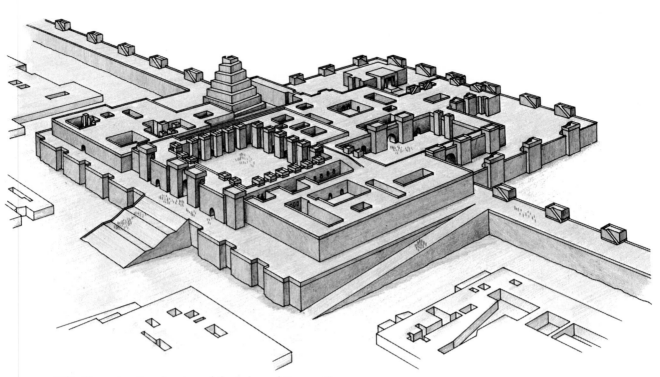

297. *Reconstruction drawing of the palace of Sargon II, Khorsabad, Iraq. c. 720 B.C.*

a ziggurat with a spiral ramp. Unlike the huge Sumerian Ziggurat at Ur, however, the Assyrian mountain to the gods, similar to the ziggurat form, was reduced to a small temple.

The Assyrians were depicted primarily as warriors and hunters; they commissioned their sculptors to show expeditions, hunting scenes, and the lives of kings and the military. The combative Assyrian spirit is reflected in their realistic carvings, such as a relief decorating the palace of Ashurbanipal at Nineveh **[298]**. The sculptor portrays the death of a wounded lioness, showing a strong sense of action, knowledge of animal anatomy, and even a sensitivity to the pain of the animal, a concern rarely directed toward people in Assyrian art. Many animal sculptures were nonrealistic. For example, each of the pair of stone guardians that stood at one of the entrances to the palace of Sargon II at Dur Sharrukin has a human head, the headdress of a god, the wings of a bird, and the body of a lion **[299]**. It also was made with five legs, so that when seen from the front it would appear to have four legs, and as one walked past it into the palace, it would still seem to have four legs. The extra leg represents an effort to make the animal appear as complete as possible. In the same way the

Egyptians drew the human figure from several points of view in an attempt to present a total image.

Persian Art The final period of ancient Near Eastern art, when the area was dominated by Persia (modern Iran), overlaps Greek civilization, and its architecture was stimulated by contact with Greece. Darius, the Persian emperor whose effort to conquer Greece was defeated at the Battle of Marathon in 490 B.C., built a massive stone palace in the city of Persepolis. Its great halls, with roofs supported on slender 60-foot (18.28-meter) pillars, show the influence of Greek architecture. Unlike earlier Mesopotamian palaces, the Persian palace did not look like a fortress; instead, it was open and inviting with many stairways, ramps, and columned waiting rooms. Perhaps this huge capital with two noble bulls' heads placed back to back **[300]** is symbolic of the historical role played by the Persian empire; one head looks back to the civilization of the Fertile Crescent upon which much of the Judeo-Christian tradition is based, while the other head looks toward the Mediterranean and the civilization of Greece, whose philosophy and art have so strongly influenced the West.

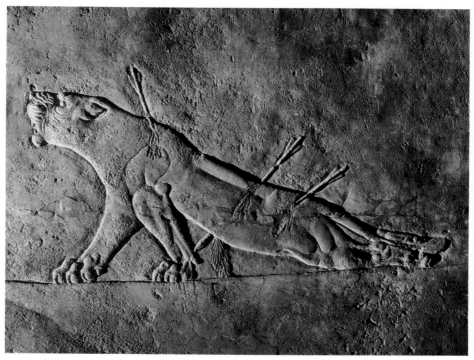

above: **298.** Dying Lioness. *Nineveh, c. 650 B.C. Limestone, height 32¾″ (60 cm).*
Reproduced by courtesy of the Trustees of the British Museum.

below: **299.** *Winged lion (guardian of the palace gate), from the palace of Ashurnasirpal II. Assyrian, 9th century B.C.*
Limestone; height 10'2½″ (3.11 m), length 9'3¾″ (2.76 m), width 2'1½″ (0.65 m). Metropolitan Museum of Art, New York
(gift of John D. Rockefeller, Jr., 1932).

right: **300.** *Double bull capital and column from Persepolis (restored). Achaemenid Period, c. 522–486 B.C.*
Black limestone, height approximately, 13' (4 m). Courtesy of The Oriental Institute of The University of Chicago.

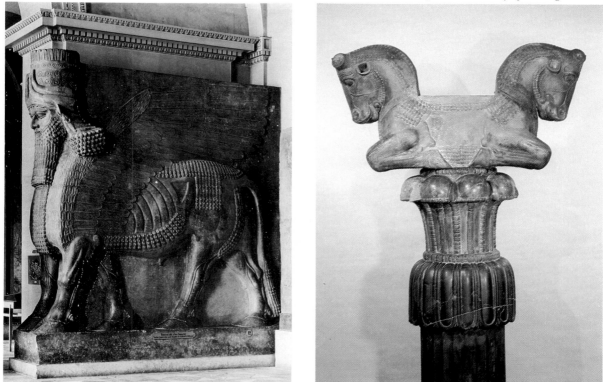

Exercises and Activities

Research Exercises

1. What do we believe were the earliest art forms? What were the materials and functions of that art? Would you consider the art of our earliest ancestors to be simple and childlike? If not, in what way do you think it was skilled and expressive?
2. Locate two examples of modern art that deal with themes similar to those of prehistoric times in the ancient Middle East. How do the modern works differ from early art, and in what ways are they similar?

Studio Activities

1. Do a simple painting based on a subject from everyday life, using some of the spatial concepts of the Egyptians.
2. From a top view, draw the plans for the three great pyramids, preserving the actual scale of these monuments and their orientations to the cardinal points.

3. Describe the construction of Stonehenge. What structural method was used?
4. What is meant by the terms "Fertile Ribbon" and "Fertile Crescent"? How were these areas important? When Herodotus stated that "Egypt is a gift of the Nile," what facts did he have in mind?
5. Contrast the architecture, sculpture, and painting of Egypt and Mesopotamia from the viewpoints of material and style. Explain the reasons for the difference.

3. Make a small model of King Kafre's pyramid.
4. Carve a model of the Sphinx with whatever material you prefer.
5. Carve from a piece of slate an incised image relating to any of the four major Mesopotamian periods that seems appropriate to your theme.

11
Gods and Heroes: The Classical World; The Americas

Leaving the waters of the splendid East, the Sun leapt up into the firmament to bring light to the immortals and to men who plough the earth and perish.

Homer, *The Odyssey*

To the Ancients, the movement of the sun and stars was the image of perfection: to see the celestial harmony was to hear it, and to hear was to understand it.

Octavio Paz, *In Praise of Hands*

[Augustus Caesar] made so many improvements in Rome, he could rightly boast that he found it brick and left it marble.

Gaius Suetonus Tranquillius

Most of us in the West have been brought up to think of the Greeks and the Romans as the wise ancients who developed within a scant thousand years the sophisticated civilization we call classical. In fact, the Greeks were fortunate in the sense that their world was far smaller and younger than ours. They were unburdened by an accumulated weight of long-established traditions. Nevertheless, the early Greeks chose not to accept even the rather simple mythological and religious beliefs with which their neighbors had explained the nature of the world. Instead, they boldly struck out for themselves to evolve new philosophies and governmental systems and different concepts of art. In contrast, perhaps, we in the 20th century seem to be the ancients, grappling with the inherited problems of a weary world that has made many mistakes. And, with it all, our legacy from the Greek and Roman culture termed classical remains incalculable.

Drama, poetry, architecture, sculpture, experiments in democracy, philosophical concepts, a rational approach to the mysteries of nature—there is hardly a facet of our lives that is not affected by Greek achievements. For instance, 2400 years later, we can still see references to the classical world in today's post-modern architecture. Greek civilization was gradually absorbed by Rome, which added its own contributions, especially in government, architecture, and engineering. Roman law, roads, arches, and their Latin language lasted for centuries after Roman political power came to an end. The combined achievements of both peoples make up the classical heritage of the West. Yet a good deal of what we used to think was original with the Greeks and Romans was in fact derived from earlier Mediterranean peoples [301].

Prehistory: The Aegean Background

The Aegean Sea is full of islands that provided stopping places for sailing ships. During prehistoric and ancient times, the constant trade and exchange of ideas among many peoples border-

The Aegean Sea; Greece; Rome; Middle and South America

THE VISUAL ARTS		HISTORICAL NOTES
	B.C.	
	prehistory	Asian nomads cross Bering Strait
		c. 2100 Aegean civilization
	2000	**2000–1200** Crete; Mycenae
		1400–300 Olmec culture, Vera Cruz
c. 1250 Lion gate, Mycenae [302]		
c. 1000 Fertility figures, Mexico [202]	1000	
		c. 800 Etruscan beginnings
		776 Olympic Games begin
		753 Rome founded
c. 750 Dipylon vase, Greece [47]		**c. 750** Homeric epics
		c. 700–500 Archaic Greek period
600–575 Kouros and kore statues, Greece [303, 304]	500	**c. 500–375** Classical Greek period
		c. 480–400 Greek playwrights: Aeschylus, et al.
c. 470 *Charioteer* [310]		
c. 460 Myron, *Discobolus* [311]		**457–429** Golden Age of Athens (Age of Pericles)
		c. 450–350 Greek philosophers: Socrates, Plato, et al.
448–432 Parthenon, Athens [307]		
410 Erechtheum, Athens [309]		
		c. 375–100 Hellenistic Greek period
c. 340 Praxiteles, *Hermes with Dionysus* [312]		**336** Alexander of Macedonia
c. 150 *Laocoön Group* [314]		
150–100 *Aphrodite of Melos* [315]		**58–49** Caesar conquers Gaul
c. 50 Pont du Gard, France [253]		**c. 6** Birth of Christ
	A.D.	
c. 72–80 Colosseum, Rome [317]		**79** Pompeii destroyed
118–125 Pantheon, Rome [257]		
c. 200–700 Temple of Quetzalcoatl, Mexico [40]	300	
310–320 Basilica of Constantine, Rome [318]		**313** Christianity a Roman state religion
		300–900 Classic Mayan cultures, Yucatán
c. 400–600 Pyramid of the Sun, Mexico	1200	**1200–1500** Aztec cultures, Mexico

ing the sea stimulated the development of Aegean civilization. The island of Crete, midway between Greece and Egypt, carried on extensive trade with Asia Minor and Egypt between 2000 B.C. and 1400 B.C. Enriched by these contacts, Crete developed a very sophisticated civilization. Egyptian post-and-lintel construction probably influenced the enormous palace at Knossos, which inspired the Greek legend of the Minotaur and the labyrinth. According to the story, the Greek hero Theseus found his way through a complex maze, perhaps representing the many rooms of the palace, to slay the Minotaur, a monster half man and half bull. The Minotaur myth probably developed from the Cretan cult of the bull, so vividly expressed in the palace frescoes of youths and maidens leaping over a running bull [104].

By the mid-15th century B.C., Mycenae, in southern Greece, had grown to rival Crete as a center of culture. Gold masks, jewelry, weapons, and cups from the beehive tombs of the Mycenaeans bring to life the lusty days of the ten-year war between the Mycenaean rulers and the Trojans in Asia Minor, described in Homer's epic *The Iliad*. The lion gate stands on the hilltop citadel at Mycenae surrounded by walls of massive stone blocks fitted together without mortar

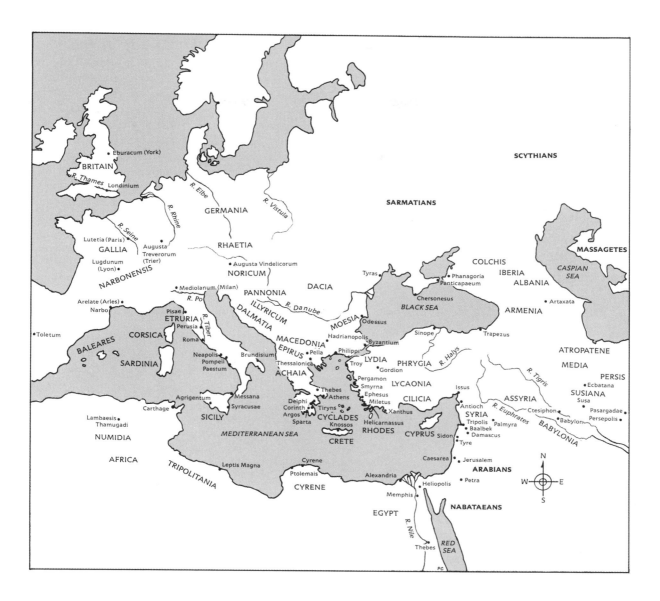

above: **301.** *The Greeks and their neighbors.*

right: **302.** *"Lion Gate," Mycenae. c. 1250 B.C. Relief, height 9′6″ (2.9 m).*

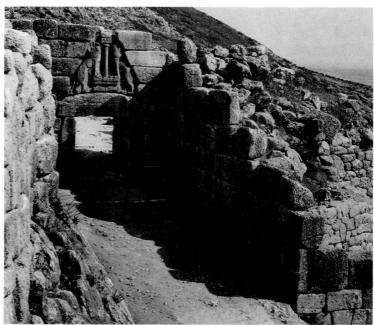

[302]. The wall paintings, the metalwork, the architecture, and the sculptures of Mycenae were forerunners of the Greek art that followed.

Greece

Greek civilization was a blend of many influences. The Dorian Greeks, who invaded the Greek mainland, Crete, and the other Aegean islands from the north about 1000 B.C., absorbed the skills of metallurgy, pottery, weaving, and building developed earlier in Mycenae and

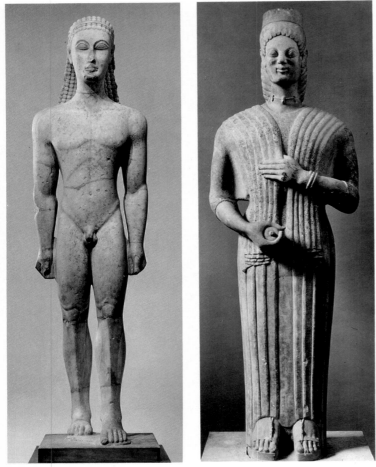

left: **303.** Statue of a Youth (Kouros). *c. 600 B.C. Marble, height with plinth, 6'½" (1.84 m). Metropolitan Museum of Art, New York (Fletcher Fund, 1932).*

right: **304.** Young Maiden (Kore). *Early 6th century B.C. Attic marble, height 6'4" (1.93 m). State Museums, West Berlin.*

Crete. The Ionian Greeks, who migrated from southern Greece to Ionia in western Asia Minor in the 11th and 10th centuries B.C., incorporated into their art and religion ideas from Mesopotamia. These many elements all contributed to form the distinctive Greek civilization we admire.

Greek art may be divided into three periods:

Archaic period, 7th and 6th centuries B.C.

Classical period, 5th century and early 4th century B.C.

Hellenistic period, late 4th, 3rd, and 2nd centuries B.C.

Sculpture of the Archaic Period

By about 700 B.C. the basis of Greek political and economic life was shifting from agricultural villages to cities dependent on trade. Wealthy cities and elite citizens commissioned statues of the gods, legendary heroes, and athletes, who took part in the Olympic Games, held to honor the gods since the 8th century B.C. Although the Greeks stood in awe of their immortal gods, they also felt close to them and imagined them in human form. Greek legends and the epics of Homer presented the gods as superhuman beings entangled in the affairs of mortals. Men and women, although weak and imperfect, were believed to resemble the gods. Therefore, Greek statues of divinities and mortals showed similarities, since athletes served as models for both. Selected features of many athletes were combined in idealized sculpture, which eventually became the standard for human beauty in the West. As a reflection of Greek philosophy, idealized sculptural proportions (Plato believed) could transform an image of the human being to a divine level.

Rigidly posed Egyptian statues must have been the models for the early Greek representation of the nude male figure, known as a **kouros** [303]. Unlike the Egyptian artists, who made static figures to serve as eternal replicas of the pharaoh and aristocracy, Greek artists were not content with stiff poses to convey the spirit of their gods and heroes. So, although the kouros is severe, he is also full of vitality, both physical and mental, illustrating the Greek ideal of a healthy mind in a healthy body. Standing with one foot advanced, fists clenched and muscles taut, the figure seems ready to burst from its bonds of stone.

The Greeks also represented a young maiden, or **kore** [304]. Her compact figure, always clothed, perhaps because the female figure was not then seen to represent the perfect ideal of beauty like the male, stares at us with an archaic smile that may not have been so much the result of artistic design as of the sculptor's difficulty in carving the mouth. This kore holds a pomegranate, regarded as a symbol of fertility because of its many seeds. Like most Greek sculpture, the kouros and kore statues were colored, and we can still see traces of their original paint.

Even in early figures of gods, heroes, and other mortals, we can perceive that quality of balance among the emotions, sensations, and intellect that became typical of later Greek art in the Classical period, when concept and imagery flowed freely.

Architecture of the Classical Period

The renowned Classical period of Greece refers to a rather short time in the 5th and sometimes the early 4th centuries B.C. when Athens was the center of a rich flowering of art, literature, and philosophy. **Classical** has since come to refer, not only to what might be considered the Greek era at its height, but also to the lasting, significant best form of any art. This moderately sized city-state produced in three generations such dramatists as Aeschylus, Sophocles, and Euripides; the philosophers Socrates, Plato, and Aristotle; the sculptors Phidias, Myron, and Praxiteles; and the outstanding political leaders Themistocles and Pericles (461–429 B.C.). During this period Athens and other city-states built many temples to their patron gods and goddesses. The crowning achievement of Greek architecture of the Classical period was marble temples. They adhered to the same general floor plan—a **cella,** or room housing the statue of the god, entered through a porch with columns. Some temples had also variously a porch in back, a treasure room behind the cella, and a colonnade on all four sides. Temples were approached by three steps and covered with a gable roof. Every architectural element was subtly related to the whole composition.

Greek marble temples reveal Egyptian influence as well as of earlier Greek temples in wood. For example, the marble columns were placed at what were originally the meeting points of wooden beams, and an **abacus,** or square form originally interposed between the capital and the beams to strengthen the joining point, was retained. Other decorative details can also be traced to original wood construction.

The Orders of Architecture   Variations in temple design are mainly in the elements of the **order** of a temple. A Doric order consists of a column, or post (including base, shaft, and capital with abacus and echinus), and an **entablature,** or lintels, above it (including a plain **architrave,** a decorated **frieze,** and the **cornice** of the roof) [305]. All the elements were refined to create a satisfying and harmonious relationship.

305. *Orders of architecture.*

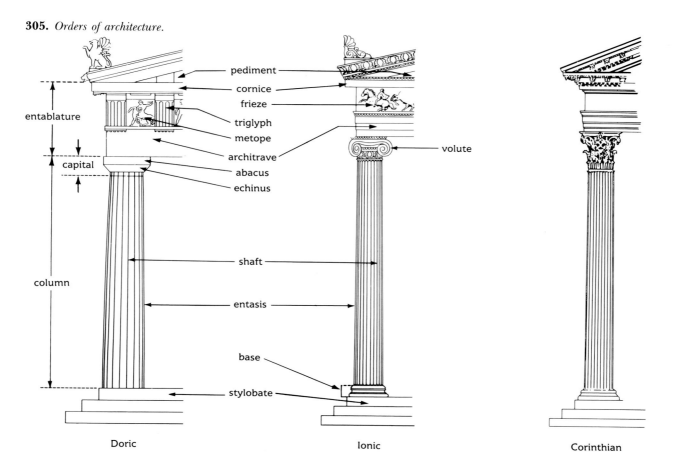

entablature

capital

column

pediment
cornice
frieze
triglyph
metope
architrave
abacus
echinus
volute

shaft

entasis

base

stylobate

Doric   Ionic   Corinthian

Importance was given to the number three. As the ideal, perfect male body is basically made of three parts, so also are the components of architecture. There were three kinds or orders, each with its own proportions and decorative scheme. The simple, early Doric order was named for the Dorians, although it may have originated in Crete. It had an unadorned cushionlike **echinus** and square **abacus** for a **capital** and a sturdy, widely **fluted** (grooved) shaft. The frieze was decorated with **triglyphs,** stone copies of the grooves in the clay tablets that once covered the ends of the wooden beams to protect them from the weather and probably to drain off rainwater. The square spaces between the triglyphs, called **metopes,** were sometimes filled with sculpture. The Doric order gave an air of massive grandeur to early temples.

The Ionic order, which had **volutes** (spirals) on the capitals and a slender shaft, with delicate, narrow fluting to emphasize its height, gave a temple a lighter effect that was more open and inviting. The continuous frieze was often ornamented with sculpture. The Ionic order can be traced through Ionia to earlier forms used in Asia Minor, where spiral decoration is believed to be derived from sheaves of rushes native to Mesopotamia but unknown in Greece. Some scholars, however, believe the capital derives from ram's horns.

The later, more ornate Corinthian order had a capital shaped like an inverted bell, usually with overlapping rows of acanthus leaves. It was adopted by the Romans and eventually influenced Romanesque, Gothic, and Renaissance builders.

Since the Renaissance, Western architects have borrowed and adapted all three orders, which still can be seen. Look for them especially on libraries, courthouses, and banks, copied in wood, marble, or even concrete.

The Acropolis Some of the most famous Greek temples were built on the Acropolis overlooking Athens and the Aegean Sea. An **acropolis** is a fortified hill, which originally provided defense in most Greek cities. This artist's reconstruction shows the Athenian Acropolis during the Golden Age of Pericles, when it was at its height as a civic and religious center [306]. Tem-

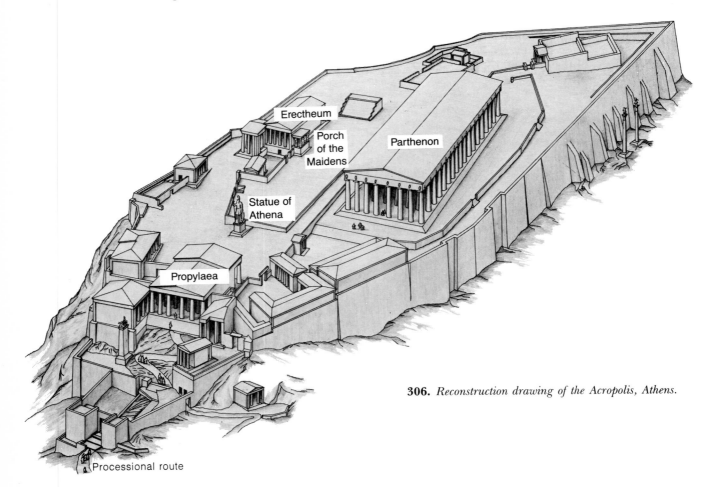

306. *Reconstruction drawing of the Acropolis, Athens.*

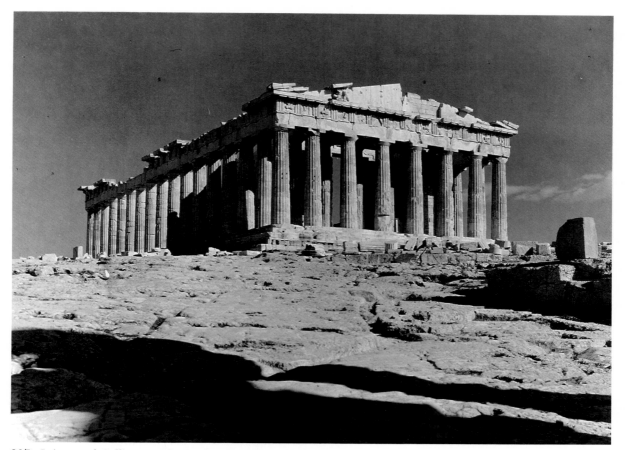

307. *Ictinus and Callicrates. The Parthenon, Athens. 448–432 B.C..*

ples, a storehouse, and commemorative statues were reached through the **Propylaea,** a ceremonial gateway at the head of a steep, twisting path with steps.

The Parthenon The best-known Acropolis temple, although not necessarily the most refined, was the Parthenon. Commissioned by Pericles and designed by the architects Ictinus and Callicrates, it was dedicated to Athena during the Panathenaic Festival of 438 B.C. Its sturdy Doric form reveals the subtle architectural relationships that have influenced so many later architects. The precise proportions, the interplay of vertical and horizontal forms, the contrast of the solid cella against the many columns of the two porches and surrounding colonnade, all combine to create a harmonious design that appears simple but that is actually extremely complex.

The columns were designed to bulge slightly in the center, a distortion called **entasis,** intended to counteract the optical illusion that causes parallel straight lines to appear to curve inward. In addition, the horizontal line of the top step of the porch and the line of the architrave were also curved slightly upward to avoid the appearance of sagging. In the space formed by the columns and architrave at the end of the colonnade we can see a graceful shape like an inverted vase [**307**]. Was it created by chance or by careful planning, perhaps as a symbol whose meaning is lost?

The Parthenon, like all Greek temples, was built to be visually satisfying from all sides. Its carefully proportioned form presents an impressive silhouette, which dominates the Acropolis. Let us imagine ourselves part of a procession of Athenians making our way up the rock of the Acropolis through the Propylaea to the Parthenon. Instead of entering the temple at the near, west end, the procession will wind around to approach from the far, east end. We can look up and see struggling figures, such as gods and giants, Greeks and Amazons, and Lapiths and Centaurs carved in high **relief** in the metopes of the **frieze** above the colonnade.

Preserving the Crumbling Parthenon

During the last decade, scientists from many nations have gathered their resources in Athens to salvage a precious monument of the classical world from the ravages of time, tourists, and, worst of all, technology gone awry. The temple sacred to Athena Parthenos, surviving centuries of war and nature's elements, now is attacked by *nefos,* an eye-stinging cloud of sulfur dioxide, a byproduct of petroleum fuel combustion. As rain, dew, and *nefos* mix, the gleaming marble of the Parthenon turns into crumbling plaster.

Crowning the Acropolis, the renowned citadel of Athens, the temple to Zeus' daughter Athena the Virgin has outlasted the Romans, who set fire to the colossal gold and ivory statue of Athena by Phidias that was housed in the sacred inner chamber. A thousand years later, the Parthenon still stood after Turkish-stored gunpowder blew off fourteen of the outside columns. But the temple's continued existence in the 20th century is more precarious than ever.

In the past one hundred or so years, bungled restorations have jeopardized some of the 12,500 white marble blocks hewn from Mount Pentelicus to the north that make up the temple. Adding new iron clamps and reinforcing rods to the stone, restorers overlooked the ancient design of sculptor Phidias and architects Ictinus and Callicrates. To eliminate rust-producing moisture, the original rods had been tightly wrapped in a sheath of pliable lead that had also permitted expansion in heat and contraction with cold. The new rods installed only eight decades ago have already rusted and caused cracks in the stones with temperature changes.

The present Committee for the Preservation of the Acropolis Monuments, with native-born architect Mangolis Korres, specialist in restoration, in charge, has nearly completed the seven-year project involving the nearby Erechtheum. Its caryatids, which for two millennia stood under roof carvings that acid rain has obliterated, have been replaced with copies. The original sculptures have been taken to the Acropolis Museum to be placed in a nitrogen-filled glass chamber where they can be preserved. The Erechtheum walls have been torn down and replaced with today's technology.

Restoration of the eight-times larger Parthenon has proven more difficult, since the 24,000-square-foot (2230-square-meter) structure is far more devastated. Thousands of the Parthenon's stones have toppled to the ground, presenting a source of danger to the remaining structure as well as to the hordes of visitors, who have therefore been denied access to the temple for decades. Yet, enough of the old marble stones, numbered and catalogued—some weighing as much as 12 tons (10.9 metric tons)—still remain to rebuild much of the Parthenon's inner chamber, or cella. Architect Korres argues against a rebuilding to mint condition. His summation makes it clear: "We are obliged to accept that the perfect lines and surfaces have been lost forever and that the monument has a new character—that of a ruin."

Approaching the east end, we may stop to admire the sculptured figures of the three goddesses on the **pediment [308]**, the triangular space between the frieze and the gable. The quarrel between Athena and the sea god Poseidon for the patronage of Athens occupies the west pediment. The figures in the middle of the pediment have enough space to stand erect, but as the roof slopes down, the tapering space dictates figures with crouched and extended poses. These pedimental sculptures, now in the British Museum, were designed by Phidias, who supervised all the architectural projects ordered by Pericles. We must remember, when we think of white marble statues and temples, that many were once brightly painted.

As we pass through the colonnade, we can see above us the low-**relief frieze** honoring Athena, surrounding the cella, which may depict the Panathenaic procession held every four years. We may look for fellow-citizens represented in the frieze, but the idealized faces have a dignity appropriate to the occasion that makes them difficult to recognize. Perhaps only priests can enter the sanctuary, but if we stand at the door of the cella, we may be able to glimpse the magnificent gold and ivory statue of Athena Parthenos by Phidias.

Now the gold and ivory figure is gone, as well as the pediment marbles. Of Athens' foremost temple, only the basic structure and its reliefs remain, and these are in precarious condition.

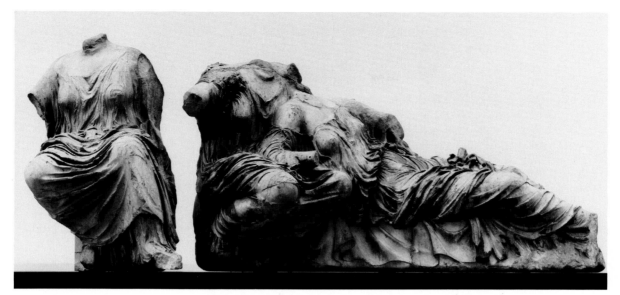

above: **308.** *Three Goddesses, from Parthenon east pediment. c. 438–432 B.C. Marble, over life-size. Reproduced by courtesy of the Trustees of the British Museum.*

below: **309.** *The Erechtheum, Acropolis, Athens; view from the west. c. 410 B.C. Height of caryatids 7'9" (2.36 m).*

The Erechtheum On the north side of the Acropolis is the Erechtheum, a temple built on the site of one of the most ancient shrines, sacred to Athena, the early Athenian king and snake god Erechtheus, and Poseidon. This multiple dedication explains the complicated and unusual plan of this early split-level temple. Its four levels are marked by three differently proportioned sets of Ionic columns and the **caryatids** (figures of women) that form the Porch of the Maidens **[309]**.

Sculpture of the Classical Period

Sculptors of the Classical period learned to distill the essence of beauty from the world around them, idealizing the body but retaining qualities that allow us to identify with the figures. While no particular individual is ever portrayed, enough humanity remains in the figures to express the Greek intent of serenity. Reflecting the ideal of moderation, the body is shown in a state of balance between energy and repose. Greek Classical figures demonstrate the features we still admire: balance, containment, moderation, universality, and idealism.

The bronze *Charioteer* from Delphi, cast about 470 B.C., stands stiffly like a kouros, but there is a lifelike quality in his head with its curly hair held by a headband and its inlaid stone eyes

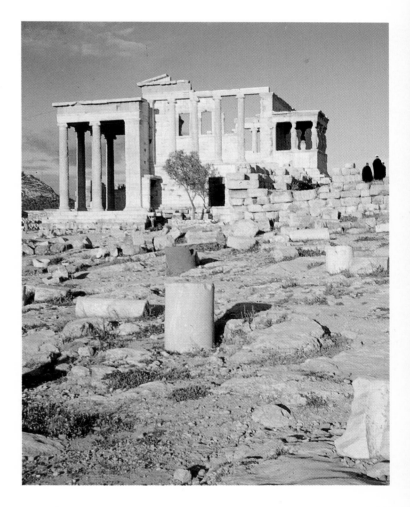

Phidias (c. 490–c. 430 B.C.)

A native-born Athenian sculptor, Phidias has had an abiding influence on Greek sculpture, past and present. Chief designer of the sculptures of the Parthenon and of colossal statues throughout the Greek world, his reputation was built as chief sculptor of Athens under Pericles. After training with Hegias of Athens and Argos, his first works were 13 figures at Delphi, commemorating the Greek victory at Marathon. To this early period is also ascribed the *Athena Promachus*, a bronze colossus set on the Acropolis and visible for miles. Evidence of this figure, of which only the pedestal remains, was discovered in 1845; the statue, dated 460–450 B.C., was probably more than 30 feet (9.14 meters) tall, the largest bronze ever made in Athens.

By 444 B.C. Phidias must have been in Athens and closely associated with Pericles, who, during the Greek Golden Age, transformed the city. Most of the great monuments of Athens, including the Parthenon, were erected in this twenty-eight-year interval. The 38-foot (11.5-meter) standing *Athena Parthenos*, finished in chryselephantine (gold and ivory), was consecrated in 438 B.C., paid for with money extracted from allies of Athens. The huge expense of these works brought both Phidias and Pericles into political and financial difficulties. Phidias was accused of sacrilege in that he represented himself and Pericles on the shield held by Athena. The practice of incorporating artist and patron in religious works was long established in traditions that have persisted to the present time, so the probability remains that the condemnation of Phidias was politically motivated.

The sculptures of the Parthenon—the metopes, frieze, and large pedimental figures—are associated with Phidias and are almost universally regarded as masterpieces of art [308]. In the words of Pliny, "[Phidias] opened up new possibilities in metalwork [and all art]."

---

[310]. Probably the statue was commissioned to celebrate the victory of King Polyzalos of Gela in religious games. Whether it was a portrait or an expression of a healthy mind and healthy body is not known, but we see the beginnings of the idealization and refined proportions that characterize art of the Classical period.

Myron's bronze *Discus Thrower* [311], cast about 460 B.C., now existing only in a Roman copy in marble, shows how far sculptors had moved from the stiff pose of the kouros. Myron successfully solved the sculptural problem of rendering movement in space by showing the athlete critically poised. We see him just as he bends down to swing his arm back to throw the discus with all his force. From whatever angle we regard the work, a rhythm develops that draws us into the sculpture and encourages us to examine it from all sides. Our eyes move from the discus to the arm, up to the head, down to the knee, and back to the heavy discus to begin the cycle again.

Hermes and the Infant Dionysus by Praxiteles is a work of the late Classical period, which prefigures Hellenistic trends. When we say that someone has the body of a Greek god, we are probably thinking of such a sculpture as *Hermes* [312], noted for the soft, sensuous appearance of the skin and the graceful pose, which contrasts so sharply with the stiff kouros of two hundred years earlier. Hermes, messenger of the gods, stands relaxed, his weight flowing from his torso to the reversed **(contrapposto)** direction of his hips in a gentle S-curve. On one arm he holds the infant god of wine, and his missing arm probably held a bunch of grapes toward which the baby is reaching.

Painting of the Classical Period

Unfortunately, the great wall paintings that adorned the temples and civic buildings of the Classical period have disappeared, and we know of them only through literature. But the creativity of Greek painters has been preserved for us in the refined and expressive decorations on pottery.

Greek pottery, famous throughout the ancient world because of its varied shapes and skillful paintings, was a major export item, contributing importantly to the Greek economy. Modern divers have found pieces of Greek pottery on sunken ships as far from Greece as southern France.

Potters and vase painters were highly regarded and often signed their works. Designing specific shapes for specific functions [206], painters imaginatively decorated pottery with

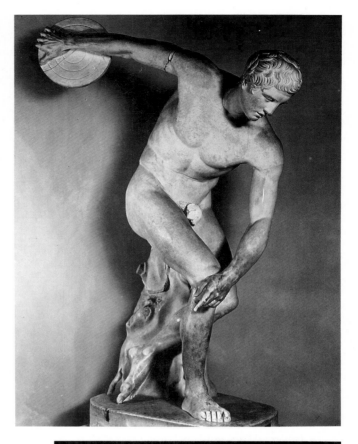

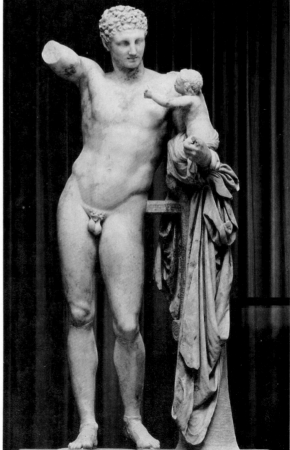

above: **310.** Charioteer, *from Sanctuary of Apollo, Delphi. c. 470 B.C. Bronze, height 6'11" (2.11 m). Archaeological Museum, Delphi.*

above right: **311.** *Myron.* Discobolus (Discus Thrower). *Roman copy after bronze original of c. 460 B.C. Marble, life-size. National Museum, Rome.*

below right: **312.** *Praxiteles.* Hermes with the Infant Dionysus. *c. 340 B.C. Marble, height 7'1" (2.16 m). Archaeological Museum, Olympia.*

myths of gods and heroes and activities of daily life. Just as sculpture evolved from the simple forms of the Archaic period to the graceful complexities of the Classical period, so vase painting developed in stages. Early pottery decoration was geometric **[47]**. In the Archaic period vases had lively black figures painted on red clay with details scratched through the black. In an amphora by the painter Exekias (late 6th century

B.C.) we see the heroes Ajax and Achilles sitting on stools intently bent over a game [313]. Note the fine proportions and new use of foreshortening in the shoulders. The design shows a strong sense of order, and the delicately incised lines of the hair and elaborate cloaks testify to the artist's skill.

Vases in the Classical period were in a freer, more sophisticated style in which red figures stand out from a black ground and details are applied with a brush.

Sculpture of the Hellenistic Period

In the late 4th century B.C., Alexander the Great, a Macedonian king, forged an empire that included Greece and the lands of the eastern Mediterranean. As a result of Alexander's enthusiasm for Greek civilization and the military, Greek influence dominated this region, and continued even after his death in 323 B.C. Then, his empire was broken into small states ruled by his generals, who competed with one another in commissioning extravagant art. The art of this period, which lasted until the Roman conquest, is called Hellenistic because Greece, which inspired it, was known as the land of the Hellenes.

Sculptors of the Hellenistic period became more interested in portraying detailed specific individuals than in creating serene idealized figures. The marble group of *Laocoön* and his sons in the agony of their death is typically Hellenistic in its exaggeration of emotion [314]. According to legend, the Trojan priest Laocoön was strangled by snakes sent by the gods because he revealed to the Trojans that the wooden horse given them by the Greeks was a trick designed to defeat Troy. The sons were grown men, but the sculptor made them smaller to indicate that they were sons.

Influenced by the 4th-century taste for sculpture of nude women was an *Aphrodite* from Melos, better known by its Italian name as the *Venus de Milo* [315]. She has captured the imagination of the public ever since she was discov-

below left: **313.** *Exekias.* Ajax and Achilles Playing Draughts, *black figure amphora. 550–525 B.C. Terracotta, height of amphora 24" (61 cm). Vatican Museums, Rome.*

below right: **314.** *Agesander, Athenodorus, and Polydorus of Rhodes.* Laocöon Group. *c. 150 B.C. Marble, height 8' (2.44 m). Vatican Museums, Rome.*

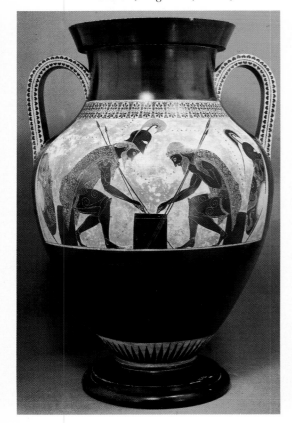
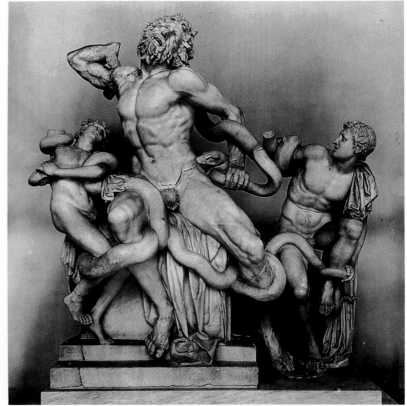

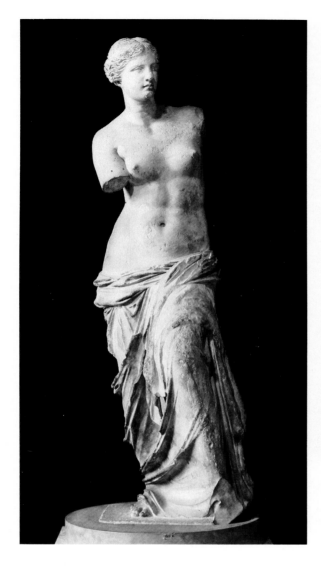

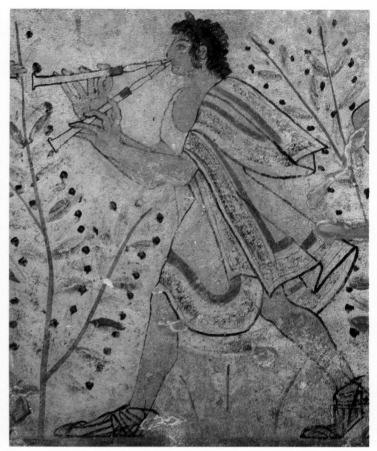

left: **315.** Aphrodite *from Melos. c. 150–100* B.C. *Marble, height 6'8" (2.03 m). Louvre, Paris.*

above: **316.** *Aulos player, detail of fresco from the Tomb of the Leopards, Etruscan, Tarquinia, Italy. c. 470* B.C.

ered in 1820. Some scholars say she was holding a shield in which she was gazing at her reflection. Her **wet drapery,** marble carved to resemble wet cloth, reveals as much as it conceals.

Rome

Originally an Italian city-state on the Tiber River, Rome eventually ruled the greatest empire of the ancient world. The expanding Roman culture first overwhelmed the Etruscans, who had developed a civilization in west central Italy north of the Tiber, in the 3rd century B.C. Rome next absorbed the Greek colonies that had been founded in southern Italy and Sicily in the 8th century B.C., and in 146 B.C. defeated the Greeks at Corinth in their own homeland.

Like the Greeks before them and the rest of us since, the Romans borrowed ideas from earlier peoples to incorporate into their civilization.

One source of ideas was the Etruscans, who had earlier absorbed elements of Greek, Mesopotamian, and perhaps ancient Italic culture. Many Roman concepts of religion and government began with the Etruscans. The Romans employed Etruscan artists and probably learned from them how to build arches, cast in bronze, and carve in stone. Roman art was also influenced by the vigorous clay portrait figures the Etruscans placed on the lids of their coffins and the lively frescoes of banquets and festivals which they painted on the walls of their tombs [316]. Etruscan figures are generally heavier than those of the Egyptians [86], Cretans [104], and Greeks who preceded them.

The strongest influence on the Romans was surely Greek civilization, first encountered in southern Italy and then later as Romans studied with Greek teachers. They also commissioned Greek artists to work for them in Italy and col-

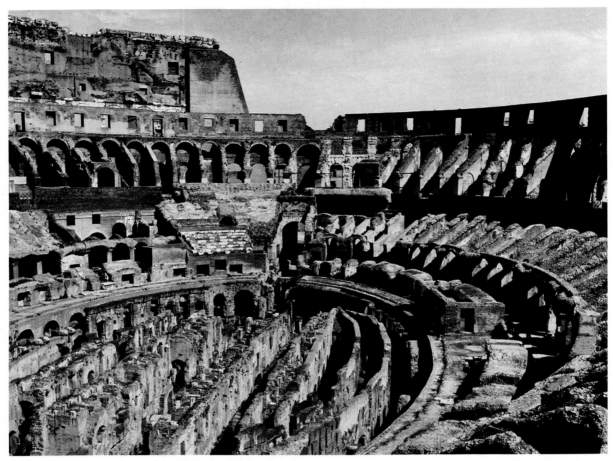

317. *The Colosseum, Rome. 72–80* A.D.

lected Greek works. The Roman town of Pompeii was filled with art objects in the Hellenistic style. Indeed, the art of Italy in the 3rd and 2nd centuries B.C. is called Greco-Roman.

The Romans, however, added their own genius in military affairs, government, and engineering to the arts of the Etruscans and Greeks. Roman law and Roman construction was spread over a wider area than that achieved by any prior civilization. Under the *Pax Romanum,* or Roman Peace, the Roman army maintained law and order and assured conquered peoples of security from other invaders. Roman governors wisely allowed subject peoples to continue to worship local gods as long as they recognized the supremacy of Roman gods. Roman builders, refining the arch and the vault, provided every city under Roman jurisdiction with roads, bridges, aqueducts, temples, basilicas, forums, and baths—amenities that helped unite the empire. Temples in North Africa, the Pont du Gard, which brought water to Nîmes, France **[253]**, and Roman ruins in northern Britain remain as examples of their imperial expansion.

Architecture

The Romans had a taste for large-scale building and lavish decoration. The Roman Colosseum, of concrete faced with stone **[317]**, was the largest structure for public assemblies built up to that time. It seated 50,000 spectators, who were protected by canvas awnings from the sun and rain as they watched the bloody battles between men and wild beasts. Like many other Roman buildings, the Colosseum combined columns of all three Greek orders.

Another large, richly decorated building is the Pantheon, the only temple of classical antiquity that has always remained a house of worship **[257]**. Originally designed to hold statues of the seven major planetary Roman gods under one roof, it is now a Christian church. The building, of brick and concrete, was once faced with marble. In its huge dome, the largest of antiquity, with a diameter of nearly 140 feet (42.67 meters), we see the Romans' great skill in engineering. The walls of the building are 20 feet (6.9 meters) thick in some places to support the heavy weight of the dome, symbolically representing the heavens, which had an open central *oculus,* or eye, to admit light. As the sun moved across the sky, it spotlighted in turn every niche holding a statue of a god.

Also large and ornate were the public baths, which included spacious halls and gardens as well as cold and hot rooms, dressing rooms, gymnasiums, open-air swimming pools, and libraries. The baths were heated by furnaces. Lead pipes, which carried the hot water, can still be seen in the ruins. The vast, cross-vaulted Baths of Caracalla in Rome, resplendent in marble, murals, and carving, are an outstanding example.

Adopting the **basilicas** of the Hellenistic Greeks, the Romans built long, colonnaded halls throughout the empire as law courts and places of assembly. Most of them had a high central nave flanked by lower aisles. They were entered from the long sides. At one or both ends was a raised semicircular area, or **apse,** where the judges sat behind an altar for the sacrifices that preceded judicial deliberations. Although many had wooden gabled roofs, the Basilica of Constantine [318] was vaulted. Even larger than the Pantheon, it rose 114 feet (34.74 meters) and glowed inside with rich marble facing. This basilican plan was used for Christian churches, as we shall see in Chapter 12.

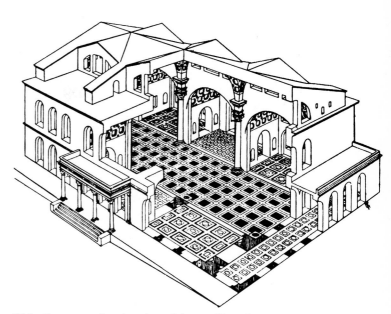

318. *Reconstruction drawing of the Basilica of Constantine (after Huelsen), Rome. c. 310–320* A.D.

Typically Roman was the ornate triumphal arch, built by successful generals to celebrate their victories, and constructed in areas conquered by Rome to symbolize Roman glory. The triple Arch of Constantine [319] was an important gateway to Rome when the city was still

319. *Arch of Constantine, Rome. 312* A.D. *Height 67'7" (20.6 m), width 82' (25 m).*

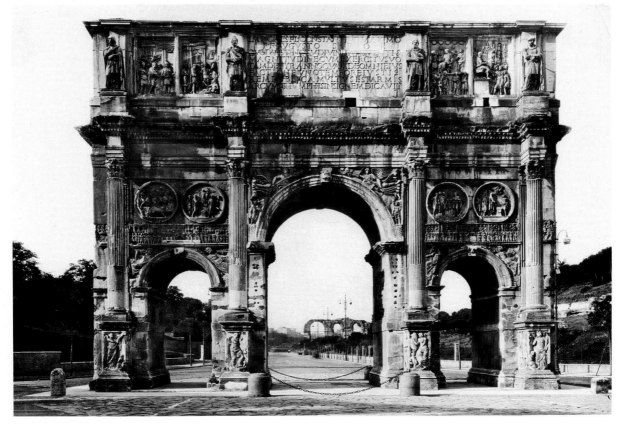

walled for protection. Much later, Roman arches were copied in Paris, London, Berlin, and even in Washington Square in New York.

Roman emperors, senators, and other rich citizens lived in luxurious palaces and country villas with elaborate fountains and gardens. Well-to-do city dwellers had pleasant town houses built with post-and-lintel construction around a formal court with a pool for rainwater. Many included a colonnaded rear court with a fountain and garden. The House of the Vettii in Pompeii, buried in the volcanic lava and ash that erupted from Mount Vesuvius and now restored, shows how elegant such homes could be [320]. Urban citizens often climbed several stories to their rooms in a large apartment house, as noted in Chapter 9.

Murals

Larger villas and houses were decorated with colorful wall paintings, many of which still can be seen in Pompeii. These murals give us some idea of what ancient Greek painting must have been like, for most of them were done by Greek artists. Landscapes, intimate scenes, ceremonies such as weddings, mythological figures, and still life were favored subjects, sometimes set in panels of flat color. Painted with lively brush strokes and often a sense of architectural perspective, **illusionistic** murals gave the effect of a view beyond a window.

Mosaics, made of small pieces of marble set in mortar, were also popular for wall and floor decoration, depicting battle and hunting scenes alive with exotic animals and birds from as far away as Egypt. One example shows the Nile with crocodiles, lotus buds, and a hippopotamus.

Sculpted and Painted Portraits

Perhaps the most typical Roman contribution to art was portraiture. In contrast to the Greek idealization of the face, Roman portraits were **veristic,** duplicating real people with warts, wrinkles, and other disfigurements. Realistic

320. *House of the Vetti, Pompeii. 63–79* A.D.

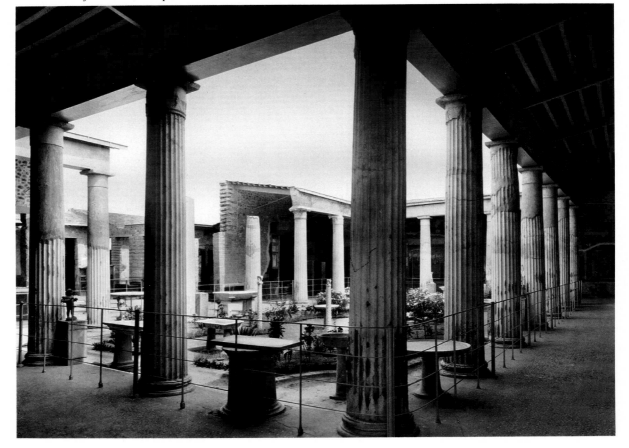

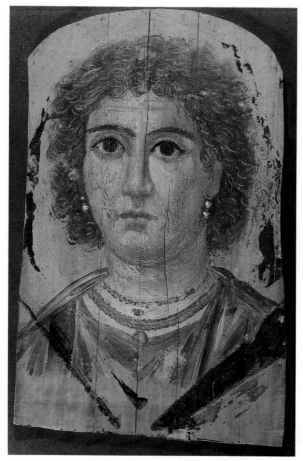

321. *Mummy portrait of an elderly woman, from the Faiyum, Egypt, 1st–2d century A.D. Encaustic on panel, 14⅞ × 9" (38 × 23 cm). State Collection of Egyptian Art, Munich.*

marble busts of stern-looking Roman generals and rulers were placed in local forums to represent Roman authority to the conquered peoples. These, along with faces depicted on Roman coins, spread the imperial image throughout the Roman world. Perhaps this ancient form of mass media contributed to the success of Roman government.

The same Roman taste for realistic portraiture appeared in a group of funerary paintings of Romans who had settled in the Faiyum district in Egypt. When they died, their bodies were wrapped in linen and a colorful portrait of the deceased was inserted over the face, according to Egyptian custom [**321**]. Painted on wood panels in **encaustic,** an exceptionally durable mixture of pigments and hot wax, these informal individualized portraits are so full of life that they seem to have been painted while the sub-

jects were still alive. Such vitality in portraiture was not to be seen again for a thousand years.

Pre-Columbian Americas

In prehistoric times, most scholars believe, waves of adventurous Asians crossed the land mass from Siberia that has since been covered by waters known as the Bering Straits. These nomads gradually filtered from the area of modern Alaska down through the Western corridor along the coast into modern-day Mexico, Central America, and, finally, South America. They left scattered distinctive Indian cultures; in North America these were clear-cut more or less independent units, shaped by local geographic conditions.

Middle America was the intellectual and artistic cradle of complex Indian civilization in the American hemisphere, much as the Nile Valley was for Africa, the Aegean Islands for Europe, and the Yellow River for eastern Asia. Hundreds of miles to the south, the Central Andes of Peru and Bolivia served as focus for high civilization in South America. Nevertheless, Middle American Indian achievements in astronomy and the calendar, mathematics, metallurgy, hieroglyphic writing, and the corbelled Mayan arch, along with architecture, mural painting, and sculpture, were unsurpassed in the New World. There must have been many contacts and mutual influences throughout because North, Middle, and South American Indians share important features such as maize, cotton, and tobacco, irrigation systems, weaponry, metal work, feather work, basketry, and textiles. As in early China, the various nations seem to have contended with both pressures from the nomadic barbarians at their northern frontiers and with periods of warfare with each other.

While the southern half of Central America, from Nicaragua through Panama, is closest to South Amerian cultural traditions, the scholarly term **Mesoamerica** culturally differentiates the area below the contemporary northern boundary of Mexico, and includes Guatemala, El Salvador, and Honduras. These regions of Mexico, Central America, and South America were occupied in prehistoric times by peoples whose societies were heavily weighted with ceremonial rituals and worship of the plumed serpent divinity Quetzalcoatl, noted earlier, societies marked by the development of impressive stone religious architecture [**40**], and an elaboration of the arts and crafts. The influence of Middle America, a somewhat broader term that includes the islands east of Central America, spread far and wide—north to the Mississippi Valley and southwestern United States, to the Antilles, and into Central and South America, even briefly through Ecuador and possibly Peru. So advanced was intercommunication between these peoples that, according to Indian accounts, within a few hours of Columbus' arrival in the New World, on the island called San Salvador, Montezuma, the Indian king of Mexico, had been notified.

Middle America

Traces of primitive hunters on a preagricultural, preceramic level in Mexico identify the Tepexpan man. Somewhat later, fine ceramics appeared that included fertility figures from Tlatilco that date from 1000 to 600 B.C. in the Valley of Mexico with eye details that seem Oriental [202]. These figurines were buried under a thick cover of lava, fortuitously, perhaps, like the many artifacts preserved when Mount Vesuvius blanketed the city of Pompeii in Italy. In fact the site called El Pedregal is close to the land made habitable once again by Luis Barragán near Mexico City [273].

Peoples of Mesoamerica included the Olmec civilization in eastern Mexico between 1000 and 600 B.C., the Toltec in the north, the Maya in the southeast, the Zapotec and Mixtec in the southwest, and the people of Teotihuacán and the Aztec, the last best known because of their dramatic conquest by Spain, in the central Valley of Mexico. All their economies were based on growing maize. Since there are extremes of climate throughout the region, the Indians probably felt overwhelmed by the forces of nature, personified as gods, on which their crops depended. Their efforts to appease the gods directed their social, political, and artistic life.

South America

In the Andean region of South America other Indian peoples were raising maize and building ceremonial centers with pyramid temples before 800 B.C. Somewhat later, pottery, weaving, and goldwork reached a highly sophisticated level. The Paracas and Nazca peoples and their descendants on the south Peruvian coast wove and embroidered magnificent garments with colorful stylized patterns of animals and divinities.

Exercises and Activities

Research Exercises

1. Discuss the Greek architectural principles of unity and proportion that are demonstrated in the design and decoration of the Parthenon.
2. List and define the different parts of a Greek order. How do the three orders differ?
3. Explain the concept of ideal beauty in relation to Greek art, naming specific works. In what way is that ideal expressed in the sculpture and architecture of the Golden Age of Greece? How did the sculpture of the Hellenistic period differ from that of the Golden Age?
4. What features did Greek and Roman art have in common? What elements from other civilizations did the Romans incorporate into their art? What are some of the Roman engineering innovations?
5. Explain the origins of the arch, its construction, and how it was used in Rome.

Studio Activities

1. Draw a diagram to show construction of the arch.
2. Create in clay, wax, or soap a sculptural work of art inspired by Greek or Roman art.
3. Shape a piece of pottery or clay in the form of a Greek cup (kylix) or a jar (amphora).
4. Carve from soap a sculpture of a head reminiscent of Roman portraits.
5. Form a fertility figure of clay close to the Tlatilco figurines.

12
Faith:
The Middle Ages

Between the city in which it is promised that we shall reign and the earthly city there is a wide gulf—as wide as the distance between heaven and earth. Yet . . . there is a faint shadowy resemblance between the Roman empire and the heavenly city.

St. Augustine, *City of God*

To adore images is one thing; to teach with their help what should be adored is another . . . what scripture is to the educated, images are to the ignorant. . . .

Pope Gregory I

In the broad sense anyone is a pilgrim who is outside his fatherland . . .

Dante Alighieri, *La Vita Nuova*

As the light of "Eternal Rome" flickered low in the 4th century A.D., in its place throughout the Mediterranean world altar lights glowed softly as the new Christian faith attracted converts. The power of Rome was fading, but images of classical times lingered on through Early Christian religious art, and were later perpetuated in Carolingian, Romanesque, and Gothic art during the period we call the Middle Ages.

Early Christian Art

For the first three centuries after the birth of Christ the Early Christians worshiped in private homes or, during times of persecution, in the **catacombs,** underground tunnels in and near Rome that honeycombed the soft volcanic rock and were used by both Christians and pagans as cemeteries.

Christian fortunes changed markedly in the 4th century. The Roman emperor Constantine, who became a Christian in A.D. 303, recognized Christianity as one of the official religions of the empire in 313. In 330, to strengthen the empire,

threatened by barbarians from the north and east, he moved the capital from Rome to Constantinople (Byzantium, or modern Istanbul) in the East. Christians, as inhabitants of the far-flung Roman empire, were already diverse in origin, language, and point of view. Some were Romans, living in the West. Some were Gauls and Goths in the North. Some were Jewish converts, Syrians, and other Eastern peoples. The shift of the capital, which resulted in a division of the empire into a Latin-speaking West and Greek-speaking East, intensified their differences. Early Christian art reflects this history.

Symbolism in Sculpture and Murals

The linguistic diversity of the Early Christians encouraged them to express their common faith through visual symbols whose meaning was clear to all Christians. Symbols also had the advantage of hiding a religious message so that the Romans would be less likely to persecute believers. For example, the Romans might not recognize the cross as a symbol of the crucifixion of

THE VISUAL ARTS		HISTORICAL NOTES
		c. 105 Chinese invent paper
c. 225 *Good Shepherd* fresco [322]		
c. 200–700 Temple of Quetzalcoatl, Mexico [40]	300	
		306 Constantine crowned emperor
		330 Constantinople capital of Roman Empire
c. 333 Old Basilica of St. Peter [325]		
c. 300–350 *Good Shepherd* sculpture [323]		
		410 Visigoths sack Rome
c. 450 *Good Shepherd* mosaic [324]		
		455 Vandals sack Rome
		476 Ostrogoths sack Rome
	500	
526–547 San Vitale [326]		
532–537 Hagia Sophia [258]		
607–637 Horyuji Temple, Nara, Japan [261]		
c. 698 Lindisfarne Gospels [96]		
		c. 700–800 Printing begins in China
		c. 700 Arabs market Oriental spices (cinnamon, cloves, pepper)
		c. 710 Tea becomes popular in Orient
c. 795 Chapel of Charlemagne [333]		
	800	800 Charlemagne crowned emperor
		962 Otto I crowned emperor
	1000	
		1066 Norman conquest of England
1073–83 Bayeux Tapestry [230]		
		1095 First Crusade
1120–32 Vézelay church [335]		
1144 St.-Denis church [60]		
1163–1250 Notre Dame de Paris [338]		
c. 1250–1500 Codex Vaticanus B (Mixtec Calendar) [186]	1200	c. 1200 Paper produced in Europe
		1275–92 Marco Polo travels to Orient
		1290 Spectacles (eyeglasses) invented
		1300–1400 Italian city-state conflicts
c. 1325–50 Traini frescoes [339]		1348 Bubonic plague (Black Death)
1354–91 Alhambra, Spain [329]		1385 Chaucer, *The Canterbury Tales*
	1400	
c. 1475 Coatlicue [39]		
c. 1500 Machu Picchu, Peru [452]		

Christ if it were combined with the Greek letters *chi* and *rho*, the first two letters of the word *Christ*. They would not know that the fish stood for Christ and the sacrament of baptism. The early images of Christ that appeared within two hundred years were also developed as symbolic representations.

Early Christian art used classical images with new religious meaning. No pagan could object to paintings or sculpture of the Good Shepherd, for this was a popular subject in classical art; but in Christian art the shepherd surrounded by his flock symbolized Christ with his disciples or other devout followers. Posed like earlier Greek figures, Christ is beardless and wears a Roman tunic. In a fresco of *The Good Shepherd* from one of the catacombs, Christ is seen as a clean-shaven Roman youth [322]. The circle that surrounds the figure signifies eternity. Christ as a Good Shepherd also appears in sculpture [323] and mosaic [324].

Just as pagan festivals were reconstituted as Christian holy days, so Early Christian frescoes painted on the walls and ceilings of the catacombs used images of grapes, animals, birds, and fish, borrowed from classical art, to convey new Christian significance. For example, grapes, a pagan symbol of the cult of Bacchus, the Roman god of wine, now represented wine as the sacramental blood of Christ. The peacock,

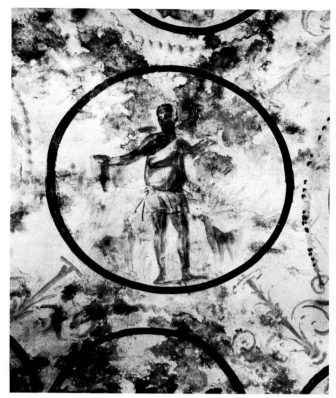

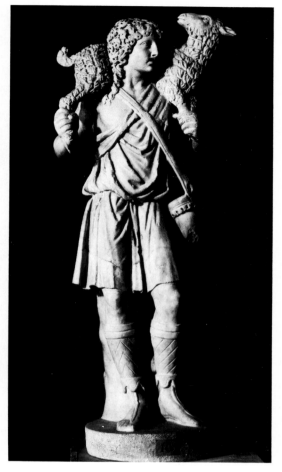

above: **322.** The Good Shepherd. *Early 3d century* A.D. *Fresco. Catacomb of Domitilla, Rome.*

right: **323.** The Good Shepherd. *c. 350. Marble, height 39" (99 cm). Vatican Museums, Rome.*

originally meaning wisdom, became a symbol of eternal life because its flesh was believed to be incorruptible.

Frescoes and mosaics on the walls and ceilings of tombs and, later, churches were created to tell the story of Christ's life, death, and resurrection, serving as a pictorial narrative for the illiterate. Artists became progressively less concerned with realistic representations of human forms and more concerned with expressions of religious truths. As a result, images became simplified and spiritualized. Christ appeared as a middle-

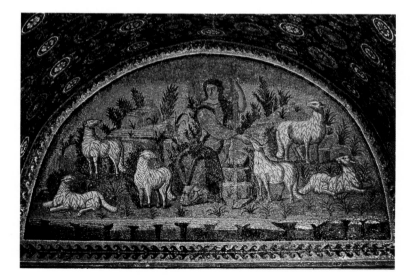

324. The Good Shepherd, *from the Mausoleum of Galla Placidia, Ravenna. 5th century. Mosaic.*

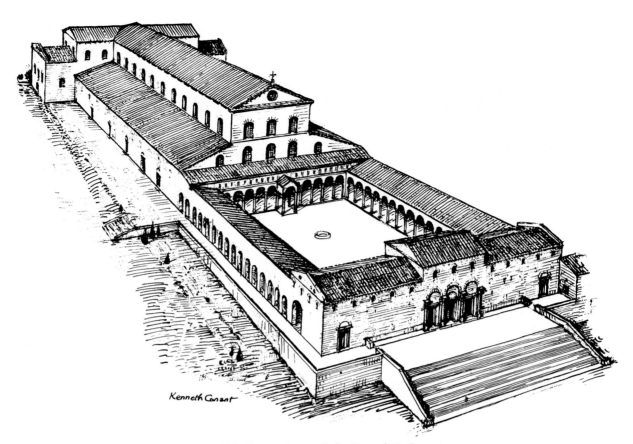

325. *Old St. Peter's Basilica, Rome. c. 333. Restoration study by Kenneth J. Conant.*

aged man and acquired a long Middle Eastern robe and beard and a **halo,** a gold circle around his head signifying his holiness.

So he has been depicted ever since. This abstract style and the use of the halo were especially effective in mosaic, a process involving small pieces of glass set into cement and carefully placed to reflect the light that filtered through the small windows and flickered from the altar candles. The walls seemed to lose their solidity in an almost supernatural glow, well suited to express the spiritual messages of early Christianity. The shimmering gold and colored-glass pictures suggested heaven, and as the congregation entered the mysteriously lit interior of early houses of worship, they must have felt as if they were already transported there.

Architecture

As the Christians increased in numbers, the catacombs were abandoned and new places for worship had to be provided. These could not be modeled on pagan temples, for the ritual of the Christian Church differed fundamentally from that of ancient religions. The cella of a pagan temple was reserved for the gods and their priests. The faithful, who processed around the outside of the temple, could only glimpse the sanctuary through the doors. The sacrificial altar was placed outside where they could see it, and the exterior of the building was decorated with sculpture. In contrast, Christian ceremonies took place indoors and the congregation participated. Space was needed to allow people to participate in the mass and later to move toward the altar to receive communion.

Since Roman basilicas [318] and lavish villas were large secular buildings not associated with pagan religion, their layouts (floor plans) were adapted for the new places of Christian worship. Just as various rooms in a Roman home satisfied different functions, the spaces of the church did also. The apse, placed at the eastern end, was retained for the altar and clergy, and the main entrance was moved to the west end. This arrangement gave a powerful linear orientation, focusing attention on the altar. Sometimes the builders used columns taken from older pagan structures.

The restoration study of Old St Peter's Basilica in Rome, an important Early Christian basilica, shows us how the needs of Christian worship were met [325]. The faithful first entered through a gateway into a walled courtyard, like the atrium, with a pool used for baptism, before entering the church, an oblong hall divided by columns into a high nave and four side aisles for the sharing of the scriptures. The low aisles increased the floor space while allowing light to come through the windows of the **clerestory,** the upper part of the walls of the **nave,** which could be seen from the exterior. At the east end was a **crossing** (transept), or horizontal space, that intersected the nave and beyond it the **apse** with an altar for the Eucharist (breaking of the bread).

Christ had preached that riches on earth were less important than salvation. The churches symbolized this belief with plain exteriors and interiors lavishly decorated with richly colored mosaics or paintings representing the spiritual riches of the kingdom of heaven [326]. Such interiors were suitable settings for ornate and gem-studded altar furnishings—chalices, screens, candle holders, and **reliquaries,** containers that held the relics of martyrs. Many Early Christian churches were constructed over crypts or relics of martyrs because such areas were believed by the faithful to be sacred, and some churches offered a **narthex,** or gateway into the new spiritual city.

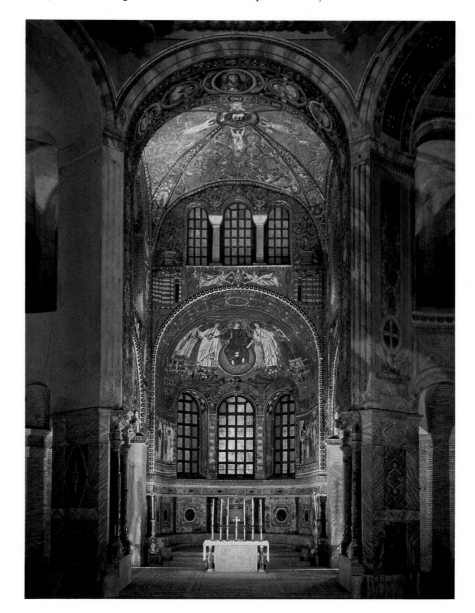

326. *Choir and sanctuary, San Vitale, Ravenna, Italy. c. 530–548.*

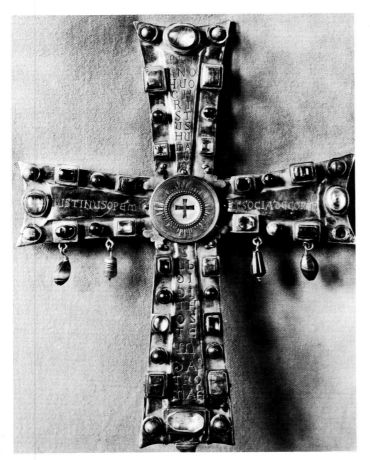

327. *Cross of Justinian. 527–565 A.D. Vatican Museums, Rome.*

Byzantine Art

Before the 6th century, Early Christian art was a blend of its Western Roman and Eastern Byzantine roots. As the Western Empire weakened, the leadership tended to shift more and more to the East. During the reign of Justinian (527–565), the center was firmly established far to the East in Constantinople. There the emperor launched a building program destined to enrich the Eastern Orthodox Empire.

Architects in the East had been using domes, symbols of heaven, to roof square or cross-shaped churches for many years. In 532 Justinian commissioned the church of Hagia Sophia, or Holy Wisdom, which had a great central dome that seemed to float over the interior space [258]. The Byzantine historian Procopius, who saw it being built, said it hung "as if suspended by a golden chain from heaven." The weight of the dome, carried by four piers at the corners of the square space below it, rested on **pendentives [256]**, a brilliant structural innova-

tion, described as spherical triangles, or sections of domes. The ribbon of small arched windows around the base of the dome let in a stream of light that must have been dazzling as it played over the original gold and colored mosaics.

Domes and mosaic decoration were characteristic of Byzantine architecture, as may be seen in San Vitale, a church built by Justinian in Ravenna [326], a Byzantine focus of culture in Italy. Octagonal in shape with a central dome, its interior was covered with marble and rich mosaics that echo the imagery of the catacomb paintings while heralding the new Byzantine style. The tall, thin, large-eyed figures, high above the heads of the congregation, added to the sense of awe and mystery that would have been felt by the worshippers. The Byzantine love of rich decoration may also be seen in the cross of Justinian, a jeweled reliquary believed to contain a fragment of the true cross, on which Christ suffered and died [327].

The Islamic World

Almost one-fourth of the world, including the vast area of North Africa and the Middle East, is dominated by Islam, the religion founded by the prophet Mohammed in Arabia in the early 7th century A.D. In its first forty years the new faith spread through the Mediterranean world, drawing more converts than Christianity had won in the previous three centuries. Devout Muslim warriors occupied Spain in the 8th century and in the 16th and 17th centuries controlled northern India. Medieval Christian Crusaders, who drove the Muslims from Spain and fought them in the Holy Land, learned much from their highly civilized adversaries. From Arabic numerals, scholarship, and arabesque ornament to the manufacture of paper, Islamic art, learning, and craftsmanship profoundly affected the European Middle Ages. How can we account for the phenomenal Islamic conquests? Beyond their immediate triumphs by the sword, the new faith must have satisfied the needs of millions of Muslim converts more fully than any of the surrounding older religions.

Architecture

Throughout the Islamic world the Muslims built **mosques** as houses of worship. A mosque usually consisted of a courtyard and fountain for ritual washing and a spacious columned or vaulted hall where men knelt on rugs in prayer.

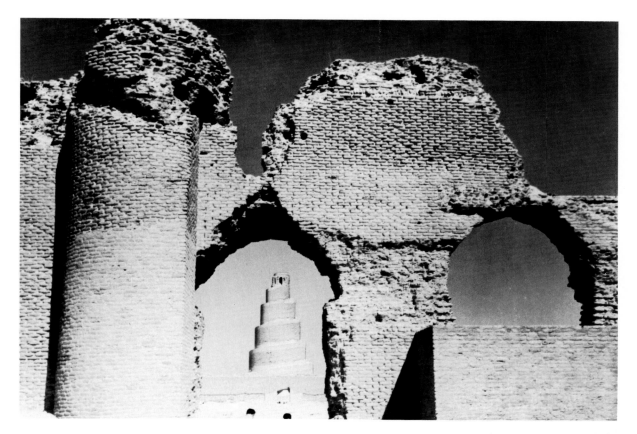

above: **328.** *Mosque of Mutawakkil, Samarra, Iraq.*
848–852 A.D.

right: **329.** *Court of the Lions, Alhambra, Granada,*
Spain. 1309–1354. 115 × 66′ (35.05 × 20.12 m).

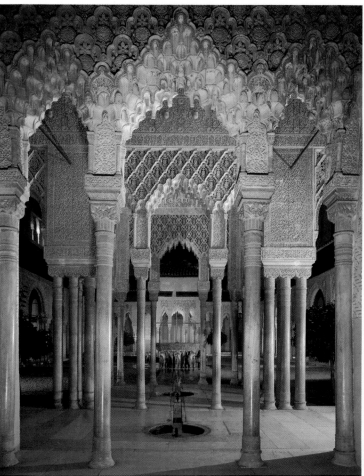

Most mosques had **minarets,** or towers, from
which the faithful were called to prayer five
times a day. In the great 9th-century mosque
built by the caliph Mutawakkil in Samarra (in
modern Iraq), the largest ever built, you may
recognize the influence of the ancient Mesopotamian ziggurat **[294]** in the minaret, which is
encircled by a steep ramp **[328]**.

The Muslims also built religious schools, palaces, and tombs. One of the most magnificent
palaces is the 14th-century Alhambra, or red
castle, in the **Moorish** (North African and Spanish) city of Granada in southern Spain. Its lion
court **[329]**, enlivened by a fountain, is surrounded by brilliantly tiled walls and an arcade
of slender columns supporting high arches in a
lacelike wall. The interior walls are enhanced by
an endless-appearing variety of perforated **arabesque** detail, yet disciplined by the rhythmic
design that courses through it all. The Alhambra set a style copied throughout the Islamic
world.

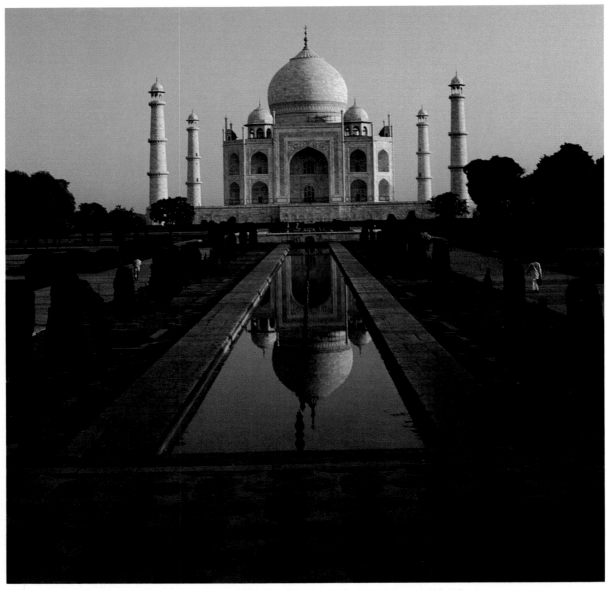

330. *Taj Mahal, Agra, India. 17th century. 186′ (56.69) square, height of dome 187′ (57 m).*

Probably the best-known Islamic structure is the Taj Mahal in Agra, India, built in the 17th century by the Mughal emperor Shah Jahan as a loving memorial to his favorite wife [330]. The onion-domed, white marble tomb, standing on a square platform with slender minarets at each corner, seems to float above its reflecting pool.

Other Art Forms

Since orthodox Muslim tradition forbade representation of the human figure in religious art, there is little Islamic sculpture. Most figure painting consists of delicate miniature illustrated secular books by Persian court artists. The Mus-

lims excelled, however, in nonrepresentational decoration, which appeared on mosques and other buildings, in copies of the Koran, and in glazed pottery and tile, metalwork, glass, and rugs. Some motifs were geometric; others were flowing abstractions of flowers and plants—arabesques. Much favored were inscriptions in Arabic from the Koran [16].

China and Japan

Because Chinese civilization greatly influenced that of Japan, we will review Chinese and Japanese art side by side. In both countries, society was structured into rigid classes. Daily life was ruled by the extended family, respect for the ancestors, and custom. With this conservatism, art styles remained much the same for long periods of time.

Architecture

Traditional buildings of the Far East used post-and-lintel construction and were made of wood. Conservative architecture changed little over the centuries. Chinese temples, palaces, and houses, as we know from clay models found in tombs of about 200 B.C. and from later paintings, consisted of a complex of low buildings built around a series of courts. Each building stood on a masonry platform. Columns topped by brackets, all carved and painted, supported the tiled roof. The sliding curtain walls of the Japanese could be adjusted according to climate. Multistoried pagodas were derived from a combination of elements from the Indian stupa and the Chinese watch tower. The spires on both the stupas and the pagodas were symbols of aspects of the Buddha.

Japan accepted Chinese architecture along with Buddhism, imported from China via Korea in the 6th century. Japanese temple complexes such as the Horyuji in Nara include pillared halls, a pagoda [261], and wooden gates. Japanese craftsman developed wooden architecture to its finest expression. The house or palace with its sliding paper screens for walls, opening onto a deep porch and garden, permitted great flexibility in interior design and the integration of indoor and outdoor space. Through the work of Frank Lloyd Wright, who built the Imperial Hotel in Tokyo in the 1920s, concepts of Japanese domestic architecture influenced the modern glass and steel architecture of the West, as in Mies's German Pavilion [242] and Philip Johnson's glass house [243].

Sculpture

Early Chinese and Japanese sculpture was generally religious, with many examples related to tombs. The Chinese carved reliefs on tomb walls and later in the 7th and 8th centuries filled tombs with lifelike glazed pottery figurines of courtiers, horses, and camels. Early Chinese tombs were guarded by large hollow clay figures of people and animals buried in the ground [287].

Buddhism and its accompanying Indian mythology was a major influence, as we saw in Chapter 10. From the 5th to the 8th centuries the Chinese carved Buddha figures in the walls of caves, some of them 70 feet (21 meters) tall. Their austere attitudes emphasized the otherworldly qualities of the Buddha. Sculptors made smaller, more graceful images in gilded bronze or wood for temple altars. Some were of **Boddhisattvas** (Buddhas-to-be), also known as deities who represented enlightenment. A Boddhisattva figure represents one who is capable of Buddhahood but who renounces it, dedicated to acts of salvation, offering again and again to be sacrificed in some way in order to save humanity. Though Boddhisattvas are usually male, one was Guanyin, the Chinese goddess of mercy, known for her gentleness and compassion [331]. The Japanese made Buddhas of wood and bronze as well as realistic wooden portraits of guardian spirits and priests.

331. *Seated* Shui-Yüeh *(Water-Moon). Guanyin. Late Yüan or early Ming. 14th century. Gilt bronze; height 13″ (33 cm), width 8″ (20 cm). Asian Art Museum of San Francisco (Avery Brundage Collection).*

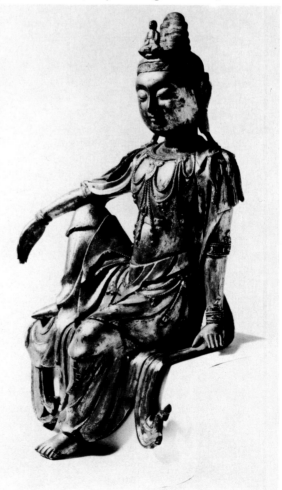

Painting

The Chinese and Japanese considered painting and calligraphy the most important forms of artistic expression. Both arts demanded great skill with the brush, requiring years of training. In calligraphy the quality of the brush strokes and the formation of the characters became as important as the story or poem they conveyed [167]. Most Chinese painters were also poets.

Except for early murals in caves and other temples, most Oriental paintings were on vertical or horizontal scrolls. The latter, held in the hands and unrolled a little at a time, allowed the viewer to "travel" through the painting, moving from scene to scene. Some Oriental paintings depicted the natural world, often, in Japan, verging on caricature. Others under the severe influence of Buddhism and Chinese Confucianism and Daoism, were more philosophical. They were less concerned with details of outward reality than with the essence of an object or a scene in order to arouse a response in the viewer.

Chinese scroll painting, which began in the 4th century, included elegant scenes of court life, realistic horses, and the first landscapes. In the Sung dynasty in the 12th and 13th centuries many gentlemen retired to the country where they painted soft poetic landscapes inspired by the Daoist search for unity in nature. In their ink and watercolor scrolls tiny human figures seem overwhelmed by the grandeur of mountains, forests, and seas. Sung painters worked in gray ink washes and a few spontaneous, brisk brush strokes, reflecting the Chan ideal of flashes of sudden enlightenment after meditation. The oneness of the universe was also a theme of Chan (better known as Japanese Zen) Buddhism. "The branch drooping in the fog, the butterfly on a blossom, the beggar in the filth of the courtyard—they are all Buddha," said the painter Xia Gui (c. 1195–1224).

Japanese painting shows strong Chinese Buddhist influence but is infused with a native vitality and decorative quality all its own. Scrolls of the 9th and 12th centuries, inspired by Chinese art, depict Amida, the Buddha of the Western Paradise, in a delightful but quite worldly paradise surrounded by lovely Boddhisattvas playing musical instruments and dancing. Other scrolls portray terrifying Buddhist guardian deities. Later scrolls present colorful scenes narrating tales from Japanese history or literature or social satires. In the 14th to 16th centuries, Japanese Zen Buddhist painters, influenced by Chinese Chan art, used a few quickly splashed lines and washes of ink to express their responses to the natural world and their experiences with Zen. Oriental landscapes [101] richly deserve the high place they are accorded in world art; they are noted for their strong brush work, brilliantly sparse imagery, and consummate artistry in handling ink on paper.

Woodcuts

Papermaking began in China in the 2nd century; it did not begin to spread throughout Europe until the 12th century. The art of printing from wood blocks developed in China in the 6th century, permitting inexpensive images of the Buddha to be mass-printed for popular distribution. By the 8th century, Japan had absorbed the technique somewhat, transforming printmaking into an expression of its own culture. The influence of Chinese civilization so strongly affected Japan that the graphic and other arts of China and Japan can be best understood when considered together. In both countries the scholarly elite, who (in China, primarily) had demonstrated their ability in arduous examinations, were the transmitters of culture and were often artists in their own right, whether painters, poets, or musicians. The liberal arts of calligraphy, painting, and music, practiced for personal enjoyment, were generally exalted above sculpture and architecture. Artists frequently copied past works in homage to their forebears, and women, it seems, were often as highly regarded for their artistic skills as men—as demonstrated by the scroll of Lady Kodai [167].

Decorative Arts

Traditions that had evolved from Neolithic eras in China persisted for almost five thousand years. The arts of metalwork, ceramics, and jade carving, developed for ritual use, flowered in the Orient. Chinese bronze ritual vessels are alive with stylized animal forms. The background and figures are often decorated with **lei-wen,** spiral designs signifying the clouds, thunder, and water necessary to an agricultural people.

Ceramics was refined into a high art in both China and Japan. From earliest times, clay pottery in China was associated with religion. The bowl or jar, made from "divine earth" and hardened by "divine fire," itself became a religious expression. From a Neolithic earthenware pot decorated with spirals to subtle monochrome Ding [207] celadon platters to elegant blue-flowered white porcelain vases of the Ming period in the 14th century, Chinese ceramics have shown extraordinary sensitivity to shape, color, glaze, and decoration. Japanese potters adapted Chinese techniques and designs.

Art of the New World

North America

Eskimos in the North lived by hunting and fishing, moving from one area to another with the seasons and the migrations of game. Life was hard, yet artists found time to carve utensils and imaginative masks from driftwood and small figures and harpoon heads from ivory, bone, and stone.

Indians along the Pacific Northwest Coast lived in settled villages. Abundant supplies of fish, wild plants, and berries allowed them some leisure to build large wooden plank houses and carve boats, masks, and furnishings. Each family or clan had a set of songs and myths and a heraldic crest, or **totem,** which was displayed on its possessions [197].

Dugout canoes, so important to a fishing and whaling economy, were shaped with stone tools and sometimes decorated with carved figures of protective spirits. The complex multiple masks of the Northwest Coast are among the most arresting in the world. Often they illustrated myths enacted by the dancers who wore them. Some were sophisticated masks within masks. During a dance, the wearer could expose several images, one after the other, by pulling the strings that operated the hinges. Other masks had moving parts that made noises. Most of these carved and painted masks were designed to be seen in ritual by the light of a flickering fire to heighten their effectiveness [196].

The Northwest Coast Indians also carved utensils such as the oversize ladle [224] used in a community potlatch ceremony. These unique gatherings were ritual occasions for feasting, poetry, and dancing at which a person of rank gained prestige by giving food, drink, blankets, tools, and utensils, sometimes to an entire invited village. While the custom inspired much art, it also ruined village economies.

Indians in the West, relying mainly on hunting and gathering, wove delicate baskets in intricate patterns that, like geometricized textiles, reflected the weaving process [225]. The Navajos in the Southwest, who herded sheep brought by the Spanish, wove distinctive blankets.

Indians in the Southwest settled in communities called pueblos and irrigated fields of maize.

The pueblos, as we saw in Chapter 9, were cliff dwellings [262] or free-standing adobe buildings built on mesas or near riverside fields. Each one had a **kiva,** or underground sacred room, symbolizing the underworld, where the Indians believed their ancestors originated and they themselves would return. Part of the kiva ritual included sand painting, done by pouring different colored sands on the floor in traditional patterns. Such ceremonies reaffirmed the contact of people to the earth and the brevity of the human lifespan. After every ritual the sand painting was destroyed.

The Anasez cultures flourished from about A.D. 500 to 1200 [274]; the Pueblo and later Zuñi cultures followed. The settled communities have all left pottery remains; some **shards** date back to A.D. 500. The arts of the North American Indian were largely animal-centered. Much of the pottery, basketry, painted hides, and metalwork found at various sites (different materials at different sites) represent arts that remained consistent for centuries.

Middle America

As we have seen, in the years before Columbus arrived on these shores, Indians living in Central America and Mexico developed cultures that included accurate calendars, written communication, skilled metallurgy, and stone ceremonial architecture.

Architecture The Indians of Middle America were not so much concerned with enclosing space as with building impressive stepped pyramids with a temple on top as the focus of religious rituals [40]. The pyramids were faced with stone that was often ornately carved or covered with painted stucco. The pyramids stood in the midst of ceremonial centers surrounded by palaces for official functions. The masses probably occupied simple adobe houses on the outskirts. Teotihuacán, however, near present-day Mexico City, covered more than 20 acres (8.9 hectares) and supported a large population. Its most imposing structure is the 300-foot- (65-meter-) high Pyramid of the Sun, still standing. The city flourished for about six hundred years, attracting sculptors, painters, potters, and other artists.

All these Middle American groups followed a similar calendar based on cycles of fifty-two years instead of the cycles, or centuries, of one hundred years that we follow. The Mayas kept annals for hundreds of years. Each cycle usually was celebrated by a building, often a temple or pyramid built upon an existing one. Memorial **stelae** were set up in the plazas to mark the time of dedication, as modern cornerstones date Western buildings. The Spanish conquerors, following Indian practice, built their churches over Indian holy places. By digging through layers of construction, archaeologists have been able to trace a history of Middle American architecture. Scholars have correlated the Middle American calendar with that of the West so we can study Middle American architecture in relation to our own dating systems.

Most of these peoples built walled stone courts for highly competitive ritual ball games in which the ball symbolized the sun. To encourage the sun god to make his daily journey across the heavens, Aztec priests made sacrifices of prisoners of war to supply him with human blood. The rain god was also important. Some groups believed that his attention could be attracted by the tears of sacrificed children. The Toltecs and Aztecs worshipped Quetzalcoatl, a symbol of the life force represented by an image that combined the beautiful feathered quetzal bird and the coatl serpent.

Sculpture and Other Arts   Much Middle American sculpture was architectural—reliefs of gods and priests and geometric designs on pyramids and temples as in the Temple of Quetzalcoatl at Teotihuacán [40]. There were also small stone and clay figures of gods, humans [202], and animals. Filled with vitality, they give us a glimpse of the daily life of the people.

The Mayas and other peoples painted murals of warriors [105] and religious scenes inside palaces and tombs. Other forms of painting were on pottery and accordion-folded bark paper books (codices) [186]. Beautifully designed jewelry of gold and jade and ritual objects of inlaid shell, turquoise, and other stones attest to the great skill of Middle American craftsmen. They also wove fabrics [225] and made elaborate feather mosaic headdresses and cloaks for priests and nobles.

South America

Mochican potters made clay vessels molded in the shapes of people and animals or painted with animals or scenes. Mochica, Quimbaya, and Chimú craftsmen made fine gold jewelry set with turquoise, and gold cups. The Chimús and the Incas built great cities, such as the 15th-century Inca stronghold of Machu Picchu high in the Andes [452]. The Incas, who ruled a large empire at the time of the Spanish conquest, constructed large plazas, temples, and palaces of massive stone blocks.

Although the Spanish disrupted the pre-Columbian civilizations for centuries, many present-day artists work close to the artistic mainstream of their ancestors.

Art of Northern Europe

In contrast to the sophisticated art of the Byzantine Empire and the diverse arts of New World Indians, art in northern Europe during the 6th and 7th centuries was an eclectic mixture of Christian and classical elements and pagan influences from central Asia. Celtic peoples occupied central and northwestern Europe. Teutonic peoples from the east had been sweeping across the vast network of Roman roads into Europe ever since the later years of the empire. The highly civilized Romans called both groups barbarians, but the northerners' art, though simpler than that of southern Europe, was far from unskilled.

Teutonic craftsmen worked in iron, gold, enamel, and wood, which they ornamented with stylized animals both real and mythological. The **animal style,** as it is called, originated in Asia, where it had developed among the nomads of the steppes. In northern Europe, the style was combined with elaborate patterns of interlaced elements borrowed from Christian art in Italy, Egypt, and the Byzantine Empire. The dragons on the front of this Ostrogothic iron helmet protect the wearer's eyes with magic powers, while another dragon on the top reaches down toward the nose, thereby protecting the skull [332]. The decoration was planned to guard against demons, which seemed very real to the wearer, but the helmet was clearly designed to ward off actual deadly sword blows as well.

Celtic craftsmen also worked in metal and enamel and carved monumental stone crosses. They mixed animal forms, geometrics, spirals, and interlacing into a richly ornamental **Hiberno-Saxon style** that reached its height in the manuscripts of the Gospels and other books. Celtic monks laboriously copied these by hand in monasteries. The Lindisfarne Gospels [96] and the Book of Kells, were, in a practice called ***horror vacui,*** or "fear of emptiness," lavishly decorated over every bit of space with swirling designs of plants, animals, birds, and humans that seem to merge into and out of one another. A beast may dissolve into a snake, which turns into a fish, the whole sequence perhaps forming the letter *T*.

Carolingian Art

In the late 8th century Charles the Great, or Charlemagne (c. 742–814), a vigorous and wise king of the Franks, tried to revive the Roman Empire in the West and to restore Roman civilization. Choosing Aachen, probably his native city, now in West Germany, as his capital, he transformed it into a cultural as well as a governmental center. There he encouraged a blend of Christian and classical scholarship, Byzantine traditions in art and architecture, and Celtic and Teutonic skills in metalwork, which fused into the **Carolingian style.** As a reward for helping the popes in Rome against their enemies, he was crowned emperor of the Roman Empire in Rome in 800.

As part of his building program, Charlemagne constructed a two-storied Palace Chapel at Aachen [333], where he worshipped and was buried. Its massive stone walls were inspired by Roman architecture as well as northern severity, but its octagonal central space, surrounded by an **ambulatory** (passageway) and covered by a dome, was influenced by San Vitale in Ravenna [326] and other Byzantine buildings. Roman elements also appeared in the barrel vaulting, the three levels of round arches enclosing the central space, and the marble Corinthian columns that divided the arches of the upper levels into three sections. The columns themselves had come from Ravenna.

The richly decorated surfaces echoed Byzantine influence, and the contrasting colors of the stones in the uppermost arches were typical of Islamic art in Spain. The emperor's throne was in the second-story gallery, where Charlemagne appeared to the congregation below as a representative of Christ on earth. From that position he was close to the Lord, pictured in a mosaic in the dome above. In its energetic combination of these different elements, the Palace Chapel embodied the Carolingian style. This and other churches sponsored by Charlemagne were an important influence on later architecture.

Charlemagne also encouraged the building of monasteries. Each included a church, living quarters for the monks, workshops, guesthouse, hospital, and surrounding farms, and was a large, self-sufficient community. Originally

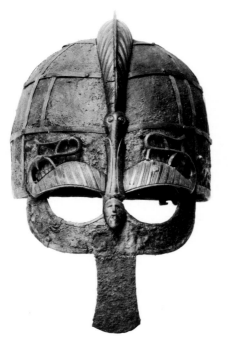

above: **332.** *Ostrogothic helmet. 7th century. Iron. Museum of National Antiquities, Stockholm.*

right: **333.** *Interior of the chapel of Charlemagne, Aachen. c. 795.*

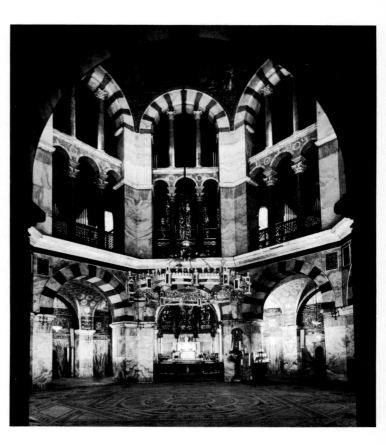

founded as quiet retreats in a turbulent world, the monasteries became bustling centers of learning and the arts. In **scriptoria,** or writing rooms, in monasteries or the palace school, copies of Christian and classical manuscripts, which might otherwise have been lost, were made. These manuscripts were illustrated with miniature paintings inspired by Byzantine art and richly ornamented with covers of gold, gems, and carved ivory. Many demonstrated the continuing Northern influence in the linear qualities of the drawn decorations.

Romanesque Art

During the Romanesque period, about 1050 to 1200, after pagan Viking invaders had settled and been converted and after Christians had recovered Spain from the Muslims, art and architecture flourished. A new Romanesque style emerged, so called because it was inspired by Charlemagne's revival of Roman styles. Romanesque architecture blossomed quite suddenly when a medieval prophecy foretelling the end of the world in 1000 failed to come true. Many Christians emerged from caves where they had hidden and, as one medieval historian put it, showed their gratitude by covering Europe with a "white mantle of churches."

These churches varied in local detail according to whether they were built in Italy, Spain, Germany, or France, but they all shared a similar floor plan—the central nave and side aisles that originated in the Roman basilica and were

334. *Sant' Ambrosio, Milan, from west. c. 1181. Length, including atrium, 390′ (118.87 m); width 92′ (28.04 m).*

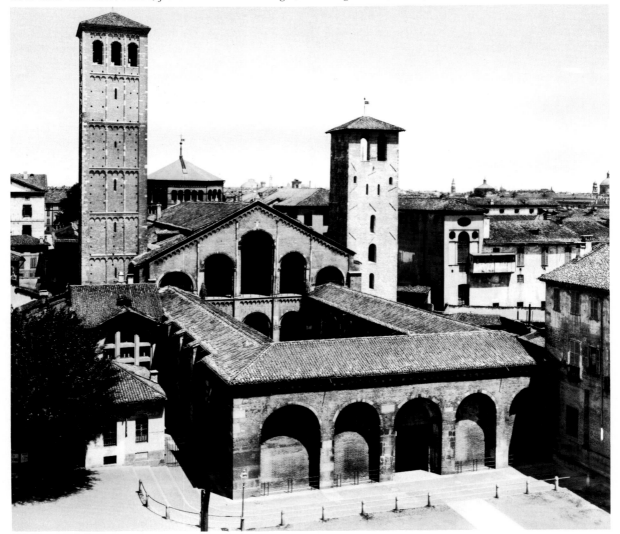

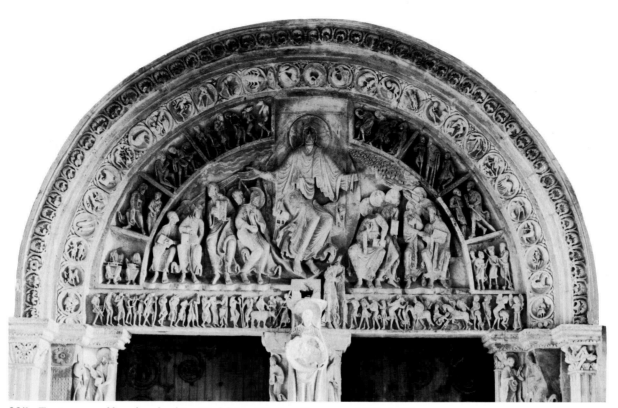

335. *Tympanum, abbey church of La Madeleine, Vézelay, France. c. 1120–1132.*

adapted by Early Christian churches. Builders used Roman techniques of masonry and adopted the Roman vocabulary of arches and barrel vaults. These stone vaults spanned large areas and lessened the danger of fire, which destroyed so many wooden roofs, but they required heavy walls to support them. As a result, Romanesque churches were often dark because windows were few and small to avoid weakening the walls. Sant' Ambrogio, Milan, is an early example, incorporating also an enclosed courtyard [334] modeled after the Roman atrium.

Sometimes walls and vaults were brightened by murals, and columns also often were painted. Many columns had elaborately carved capitals, which depicted Bible stories or portrayed the constant battle between Christians and evil demons representing the seven deadly sins. In the **tympanum** (semicircular space) over the entrance doorways, sculpture often depicted the Last Judgment. Perhaps the most beautiful of all Romanesque tympanums is in the church in Vézelay, France, depicting the Mission of the Apostles—exhorting Crusaders to spread the gospel. A large figure of Christ Ascending disperses rays of the Holy Spirit on the Apostles, each equipped with copies of the scriptures

[335]. Eventually the entire church became a sermon in stone.

Gothic Art

As Europe's population grew, many people moved from sparsely populated rural areas dominated by local barons and monasteries into towns. Town dwellers, or burghers, usually organized into guilds, took part in lively commercial exchanges of goods and ideas. Travel became easier, and Crusaders, who went to rescue the Holy Land from the Muslims, brought back new ideas from the Middle East. Universities in cities such as Paris, Bologna, and Padua attracted students from all over Europe. Teaching was in Latin, the universal language of educated men and women in the West. Pilgrims moved freely from town to town on their way to visit shrines, while burghers competed for their business. At the same time, ambitious bishops planned impressive cathedrals whose vaults often rose to awesome heights.

These new **Gothic** cathedrals expressed not only local ambition but also the pious desire of Christians to strive toward the kingdom of heaven. They were soaring, towered structures

Villard de Honnecourt (c. 1225–1250)

Born in Picardy, France, Villard de Honnecourt is mainly remembered for the remarkable sketchbook that he assembled as a traveling master mason in search of work in the great cathedrals of France. The notebook is a compendium of diagrammatic representations of architectural practices of the 13th century, supplemented by carefully phrased injunctions on what (and what not) to do in constructing churches.

As we scan the pages, the centuries slip away and we are swept into the medieval world, where itinerant specialists were the rule. News of the outside world came largely by word of travelers such as minstrels, crusaders, and messengers. The written word was prized, so first-hand knowledge gleaned through travels to such places as Rheims, Chartres, Laon, Meaux, and Lausanne was incorporated into the architect's sketchbook and valued.

Eventually Honnecourt converted his notes into a manual that provided precise instructions for building construction. In his writings, he fused principles derived from ancient geometry with workshop techniques from the Middle Ages. Honnecourt includes sections on technical processes, from mechanical subjects to human and animal figures [336]. Having visited Hungary in 1255, his sketches demonstrate the depth of his understanding of the great churches built during his lifetime even outside his native France.

The notebook of Villard de Honnecourt indirectly documents the spread of Gothic

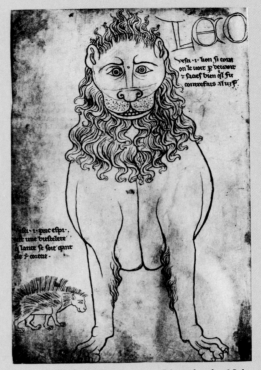

336. *Villard de Honnecourt. Lion sketch. 13th century. Bibliotheque Nationale, Paris.*

architecture in Europe, no mean achievement considering that the architect is believed to have lived only twenty-five or so years.

---

whose interiors were filled with an unearthly light filtered through stained-glass windows. The term **Gothic** was originally used by the Romans derisively to describe the "bearded barbarians to the north." Though intended as a slur, the word soon lost its negative associations.

The requirements of this style led builders to experiment with higher vaults and other ways than walls to carry their weight. Groin vaults were strengthened with ribs, which transferred the weight of the vaults to piers at the corners of the bays and thence to the ground, as we saw in Chapter 9 [254*b*, 255, 254*c*].Buttresses against the outside walls, positioned where the ribs met the piers of the wall, provided a counter-thrust

against the pressures of the vaults, while pointed arches made it possible to roof spaces that were not squares.

These elements—pointed arch, ribbed vault, and buttress—used independently in Romanesque churches, were combined for the first time in the rebuilt abbey church of St.-Denis outside Paris in the mid-12th century by the dedicated Abbot Suger. At the head of the nave Suger added a new **choir** behind the apse, surrounded by the columns of a double **ambulatory** from which radiated seven wedge-shaped chapels. Although St.-Denis was rebuilt after more than one fire, Suger's design of ribbed vaults, pointed arches, thin interior columns, and exterior buttresses was adopted throughout the church [60]. The nonsupporting walls between the buttresses of the choir were filled with glass. They were described by Suger as a "string of chapels, by virtue of which the whole [church] would shine with the wonderful and uninterrupted light of the most luminous windows, pervading the interior beauty."

And so the Gothic style was born. It spread throughout Europe during the next two hundred years and in time became more ornate. The late Gothic style is called flamboyant because the stone **tracery** separating sections of windows was elaborated into curved, flamelike patterns that masked the basic structure. Because cathedrals often took a hundred or more years to build, their plans frequently changed. One section, for example, might be in the early Gothic style and another in the flamboyant style.

Despite local variations in design and detail and stylistic changes over time, all Gothic churches used the same self-supporting system of ribs and buttresses to frame large stained-glass windows. The windows were made of small pieces of glass colored in the molten state, given details with a paint brush, fitted together with lead strips, and placed in an iron frame. Like Romanesque murals, they told biblical and other Christian stories. Particularly fine windows were made for the cathedral at Chartres [337].

The exterior of a church was decorated with deeply carved sculpture. The great portals through which the congregation entered were flanked by statues of biblical figures and saints. The tympanum, no longer dominated by Romanesque preoccupation with the Last Judgment, heaven, and hell, showed a broader range of subjects, such as scenes from the life of the Virgin. Greater emphasis on the Virgin led to gentler treatment of figures in general with softer, more graceful poses and drapery.

The Gothic cathedrals were communal efforts in which all the devout participated in whatever way they could—carrying stones, cutting them

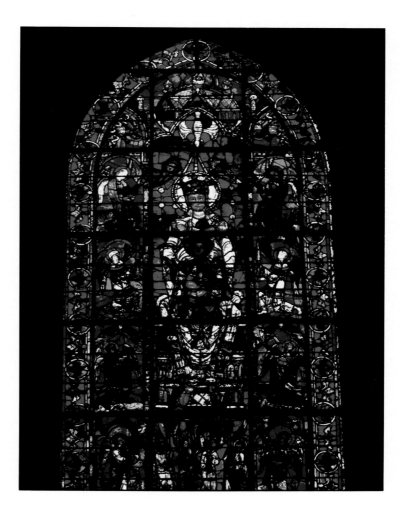

337. Notre Dame de Belle Verrière, *Chartres Cathedral. Early 13th century.*

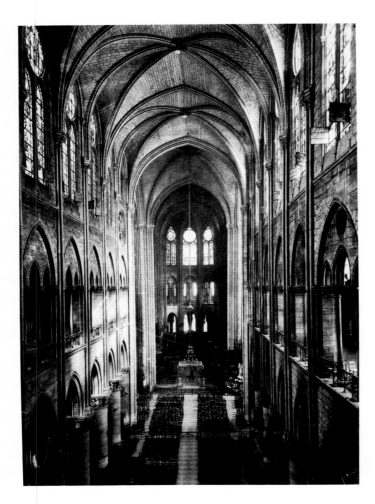

into shape, hauling them up to the masons working on the high scaffolds, or contributing money. Skilled craftsmen who could carve the stone sculpture and wooden choir stalls and fashion gold and enamel reliquaries were in great demand. Their combined efforts produced magnificent structures towering over the houses and shops huddled at their feet. Auxiliary structures, like the Campo Santo at Pisa, were often decorated with painted murals.

Inside, the vaults soared into a dim blue twilight representing heaven, the windows sparkled like jewels, and on feast days, hundreds of candles glowed on the gold and jewels of altar screens, chalices, and candlesticks and on the gold-embroidered vestments of the priests. The vision of holiness [338] enhanced by the singing of the liturgy, must have uplifted worshippers from the harsh realities of daily life and transported them to new realms of devotion. Yet it was at this time, when the Church dominated almost every phase of life, that the forces which led to a totally different spirit in a new era were already at work.

338. *Interior, Cathedral of Notre Dame, Paris. c. 1163–1250.*

Exercises and Activities

Research Exercises

1. List the historical reasons why Early Christian art incorporated so many cultural influences. Give examples of images that derived from other cultures and were absorbed into Christian art.
2. Explain how the Romanesque style of architecture originated and whether it varied throughout Europe. What earlier structural systems influenced it?
3. Locate examples of Romanesque and Gothic Revival churches in your community. De-

scribe how they use the elements of these styles.
4. Contrast a floor plan of Romanesque style with the Gothic style. Is it the floor plan or the stained glass that accounts for the differences in impact between the two systems? Explain.
5. The Gothic cathedral provided more than religious experiences for medieval populations. Describe the social, economic, technological, and cultural values that you believe were derived from the Church.

Studio Activities

1. Using colored chalks to suggest the effect of a fresco, sketch some Early Christian symbols.
2. Cut out tiny squares from magazine illustrations, searching for varied colors and tex-

tures. Paste these small pieces on cardboard to form a mosaic of geometric designs or human figures. Notice how you must simplify forms in order to represent them with mosaic squares. Study an Early Christian mosaic and see how form was developed.

Exploring Art Through Technology

The *Triumph of Death* Frescoes in Pisa

Constant warfare among the Italian city-states and among factions backing either the Pope or the Holy Roman Emperor, and pestilence on a scale quite equal to our threat of nuclear annihilation—these were facts of life for Italians in the 14th century. In 1348 the bubonic plague, or Black Death, as it was called, killed almost half the population of Italy, not to mention the rest of Europe. The frescoes attributed to Francesco Traini at the Campo Santo in Pisa are the most striking, dramatic, harrowing depictions of the anxiety and of the ever-present reminders of death Italians were experiencing at the time.

The Campo Santo, or cemetery buildings bearing this *Triumph of Death* fresco cycle, next to the Duomo and near the famous Leaning Tower of Pisa, were themselves victims in 1944. Allied bombings near Pisa reached the Traini frescoes, causing fires which damaged them. In order to prevent complete deterioration, the frescoes were detached from the wall after the war by a technique developed in this century. Once again a disaster called forth at least one unexpected beneficial result: the technology of conservation that facilitated the detachment of the frescoes from the wall brought to light the **sinopie,** or underdrawings, beneath the frescoes. These sinopie were remarkably clear and complete and reveal to us information not only about 14th-century artists' working methods but also about life at that time beyond what the frescoes tell us. The powerful, forceful sinopie underline the importance of these monumental underdrawings and confirm the belief that the frescoes themselves were probably largely executed by assistants.

There are also figures in the sinopie that did not make their way into the finished painting. For instance in the scene depicting the Last Judgment [339], in which Christ damns the sinners who are spirited off to Hell, we can definitely make out a pope,

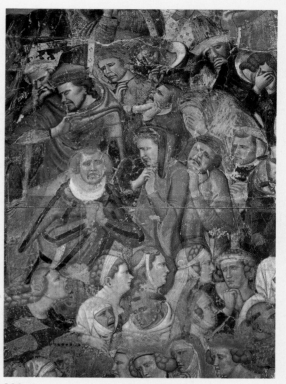

339. *Francesco Traini.* The Damned, *detail of* Last Judgment, *Campo Santo, Pisa. c. 1350. Museo del Duomo, Milan.*

bishop, and a cardinal in the sinopie, whereas these figures disappear and are replaced by two friars in the frescoed version. Whatever animosities against Rome and its hierarchy were freely expressed in the sinopie, for some reason they were toned down for the final version. We don't know the explanation for this change, but it may well be that the artist's superior, the local church, or the community required modifying the potentially inflammatory images. You can compare for yourself the sinopie and the fresco in the museum of the cloisters of the Campo Santo as they appear side by side.

3. Locate old dishes and bottles of different colors. Wrap them in many newspapers and break them into fragments with a hammer. Glue them onto a wooden surface in a satisfying mosaic design.
4. Draw a diagram of the Gothic structural system. Name and explain the function of the parts.
5. Using pieces of colored tissue paper, paste up a design for a stained-glass window. Use this as a guide to make a window from colored glass and leading available in craft shops.

13

Crossroads: Renaissance, Baroque, Rococo

Thy will is free and whole and upright and now it would be wrong to rein it in. Be thine own Emperor and thine own Pope.

Dante, *The Divine Comedy*, 1321

In his hands I saw a long golden spear and at the end of the iron tip I seemed to see a point of fire. With this he seemed to pierce my heart several times so that it pierced my entrails. When he drew it out, I thought he was drawing them out with it and he left me completely afire with the love of God.

St. Theresa, *Vida*, c. 1550

This goodly frame, the earth; . . . this most excellent canopy, the air; . . . What a piece of work is man! How noble in reason! How infinite in faculty! In form and moving how express and admirable! In action how like an angel! In apprehension how like a god!

Shakespeare, *Hamlet*, 1602

History does not unfold conveniently in chapters, and the Gothic Age had not dramatically vanished when the Renaissance came to life. The Church still dominated much of medieval life, but urbanization and commerce gave rise to the self-confidence expressed in Dante's epic poem. Similarly, the new Renaissance humanism led to the turbulent, theatrical spirit of the Baroque Age and the intimate Rococo period that followed.

During the late Middle Ages trade in Europe, with Africa, and with the East continued to increase. The merchants and bankers from prosperous cities of Italy and Flanders (modern Belgium) formed a well-to-do middle class that threatened the declining authority of the Church. The cities situated on trade routes competed as textile centers. At the same time, intellectuals began to abandon medieval scholastic philosophy. Instead they adopted a humanist view, which emphasized the abilities of the individual and the importance of life in this world.

With these humanist eras, **Renaissance, Baroque,** and **Rococo** art turned from its base in religion to the modern focus of human beings who saw themselves as important parts of the universe.

African Cultures and Art

Since Graeco-Roman times, Africa had been known to Europeans through travel and, in particular, through the Muslim expansion of the 7th century. But not until the 14th century, with a newly expanded mercantilism, did Europeans arrive in numbers on African shores. The first to come were the Portuguese, followed in the 1450s by the Spanish, and near the end of the century by the English and French. The Dutch were next, and by the end of the 16th century they had challenged the lead of the Portuguese.

The reasons for this surge of interest were partly political, but largely economic. In the beginning, trade between Europeans and Africans

Europe and Africa

	THE VISUAL ARTS		HISTORICAL NOTES
		1100	**c. 1100–1500** Ife and Benin kingdoms, Africa
		1200	
	c. 1250 *Enthroned Madonna and Child* **[343]**	1300	
	1304–13 Giotto's frescoes, Scrovegni Chapel **[342]**		**1309–20** Dante, *The Divine Comedy*
	1333 Martini, *Annunciation* **[341]**		**1385** Chaucer, *The Canterbury Tales*
	1395–1406 Sluter, *Well of Moses* **[344]**	1400	
	1424–52 Ghiberti, Doors, Baptistery, Florence **[346]**		
	1425 Masaccio, *The Trinity* **[348]**		
	1425–30 Merode Altarpiece **[38]**		**c. 1430** Portuguese traders invade Africa
	1430–32 Donatello, *David* **[347]**		**1431** Joan of Arc executed
	1434 Van Eyck, *Marriage of Arnolfini* **[361]**		
			c. 1450 Alberti, *De re aedificatoria*
			1456 Gutenberg prints first book
	c. 1478 Botticelli, *Primavera* **[350]**		
			1492 Columbus reaches America
	1495–98 Leonardo, *The Last Supper* **[80]**	1500	**c. 1500** Oil painting replaces tempera
	1500 Dürer, *Self-Portrait* **[124]**		**1503** Julius II elected pope
	1502–05 Leonardo, *Mona Lisa* **[18]**		
	1502–05 Bosch, *Garden of Delights* **[364]**		
	1508–11 Michelangelo, Sistine Chapel ceiling **[106], [352]**		
	1509–11 Raphael, *The School of Athens* **[353]**		
	1513–15 Michelangelo, *Moses* **[193]**		
			1520 Luther excommunicated
			1532 Calvin begins Reformation
	1546–64 St. Peter's Basilica and Vatican **[370]**		
			1550 Vasari, *Lives of the Artists*
			1558 Elizabeth I becomes queen of England
			1590–1613 Shakespeare's plays
	c. 1500–1600 Ivory pendant, Benin, Africa **[340]**	1600	
	1601 Caravaggio, *Conversion of St. Paul* **[367]**		
			1605 Cervantes, *Don Quixote*
	1620 Gentileschi, *Judith Beheading Holofernes* **[23]**		
			1632 Galileo Galilei, *On Copernicus*
	1636–37 Poussin, *Rape of the Sabine Women* **[373]**		
	1642 Rembrandt, *The Night Watch* **[376]**		
			1643 Louis XIV becomes king of France
	1645 Bernini, *Ecstasy of St. Theresa* **[369]**		
			1648 Académie Royale founded
	1669–85 Palace of Versailles **[372]**		
	1675–1710 Wren, St. Paul's Cathedral **[377]**	1700	
	1734 Hogarth, *The Rake's Progress* **[37]**		
			1772 Diderot and d'Alembert, *Encyclopédie*

took the form of barter. The Portuguese and later invaders found highly developed arts of gold and ivory, as well as lucrative trade in slaves. By the end of the 15th century, gold and slaves had superseded all other exports.

Travelers from north to central Africa found a continent criss-crossed with caravan routes and cart trails. Their chronicles tell of the glories of busy cities like Songhai and the legendary Timbuktu and of African empires that rose and fell.

By the late 15th century, Timbuktu had developed into the central educational and commercial metropolis of western Africa—a sophisticated city that included doctors, judges, priests, and scholars maintained by the king, assisted by a council of ministers.

In rural areas, however, traditional animistic beliefs, cults, and rituals were perpetuated, as was a social structure that can still be found in many African communities today. People are

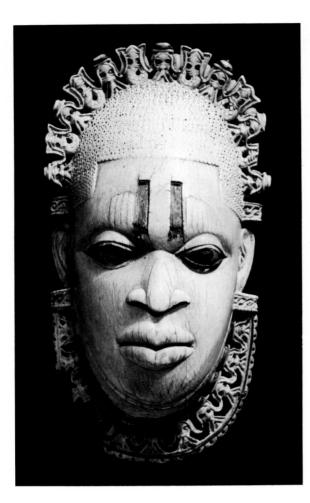

grouped in extended families consisting of several generations and many cousins, on whom they depend heavily for support. Important in Africa and other traditional societies, these extended families are parts of clans united by blood ties in devotion to their ancestors. The clans in turn form groups that share a common language and culture.

African sculpture was highly developed. Although most of it is wood, Africans also used other materials. The earliest sculptures are small clay heads from Nok in Nigeria, made about two thousand years ago. Metalworking was known by about 500 B.C. From the 12th century A.D. rulers in the kingdom of Ife and from the 16th century the Benin kingdom in Nigeria commissioned cast bronze and brass relief plaques and portrait heads, which were realistic representations of rulers. The Benin people also worked in ivory. If you closely examine this 17th-century ivory mask for a belt, you will see tiny heads of Portuguese soldiers in the scalloped beard and pierced headdress. Thus, with typical wit and inventiveness, the African artist created a work of art expressing deep feelings about the Portu-

left: **340.** *Pendant of belt mask. Nigeria. c. 1600. Ivory, height 9⅜" (24 cm). Metropolitan Museum of Art, New York (Michael C. Rockefeller Collection, gift of Nelson A. Rockefeller, 1972).*

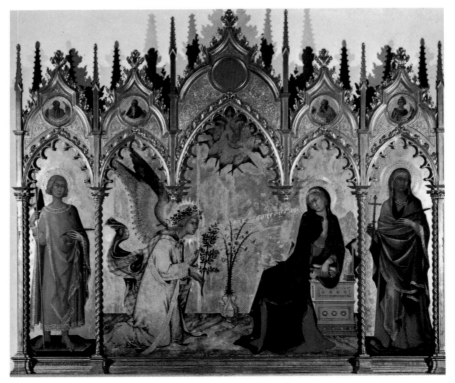

341. *Simone Martini.* Annunciation *(saints in side panels by Lippo Memmi). 1333. Tempera on wood, 8'8" × 10' (2.64 × 3.05 m). Galleria degli Uffizi, Florence.*

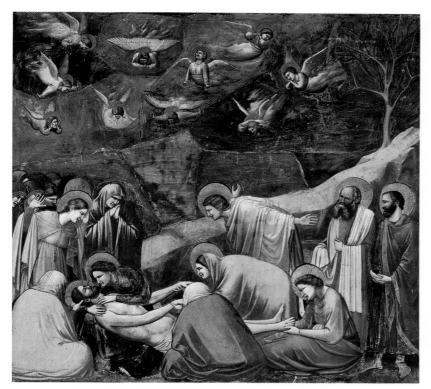

342. *Giotto.* Pietà (Lamentation). *1305–1306. Fresco, 7'7" × 7'9" (2.31 × 2.36 m). Arena Chapel, Padua.*

guese invasion of the African homeland [**340**]. European accounts describe the skill shown in goldwork and the precise accuracy of the Africans in measuring gold. Note is made of the **cire perdue** gold weights produced by African artists at the time of the early Renaissance.

Forerunners of the Renaissance

We can see a new spirit reflected in the work of three 14th-century artists. In Italy the Sienese painter Simone Martini (1284–1344) retained the Gothic spirit in his *Annunciation,* with its Byzantine gold background and decorative detail. But he depicted the Virgin, for the first time, as a real woman, startled by the appearance of the archangel with his fateful message [**341**].

The Florentine painter Giotto (c. 1266–1337) also illustrated religious subjects, but his brush brought the warmth of humanism into these Christian works. In his frescoes of the *Life of Christ* in the Arena Chapel, Padua, and the *Life of St. Francis* in the church in Assisi he expressed human emotions in a new and striking manner, depicting the founder of the Franciscan Order—noted for his love of nature—in simple communion with the birds. Again, if we compare the lifelike figures in his ***Pietà*** [**342**] with those in an altarpiece in the Byzantine style [**343**], we can see how the drapery in Giotto's work suggests

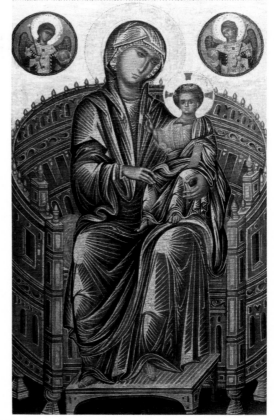

343. *Byzantine School.* Enthroned Madonna and Child. *13th century. Tempera on wood, $32\frac{1}{8} \times 19\frac{3}{8}$" (82 × 49 cm). National Gallery of Art, Washington. (Andrew W. Mellon Collection, gift of Mrs. Otto H. Kahn).*

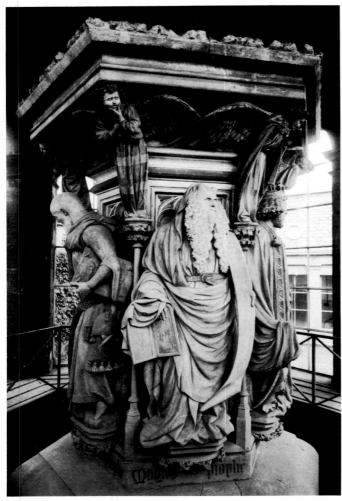

344. *Claus Sluter.* Well of Moses. *1395–1406. Marble, height of figures approximately 6' (1.83 m). Chartreuse de Champmol, Dijon, France.*

(1380–1406), who worked at the court of the Duke of Burgundy. In his notable *Well of Moses* [344] he portrayed the biblical prophets as real human beings expressing individual personality. Sluter's deep piety belongs to the Middle Ages, but the striking illusion of life that he created points to the Renaissance. Sluter was also the first major sculptor to abandon the tradition of placing sculpture in an architectural setting, such as above the door of a church [335], and to produce free-standing sculptures of monumental size. His innovations and masterful realism influenced later sculptors.

Renaissance in Italy

The term *Renaissance* means rebirth. It refers to the renewed interest in classical learning, philosophy, and art that developed in Italy in the 14th and 15th centuries and later spread throughout Europe.

During the Gothic period, France had been the spiritual and intellectual center of Europe. Italy, where classical traditions and monuments still remained, generally resisted the extremes of Northern religion and Gothic architecture. The humanistic spirit of the Greeks and Romans never quite faded, and Italian Gothic architecture never lost some sense of classical proportion and balance. In the 14th century enthusiastic Italian humanist scholars, joined by artists and princes, "rediscovered" ancient Rome by locating classical manuscripts and digging in ruins to find precious lost statues. These Italians were acutely aware that Rome had once been the center of power in the Western world. The Middle Ages seemed like a barbaric interlude to those who longed for "the glory that was Rome."

Early Renaissance

Italian Renaissance art first flowered in Florence, a mercantile and banking city. Rich families built fine palaces and churches and commissioned paintings and sculpture to decorate them. The most prominent was the Medici family, who gained control of the city and the surrounding territory and founded a powerful dynasty of princes to rule it. The Medici were great art patrons, maintaining courts that employed poets, scholars, musicians, and artists. They commissioned Benozzo Gozzoli to enrich their family chapel with frescoes of *The Journey of the Magi* [226], in which their own portraits appear.

No longer was art the expression of unknown artists dedicated to the Church. Private patron-

the solid shape of the body beneath. The low horizon, the grief-stricken mourners, the frantic angels, and the severely descending slope of the hill all direct us to the lifeless figure of Christ and the somber Virgin.

The impact of that drama is heightened by Giotto's daringly original approach. No wonder that, a generation later, the poet Petrarch, accustomed to stylized Byzantine painting, asserted that Giotto depicted nature so faithfully that his paintings could be mistaken for reality. About the same time, the poet Giovanni Boccaccio, familiar with classical art, hailed Giotto as the artist who had "restored to light this art which has been buried for many centuries." Indeed, Giotto is still regarded as the father of a new era in art.

The third artist to foreshadow the change in art style was the Northern sculptor Claus Sluter

age combined with the individual artist's own sense of accomplishment to open a new era. From the time of Giotto on, we will be able to trace the history of individual artists.

Architecture Italian Renaissance architecture, related to a human scale like Greek and Roman structures before it, was more concerned with the aesthetic questions of proportion, balance, and unity than with developing innovative construction methods.

The young Florentine architect and sculptor Filippo Brunelleschi (1377–1446) and the sculptor Donatello (1386–1466), fascinated by ancient art, traveled to Rome to find buried temples and ancient sculpture or columns. On his return to Florence, Brunelleschi was chosen from many applicants to complete the city's Gothic cathedral. Inspired by the Pantheon of Rome [257], he awed Florence with the design and completion of a giant dome over an area so large that no one in the hundred years of the church's construction had dared to undertake the assignment. In the dome and other designs, he incorporated classical columns, pilasters, and

arches to achieve balance and symmetry. Also a theorist, Brunelleschi tried to explain the world in a scientific manner, sought laws of mathematical proportion, and discovered the laws of linear perspective (see Chapter 2). His work helped bring about the change from Gothic to Renaissance style in both architecture and painting.

After the death of Brunelleschi, Leon Battista Alberti (1404–1472), well educated in classical literature, philosophy, and law, became the foremost architect of Florence. The first man of his time to study Roman buildings in depth, he wrote the famous *De re aedificatoria*, in which he discussed the rules of proportion envisioned by Brunelleschi. This treatise on architecture was one of the most influential works of the Renaissance. Inspired by the Colosseum in Rome, Alberti designed a façade for the Palazzo Rucellai [345], which consisted of three horizontal bands decorated with pilasters freely adapted from the Greek orders [305]. This was perhaps the first time an architect had applied an ornamental classical system to the outside of a nonclassical building, while subordinating the classical elements to the wall itself.

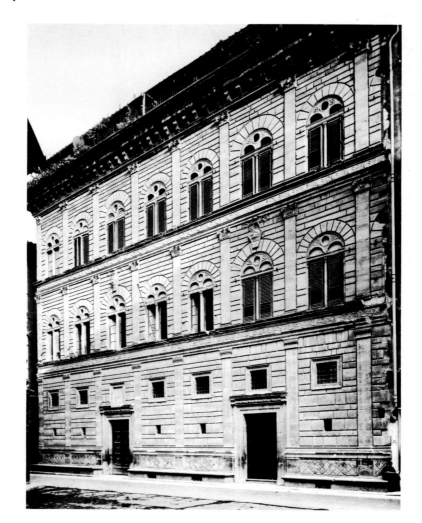

345. *Leon Battista Alberti. Palazzo Rucellai, Florence. 1446–1451.*

Sculpture The Renaissance spirit of individualism was exemplified by a contest in 1402 to design the bronze doors on the north side of the Baptistery of Florence. Lorenzo Ghiberti (1378–1455) described his victory triumphantly: "To me was the honor conceded universally and without exception. . . . I had at that time surpassed the others." For an artist to have expressed this kind of self-congratulation would have been unthinkable when cathedrals were built by humble, unknown artisans. Ghiberti's design consisted of a series of panels depicting biblical scenes in low relief [346]. In *The Annunciation* he used **aerial perspective** (Chapter 2), in which forms become fainter the farther away they are from the viewer, to give a greater sense of illusionistic depth than had ever been achieved before in such a shallow space.

It was Donatello, however, who made a complete break with medieval traditions by founding a new aesthetic rationale. Following the lead of the Greeks and Romans he admired, he studied the human body carefully and sculpted from models in his studio. In this way, he created the bronze *David*, perhaps his most revolutionary

346. *Lorenzo Ghiberti.* The Annunciation, *detail from the north doors of the Baptistery, Florence. c. 1435. Gilt bronze, 31¼" (79 cm).*

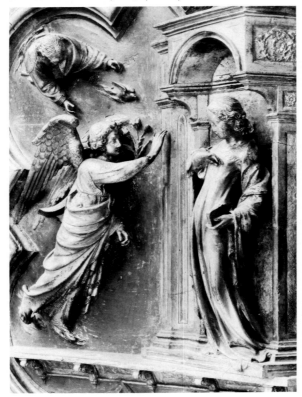

achievement, for an aristocratic patron [347]. Donatello chose to represent David, the first lifelike, life-size nude statue since antiquity, as a young Italian boy, rather than as a fully developed Greek athlete. Looking at a crucifix sculpted by the more intellectual Brunelleschi, Donatello is said to have remarked, "To you is given to make Christs . . . to me peasants." Perhaps this explains the somewhat incongruous shepherd's hat and well-made boots worn by David.

Painting Departing from medieval spiritual preoccupations, painters following Giotto were fascinated with the problem of representing three-dimensional objects in flat space. Influenced by Brunelleschi's discoveries of the laws of perspective, they applied them to painting (see Chapter 3).

One of the first painters to employ the laws of perspective was Masaccio (1401–1428). He astonished his fellow Florentines by representing space in *The Trinity* [348], a fresco in Sta. Maria Novella, as realistically as if the Crucifixion were taking place in one of Brunelleschi's chapels. Shown kneeling outside the chapel, the wealthy donors are as prominent as the religious figures and so life-like that we feel we can almost touch them. The grandeur of scale, the solid masses, and the simple draping of garments on the figures show the influence of Roman architecture and sculpture on Masaccio. His vision was of the new Renaissance man who saw himself as an important part of the universe. The three-dimensional solidity of Masaccio's figures [88] reminds us of both Giotto and early Renaissance sculpture. The relationship between sculpture and painting was important throughout the Renaissance.

As part of their effort to understand and portray the real world, Renaissance painters learned how to show the human body by **foreshortening,** or contracting its forms. They also studied anatomy in order to depict figures more naturally. Their paintings of saints and other religious characters show them as real men and women, unlike the stylized and symbolic figures of earlier medieval painting. Frescoes by Andrea Mantegna (c. 1431–1505) for the Ovetari Chapel in Padua illustrating the life of St. James show the influences of Donatello, Masaccio, and classical sculpture. His boldly foreshortened figures, as in *The Dead Christ* [349], inspired many later artists.

Italian painters were interested not only in observing and portraying the world around

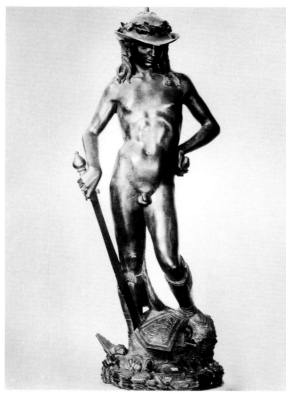

above: **347.** *Donatello.* David. *c. 1430–1432.*
Bronze, height 5'2¼" (1.58 m).
Museo Nazionale, Florence.

right: **348.** *Masaccio.* The Trinity
with the Virgin, St. John, and Donors. *1425.*
Fresco, 21'10" × 10'5" (6.68 × 3.18 m).
Sta. Maria Novella, Florence.

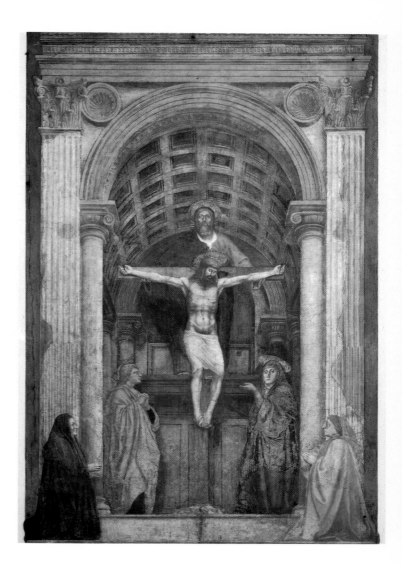

349. *Andrea Mantegna.*
The Dead Christ. *c. 1490–1500.*
Oil on canvas, 27 × 32" (69 × 81 cm).
Brera Gallery, Milan.

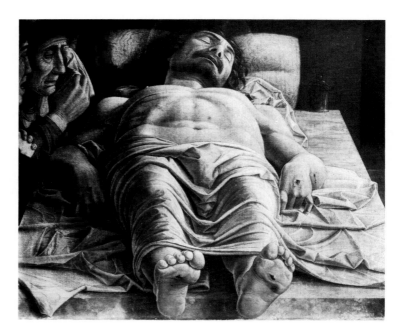

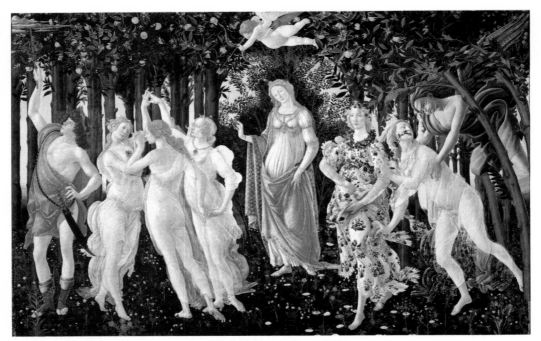

350. *Sandro Botticelli.* Allegory of Spring (Primavera). *c. 1478.*
Tempera on wood, 6'8" × 10'4" (2.03 × 3.15 m). Galleria degli Uffizi, Florence.

them but also in making formal compositions of almost mathematical precision. Artists such as Piero della Francesca (1420–1492), who worked at Arezzo, found beauty in the relationship of each part to the whole, according to the Golden Section of the ancient Greeks **[93]**, mathematically determining the architectural details he rendered in his paintings.

As Christians and classicists, Italian painters chose both religious and mythological subjects. Sandro Botticelli (1444–1510), who worked for the Medici, painted madonnas and goddesses. He was not, however, so much interested in giving an illusion of reality as in suggesting an unearthly quality. Influenced by Byzantine and Gothic painting, such as that of Simone Martini, he used elongated shapes to suggest the ethereal quality of his figures. Botticelli also expressed in his work the platonic view, originating in Greece, that everything on earth participates in an ideal form, such as he rendered in the *Primavera* **[350]**. The *Primavera*, for instance, is a symbolic allegory. The classical "Venus," centered but not the focus, represents "love," which produces life, as well as unity between the physical and the intellect. She is expressed in a trinity, the triad of graces at the left, who give, receive, and return love. Some scholars also believe that Botticelli is depicting divine love that was given to humans, is accepted, and then returned to

God as adoration. Flora on the right holds flowers born of passion, representing the flowering spring.

By this time, Italian painters had learned from Flemish painters how to work with oil glazes (see Chapter 3). In addition to working in fresco on plaster walls, they painted in tempera and in oil on wood panels and canvas.

High Renaissance

Most scholars consider the brief High Renaissance to have lasted only twenty years in the early 16th century (although some may include the very late 15th century). It is characterized, in part, by order, balance, and symmetry and represented, like the Greek Golden Age, the climax, the classic phase, of Renaissance art.

Painting Leonardo da Vinci (1452–1519), who demonstrated vast scope as both artist and scientist, came to symbolize the Renaissance ideal of the universal man. Filling many notebooks with his findings, he investigated scientific subjects from hydraulics to war machines to botany. He became an accomplished musician and a brilliant engineer. After a career of painting at the court of Milan, he spent his last years on court assignments for Francis I of France.

Exploring Art Through Technology

Nativity with the Visitation and Archangel Presenting the Donor

A remarkable discovery was made in 1984 when conservators from the Detroit Institute of Arts used infrared reflectography to study a triptych by the Master of the St. Ursula Legend [351]. Since the naked eye can make out some underdrawing in the lighter, more transparent areas, experts were aware that the painting had undergone compositional changes. Earlier infrared photography had confirmed that lines existed below the surface that did not correspond to the finished composition.

What the more sensitive reflectography revealed was underdrawing not only for the painting on the surface, but also for an entirely different three-panel scene which lay beneath it. By placing a sheet of acetate over the reflectogram and tracing the lines which bore no relation to the surface composition, historians were able to analyze the underlying work. In the triptych's center panel, a female figure kneels in a position similar to that of the Virgin Mary in the surface *Nativity*; a bearded male figure stands before her to the viewer's right. This scene has been identified as the *Coronation of the Virgin*. In the right panel, a single female figure stands where on the surface the archangel presents the kneeling donor; the female is probably St. Gertrude of Nivelle. The left panel contains a standing male saint who has not been identified. Both underlying side panel scenes are set in cathedral-like interiors rather than under the open sky. Six layers were found to exist atop the original oak panel: an initial ground preparation, an underdrawing of the underlying composition, a paint stage, a blocking layer which served as a new ground preparation, an underdrawing of the surface composition, and the final paint layer. Thus what museum-goers see as *The Nativity with the Visitation and Archangel Presenting the Donor* actually holds beneath its surface an unfinished *Coronation of the Virgin with Saints*.

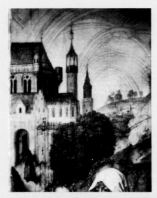

351. *Master of the St. Ursula Legend.* Triptych of the Nativity with the Visitation and Archangel Presenting the Donor. *After 1493/before 1499. Paint on wood panel, overall (with frame) 2′5⅜″ × 4′4½″ (.75 × 1.33 m). Detroit Institute of Arts (gift of the Metropolitan Opera Benefit Committee).* **Left:** *Infrared reflectograph, detail of left panel.*

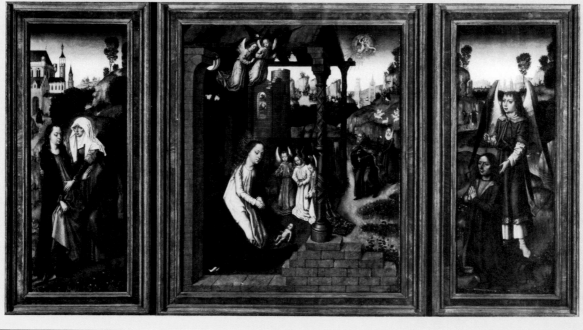

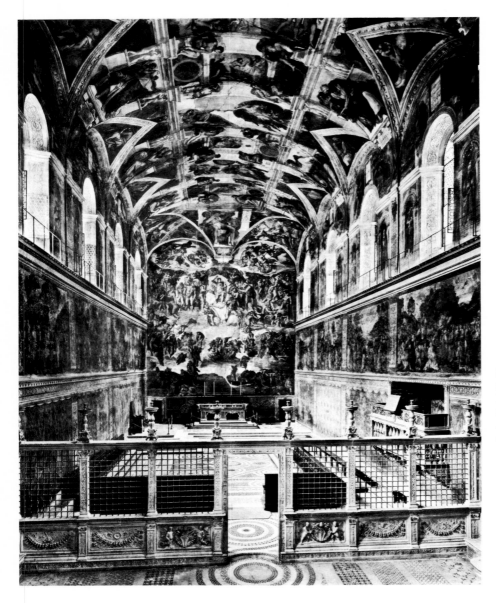

352. *Sistine Chapel, view toward Michelangelo's* Last Judgment *over the altar. Ceiling paintings, 1508–1511. Height of ceiling 68' (20.73 m). Vatican, Rome.*

Beyond his scientific interest, Leonardo was much concerned with humanity. He drew a man at the heart of the universe, represented by a combined square and circle **[94]**, reflecting the humanist view that man is the measure of all things. His largest extant work is the life-size *The Last Supper* on the walls of the monastery of Sta. Maria delle Grazie in Milan **[80]**. It was commissioned by a patron who wished to be in the company of the Lord while joining the monks at dinner. The painting reveals the individual personality of each man as Leonardo deduced it from biblical accounts, achieving the Renaissance ideal of harmony, balance, and beauty through carefully developed intellectual and technical means. The design of the painting (Chapter 2) was mathematically planned, the

figures painstakingly researched, and the fresco technique an exploration into new Renaissance technology. The technique did not hold up, and the painting fell into near ruin. In recent years, however, it has been again extensively restored.

If *The Last Supper* is Leonardo's best-known religious work, the *Mona Lisa,* or *La Gioconda,* showing the wife of a Florentine banker, is probably the world's favorite portrait **[18]**. Here, Leonardo, the intellectual who claimed there was no science that could not be translated into mathematical symbols, painted one of the world's most intriguingly poetic paintings and possibly the earliest psychological study. Some say that the soft play of light and shade that models the woman's face accounts for her cryptic smile. But since Leonardo was a master of his art and a similar smile appears in others of his portraits, it is likely that he intended to paint the mysterious expression just as it appears.

Michelangelo (1475–1564), twenty-three years younger than Leonardo, paved the way through the High Renaissance to the Mannerist and Baroque periods that followed. During his eighty-nine years he created masterpieces of painting, sculpture, and architecture in Florence and Rome. Apprenticed at thirteen, as was the tradition, he learned essential skills from his master, the accomplished mural painter Domenico Ghirlandaio (1449–1494). By the time Michelangelo was thirty, his reputation had attracted the attention of Pope Julius II, a worldly prince of the Church. Julius selected the Florentine to carry out the ambitious plans for marble sculpture for the pope's tomb. When the work was scarcely begun, however, Julius persuaded Michelangelo to undertake an even more exacting commission.

The ceiling of the Sistine Chapel, built earlier by Pope Sixtus IV in the Vatican, was unpainted, although the walls held murals by earlier artists. The pope asked Michelangelo to paint the vault of the ceiling with religious frescoes. Reluctantly agreeing, Michelangelo, who until then had considered himself more sculptor than painter, refused any help and spent the next four years almost in solitude on his back on a scaffold, creating hundreds of figures 60 feet (18.28 meters) above the floor [352]. In this huge work, figures of Old Testament prophets alternate with oracles of classical mythology. As a practicing sculptor, Michelangelo believed that the more painting resembled sculpture the better it was. He therefore accentuated the volume of his figures to create the effect of biblical reliefs ranging from the book of Genesis to the Flood. We may note that in the spirit of humanism, Michelangelo placed the figures of God and Adam almost facing each other as if on equal terms. As Adam awakens from sleep and gazes directly at God the Father, we sense energy vibrating between their outstretched fingers [1].

While Michelangelo was painting the Sistine ceiling, a young rival, Raphael Sanzio (1483–1520), was completing a series of frescoes in the Vatican. Deeply concerned with the universality of human experience, he tried to find a balance between the religious and profane aspects of the High Renaissance. He set on opposite walls of the Stanza della Segnatura theological themes in the *Disputà* and classical subjects in *The School of Athens* [353], creating a deep, three-dimensional

353. *Raphael.* The School of Athens. *1501–1511. Fresco, 26 × 18' (7.92 × 5.49 m).*
Stanza della Segnatura, Vatican Palace, Rome.

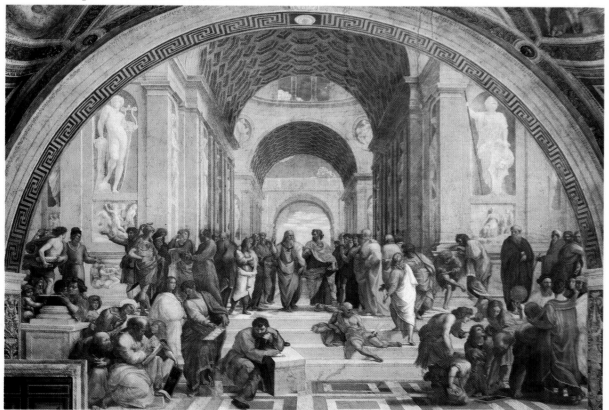

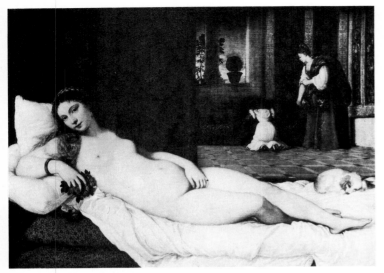

354. *Titian.* The Venus of Urbino. *1538.*
Oil on canvas, 3'11" × 5'5" (1.19 × 1.62 m).
Galleria degli Uffizi, Florence.

space as a setting for the figures. Famous classical teachers with their pupils are grouped around symbols by which we can recognize them; Plato and Aristotle are silhouetted against the sky framed by a central arch. The formal, one-point perspective lines lead our eyes to their figures, while the assembly of philosophers and pupils is split into two groups representing the Platonic and Aristotelian schools. In his short lifetime Raphael became famous for these large, formal, intellectual paintings, and many consider him the most typical artist of the High Renaissance.

Another great center of Italian art, second only to Florence, was Venice, a wealthy maritime power since medieval times. Classical ideals of form and proportion had never taken hold in the floating city built on canals. Instead, glowing mosaics such as those of the Byzantine cathedral of San Marco, ornate Gothic palaces, and the dazzling colors and sensuous textures of fabrics imported from the Orient dominated Venice. The city produced some fine painters, in particular Titian (1477–1576), a great colorist. Titian reflected the secular spirit of the Renaissance in *The Venus of Urbino* [354], a worldly version of an earlier work by Giorgione (c. 1475–1510).

The rhythmically ordered stability of Renaissance painting usually depended on a tri-part division of space—the subject in the foreground against a strongly architectural middle ground, framed by a distant background. Breaking away from such limitations Titian introduced a new

diagonal thrust into many of his works. For example, although our attention lingers on the idealized form of the Duchess of Urbino, our eyes flicker to the maids in the background, positioned not, as was customary, behind the central figure, but diagonally off center. Also, Titian portrayed gods and goddesses as distinctly mortal, such as this languid nude, who awaits the assistance of her maids to dress—and, surprisingly for a Venus figure, if indeed she is, regards us unabashedly in her nakedness.

Sculpture and Architecture After Michelangelo finished the Sistine frescoes, he continued to work on Julius' tomb, for which he carved the mighty Moses [193]. He also carved tomb figures for the Medici in Florence and for his own tomb. In some works the figures seem to struggle to release their stretched and contorted limbs from the stone. At the same time, the tension between those opposing forces and the larger-than-life scale of the sculptures increases their sense of power and movement. Such characteristics influenced many later Baroque artists, who often exaggerated the scale and movement of their works.

Michelangelo's last great undertaking was the continuation of work on St. Peter's in Rome, notably the dome [264]. The overpowering scale and the strong contrasts that exist between its diverse architectural elements mark this church as one of the most significant monuments of the High Renaissance and a herald of the Baroque era to come.

Mannerism and Late Renaissance

The 16th century was a period of contradiction and stress during which Italy was invaded by foreigners. In this changing world the equilibrium of the High Renaissance, like the Classical period in ancient Greece (see Chapter 11), was difficult to maintain. Even Leonardo and Michelangelo, typical as they were of the High Renaissance, signaled in their work the approaching Mannerist style. For example, Leonardo's preoccupation with light affected the balance of his compositions, and Michelangelo distorted his figures for expressive purposes [193]. By the 1530s the formal boundaries within which Leonardo and Michelangelo had produced their greatest works had broken down. The unrest of the time was reflected in the work of artists who consciously altered the ideals of the High Renaissance, evolving an exaggerated, theatrical **Mannerist** style.

Painting Mannerist painters were not interested in the logic of real space. They experimented with elongated proportions like those of Botticelli's goddesses, the twisting forms preferred by Michelangelo, and asymmetrical compositions often used by Titian. Such effects were probably as startling to 16th-century Italians as the works of experimental 20th-century painters are to the public today.

Parmigianino (1503–1540) shocked his fellow citizens of Parma with the elegance of *The Madonna with the Long Neck* [355]. The Madonna, her squirming baby, and attendant angels are crowded on one side, leaving a row of unfinished columns on the other. The contrast between the tightly compressed space and the open, abruptly receding space gives us a sense of instability, as does the artist's striking self-portrait [110]. These figures are elongated, ivory-smooth, and demonstrate an ideal of beauty not to be measured by the standards of reality.

The Venetian painter Tintoretto (1518–1594), influenced by Titian, altogether discarded the laws of classical structure. Tintoretto increased the sense of motion and contrast in his compositions to give the effect of floating masses lit by flickering light. His most famous work is *The Last Supper* [356], which provides a striking

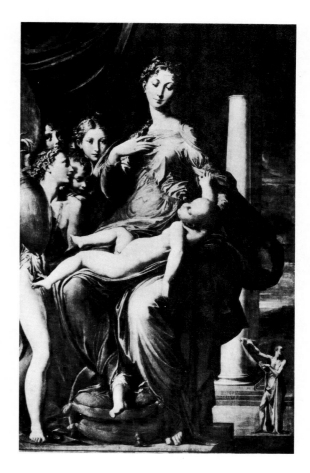

above right: **355.** *Francesco Mazzola (Parmigianino).* The Madonna with the Long Neck. *c. 1535. Oil on canvas, 7'1" × 4'4" (2.16 × 1.32 m). Galleria degli Uffizi, Florence.*

below: **356.** *Tintoretto.* The Last Supper. *1594. Oil on canvas, 12' × 18'8" (3.66 × 6.69 m). San Giorgio Maggiore, Venice.*

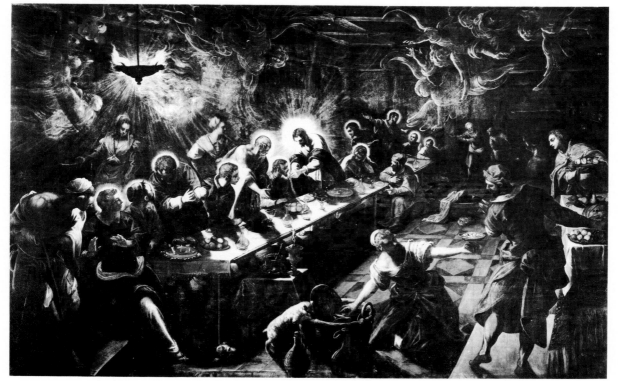

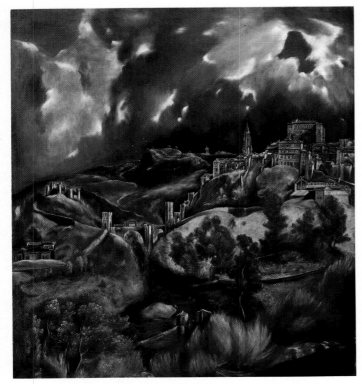

357. *El Greco.* View of Toledo. *c. 1604–1614.*
Oil on canvas, 47¾ × 42¾" (121 × 108 cm).
Metropolitan Museum of Art, New York
(bequest of Mrs. H. O. Havemeyer, 1929;
H. O. Havemeyer Collection).

tain a link with the Byzantine style. He painted the city of Toledo [357] illumined with the eerie light of an impending storm. The acrid green landscape is charged with emotion as dramatic clouds contrast with jagged hills and deep river valleys. In this work the Renaissance ideals of formal balance are totally rejected.

By the late 16th century a few women, usually born into families of painters, became known as artists. Among the first to attract attention was Sofonisba Anguissola (c. 1528–1625), one of six sisters all trained in art. Sofonisba is noted by the 16th-century historian Giorgio Vasari for her skill in portraiture, a favorite subject of the Renaissance as shown in her *Husband and Wife* [358]. Despite the simplicity of the composition, the psychological rapport between the two subjects is remarkable for this period. Perhaps this quality and her conservative, sensitive observations account for Sofonisba's favored position at the court of Phillip II of Spain.

Sculpture and Architecture Mannerism's concern with effect rather than content or intellect was typical of the work of the Florentine goldsmith and sculptor Benvenuto Cellini (1500–1571). His lively autobiography reveals expert craftsmanship and extreme egotism. Cel-

contrast to Leonardo's mural of the same subject [80]. Gone is the classical ideal of balance expressed by Leonardo's one-point perspective and symmetrical composition. Tension and drama now dominate. Judas has been set aside in the shadows, while the remainder of the painting is filled with lights and half lights. This striking interpretation portends the dramatic Baroque style soon to come.

One of the most important Mannerists was Domenico Theotocopulos, known as El Greco (c. 1548–1614). Born on the Greek island of Crete, he was familiar with **icons** (panel paintings of holy subjects) in the Byzantine style. Traveling to Venice, he studied the achievements of Titian and Tintoretto in using light, shade, and rich color. But he retained the elongated figures of Byzantine art and developed his own strong colors to create an unreal world unlike that of other Venetian painters. After a period in Rome, he settled in Spain, where his richly expressive style was in keeping with Spanish piety. His tall figures of saints in swirling drapery of violent rose, blue, and yellow main-

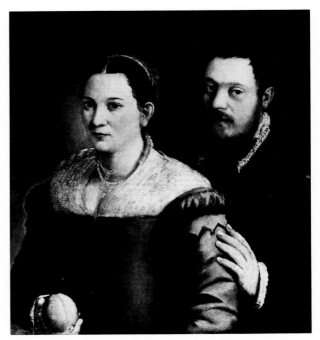

358. *Sofonisba Anguissola.* Husband and Wife.
Oil on canvas, 28¼ × 15½" (72 × 65 cm).
Galleria Doria Pamphili, Rome.

lini was clearly delighted with his own virtuosity, displayed in the gold and enamel saltcellar he made for Francis I [359]. He wrote of this feat:

The Sea, fashioned as a man, held a finely wrought ship which could hold enough salt, beneath I had put four sea horses, and I had given the figure a trident. The Earth I fashioned as a fair woman. . . . Beside her I placed a richly decorated temple to hold the pepper.

Such novelty appealed to princes and other rich patrons.

Similarly, architects such as Andrea Palladio (1518–1580) were determined to display inventive skill as well as classical knowledge. His Villa Rotonda, near Vicenza, was intended to duplicate ancient Roman styles, but there is no classical counterpart to this square mansion distinguished by four identical porches grouped around a central hall [360]. The low dome, however, is reminiscent of the Pantheon. Details of other Palladian buildings—columns, pediments, and three-window groupings—influenced later architecture in Italy and the 18th-century Georgian style in England. Even wooden copies of Georgian-style houses in far-off New England were often graced with Palladian windows.

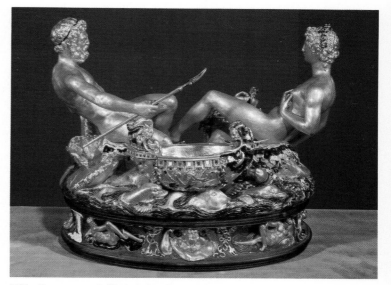

359. *Benvenuto Cellini.* Saltcellar of Francis I. *1540–1543. Gold, chased and partially enameled; base made of ebony; 10¼ × 13" (26 × 33 cm). Kunsthistorisches Museum, Vienna.*

Renaissance in the North

By the 15th century, the cities of Flanders, part of the duchy of Burgundy, were developing a wealthy middle class. Bankers and merchants

360. *Andrea Palladio.* Villa Rotonda, Vicenza. *Begun 1550. 80' (24.38 m) square, height of dome 70' (21.34 m).*

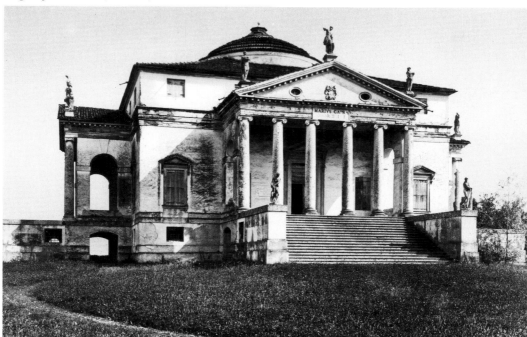

made fortunes, guilds of tapestry weavers and other skilled craftspeople prospered, and women began to appear on guild lists. Gradually, through increased trade and travel between North and South and the development of printing (see Chapter 4), the Flemish absorbed some of the artistic heritage of Rome and humanism.

15th Century

Flemish painters made revolutionary technical discoveries in oil painting (see Chapter 3). By underpainting in black or brown and white tempera, drawing details in white, and overlaying thin oil glazes in color, they evolved a new technique that combined the precision of tempera with the depth of oil. It was ideally suited for rendering the rich fabrics and shining brass furnishings of the comfortable houses of Flemish burghers and the soft blue depth of Flemish landscapes used as background.

Such painters as the Master of Flémalle (?Robert Campin, 1406–1444) and Jan van Eyck

(?1370–?1440), who worked for the Duke of Burgundy, depicted religious and secular subjects in the new technique, often combining realistic detail with medieval religious symbolism. We have already discussed the religious symbolism of the Mérode Altarpiece [38] and may note that the work breaks with tradition. The setting for this Annunciation, a supernatural event, is depicted as the home of a well-to-do citizen. However, most of the furnishings carry an extra symbolic message, as with Van Eyck's work. Van Eyck, in his *Arnolfini Wedding*, shows the Italian silk merchant and his shy Flemish bride surrounded by symbols of the religious aspects of marriage [361], as analyzed by scholars well versed in the period. The solitary lighted candle in the chandelier represents the presence of God, placed to remind the couple that their vows were made before Him. They stand on hallowed ground, their shoes discarded. The fruit on the windowsill represents the delights of lost paradise, while the dog symbolizes fidelity and possibly fertility. This Flemish room, therefore,

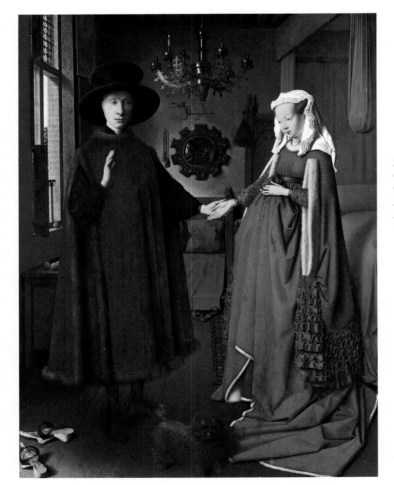

361. *Jan van Eyck.* Marriage of Giovanni (?) Arnolfini and Giovanna Cenami (?). *1434. Oil on wood, 32¼ × 23½″ (81.8 × 59.7 cm). Reproduced by courtesy of the Trustees, The National Gallery, London.*

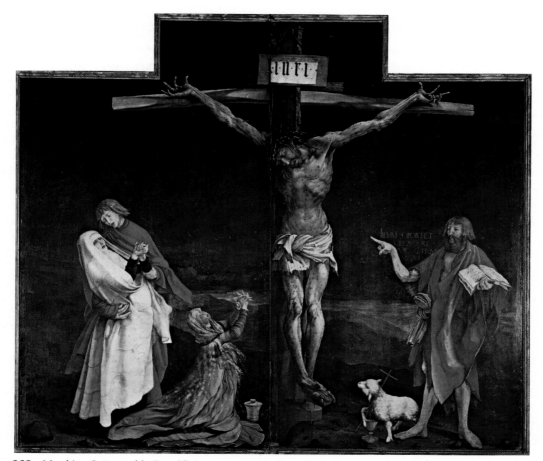

362. *Matthias Grünewald.* Crucifixion, *center panel exterior of* Isenheim Altarpiece. *Completed 1515. Oil on wood, 8'9⅞" × 10'⅞" (2.69 × 3.07 m). Musée d'Unterlinden, Colmar.*

had a deep meaning to those who understood its symbolism. The artist himself can be seen in the mirror, which repeats the uncompromising reality of the scene. He also inscribed in Latin above the mirror, "Jan van Eyck was here," a witness to the marriage!

16th Century

By the early 16th century the states of Germany were in transition from medieval piety to Renaissance humanism and the new Reformation teachings of Martin Luther and other Protestant leaders. The basic spiritual conflicts produced an intensity of emotion, typified in Matthias Grünewald (1470–1528). His monumental Isenheim Altarpiece was Gothic in spirit and, like most medieval religious art, preached a visual sermon. When the wings are closed on the central panel, we see the *Crucifixion* [362], a stark scene of suffering. Christ's dying body, painted

in heroic scale, is distorted by his wounds, and his pain is reflected in his mother's face. In contrast to this scene of suffering, in an expression of hope for the world the opened panels reveal the *Annunciation*, the *Virgin and Child with Angels*, and the *Resurrection*. These scenes are filled with mystical beauty and radiant light. In this work, Grünewald stepped beyond his medieval traditions, and through his use of solid forms and dramatic expression of personal emotions, influenced many later painters.

Albrecht Dürer (1471–1528) in his portraits and landscapes showed Northern painters how to adapt Italian Renaissance ideas without losing their own traditions. As an apprentice to a painter and an engraver, he developed the meticulous draftsmanship that characterizes all his work and makes memorable even so simple a subject as praying hands [103]. Already familiar with the paintings of Van Eyck, Dürer traveled to Italy, where he saw works by Mantegna and

Michelangelo. He brought back to Germany the Renaissance concern for science and wrote treatises on perspective and anatomy.

In printmaking, however, Dürer truly excelled. The development of printing in the previous century had increased the demand for woodcuts and copper engravings, as we saw in Chapter 4. In these media he showed his mastery of light and shade and his devotion to the traditional faith. The classical architectural detail of the enormous *Triumphal Arch of Maximilian* also reveals a strong Renaissance interest in ancient Rome even in Germany [123]. The emperor Maximilian, convinced of the value of art in service to the crown, cleverly entrusted Dürer with celebrating his royal deeds in a woodcut on paper rather than commissioning an architect to produce such a work in costly stone.

Other artists were less comfortable with the new ideas. For example, Lucas Cranach (1472–1553) illustrated pagan myths with nude figures of German beauties self-consciously acting the part of classical goddesses. In his jewel-like, decorative color surfaces Cranach is closer to 15th-century Flemish traditions. His spiritual conflicts between pagan morality and the religious teachings of the Reformation appear in the awkward forms and poses of his figures [363].

While 16th-century Italians were delighting in light, color, texture, and experiments in perspective and composition, Northern Europeans were undergoing the Reformation, which discouraged the visual arts. Because the Protestant churches were opposed to religious paintings as idolatrous and the mercantile class had little interest in classical myths, Northern artists sought more prosaic subjects. Since interest was waning in large altarpieces or church frescoes, many painted on small panels, "in-hand" paintings, which could be hung on the walls of a patron's home. Landscape made its appearance as an important subject at this time. Another theme was portraiture. However, for the strictest Calvinists, all decorative objects were considered dispensible luxury, which left only portraits, small panels, and book illustration through which most artists could make a living.

A unique example of religious panel painting is the work of the early Renaissance painter Hieronymous Bosch (1450–1516), who drew on his imagination to point out a moral lesson in *The Garden of Earthly Delights* [364]. On the left panel, fantastic creatures inhabit the Garden of Eden. On the right panel, fearsome demons—half animal, half machine—punish sinners in hell. In the center, nude figures innocently enjoy sexual pleasures in a garden that may represent earth or paradise.

One of the foremost Northern portraitists was Hans Holbein the Younger. Born in Augsburg, Germany, he went to England, where he became court painter to Henry VIII. There he completed many portraits of the English nobility and was among the first to combine the Northern interest in the precision of tempera and oil glaze with the Italian interest in perspective and rich color. In his glowing portrait *Sir Brian Tuke* [365] every detail of shape and texture has been painstakingly recorded.

Scenes of the everyday world of kitchen or tavern and still-life themes consisting of tables stocked with food and flowers were favored by Dutch painters. Pieter Brueghel (c. 1525–1569) set even biblical stories, such as the *Tower of Babel* [295], in the local Dutch countryside populated with peasants going about their daily activities. For all his apparent taste for country-bumpkin humor, Brueghel was really a sophisticate who had traveled to Italy. In his landscapes, humans are depicted as tiny figures, conveying the lesson of human insignificance in the scheme of the

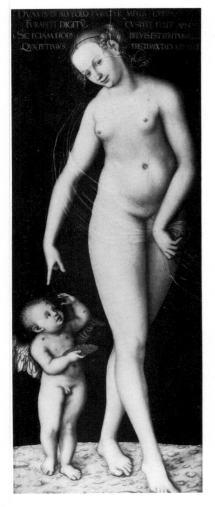

363. *Lucas Cranach the Elder.* Venus and Cupid. *c. 1531. Wood, 5'8⅞" × 26" (1.75 × 0.66 m). Art Gallery of the National Museum of Prussian Culture, West Berlin.*

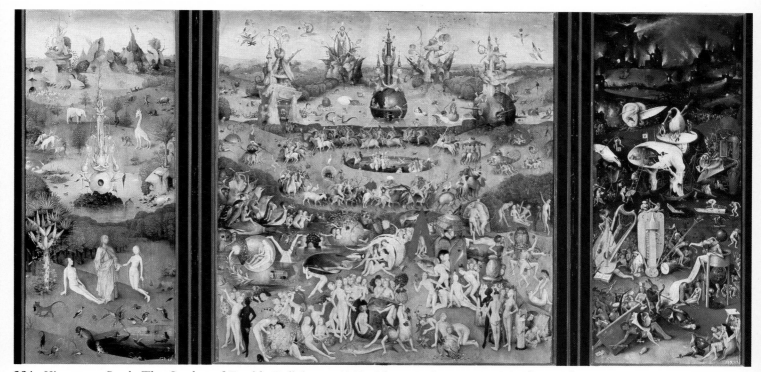

364. *Hieronymus Bosch.* The Garden of Earthly Delights. *c. 1500. Oil on panel; center panel, 7'2⅝" × 6'4¾" (2.2 × 1.95 m), each wing 7'2⅝" × 3'2¼" (2.2 × 0.97 m). Museo del Prado, Madrid.*

universe. While many of his paintings are religious allegories, they also reveal his personal joy in nature—in the hot sun on hay fields, and in frozen, snow-covered fields at dusk.

Baroque in Italy

The extraordinary achievements of the Renaissance were, perhaps, possible only at a time when traditional religious beliefs still had meaning and artists in a new spirit of inquiry and observation found fresh means to express them. During the Age of the Baroque, the 17th and early 18th centuries, the religious unity of Europe was destroyed, and the growing scientific spirit of the new age encouraged a secular outlook. It was a period of confusion and longing for a more perfect world that beckoned out of reach. Artists of the Baroque period went beyond the limits set by the Renaissance in their desire to express fresh ideas in unusual ways. Sometimes their individualism spilled out of strict stylistic categories, but their innovations foretold similar developments in later times.

By the 17th century the exodus of converts from Catholicism to Protestantism had been halted, while the Roman Catholic Church sustained a period of renewal called the Catholic or Counter Reformation. Much-needed Church

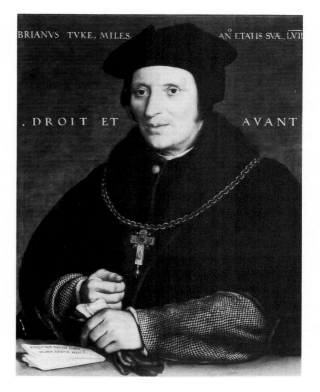

365. *Hans Holbein the Younger.* Sir Brian Tuke. *c. 1527. Oil on wood panel, 19⅜ × 15¼" (49 × 39 cm). National Gallery of Art, Washington. (Andrew W. Mellon Collection, 1937).*

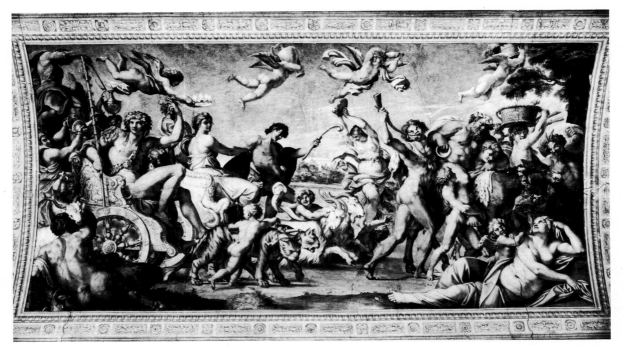

366. *Annibale Carracci.* Triumph of Bacchus and Ariadne. *1597–1601. Ceiling fresco. Galleria Palazzo Farnese, Rome.*

reforms were instituted, and in Italy a great program of renovation and rebuilding was launched to make Rome once again the center of the world. This program continued in the Baroque period. The papacy spared no expense to proclaim the authority of Rome and authorized architects to build palaces and churches and to lay out piazzas, fountains, and gardens on a grand scale. Paintings and sculptures were commissioned to decorate the architecture. Much of this art was intended for the aristocracy, but some, such as the piazza in front of St. Peter's, added a new dimension to the life of the ordinary citizen.

The word *Baroque* originated from a Portuguese derisive term used to mean "absurd" or "grotesque" because many considered Baroque art a degeneration from the restraint of the High Renaissance. In Baroque painting and sculpture emphasis was placed on light and dark contrasts, turbulent compositions, and exaggerated emotion. In Baroque architecture classical elements were freely handled to create the effects of painting and sculpture. Dramatic and mysterious effects were preferred.

Painting

One of the first to work in this new style was Annibale Carracci (1560–1609), a member of a family of painters from Bologna. Distrustful of Mannerist distortion, in his frescoes for the ceil-

ing of the Farnese Palace in Rome he combined a sense of realistic anatomy and foreshortening with dramatic light and energetic movement **[366]**.

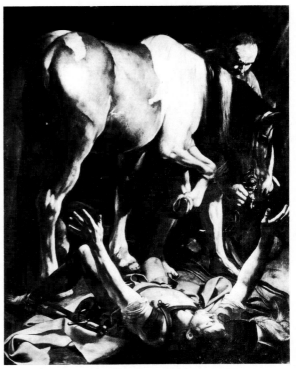

367. *Caravaggio.* The Conversion of St. Paul. *1601–1602. Oil on canvas, 7'6½" × 5'9" (2.3 × 1.75 m). Cerasi Chapel, Sta. Maria del Popolo, Rome.*

The Carracci family founded an academy of art in Bologna, the very first art school. Later, as other academies appeared, aspiring artists no longer were apprenticed to a master painter but could enroll for instruction to study art.

Also opposed to Mannerism but more strikingly dramatic than the Carracci was Michelangelo Merisi da Caravaggio, who used highly exaggerated lighting to dramatize biblical stories in ordinary settings of his day. In *The Conversion of St. Paul* [367] traditional images are gone. St. Paul is shown as an armored man flat on his back, almost trampled beneath his horse. The striking perspective and extreme contrasts of

---

Focus on the Artist

Michelangelo Merisi da Caravaggio (1573–1610)

Michelangelo Merisi, better known as Caravaggio from the name of the Italian town where he was born, was the son of a local architect. Revolutionary in his approach to art in his relatively short and quite troubled life, he is best known for his shadow-painting technique called *tenebroso* and for his ability to portray miraculous events as though they were happening before the eyes of the viewer.

After an apprenticeship of five or so years to a popular Milanese painter, by 1592 Caravaggio was in Rome, turning out works for established artists. This period was brief because he preferred to eke out a precarious art existence independently. The works of this period, light in tone, predominantly composed with earth colors, demonstrated early a direct approach to the subject, eschewing all idealization. Using models from the street, he painted his subjects realistically, as if to convince the observer that his themes had occurred just as they were described in myths and in biblical records. The works he turned out in this period show astonishing pictorial creativity, with a craftsmanship in strong contrast to his own disorderly and dissipated lifestyle. Through the efforts of Cardinal Del Monte, a prelate of great importance in the papal court, Caravaggio obtained a commission to render an imposing three-painting cycle of the life of St. Matthew. This work established him, at twenty-four, as a "pictor celeberrimus," a "renowned painter." The dramatic realism of the works astonished the public, accustomed to idealized rendering of sacred narratives. Light itself became the medium of Caravaggio's revolution. A 20th-century Italian scholar, Roberto Longhi, explains Caravaggio's illumination of form out of deep shadow "as a magical light from above, at the onlooker's shoulder, that, unlike natural light, modifies the color scheme and eliminates subtleties in its path, much like today's theatrical spotlights."

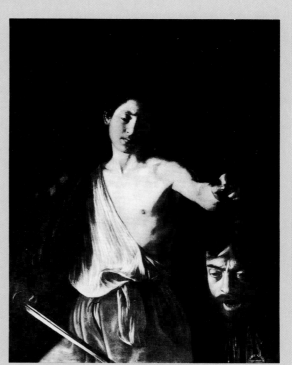

368. *Caravaggio.* David with the Head of Goliath. *c. 1609–1610. Oil on canvas, 49¼ × 39¾" (125 × 101 cm). Galleria Borghese, Rome.*

Despite his inventive solutions to traditional art concerns [367], however, Caravaggio was not universally appreciated. He was quick to take offense at criticism and was involved in a stream of conflicts until, in 1606, he killed a man in a brawl. Fleeing from town to town to avoid arrest, he contracted a fatal case of malaria in 1610. Thus did an unfortunately common end come to a most uncommon man, who left us his self-portrait in the form of the features of the decapitated head of Goliath [368]. His earthy realism and *tenebroso* herald a new phase of the era of Baroque, so important that Longhi likens Caravaggio's unique use of light to that of the Renaissance discovery of perspective!

dark and light draw us into the event. It is obvious why many of Caravaggio's conservative contemporaries were appalled by this work, which presented sacred figures in such untraditional ways.

The foremost woman painter of the Baroque period was Artemisia Gentileschi (c.1597–c.1651), the daughter of a painter. Influenced by Caravaggio, a friend of her father, she painted biblical scenes, portraits, and nudes. Her first major work, *Judith Beheading Holofernes*, portrays a heroic woman performing an atrocious duty with quiet courage [23]. The strong diagonals all lead to the sword blade and drops of blood which brilliantly contrast with the snow-white bosom of Judith. Gentileschi chose to outdo all her predecessors by showing the ferocity with which Judith destroyed the general who was attacking her beloved city.

Sculpture and Architecture

The most outstanding sculptor-architect of the Baroque period was Giovanni Lorenzo Bernini (1598–1680), who is probably best known for his extraordinary *The Ecstasy of St. Theresa* [369], influenced by emotional Hellenistic works. This sculpture of religious mysticism epitomized the spirit of the Baroque. In the saint's own words, at the moment of ecstasy she felt such a great love of God that "the pain was so great that I cried out, but at the same time, the sweetness which the violent pain gave me was so excessive that I could not wish to be rid of it." The drapery falling in a cascade of agitated folds rejects the solidity of the marble from which it was carved, revealing Bernini's technical skill and preoccupation with detail.

Bernini's religious intensity led him also to create a spectacular design for the piazza of St.

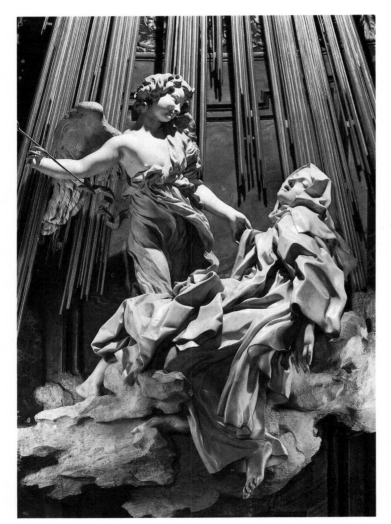

369. *Giovanni Lorenzo Bernini. The Ecstasy of St. Teresa. 1645–1652. Marble and gilt bronze, life-size. Cornaro Chapel, Sta. Maria della Vittoria, Rome.*

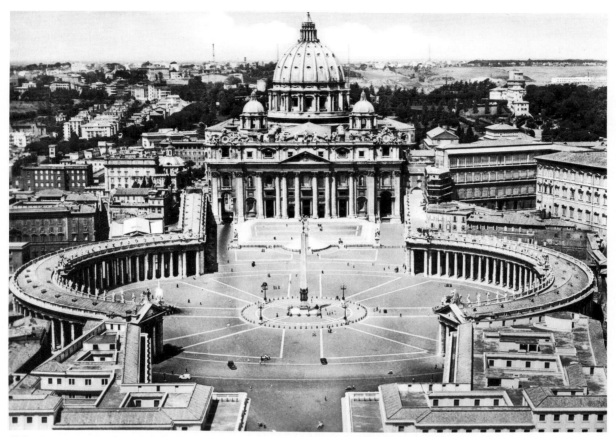

370. *St. Peter's Basilica and the Vatican, Rome. Apse and dome by Michelangelo, 1547–1564; dome completed by Giacomo della Porta, 1588–1592; nave and façade by Carlo Maderno, 1601–1626; colonnades by Giovanni Lorenzo Bernini, 1656–1663.*

Peter's Basilica in Rome [370]. Designed to hold crowds of worshippers at Easter and Christmas time, the piazza is said to accommodate half a million people. Bernini intended the two curving colonnades to represent the arms of the Church, which "embrace Catholics to reinforce their belief, heretics to reunite them with the Church, and agnostics to enlighten them with the true faith."

Baroque in Spain and the North

Born in Italy, the showy Baroque style soon spread to Spain, France, Germany, the Low Countries, and England. In each country, Catholic or Protestant, it was modified by local circumstances. Princes and nobles competed to build magnificent palaces and gardens, redesign cities, and amass works of art. Even functional objects soon acquired Baroque curves and elaborate decoration.

Spain

With the immense wealth derived from their colonies in the New World, the kings of Spain maintained an impressive court in keeping with the role in which they saw themselves, as divinely appointed rulers of their people and representatives of the Church in Spain. Continuing the 16th-century practice of commissioning works from foreign painters, such as El Greco and Titian, they also favored Spaniards.

The most illustrious Spanish court painter was Diego Velázquez (1599–1660), who excelled in portraiture and grandiose historical scenes. Although influenced by Caravaggio's lighting and by Titian and the Flemish Baroque painter Peter Paul Rubens, Velázquez evolved his own personal style. His canvases are Baroque in color, depth of space, and light and dark contrasts, but he applied his paints in separate brushstrokes that presaged 19th-century Impressionism. With this technique, Velázquez could recreate the play of light over the rich garments of his royal subjects and the luxury of their palaces. In *Las Meniñas,* he painted his own portrait standing at the canvas near the small Infanta surrounded by her maids of honor **[371]**. Tiny portraits of the king and queen, who came to watch the artist at work, appear in the mirror behind him. He must indeed have felt secure as court artist to record himself more prominently than his royal employers.

France

The most outstanding example of French Baroque art was the Palace of Versailles **[372]**, built by Louis XIV outside Paris to reflect France's position as the major power in Europe. The king assembled a team originally consisting of the architect Louis Le Vau (1612–1670), the landscape architect André Le Nôtre (1613–1700), and the painter and decorator Charles Lebrun (1619–1690) to integrate all aspects of

371. *Diego Velázquez.* Las Meniñas (Maids of Honor). *1656. Oil on canvas, 10'5¼" × 9'3¾" (3.18 × 2.76 m). Museo del Prado, Madrid.*

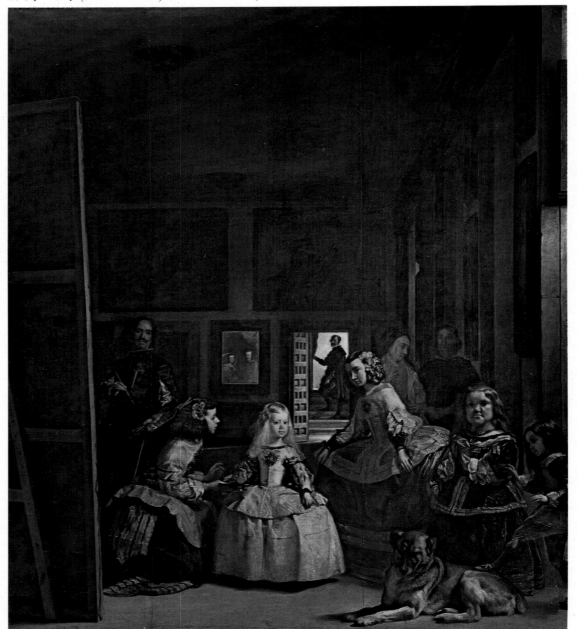

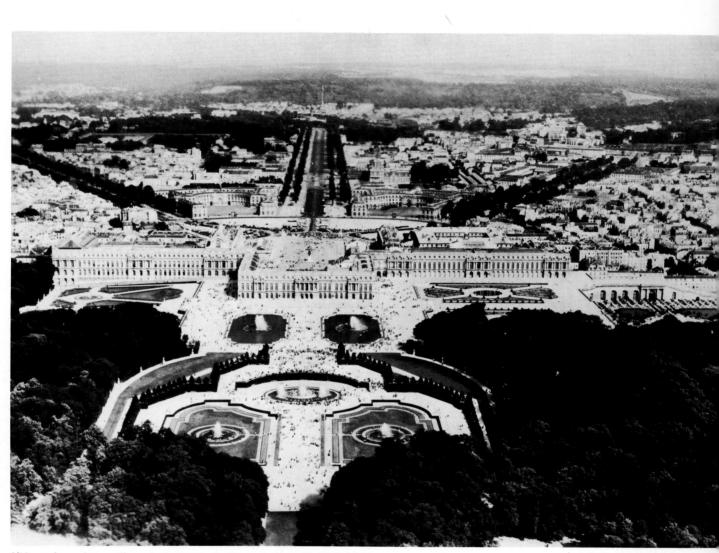

372. *Palace of Versailles. 1669–1685. Palace width 1935' (589.79 m).*

the design. Although a new wing for the old Louvre Palace in Paris had been a collaborative effort, Versailles was the first design and construction of such tremendous scope to be a group effort.

In its magnificent scale Versailles resembled Bernini's piazza in Rome [370], but its restrained, intellectual style defined characteristic qualities of French Baroque. Unlike most Italian Renaissance palaces, which looked inward on central courtyards. Versailles' long, windowed galleries overlooked broad terraces and formal gardens full of pools, splashing fountains, and marble statuary in the classical style. The palace with its gardens and park covered about 20 acres (8.9 hectares). A small city in itself, it held a thousand brilliantly dressed courtiers and the servants needed to maintain the palace.

Louis, who expected all French culture to serve the state, was responsible for the founding of royal academies of literature, science, and the arts. Other rulers founded similar institutions. These powerful, conservative state academies set official standards and dispensed honors upon only those who followed their dictates. Artists who opposed their rigid rulings usually had a difficult time finding work. Perhaps the greatest French painter of the century, with international renown, was Nicolas Poussin (1593/ 4–1665), leader of the Neoclassic style established by the Royal Academy of Painting. Poussin stoutly maintained that "the highest aim of painting is to represent noble and serious actions!—not as they really happened, but as they would have happened if nature were perfect." We encountered the same philosophy a century

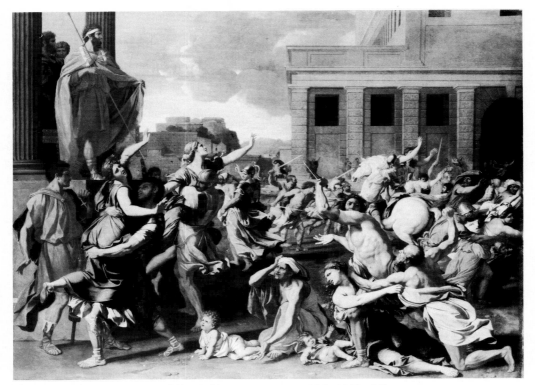

373. *Nicolas Poussin. Rape of the Sabine Women. c. 1636–1637. Oil on canvas,
5′1″ × 6′10½″ (1.98 × 2.1 m). Metropolitan Museum of Art, New York
(Harris Brisbane Dick Fund, 1946).*

later with the art critic Diderot (Chapter 1). *Rape of the Sabine Women* **[373]** is so carefully composed, with evenly distributed colors and directional forces, that the emotion and turmoil of the event seem frozen in action, but the rational clarity of Poussin's work served to reinforce Neoclassic views.

Low Countries

Peter Paul Rubens (1577–1640), a prolific painter trained in Flanders and Italy and a worldly, well-traveled ambassador at home in many European courts, helped spread the Baroque style. During his years in Italy he learned to make full use of color and light. Huge, movement-filled canvases reflect his delight in painting rich drapery, the sheen of armor and jewels and the glowing skin tones. His work, such as the *Garden of Love* **[374]**, was tremendously popular, bringing him great wealth and a studio in Antwerp with many assistants. He kept such tight control over the art, however, that when a painting was almost completed by his helpers, he had only to take a brush to a detail here or there to make the work his own.

Meanwhile, Dutch painters were producing for a Calvinist merchant class unassuming works that emphasized middle-class daily life. Frans Hals (1580–1666), a Protestant from Haarlem, was a popular portraitist of Dutch burghers, whom he often depicted in official group paintings. He was innovative in his method of finishing his paintings in loose, distinct brush strokes. In *The Bohemian Girl* **[111]** he catches a momentary expression to give the impression of quick work, which was in fact the product of long, calculated effort. Hals's rough naturalism is, however, quite different from the smooth realism of Caravaggio's *The Conversion of St. Paul* **[367]**.

Hals greatly influenced his fellow citizen Judith Leyster (1609–1660), whose substantial body of work is somewhat similar in style. Several of her paintings, such as *The Jolly Companions* **[375]** and *The Jolly Toper,* which has her monogram, were sold as the work of Hals. Although the themes of the two artists are similar, there are differences in their work. Leyster's compositions are generally more intricate, the brush work perhaps more sensitive, and the mood less exuberant.

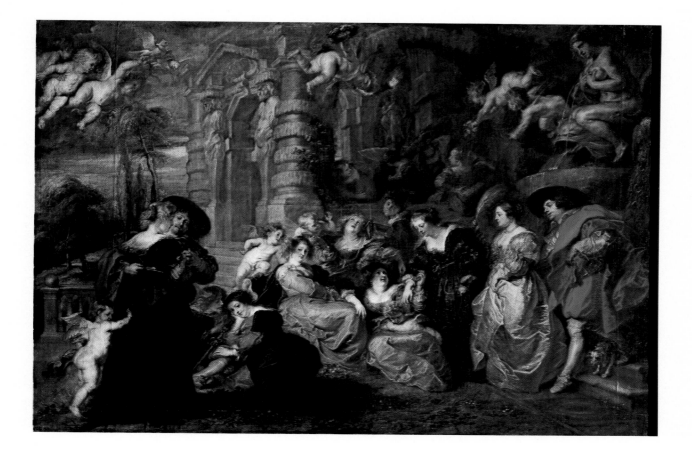

above: **374.** *Peter Paul Rubens.* Garden of Love.
c. 1632–1634. Oil on canvas, 6'6" × 9'3½"
(1.98 × 2.83 m). Museo del Prado, Madrid.

right: **375.** *Judith Leyster.* The Jolly Companions.
1630. Oil on wood, 26¾ × 21¾" (68 × 55 cm).
Louvre, Paris.

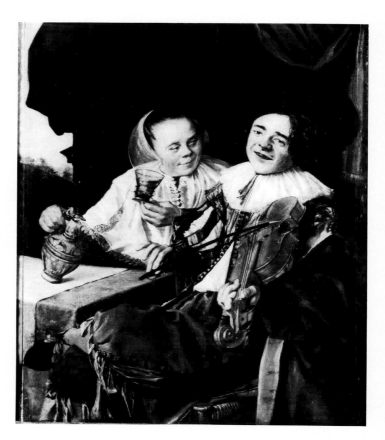

While Hals and Leyster painted their subjects
as if caught in a passing moment, Rembrandt
van Rijn (1606–1669), working in Amsterdam,
studied his subjects with psychological penetra-
tion, searching for the essential core of each one.
His portraits reveal such depths that at times we
turn from the embarrassing intimacy of his insights. To find authentic models for the biblical
themes of his works, he frequented the Jewish
quarter of Amsterdam.

Rembrandt used strong contrasts of light and
shade like Italian Baroque painters, but with
more restraint. His unconventional approach to
group portraits is evident in *The Night Watch*, in
which he strengthened the overall composition
with light and shadow at the expense of detailed

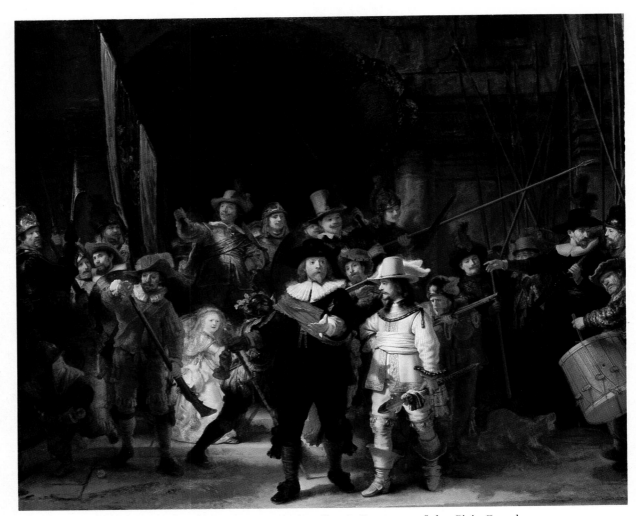

376. *Rembrandt.* The Sortie of Captain Frans Banning Cocq's Company of the Civic Guard (The Night Watch). *1642. Oil on canvas, 12'2" × 14'7" (3.71 × 4.45 m). Rijksmuseum, Amsterdam.*

likenesses **[376]**. So titled because darkened layers of varnish made it look like a night scene until it was cleaned in the 1940s, *The Sortie of Captain Frans Banning Cocq's Company of the Civic Guard,* as it is properly called, actually represents a volunteer military company called together to honor visiting royalty.

Rembrandt was also a master at graphics. He preferred etching to engraving because etching gave him more freedom to change a plate in preliminary states (see Chapter 4). With only a few lines he could express the essence of a scene, a gesture, or a pose.

In contrast to Rembrandt's uncluttered, deep-shadowed works, paintings by Jan Vermeer (1632–1675) of Delft appear clearly detailed. He portrayed the interiors of Dutch households with loving concern for meticulous accuracy, using mellow colors that reflect Dutch Baroque taste. The strong compositions brought atten-

tion to the sensuous colors and textures of everyday objects **[59]**. If the paintings were reduced to abstract shapes and flat colors in the 20th-century style of Mondrian **[46]**, we could see the careful plan of the composition. Vermeer's skill in framing his scenes with draperies, combined with his innovative device of cutting off figures at unusual levels, presaged a different way of depicting the world.

England

Separated from the mainland of Europe by the English Channel and conservative tradition, England was slow to accept Renaissance and Baroque art. English Baroque, exemplified by two London buildings, the Banqueting Hall at Whitehall by Inigo Jones (1573–1652) and St. Paul's Cathedral by Sir Christopher Wren (1632–1723), is not so ornate or luxurious as

Italian Baroque. Jones was influenced by Palladio. Wren's restrained forms link St. Paul's more closely to Italian and French Renaissance styles than to exuberant Italian Baroque [377]. The dome and façade were probably influenced by the late Renaissance St. Peter's in Rome [264], and the double rows of paired columns are reminiscent of the classical Louvre in Paris.

St. Paul's was the largest of many churches that Wren designed after the Great Fire of London in 1666. Their pillared porches, classical pediments, and single, slender steeples, imaginatively combined to give an effect of dignity and strength, influenced 18th-century churches in the English colonies in North America.

Age of Reason

The restless Baroque period passed quietly into the Age of Reason. Sir Isaac Newton had discovered laws of physics that led to a Scientific Revolution in the 18th century. Later, writers such as Voltaire in France expressed questions about the gap between the brilliant court life of the aristocracy and the poverty of the masses. Reflecting the times, art also underwent changes. Whereas the Baroque taste had favored theatrical arts of sensuous color and huge scale, French designers now created an intimate **Rococo** style, smaller in scale, and characterized by subtle colors and a profusion of curved ornament. Palaces and country estates were soon filled with paintings, tapestry, porcelain, and silver, intricately decorated.

Rococo Painting

Painters in the new style chose as subjects classical divinities and the aristocracy, in classical or rich court dress. Their palette was light—white, gold, pink, blue, and other clear hues. The work of Jean Antoine Watteau (1684–1721), who, like most court painters, was also an interior designer, shows us the Rococo style at its best. He was especially successful at recording the open-air entertainments so popular at court, making quick sketches at the scene and then painting the event in silvery tones in his studio. *The Em-*

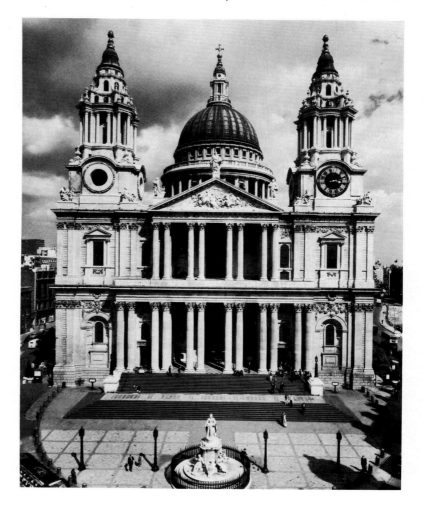

377. *Christopher Wren. St. Paul's Cathedral, London. 1675–1710.*

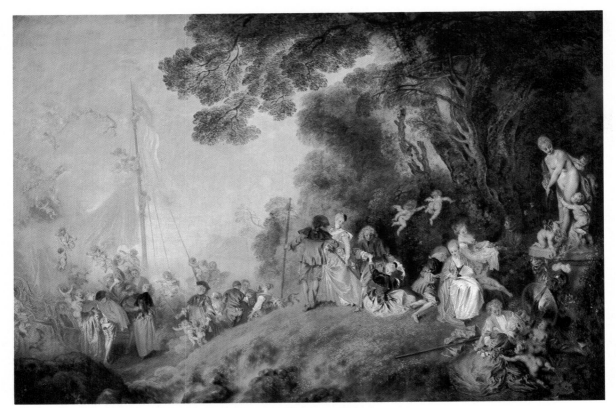

378. *Jean Antoine Watteau.* The Embarkation for Cythera. *1717. Oil on canvas, 4'3" × 6'4½" (1.3 × 1.94 m). Louvre, Paris.*

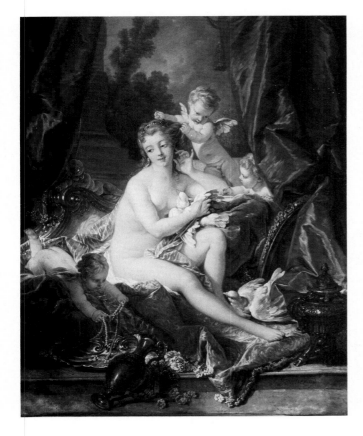

barkation for Cythera [378], a dreamy landscape peopled by courtiers leaving (in spite of the title) the mythological island of love, may have been inspired by a court fête. Adapting painting techniques from Rubens' more robust works, Watteau also borrowed ideas from the theater. His subjects, who included actors, seemed to act out their parts like tableaux in a stage setting as artificial as their lives. By focusing on the departure of the young couples from the island of love, he perhaps wistfully foreshadowed the coming changes that ended in Revolution.

François Boucher (1703–1770), painter to Louis XV's mistress Madame de Pompadour, was also known for allegories. Typical of his sprightly fantasies is *The Toilet of Venus* [379]. The glowing skin tones, carefully rendered textures, and coquettish eroticism give us an idea of how aristocratic patrons chose to decorate the walls of their salons and boudoirs.

left: **379.** *François Boucher.* The Toilet of Venus. *1751. Oil on canvas, 42⅝ × 33½" (108 × 85 cm). Metropolitan Museum of Art, New York (bequest of William K. Vanderbilt, 1920).*

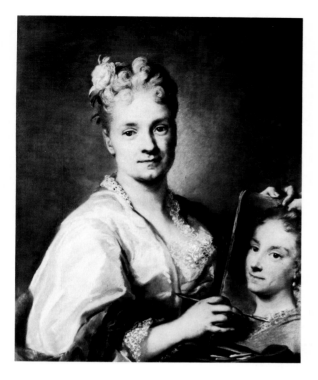

380. *Rosalba Carriera.*
Self-Portrait, Holding Portrait of Her Sister.
1715. Pastel, 28 × 22½" (71 × 57 cm).
Galleria degli Uffizi, Florence.

Portraiture

One of the most popular subjects of Rococo painters was portraiture, Rosalba Carriera (1675–1757) gained a reputation for life-size and miniature portraits in her native Venice. Many were in pastel, a new medium, which she introduced to Paris on a trip there in 1720. Her pastels, which range from simple studies to complex group compositions, illuminate the character of her subjects. They were so popular with Paris society that she was elected to the French Royal Academy of Painting and Sculpture. Her self-portrait [380] is a typical example.

Another member of the Royal Academy was Elisabeth Vigée-Le Brun (1755–1842), the daughter of a painter. Of the more than twenty portraits to her credit, the best known, a self-portrait with her daughter Julie, is a rhythmic composition well suited to aristocratic demands [381]. In fact, she pleased royal tastes so well that Queen Marie Antoinette sponsored her election to the Royal Academy.

The art of portraiture flourished especially in England. One of the foremost portraitists of his day was Sir Joshua Reynolds (1723–1792), who had studied in Italy. As co-founder and first president of the Royal Academy in London, he laid down rules governing the creation of art in

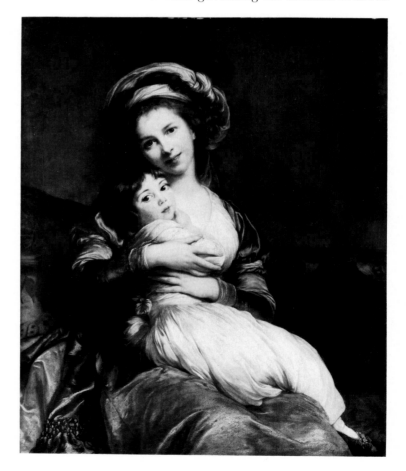

381. *Elisabeth Vigée-Le Brun.*
Self-Portrait with Her Daughter.
Oil on wood, 51⅛ × 37"
(130 × 94 cm). Louvre, Paris.

accordance with Italian and French academic principles. Although his writings on art were somewhat pompous, his portraits have grace and dignity. Flattering to their subjects, they appealed to aristocrats and set a style in fashionable portraiture [382].

In contrast to Reynolds' formal compositions are the freer works of Thomas Gainsborough (1727–1788), which point forward to the Romantic style. He had a talent for posing his subjects with an easy grace [383], against a landscape that suggested their luxurious estates. His colors are delicate, and his light-filled canvases sparkle with an elegance that evokes aristocratic life.

Genre and Still Life

The middle classes, like the aristocracy, also enriched their surroundings with art. Some chose allegories by Boucher, Jean Honoré Fragonard (1732–1806), and others, but many preferred subjects that reflected their own world—comfortable household scenes and boisterous drinking parties or tables laden with food and flowers. In short, their tastes were much like those of 17th-century Dutch burghers.

The foremost French painter of **genre** and **still life** was Jean Baptiste Chardin (1699–1779). His refined arrangements of food and cooking implements [384] reveal subtle color harmonies and textures, and, despite the sim-

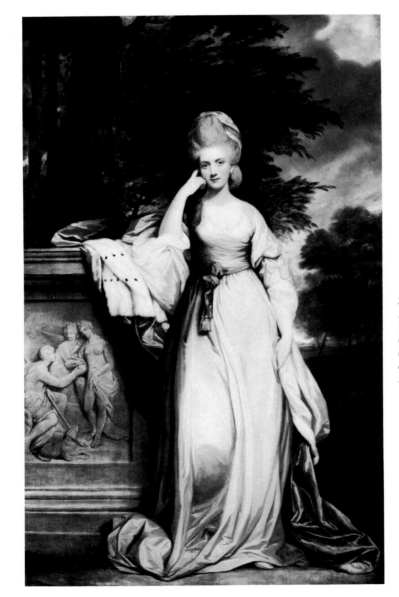

382. *Joshua Reynolds.*
Anne, Viscountess, Afterwards Marchioness of Townsend. *c. 1780.*
Oil on canvas, 7'11" × 4'10"
(2.41 × 1.47 m). Fine Arts Museum of San Francisco (gift, Roscoe and Margaret Oaks Collection).

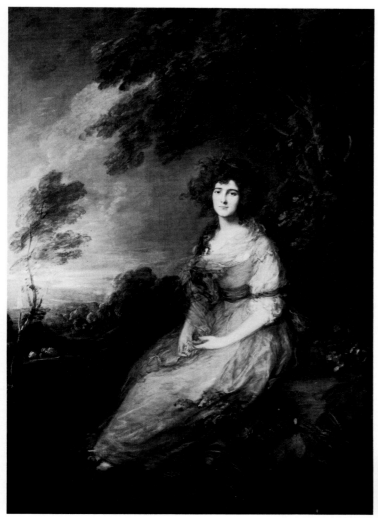

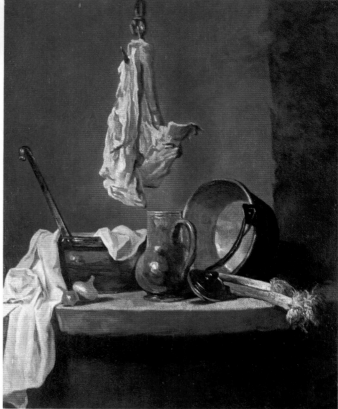

left: **383.** *Thomas Gainsborough.*
Mrs. Richard Brinsley Sheridan.
1785–1786. Oil on canvas, 7'2½" × 5'1½"
(2.2 × 1.54 m). National Gallery of Art,
Washington. (Andrew W. Mellon
Collection, 1937).

below: **384.** *Jean Baptiste Simeon Chardin.*
Still Life. *c. 1728–1730. Oil on canvas,*
15¾ × 12⅜" (40 × 31 cm).
Norton Simon Museum, Pasadena, California.

plicity of the subjects, they satisfied even the
most conservative patrons. Through his ability
to infuse a quiet dignity in domestic scenes, he
reminds us of Vermeer [59]. Chardin's paintings
were even enjoyed by the aristocracy, who liked
to play at living a simple life.

Still-life painting, called *nature morte* ("dead
nature") by the French, did not, however, rank
high by the standards of the academies, which
insisted that narrative content was a painting's
major justification. Since few women were encouraged to try their hands at "noble narratives"
or were admitted to the academies for the requi-
site anatomical training, still-life subjects, and in
particular flower painting, had obvious appeal
for them. One of the great still-life painters of
the time was Anne Vallayer-Coster (1744–
1818), the daughter of a goldsmith. She reveals
a delight in her subject, even in such early work

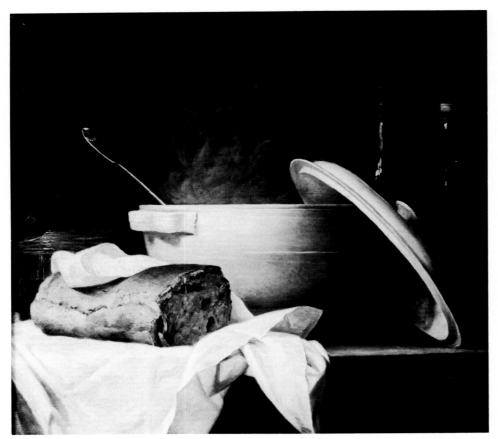

385. *Anne Vallayer-Coster.* The White Tureen. *1771.*
Oil on canvas, 19⅝ × 24½" (50 × 62 cm). Private collection, Paris.

as *The White Tureen* [385]. The composition, setting directional forces with the napkin, the ladle, and the tureen lid, is masterful, the silvery tones sensuous, but it is likely that her skill in portraying texture determines the appeal of the work.

Life in the 18th century had its problems, even among the privileged. The unpleasant side was told by William Hogarth in bitingly satirical works such as *The Harlot's Progress* and *The Rake's Progress* [37], a moralizing series of engravings narrating the downfall of a young man and woman. The rake comes to a pathetic end as a raving maniac in Bedlam, London's insane asylum, where his demented companions include a grimacing fiddler and a schizophrenic wearing an impromptu crown. Engravings had become a popular and inexpensive form of art, and a series like this reached large audiences. With Hogarth, the graphic arts had become an important propaganda tool for arousing indignation against social injustices, the vices of the rich, and the uneducated tastes of the new patrons. As the century progressed, the rising tide of democratic ideals presaged a new age.

Exercises and Activities

Research Activities

1. What factors were responsible for the development of the Renaissance attitude? How was it reflected in art? Describe one example of Renaissance sculpture, painting, or architecture and contrast it with one work of art from the Middle Ages.

2. How did the Renaissance discovery of the mathematical laws of perspective change the character of Western art? Using examples from this book, discuss the effect of this discovery of perspective on painting and on relief sculpture. How did the Italian concern

with perspective and idealized form affect the art of northern Europe?

3. Study of *The Last Supper* [80] by Leonardo reveals he viewed this event in terms of both the everyday world and divine harmony. Explain how the painting depicts the unity of both concepts.

4. In *The Night Watch* [376], Rembrandt includes a few formal portraits but many were painted in a process of action. Was this a typical group portrait? Explain.

5. What is meant by the statement "Michelangelo was born with one foot in the Renaissance and the other in the Baroque era"? Cite examples of his work that support this statement.

Studio Activities

1. Renaissance architecture was influenced by Greek art. Find a building in your community and sketch some of its Renaissance details.

2. Analyze the use of perspective in Renaissance paintings or prints, one each from northern and southern Europe. Trace each work and make a diagram of its perspective, using paper wide enough to incorporate both right and left vanishing points. Can you see the differences in the way southern and northern Europeans used perspective?

3. Select a Renaissance work such as Raphael's *School of Athens* [353]. Using colored chalk or pens, create a new composition from it in which Renaissance colors are changed and the subject is reorganized in the Baroque style.

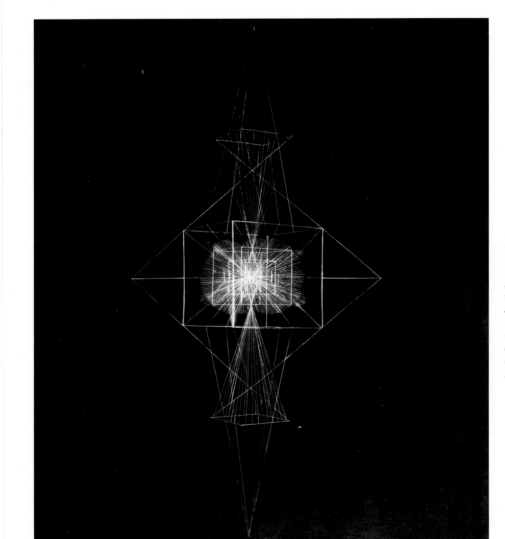

386. *Richard Lippold.*
Variation No. 7:
Full Moon. *1949–1950.*
Brass rods,
nickel-chromium, and
stainless steel wire.
10 × 6′ (3.05 × 1.83 m).
Collection, Museum
of Modern Art, New York
(Mrs. Simon Guggenheim
Fund).

Part Five
THE MODERN AGE

The Age of Reason promised to resolve all problems through the application of a scientific approach. With the growing revolutionary spirit in Europe and America, the modern world was born.

Confidence in science and progress ran high. Industrialists and the growing middle class lived comfortably side by side. The United States survived a Civil War. For the lower classes, however, industrialization often meant low wages, uncertain employment, and disagreeable living conditions in crowded, dirty factory towns. The traditions of a rural society and the comforts of religion were often destroyed for them, and socialism, anarchism, and labor movements provided poor substitutes.

As the 20th century replaced the 19th, world war, economic exploitation, and dehumanizing labor enveloped many who crowded into smoky towns. The rate of change has accelerated enormously over the last eighty years. Advances in technology reflected in our art [386]—airplanes, cinema, television, and computers—follow so quickly that we reel from the shock of rapid change. Our slow biological rhythms are upset by the speed of modern transport and communication. The mass media help to create a society to which millions are persuaded to conform, while their survival is threatened by its pace. Much of the world still faces famine. Wealthy countries find that they can no longer deny entire nations or races an equal share in the profits of their labor. Our natural resources are being depleted, and even remote areas are affected by our abuse of this earth. For example, penguins in Antarctica have been found with internal insecticide residues, while satellite photographs show huge smudges of smog covering continents. Against this background of change we will view the art of modern times.

14
Revolution and the Modern World: 1776–1900

Revolution is the larva of civilization.

Victor Hugo

It is not easy to retain the imagination's immediate, transitory intention and the harmony of the first execution.

Francisco Goya, c. 1785

There is nothing ugly in art, except that which is without character, that is to say, that which offers no outer or inner truth.

Auguste Rodin

Philosophy is dull if it does not touch my instinct. . . . It dares not manifest itself as a reality, but as an image even as a picture is—admirable if the picture is a masterpiece.

Paul Gauguin, *Avant et Après*

By the mid-18th century, absolute monarchies ruled almost everywhere. Aristocrats were insulated from the real world where most people lived in abject poverty. But the farther the wealthy retreated to their country estates, the stronger the revolutionary spirit that grew through Europe and the New World. The modern age began with revolution—political, social, and artistic.

Age of Revolution

As the 18th century drew to a close, the French ruling classes retreated from signs that the monarchy was shaky and isolated themselves from the needs of their subjects. Despite the example of the American Revolution against British rule in 1776, most were unprepared for the violence of the French Revolution in 1789, which cost the king and scores of nobles their lives. A new spirit of democracy and reform was sweeping the land, to which many artists were sympathetic.

Neoclassicism

Long before the Revolution, Rococo art was displaced by another style. Rediscovery of the buried cities of Pompeii and Herculaneum in the 1730s and 1740s and their study through archaeology led to renewed interest in classical Greece and Rome. The earlier **Neoclassical** movement **[373]** grew and, combined with the new scientific approach, appealed to intellectuals, who believed in the power of reason to uplift society. The style eventually became associated with the republican ideals of the Revolution and the early career of Napoleon Bonaparte and merged with the Romanticism that followed.

The Neoclassical style stressed straight lines and classical ornament in architecture and decorative arts. Neoclassical paintings emphasized balanced formalism, precise linear drawing, and often classical subjects. In England, Neoclassicism appeared in Georgian architecture and in the interior decoration of great houses by Rob-

THE VISUAL ARTS		HISTORICAL NOTES
1770–84 Jefferson, Monticello [387]		**1772** Diderot and d'Alembert, *Encyclopédie* **1773** Boston Tea Party
	1776	**1776** American Declaration of Independence **1776–79** James Cook's voyage to the New World and Hawaii
1787 David, *Death of Socrates* [388]		
		1789 Fall of Bastille, Paris **1789–97** George Washington first U.S. president **1791** Thomas Paine, *Rights of Man* **1793** Execution of Louis XVI
1800 Benoist, *Portrait of a Negress* [20]	1800	
		1804 Napoleon crowned emperor
1814–15 Goya, *Third of May* [53]		
		1815 Napoleon defeated at Waterloo
1818 Géricault, *The Raft of the "Medusa"* [391] **1821** Constable, *The Hay Wain* [390] **1823** Hokusai, *Great Wave* [121]		
		1829 Invention of photographic Daguerrotype
1830 Delacroix, *Liberty Leading the People* [392]		
		1837 Victoria becomes queen **1847** Karl Marx, *Communist Manifesto*
	1850	
		1851 Crystal Palace, London **1852** Harriet Beecher Stowe, *Uncle Tom's Cabin* **1853** Matthew Perry opens Japan
1855 Courbet, *The Studio* [394] **1857** Hiroshige, *Maple Leaves* [122]		
		1861–65 American Civil War **1860 on** American expansion to Pacific
1863 Manet, *Luncheon on the Grass* [401]	1865	**1865** Lincoln assassinated **1884–1957** European colonization of Africa
1867 Manet, *Execution of Emperor Maximilian* [66] **1871** Whistler, *Arrangement in Gray and Black* [406] **1872** Monet, *Impression: Sunrise* [403]		
	1880	
1884–86 Seurat, *Sunday on La Grande Jatte* [71], [72] **1889** Van Gogh, *The Starry Night* [22] **1892** Gauguin, *The Spirit of the Dead Watching* [410] **1892** Toulouse-Lautrec, *At the Moulin Rouge* [413] **1893** Munch, *The Scream* [128] **1894** Cézanne, *Still Life with Peppermint Bottle* [112] **1894–95** Sullivan, Guaranty Building		**1889** Eiffel Tower, Paris
	1900	
		1901 Queen Victoria dies

ert Adam (1728–1792), who made his own interpretation of classical motifs. Neoclassicism also affected American architecture, for example, Monticello, Thomas Jefferson's home that he designed himself near Charlottesville, Virginia [387], and most government buildings in Washington.

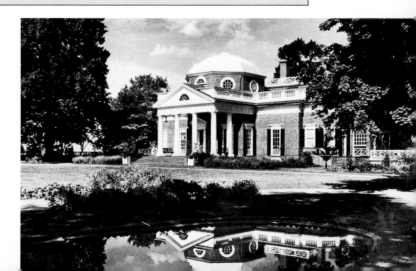

right: **387.** *Thomas Jefferson. Monticello, Charlottesville, Virginia. 1770–1784; 1796–1809.*

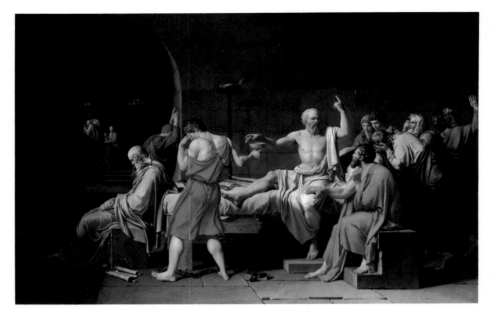

388. *Jacques Louis David.* The Death of Socrates. *1787. Oil on canvas,*
4'3" × 6'5¼" (1.3 × 1.96 m). Metropolitan Museum of Art, New York
(Wolfe Fund, 1931; Catharine Lorillard Wolfe Collection).

The most prominent Neoclassical painter was Jacques Louis David (1748–1825), who celebrated in his work the French Revolution and the rise of Napoleon. David portrayed classical themes as dictated by the Royal Academy while expressing republican ideals and the moral strengths of Greece and Rome. In *The Death of Socrates* [388] he retold the self-sacrifice of the ancient Greek philosopher who preferred to die rather than to give up the freedom to teach what he believed. In a formal composition he shows Socrates addressing his followers in prison. Vertical and horizontal shapes dominate the rigidly composed painting, giving it a structured quality of shallow space, not very revolutionary by our standards. David, however, felt that these classical forms were the best way to express the ideals of liberty, equality, and fraternity that were the watchwords of the Revolution. His emphasis on two-dimensionality became increasingly important in later 19th-century painting.

Belonging both to the Age of Reason and the Age of Revolution, Francisco Goya (1746–1828) was one of the foremost painters of the modern age. He was a skillful portraitist in the tradition of Velázquez, adept at depicting both the personality and fine costumes of the Spanish aristocracy and the court. He was most popular with his subjects, who apparently did not realize that beneath the elegance of his paintings he was commenting on court vanity and corruption.

Goya witnessed Napoleon's invasion of Spain in 1808. The artist depicted the violence and human capacity for evil in a series of etchings, *The Disasters of War*, which presented an uncompromising view of slaughter, rape, and distruction. Some of his paintings delved into the same themes, such as *Execution of the Madrileños on May 3, 1808* [53], which marks an incident of the war. This work strongly influenced Edouard Manet in France a half century later.

Disillusioned in his last years, Goya lived in seclusion and produced dark Romantic images of horror and despair. They might be taken as indications of the greed of the court feeding on its children, the masses [389]; or possibly, as works of the artist's old age, they were an allegorical reference to time, which consumes all.

Romanticism

Reacting against early-18th-century confidence in reason and the artificiality of court life was the **Romantic** movement, which began in the late 18th century and continued into the 19th century. It was characterized by the great value placed on strong emotion, the sublime, and a fascination with untamed nature, country folk in natural settings, and the picturesque or exotic.

English Landscape Romanticism flourished in England, which was not torn by revolution

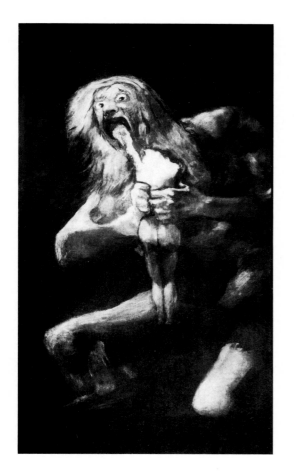

and had little need for an art of propaganda. John Constable (1776–1837) devoted himself to the study of nature. His picturesque English landscapes, painted in rich earth tones, shocked people accustomed to pretentious academic art. Constable said he wanted to capture the "light—dews—breezes—bloom—and freshness" of the English countryside. He sketched outdoors, and his quick studies are bolder than the paintings that he later composed in his studio. Nevertheless, he tried to keep the freshness of nature in his work and to portray what he saw, without contriving compositions to fit academic rules. *The Hay Wain* [**390**], typical of Constable's rural subject matter, was painted with a real love of the countryside and an ability to show atmospheric effects with a free brushstroke. The idea of landscape without allegorical or religious references attracted other artists, and the technique paved the way for the Impressionists, at midcentury.

Another landscape painter, J. M. W. Turner (1775–1851), had visions of painting the "unpaintable" and was possessed with a determination to record the changes of nature's atmosphere. In many ways, Turner was ahead of his age, reducing air, water, and even fire to undetailed color arrangements. When Turner

above: **389.** *Francisco Goya.* Saturn Devouring One of His Sons. *c. 1821. Fresco detached on canvas, 4'9½" × 2'8⅛" (1.46 × 0.83 m). Museo del Prado, Madrid.*

below: **390.** *John Constable.* The Hay Wain. *1821. Oil on canvas, 4'2½" × 6'1" (1.28 × 1.85 m). Reproduced by courtesy of the Trustees, National Gallery, London.*

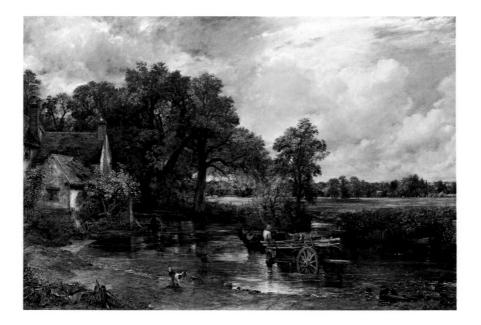

watched the fire that destroyed the Houses of Parliament in 1834, he was inspired to paint a series of remarkable pictures of the disaster. Images of flames, smoke, reflections in the river, and crowds of people watching all dissolve into one another. Occasionally applying paint with a palette knife, Turner suggests turbulence with spontaneous, bold streaks and dabs, as in his scenes of Venice [108].

Turner was a forerunner of the Impressionists and was rediscovered by two of them, Pissarro and Monet, after his death. But Turner was affected by the poetic quality of light; he had more interest in abstract patterns than the Impressionists, who were mainly concerned with the effects of light on objects. A poem by Turner about Switzerland, where it was fashionable for English artists and lords and ladies to go to contemplate the grandeur of the Alps, tells us a good deal about his attitude toward nature:

> . . . its pine clad forests
> And towering glaciers fall,
>   the work of ages
> Crashing through all . . .

French Romanticism In the spirit of Romanticism the French painters Théodore Géricault (1791–1824) and Eugène Delacroix chose faraway and exotic subjects. Géricault's *The Raft of the "Medusa"* [391] was also an indictment of mismanagement and corruption in the French government, which had sent a shipload of emigrants to North Africa without life-saving equipment. Géricault depicts in realistic detail the makeshift raft crowded with desperate, starving, shipwrecked passengers and crew. But the protest went unheeded. Instead, the public was outraged by the artist who used naked figures in unclassical poses to convey his message. This was a revolutionary painting in its dramatic championing of a current political cause and in the use of colors and composition to intensify emotion. Compare its complex arrangement of turbulent forms with David's Neoclassical painting [388] to see how strongly Géricault was rebelling against academic constrictions.

Described as a Romantic and a Neoclassicist, while straddling both camps, was the fiery Eugène Delacroix (1798–1863). Romantic extremes of emotion and a brilliant palette, fused

391. *Théodore Géricault.* The Raft of the "Medusa." *1818. Oil on canvas, 16′1¼″ × 23′6″ (4.91 × 7.16 m). Louvre, Paris.*

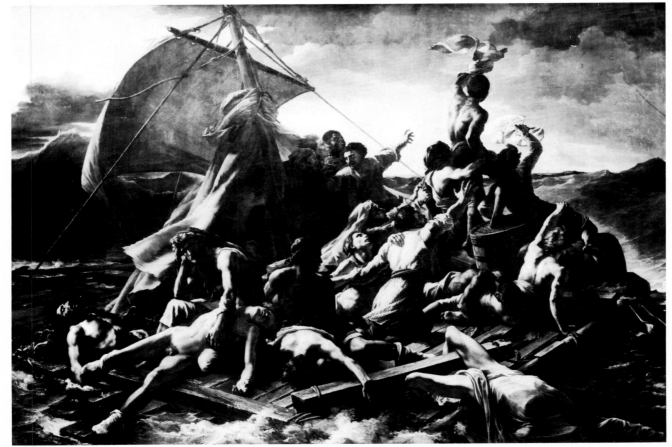

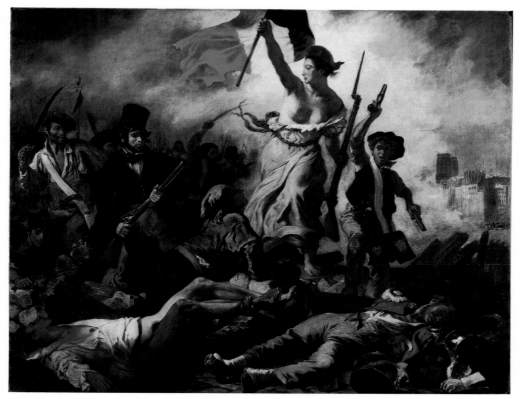

392. *Eugène Delacroix.* Liberty Leading the People, 1830. *1830. Oil on canvas, 8'6" × 10'10" (2.59 × 3.3 m). Louvre, Paris.*

to the purity of form and nobility of subject typical of Neoclassicism, were both present in *Liberty Leading the People* **[392]**. High drama can be found in the radical linking of rich and poor, male and female, young and old in a communal cause. Turbulent though the content was, the traditional triangular composition with liberty at the apex produced stability, reinforced by the huddled masses at her feet.

Also rebelling against tradition was Rosa Bonheur (1822–1899), daughter of a painter, who studied at the École des Beaux Arts. From her childhood, Rosa had adopted masculine dress, which freed her to travel (and paint) in public places. Her reputation as a painter was established by *The Horse Fair* **[42]**, which won her the rank of Chevalier de la Légion d'Honneur. Although animals and flowers were considered suitable subjects for women, Bonheur's work was outstanding for its power and scope.

Realism and Social Protest

During the 19th century the Industrial Revolution encouraged a capitalist economy in which hard-driving entrepreneurs used the productivity of workers for personal gain. Peasant families

crowded into industrial towns to find work and settled in cheap housing near factories, which quickly became slums. Even children were forced to work long hours in factories and mines. Although the British abolished the slave trade early in the 19th century and slavery was ended in the United States by the Civil War, the exploitation of industrial workers continued.

Newly rich industrialists and bankers, if they bought art at all, chose academic, Neoclassical paintings such as those of David or of Jean Auguste Dominique Ingres (1780–1867), whose portraits and exotic scenes show his mastery of line and classical composition. Few were interested in the social criticism of Géricault or the political commentary of satirist Honoré Daumier (1808–1879), who earned his living as a cartoonist and illustrator. His lithographs were sympathetic to the poor and disadvantaged while presenting brutal caricatures of the ruling classes. Critical of the French political, judicial, and police systems, these prints appeared in newspapers, where they influenced political cartooning for years to come. In addition to his graphic work, Daumier painted the slum dwellers of Paris in their squalid surroundings. His

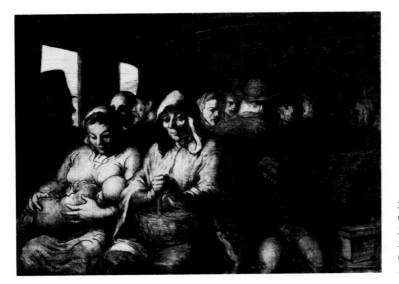

393. *Honoré Daumier.* The Third-Class
Carriage. *c. 1862. Oil on canvas,*
25¾ × 35½" (65 × 90 cm).
*Metropolitan Museum of Art, New York
(bequest of Mrs. H. O. Havemeyer,
1929; H. O. Havemeyer Collection).*

The Third-Class Carriage [393] and its companion
The First-Class Carriage make strong statements
about the gulf between the rich and the poor. At
the same time, the three generations represented in the third-class coach, all trapped in the
economic system, reflect Daumier's view of the
power of the proletariat.

Another French painter who rejected the
standards of the Academy was the independent
Gustave Courbet (1819–1877). His paintings

did not depict graceful poses or rich textures,
but, like those of Caravaggio two centuries earlier, were realistic portrayals of daily life. He
gathered students to him and even brought a
bull into the studio for them to draw.

Refused entry to the Paris Exposition of 1855,
Courbet set up in a nearby wooden shed his own
exhibit entitled "Réalisme, G. Courbet." His
most ambitious painting, *The Studio: A Real Allegory of the Last Seven Years of My Life* [394], was

394. *Gustave Courbet.* The Studio: A Real Allegory of the Last Seven Years of My Life. *1855.
Oil on canvas, 11'9¾" × 19'6⅝" (3.6 × 5.96 m). Louvre, Paris.*

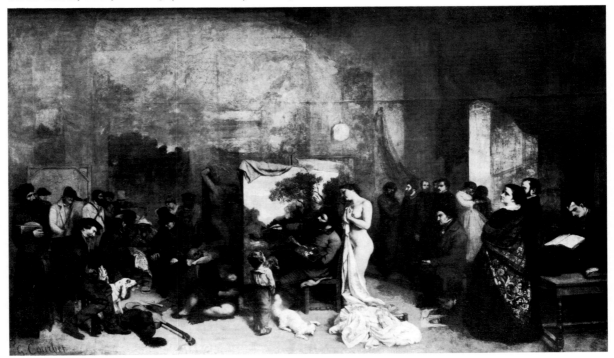

featured. Among the figures were a nude, Courbet himself at the easel, a small boy, famous critics, and a cadaver. Courbet issued a *Manifesto of Realism* supporting this work. Thus he addressed an issue central to avant-garde artists as they struggled against the rigid control of the Academy. Accused of socialist political activities, Courbet was exiled in 1873, but his independent spirit continued to influence young artists.

Other Views of Reality

In the mid-19th century, fresh views of reality expanded European artists' traditional depictions of nature. Exposure to the world outside the West, to Oriental, African, and Oceanic art, opened new possiblilities in the two-dimensional rendering of three-dimensional space, possibilities not based on the Renaissance "window view" of reality.

The Orient

Japan had been isolated from the outside world for more than two hundred years. In 1857, actions of the United States Navy supporting an "Open Door" doctrine opened more than Oriental ports to trade with the West. Europeans excitedly brought back the newly discovered arts of Japan, as well. In addition, even the packing used to protect products for shipping showed new ways of representing form, for it often consisted of discarded woodcuts used as wrappings.

Woodcuts   From the 17th century on, woodblock printing was a mass medium that all Japanese could afford. Illustrations of folktales appeared in widespread inexpensive editions, along with topical images of the day in the 19th century, when prints of courtesans and actors were banned.

The popularity of these **woodcuts** depended on the styles of the moment; a new hair style could suddenly outdate a whole edition of prints. When the woodcuts reached Europe in the mid-19th century, their flat shapes with little depth and diagonal composition profoundly affected French Impressionist painters. The refreshing variety of themes expressed in a new way proved inspiring. For example, in the woodcut showing an unusual view of Mount Fuji, Hokusai created a bold composition in which a huge wave curls up and breaks in the foreground, dwarfing the distant mountain [121]. A traditional Western landscape artist would probably have emphasized the mountain, not the off-center wave, and would have shown Fuji in realistic perspective. In addition, the Japanese approach to portraiture, which also reduced form to flat images, appeared strange, though fascinating, to Western eyes.

Pottery   Oriental procelains were imitated by Western potters from the 17th century on [207].

The Japanese also developed a rough, simpler pottery, influenced by Zen Buddhism, as we saw in Chapter 7. Its spontaneous shapes, variety, earth-colored glazes, and quickly brushed-on decoration have appealed greatly to 20th-century potters in the West.

Because Zen Buddhists considered everyday living to be as important as the spiritual, many took delight in the process of making pots, stressing that uniformity and repetition were fatal to imagination [208]. The Zen tea ceremony, a religious ritual, traditionally takes place in a simple teahouse designed to recreate the peace and purity one might feel alone by a mountain waterfall. Everything used in the ceremony is intended to induce serenity. The subtle response of the tea drinker to the shape of a bowl, the sound of the bamboo whisk stirring the tea, or the color of a flower in a vase characterizes for us the essential difference between the art of the Far East and the art of the West.

By the 19th century, after two thousand years of largely Greek and Roman inspiration, many Western artists began to question their goals. The spiritual essence of much Oriental art profoundly affected Western concepts, while from Africa came part of the Cubist impulse for Picasso and others. Beyond the Church and our classical heritage existed a whole world we knew little about. The art of our 20th century took part of its legacy from that other world.

Africa

Africans of the 19th century continued to live much as they had for centuries, grouped in extended families. Africans who continued in this traditional way of life lived in villages of a few families, raised crops for the community, and believed in an animistic religion. They thought of the world around them and the forces of nature—sun, rain, fertility of crops and humans, and death—as determined by powerful spirits, or divinities. African art expresses human responses to those forces with great emotion and vitality.

The Western division between fine and functional art never existed in traditional African (or

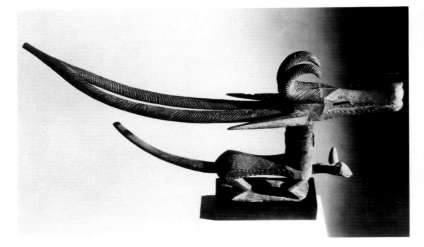

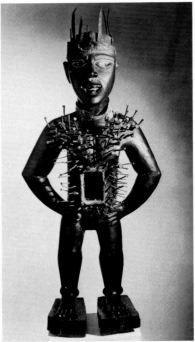

above: **395.** *Antelope headpiece, from Mali. 19th century. Wood, length 24¾" (63 cm). Whereabouts unknown.*

right: **396.** *Nail fetish, from Zaire. 19th century. Wood, height 32¼" (82 cm). Whereabouts unknown.*

any other preindustrial) society. Some art objects, such as masks and headpieces [395], were created for religious ceremonies held by secret organizations, so our knowledge of their use is scanty. Houses and furnishings were decorated with carving and color. Africans also enhanced their own bodies with paint, tattoos, and scars [26], both as decoration and as symbolism. For the Africans, as for the ancient Greeks and many other peoples, art was an important part of life.

Expressing an emotional response to the world was vital to African artists, who usually considered realism in art an infringement on the powers of the divine. Therefore, they emphasized and exaggerated the characteristic shapes of humans, animals, or imagined spirits, sometimes so strongly as to startle Western eyes. Perhaps that is why many artists looking for new approaches have found African art so appealing.

Wood Sculpture In Africa as in the West, the human figure has been a constant source of inspiration. Sculptured forms, usually carved from wood, range in height from 3 inches to 6 feet (7.6 to 183 centimeters). Most figures were left uncolored or painted solid red or black. Some present-day Yoruban art from Nigeria and sculpture from East Africa is multicolored. Male and female figures were carved from tree trunks for ancestor rites as commemorative statues or as mendicant figures holding bowls for contributions [27]. Many of these figures were

status symbols made for the well-to-do in each community.

Like Christian sculptures of religious figures, African images evoke ancestors and gods. Some of the sculptures are fetishes, which were designed both to make contact with the gods for help and to ward off evil spirits. For example, in this fetish from Zaire [396], each nail represents an attempt to reach a divinity. If there had been no rain for weeks, a priest might drive a nail into the figure to attract the power of the rain god. Or if someone were ill, a fetish would be used to reach a spirit for help in effecting a cure. An unsuccessful fetish would soon be discarded. Such rituals might be distantly compared with Christians lighting a candle before an image of a saint in a plea for help.

Besides figures, African sculpture includes ceremonial thrones (stools), neck rests, masks, and other furnishings. Most were ornamented with carving, paint, or materials such as feathers, shells, hair, and stones. Typically, a wooden throne from Cameroon was completely covered with a geometric design of beads and cowrie shells [397]. Thrones were important to Africans. In some regions people believed that a person's soul occupied the throne that he cherished during his lifetime. In other regions, certain stools were reserved for important personages. The Ashanti people of Ghana preserved a myth about a golden throne that fell miraculously from heaven and brought good fortune. Royal Ashanti thrones were often covered with gold,

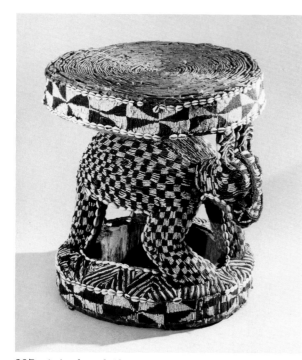

397. *Animal stool (throne), Bamum or Bamileke tribe, Cameroon. 19th or 20th century. Wool, glass beads, cowrie shells, burlap, cotton cloth; height 19¼" (49 cm). Metropolitan Museum of Art, New York (Michael C. Rockefeller Memorial Collection, bequest of Nelson A. Rockefeller, 1979).*

Sculptural styles and decorative patterns varied widely. Often certain objects were unique to an area. An example from Ghana is the disc-headed Akua'ba figure similar to those worn by young Ashanti girls as fertility charms to ensure a good marriage and children [398].

Masks African ritual masks played an important role in community life. Elaborate masks were worn in ceremonial dances to heighten the emotional effect on the spectator as well as to draw power from the spirits. Masks also emphasized the strong emotional ties that exist among humans, animals, and nature. Some masks were made to fit on top of the head, others to cover the face, and still others to fit over the head and shoulders. In order to help dancers keep their masks on, they were often fitted with a bar inside for the wearer to grip with his teeth [399].

In addition, the body of the masked dancer was usually decorated with paint or costumed in feathers, skins, cloth, or vegetable fibers. Representing a particular god or spirit, masked ritual dancers often felt themselves to be psychologically identified with the power of the spirit. And, in turn, they were identified as that spirit by the community. Similarly, masks for identification and emotional effect were used in ritual dances in Oceania and pre-Columbian North America and in Chinese and Japanese theater.

Many African dance masks were designed to celebrate the rites of passage through life—particularly birth, puberty, marriage, and death. Since ancestor worship was strong in African cultures, death was a constant preoccupation, and masks reflected its importance. Thus, a white mask might be worn to attract the power

once so abundant that Europeans called Ghana the Gold Coast. Neck rests were used to support the head of a sleeping person without disturbing an elaborate hair style. Most decorations on these rests were geometric, but designs differed from place to place.

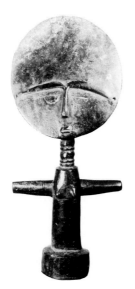

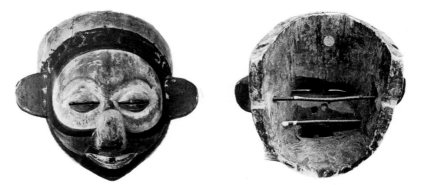

left: **398.** *Akua'ba statue, from Ghana. Ashanti. Wood, height 11" (28 cm). Segy Gallery of African Art, New York.*

above: **399.** *Bayaka mask (front and back views), from Lower Congo. 19th century. Painted wood, 13 × 12 × 9" (33 × 30 × 23 cm). Collection the author.*

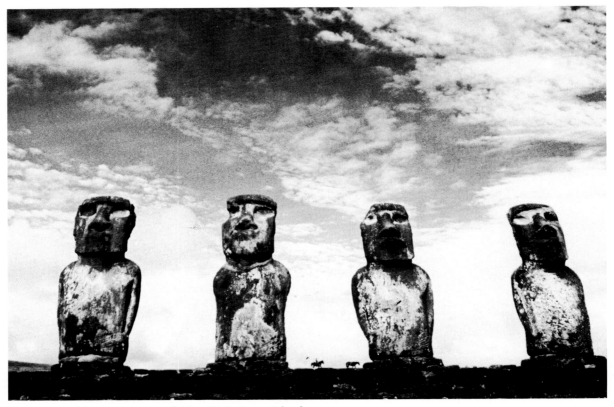

400. *Four of the seven statues of Ahu-Akivi, Easter Island.*

of ancestral spirits because white symbolized dead flesh. In this Bayaka puberty mask from the Congo [399], the color white signifies the death of the child and the initiation of the young adult into community life.

African Influences on 19th- and 20th-Century Art In the 19th century, European traders began to bring African sculptures home with them in significant numbers. Artists in Paris soon discovered these exotic objects. Searching for new ways to depict the world and express their emotions, they were impressed by the uncanny ability of African sculptors to emphasize the essentials of a subject while simplifying and distorting it. Picasso and Braque, influenced by African sculpture, developed **Cubism.**

Oceania

The islands of the south Pacific Ocean are grouped into three cultural areas: Micronesia (including the Caroline and Marshall Islands), Melanesia (including New Guinea), and Polynesia (including Hawaii, New Zealand, and Easter Island). Sometimes Australia is considered part of Oceania. Although each area and island had a distinctive culture, many elements were common to all.

Most Oceanic peoples came originally from the Asian mainland and traditionally belonged to extended families and clans. They farmed and fished for a living and worshipped their ancestors and other spirits. Since wood was plentiful, it was the most common material for building tools and war implements, often fitted with blades of shell or stone. Each island had its particular form of war club, all of them lethal. Wood was also used for carved stools, house posts, and figures of the gods.

Oceanic art objects, such as carved and painted shells, reflect the constant warfare between the islands. Many were part of elaborate religious ceremonies. Most art was made to be seen in action—masks moving with the rhythms of ceremonial dancers, weapons wielded in battle, the carved paddles and prows of Maori canoes moving over water.

The famous statues on Easter Island in Polynesia, made from volcanic tufa, are an exception to the liveliness of most Oceanic art [400]. These large, brooding sculptures, originally set on ceremonial stone platforms, were discovered on Easter Sunday by 19th-century missionaries.

The islanders had then lost all recollection of the origins of the sculptures, and archaeologists are still uncertain of the religion they served.

The Reality of the Camera and Protoimpressionism

As a result of the invention of the camera, a 19th-century Western painter, trained to believe that the purpose of art was an imitation of nature, faced a new dilemma. Because the camera could capture a sitter, an event, or a scene more quickly and more realistically than the painter could, no artist was needed to transcribe reality. Relieved of having to transpose solid forms onto a flat surface, many painters were forced to find new outlets for artistic expression.

Edouard Manet (1832–1883) faced this delemma creatively; instinctively combining many influences, he transformed them into a new style sometimes called **Protoimpressionism.** Schooled academically, he was, however, a Romantic in his choice of exotic subjects and use of rich color and texture. He often chose Spanish themes in paintings that show his admiration for Velázquez [371] and Goya [53], and he was fascinated by the flat areas of color in Japanese art. His broad areas of paint, reminiscent of early photographic effects, and his occasional spots of brilliant color shocked a public accustomed to academic painting [401]. In addition, Manet was attacked as a heretic because he did not follow the traditional method of modeling forms, going back to the time of Giotto, by painting dark values, middle values, and then building up lights and reinforcing darks. Instead, he adopted a radical approach of trying to duplicate sunlight by preserving the natural brilliance of the primed canvas and gradually adding darker tones.

Manet's large painting, originally titled *The Bath* and dubbed by critics *Luncheon on the Grass,* presented a nude woman picnicking with two fully clothed men in a woodland glen [401]. The painting was a reworking of the Renaissance painting by Giorgione, *Sacred and Profane Love,* an allegory referring to the Muse, who must be present to inspire art. Manet included a figure bathing in a pool in the background to justify his posing nudes outdoors and used a well-known courtesan as a model, presenting her as a naked picnicker gazing boldly at the viewer. The public was scandalized. Moreover, his painting of skin tones under strong natural light was not

401. *Edouard Manet.* Luncheon on the Grass (Le Déjeuner sur l'Herbe). *1863. Oil on canvas, 7'3¾" × 8'10⅜" (2.15 × 2.7 m). Musée d'Orsay, Paris.*

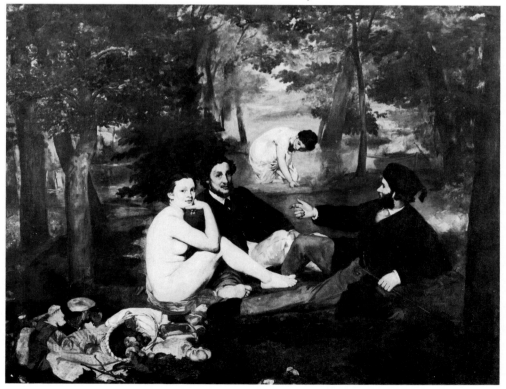

considered sound academic practice. The Academy refused to exhibit his painting in the official Salon of 1863. The protests of Manet and other rejected painters led to the government's forming a separate *Salon des Refusés,* which eventually broke the hold of the Academy on artists.

In 1865, Manet's masterpiece, *Olympia* [402], today a favorite in the Musée d'Orsay, created an even greater scandal than *Luncheon*; in fact, it was considered pornographic by some of the artist's contemporaries! Actually, Manet based *Olympia* on Titian's *The Venus of Urbino* [354], but Manet's figure does not appear goddess-like. Obviously a courtesan of the Paris demimonde (a world of questionable morals), she lies on her rumpled bed, with no signs of modesty when her maid brings an admirer's flowers. Although figures of goddesses were traditional subjects, Manet's suggestion in *Olympia* that Venus was an ordinary woman was badly received by the public. The flat silhouette of her body further shocked traditionalists. Manet never hesitated to paint as he believed, but he disliked the criticism that came his way, and he rejected for himself the term *Impressionist,* which his followers were beginning to apply to him.

Impressionism

Several young artists were influenced by Manet's attempts to capture the immediacy of a moment, his use of flat areas of color, and his efforts to depict natural light. Rejected by the official Salon of 1874, these rebellious painters organized their own exhibit in the studio of the photographer Nadar [64]. They considered the location appropriate because they believed that photography was a vital new art medium, just as they hoped their own work marked a new direction in painting. The name **Impressionism** was provided by a journalist who laughed at a painting exhibited by Claude Monet (1840–1926) entitled *Impression: Sunrise* [403]. The critic's statement that "these are not artists, they are Impressionists" seemed to describe the common trait in their work. Although it was meant as an insult, the painters adopted the label for their new style.

Theory and Technique

The Impressionists were more interested in the fleeting light and color reflected from an object than in form or content, and they had little interest in story-telling. To capture the effects of movement and atmospheric vibration over landscape and figures, Monet and other Impressionists such as Camille Pissarro (1830–1903) and Auguste Renoir (1841–1919) painted *en pleine air* ("in the open air"). This practice, begun by painters who took to the Barbizon forest near Paris in the 1830s, was a radical depar-

402. *Edouard Manet.* Olympia. *1863. Oil on canvas, 4′3¼″ × 6′2¾″ (1.3 × 1.9 m). Musée d'Orsay, Paris.*

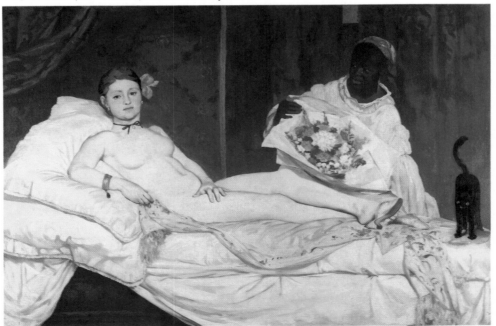

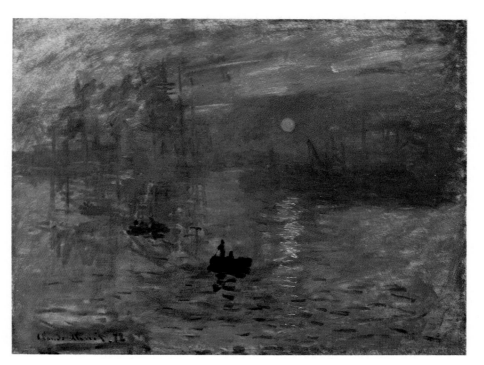

403. *Claude Monet.*
Impression: Sunrise.
1872. Oil on canvas,
19½ × 24½″ (60 × 62 cm).
Musée Marmottan, Paris.

ture from the academic custom of making only sketches outdoors and developing them traditionally into paintings in north-lighted studios. Another departure was the Impressionists' determination to paint directly on primed canvas without the traditional underpainting in an umber (brown) tone. Also revolutionary was the Impressionists' use of the **broken-color** technique, in which they painted with pure colors taken directly from the tube. Instead of, for example, mixing blue-green and yellow on their palettes to make green, or yellow and red to make orange, they placed small brushstrokes of analogous colors [70] next to each other, intending the eye to mix them. They sometimes juxtaposed strokes of complementary colors to intensify their effect [72]. When viewed from a distance, these areas of color became images of trees, flowers, figures, and buildings. Such techniques enabled many Impressionists and some Post-Impressionists like Georges Seurat to produce works that seemed to vibrate with color.

Broken colors, emphasis on visual sensation, flat shapes, and unusual perspective, the last two borrowed from the Japanese, were common traits of Impressionism, but individual painters varied considerably in their styles. Some, such as Monet and Pissarro, remained dedicated Impressionists all their lives. Others, Cézanne, Gauguin, and Van Gogh, for example, briefly practiced Impressionism but developed different approaches very soon afterwards.

Painters

Most typical of the Impressionists, perhaps, was Monet, who was chiefly concerned with the appearance of objects in changing light. Intrigued by the dancing patterns of sunlight through mist on the water at dawn, he created the controversial *Impression: Sunrise* [**403**]. Influenced by Hokusai's *Thirty-six Views of Mt. Fuji* [**121**], he explored the effects of light at different times of day in twenty-six canvases of Rouen Cathedral. As Monet continued to refine the broken-color technique, he became more and more absorbed in light. Saying that he wished he had been born blind so that he could regain his sight and paint objects without knowing what they were, he painted solid forms that dissolved into mists of color. Monet produced hundreds of studies of the shimmering surface of water and light on the shiny leaves and delicate blossoms of the water lilies of the Japanese-style pool in his garden at Giverny. In his last, large paintings done just before his death, the water lilies are almost completely abstract. These loose, much-admired paintings, like his Japanese garden, have become aesthetic environments that were forerunners of the large field paintings of Jackson Pollock [**10**] and other **Abstract Expressionists** in the 1950s.

Academic tradition was also questioned by Pissarro in such works as the *Boulevard des Italiens, Morning, Sunlight* [**29**], when he captured a busy Paris street scene on canvas. According to the

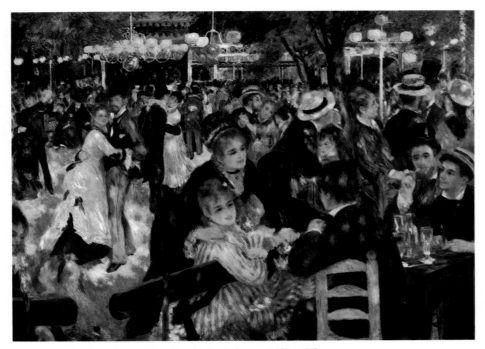

404. *Auguste Renoir.* Le Moulin de la Galette. *1876. Oil on canvas,*
4'3½" × 5'9" (1.31 × 1.75 m). Musée d'Orsay, Paris.

Academy, beauty was achieved through the careful, rational rearrangement of nature and the elimination of the accidental. But Pissarro, influenced by the unusual perspectives of Japanese prints, chose the reality of a bird's-eye view of a boulevard from his room under the roof. The critics condemned *Boulevard des Italiens* as having no center of interest; no foreground, middle ground, or background; no ordered path through which the eye could travel. They also criticized Pissarro's technique because one could see the strokes of color. Today, we find it difficult to imagine that people once found it shocking, but we must remember that we have become used to the Impressionist way of looking at the world.

Auguste Renoir (1841–1919), who was first apprenticed to a painter of Rococo ornament and flowers on porcelain cups and plates, loved color, flowers, beautiful women, and charming children. He sincerely wished to please himself and his viewers. Because Renoir would not undertake commissions from those he found unappealing, all his works show similar delight in their aesthetic subject.

The traits we identify with Impressionism can be seen in Renoir's *Le Moulin de la Galette,* a painting of a Parisian outdoor dance hall **[404]**. The scene is informal. Color is broken. The vertical and horizontal shapes, such as the pavilion

in the background, are emphasized so that our eyes stay on the surface of the painting, for depth in space was not important to Impressionists. We may compare this shallow space with the deep space in a Renaissance painting such as Leonardo's *The Last Supper* **[80]**. In spite of his early dedication to Impressionism, Renoir, as much as Degas, was concerned with composition in his paintings, and his later canvases, especially those of bathers, were influenced by Titian and other Venetian painters.

Degas carried the idea of painting figures in momentary poses even further than Manet. Like most Impressionists, he was intrigued by movement, and horses and dancers were among his favorite subjects. He liked to catch ballet dancers in unusual positions or moments of action on stage, lit by bright footlights **[405]**. His paintings appear to capture movement like candid shots with a camera, with which he experimented. Inspired by Japanese prints, he also depicted his subjects from unusual views.

Degas, however, was deeply concerned with composition and worked out his paintings carefully in sketches and studies. While he exhibited with the Impressionists, he never considered himself one of them because of his formal interest in composition. He supported Impressionist efforts to change the rules of the Academy primarily because he believed in the right to question restrictive attitudes. He could afford to give them his support, for he was a wealthy aristocrat by birth, had been trained in the tradition of the Academy, and had been accepted to exhibit in the Salon. Set apart from the Impressionists also because of his concern for faithful draftsmanship, Degas might have become one of the greatest portraitists of his day. But he would paint only friends with whom he felt empathy.

Also responding to the influence of Japanese art, James Abbott McNeill Whistler (1834–1903) was particularly impressed by the apparent simplification of planes and colors which he identified in Oriental woodcuts and paintings. As an expatriate American who from an early age was exposed directly to European art, he managed somehow to detach himself, like Degas, from the Impressionist movement around him. Rejecting the brilliant colors of his Impressionist friends, Whistler used muted grays and subtle harmonies with only touches of gold and red. He called his paintings "nocturnes," "symphonies," and "arrangements" to emphasize his belief in the importance of the abstract qualities of painting, which he compared to music. Unlike artists such as Pissarro and Monet, who painted the momentary light effects they saw before them, Whistler believed that "Nature contains the elements, in colour and form, of all pictures, as the keyboard contains the notes of all music." Form and color,

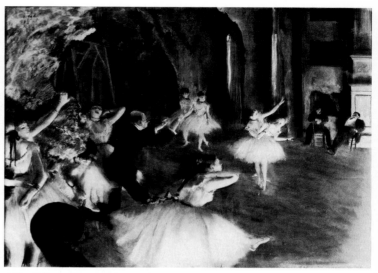

405. *Edgar Degas.* The Rehearsal of the Ballet on the Stage. *1878–1879. Oil colors freely mixed with turpentine with traces of watercolor and pastel over pen-and-ink drawing on paper mounted on canvas; 21⅜ × 28¾" (54 × 73 cm). Metropolitan Museum of Art, New York (gift of Horace Havemeyer, 1929).*

rather than subject matter, were elements he considered important. He called his famous portrait of his mother *Arrangement in Gray and Black No. 1* [406] because he saw no reason why the public should be interested in the identity of the

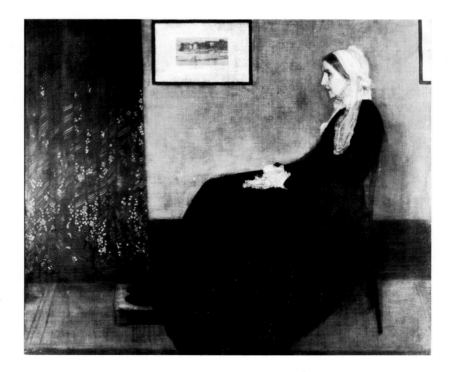

406. *James Abbott McNeill Whistler.* Arrangement in Gray and Black No. 1 (The Artist's Mother). *1871. Oil on canvas, 4'9" × 5'4½" (1.45 × 1.64). Louvre, Paris.*

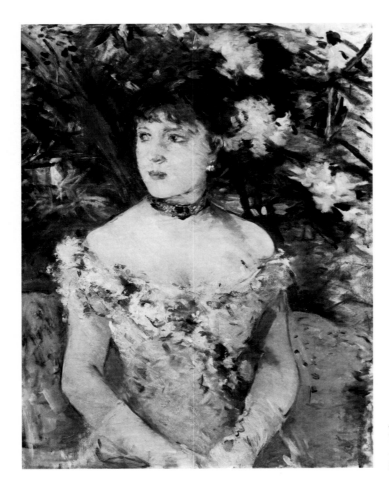

407. *Berthe Morisot.*
Young Woman in a Ball Dress.
*1879–1880. Oil on canvas, 28 × 21¼″
(71 × 54 cm). Musée d'Orsay, Paris.*

sitter. Whistler's concept of a painting as an arrangement of color, value, and shape had an important influence on later painters and on the development of abstract painting in the 20th century.

We have seen the number of women in the art world gradually increase since the Renaissance. Although they were often denied entrance to the academies for instruction, some of them traveled to distant lands to paint the exotic scenes popular during the Romantic period.

The youngest of the Impressionists was Mary Cassatt (1845–1926). After a comfortable childhood in a rich Philadelphia family and training at the Pennsylvania Academy of Art, she studied in Europe. Although she is best known for her sensitive paintings of women and children [126], it is in her etchings and aquatints that she is most original and free. They show the influence of Degas, whom she greatly admired, and an unusual perspective, reminiscent of Japanese prints.

An important figure in the Impressionist group was Berthe Morisot (1841–1895). She began early to experiment with the technique of capturing fleeting impressions. Her portrait of a

young woman with its sketchy brush strokes [407] shows characteristics similar to Monet's later work. Dedicated to Impressionism, Morisot tried to keep the early group functioning while continuing to employ the style after most had abandoned it.

English Arts and Crafts; Art Nouveau

As a result of the Industrial Revolution, with its cheap, over-decorated factory-made goods [238], people like the critic John Ruskin and the painter and designer William Morris (1834–1896) campaigned for a new attitude toward art and crafts. Attempting to reinstate the traditional skills of the medieval guilds, they turned toward stained glass, decorative wall paintings, and handcrafts. They were associated with a group of painters who called themselves Pre-Raphaelites because they were inspired by the forms of art created just before the High Renaissance of Raphael. Morris, who was also a writer and social reformer, was a Romantic in his desire to return to the Middle Ages, but with his competent technical knowledge he inspired a revival of interest in the crafts that led to such Art Nouveau designs as Louis Comfort Tiffany's lamp [239] and handmade ceramics, jewelry, weaving, and book printing. Genuinely appalled at the ugliness of the pompous furniture and household implements exhibited at the Crystal Palace [265] in 1851, he designed the Morris chair in an attempt to simplify furniture and make it more functional. Although his approach to wallpaper [187], fabrics, and glassware looked toward the past, Morris was progressive in his beliefs. His English Arts and Crafts Movement was one of several that led to **Art Nouveau,** which evolved from about 1895 to 1905; this was a decorative style derived from plants that was applied to jewelry, furnishings, and architecture.

Architecture and Sculpture

Architecture of the 19th century at first continued the Neoclassical style exemplified by Jefferson's Monticello [387]. Soon a nostalgia for all things past produced an eclectic mixture from Assyrian to Gothic. Revivalists built banks, stock exchanges, and government buildings patterned on Greek and Roman temples. Engineers, however, were using their new prefabrication skills, introduced in Joseph Paxton's Crystal Palace [265], to build bridges, railway stations, and monuments such as the Eiffel Tower. By the end of the century, some architects were following their lead. The pioneer American architect Louis Sullivan, despite his traditional training, turned to the new structural systems in his designs [266]. His ideas led the way to the skyscrapers of the 20th century, in keeping with an aesthetic interpretation of the new technology (Chapter 9).

In contrast to the static academic sculpture at this time, Auguste Rodin (1840–1917) restored sculpture to a major art form while creating a style leading to **Expressionism.** Born in a working-class quarter of Paris, Rodin first earned his living as a goldsmith and a maker of plaster decorations for buildings. When he visited Italy, he was influenced by the sculpture of Donatello and Michelangelo. Fascinated by the human body in action, he made quick drawings and clay sketches of dancers to catch their momentary poses. In this way he became familiar with the natural movements of the nude human body instead of repeating the stiff stances approved by the Academy. Rodin's rather Romantic figures are often carved or modeled so that the solid stone or bronze appears like living

flesh. The influence of Impressionism can be seen in the way the light plays over the textured surfaces so that they seem to vibrate [194]. He himself called sculpture "quite simply the art of depression and protuberance."

Post-Impressionism

By the mid-1880s, the Impressionists were accepted as serious artists by critics and a large portion of the public. But many of their colleagues and younger followers came to feel that in the search for momentary sensations of light and color, traditional elements of picture-making had been neglected. The **Post-Impressionists,** as they came to be known, all worked for more solid structure in art, which each, in his or her own way, found by a method essentially personal.

One of the most important of these artists was Paul Cézanne (1839–1906), who exhibited in early Impressionist shows, although he disagreed with their aesthetic theories. He thought that Impressionistic works were brilliant renderings of natural light and color, but lacked clarity and order. He determined "to make of Impressionism something solid and durable like the art of the museums." By emphasizing horizontal and vertical shapes and other classic devices of composition, he brought formal order and sculptural grandeur to his paintings. To further his knowledge, he studied great paintings of the past, stating that a museum is "the book in which we learn to read." Cézanne very early discarded the idea of capturing transient light effects. His paintings, although colorful, are made up of forms that exist in a timeless light rather than in the glancing sunlight seen by Monet or Renoir.

In order to develop solidity, Cézanne modeled his masses in a series of planes of color. This approach made him one of the most innovative painters of the 19th century and led directly to the art of the 20th-century Cubists. "Treat Nature by the cylinder, the sphere, the cone," he wrote, applying this rule to his painting by breaking down the most complex objects into geometric-like forms. In his later paintings Cézanne treated masses in small planes of color, using warm yellows and oranges to bring planes forward and cool blues, violets, and greens to push them away from the viewer. He also distorted perspective and shapes to achieve the composition he wanted, disregarding realistic appearances. Deliberate and careful, he painted Mont Sainte-Victoire near his home in the South

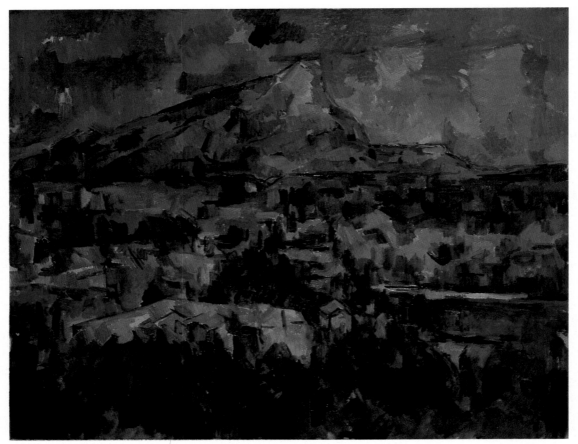

408. *Paul Cézanne.* Mont Sainte-Victoire. *1904–1906. Oil on canvas, $27\frac{7}{8} \times 36\frac{1}{8}''$ (73 × 92 cm). Philadelphia Museum of Art (George W. Elkins Collection).*

of France over and over again, gradually abstracting the familiar view [408]. The mountain, valley, trees, and houses in his later paintings of the mountain are no longer treated as recognizable themes but become simply planes of color. In essence, he diminished the subject's importance to stress the objective character of his art and the totality of his painting.

Thus Cézanne, although he lived most of his life in the 19th century, was one of the strongest painters of the modern period, and from him we can move easily into the daring art of the early 20th century. We have only to compare *Mont Sainte-Victoire* with a loose, Romantic landscape such as Constable's *The Hay Wain* [390] and with later geometric, Cubist paintings by Picasso [19] to see how important Cézanne was as a bridge between the old and new ways of looking at the world. Without the influence of Cézanne's experiments, the radical 20th-century view that art need not imitate nature could never have developed.

While Cézanne searched for new ways of depicting form, Georges Seurat (1851–1891) was also trying to develop more ordered compositions than those of the Impressionists. Seurat extended earlier ideas of broken color into a scientific process called **Divisionism,** or **Pointillism [71]**. He studied scientific theories of light and color in order to separate colors, trying to analyze the exact amounts of each color complement. Then he meticulously placed dots of different colors side by side on the canvas, letting the eye blend them. Seurat was also concerned with the silhouettes of objects, simplifying them into simple shapes. He assembled his figures into large compositions, which, despite the vibrations of the color, appear stable because of the quiet shapes and poses. This reduction of form and strong composition, even more than his use of broken color, make Seurat historically important and an influence on the 20th century.

A young, enthusiastic Dutchman, painting in the blazing sunlight of southern France, also searched for new color techniques. But, unlike Cézanne and Seurat, who had used color to define planes in space, Vincent van Gogh (1853–1890) used hot color to express his very personal, emotional response to the world. Van Gogh was deeply religious, concerned about all of humanity. Indeed, at the start of his painting career he had lived with coal miners and had painted their poverty in dark, depressing colors. He had also hoped, with the help of his brother Theo, to establish a community of artists dedicated to spiritual values, in rebellion against the commercialism produced by the Industrial Revolution.

In a frenzy of creation, Van Gogh painted the grandeur of nature [22] and the simple objects of his daily surroundings. Primarily concerned with a fresh response to familiar objects, he used bright colors to intensify the mood of joy and somber colors for pain. A painting of his bedroom [409] shows how strongly color can affect us. He wrote about this bedroom: "I had a new idea in my head and here is the sketch to it . . . this time it's just simply my bedroom, only here colour is everything."

Along with many 19th-century painters influenced by Japanese prints, Van Gogh, like Cézanne, was unconcerned with linear perspective. However, his interest was not in portraying the structure of objects as was Cézanne's. Van Gogh saw the outer world in emotional terms, which he expressed with strong, slashing brushstrokes and brilliant color. In this approach he was a forerunner of 20th-century Expressionism.

Distrustful of conventions in art and impatient with academic emphasis on technical skills, Paul Gauguin was as idealistic as Van Gogh. To escape the harsh realities of an industrial society, he retreated to the island of Tahiti in the South Seas. There Gauguin sought the simplification

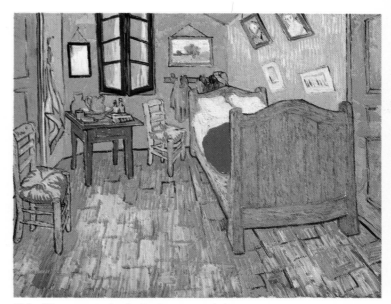

409. *Vincent van Gogh.* Bedroom at Arles. *1888. Oil on canvas, 29 × 36¼″ (73.6 × 92.3 cm). Art Institute of Chicago (Helen Birch Bartlett Memorial Collection). © 1988 The Art Institute of Chicago. All rights reserved.*

of reality that he believed could exist only where life was stripped to its essentials. Many were attracted to such remote cultures, believing they could lose themselves and avoid worldly problems. We, as viewers of their exotic works, are also momentarily diverted from our daily pressures. In *The Spirit of the Dead Watching* [410] we can vicariously experience a simple lifestyle in a romantic setting. The drama is heightened for us by a juxtaposition of tropical flowers with the dark figure from the spirit world.

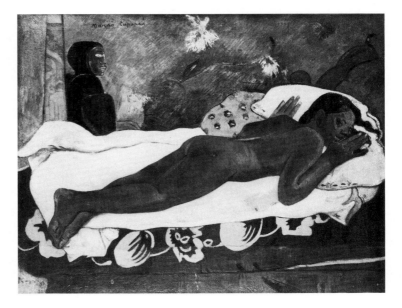

410. *Paul Gauguin.* The Spirit of the Dead Watching (Manao Tupapau). *1892. Oil on burlap mounted on canvas, 28½ × 36⅜″ (72.4 × 92.5 cm). Albright-Knox Art Gallery, Buffalo (A. Conger Goodyear Collection, 1939).*

Focus on the Artist

Paul Gauguin (1848–1903)

The story of Paul Gauguin's life reads like a best-selling novel, and the novel about him by W. Somerset Maugham that appeared in 1919 was indeed a best-seller. Titled *The Moon and Sixpence,* it was followed in 1943 by a film that also was successful. We can begin to piece together the reasons for the continued popularity of both book and film.

This French painter and woodcut artist, born in Paris, was the son of a journalist and a French-Peruvian mother. Gauguin went to sea at an early age, but soon gave up the maritime life for marriage and a settled career in banking. Neither held him very long; by 1883 Gauguin had left his wife and five children and the bank to take up the uncertain life of a painter.

Allying himself with the Impressionists, by 1886 he had exhibited with them in four shows. The next year, he sold all his possessions and left for the tropics as a protest against the demands of civilization. Convinced of the purity of simple cultures, he settled in Martinique in the West Indies. Illness forced him to return the next year to France, where he had a brief but tragic interlude in Arles with Vincent van Gogh. Instead of establishing the artists' colony they had intended, Gauguin and Van Gogh quarreled violently, and Gauguin's visit to Arles was aborted.

In 1888 Gauguin and Emile Bernard, an artist in enamel and stained glass, proposed a bold **Synthetist** theory of art, emphasizing the use of flat planes and bright unrealistic color to render religious and non-Western themes. This style, which had many adherents, characterized most of Gauguin's works for the rest of his life. His autobiographical novel *Noa Noa* appeared in 1895 (English translation, 1947), while he lived in Tahiti in the South Seas, producing some of his finest work. In despair and in considerable physical suffering from tropical maladies contracted in the Islands, he painted until the very end.

As the 19th century came to its close, clearly, painting had become less of a dependable livelihood and more of a lifetime commitment for him. Gauguin noted: "The painter's art calls for too great a body of knowledge. It requires of the artist a higher, dedicated life, especially when instead of going along with the general run he rises above it and becomes an Individual, having to take account of the peculiar nature of the creative artist, and to take account too of the surroundings in which he lives and his education." The painter is alone: "In front of his easel, he is the slave neither of past or present, neither of nature or his neighbour. He contends with himself, only himself." To make the painter's art express something, "it has got to be searched into unremittingly by searching into oneself" [411].

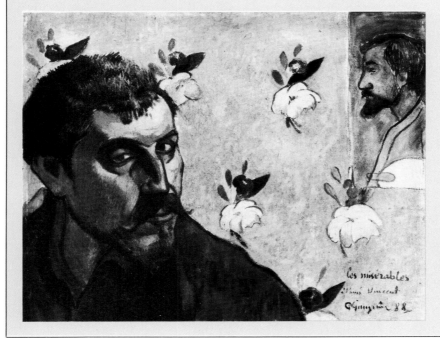

411. *Paul Gauguin.* Self Portrait with the Portrait of Emile Bernard (Les Miserables). *1888. Oil on cloth, 17¾ × 22" (45 × 56 cm). Rijksmuseum Vincent van Gogh/ Vincent van Gogh Foundation, Amsterdam.*

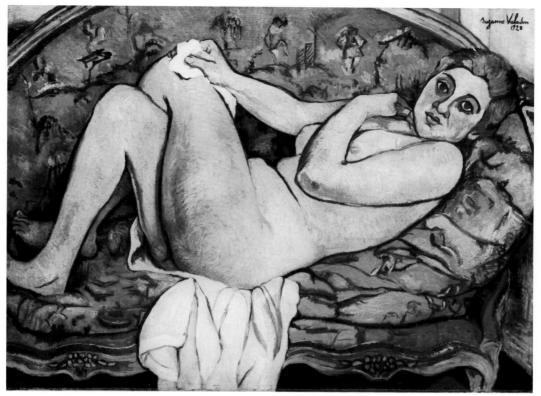

412. *Suzanne Valadon.* Reclining Nude.
Oil on canvas, 23⅝ × 31¾″ (60 × 80.6 cm). Metropolitan Museum of Art, New York (Robert Lehman Collection, 1975).

Gauguin was influenced by Japanese prints, and he also studied the art of Polynesian craftspeople in the village where he lived. He developed a decorative style of painting, making use of flat areas of pure, often unrealistic, color. Gauguin believed that the Impressionists used color without freedom, constrained by the needs of reality and probability. He simplified the outlines of figures and objects until they often appeared unrealistic or symbolic. He believed that a painter should study the silhouette of every object—as he saw it—for distinctness of outline comes from sure knowledge. Aside from their own beauty, Gauguin's paintings are important also for their influence upon later Expressionists.

Another noteworthy Post-Impressionist was Suzanne Valadon (1865–1938), a former artist's model and mother of the **Fauvist** painter Maurice Utrillo (1883–1955). She had no formal art training but great skill in drawing [412]. She worked in the spirit of the Impressionists, especially Degas, although she painted at the beginning of the 20th century. The heavily defined contours, simplification of form, and nonrep-

resentational colors of her vigorous paintings link her also to Gauguin and the Expressionists.

The dissatisfaction of Van Gogh and Gauguin with Western society was a point of view shared by others at the end of the 19th century. Henri de Toulouse-Lautrec, an artist of great talent, led a dissolute life on the fringes of society, illuminating the café scene in the flat, patterned Japanese style he so much admired. *At the Moulin Rouge* is a fine example of his work.

The turn of the century found many European artists preoccupied with decadence and despair. For example, Edvard Munch (1863–1944), a Norwegian with a tragic sense of human isolation, expressed alienation, anxiety, and despair in both paintings and prints. His remark, "I hear the scream in nature," is vividly illustrated in *The Scream* [128]. The open mouth of the central figure suggests howls of fear or pain, while the anonymous silhouettes on the bridge portray the coldness and indifference of the world. The torment of the lonely figure fills the atmosphere with expanding waves of terror, which are repeated in the water and sky. Munch's figures, isolated from one another and

At the Moulin Rouge by Henri de Toulouse-Lautrec

The life of Henri de Toulouse-Lautrec (1864–1901) was the material out of which legends are customarily made. A wealthy French aristocrat, as a child he injured his legs so severely in a fall that his growth was permanently stunted. He rejected the social circle of his birth in favor of the bohemian nightclubs and cafés of Montmartre in Paris in the 1880s and 1890s, recording this demimonde in his paintings, prints, and posters. His untimely death in 1901 of a stroke related to his alcoholism left a legacy of more than three hundred lithographs and posters.

One of Lautrec's most celebrated paintings, *At the Moulin Rouge,* has served for years as an icon of the world that the painter immortalized, and just as myth has attached itself to Lautrec's life, so, too, with the painting [413]. In *At the Moulin Rouge* we see five figures, including the artist himself and his cousin, seated around a table in the middle ground, four standing figures in the background, repeating Lautrec and his cousin, and a woman lit as if by footlights in the foreground at the far right, part of whose electric blue face is cut off at the edge of the painting. It is apparent to the naked eye that the picture is composed of two joined canvas segments, a rectangle comprising the figures seated at the table and the figures in the background, and a backward-L-shaped segment of canvas consisting of the right and lower borders with the foreground figure on the right.

For years it was believed that the rectangular canvas segment was the original and that the L-shaped canvas with the head of the woman had been added later. Not until the fall of 1985 was the painting painstakingly examined by the conservator at the Art Institute of Chicago, where the painting has been exhibited since 1928. The conservator's x-ray examinations provide us with information causing us to draw completely different conclusions from what was formerly believed. The original painting indeed was comprised of both fragments, which were later cut up. The rectangular portion was exhibited as a painting in its own right, and the L-shaped part of the canvas was probably rolled up and stored until the two were reunited. We can only conjecture why the canvas was cut apart and when, but it may well have had to do with combating the outrage which some of the public expressed about the lack of convention surrounding the artist's life. Soon after Lautrec's death the remarkable face on the right, depicted in shocking complementary colors, may have seemed to lend fuel to the tales of the excesses of the artist's existence. Later, when his artistic stature was more widely recognized and public indignation had subsided, the two segments could have been reunited. When they were, the greatness of the work was able to speak for itself and for the genius of the artist, who displayed therein a bold use of space, inventive composition, and expressive color unique in his time.

caged in their separate terrors, are ageless, sexless, classless symbols of late-19th-century humanity.

18th- and 19th-Century America

Across the Atlantic Ocean, in the Americas, art was for the most part a distant and late echo of European models. The rambunctious spirit of the New World was missing in the realm of art. Patrons of art, like their British and Dutch counterparts, looked for traditional portraits, or for painted shop signs—even an occasional painter to repaint a house wall or a barn. Most itinerant artists were anonymous craftspeople who made their way from house to house and plantation to plantation. Remarkably few were known by name—black or white. Still fewer Afro-Americans became established portrait painters, but Scipio Morehead (18th century) and Joshua Johnston were indeed successful. Though Johnston's commissions during the period we know most about, from 1796 to 1824, were mainly from middle-class whites, the somber *Portrait of a Cleric* is an exception, and, accounts state, "a fine likeness," typical of Early American portraiture [414].

Most 19th-century American artists continued to look to Europe for standards in art. Those who could afford it received their art education in England and France, as did Benjamin West, John Trumbull, Mary Cassatt, and James Whistler.

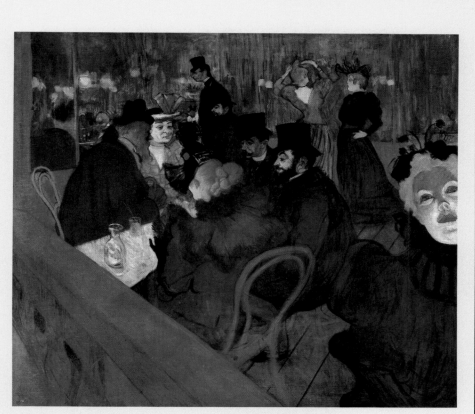

413. *Henri de Toulouse-Lautrec.* At the Moulin Rouge. *1892.*
Oil on canvas, 4'3⅜" × 4'7½" (1.23 × 1.41 m).
Art Institute of Chicago (Helen Birch Bartlett Memorial Collection).

Hudson River School

American patrons became increasingly more sophisticated as the 19th century drew to a close. Portraits remained popular, but there was a growing interest in genre and landscape subjects that expressed a patriotic enthusiasm for the natural beauty of a growing America. The traditions of what came to be called the **Hudson River School** began when Thomas Cole (1801–1848) and Asher Durand (1796–1886) set out easels in the Catskills near the Hudson. Soon

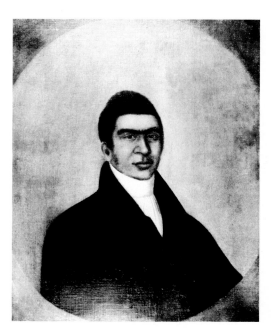

right: **414.** *Joshua Johnston.* Portrait of a Cleric. *1805–1810. Oil on canvas, 28 × 22" (71.1 × 55.9 cm). Bowdoin College Museum of Art, Brunswick, Maine (Hamlin Fund).*

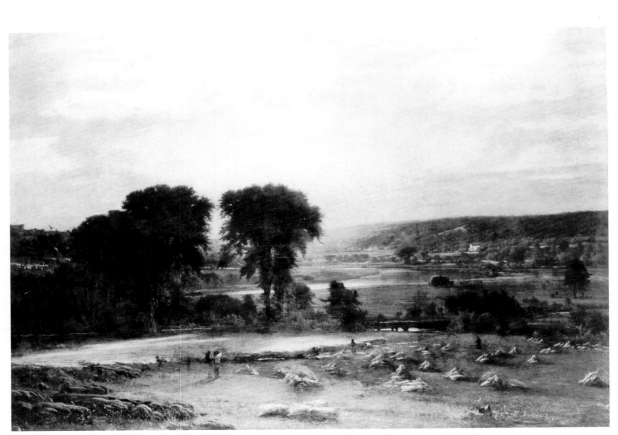

415. *George Inness.* Peace and Plenty. *1865. Oil on canvas, $77\frac{5}{8} \times 112\frac{3}{8}''$ (197 × 285.75 cm). Metropolitan Museum of Art, New York (gift of George A. Hearn, 1894).*

landscape enthusiasts found other vistas. As it had for the French who had taken to Barbizon woods forty years earlier, a romantic nostalgia developed in America for grand landscape painting, of which the post-Civil War *Peace and Plenty* [415] by George Inness (1825–1894) is a fine example. "The purpose of the painter," Inness concluded, "is simply to reproduce in other minds the impression which a scene has made upon him."

Technological developments of the 19th century had succeeded in focusing artists the world over on their new role in an age that no longer required large numbers of realistic portraits. The Age of Revolution had signaled the growing movement toward freedom for personal expression in the subject matter, technique, and style of art. The styles of Post-Impressionism, with which the century closed, anticipate the bold individuality of art in the 20th century.

Exercises and Activities

Research Exercises

1. Select a passage from the *Discourses* by Sir Joshua Reynolds that seems particularly relevant to today's world. Explain your reasons for choosing that passage.
2. Locate some buildings or photographs of buildings that show Palladio's influence on architecture.
3. How were such artists as Goya and Turner influenced by the earlier works of Velásquez and Rembrandt? How were they affected by the new spirit of the age?
4. Discuss some art movements of the 19th century that expressed the conflict between industrialization and nostalgia for the past. Analyze two artworks.
5. The Impressionist painters of the 19th century developed a technique that created the illusion of light, color, and atmosphere. How did it differ from earlier painting techniques? Give examples.

Studio Activities

1. Draw a still life in outline. Using poster paints, create an illusion of light on the objects, applying dabs of pure color next to each other. See if your eye mixes the dots to form an area of color. If it does not, alter the proportions of the colors until you achieve the effect you wish.
2. Sketch a view of part of a room. Paint it, using dabs of poster, oil, or acrylic paint to simulate either the Impressionist or Post-Impressionist technique.
3. In the spirit of Whistler, organize a cityscape in charcoal based on a division of space, respecting the Golden Section. Does this principle apply to a composition of houses and sidewalks?
4. On a simple loom made from a picture frame with yarn stretched between nails, interlace yarns, using American Indian motifs as a guide.
5. Create in clay or soap a three-dimensional figure reminiscent of the art of the Orient.

15
Tradition and Innovation: 1900–1935

If you bring a mirror near to a real picture, it ought to become covered with steam, with living breath, because it is alive.

Pablo Picasso

Every work of art is the child of its time; often it is the mother of our emotions. . . .
Wassily Kandinsky

To become truly immortal a work of art must escape all human limits; logic and common sense will only interfere.

Giorgio de Chirico

One of the main causes of our artistic decline lies beyond doubt in the separation of art and science. Art is nothing but humanized science.

Gino Severini

The clown is not I, but rather our monstrously cynical and so naively unconscious society that plays at the game of being serious, the better to hide its own madness.

Salvador Dali

As we approach the art of our own time, the pace quickens and diversity becomes the rule. Changes occur so rapidly that despite the perspective of almost a hundred years we are shaken by the explosion of styles.

The 1920s and 1930s were a period of broad disillusionment and unrest. Nineteenth-century promises of peace and prosperity had dissolved in World War I and the Great Depression of the 1930s. Numerous writers and artists saw this era as one of mass exploitation, dehumanization, and irrational political leadership. Social confusion led to considerable artistic experiment. It was a period when modern art flourished, and some critical artists even produced works that were anti-art.

The spirit of artistic freedom that had developed in the 19th century with the efforts of

Courbet and Whistler to choose their own styles, subjects, and titles of works increased in the 20th century. By the second and third decades a half-dozen or so manifestos had been issued, and artists, who generally resisted grouping, had developed several art currents. By the early 1930s, however, the many confusing styles or "-isms" could be sorted out into the following general trends, which have persisted to the present time: formalism, Expressionism, fantasy, and realism.

Formalism refers to an intellectual approach popular in the modern period that is more concerned with form—the spatial arrangement of such elements as line, shape, and texture—than with content from the real world.

Expressionism refers to a concern with the intensity of the artist's emotions as opposed to his or her representation of external reality, an

THE VISUAL ARTS		HISTORICAL NOTES
1897 Rousseau, *The Sleeping Gypsy* **[436]**		
	1900	**1900** Sigmund Freud, *Interpretation of Dreams*
		1903 Wright brothers, powered flight
1905 Matisse, *Madame Matisse* **[424]**	1905	**1905** *Die Brücke* formed in Dresden
1906–07 Modersohn-Becker, *Mother and Child* **[427]**		**1907** Cubism appeared
1907 Picasso, *Demoiselles d'Avignon* **[446]**		
		1908 Model T Ford
1907–09 Wright, Robie House **[457]**		**1909** Futurism appeared
	1910	
		1911 *Der Blaue Reuter* formed in Munich
1912 Duchamp, *Nude Descending Staircase (No. 2)* **[91]**		**1912** Kandinsky, *Concerning the Spiritual in Art*
1913 Boccioni, *Unique Forms of Continuity* **[444]**		
1914 De Chirico, *Melancholy of Departure* **[437]**		**1914** World War I begins
	1915	
		1916 Einstein, General Theory of Relativity
		1917 USA enters war
		1918 World War I ends
	1920	**1920** First public radio broadcast
1922 Klee, *Twittering Machine* **[438]**		**1922** James Joyce, *Ulysses*
		1923 USSR established
1925 Eisenstein, *Potemkin* **[157]**	1925	**1925** Adolf Hitler, *Mein Kampf*
1925–26 Gropius, Bauhaus **[455]**		
1929–30 Le Corbusier, Villa Savoye **[458]**		**1929** Wall Street crash: Great Depression
	1930	
1931 Dalí, *Persistence of Memory* **[439]**		
		1933 F. D. Roosevelt becomes president: New Deal
		1933 Hitler becomes chancellor of Germany
1934 Kollwitz, *Death Seizes a Woman* **[429]**		
	1935	

approach that often results in distortions of color and shape. The term was perhaps first applied to the art of Van Gogh.

Fantasy refers to art derived from the artistic imagination. It may be expressed either realistically or with abstract symbols.

Realism refers to the artist's use of light, shade, color, and perspective to reproduce as closely as possible the appearance of objects in nature. As proposed by Courbet in the 19th century, the trend never took hold in most of the European world, but it never quite disappeared in America.

If we remember that the many styles and "-isms" discussed in Chapters 15 to 18 are loosely grouped within the general trends, perhaps the first decades of modern art will be easier to follow.

Formalist Painting

For centuries artists were concerned with how to paint the illusion of three-dimensional objects in deep space on a flat, two-dimensional surface. The Greeks and Romans used a limited form of linear perspective, which Renaissance painters developed into a science. They held up a mirror to nature and then surrounded the painting with a frame, making the painting a window on reality. This concept prevailed until the mid-19th century, when the invention of the camera released Western artists from the need to reproduce nature. Cézanne and Gauguin began to take advantage of this freedom, as we saw in Chapter 14.

The public is always slow to change. Few people in 1910 understood the new views of the world, and many artists continued to cling to tradition, comfortable as skillful recorders of society. But in the early 20th century, avant-garde artists plunged ahead to explore new horizons, especially in styles of formalist painting. Their work in **Cubism, Futurism, Nonobjectivism, De Stijl,** and **Suprematism,** all of which we shall now examine, has come to be recognized for its outstanding creative achievement.

Cubism

The young painters and sculptors who gathered in Paris from all over Europe from the 1880s on discussed Cézanne's efforts to reduce volume and space to simple cones, cylinders, and planes to make objects appear to be seen from several vantage points [408]. Many of these young rebels also looked to the arts of Africa [398], with their exaggerations and simplifications of forms, as an escape from the binding rules of the Academy, as well as from the Impressionists' preoccupation with fleeting light. Under these major influences two young artists, Georges Braque and Pablo Picasso, "roped together like mountaineers" as Braque put it, developed a new kind of pictorial space in which objects were presented as if seen from several angles. Some observers believe that they also added a temporal dimension to space by representing objects in sequential moments of time. A startled critic gave the name **Cubism** to this new style. Braque and Picasso later said, "We had no intention of creating Cubism but simply of expressing what we felt inside."

Leaving Cézanne behind, in 1907 Picasso explored the essential elements of Cubism in a major experimental work, *Les Demoiselles d'Avignon,* or *The Young Ladies of Avignon* [416]. In this painting artistic rebellion became outright revolution. First planned as an allegory of vice and virtue, the painting became intense and stark. The figures and faces of the women are distorted in angular, jagged forms. The girl on the left is depicted in a series of overlapping planes; the central figure has eyes that look directly at us, but the nose is in profile; and the faces of the figures on the right are like African masks. *Demoiselles* attacked long-held Renaissance concepts of space and the idealized nude. That Picasso may also have been representing women from the red-light district of Avignon, as many believe, had a tremendous effect on the course of 20th-century Western art.

Both Picasso and Braque recorded the world in a startling way, as if they echoed the weakening in social patterns and the uncertainty of the new age. Just as the political radicals tried to find a new order to restructure an unjust society, so too did the Cubists search for a new way to rearrange visual images. Familiar objects—tables, wine bottles, violins, sheet music, and the human figure—were reduced to geometric abstractions, simplified, and then restructured. Picasso said, "We have kept our eyes open to our surroundings, and also our brains." The Cubists abandoned conventional linear perspective, replacing it with a new surface perspective that

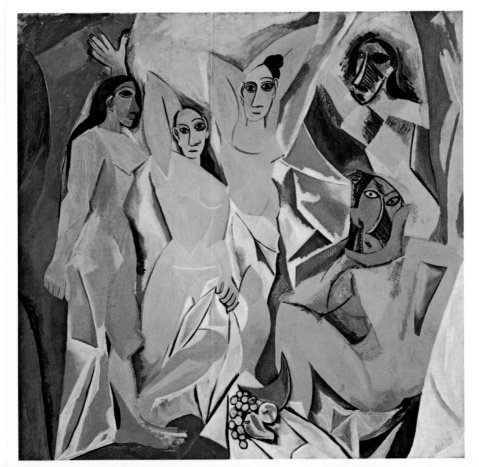

416. *Pablo Picasso.* Les Demoiselles d'Avignon. *1907. Oil on canvas, 8' × 7'8" (2.44 × 2.36 m). Collection, Museum of Modern Art, New York (acquired through the Lillie P. Bliss Bequest).*

does not create a sense of depth in the canvas but rather seems to advance from the frame. A comparison of *Ma Jolie* [19] with Leonardo's *The Last Supper* [80] demonstrates the revolutionary manner in which these young painters handled perspective.

The Cubists painted not only what they saw but also what they knew was there. For instance, a wine bottle might be painted as seen from the side, back, and top, all these views organized into a single, complex, intellectually analyzed composition in muted colors. Because of the intellectual and disciplined nature of these paintings, the early stages of the style are described as **Analytical Cubism [74]**, a collage. Gradually, however, the object itself was lost, and the Cubists became more interested in the design formed by bright-colored, overlapping shapes in a shallow space. This mingling of the decorative aspects of an object by taking its various parts and combining them into compositions that may only remotely resemble their origins is described as **Synthetic Cubism.** Picasso's *Girl Before a Mirror* [417] is a remarkably direct Synthetic Cubist work. It presents a psychological study of a young girl considering her impending sexual maturity with apparent fear and anticipation. Her arm, stretched into the mirror, forms a bridge from the present time to what will be.

Along with Cubist paintings, Picasso, Braque, and others made collages [74] and, then, paintings that looked like collages [85]. The colors, shapes, and volumes of the language of Cubism were used more inventively and expressively, often with humor. The rules of academic art were totally shattered. Even painters who used the academic devices of perspective and light and shade to create the illusion of three dimensions used them more freely. Art was never again the same.

Although Picasso was one of the founders of Cubism, he also worked in a number of different styles. Cubist, Expressionist, Neoclassical, Surrealist—any of these labels suit some of his work, but none could describe it all. Born in Spain but working in France, Picasso was an artist of vitality and inventiveness. In his long life he produced thousands of paintings, drawings, etchings, lithographs, sculptures, and ceramics in a rich and varied outpouring of artistic expression [19, 31, 85, 417]. In his work, lush colors alternate with muted soft tones, sketchy images of bullfights contrast with amusing ceramics or play with light [95]. But it is probably for his large painting *Guernica* [35] that he will be best remembered.

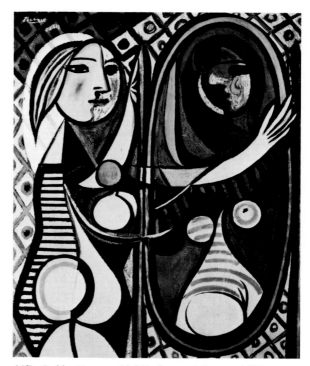

417. *Pablo Picasso.* Girl Before a Mirror. *1932. Oil on canvas, 5'3¾" × 4'3½" (1.62 × 1.31 m). Collection, Museum of Modern Art, New York (Mrs. Simon Guggenheim Fund).*

Guernica was painted during a few weeks in the spring of 1937 after German planes supporting General Francisco Franco attacked the village of Guernica in a test run of saturation bombing. The village was totally destroyed. Picasso's 26-foot (7.92-meter) -long black, white, and gray mural was his memorial to those who had perished—his agonized protest against senseless destruction of human lives. The many studies that Picasso made for the painting [35] show the gradual evolution of the images—from three-dimensional drawings of distorted, screaming mouths and fragmented bodies to the flat, abstracted shapes of the final painting. In the finished work a mother clutches a dead child, a woman falls from a flaming house, and a horse dies from the thrust of a spear. The bull, sometimes a symbol of evil and sometimes of resurgent Spain in many of Picasso's etchings, stands triumphantly over the dead and dying villagers, while a single glaring light bulb stares down like a cold eye on the scene of death. It is difficult to experience from reproductions the full impact of one of the strongest antiwar statements of our century. Universal in its images, this painting could represent a village in Vietnam, the Middle East, or Northern Ireland—

anywhere the horror of war destroys the innocent.

Picasso summed up the confused reactions to Cubism (and to all his art) by saying, "Everyone wants to understand art. Why not try to understand the song of a bird?" Spontaneously creative, he could paint a charming young girl in a lyrical Neoclassical style, capture the pathos of starving beggars with a few lines, and then assemble a bicycle seat and handlebars into a humorous bull [31]. With such works, Picasso introduced playfulness and humor into art that was a refreshing change from the stuffy gravity of David's academic painting [388] and the intellectualism of Analytical Cubism. But the impact of Cubism on painting was so powerful that it affected sculpture and architecture as well, as we shall discover shortly.

Futurism

In 1908 the American inventor Wilbur Wright flew across the English Channel at about the same time that Ettore Bugatti was designing racing automobiles in Italy. Many artists were intrigued by concepts of motion, and a group of young painters eager to escape tradition founded the **Futurist** movement. In their painting and sculpture they tried to reconcile the human being with the new machines and to express their joy in the glorious speed of steam engines, automobiles, and airplanes. Influenced by the Cubists, some of these artists reduced forms to planes and painted almost abstract canvases with titles such as *Dynamism of the Automobile*. Robert Delaunay (1885–1941) and his wife Sonia Terk-Delaunay (1895–1979) experimented with the mechanics of light, merging Pointillist techniques with Cubist and Futurist forms in a short-lived style that became known as **Orphism [418]**.

Others, such as Gino Severini (1883–1966), who painted multiple images to show movement, may have been influenced by the new art of the motion picture. In *Dynamic Hieroglyphic of the Bal Tabarin* [419], for instance, Severini expressed the swirling movements of cancan dancers in a brilliantly colored painting whose forms have been broken down into Cubist planes. Only the dancers' ringlets and red lips remain recognizable; added touches of painted lace and real sequins suggest their costumes. The Futurist movement broke up under the stress of World War I, but Futurist influence continued in works by Fernand Léger (1881–1955), Marcel Duchamp [91], and later machine-oriented paint-

below: **418.** *Robert Delaunay.* The Eiffel Tower. *1910. Oil on canvas,* 79½ × 54½″ *(201.9 × 138.4 cm). Solomon R. Guggenheim Museum, New York.*

below right: **419.** *Gino Severini.* Dynamic Hieroglyph of the Bal Tabarin. *1912. Oil on canvas with sequins, 5′3⅝″ × 5′1½″ (1.62 × 1.56 m). Collection, Museum of Modern Art, New York (Lillie P. Bliss Bequest).*

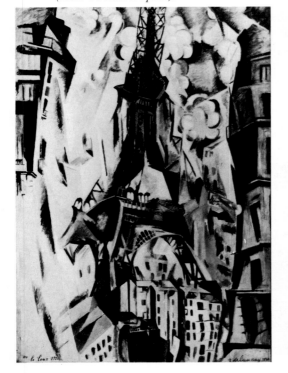

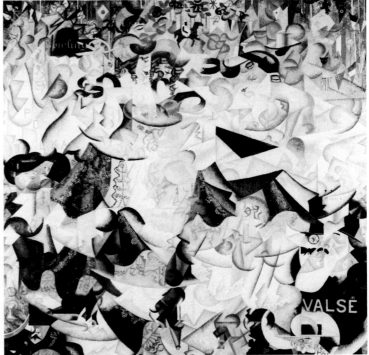

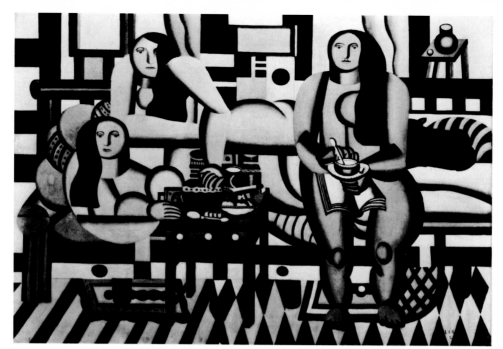

420. *Fernand Léger.* Three Women. *1921. Oil on canvas, 6'1¼" × 8'3"
(1.84 × 2.51 m). Collection, Museum of Modern Art, New York
(Mrs. Simon Guggenheim Fund).*

ers. Duchamp's Cubistic, machinelike walking
nude parodies the idealized Venus figure of
Renaissance art.

First affected by the Cubists, Léger moved
slowly toward a style that related human beings
to machines. In his paintings he turned city
buildings, smoking factories, machine parts, and
human bodies into simplified cylinders, rectangles, circles, and cubes, painted in brilliant blue,
yellow, and red against stark white and black.
His figures are static robots surrounded by machine parts. The colors and forms of Léger's
painting directly influenced furniture design
and advertising art in the United States in the
1940s, for his simplified forms lent themselves
well to graphic poster art [420].

De Stijl and Other Nonobjective Art

During the years of World War I the neutral
Netherlands remained one of the few countries
where creative design and construction could
continue uninterrupted. As a consequence, this
country became a center of innovation. The
architect Gerrit Rietveld (1888–1964) and the
painters Theo van Doesburg (1883–1931) and
Piet Mondrian (1877–1944) worked closely together and in 1917 evolved a movement they
called **De Stijl** ("The Style"). Convinced that realistic or even semiabstract images had no place
in the machine age, the painters of De Stijl reduced their images to simple horizontal and ver-

tical shapes. Later, Van Doesburg's studies of a
cow reveal clearly the process of abstraction
[421]. In most canvases by Mondrian [46] and
Van Doesburg, the object that may have originally inspired the works has completely disappeared, leaving only flat rectangles of color and

421. *Theo van Doesburg.* The Cow
*(series of 8 pencil drawings). Undated.
Nos. 1, 2, 4, 5, 6, 7: 4⅝ × 6¼" (12 × 16 cm);
nos. 8, 9: 6¼ × 4⅝" (16 × 12 cm). Collection,
Museum of Modern Art, New York (purchase).*

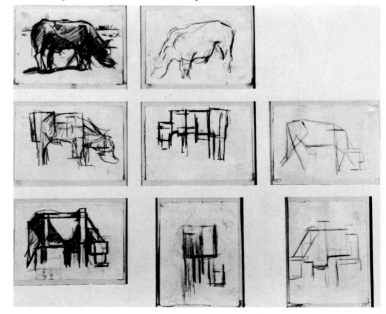

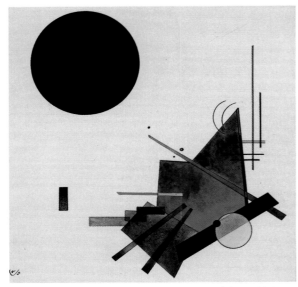

422. *Wassily Kandinsky.* Black Relationship. *1924. Watercolor, 14½ × 14¼" (36.8 × 36.2 cm). Collection, Museum of Modern Art, New York (acquired through the Lillie P. Bliss Bequest).*

strong dark lines placed in harmonious compositions. Applied to painting, architecture, and all areas of design, De Stijl affected creative expression in many countries for decades, as evidenced by Rietveld's straight-lined chair [233]. While some see De Stijl art as "pure" and tranquil, others find the style harsh and rigid.

Another painter who helped develop nonobjective art (see Chapter 2) was the Russian Wassily Kandinsky (1866–1944). Studying in Munich and visiting Paris, he was exposed to various kinds of avant-garde art. He painted his first nonobjective work, a watercolor of pure color and line, in 1910, about the time he also became a leading figure in Expressionism. He claimed that what is most important in art is what the viewer feels while under the effect of the combinations of form and color in a painting. Like Whistler before him, he wanted painting to approach pure music. He called his compositions "improvisations" to emphasize their lack of literal subject matter. His later works in the 1920s and 1930s, when he was teaching at the Bauhaus, became entirely geometric [422].

Nonobjective art was also being developed in Russia about the time of World War I by such artists as Kasimir Malevich (1878–1935). In 1913 he exhibited a painting of a black square on a white background. Describing this work Malevich stated, "It was not just a square I had exhibited but rather the expression of nonob-

jectivity." Malevich spent years exploring squares and their relationships to each other. In 1918 he painted *Suprematist Composition: White on White* [423] in which he believed he had attained the ultimate in purity of art. Many agreed.

In Russia at this time nonobjective painting and other experimental art were encouraged by the Communist party, which came to power in 1918. By 1920, there were more museums of abstract art and more artists working in a nonobjective manner in Russia than anywhere else in the world. As with Courbet in France, political radicalism was again linked with artistic radicalism. Soon, however, the new regime outlawed experiment and insisted on realistic works that glorified the state. Avant-garde artists chose either to stay in an environment that was hostile to innovation or to leave the country. Kandinsky, for example, who had taught in Russia during World War I, left in 1921 and joined the faculty of the Bauhaus, an innovative school of design we shall soon examine.

Expressionist Painting

Also innovative but quite different in their approach to art were the Expressionists, who worked in France and Germany. Of course, emotional expression has existed as long as art. Certainly Romanesque sculptors expressed religious emotion [335]. In the 19th century, Goya expressed his horror at the cold-blooded murder of hostages by Napoleon's troops [53]. Later, Géricault, in *The Raft of the "Medusa,"* protested against the callous disregard for human life by the authorities [391]. Van Gogh poured his emotions into his vigorously brushed, vibrantly colored paintings [22]. Munch expressed his personal distress in woodcuts and lithographs [128].

Troubled by the dehumanized and materialistic world they saw around them, many early-20th-century painters worked in a variety of styles that are loosely classified as Expressionist. Those in France are known as the **Fauves.** Those in Germany are called **German Expressionists.**

Fauvism

In 1905 a new movement burst on the Paris scene with an astonishing exhibit by Henri Matisse (1869–1954) and eleven other artists. Among the rooms filled with brilliantly colored canvases a bewildered critic noticed a small bronze sculpture in Renaissance style, which, he

423. *Kasimir Malevich.*
Suprematist Composition:
White on White. *c. 1918.*
Oil on canvas,
31¼″ (79 cm) square.
Collection, Museum of
Modern Art, New York.

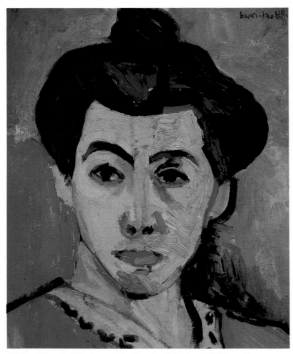

424. *Henri Matisse.* Madame Matisse (The Green
Line). *1905. Oil on canvas, 16 × 12¾″ (41 × 32 cm).*
Statens Museum for Kunst, Copenhagen.

remarked, was like "Donatello among the wild beasts." Consequently, the term *les Fauves* ("the wild beasts") was applied to artists of this movement, called Fauvism. It lasted only three years or so, but had far-reaching effects.

Matisse's innovative use of color and strong, simplified forms was startling. For example, in his *Madame Matisse (The Green Line)* **[424]** he arbitrarily painted one of his wife's cheeks a warm yellow-ochre, the other a cold pink, and then separated them with a line of green down her face and a background of color complements. Here he used color with minimal reference to reality, and, like other Fauves, in its fullest intensity. The features were simplified into a mask.

Throughout his long life, Matisse showed an impressive ability to put colors together successfully in unusual ways. As an accomplished pictorial designer, he could define space by overlapping planes of flat color. As a fine draftsman, through extreme simplification and elimination of detail, he, unlike many other Expressionists, represented a serene world where line, color, and shape could be enjoyed independently of the subject matter.

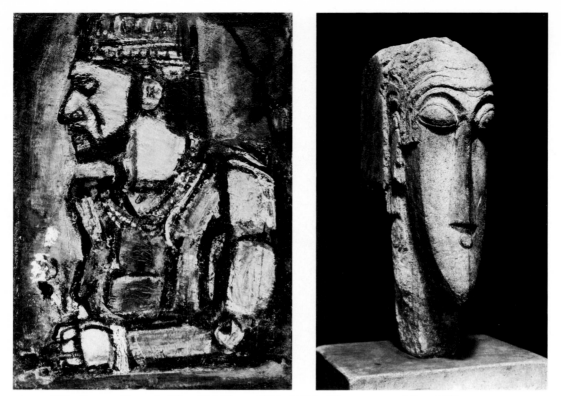

above: **425.** *Georges Rouault.* The Old King. *1916–1936. Oil on canvas, 30¼ × 21¼″ (76.8 × 54 cm). Carnegie Museum of Art, Pittsburgh (Patrons of Art Fund, 1940).*

above right: **426.** *Amedeo Modigliani.* Head. *c. 1915. Limestone, 22¼ × 14¾″ (57 × 18 × 37 cm). Collection, Museum of Modern Art, New York (gift of Abby Aldrich Rockefeller in memory of Mrs. Cornelius J. Sullivan).*

The Fauve painter Georges Rouault (1871–1958) was haunted by the poverty and misery of his day. His paintings depicted the degradation of prostitutes and tragic circus clowns as symbols of the cruelty of people toward each other [425]. Deeply religious, Rouault also painted many biblical characters and Crucifixions. His youthful apprenticeship to a maker of stained glass is reflected in the glowing colors and black outlines of his paintings. As an experimental printmaker, commenting on the horror of war, Rouault developed daring graphic techniques. For instance, he combined etching and engraving in one print and worked on the plate with files, sandpaper, and anything else that would mark it. This free approach helped expand the limits of 20th-century printmaking.

An Expressionist painter and sculptor who lived in Paris but was not a Fauve was the Italian-born Amedeo Modigliani (1884–1920). He used the distortions of African art as well as strong, often somber colors to express the restlessness of his life. Handsome, poor, dissipated, and dying of tuberculosis, he nevertheless carved fine abstract figures [426] and painted portraits and nudes that echoed the work of Bot-

ticelli in their graceful elongation of the female form.

German Expressionism

Before World War I, Dresden, Munich, and cities in northern Germany were centers of artistic innovation, where avant-garde artists formed groups to promote their Expressionist ideas. They used harsh, brutally simplified forms and strong, clashing colors to express the intensity of their inner sense of conflict, violence, and tragedy.

Paula Modersohn-Becker, a gifted and strongly motivated painter, after marriage was torn between her artistic aspirations and her maternal responsibilities. Of all her 259 paintings, many of them intense reworkings of images of motherhood, she sold only one. The maternal bond of protection in *Mother and Child* [427] is emphasized by the mother's arms, strong forces of tenderness cradling the small baby.

The German Expressionists used distortion and exaggerated color not only to convey their own feelings but also as symbols of emotion.

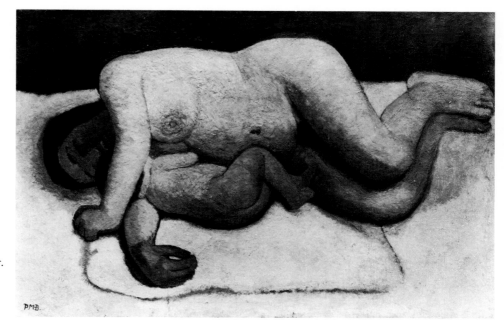

427. *Paula Modersohn-Becker.*
Mother and Child. *1907.*
Oil on canvas, 32¼ × 49″
(82 × 124.7 cm).
Private Collection.

Emil Nolde (1867–1956) in his violent religious and moral paintings distorted the physical features of his figures to the point where they resemble animals, driven by greed, anger, or grief [428]. Some of these artists may have reached their greatest heights in their prints. Inspired by Japanese prints and perhaps drawing on their own medieval graphic tradition, they began to experiment with woodcuts, often using color in conjunction with strong black and white. They distorted figures to bring intense emotion to printmaking. Käthe Kollwitz (1867–1945) made drawings and lithographs chiefly in black and white [429]. A champion of the poor and ex-

below: **428.** *Emil Nolde.* Prophet. *1912. Woodcut, 12¾ × 9″ (32 × 23 cm).*
National Gallery of Art, Washington (Rosenwald Collection).

below right: **429.** *Käthe Kollwitz.* Death Seizes a Woman. *1934. Lithograph,*
20⅛ × 14⅜″ (51 × 37 cm). Courtesy of The Harvard University Art Museums,
Fogg Art Museum (purchase from the Francis Calley Gray Fund for Engravings).

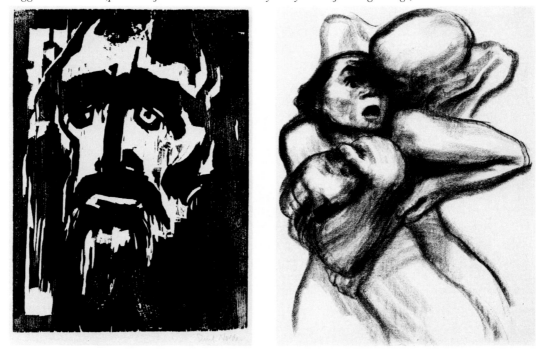

ploited, she poignantly depicted agonized mothers clutching starving children and peasants revolting against rapacious landlords. Other German Expressionists tempered in the crucible of war like George Grosz (1893–1959) screamed their hatred of social apathy, militarism, and corruption in their works [430]. Thus the Expressionists continued the tradition of social protest introduced by Goya and Daumier a century earlier.

Fantasy in Art

During World War I and in the uneasy years afterward, when Europe was gripped by political tension, anxiety, and fear of revolution, many intellectuals and artists became disillusioned by traditional values. While Cubists, Futurists, and Expressionists sought different ways to represent the world and their feelings, others reached nihilistic conclusions. Their rejection of the world took the form of **Dada, Surrealism,** or other expressions of fantasy.

Dada

The movement known as Dada arose among European poets, experimental writers, and artists arriving in neutral Zurich in 1915. To express their rebellion at the uselessness of war and the meaninglessness of all past art they called their movement Dada, meaning nonsense like the babble of babies. The word was supposedly found by opening a dictionary at random, but probably it was carefully chosen. The founders were laughing at the pompousness of traditional artists and at the society that supported them. Unlike artists of the past, who presented viewers with images from their own culture, which they were expected to understand, Dadaists did not care to be understood. They felt they were living in an incomprehensible world bound for destruction. Nevertheless, they began to publish the journal *Dada* in 1917. Dada also flourished in New York, where European artists had settled during the war, and later in Paris. The movement ended in the 1920s, but its influence continued in Surrealism.

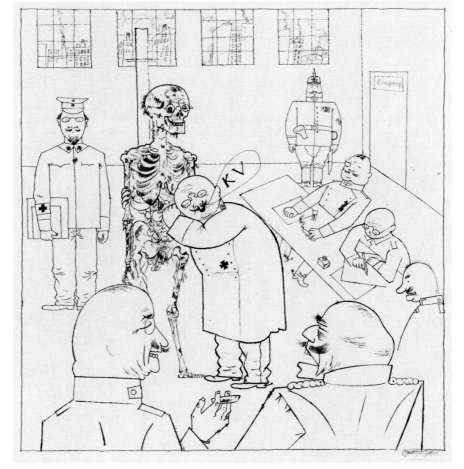

430. *George Grosz.*
Fit for Active Service.
*1916–1917. Pen and brush
and india ink on paper,
20 × 14⅜" (50.8 × 36 cm).
Collection, Museum of
Modern Art, New York
(A. Conger Goodyear Fund).*

Focus on the Artist

Paula Modersohn-Becker (1876–1907)

Born in Dresden, Germany, Paula Becker became interested in art when whe was given art lessons at the age of sixteen, as part of her finishing school education. Overcoming her parents' resistance, she enrolled at twenty in the same art school for women attended nine years earlier by Käthe Kollwitz.

After two years of this traditional instruction, like many other artists seeking a more natural way of living outside of civilization's pitfalls, Becker joined an Expressionist artists' colony at Worpeswede in northern Germany. On New Year's Eve, 1900, and also on other occasions over the next seven years, she went to Paris, the acknowledged center of the art world (perhaps since Louis XIV in 1666 had founded the Académie Royale). She joined other women working at the Académie Colarossi and later at the École des Beaux-Arts, previously restricted to male artists.

With renewed confidence in herself, Becker returned to Worpeswede, to the school founded by Fritz Mackensen and Otto Modersohn. Amidst pressure from her parents to abandon art and giving in to the recently widowed Modersohn's needs for a wife and mother to his children, in 1901 she was married. The marriage was not particularly fulfilling for her, and in 1903, she returned to Paris. Still under the spell of Cézanne, as can be seen by her own still-life paintings of this period, she also discovered the arts of Japan, India, and Persia. When she saw the work of Van Gogh and Gauguin, she recognized a kinship with their interest in workers and people of the earth and is probably the first German artist to incorporate **post-Impressionist** ideas into her work. During her third visit to Paris, she encountered the works of the Nabis, a radical group of artists and writers, attracted to Gauguin's primitivist-Synthetist theories, and made plans to visit their studios, which was quite bold for a single, unescorted woman at this time.

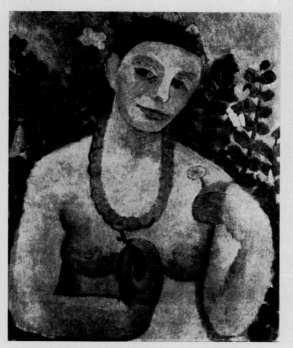

431. *Paula Modersohn-Becker. Self Portrait (Half-length with Amber Necklace). 1906. Oil on board, 24½ × 18⅝″ (62.2 × 48 cm). Private collection.*

Letters from Modersohn, whom she loved, brought her back briefly to Worpeswede and a group exhibition in which she was moderately praised by the local critic and by the poet Rainer Maria Rilke, also a resident of the small village. Becker's use of simplified shapes, heavily outlined contours, and modified color reveals her post-Impressionist style, but her strong feeling for maternity is unique.

Perhaps this self-fulfilling entry in her 1901 journal foretold her untimely death with the birth of her only child, at thirty-one: "I know I shall not live very long. But why should this be sad? Is a festival more beautiful for lasting longer? For my life is a festival. My sensual perceptions grow sharper, as though I were supposed to take in everything with the few years that will be offered me . . . " [431].

One of the founders of Dada in Zurich, who was later a Surrealist, was the painter and sculptor Hans (later Jean) Arp (1887–1966). He created artworks by tearing or cutting paper and attaching the rectangular pieces as they dropped onto a sheet of paper. He also favored paintings and then wood reliefs of amoeba-like forms with curving contours, mushroom-shaped heads, and round-dot eyes or simplified egg or navel shapes. He abhorred contrived art. To him, art was "a fruit which grows out of a man like a fruit out of a plant or like a child out of a mother." In *Objects Arranged According to the Laws of Chance or Navels* he used flat, organic shapes of painted

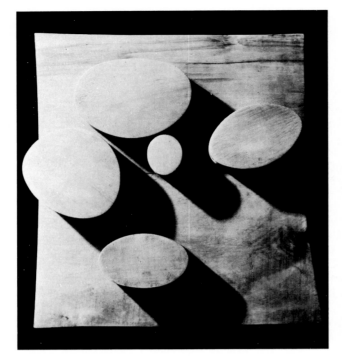

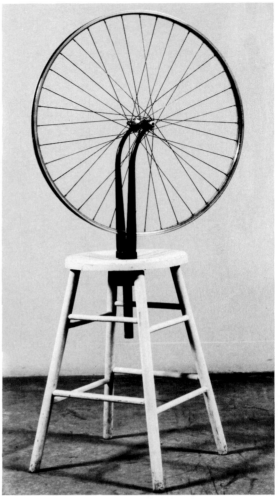

above: **432.** *Jean Arp.* Objects Arranged According to the Laws of Chance or Navels. *1930. Varnished wood relief, 10⅜ × 11⅛″ (26 × 28 cm). Collection, Museum of Modern Art, New York (purchase).*

right: **433.** *Marcel Duchamp.* Bicycle Wheel. *1951. Third version, after lost original of 1913. Assemblage: Metal wheel, diameter 25½″ (65 cm), mounted on painted wood stool, height 23¾″ (60 cm); overall height 4'2½″ (1.28 m). Museum of Modern Art, New York (Sidney and Harriet Janis Collection, gift).*

wood to make a small construction [432]. His love of nature is perhaps best expressed in his later stone sculpture, influenced by Surrealism, with its sensuous and organic forms as smooth and simple as water-worn rocks. Arp's free-form shapes have inspired contemporary industrial design such as that of cocktail tables, but they have been so much modified that much of their early impact has been lost.

Working with similar motifs from her paintings, Sophie Taeuber-Arp (1889–1934), wife of Hans Arp, also created a prodigious range of works, including weaving, embroidery, stained glass, collage, and wood reliefs. She and her husband shared a creative relationship that inspired productivity in both.

A leading contributor to Dada who worked both in New York and in Paris was Marcel Duchamp (1887–1968). According to him, "Dada was a way to get out of a state of mind, to get away from clichés—to get free." He had left

behind his Cubist- and Futurist-inspired paintings like *Nude Descending a Staircase (No. 2)* [91] to comment on the results of the machine age. Like Picasso and Braque, he also worked in collage. In 1913 he had glued string onto a canvas and combined it with paint and varnish to recreate the childhood memory of a chocolate-grinding machine repeated as part of *The Bride Stripped Bare by Her Bachelors, Even* [495]. This *Large Glass,* as it is also known, is in reality a mixed media narrative about six bachelors courting the same pretty young woman—the eternal chase of male/female—and the lure of the bride who is not what she purports to be. Duchamp's art statements were there to be consulted and deciphered rather than glanced at. Out of such experiments he combined ordinary mass-produced objects into constructions, which he called ready-mades. His first construction consisted of a bicycle wheel fastened to a kitchen stool so that the wheel could be spun easily—a spoof on activity (possibly referring to the government) that goes nowhere, ending where it starts [433].

With this new method of absorbing actual objects into compositions, painters had moved away from the mere representation of reality. The question became, "Where does reality end and art begin?" Dadaists believed art was created by the very process of the artist's selection. Duchamp's ready-mades emphasized his belief that there is no boundary between life and art, and his constructions expressed his disgust with the assembly-line production of material goods. In bringing together everyday experiences and common objects in new combinations, Duchamp was reflecting on the absurdity of human attachments to the mundane in a world he saw as illogical. He considered the creating of art the only rational act.

Mocking human attempts to find salvation through materialism, the New York Dadaist Man Ray (1890–1976) transformed a flatiron into a work of art by gluing a row of tacks to it [434]. Here, a useful object in the hands of a Dadaist becomes nonfunctional, leading us to consider whether people today may also become nonfunctional because of dependency on machines. Dadaist objects like these also posed another question—whether a culture that produces masses of material goods has provided for disposal of that mountain of junk society soon discards.

The outstanding German Dadaist was Kurt Schwitters (1887–1948), who deliberately threw out traditional notions of beauty as a gesture against artistic authoritarianism. He collected crumpled trash to make collages that hint at the disintegration of our civilization and perhaps of our personal values. In his home in Hanover about 1925 he built the first of three *Merzbau*. It was a spatial environment of little grottoes, assembled from refuse, which filled a whole room and the one above. Titled a "cathedral of erotic misery" and dedicated to his friends, it even incorporated bits of their discarded clothing cast in plaster [435].

below: **434.** Man Ray. Cadeau (Gift). *c. 1958. Replica of 1921 original. Painted flatiron with row of 13 tacks, heads glued to bottom, 6⅛ × 3⅝ × 4½" (16 × 14 × 11 cm). Collection, Museum of Modern Art, New York (James Thrall Soby Fund).*

below right: **435.** Kurt Schwitters. Hanover *Merzbau. c. 1923–1936. (Photograph c. 1933). Height 13' (3.93 m). Destroyed.*

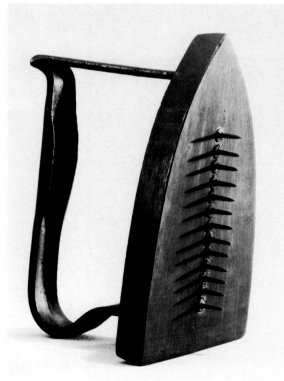

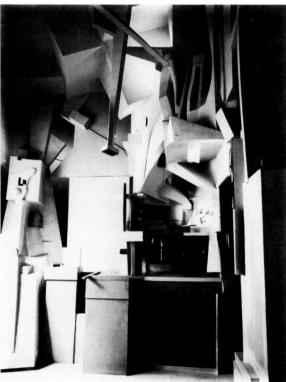

Surrealism

In Paris in the 1920s a few Dadaists like Francis Picabia (1879–1953) and Max Ernst (1891–1976) and avant-garde writers like André Breton brought their ideas together in a new literary and artistic movement called Surrealism. According to Breton's *Manifesto of Surrealism* (1924), the movement was based on the conviction that dreams and other nonrational mental processes were the most important way to deal with life.

Influenced by the Austrian psychologist Sigmund Freud and the Swiss psychologist Carl Jung, Surrealist poets and painters tried to strip away the façades that often conceal our unconscious desires. They advocated spontaneous or automatic scribbles, doodles, or drips as a means of bringing such desires to light, and they gloried in the unexpected, the contrary, and the element of shock for shock's sake. In 1925 the Surrealists held their first group exhibition, including works by Jean Arp, Man Ray, Picasso, Giorgio de Chirico, Paul Klee, and Joan Miró. Not all these men continued to paint in the Surrealist manner, and others such as Dalí joined Surrealism later, but these painters formed the core of the movement.

Long before the appearance of Surrealism as a recognized style, people were interested in art inspired by dreams and the subconscious, as depicted in the early Renaissance *Garden of Earthly Delights* [364]. Later in the 19th century the self-taught artist Henri Rousseau (1844–1910) painted an enchanted dream world. A customs inspector, unspoiled by exposure to traditional artistic conventions, Rousseau painted exotic canvases, such as *The Sleeping Gypsy,* which anticipated the limitless space of Surrealist paintings [436]. We delight in the paradoxical relationship of the woman and the lion, brightly illumined by the moon-face in the deep azure sky.

An early-20th-century forerunner of Surrealism was the Italian poet, novelist, and Metaphysical painter Giorgio de Chirico (1888–1978). He wrote, "Everything has two aspects: the current aspect we see and the ghostly which only rare individuals see in moments of clairvoyance and metaphysical abstraction." Strongly affected by the classical architecture of his homeland, De Chirico believed that an understanding of architecture was vital to the painter and that a landscape enclosed in an arch acquired "a greater metaphysical value, because it is solidified and isolated from the surrounding space." He frequently used arches in his urban scenes to suggest timelessness. These works also convey a

436. *Henri Rousseau.* The Sleeping Gypsy. *1897. Oil on canvas, 4'3" × 6'7"*
(1.46 × 2 m). Collection, Museum of Modern Art, New York (gift of Mrs. Simon Guggenheim).

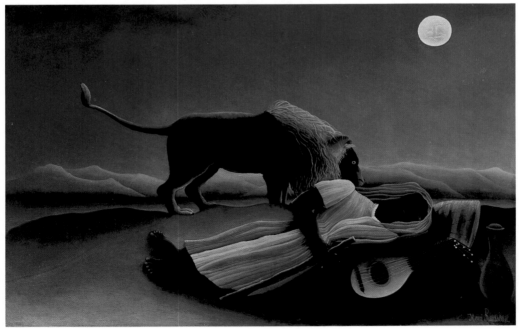

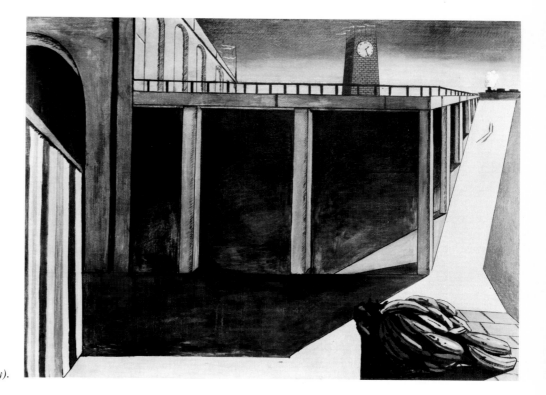

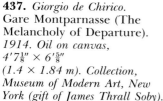

437. *Giorgio de Chirico.* Gare Montparnasse (The Melancholy of Departure). *1914. Oil on canvas, 4'7⅛" × 6'⅝" (1.4 × 1.84 m). Collection, Museum of Modern Art, New York (gift of James Thrall Soby).*

sense of loneliness and menacing supernatural power. In *Gare Montparnasse* distorted linear perspective creates an eerie space, broken only by shadows cast by empty buildings, with tiny figures, a train, and a clock ticking off the minutes before departure **[437]**. These same images are repeated in other works where a distant horizon and empty city express the infinite time and space of the subconscious mind.

The Swiss artist Paul Klee (1879–1940), who taught at the Bauhaus, combined nonobjective tendencies, Expressionistic color, and elements of fantasy and humor that link him with Dada and Surrealism. He believed there is a kind of laughter that "can be put on the same dignified level as higher lyrical emotions." Certainly his water color *Twittering Machine* **[438]** and his many etchings make us smile with a sense of delighted discovery. As a Surrealist, Klee believed in the importance of intuition as opposed to analysis. He tried to avoid the burden of historical styles by dipping into the art of children and "primitives," that is, people without art training. He wrote, "Everything vanishes around me and good works rise from me of their own accord. . . . It is not my head that functions but something . . . more remote." To keep in touch with his subconscious, Klee left himself open to new associations throughout the painting process.

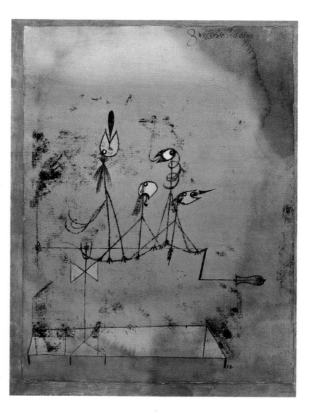

438. *Paul Klee.* Twittering Machine. *1922. Watercolor, pen and ink, 16¼ × 12" (41.3 × 30.5 cm). Collection, Museum of Modern Art, New York (purchase).*

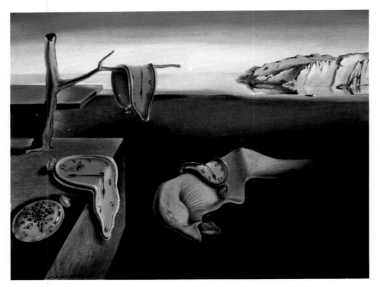

439. *Salvador Dalí.* The Persistence of Memory. *1931. Oil on canvas, 9½ × 13" (24 × 33 cm). Collection, Museum of Modern Art, New York (given anonymously).*

He rarely knew at the start of a work what might emerge, but developed in a splash of color or a line images as they suggested themselves. He titled the work only after he had finished it.

The Spanish painter Salvador Dalí (b. 1904), whose explanations of his paintings are purposely enigmatic, declared, "All men are equal in their madness." His paintings reflect this view. Brilliant and arrogant, Dalí has been a master at publicizing himself and is, therefore, the best known of the Surrealists. He joined the movement late, and many consider him too theatrical to be taken seriously. Technically skilled, he creates precisely delineated, dreamlike landscapes filled with unexpected images. In *The Persistence of Memory* [439], time wilts in a limitless desert; ants cavort in an empty watch case; and a warped headlike image in the foreground, said to be a self-portrait, suggests the last remnant of a vanishing humanity.

Another Spaniard, Joan Miró (1893–1983), used abstracted images in his inventive, poetic paintings, which Surrealistically combine humor and horror. Some of the images are recognizable, while others are strange forms, which he said he saw in hallucinations as a starving young artist. About *Carnival of Harlequin* [92] he wrote, in flamboyant Surrealist prose,

The ball of yarn unraveled by the cats dressed as Harlequins of smoke . . . throbbing like the throat of a bird at the contact of a woman . . . at this period I plucked a knob from a safety passage which I put in my eye like a monocle . . . which dives

into the phosphorescent ocean after describing a luminous circle.

Miró was trained in Spain in the academic tradition, and there is nothing undisciplined about his seemingly childlike paintings. Although he was anti-intellectual, passionately fond of color, and hostile to tradition, he produced paintings, sculpture, lithographs, and ceramics that are subtle and brilliantly composed. He was also active in theater and ballet, designing sets and costumes for the famous ballet company of Serge Diaghilev, and it is from this period that *Carnival of Harlequin* dates. Of all the Surrealists, Miró perhaps had the strongest influence on painters of the later **Abstract Expressionist** movement.

Instead of expressing Surrealist anxiety and pessimism, Marc Chagall (1889–1985) painted his feelings of joy, festivity, and love with a sensuous delight in color and texture. His works, based on memories of his childhood in a Russian Jewish family, are steeped in folklore and the mystical Hasidic tradition. He filled his canvases with fiddlers, Talmudic scholars, peasant women, and floating cows and roosters. In his fantasies, Chagall is close to Henri Rousseau, and his works are richly personal. His portrait of

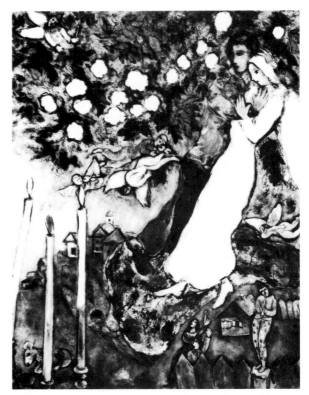

440. *Marc Chagall.* Three Candles. *1938–1940. Oil on canvas, 4'3¼" × 3'2" (1.3 × .965 m). Collection, The Reader's Digest Association, Inc.*

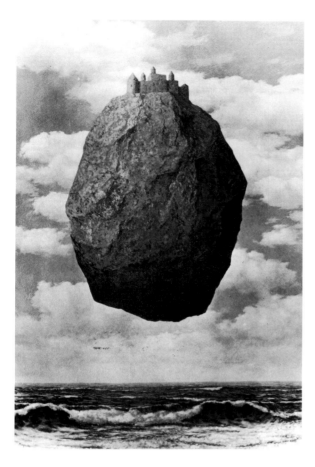

himself with his wife expresses the perennial euphoria of love [440].

The Belgian Surrealist René Magritte (1898–1967) used unexpected and disturbing images in his paintings. Heavy rocks float lightly through soft blue skies [441]; or a room as perfect in scale and detail as a Van Eyck interior [361] may contain a huge apple, which almost reaches the ceiling. A closet full of discarded clothes may bulge with invisible human forms, becoming a chronicle of past events. Painted in a meticulous, realistic style, most of Magritte's works present the incredible as an accomplished fact. Alternating truth with illusion, Magritte makes us suspicious of both the painted and the real world. He presents us with a world in which we see his dreams become real objects and his objects become dreams.

Meret Oppenheim (1913–1985) emphasized the Surrealists' sense of the absurd. In the spirit of Man Ray's *Gift* [434], her *Object*, a fur-covered cup and saucer, mocked a pretentious society whose products could no longer function [442].

left: **441.** *René Magritte.* The Castle of the Pyrénées. *1959. Oil on canvas, 6'6¾" × 4'9⅛" (2.0 × 1.45 m). Israel Museum, Jerusalem (gift of Harry Torczyner, New York, to the American Friends of the Israel Museum, 1985).*

442. *Meret Oppenheim.* Object. *1936. Fur-covered cup, saucer, spoon; diameter of cup 4⅜" (11 cm); diameter of saucer 9⅜" (24 cm); length of spoon 8" (20 cm); overall height 2⅞" (7 cm). Collection, Museum of Modern Art, New York (purchase).*

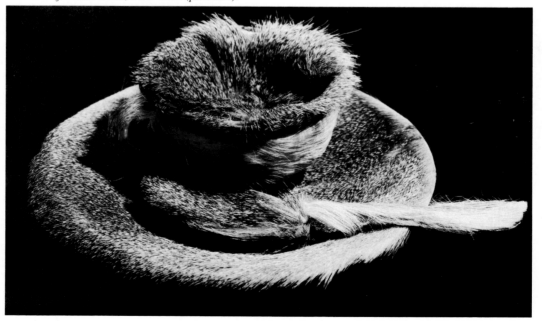

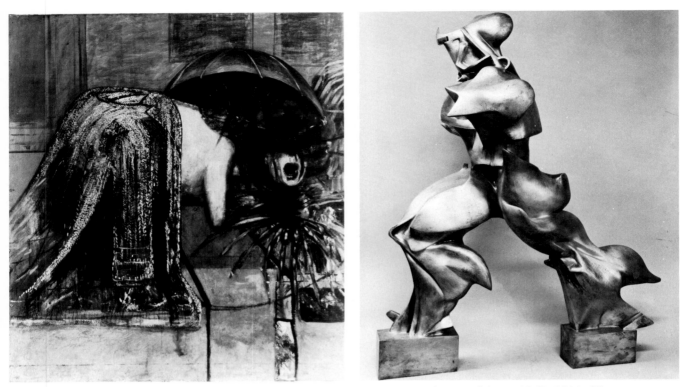

above: **443.** *Francis Bacon.* Figure Study II *(previously known as* The Magdalene) *1945–1946. Oil on canvas, 4'9¼" × 4'2¾" (1.45 × 1.29 m). Huddersfield Art Gallery, Kirklees Metropolitan Council, West Yorkshire, England.*

above right: **444.** *Umberto Boccioni.* Unique Forms of Continuity in Space. *1913. Bronze (cast 1931). 43½ × 24⅞ × 15¾" (101 × 88 × 40 cm). Collection, Museum of Modern Art, New York (Lillie P. Bliss Bequest).*

The Surrealist current continues in the paintings of the Irish-born Francis Bacon (b. 1910), who uses the past as a basis for his works but transforms them through his own inward vision of personal torment. As part of a series of works on the Crucifixion, one of his characteristic themes, he painted a *Magdalene* [**443**]. The figure's solid form recalls Giotto. Under an umbrella and veil the gaping mouth howls in grief. This work reveals Bacon's superb skills as a painter, his foundation in realist tradition, and the acute sense of the horrors of his world.

Sculpture

Until the 20th century, sculptors had carved or cast figures that relied on visually solid volumes surrounded by space. At the beginning of the century, many sculpters continued that tradition, exemplified by Rodin. In the new age, however, the changing concepts of space and motion that affected painting also affected sculpture. Avant-garde sculptors reached for different images, techniques, and materials, as we saw in Chapter 7.

One of the first sculptors to break with the past was Umberto Boccioni (1882–1916), whose *Manifesto* of 1912 announced Futurism. His *Unique Forms of Continuity in Space* [**444**] depicts a figure rushing forward in violent motion. Expressive as it is, with strong, forward-thrusting diagonals, the cubistic figure is impersonal. Boccioni was interested in movement in the abstract and arranged the shapes to convey the impression of action. The Futurists set out to make of Italy, where the style was born, a Utopia of tension and transformation whose god was machine-created movement (and speed).

Cubism

The Cubist movement freed many sculptors from traditional imagery. Jacques Lipchitz (1891–1973) at first created flat forms that seemed to be almost literal translations of Cubist paintings into sculpture. Later he developed a personal style in which he combined Cubist simplification with his own ideas about birth, growth, and death. Also affected by African art, he searched for a way to reconcile human forms with the new geometry of the machine. His bronze, robotlike *Figure* [445] of 1926–1930 is composed of biomorphic (organic) shapes, yet in its stark simplicity suggests an ominous, machinelike force.

An academically trained Rumanian, Constantin Brancusi (1876–1957), joined the radical young artists working in Paris. Although he was concerned with the machine age, African art, and Cubism, he never gave up his deep involvement in the natural world. His famous *Bird in Space* [446] deals with organic subjects at the same time that it explores Cubist simplification of masses.

Related to the Cubist simplification of form and to the elongation of features seen in Sudanese masks, Amedeo Modigliani's works [426]

demonstrate the influence of African art while expressing a unique sensuous quality of their own.

Constructivism

An even more radical break with tradition was Constructivist sculpture. No longer dependent on carving, modeling, or casting but moving into a new technical area, these sculptures consisted of constructions, or assemblages, of pieces of wood, metal, plastic, or other materials. Constructivist space between solid forms and seen through transparent planes was composed as carefully as the forms themselves.

Constructivism began in Russia, where two brothers, Naum Gabo (1890–1977) and Antoine

below: **445.** *Jacques Lipchitz.* Figure. *1926–1930. Bronze (cast 1937), 7′1¼″ × 3′2⅝″ (2.17 × .99 m). Collection, Museum of Modern Art, New York (Van Gogh purchase fund).*

below right: **446.** *Constantin Brancusi.* Bird in Space. *c. 1928. Bronze (unique cast), height 4′6″ (1.37 m). Collection, Museum of Modern Art, New York (given anonymously).*

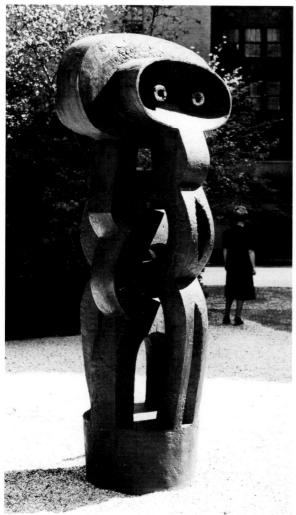

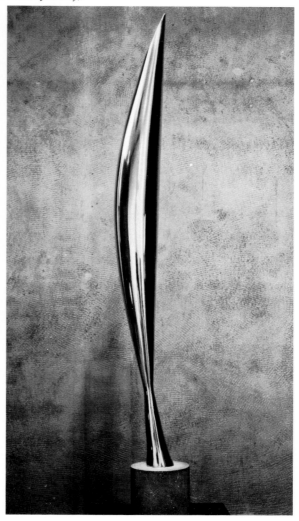

Pevsner (1886–1962), were attracted to the analytical approach of Cubism and to new areas of technology. In 1920 they wrote a *Realistic Manifesto,* in which they declared that sculpture must no longer describe reality but must be in harmony with engineering technology. When the Soviet government insisted on a return to conservative art, they, like Kandinsky, left for the West, where their ideas were well received by avant-garde artists. Pevsner's *Torso* [447] used Cubist-inspired planes to recreate the concave and convex forms of the human body out of sheets of copper and plastic. The transparency of the plastic denied the solid aspects of traditional sculpture. Even more revolutionary was Gabo's *Linear Construction No. 1* [448], which consisted of a plastic frame threaded with nylon. Like Cubist painters, both sculptors were concerned with overlapping and combining multiple views of the same, usually geometric, subject as well as with the relation of mass and interior and exterior space.

Both Cubism and Constructivism influenced the work of the outstanding British sculptor Barbara Hepworth (1903–1975). Using highly polished marble, wood, and bronze, she sculpted abstract geometric forms, which were usually pierced or hollowed out in order to incorporate space within their design. Her *Single Form* (Dag Hammarskjöld memorial) [449] is a fitting testimonial to her powers. She wrote of it:

I had to work to the scale of twenty-one feet and bring into my mind everything . . . taught me about stress and strain and gravity and wind force. Finally all the many parts were got out of St. Ives safely, and when assembled, . . . they stood in perfect balance. This was a magic moment.

Realism

The human body has been the main subject of figurative sculpture since ancient times. It has been treated in a variety of ways. Egyptian sculp-

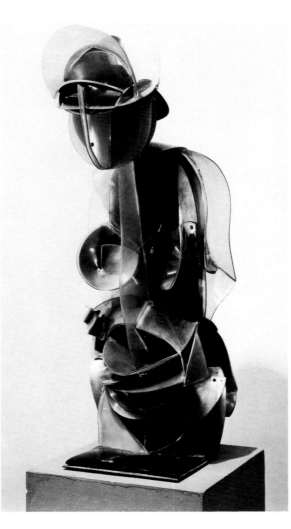

left: **447.** *Antoine Pevsner.* Torso. *1924–1926. Construction in plastic and copper, 29½ × 11⅝″ (75 × 30 cm). Collection, Museum of Modern Art, New York (Katherine S. Dreier Bequest).*

below: **448.** *Naum Gabo.* Linear Construction No. 1 (Smaller Version). *1942–1943. Plexiglass and nylon thread on plexiglass base, 12¼ × 12¼ × 2¾″ (31 × 31 × 6 cm). Hirshhorn Museum and Sculpture Garden, Smithsonian Institution, Washington (gift of Joseph H. Hirshhorn, 1966).*

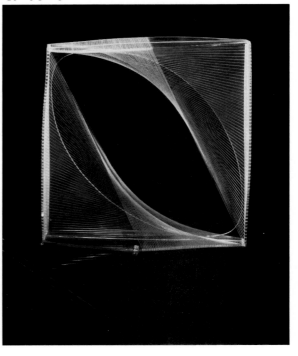

tors carved massive stone statues [55], abstracted in form and exaggerated in scale, to glorify their rulers and gods. Classical Greek statues of gods and heroes, subtly elegant examplars of moderation, show the body in a state of balance between energy and repose [310]. Medieval sculpture, chiefly for the Church, portrays the human figure symbolically [335] in conflict between yearning for heaven and earthly temptation. The open sexuality of an Indian goddess was intended to remind the viewer of his or her oneness with the universe [286]. In 19th-century Europe, Rodin's sculpture expressed his interest in psychology and movement [194].

In the 20th century, the concept of the figure changed radically, as we have seen. Reflecting the machine age, the body was abstracted and almost dehumanized by Cubist sculptors and

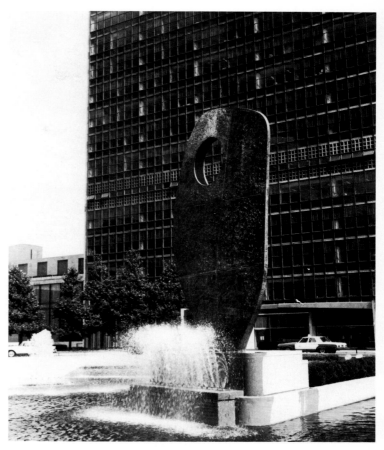

right: **449.** *Barbara Hepworth.* Single Form. *1964. Bronze, height 25' (6.4 m). United Nations Plaza, New York.*

below: **450.** *Gaston Lachaise.* Standing Woman. *1932. Bronze, height 7'4" × 3'5⅛" × 1'7⅛" (2.24 × 1.04 × 0.48 m). Collection, Museum of Modern Art, New York (Mrs. Simon Guggenheim Fund).*

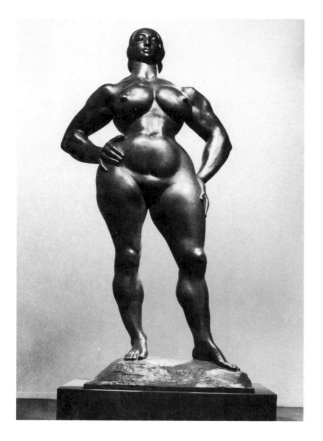

ignored by Constructivists. Other sculptors, however, remained closer to the figurative tradition.

The fertility symbol first seen in the prehistoric *Venus of Willendorf* [25] reappears in the work of Gaston Lachaise (1882–1935). Throughout most of his career he was obsessed by the image of the female nude. He modeled her as a gross maternal figure with mountainous breasts and thighs, but her delicately tapered arms and legs give her an almost classical elegance. She sits in a chair, floats on a high pedestal, or stands [450] and [62].

One of the most creative of the figurative sculptors was Henry Moore (1898–1981), the son of an English coal miner. Unlike the work of his friend and colleague Barbara Hepworth, Moore's work is highly organic. He was interested in the biological structure of the body and the connections between its forms and the natural world. He explored these relationships in wood, stone, and bronze, handling each with a deep sensitivity to its innate characteristics.

Moore developed his style to express an association of the body with the universal mystery of life and to separate it from the emotions of the

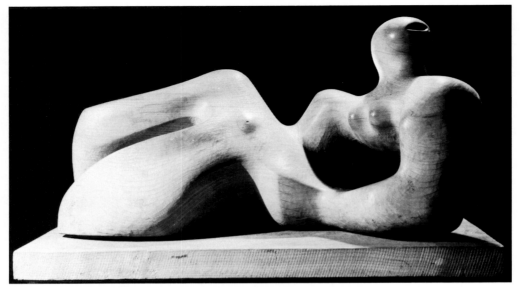

451. *Henry Moore.* Reclining Figure. *1935. Elm wood, 19 × 35 × 15" (48 × 89 × 38 cm). Albright-Knox Art Gallery, Buffalo (Room of Contemporary Art Fund, 1939).*

individual. Often he reduced the head, concentrating instead on the shafts and terminals of the body structure, which is often shown reclining [451]. Like the Constructivists, he brought space into sculpture. He created great hollows in the middle of his figures, sculpting strong rhythmic volumes and spaces that suggest the openings of the living body and emphasize sexual associations but may also recall caves and holes in rocks and trees. These forms reflect one of the most pervasive influences in Moore's work, the *Chac Mool* [452], a massive pre-Columbian stone figure of a rain god from Mexico that lies on its back and has a hollowed-out abdomen. The sim-

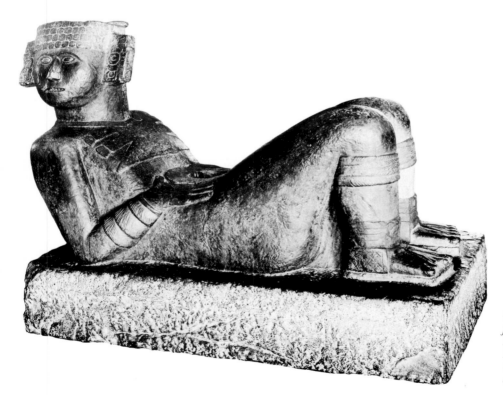

452. Chac Mool, *rain god, from Chichén-Itzá, Mexico. Mayan-Toltec, 900–1300* A.D. *Limestone, height 42⅛" (107 cm). National Museum of Anthropology, Mexico City.*

plified forms of his figures and groupings suggest timeless mountains as well as the solidity of the bony structure under the flesh.

Two influential Continental sculptors, Marino Marini (1901–1980) and Alberto Giacometti (1901–1966), used the human figure expressively to comment on human isolation and fear. In the tradition of Rodin, both emphasize surface textures. Having absorbed Surrealist attitudes as well as influences from early Italian figure sculpture, their styles are nonetheless quite personal.

Although Marini's subjects included female figures and portraits, he is known for his bronzes of men on horses—forms that seem linked to the Etruscan sculpture of his native Tuscany. The sense of isolation and fear projected by these anonymous riders is not accidental. Marini watched Italians fleeing from wartime air raids; the frightened way they looked upward to watch the sky for bombers became an important gesture in his sculpture—expressing human helplessness [453]. In his later years his images became increasingly violent. The stumplike vestiges of feet and hands suggest mutilation of bodies by war and make his figures appear even more isolated and mute.

Giacometti, the son of a Swiss painter, created a new human image in his emaciated bronze figures that stand so stiffly and face us so directly. The attenuated forms in *City Square* [63] appear almost like shadows that float across the flat plane of the street. The five figures, captured in a momentary encounter, seem unable to experience any real interchange. Large or small, in groups or by themselves, Giacometti's forms seem lonely and alienated. He has exaggerated the distance between subject and viewer by erasing the nonessential details of the body, thereby increasing its sense of isolation.

Architecture

We saw in Chapter 9 how consideration of structure, function, and space was related to the development of new building materials and engineering methods in the 19th century. Louis Sullivan, who used new techniques in his tall steel-frame buildings [266], made a statement that widely influenced 20th-century architecture: "Form follows function." That is, an architect should consider the function of a building and then design a form to suit the function rather than deciding on a Neoclassical temple design, for example, and forcing a modern bank to fit into it.

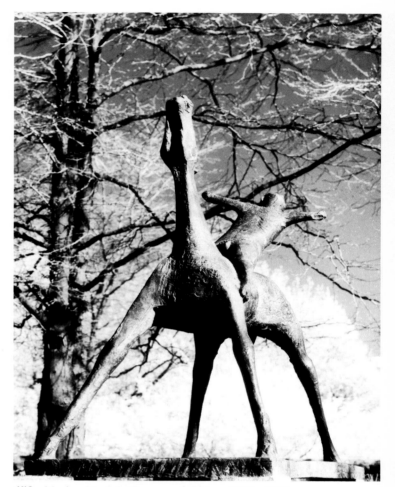

453. *Marino Marini.* Horse and Rider. *1952–1953. Bronze, 6'10" × 6'9" × 3'10½" (2.08 × 2.06 × 1.18 m). Hirshhorn Museum and Sculpture Garden, Smithsonian Institution, Washington.*

In the early 1900s in France, Auguste Perret (1874–1954) was using reinforced concrete frames and nonsupporting, or curtain, walls, which left building interiors free to be divided into a combination of rooms. In Germany, Peter Behrens (1868–1940) and Walter Gropius (1883–1969) were using the same technique to construct functional buildings with clean, almost mechanical lines. Gropius in collaboration with Adolf Meyer (1881–1929) carried a curtain wall of glass windows out to the corners of the Fagus Shoe Factory in Alfeld-an-der-Leine. This device made possible simultaneous views of the interior and exterior, as in the shifting planes of a Cubist painting, and at the same time achieved an appearance of lightness. In the United States, Frank Lloyd Wright was experimenting with functional buildings, Cubist planes, and cantilevering [260]. This ferment of new ideas in

Exploring Art Through Technology

From Obsolete Station to Grand Museum

The majestic Gare d'Orsay in Paris, a luxurious railroad station when it was finished in 1900, slid slowly into disuse as trains were replaced by cars and planes. Now it has reemerged as a splendid museum [454]. This is not so surprising a metamorphosis if we consider this March 22, 1900, journal entry by an artist, Edouard Détaille: "The station is superb and gives the impression of a Beaux Arts palace. I suggest to Laloux [the architect] to exchange them if there is still time." Eighty-six years after its construction, Détaille's recommendation was fulfilled when the train station opened on December 9, 1986, renovated as a museum dedicated to 19th-century art. And, coincidentally, a work by Détaille himself hangs in the gallery.

The Musée d'Orsay, as it is now called, taps the French government's vast collection of 19th-century art previously housed in various museums in Paris. The quality of the collection is impressive, consisting of the finest 19th-century European art seen anywhere.

The whole venture, which began to take shape in 1977, has evolved under the firm guidance of Italian architect Gae Aulenti into what is actually the second remodeling of the building's history. In 1897, the Paris-Orléans rail company had bought the site of the former Palais d'Orsay. Victor Laloux entirely covered the metal framework of the palace and the train station behind a stately classical facade of stone to relate as a neotraditional structure to the nearby Louvre museum.

The current renovation retained the vast semicircular barrel vault of iron and glass, arching 100 feet (30 meters) above the floor. Aulenti faced formidable problems in this assignment, one of the largest she had ever undertaken. There were 323,000 square feet (30,000 square meters) of floors and almost no walls. Her design shows a new building inside the old, encouraging constant reference historically while scrupulously displaying the art functionally, each piece in tune with its own time. Further, at least in the first exhibitions, academic artworks and the historic avant garde, which defied them, appeared to coexist comfortably, each suitably "tracked" in separate but equal galleries—a pattern to consider in the design of museums of the future.

454. *Interior, Musée d'Orsay, Paris.*

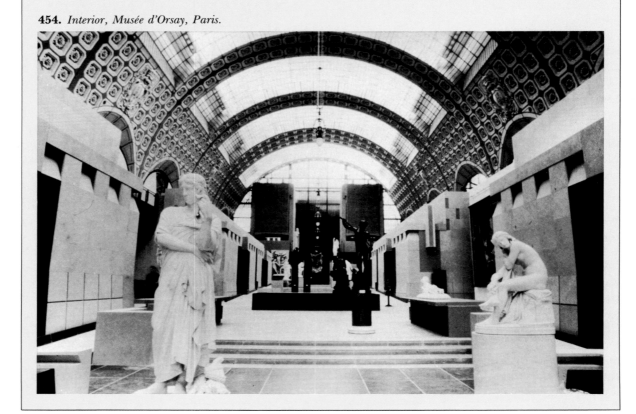

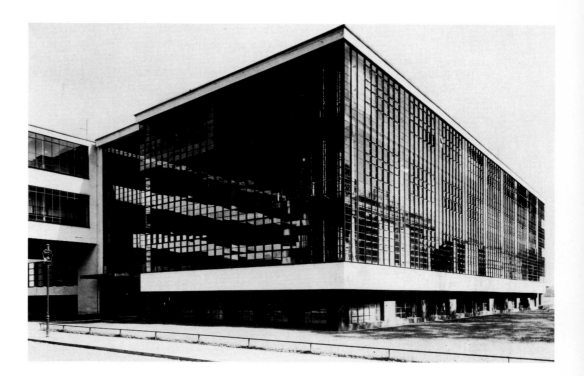

455. *Walter Gropius, Workshop wing, Bauhaus Building, Dessau, East Germany. 1925–1926.*

architecture influenced artists, who in turn influenced architects. In fact, architects, artists, and designers often knew one another or at least were familiar with one another's published works.

The Bauhaus and the International Style

Many of these ideas flourished in the **Bauhaus,** a school of design founded by Gropius in Weimar, Germany, in 1919 from two earlier schools of arts and crafts. Here art, technology, and business were brought together in an attempt to apply principles of good design to industrial production. Artists from Germany, Russia, the Netherlands, and Switzerland joined the faculty to develop an **International Style** of architecture and design, which gradually spread throughout the industrialized world.

Fundamental to Bauhaus teaching was Sullivan's principle that form follows function and William Morris' belief that utility and aesthetics could be integrated. Rather than returning to old craft-guild concepts, however, the school looked forward, embracing modern technology and materials. It explored new approaches to printing, metalwork, weaving, pottery, and stagecraft, as well as architecture. The faculty included such prominent figures as the painters Kandinsky and Klee and the designers and architects Ludwig Mies van der Rohe and Marcel Breuer. Gropius declared:

We want to create a clear, organic architecture whose inner logic will be radiant and naked, unencumbered by lying façades and trickiness; we want an architecture adapted to our world of machines, radios, and fast motor cars, an architecture whose function is clearly recognizable in the relation of its form.

A structural base of the new style was the use of a weight-bearing cage, or frame, on which the outer, non-weight-bearing walls could be hung. These **curtain walls** could be made of any material that would serve to enclose space. As a result, windows and doors could be enlarged almost indefinitely, while the reduction of interior supports allowed the inside of the building to be rearranged at need. Fundamental to the new International Style was an avoidance of applied decoration. Gropius believed that aesthetic satisfaction in a building could be achieved through a balance of solids and spaces. Nothing more was needed to make a building beautiful.

When the Bauhaus was moved to Dessau in 1925, new administrative offices, classrooms, studios, workshops, a library, and living quarters for faculty and students were needed. Instead of attempting to fit these varied areas into a group of Gothic or Neoclassical buildings, Gropius designed a new building, using new engineering methods, that honestly served its varied functions and reflected them in its design [455]. Beginning with an open box as the basic unit, Gropius varied its volume according to its potential use and then grouped the boxes into a pleasing three-dimensional composition that suggested the crisp rectangles of a Mondrian painting.

Ludwig Mies van der Rohe (1886–1969), who became director of the Bauhaus after Gropius, refined the International Style, bringing it an elegance through the use of light-reflecting materials and subtle detail. His German Pavilion at the International Exhibition in Barcelona in 1929 (since destroyed) was the archetype of the International Style [242]. The long, low, open building conveyed a quality of serenity through its clean lines, refined details, and sensitive use of materials. Its interior spaces were defined, without being isolated, by chrome-plated steel supports, glass walls, and marble panels. These surfaces contrasted with one another and with the open expanse of the pool in the court. Mies's famous Barcelona chair [240], designed for this pavilion, can be seen through the glass wall, expressing the Bauhaus ideal of carrying good design through all aspects of a building.

When Hitler closed the Bauhaus in 1933, many faculty members came to the United States, where they taught Bauhaus principles and continued to work in the International Style. In his buildings for the Illinois Institute of Technology in Chicago, his Lake Shore Apartments in Chicago, and the Seagram Building in New York [268], Mies integrated concrete, steel, and glass into refined, rational compositions. Gropius and Marcel Breuer (1902–1981) designed low, cubistic houses. Breuer's tubular metal chair [456], first made in Germany, and Mies's Barcelona chair were mass produced, as were lamps and other objects that showed Bauhaus influence. Herbert Bayer (1900–1985), also from the Bauhaus faculty, influenced typography and advertising design.

Frank Lloyd Wright and the Organic Style

An American pioneer in early-20th-century architecture was Frank Lloyd Wright (1869–1959). Although he affected the International Style, he despised it and developed a personal style that never fit into any category. Brilliant, rebellious, and innovative, he was influenced by Sullivan, with whom he studied. Like Sullivan he believed that buildings should openly reflect the functions they are intended to perform. He deplored, however, the ferroconcrete boxes produced by the International Style. Wright designed the Imperial Hotel in Tokyo around an open court, adapting Oriental decorative details; he also built it according to a structural system that enabled it to withstand the devastating earthquake of 1923. (It was razed in 1968 to make way for a larger hotel.) Wright also be-

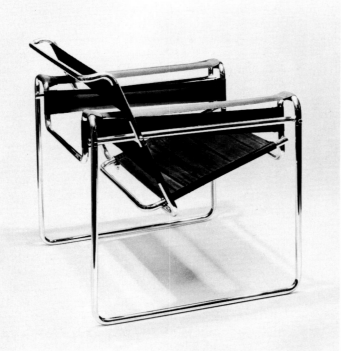

456. *Marcel Breuer.* Club Armchair. *1925. Chrome-plated tubular steel with canvas slings, 28⅛ × 30¼ × 27¾″ (71 × 76.8 × 70.5 cm). Collection, Museum of Modern Art, New York (gift of Herbert Bayer).*

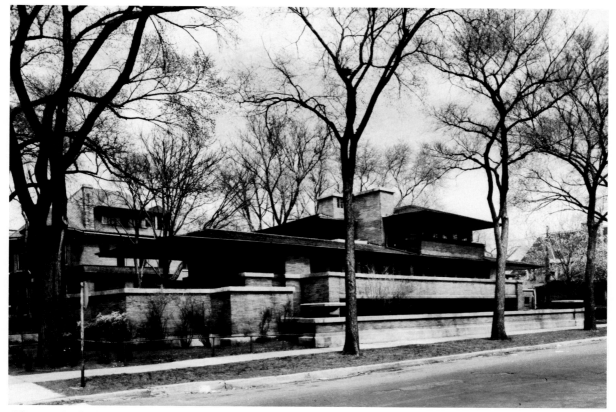

457. *Frank Lloyd Wright. Robie House, Chicago. 1909.*

lieved that a building should reveal the materials with which it is constructed. For example, stone should look like stone and be used as a means of support rather than to conceal modern structural systems. In the same way, ferroconcrete building blocks should not pretend to be anything else.

In addition, Wright was always concerned for natural surroundings and people's spiritual needs. Rejecting the European idea that buildings should function like machines, he believed that a house should provide for the spirit as well as the body. Strongly influenced by Japanese architecture, he was convinced that people must keep alive their relation to the natural world. Therefore he gave his houses an organic growing quality by often using wood and stone, and designing them to fit naturally into their surroundings. The long, low lines of the early ranch-style Robie House in Chicago [457] are integrated with the flat site, and the later Kaufman House in Bear Run, Pennsylvania, is cantilevered over a waterfall [260].

Wright's designs evolved over the years. In the 1920s, for example, his buildings were massive rectangular forms as a result of his experiment-

ing with poured concrete and patterned concrete blocks. Decorative elements were provided by the texture of the materials and the interplay of blocklike masses and open space. The glass and cantilever construction of the Kaufman House suggests the machine-oriented International Style. Nevertheless, his basic philosophy was maintained.

Wright was once asked by a student how to develop an original personal style. He responded briefly, "You can't. I invented the new architecture at the turn of the century. All you can do is learn its principles and work them." Arrogant though the statement was, there was truth to it; Wright's buildings radically altered the course of architecture in the 20th century.

Le Corbusier and the Functional Style

In France, Le Corbusier (1887–1965), who had worked with Behrens, was also designing innovative, functional buildings in the International Style. He used his knowledge of modern engineering techniques to open up his buildings and introduce light, air, and sun. He saw a house as "a machine for living in," believing it

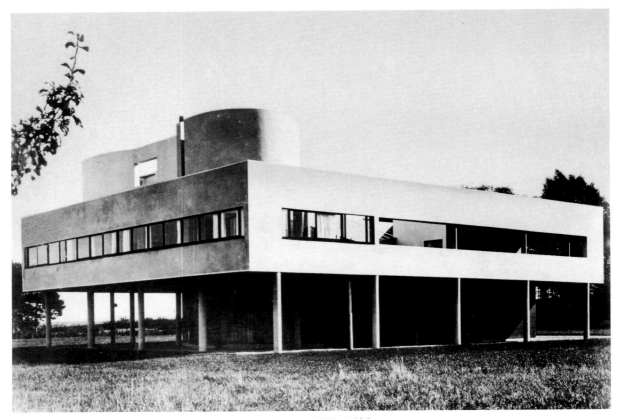

458. *Le Corbusier. Villa Savoye, Poissy-sur-Seine, France. 1929–1930.*

should function no less than a machine. In his influential book *Towards a New Architecture* (published in French in 1923), he urged architects to move away from an architecture stifled by custom and to study ocean liners, airplanes, and automobiles instead. His Villa Savoye in Poissy, France [458], one of the outstanding examples of the International Style, illustrates these beliefs.

The concrete and glass structure is close to the purist ideals of Mondrian, and the combination of its curved forms and rectangles suggests Le Corbusier's interest in ocean liners. The Villa Savoye has none of Wright's respect for site; instead, raised on posts, it seems to float above the earth, suggesting the rootless, transient quality of modern life. Many of its features, such as the posts and the windows in horizontal strips, were adapted by later architects. Wright derisively referred to Le Corbusier's buildings as "boxes on stilts," but they may have influenced his Kaufman House [260].

Le Corbusier's influence on architecture was immense, but perhaps in the long run he will be remembered best for his social philosophy. He believed that not only the rich, who could afford houses like the Villa Savoye, but *all* human beings are entitled to live in buildings that will surround them with space and beauty. Dedicated to this ideal, he planned groups of inexpensive, mass-produced houses made of reinforced concrete. These houses were designed to provide comfortable living in units, which could be divided inside according to the needs of each family. As the movement of population to cities progressed and space became scarce, he gave up his early row-house concept and built vertical apartment towers surrounded by open space. These structures are discussed in Chapter 9.

The work of these internationally active architects, and others who adopted their philosophies, has profoundly affected our lives. Thousands of useful objects and buildings in the last several decades have been influenced by them. Out of the chaos of changing needs, changing materials, and changing art of the 20th century, these creative minds brought a measure of logical order, through architecture, into our world.

Exercises and Activities

Research Exercises

1. Trace the growth of one new style of art that emerged during the first two decades of the 20th century. Discuss in detail two artists who worked in that style.
2. Explain in what way exposure to African art was an important force in the development of 20th-century art; give examples. Explain what aspects of Oriental art influenced 20th-century artists.
3. Search for and quote passages of poetry or fiction that deal with the same themes as those that appear in Surealism and Dadaism.
4. What is the International Style? How did the style start, and how did it influence painting, architecture, sculpture, and the industrial arts?
5. What was the Bauhaus? How did it influence 20th-century art? Cite examples.

Studio Activities

1. Draw a composition in the style of Cubism, superimposing in one drawing at least three views of an object. Include interior and exterior aspects and top, side, and front views, presenting a familiar object in a new way.
2. Create a construction of objects emphasizing nonart values.
3. The creation of the illusion of deep space has appeared throughout art history. What Surealist painters used this technique? Create a composition in color or in black and white using perspective, changing hues, and values to create an illusion of deep space, but using images from the world of dreams and fantasy.
4. Using poster paints, create a simple still life in at least two of the styles that developed in the first quarter of the 20th century.
5. Draw a floor plan of the Bauhaus in Dessau, Germany.

16
America Ascending: 1900–1945

For it is ultimately the function of art in imposing a credible order upon ordinary reality, and by eliciting some perception of an "order in reality" to bring us to a condition of serenity, stillness and reconciliation.

T. S. Eliot, "Poetry and Drama," post 1940s

Born into a place and an age in which space and time are our principal companions-in-concern, I find it inevitable to love them more than the solid materials with which my ancestors were involved.

Richard Lippold, 1973

The four large systems of commerce, museums, education and great bureaucracy exist, requiring art and artists. The integration of art into bureaucratic society . . . may destroy art.

Donald Judd, 1984

After a brief euphoria following World War I, the world slid into the Great Depression of the 1930s. Paris, where the arts had continued during the international conflict, resumed its position as the art capital, but an ocean away, America's growing isolation had led our artists to develop their own art forms. As bankruptcy and unemployment gripped much of the country, social problems multiplied. In response, the arts in the United States became more socially conscious, increasingly realistic, and often nationalistic. The diversity of European art did not exist in this country. We can identify for the most part, however, the same basic trends that characterized European art—realism, derived from what already existed in traditional American art; Expressionism, with strong emotional overtones comparable to the European currents; formalism, with a concentration on design and color; and fantasy.

Realist Painting

The *Réalisme* of Gustave Courbet (Chapter 14) found few European adherents, but American tastes were more conservative. By the turn of the century Thomas Eakins (1844–1916), trained in America but much influenced by historical painters of Europe, was established as an uncompromising realist. His fascination with photography led to many experiments; he used some of his camera studies to prepare his paintings and others—like the series by Eadweard Muybridge **[89]**—to investigate movement. Eakins' style of precision and realistic details, as revealed in his portraits, were no doubt inspired by photography and influenced many American realist artists of the early 20th century. In brilliant, raking light from the left, Susan Eakins **[459]** confronts the viewer with firmness and strength. Eakin's admiration for his wife at forty-seven appears as uncompromising as are the details he rendered of her dress, the open coat with the light on it and the scarf pinned in place.

During the first decades of the 20th century, conservative American artists continued to follow the rules established by academies of art. These American academies were modeled after

America in the World

THE VISUAL ARTS		HISTORICAL NOTES
1899 Eakins, *Mrs. Thomas Eakins* **[459]**		
	1900	
		1914 World War I begins
		1917 USA enters war
		1918 World War I ends
	1925	**1925** Scott Fitzgerald, *The Great Gatsby*
1927 O'Keeffe, *Calla Lily with Red Roses* **[461]**		**1927** Al Jolson, *The Jazz Singer*
1930 Hopper, *Early Sunday Morning* **[463]**		**1929** Wall Street crash: Great Depression
1930 Wood, *American Gothic* **[466]**	**1930**	
1931–32 Shahn, *The Passion of Sacco and Vanzetti* **[464]**		**1933** F. D. Roosevelt becomes president: New Deal
1934 Douglas, *Aspects of the Negro Life* **[468]**		
	1935	
1936 Chaplin, *Modern Times* **[479]**		**1936** Spanish Civil War begins
1936 Lange, *Migrant Mother* **[144]**		
1937 Siqueiros, *Echo of a Scream* **[472]**		
1937 Picasso, *Guernica* **[35]**		**1939** World War II begins
	1940	
		1941 Japanese bomb Pearl Harbor; USA enters war
		1943 Penicillin developed
	1945	**1945** Germany surrenders
		1945 USA drops atom bomb on Hiroshima
		1945 Japan surrenders
1946 Lawrence, *Going Home* **[109]**		
1946 C. and R. Eames, plywood chair **[235]**		
1948 Wyeth, *Christina's World* **[107]**		
1948 Pollock, *Number 1* **[10]**		
1952 White, *Preacher* **[102]**		

their European counterparts, where many Americans studied.

The Ash Can School and Modernism

The high caliber of late-19th-century realist painting developed by such artists as Thomas Eakins was coupled with growing interest in the camera—leading to an early-20th-century movement (dubbed **Ash Can** by critics) that carried realism much further. Many, possibly drawing on their experiences as journalists, found themes for art in backyards, city streets, and bars. One of the most noted, John Sloan (1871–

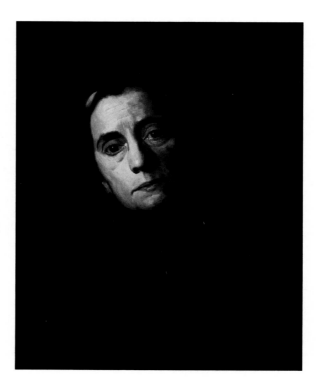

right: **459.** *Thomas Eakins.* Mrs. Thomas Eakins. *c. 1899. Oil on canvas, 20⅛ × 16⅜″ (41 × 40.8 cm). Hirshhorn Museum and Sculpture Garden, Smithsonian Institution, Washington (Gift of Joseph H. Hirshhorn, 1966).*

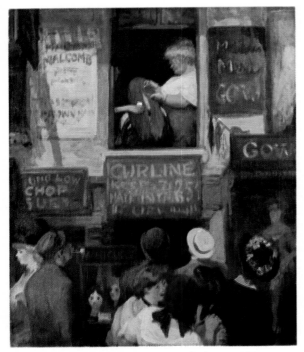

460. *John Sloan.* Hairdresser's Window. *1907. Oil on canvas, 31⅞ × 26" (81.03 × 66 cm). Wadsworth Atheneum, Hartford (The Ella Gallup Sumner and Mary Catlin Sumner Collection).*

1951), produced paintings and etchings showing New Yorkers at work and play [460].

The year 1908 witnessed a group show of "Eight Independent Painters," including Sloan, that could be termed the 20th century's first band of rebel realists committed to painting what they saw, not what society proclaimed to be aesthetic. With the Armory Show of 1913, which included the more radical European and American artists such as the Parisian Duchamp's iconoclastic *Nude Descending a Staircase* [91], America was faced with growing misgivings about academic teachings. The photographer and art pioneer Alfred Stieglitz's avant-garde art magazine *Camera Work* quoted no less an authority than the conservative Metropolitan Museum of Art's director Sir Purdon Clark addressing the mounting unrest of the art world with some support for modern art. From these beginnings, the American tradition of **Modernism** was born between 1908 and World War I with a group of young artists, newly exposed to radical European art and uninhibited in testing those modern idioms.

An early modernist, Georgia O'Keeffe, who taught in western Texas and eventually settled in New Mexico, painted barns, mountains, and bleached bones characteristic of the harsh, barren landscape of the Southwest. Other subjects included flowers, New York skyscrapers, and clouds seen from a jet plane. Well acquainted with European art currents, she presented all these objects, man-made and natural, from a distinctive point of view and in a precise personal style that gives them fresh meaning [461]. The natural smoothness of her technique and

461. *Georgia O'Keeffe.* L. K. White Calla and Roses. *1926. Oil on canvas, 2'6" × 4' (0.76 × 1.22 m). Private collection.*

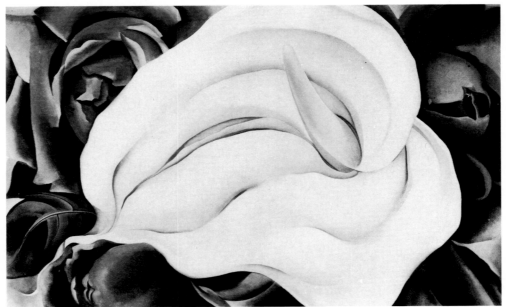

Focus on the Artist

Georgia O'Keeffe (1887–1986)

Georgia O'Keeffe was always a very private person. From her first meeting in 1914 with Alfred Stieglitz, who would later become her husband, she found him very exciting, yet watched her friends asking him personal questions and backed away, thinking, "That isn't for me. Let them talk if they want to." Early on, however, she found she "could say things" with art that she could express in no other way.

With this realization, in 1917 she sent a bundle of her drawings to a Columbia University school friend, Anita Pollitzer, with instructions to show them to no one else. Thrilled with the work, Pollitzer took them instead to photographer Stieglitz at his 291 Gallery, a showplace for avant-garde art. He included the large, sensuous organic forms O'Keeffe had called "Lines and Spaces in Charcoal" in his next group show. Despite her anger at what O'Keeffe saw as a betrayal of her trust, her relationship with Stieglitz ripened into marriage within seven years, and so, for almost thirty years, he was her chief advocate and photographer [462].

Born in Sun Prairie, Wisconsin, O'Keeffe retained all her life the spirit that burned best in vast empty space—like the six hundred acres of farmland where she grew up and the Ghost Ranch in New Mexico where she spent most of her later life. She had once remarked, after studies at the Art Students League, that "a lot of people had done this painting before I came along." She destroyed all her work at that point and quit the League.

In the 1920s, O'Keeffe began painting blown-up images of dark-tissued iris and bone-white jimson weeds. With the flower paintings for which the artist is best known— images so large they crowd the picture plane— she found the idiom she was to retain through the years. Her work over the seventy or so years of her productivity indeed shows amazing consistency. Although she varied her

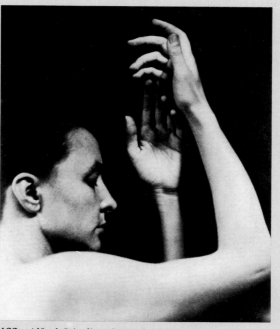

462. *Alfred Stieglitz.* Georgia O'Keefe. *1918. Photograph. Metropolitan Museum of Art, New York (gift of David A. Schulte, 1928).*

interests from nature to "ideas in her head," those first abstract "Lines and Spaces in Charcoal" can be identified even by those familiar only with her last works.

As a girl, Georgia "was already known in her family for wild notions." She retained to the end an isolation and fierce disinclination toward worldly involvement. Two years before her death, a Long Island exhibition of work of the two great matriarchs of 20th-century art, O'Keeffe and Louise Nevelson, was planned. When asked for works that might be shown, O'Keeffe is said to have responded, "You can expect absolutely no help from me." Called a new woman of the 20th century, she was known as an independent spirit to the very end.

the extreme perspective and enlarged scale of the objects tend to convert most of her work into almost abstract images, which may be terrifying in their starkness and intensity.

Closer to the mainstream of 20th-century American realist art, Edward Hopper (1882–1967), perhaps influenced by the Ash Can school, adhered to American realistic traditions, commenting on human isolation with paintings

of empty city streets and lonely houses. Hopper, who supported himself for years as a commercial artist, insisted that his aim in painting was always "the most exact transcription possible of my most intimate impression of nature." While that may have been true, his sensitive eye carefully selected and reorganized colors, forms, and light patterns in order to convey a sense of poignancy. His point of view is that of a traveler who stands in the street watching the lives of other people through the windows of all-night cafés and empty-looking, flatly lit rows of apartments. In *Early Sunday Morning* [463], without seeing a single person, we sense the silent world of individuals caught in their own cycles of life and death. Each area of the painting is reduced to the essentials, and the bare windows and empty shops are organized into a quiet, almost formal vertical and horizontal composition which implies, rather than depicts, the loneliness behind drawn shades.

Social Protest

With the Depression, Americans turned inward, frightened and disillusioned by the failure of the economy. The stock market crash of 1929 meant that people could no longer depend on limitless material progress to provide security. Businesses failed and unemployment spread. Artists stood in bread lines with factory workers. To give some artists employment the Works Projects Administration (WPA) commissioned them to paint murals in public buildings. This was the first broad governmental program of support for the arts in U.S. history.

Many artists turned to social issues for their subject matter. Before the 1930s, most artistic expressions of political and social criticism in the United States had been limited to cartoons. But the Depression inspired the first American movement that combined serious art with social protest in the tradition of Goya and Daumier. One artist involved in this movement was Ben Shahn (1898–1969), whose work powerfully expressed the tragedy of human degradation and social injustice. Experienced as a mural painter and illustrator, he depicted isolated city dwellers, victims of official inequity, and the starving wives and children of coal miners. Shahn, like other American artists, incorporated the influences of Cubism and Expressionism into his protest paintings. In *The Passion of Sacco and Vanzetti* [464] he condemned the execution of two Italian immigrants who he, and many other Americans, believed were victims of personal and political prejudice.

From a strongly personal viewpoint, Ivan Le Lorraine Albright (1897–1983) used an almost microscopic form of realism to express his response to the disintegration of the individual in a hostile world. Of *Poor Room* [465], which shows a clutter of Victorian decadence seen through a broken basement window, Albright gave as a title, *"Poor Room—There is No time, No end, No Today, No Yesterday, No Tomorrow. Only the forever and forever and forever without end."* The sense of gray-green decay and rotting flesh that pervades Albright's still lifes and figure paintings turns them into intense statements about the impermanence of material possessions and of life itself.

Isolationism was especially strong in the Midwest, where a combination of erosion, caused by years of poor farming practices, and prolonged drought created dust-bowl conditions in many areas. At first, Midwestern artists depicted the world around them with a satirical eye. As the Depression wore on, they became more nation-

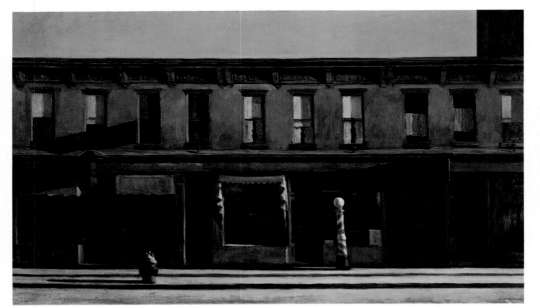

463. *Edward Hopper.* Early Sunday Morning. *1930. Oil on canvas, 2'11" × 5' (0.89 × 1.52 m). Whitney Museum of American Art, New York (purchase, with funds from Gloria Vanderbilt Whitney).*

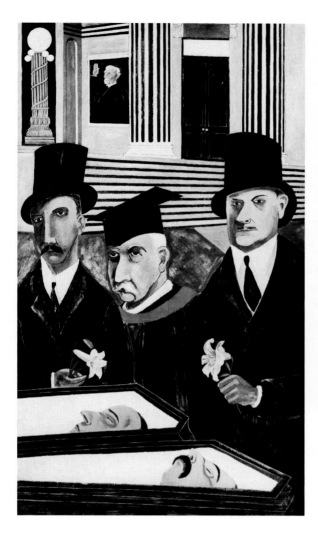

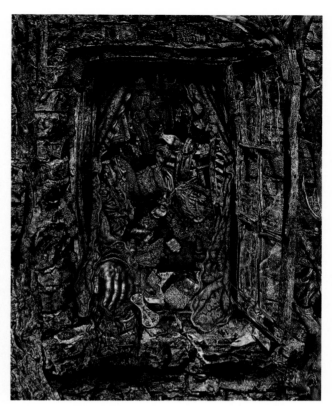

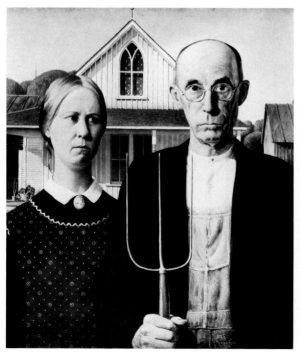

above left: **464.** *Ben Shahn.* The Passion of Sacco and Vanzetti. *1931–1932. Tempera on canvas, 7'$\frac{1}{2}$" × 4' (2.14 × 1.22 m). Whitney Museum of American Art, New York (gift of Edith and Milton Lowenthal in memory of Juliana Force).*

above: **465.** *Ivan Le Lorraine Albright.* Poor Room— There Is No Time . . . *1941–1962. Oil on canvas, 4' × 3'1" (1.22 × .94 m). Art Institute of Chicago (gift of Ivan Albright, 1977). © 1988 The Art Institute of Chicago. All rights reserved.*

below left: **466.** *Grant Wood.* American Gothic. *1930. Oil on beaver board, 29$\frac{7}{8}$ × 24$\frac{7}{8}$" (76 × 63 cm). Art Institute of Chicago (Friends of American Art Collection, 1930). © 1988 The Art Institute of Chicago. All rights reserved.*

alistic, turning their anger toward foreign influences rather than toward the absurdities of provincialism and conservatism. Many rural and small-town Americans viewed European culture with distrust, even though their own ancestors had come from the Old World. Fearful that what they had worked so long to achieve might be lost in the Depression, they clung to their possessions and their beliefs. Grant Wood (1892– 1942) in *American Gothic* [**466**] combined humor with a respect for the hardships of farm life. He depicted a farmer and his wife as solemn, suspicious provincials.

A painter who has balanced realistic recording of the world with poetic invention is Loren Mac-Iver (b. 1909). Whether her themes are urban life or ephemeral aspects of the natural world, her work reveals both formal sophistication and control and expressive delicacy and pictorial suggestion. *Venice* [467], for example, implies transparent views of sails and, perhaps influenced by Cubism, projects the exhilaration of light and movement through the varying blues of the water.

The Harlem Renaissance

The new spirit of the 20th century produced optimism for all, with a hint of new opportunity for blacks, at least for Northern blacks, that culminated in the **Harlem Renaissance,** a cultural movement that flourished in the Harlem section of New York City and included writers, jazz musicians, and entertainers, as well as painters. Not until then, the 1920s and 1930s, did black artists develop an art based on appreciation of their own heritage. Black artists of the Harlem Renaissance took pride in their roots and expressed that pride in their work. For example, Archibald Motley (1891–1981), Lois Mailou Jones (b. 1905), who painted in France and Haiti, and Hughie Lee-Smith (b. 1914) dealt with African themes. Aaron Douglas (1899–1979) combined African simplification of forms with a personal symbolic style in his murals for a Harlem branch of the New York Public Library.

His paintings were emotional stylizations, employing extreme elongation, distortions, and circles of mystical light to honor his racial heritage [468]. In 1925 Douglas collaborated with the author Alain Deroy Lock to produce *The New Negro,* an illustrated anthology of writings by black sociologists and political scientists. That book encouraged the African orientation of American blacks.

The rediscovery of African culture inspired many black American artists, who cultivated a close kinship with it. Douglas was soon followed by Charles White (1918–1979) [102] and others. These artists, sponsored by the Works Project Administration, contributed significantly to the development of American art of the 1930s. Hale Woodruff (1900–1980) evolved a highly personal style, which resulted from many influences—his studies of Cézanne in Paris, his work in Mexico with Diego Rivera, and, of course, African art. By the 1940s and 1950s, Woodruff's work had achieved a lyrical abstraction [469]. Other artists, such as Romare Bearden (1914–1988) [43] and Richard Mayhew (b. 1924), were inspired by what they knew best—their own experiences and dreams.

By 1941, Jacob Lawrence (b. 1917) had emerged as a vigorous artist who drew material from the historical background of his race as well as from everyday life. His subject matter, his flat, vividly colored shapes, and his originality established him as an exceptional painter. In his gouache painting *Going Home* [109] the

467. *Loren MacIver. Venice. 1949. Oil on canvas, 4'11" × 7'9" (1.50 × 2.36 m). Whitney Museum of American Art, New York (purchase).*

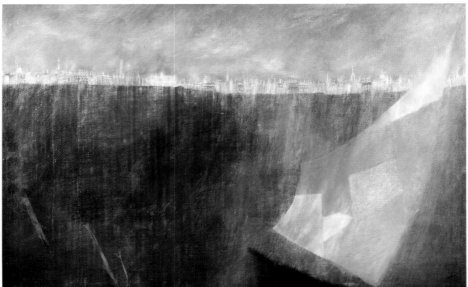

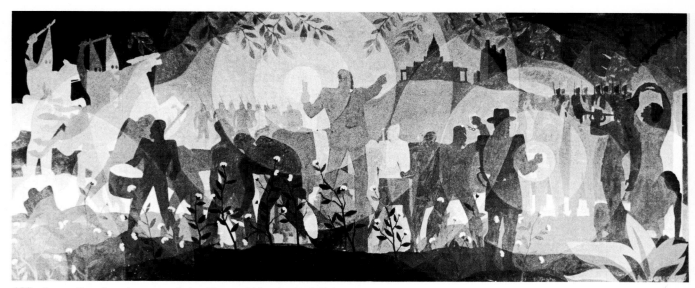

468. *Aaron Douglas.* Aspects of the Negro Life, *detail. 1934. Oil on canvas, entire work 5 × 11' (1.52 × 3.35 m). Schomberg Center for Research in Black Culture, New York Public Library (Astor, Lenox and Tilden Foundations).*

drooping shapes of the fatigued train travelers contrast with strong horizontal and vertical lines. The only active figure is the man reaching hurriedly for his suitcase as the train nears the station.

Only since the 1960s have blacks achieved fuller access to the art world. Many remain concerned with aiding their people in their struggle for justice. However, most black artists, like other minorities, are part of the mainstream of American art, exploring personal creative avenues.

Mexican Protest Art

The Spanish conquistadors brought with them to the New World the typical colonizer's attitude that the only worthwhile culture came from their homeland. Consequently, Mexican colonial art after the 16th century was generally modeled on that of Baroque Spain. The vitality of the Indian tradition, however, contributed to the rich decoration of Mexican churches. The culture of the Mexican people was influenced by pre-Columbian traditions. Such artists as José Guadalupe Posada (1852–1913) were passionate in their support of working-class Mexicans against an oppressive dictatorship, combining

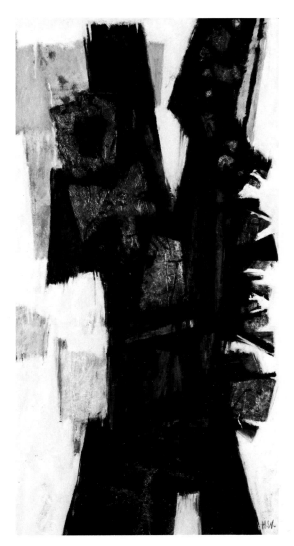

right: **469.** *Hale Woodruff.* Shrine. *1967. Oil on canvas with gold leaf, 20 × 40" (51 × 102 cm). Private collection.*

fantasy, humor, religion, and protest. Their art formed a direct link between Indian culture and the painting of the three great Mexican protest muralists, who flourished in the late 1920s and 1930s—Diego Rivera, José Clemente Orozco, and David Alfaro Siqueiros.

Diego Rivera (1886–1957) studied in France, where he encountered Cubism. Then traveling in Italy, he was deeply affected by the frescoes in the churches. In fact, he was responsible for the rebirth of the fresco technique in North America, where his frescoes show the influence of Renaissance art in their formal composition.

Rivera's murals for Mexican public buildings—the National Palace, the Secretariat of Public Education, and the University of Mexico, all in Mexico City—took art from galleries and museums to places where it could be seen by large numbers of people. Convinced that his countrymen needed to develop a pride in their past, he painted scenes that chronicled the life of the peasant and drew on Mexican legend and folk custom as well as on revolutionary social and political themes [470]. Thus he used murals to teach Mexican heritage in the same way that the medieval church used art to make the Bible a familiar part of everyday life. Although his mu-

rals were decorative and at times rigid in composition, they brought a sense of community to the Mexican people.

The works of José Clemente Orozco (1883–1949) are more powerful, brutal, and political than those of Rivera. Trained in architecture as well as painting, Orozco created huge murals in which surging masses of peasants and workers struggle against tremendous odds symbolized by steel bayonets in their unceasing striving to reach their revolutionary goals. His figures echo the violence and cruelty of ancient Aztec religious practices and the conquering Spaniards, which continued in Mexican folk tradition. There is also an element of folk fantasy, for Orozco's skeletons and the tortured forms of the oppressed relate to the candy figures traditionally sold in Mexico for the Day of the Dead.

Orozco covered the walls of government buildings in Mexico with his dramatic works. Those in Guadalajara are so exaggerated in scale, so violent and twisted in form, and so savage in their masses of figures that they seem to burst from the walls. His murals at Dartmouth College in Hanover, New Hampshire, create a panorama of the history of Mexico in brilliant colors and striking symbols. The overpowering

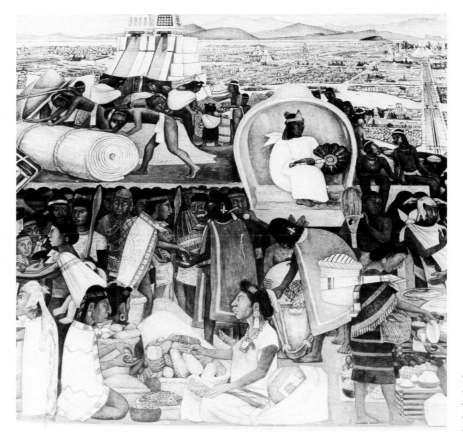

470. *Diego Rivera. 1950. Fresco. One of a series of murals, National Palace, Mexico City.*

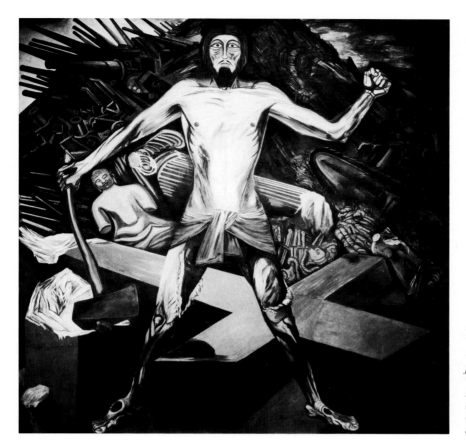

471. *José Clemente Orozco. The Modern Migration of the Spirit, panel 21 from* The Epic of American Civilization. *1932–1934. Fresco, 10'5" × 10' (3.18 × 3.05 m). Courtesy of the Trustees of Dartmouth College.*

figures tell stories of the feathered-serpent god, Quetzalcoatl, and of the coming of the Spaniards. The murals also protest the destructive forces of war and the machine age. Their climax is reached in an overwhelming figure of a militant, flayed Christ, who destroys his cross, calling on oppressed peoples everywhere to arise [471].

David Alfaro Siqueiros (1898–1974), like Courbet a half-century earlier in France, was as involved in political activities as he was in painting and was later imprisoned for his Communist beliefs. He led the organization of the Syndicate of Technical Workers, Painters, and Sculptors, which contributed much to the development of art in Mexico. Siqueiros' murals, more visionary than those of Rivera and Orozco, use Surrealist images to protest social injustices. Compare his *Echo of a Scream* [472] with Picasso's *Guernica* [35] and Munch's *The Scream* [128] to see how the three artists employed strident images in different ways to express inhumanity and horror. Si-

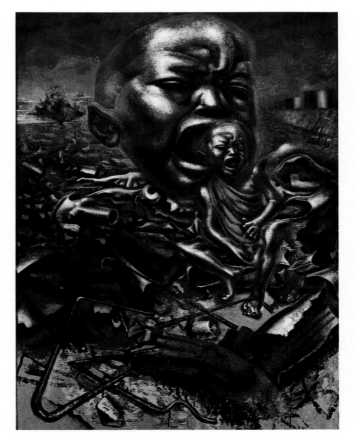

right: 472. *David Alfaro Siqueiros.* Echo of a Scream. *1937. Duco on wood, 48 × 36" (121.9 × 91.4 cm). Collection, Museum of Modern Art, New York (gift of Edward M. M. Warburg).*

queiros, like Jackson Pollock [10], also experimented with materials, using industrial enamels for his outdoor murals, which he hoped would expose his ideas to the largest possible number of people.

Artists in the United States became more interested in fresco painting in the 1930s through exposure to the works of Rivera and Orozco. Supported by the Works Projects Administration, many, such as the Dutch-born Willem de Kooning, traveled around the United States, painting murals in post offices and other government buildings. Most of the paintings were conservative, and few approach the impact of their Mexican counterparts as expressions of social protest.

Abstract Expressionism; New York School

During the Depression and World War II, New York became a center for the kind of discussion and stimulating exchange that had formerly made Paris so attractive to creative people. Artists came to New York from all over the country, from Mexico (Orozco and Rivera) and from Europe (Mondrian, Chagall, Ernst, Dalí, and Léger). Whether they settled in New York or only visited, some are loosely classified as the **New York school** because they shared a common center of artistic concern. Their work showed no uniform style. They issued no manifestos. A few of these artists were realists, such as Hopper [463], but most explored highly personalized nonobjective painting. Many developed a free-flowing style that was described by critics as **Abstract Expressionism.**

Abstract Expressionist paintings are generally nonobjective, without obvious reference to reality. Many have a raw, tough strength that is remote from the grace and finesse of the early nonobjective formalist paintings of Kandinsky [422], Malevich [423], and Mondrian [46]. Abstract Expressionist works may be grouped in two broad divisions. In **Action painting,** the physical traces of the artist's actual gestures are explicit and emphatic. In the other, known as **Color-Field painting,** the emphasis is on large planes of color. Action painting dominated the 1950s. The formalist painting of color areas developed more gradually until it emerged as one of the significant movements in the 1960s, as we will see in Chapter 17.

When we look at Action paintings, our own muscles respond with awareness of the movements of the artist's body. The canvases are very large because traditional easel-size paintings seemed too small to contain the artist's energies. The artist had to reach beyond restrictive borders to enormous areas in which to work out his or her drives. To feel this physically expressed energy we must see the paintings themselves, for their huge scale intensifies the impact, forcing us to become involved in the work.

European influences on Abstract Expressionism were the powerful transitions of color developed by such 19th-century painters as Turner [108] and Monet [403] and the various forms of Expressionism of the early 20th century, such as that of Emil Nolde [428]. Abstract Expressionism drew also on Oriental sources, notably calligraphy and Zen Buddhism. According to Zen belief, when the mind and body are in accord, or centered, the hand becomes free to serve a deeper purpose, allowing inner vitality to be released. This attitude, which inspired much of Chinese and Japanese painting for centuries [121], proved congenial to many Abstract Expressionists.

From these currents, Abstract Expressionism evolved in the late 1940s. It had a vitality that was typical of much American painting of the 20th century no matter what its style. It seems that American artists tackled art frontiers with the same fresh excitement with which their ancestors had tackled the physical frontiers of the New World.

We may consider Arshile Gorky (1904–1948), who painted abstract expressive works that recalled his childhood in Armenia, as an early Abstract Expressionist. He evolved his paintings in the automatic manner of the Surrealists, who used doodles to suggest images, drawing and painting according to impulse. In their random brush marks the Surrealists would see suggestions of a figure, which they would then encourage to emerge into a more definite image. Gorky's organic forms and erotic fantasies were influenced by the works of Kandinsky [422], Miró [92], and Picasso [35]. He brought to his painting a love of texture and especially of richness of paint. Compare, for example, Gorky's lively, free brushstrokes [473] with the tight, smooth surface of American Realistic painting exemplified by Grant Wood [466].

The free-flowing style of Gorky and other abstract organic painters was also characteristic of Hans Hofmann (1880–1966), a German-born artist whose art classes in New York became a center of Expressionism and abstraction. The apparent spontaneity of his brushstrokes was based on an unusual combination of painterli-

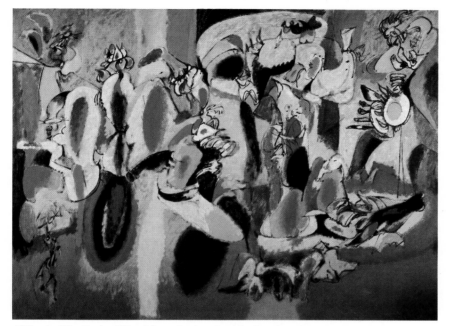

473. *Arshile Gorky.* The Liver Is the Cock's Comb. *1944.*
Oil on canvas, 6'1¼" × 8'2" (1.86 × 2.49 m).
Albright-Knox Art Gallery, Buffalo (gift of Seymour H. Knox, 1956).

ness and abstraction. In *The Golden Wall* **[474]**, rectangles of rich color are contrasted with areas of thick, loosely brushed paint. Hofmann's glowing color expresses his joyful attitude toward life. He considered the actual process of looking at a painting to be an important part of the act of

art. He felt that if this process is successful, the painting and the viewer will establish a relationship based on spontaneous feeling.

Two painters became the focal point for the new style—Willem de Kooning (b. 1904) and Jackson Pollock (1912–1956) **[10]**. In direct

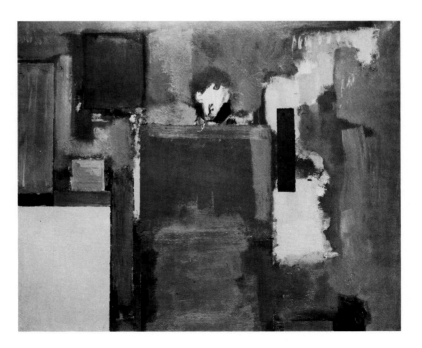

474. *Hans Hofmann.*
The Golden Wall. *1961.*
Oil on canvas, 5' × 6'½"
(1.51 × 1.82 m).
Art Institute of Chicago
(Mr. and Mrs. Frank G. Logan
Purchase Prize Fund, 1962).
© 1988 The Art Institute
of Chicago. All rights reserved.

opposition to the carefully composed geometric painting of Josef Albers (1888–1976) [475] and Mondrian [46], they brought to their work an immediacy of emotion that made the process of painting an important part of the artwork itself. For several years De Kooning painted in a broadly Abstract Expressionist style, angrily slashing wide, violent strokes onto his canvas. Later, in the 1950s, he became almost obsessed with the image of a female [476]. These paintings seem conceived in horror and depict a sense of desperate rage that was physically expressed in the brushstrokes. This use of the larger muscles of the body, typical of Abstract Expressionism, brought great energy to painting.

Pollock said, "I believe the easel picture to be a dying form and the tendency of modern feeling is toward the wall picture or mural." Because he felt the public was not ready for murals, he painted on large canvases, which he considered to be a transitional step toward wall painting. Pollock's drips, splashes, and spills appear to have been painted in an intense and undisciplined fury of action. His paintings, however, actually are carefully textured and organized. Each of his active strokes appears balanced by an opposing one. His color combinations are subtle, and the structure of each painting develops through the rhythm of his movements. Pollock, who often used industrial enamels and metallic paints, spread his canvases on the floor and dripped his paints from buckets, using sticks and large brushes. The concentration of paint on the canvas from the path of his hand forces us to note the importance of the artist's association with his materials.

Pollock's passages of color lead our eyes into the painting to wander through the canvas, finding refreshment by following the myriad paths of the paint as they build up a weblike surface. Through the involvement of our eye movements, his paintings become environments that surround us. Perhaps subconsciously expressing the fears and hopes of the mid-century, Pollock extended his painting to limitless horizons, bringing together the near and the far, the important and the trivial, to merge into a broad cosmos. Through his work we sense the tensions of all people trapped by the 20th century, as well as Pollock's own expressive personal frustrations as an artist living in a world he viewed as hostile.

Lee Krasner (b. 1908), who studied and worked with Hofmann and married Pollock, assimilated Surrealism, Fauvism, Cubism, Oriental Zen, and Action painting. Her images suggest movement, flux, and growth, reflecting energies essential to life. The rhythmic flow of her paint and the density and transparency of her surfaces identify her as an Action painter, but it is the monumental concept of even her small-scale work that marks her contribution as significant [477].

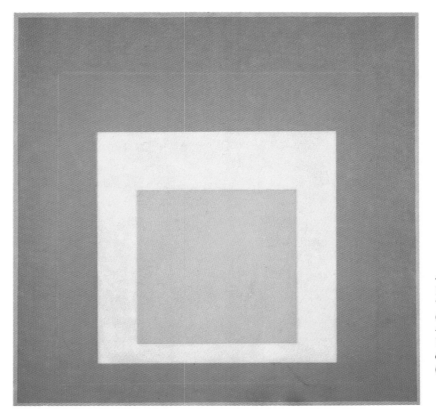

475. *Josef Albers.* Homage to the Square: "Ascending." *1953. Oil on composition board, 43½" (110 cm) square. Whitney Museum of American Art, New York (purchase).*

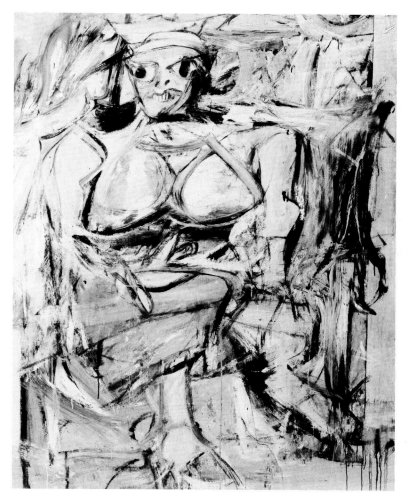

476. *Willem de Kooning.* Woman, I. *1950–1952. Oil on canvas, 6'3⅞" × 4'10" (1.93 × 1.47 m). Collection, Museum of Modern Art, New York (purchase).*

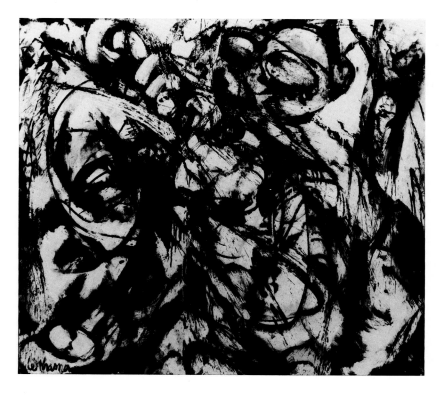

477. *Lee Krasner.* The Guardian. *1960. Oil on canvas, 4'5" × 4'10" (1.35 × 1.47 m). Whitney Museum of American Art (gift of Uris Brothers Foundation, Inc.).*

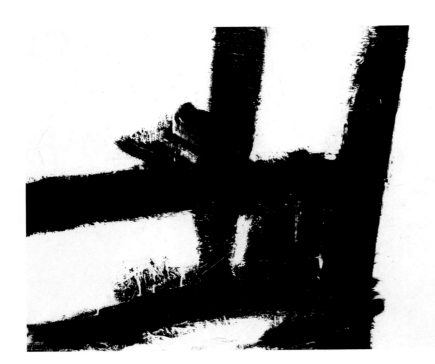

478. *Franz Kline.*
Two Horizontals.
1954. Oil on canvas,
31⅛ × 39¼″ (79 × 100 cm).
Collection Museum of
Modern Art, New York
(Sidney and Harriet
Janis Collection, gift).

The Oriental calligraphic element is particularly strong in the work of Franz Kline (1910–1962). Kline painted enormous black shapes, somewhat like enlarged Chinese characters. His large strokes of black drawn across the white surface of the canvas create tensions to which we respond physically—a pull we can feel [478]. Kline was concerned with tensions and balances of positive and negative space.

The youngest of the original Abstract Expressionists, Robert Motherwell (b. 1915), wrote in *The New Decade:* "I happen to think primarily in paint. . . . If a painting does not make a human contact, it is nothing." The act of applying paint to canvas itself was what dominated the Action painters. They did not represent their emotions but enacted them in their works.

Photographic Arts

The same spirit of freedom that inspired painters to break away from academic and realistic representation led artists and others to experiment with still photography and film in both Europe and America. Film became a big business in America as well as a major art form, often fulfilling the role of fantasy.

Still Photography

Classical American photographers such as Edward Weston and Ansel Adams explored form and light in their still lifes and landscapes (see Chapter 5). The artist Alvin Langdon Coburn (1882–1966) experimented with mirror-multiplied photographic images he called Vortographs. Skilled also in rotogravure (see Chapter 6), he made the plates used to print four of his books. László Moholy-Nagy, who founded the New Bauhaus in Chicago after the closing of its namesake in 1933 in Berlin, was convinced that photography is an indispensable tool of this century. He created photographic shadow prints and micrographs of rare scientific beauty and educational value [145].

During the 1930s photographic technology improved greatly. New lighting methods, more sophisticated lenses, and smaller cameras made for greater flexibility. *Life* magazine, which featured the new art of photojournalism, first appeared in 1936 and soon became so popular, it was rapidly followed by imitations. The Farm Security Administration of the federal government used skilled photographers to record the life of rural America during the Depression years. These sensitive and perceptive photographers produced prints that are unquestionably fine art. Dorothea Lange, in particular, commented on the tragic plight of the farmers who were driven from their homes in Oklahoma by dust storms. Her photographs of women and children from this period are classics. Realistic and objective, she never used unusual angles or lighting to increase the expressiveness of her work. *Migrant Mother* [144] is much more than a mere recording; the faces and poses speak eloquently of hopelessness and despair.

Film

In the early 20th century, avant-garde painters and writers alike were fascinated by the potentials of film-making. In Paris, Marcel Duchamp made a natural progression from the painting of a technological *Nude Descending a Staircase (No. 2)* [91] to using ready-made objects (such as the wheel) that moved [433] to his moving picture *Anaemic Cinema* (1926). Fernand Léger developed his interest in machines into moving images in his film *Ballet méchanique* (1924), and Salvador Dalí expressed his theatrical and Surrealist viewpoint in films. French film-makers created art films in an Impressionist style that brought cinema into the stream of modern art. René Clair's (1898–1981) stylized, fanciful films commented on the absurdities of our machine-dominated lives. During the 1920s film-makers in Sweden and Germany introduced innovations in visual design that made possible new intensity of emotion, unity of mood, and fuller expression of character. The Soviets refined a new system of editing by montage [157], which allowed unprecedented evolution of ideas.

Despite these achievements in Europe, the "movies" are more closely identified with the United States than with any other country. While Europe was involved with World War I and America was still neutral, Americans gained several years' lead in film-making. In contrast to European "art films" for elite audiences, Hollywood produced films for the mass market, ranging from the epic pageants of D. W. Griffith (1875–1948), culminating in *Birth of a Nation* (1915), to the disciplined lunacy of comedies by Mack Sennett (1884–1960) and British-born Charlie Chaplin (1889–1977) [479], to the classic romances starring Greta Garbo, Gloria Swanson, and others. The classic Western film such as *Stagecoach* introduced by John Ford in 1939 presents a historic image of America by which much of the world still identifies this nation. The ability to appeal to a wide variety of tastes, plus American business skills of mass production and distribution, established the American motion picture as a great commercial success and an influential art form. *Birth of a Nation* grossed an estimated $50 million, making it the top money-maker until recent years.

The major breakthrough in cinema was signaled on October 6, 1927, when Warner Brothers presented *The Jazz Singer* with Al Jolson, the first feature film with synchronized music, speech, and other sounds. Their Vitaphone system used disc recordings, which were mechanically synchronized with the projector. At the end of the 1920s there was no doubt that synchronized sound films would be the film form of the future.

In commercial cinema, the need for mass escapism during the Depression led to slick, sophisticated comedies and elaborately staged singing and dancing shows. Charlie Chaplin, however, continued to produce satirical comedies. He commented on the world of machinery [479] or on the rising European dictatorships in such films as *Modern Times* (1936) and *The Great*

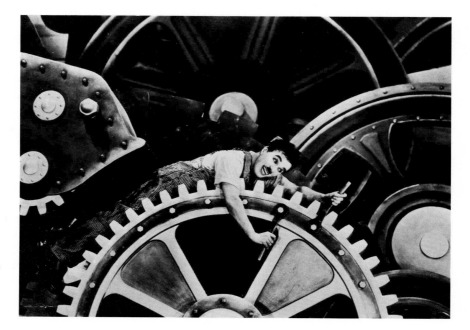

479. *Film still from Charlie Chaplin's* Modern Times. *1936. Museum of Modern Art, New York (Film Stills Archive).*

Rebirth of Film Classics

Greater performances in silent films than Lillian Gish's in D. W. Griffith's 1920 film *Way Down East* may not exist, nor finer early color films than Rouben Mamoulian's three-strip Technicolor *Becky Sharp* (1935); yet few film historians or film critics—not to speak of us, the general public—have ever had an opportunity to view these works. And they are just two of the extensive list of fading classics.

Critics and scholars have had to rely on inferior two-color prints that have drastically altered original color schemes; in the case of black-and-white films, many prints have missing or damaged frames. For example, Becky's costume that Mamoulian described as "demure pink" now appears as brilliant yellow. The restoration of disintegrating films is a painstaking process. The problems are at least two-fold. Not only are the surviving prints exceedingly fragile, perhaps from imperfect processing originally or the very nature of the film itself, but early directors' editing cuts often permitted various film versions to be circulated.

The recent restoration of Griffith's film by the Museum of Modern Art (MOMA) in New York has raised questions certain to disturb film historians for decades. Since many established film classics are available in a variety of versions, which is to be considered authentic? The shortest, the longest, or the earliest? In the case of *Way Down East,* only a year after the film was released, it had already lost footage. In the early 1930s, when a sound track was added, *Way Down East* was down approximately three reels, or 30 minutes.

When MOMA began its efforts with two silent 35 mm nitrite prints with the original tinting from the mid-1920s, the tangled web of Griffith's versions came to light. Neither print conformed to the example of the negative (with sound) already in the Museum's archives. From a complete list of shots and intertitles deposited by Griffith with the Library of Congress at the time of copyrighting the film, and by comparison with the musical score, an exact correspondence of film version and script was finally found. Perhaps the most tantalizing sequences, however, remain those carefully described in the shot list that even MOMA cannot locate!

After more than four years of technical work, including approximately $70,000 spent on chemical preservation and hand restoration, MOMA has presented a version of *Way Down East* as close as possible to that of its premiere in 1920. In the case of *Becky Sharp,* extraordinary and costly technological processes of color filtration and photocopying have produced a landmark film restored to its historic colors and clarity of detail. And the restorations of other film classics continue [480].

480. *Robert Gitt and Richard Dayton. "Restoring Becky Sharp." Before and after restoration.*

Dictator (1940). These films describe the loneliness and isolation of those who refuse to conform to the dictates of the world around them—whether it be a factory or an oppressive political regime.

Chaplin's creativity was echoed in the remarkable American phenomenon of the animated cartoon. The need for food for the spirit and escape in fantasy from daily reality perhaps explains the desire of millions to return to an adolescent state through the art of Walt Disney (1901–1966) and other animators. Mickey Mouse, imaginary subject of many short Disney cartoons, became for many people a symbol of America. The importance of music to Disney led him to create *Fantasia* (1940), a feature-length film composed of seven episodes of animated ballet set to classical music. In visual style *Fantasia* ranges from total abstraction as a background for music by J. S. Bach to romantic cartoons for most of the film. Mickey Mouse himself appears as the hapless servant in the *Sorcerer's Apprentice* by Paul Dukas.

Disney's art was determined, perhaps most significantly, by his creative organization of skilled technicians, whom some consider pioneering artists. In their hands, color is used expressively rather than illusionistically. It is bright and flat. All the best Disney films use line rather than modeling to present an image. One can recognize in them the influence of Picasso, Matisse, and even Modigliani. The Disney films ef-

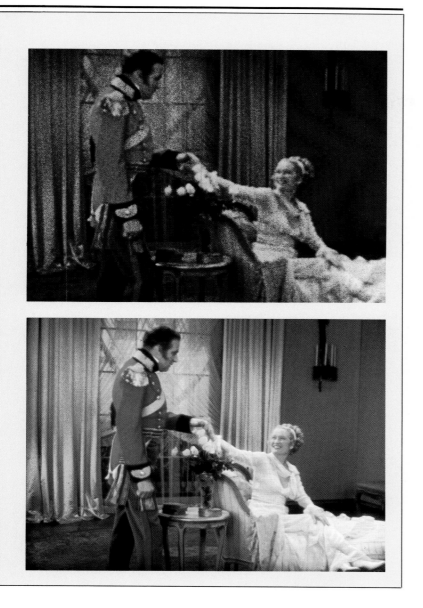

fectively convince us that art can also be entertainment and story-telling can be art.

Film seems to have given us a universal language. While cartoons can amuse people, documentaries can influence public opinion. Such films as *Nanook of the North* (1922) made audiences feel close to people struggling for existence in two difficult natural environments.

Techniques developed in these films were used in army films during World War II and have continued to influence documentaries.

The American contribution to film—in comedy, fantasy, drama, or documentary—is obvious. We will consider recent developments in cinema and the effect of television in Chapters 17 and 18.

Exercises and Activities

Research Activities

1. Abstract Expressionism was an important force in art in the 1950s. Compare and contrast the work of Jackson Pollock and Willem de Kooning. Analyze how their works are similar and how they differ.

2. The traditional fresco technique was revived by Mexican painters to serve a particular purpose. Why was the technique particularly appropriate to their work? How did they use it? How did their art influence painting in the United States?
3. Describe your reaction to a work of Orozco and to Picasso's *Guernica*.
4. How did a changing approach to the human body affect sculpture of the 20th century? Give examples.
5. Read a novel of protest that describes the social conditions existing between World War I and World War II. Discuss the art of the period in relation to the book. Does the art mirror in visual form the conditions described in the book? If so, how?

Studio Activities

1. Create in oils, acrylics, or enamels a painting in the style of Jackson Pollock. To get the full impact of the muscular involvement in his work, you will need a large area of paper or canvas.
2. Using images from magazines involving blacks, create a photo montage that concerns a theme of black interests. You may use Romare Bearden's work [43] as a reference.
3. Create a photographic essay that expresses the Depression era into which Franklin D. Roosevelt introduced his New Deal programs, using magazine cut-outs or snapshots of your own.
4. Express the changing approach to the human body in sculpture of the 20th century, using clay or any other medium of your choice.
5. Create an artwork of your own that responds to technology in the 1930s.

17
The Mid-Century World: 1945–1970

The future of art no longer seems to lie with the creation of enduring masterpieces, but with defining alternative cultural strategies.

John McHale, art critic

The dilatory pace of the ruminative critic is less and less consonant with contemporary life. Swift social change coupled with unconscious technological habits of mind . . . offer the critic countless obstacles to the measured development of his thoughts, and this situation he shares with the contemporary artist.

Dore Ashton, *A Reading of Modern Art*

Modern art has traditionally obscured the distinctions between the beautiful and the ugly, but rarely so systematically as now; it now has blurred the categories of good and bad, the indifferent and the committed.

Max Kozloff, *Renderings: Critical Essays on a Century of Modern Art*

World War II marked the end of European art leadership. The flow of art directed for hundreds of years by European tastes was now firmly centered in America. The shift in power surprised very few. The United States dominated so many aspects of living overseas—from American hamburgers, Coca-Cola, and blue jeans to the heavy industries we had set up all over the world. Other factors contributed to centering the art world in America. Several major artists had spent the war years here—Mondrian, Chagall, Ernst, Dalí, and Léger—joining Duchamp, De Kooning, and other artists, writers, and critics already on the East Coast.

It seems that few areas could compete with the stimulation of New York. Poetry, aesthetics, and the philosophies of Zen, Jung, Sartre, and Kirkegaard provoked heated discussions among artists, while exhibitions at the Museum of Modern Art and the Solomon R. Guggenheim Museum provided on-the-spot stimulation. The pioneering New York school of **Abstract Ex-** **pressionism** had established a strong medium for individualism and, in so doing, was rejecting most traditional art conventions that might inhibit "modern art." Many postwar artists became engrossed in highly personalized interpretations, such as De Kooning's involvement with the female figure **[476]**. Antibiotics, computerization, electronic transistors, and the prospect of an age of nuclear power all portended a fresh world.

Against this background of ferment, it is still possible to view 1945 through 1970 within much of the framework we have seen before—formalism, modified realism, Expressionism, and fantasy.

Formalism

As we saw in Chapter 16, America took the lead in avant-garde art all over the world at mid-century. While the more emotional side of Abstract Expressionism, called Action painting,

THE VISUAL ARTS		HISTORICAL NOTES
	1945	
1948 Pollock, *Number 1* **[10]**		
1949 Picasso, *Centaur,* light drawing **[95]**		**1949** George Orwell, *1984*
1950 Newman, *Vir Heroicus Sublimis* **[73]**	1950	**1950** Korean War begins
1952 Le Corbusier, Unité d'Habitation **[505]**		
	1955	
1956 Hamilton, *Just What Is It . . .* **[497]**		
1957 Gottlieb, *Blast II* **[482]**		**1957** USSR launches Sputnik I
1957–59 Wright, Guggenheim Museum **[276]**		**1957** Boris Pasternak, *Dr. Zhivago*
		1959 USA: first transistorized computer
1960 Tinguely, *Homage to New York* **[492]**	1960	
1961 Bontecou, *Untitled* **[117]**		**1961** USSR: first man in space
1962 Warhol, *Marilyn, Diptych* **[28]**		
		1963 Betty Friedan, *The Feminine Mystique*
		1963 President John F. Kennedy assassinated
1964 Bearden, *Prevalence of Ritual* **[43]**		
	1965	**1965** USA in Vietnam
		1965 Selma, Alabama, Civil Rights demonstrations
1966 Kienholz, *State Hospital* **[36]**		
1966 Oldenburg, *Giant Soft Fan* **[217]**		
1968 Indiana, *Love* **[499]**		**1968** Martin Luther King, Jr., assassinated
		1969 USA: first man on moon
1970 Smithson, *Spiral Jetty* **[11]**	1970	**1970** Kent State campus killings
		1970 Germaine Greer, *The Female Eunuch*

had dominated the art world in the 1960s, many artists turned to cooler, more intellectual, non-objective art whose formal aesthetic depended mainly on color, shape, and texture.

Color-Field Painting

Some Abstract Expressionist painters in the 1950s had been more interested in planes of color than in gestural brushstrokes. Their interest developed into a form of **Postpainterly Abstraction** called **Field painting,** or **Color-Field painting,** a dominant style of the 1960s. Color-Field painting avoids subject matter in order to concentrate on color relationships (see Chapter 2 on color). A painted canvas may consist of large, nonobjective areas of color on a flat-colored or white ground, with one brushstroke as large as a conventional easel painting or even as large as the viewer. Although a large area of color may have smaller shapes floating on it, they do not completely break up the major area.

Color-Field painters usually created oversized works so large that they are not meant to be seen all at once. Widths of 10, 12, or even 40 feet (3.04, 3.65, or 12.19 meters) are not unusual. Such paintings are designed to overwhelm us.

To appreciate them as the artist intended, the viewer must stand close enough to the canvas to be surrounded by the field of paint and visually led into it.

Many Color-Field painters used acrylic paints (see Chapter 3), which came into general use in the 1950s. Although they have not replaced oils, they are applied in new ways, giving painters an opportunity to create new effects. Acrylics can be used to fill in flat areas by creating a smooth surface that is glossy or matte according to the vehicle used. Since acrylics flow easily onto the canvas and dry quickly, they are more suitable than oils for painting sharp edges on forms next to each other. Also, acrylics can be thinned to give a transparent, watery look; and if used on absorbent, unsized canvas, they will sink into the fabric and produce soft edges.

A Color-Field painter who used acrylics in this way is Morris Louis (1912–1962) **[114]**. His pigments interact with the canvas, becoming part of it, rather than remaining on the surface. This technique gives depth to the color, reducing the reflective quality of the painting and producing a very different effect from that of oils. Like Louis, Helen Frankenthaler (b. 1928) **[75]** often allows her colors to soak into the canvas. Like Pollock, she lays her huge canvases on the floor,

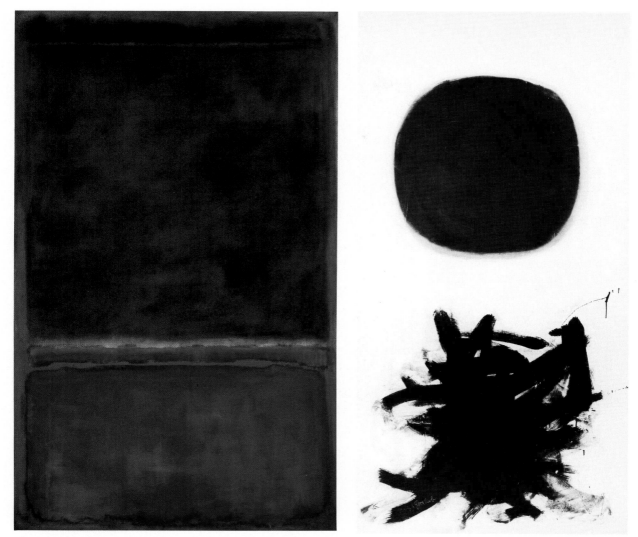

above: **481.** *Mark Rothko.* Green and Maroon. *1953. Oil on canvas, 7'6¾" × 4'6½" (2.31 × 1.38 m). The Phillips Collection, Washington.*

above right: **482.** *Adolph Gottlieb.* Blast II. *1957. Oil on canvas, 7'5" × 3'9" (2.26 × 1.14 m). Collection Joseph Seagram and Sons, Inc., New York.*

pouring and pushing her paints into the fabric until the color arrangements satisfy her.

Works such as *Green and Maroon* by Mark Rothko (1903–1970) have great impact based on color sensation and large size **[481]**. Rothko placed vaporous, rectangular patches in front of one another, and his color, unrestrained by drawn lines or hard edges, spreads from one shape to the next. Often the color areas are extremely close to each other in value. Sometimes Rothko soaked and stained the canvas with transparent paint, and sometimes he brushed on opaque pigment. Color provides both the form and the content; it is the sole carrier of his ideas, capable of endless variations.

In a series of large paintings, Adolph Gottlieb (1903–1974) produced images that remind us of explosions **[482]**. In *Blast II* the two main forms are separate, placed one above the other. The brilliant color and the rounded form of the upper shape may represent the sun or a nuclear explosion, while the somber colors below remind us of the earth. No matter what these forms may suggest to us, however, their opposition creates a visual tension in the viewer.

While tension and fury often appear in the work of Willem de Kooning **[476]**, he thinks of himself as a colorist steeped in Renaissance traditions. By 1960, he had developed his own personal aspect of Abstract Expressionism, characteristically with a delicate pastel palette of flowing color shapes [483].

Hard-Edge Painting

Other artists who came to maturity in the 1950s turned away from Action painting in favor of a form of Postpainterly Abstraction known as **Hard-Edge painting.** Their works are comprised of flat areas of color, confined within precisely delineated boundaries. In formal investigations of color and design, many approached painting methodically, using masking tape, triangles, and rulers to make straight edges. Within this climate of technical precision, the contribution of Josef Albers is prominent.

After leaving the Bauhaus, Albers continued his preoccupation with color in the United States. For more than fifteen years he worked on a series of one hundred paintings called *Homage*

to the Square [475]. Of approximately the same outer dimensions, each consists of squares that vary in size, color, and relationship to each other. Albers experimented with innumerable combinations of warm and cool, muted and intense color. The simplicity of the square shapes intensifies the visual relationships of the colors, exploiting their optical effects fully. Albers recognized that in visual perception a color is rarely seen alone but usually in relation to the colors around it. As a simple demonstration of this, look at the corner of a plainly painted room. The slight variation in the intensity of the light that hits the two walls will show some difference in the color of the two surfaces. One wall may appear nearer, while the other looks distant. If a warm light hits one wall and the other is in cool shadow, the tension between them will be further increased.

The variety in Albers' series of squares depends not only on the combinations of colors

---

Focus on the Artist

Willem de Kooning (b. 1904)

Born in Rotterdam, De Kooning experienced the early divorce of his parents and by the age of twelve was already working at a commercial art company. His evening studies were unique in Holland because they provided him an art education that blended fine and functional arts (the guild system) with intellectual philosophies (the academy). De Kooning recalls that guild and academy ideas were often fused into a single project. There was no stress on originality, which was present in the artist—or not. As part of the curriculum, the brilliant "De Stijl" group under Mondrian and Van Doesburg introduced concepts of the modern artist as a revolutionary social engineer, a viewpoint De Kooning has continued to maintain.

At twenty-one, De Kooning was in the United States, where he had finally arrived after several illegal and unsuccessful attempts to slip in through Holland-America Line ships. By 1935, he was able to commit all his energies to painting and had spent a valuable year on the Federal Arts project. De Kooning and Arshile Gorky had become friends and with other New York artists created a social milieu that in part led to the great flowering of post-war American art with the **New York school.** Few were financially successful during these years, but collegiality and mutual respect promoted serious creative growth.

About the time of his marriage to Elaine Fried, an art student [50], by coincidence he launched his series called *Women,* a theme continued from then on.

In the late 1930s and the 1940s, both De Kooning and Gorky became underground leaders in the art world, counter to the mainstream of realistic art. Like many of their friends, they reacted strongly against the aesthetics of the then dominant school of Paris. Particularly abhorrent to them was the "finish" so critical to academic practice. Their pictures instead revealed the obstacles they encountered, along with their solutions— functional parts of the image inextricably fused with the content itself. The process introduced contradictions and ambiguities that often led to unfinished work, like his house in The Springs on eastern Long Island, a major undertaking he states he is likely always to be building.

With the same devotion to ambiguity, he has concurrently maintained identification with abstraction that pushes and pulls, held to the surface by bright colors, so close in value that, in the artist Fairfield Porter's words, they "make your eyes rock." In his figural abstractions there are neither foregrounds nor backgrounds. Surfaces are continuous.

De Kooning's work cannot be divided into neat periods. He has always remained open to any possibilities and therefore to apparent inconsistencies.

483. *Willem de Kooning.* Rosy-Fingered Dawn at Louse Point. *1963. Oil on canvas, 80⅛ × 70⅜″ (203.6 × 178.8 cm). Stedelijk Museum, Amsterdam.*

but also on how the colors change in relationship to each other, the amount of each color used, and the number of squares. Albers also made use of the physical phenomenon of after-images to cause vibrations in our eyes. For him, color experiments enriched the visual experience, and since he believed that the eye is an important part of the mind, he also believed that his paintings had intellectual as well as visual content.

Two other Hard-Edge painters who were color purists were Alice Trumbull Mason (1904–1971), descendant of the American historical painter John Trumbull, and Ad Reinhardt (1913–1967), who claimed to be following her lead. Mason was a charter member of the American Abstractionists and first exhibited with the group in 1937. Both worked mainly in a geometric style after the 1930s. Mason's canvases have a haunting, poetic lyricism, which she sometimes produced with a limited range of colors **[484]**. She studied with Gorky and the graphic artist Stanley Hayter at his Atelier 17 and produced a large body of significant works that are even more highly regarded today than in her lifetime.

484. *Alice Trumbull Mason.* Shafts of Spring. *1955. Oil on gesso board, 27 × 29″ (69 × 74 cm). Collection the author.*

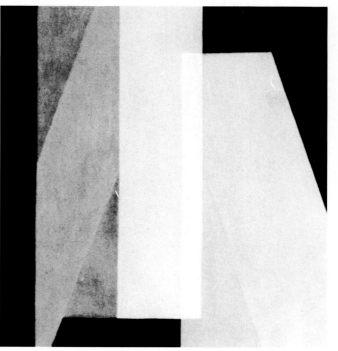

485. *Ad Reinhardt.* Abstract Painting, Blue. *1952. Oil and acrylic on canvas, 6'3" × 2'4" (1.91 × 0.71 m). Carnegie Museum of Art, Pittsburgh (museum purchase, gift of the Women's Committee of the Museum of Art, 1965).*

Like Mason, Reinhardt gradually reduced his paintings to areas of muted tones, close in intensity and value. In the late 1960s he worked only in dark monochromes, creating areas of paint on canvases as large as 5 by 5 feet (1.5 by 1.5 meters). His goal was the refinement of painting to a single, all-consuming experience. A small reproduction cannot convey the aesthetic response that a large painting elicits [485]. Experiencing such a work, we feel drawn into its depth and may have a physical sensation of floating in a lightless, soundless void. As in many Color-Field paintings, Reinhardt's canvas surfaces cease to exist, leaving a mysterious infinity of visual and spatial effects created by color. Paintings such as these are closely related to the **Minimal,** or Primary, painting of Ellsworth Kelly (b. 1923).

Other Color-Field painters, such as Kenneth Noland (b. 1924) and Frank Stella (b. 1936), also depend on large scale and color to offer a visual experience of total immersion. The concept of expanding and contracting intervals of color arranged in hard- or soft-edge stripes is dominant in their work. As in his graphics, Stella painted complex patterns of stripes separated by light lines [486]. He also used unconventional shapes for his paintings [118], fitting the pattern of the stripes into the shape of the canvas or contrasting them to set up an opposing tension. Avoiding the individualization of Action painting, the clean-cut outlines and flat surfaces of these large, bright Minimalist paintings often suggest the anonymity of mass-produced industrial products. Other Hard-Edge paintings are created by repeating hundreds of small shapes, as in the Optical Art we will examine next.

Optical Art

Art has used optical illusions since the Old Stone Age. Without illusion, we would not accept foreshortening and we could not use linear perspective to create a three-dimensional representation of a two-dimensional surface. The **Optical** artists of the 1960s and 1970s made such illusions the basis of their work (often called Op art). The Israeli-born artist Agam (Yaacov Gipstein, b. 1928) devised works that appear to change as we view them. Possibly inspired by moving billboards, which change their images by means of mechanically turning louvers, Agam incorporates similar, though fixed, projecting louvers in some of his paintings [487]. Looking at an Agam creation from one side of a room, we see what appears to be a flat painting with simple, nonobjective shapes. But if we ob-

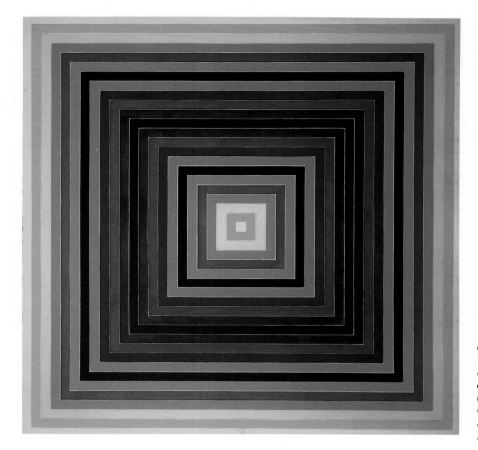

left: **486.** Frank Stella. Bijoux indiscrets. *1974. Synthetic polymer paint on canvas, 11'3" × 11'3" (3.43 × 3.43 m). Collection Rita and Toby Schreiber. Courtesy M. Knoedler & Co.*

serve the same painting from another point in the room, it looks like a different work.

Bridget Riley (b. 1931) also depends on optical illusions for the impact of her black-and-white paintings **[56]**. These illusions suggest movement where none exists and produce an intense, sometimes uncomfortable sensation as we view the works.

The tensions produced by Stella's *Bijoux indiscrets* **[486]** draw the nest of squares toward optical experiences. In this painting, titled perhaps after an indiscreet 18th-century novelette by Denis Diderot with the same title, Stella presents twenty-three concentric squares and the compositional effect of a regularly stepped pyramid seen from above. By setting hot colors in the outermost and innermost zones, the painting appears to dilate, almost erotically. The regulated geometry of the squares strives toward the flat plane, but the colors struggle to give the painting a thrust toward the third dimension.

right: **487.** *Agam (Yaacov Gipstein).* Double Metamorphosis II. *1964. Oil on corrugated aluminum in eleven parts, 8'10" × 13'2¼" (2.70 × 4.02 m). Collection, Museum of Modern Art, New York (gift of Mr. and Mrs. George M. Jaffin).*

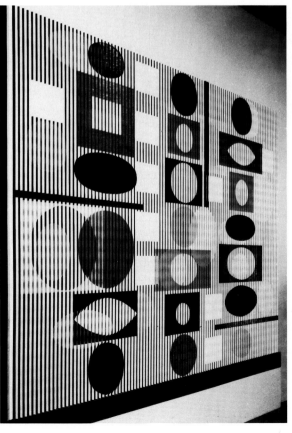

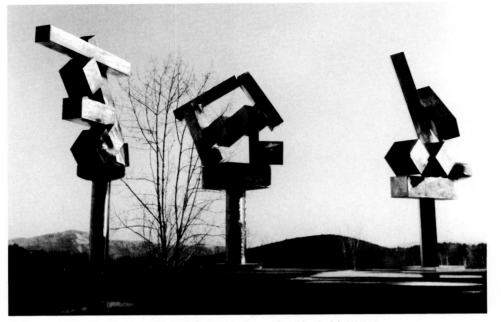

488. *David Smith.* Cubi *series. Polished stainless steel. Left:* Cubi XVIII. *1964. Height 9'8" (2.95 m); base 21¾" (55.2 cm) square. Museum of Fine Arts, Boston (gift of Susan W. and Stephen D. Paine). Center:* Cubi XVII. *1963. 8'11¾" × 5'4⅜" × 3'2⅛" (2.7 × 1.64 × .97 m). Dallas Museum of Art (The Eugene and Margaret McDermott Fund). Right:* Cubi XIX. *1964. Height 9'4¾" (2.84 m). Tate Gallery, London.*

Direct-Metal and Primary Sculpture

A logical progression from the work of early-20th-century Constructivist sculptors [61] was the **direct-metal** and **Primary sculpture** of the 1950s and 1960s. Rejecting the traditional representation of the human figure, sculpture became an extension of physics rather than a direct reflection of humanity. Architectural space became an arena for exploration by means of welded metal sheets, rods, and wires.

Richard Lippold (b. 1915) extended the spatial concepts of **constructivism.** Using taut strands of metal wire as lines that reflect light, he suspends a series of interconnecting geometric units in space. Sometimes light is focused at the heart of the structure, as in *Variation Number 7: Full Moon,* a creation of luminescent beauty 10 feet (3 meters) high that seems to float in space [386]. The shimmering quality of its overlying squares is evidence of Lippold's detailed planning, mastery of the material, and careful execution. He has produced even larger works of gold wire and metal strips that probe space in diagonal thrusts and are designed to relate art to architecture. In such works, light seems to pulsate over the geometric forms much as a musician might create subtle variations on a basic

theme. Perhaps Lippold's work suggests the positive aspects of our technological age.

David Smith (1906–1965), who had welded tanks in a wartime factory and studied the direct-metal sculpture of Picasso and other Europeans, made complex linear steel constructions in a Surrealist vein. In later work, using painted steel plates, he explored the human figure in Cubist terms [488]. John Chamberlain welded discarded automobile parts to form strong spatial constructions and to highlight our growing stockpile of debris [502].

The new inquiry into space led to a gradual reduction of nonessential details until sculptors reached a vocabulary, or system, of simple, basic geometric volumes. Their works are called **Primary, Minimal, ABC,** or **Systemic sculpture.** The shapes are usually so depersonalized that the artists can turn over their drawings to a workshop to do the actual construction. As a reflection of materialistic anonymous society, the surfaces of the shapes are mechanically finished, and they are assembled in multiples.

Primary sculpture may be placed on the floor or against the wall, suspended from the ceiling, or placed outdoors on a lawn or sidewalk. Such work enjoys the same freedom in three dimen-

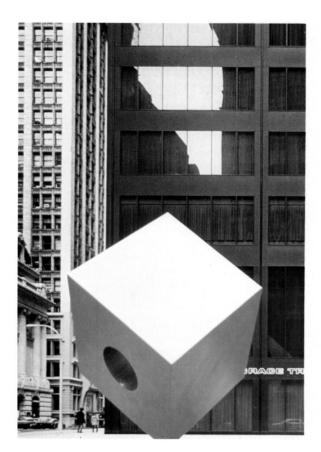

turbs us, while its huge geometric mass forces us to see it in relation to the surrounding architecture.

French-born Louise Bourgeois (b. 1911) also works in a variety of media, including wood, plaster, and marble. She traveled extensively from her childhood in Paris on and taught at the Louvre and elsewhere. Her first exhibition, in New York, was an extraordinary assemblage of forms. Wooden constructions with knobby heads stood together in clusters. A 6-foot-tall (1.83 meters) group of beams, painted purplish red and joined at cranial level by one wooden lintel, clumped unsteadily across the bare floor, a comment on modern-day witch-hunts [490]. It

left: **489.** *Isamu Noguchi.* Red Cube. *1968. Painted welded steel and aluminum. Height 28' (8.54 m). 140 Broadway, New York. Courtesy Isamu Noguchi Foundation.*

below: **490.** *Louise Bourgeois.* The Blind Leading the Blind. *1949. Painted wooden stakes, 7' × 7' × 7" (2.13 × 2.13 × 0.18 m). Copyright © 1987 Detroit Institute of Arts (Founders Society Purchase, Mr. and Mrs. Walter Buhl Ford II Fund).*

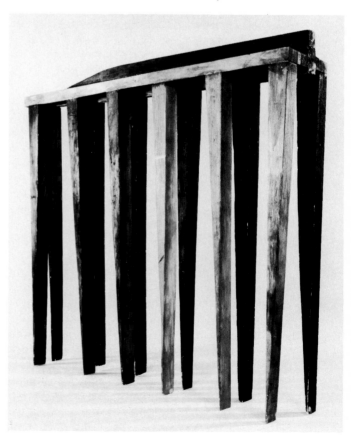

sions that nonobjective painting occupies in two. Although the physical presence of the viewer is not part of the design, his or her perceptions and responses to spatial openings, volumes, and enclosures concern the artist. Most significantly, the spectator is often invited to become part of the scene, to wander under, around, and through the sculpture.

Primary sculptors range from engineers who design by equation and computer to sculptors who create intuitively. David Smith belonged to the latter category. Just before he died, he created the *Cubi* series, which may be considered Primary sculptures in the stark simplicity of their forms and in the economy of their flat surfaces. Using only cubes and cylinders of stainless steel, he created works of endless variety, welding and finishing them himself with great technical control and sensitivity [488].

Isamu Noguchi's (b. 1904) bold red *Cube* is a Minimal sculpture that engages our attention and creates tension by the questions it raises about balance [489]. Its apparently precarious position, poised on one corner, startles and dis-

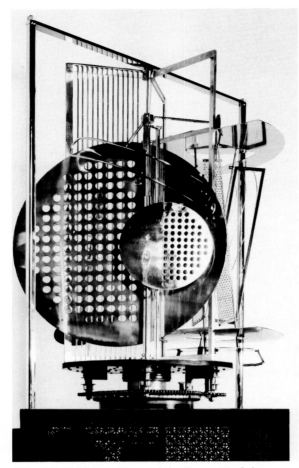

491. *László Moholy-Nagy.* Light-Space Modulator. *1923–1930. Mobile construction of steel, plastic, wood, other materials, with an electric motor. Height 4'11½" (1.51 m). Courtesy Harvard University Art Museums, Busch-Reisinger Museum (gift of Sibyl Moholy-Nagy).*

was named *The Blind Leading the Blind* and perhaps recalls Brueghel's similarly titled work, which satirized the religious cults of his day.

Motion in Sculpture

Like all animals, we are fascinated by motion. The driving rain, waving branches in the wind, the crash of waves onto a beach intrigue us as they did our ancestors. Motion is essential to life, even if it is the slow, almost imperceptible motion of a germinating seed thrusting a shoot through the earth. Today, however, we live in an age of motion unlike any the world has ever known. The speed with which our space vehicles rush toward other planets is almost beyond comprehension, while here on earth jets travel at velocities never dreamed possible. It is no wonder, then, that 20th-century artists have been fascinated with motion and have attempted to respond to it in their art.

The concept of combining sculptured figures with mechanical motion is not new. Turkish sultans had elaborate mechanical figures built for their amusement, probably inspired by Oriental creations. In medieval Europe, the bells in many clock towers were struck by mechanical figures, and during the Renaissance Leonardo designed figures for royal festivals which were moved mechanically.

The machine-oriented Futurist Umberto Boccioni expressed motion in his sculpture as early as 1913 **[444]**. Constantin Brancusi's *Bird in Space* of 1919 **[446]** minimized the material limitations of solid mass by its soaring form. But it was the constructivist sculptor Naum Gabo who, in 1920, designed the first motorized sculpture, a tall shape that vibrated. Works of this kind, often moved by a motor, are called **kinetic sculptures.** At the Bauhaus, László Moholy-Nagy (1895–1946) built the first light-and-motion sculptures, which were activated by the sun and called light modulators **[491]**.

In the 1930s and later, Alexander Calder (1898–1979) constructed moving sculpture from industrial materials such as sheet metal and wire. Although he added motors to some constructions to make them move, he preferred to leave their motion to the unpredictability of air currents. The result was a totally new sculptural form called a **mobile** by his friend Duchamp **[57]**. The cheerful elements of his mobiles remind us not of machines but of fish, animals, plants, and sometimes planets. Arranged in carefully balanced systems, they are set in motion by a passing breeze, the hot air of a furnace, or even the movement of someone walking past. Each element moves independently but within a prescribed orbit. Some strike each other like gongs and bells, adding an element of noise to the sculpture. Many of Calder's largest pieces are balanced on bases anchored to the ground, and movements of their heavy forms are slow and stately. He also built some pieces of sculpture that do not move, called **stabiles.**

Thus, over the last fifty years, motion has become an important feature of some works of art.

Kinetic sculptures often consist of nonfunctional machines, their movement existing only to provide a visual experience. Some of these machines perform complex operations perfectly, but at the same time they amuse us with their somewhat ridiculous uselessness. In our

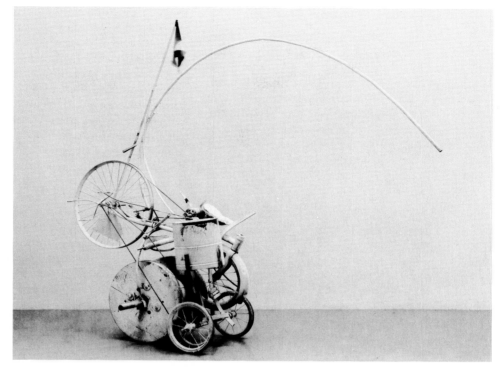

492. *Jean Tinguely. Fragment from* Homage to New York.
*1960. Painted metal, 6'8¼" × 2'5⅝" × 7'3⅞" (2.04 × 0.75 × 2.23 m).
Collection, Museum of Modern Art, New York (gift of the artist).*

mechanistic society, a machine that can do nothing but move seems laughable.

Erratic movement is expressed uniquely by the Swiss sculptor Jean Tinguely (b. 1925), who creates machine-powered kinetic sculptures that perform a series of actions. *Homage to New York* [492] was constructed of assorted discards found in dumps or second-hand stores. It made music with a battered piano, issued reports from an old typewriter, and gave birth to machine offspring. Finally one memorable evening in the garden of the Museum of Modern Art in New York, under the baleful eye of a New York City fireman and before an enthralled audience, *Homage to New York* with some frantic help from its inventor committed suicide in a flurry of movement, sound, and smoke. Its demise echoed the absurdity of Dada as it parodied modern self-destructing society.

Another example of kinetic sculpture is the work of Ernest Trova (b. 1927). All his pieces consist of an armless, sexless, featureless figure that is apparently helplessly thrust by modern technology toward a machine that threatens to destroy it or perpetuate it, unknowing, unfeeling, operating in a void, as in *Falling Man, Study No. 53* [493].

493. *Ernest Trova. Falling Man, Study No. 53.
1968. Nickel-plated bronze, 13 × 10 × 9¾"
(33 × 25 × 25 cm). Private collection.*

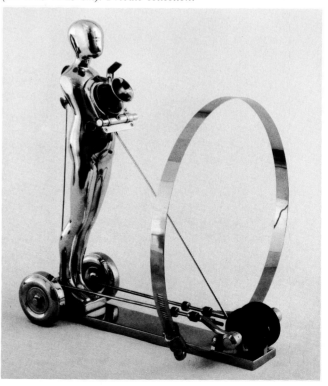

Expressionism and Realism

The emotional trend in art, identified with Abstract Expressionism in the 1940s and 1950s, all but disappeared from the scene during the 1960s and 1970s, only to reappear in new form later. For a brief time the Feminist movement became a passionate cause for some, combining personal feelings with a response to the real world that the public often found disturbing.

Feminism

The Feminist movement that gathered strength in the 1960s led to a re-examination of women's achievements in the visual arts. In the past, as we have seen, few women not born within a family of artists had any opportunity for art training or patronage. In the 1960s and 1970s, however, women's cooperative galleries mushroomed, and a few commercial dealers in art of women appeared and have continued. These galleries and dealers succeeded in informing women themselves about their groundbreaking role as artists. Much Feminist work attacked sexism, often in erotic ways that shocked many.

Judy Chicago (b. 1939), an ardent Feminist, uses hard-edge imagery to communicate her intuitions about the nature of womanhood. While she taught at the California Institute of the Arts, she initiated a Feminist art program that was highly successful in politicizing the female art community. Together with Miriam Schapiro (b. 1923), Chicago worked on projects such as Womanspace, the first cooperative women's art gallery on the West Coast, which became the Woman's Building, still functioning as a busy art center in Los Angeles. Her best-known work is *The Dinner Party* [**494**], the archetypal Feminist work. Five years in the making, it was assembled by the collective skills of four hundred women who executed Chicago's design. The format of the work is a huge triangular table with thirteen place settings on each side, referring to Christ and his disciples at the Last Supper. All thirty-nine place settings, named in honor of famous women, consist of plates, goblets, and flatware, with each one decorated with explicit female sexual symbols that affronted many anti-Feminists, as well as other women and men with moderate views. They repose on hand-worked place mats. The triangular ceramic floor bears the names of 999 other cultural heroines. *The Dinner Party* was exhibited to packed crowds and, like

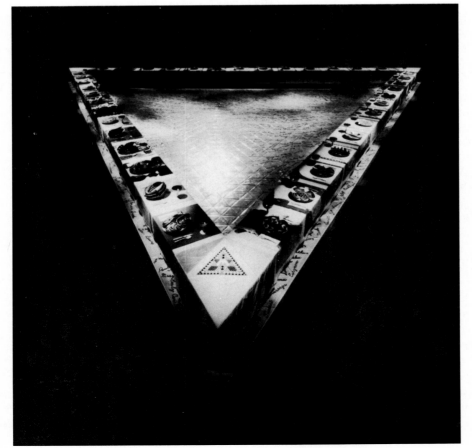

494. *Judy Chicago.* The Dinner Party. *1979. Copyright © 1979. Mixed media, each side 47' (14.34 m). Collection of the artist.*

Exploring Art Through Technology

Preserving Experimental Modern Art

Beginning perhaps with Marcel Duchamp's *The Bride Stripped Bare by Her Bachelors, Even (The Large Glass)* [495], some modern art is not likely to survive long enough ever to be considered old masterpieces. The improperly packed glassed work by Duchamp was discovered to be cracked some time after it had been removed from the Brooklyn Museum, where it had been exhibited at the International Exhibition of Modern Art in 1926. Duchamp's reputed reaction, "All the better," may have portended a carelessness about the making and preservation of art that seems to persist to this day.

Gone is the era when artists spent years in apprenticeship to learn all fundamentals of the preparation of painting surfaces, as well as the production of art finished for posterity. The very quality that makes some modern art so exciting to its viewers is its experimental nature—its violation of the traditional rules. Artists like Jackson Pollock shocked the art world by pouring house paint onto canvases that were neither stretched nor prepared for long life. Jean Dubuffet mixed bread crumbs and pieces of grapefruit rinds with his paint. Today Anselm Kiefer from Germany has glued bunches of straw onto his paintings. Arthur Page, a Washington conservator, says "Everyone acknowledges that in painting conservation, the most difficult problem we have is with modern paintings."

The *Wall Street Journal* assures us that the modern art market is in no way diminished by conservation concerns. That Willem de Kooning was suspected of mixing mayonnaise into his colors and Mark Rothko combined oils, acrylics, and substances like raw eggs in paint did not prevent collectors from spending almost 2 million dollars each for their works.[1]

The techniques of conserving impermanent arts vary with each problem, but few conservators are able to make enduring art works of those planned, it would seem, for obsolescence. Denise Domergue, president of the Los Angeles-based Conservation of Paintings, Ltd., recalls the replacement of a deteri-

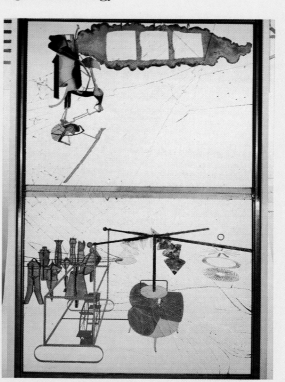

495. *Marcel Duchamp.* The Bride Stripped Bare by Her Bachelors, Even (The Large Glass) *1915–1923. Oil and lead wire on glass, 9′1¼″ × 5′9⅛″ (1.77 × 1.75 m). Philadelphia Museum of Art (bequest of Katherine S. Dreier).*

orated cigarette butt that Pollock had incorporated into one of his paintings. "Somebody had to smoke a Camel down, bend it into the right shape and stick it back," she reported.

Museums' temperature and moisture-control technological devices are a help, and Plexiglas boxes (rarely approved of by the original artists) protect some vulnerable surfaces. But who is to safeguard works against physical abuse by a few viewers provoked by modernism? Even with guards hovering nearby, Ad Reinhardt's black paintings had to be rehung ever higher out of the reach of smudging fingers!

[1] Tim Carrington, *Wall Street Journal,* January 14, 1985, p. 1.

many frankly sexual works, has received mixed criticism.

As we review the works of various women artists, it appears that women's experiences, although different from men's, do not make wom-

en's artworks similar to one another in style. Most women artists, in fact, seem to find affinity with other artists of their own **milieu** (environment) and period and work within the general mainstream of art.

Fantasy

Fantasy, like **formalism,** was partly a reaction to the emotional aspects of **Abstract Expressionism.** It pervades **Pop Art, assemblage,** and the improvisational art experiences known as **"happenings."** Two important transitional figures who drew on Abstract Expressionism but were forerunners of Pop Art were Robert Rauschenberg (b. 1925) and Jasper Johns (b. 1930).

Rauschenberg, as we saw in Chapter 3, in his desire to work in the gap between art and life, combines collage, the commercial silk-screen process, Action painting technique, and readymade objects such as an electric fan to create combine art **[116].** The prevailing theme is often nonmeaning, or like Dada, art of the absurd.

Johns painted familiar objects such as American flags **[41],** and beer cans. In *Studio I* **[496]** he follows the Renaissance theme of the artist painting his own studio while also referring to the Romantic Courbet's painting of his studio **[394],** an assertion of freedom of artistic expression. Johns' piece, consisting of several canvases nailed together to which a string of his paint cans is attached, is another early example of **combine art**: adding objects that already exist in the real world to art.

Pop Art A movement of the 1960s that combined both fantasy and realism was Pop Art. It began in London in 1956 when the Independent Group, a small group of artists, architects, sculptors, and art historians who were studying the symbolism and imagery of the art of mass society, staged the exhibition "This Is Tomorrow." It included a provocative work by one of the members, Richard Hamilton (b. 1922), entitled *Just What Is It That Makes Today's Home So Different, So Appealing?* **[497].** It was unclear whether the public was expected to consider as art this montage of ready-made motifs culled from any nonart sources and explicitly connected to **Dada.**

However, the content of Hamilton's work could also be compared with a 17th-century Dutch painting whose genre theme is brought up to date—a couple at home, served by an upstairs maid standing before a window view of an urban scene beyond. The name for the new style may be expressed in the oversize Tootsie Pop

496. *Jasper Johns.* Studio I. *1964. Oil on canvas with objects,*
6′1½″ × 12′1″ (1.87 × 3.68 m). Whitney Museum of American Art, New York.

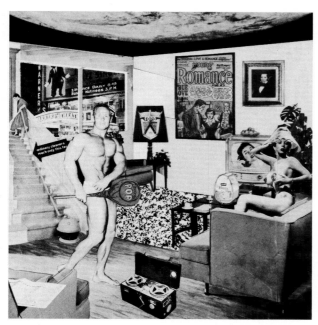

497. *Richard Hamilton.* Just What Is It That Makes Today's Home So Different, So Appealing? *1956. Collage on paper, 10⅛ × 9¾″ (26 × 25 cm). Kunsthalle, Tübingen, West Germany (Collection Professor Georg Zundel).*

many are sculptures executed in mixed media such as commercial lithography and silk-screening. In this way Warhol removed the artist's touch from the art, not scientifically like Seurat [71, 72] but by the techniques of industry. He believed that "painting is essentially the same as what it has always been. . . . All painting is fact, and that is enough; the paintings are charged with their very presence."

The work of James Rosenquist (b. 1933) [17], who initially was an outdoor-sign painter, performs the same function as the work of Warhol—magnifying images and forcing us to look at the carbon-copy quality of our lives and at the endless assembly-line products of which we have become a part. In *F-111* he covers all four walls of a room with blown-up images of food, automobile tires, spaghetti, an atomic mushroom cloud, and a little girl being initiated into the rites of grown-up artificiality. Roy Lichtenstein (b. 1923), however, may best represent Pop. He has seized standardized imagery of sentiment and violence in our popular comic strips and greatly enlarged its impact while faithfully transcribing every detail [498]. Like the carefully let-

held by the head of the house. It any event, this work ridiculed the banalities of daily life and the fantasy world depicted by mass media. The popular culture represented at this exhibition was identified as Pop Art by the British critic Lawrence Alloway, a member of the group.

Pop Art focuses on movies, billboards, machines, comic books, and advertising. Pop artists examine our everyday world and report it directly, with neither satire nor antagonism, but with such intensity that the spectator frequently becomes conscious for the first time of what he or she sees every day. Pop Art depends on large scale to increase its impact, thrusting forward in monumental size aspects of our culture we have chosen to ignore. Another characteristic of Pop Art is the repetition of images in patterns reminiscent of the rows of mass-produced packages seen in the supermarket, an emerging phenomenon at mid-century.

In the United States, Andy Warhol (1930–1987) was a pioneer in using multiple images and in container art as well. He made use of his commercial training and early career in advertising in his paintings. After 1961, his subjects included soup cans [175], Marilyn Monroe [28], and a bottle of Coca-Cola. Some of his pieces are paintings on two-dimensional surfaces, but

498. *Roy Lichtenstein.* Drowning Girl. *1963. Oil and synthetic polymer paint on canvas, 5′7⅝″ × 5′6¾″ (1.71 × 1.70 m). Collection, Museum of Modern Art, New York (Philip Johnson Fund and gift of Mrs. Bagley Wright).*

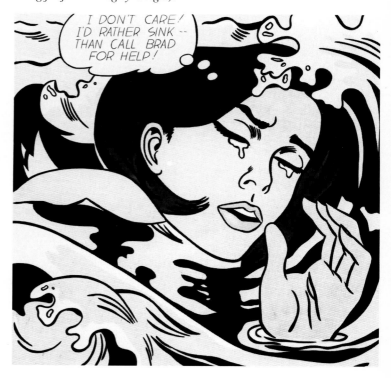

tered message which amplified the medieval illustration page of the *Symbol of Solomon as Wisdom* [166], Lichtenstein's caption pinpoints his story.

Jim Dine's (b. 1935) art, like that of Rauschenberg and Johns, draws on Abstract Expressionism [100]. Retaining the stock accessories of theater—stage-set colors and actual props—Dine uses paint and modeling materials to remind the spectator of commonplace objects. His work combines anti-art objects with the immediacy of Action painting. For instance, in one of his assemblages, Dine set a lawnmower against a canvas painted green and permitted the paint to drip off the canvas onto the mower as if art must include not only paint and canvas but also anything attached to the canvas.

Anonymity is another feature of Pop Art. Robert Indiana (Robert Clark, b. 1928) exhibits paintings of stenciled signs that reveal nothing about the artist except what can be read into his choice of subjects. Indiana is absorbed by word images that suggest the stark simplicity of flashing neon signs. The words *eat, love,* and *die* are rendered in clashing, precise, hard-edged colors. His *Love* [499] has become so much a part of the popular American scene that few are aware of its source. Many other Indiana word images are bitter indictments of modern life. Thus Pop

499. *Robert Indiana.* Love. *1968. Aluminum, 12 × 12 × 6″ (30 × 30 × 15 cm). Whitney Museum of American Art, New York (gift of the Howard and Jean Lipman Foundation, Inc.).*

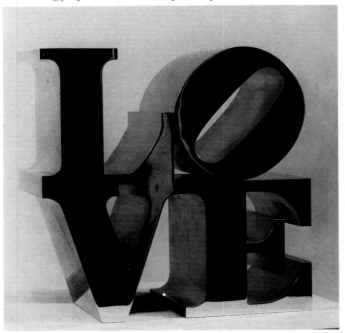

Art echoes the bland character of our commercial surroundings as contrasted with the highly individualized creations of traditional art.

The most impressive sculptor associated with Pop Art may be George Segal (b. 1924), who, like Edward Kienholz [36], will be discussed later as an environmental sculptor. After working on happenings with Allen Kaprow (b. 1927), Segal turned to building real environments into which he placed sculptured people [500]. These works, often assembled from junkyard materials, are filled with machines, oil cans, and other Pop images. But the figures are always taken directly from life. Replicas of nondescript people, they are cast from the live model into plaster as if they could be produced in multiples, like beer cans or soap boxes.

Marisol (b. 1930) has created her own style, which uses wood, plaster, paint, photographs, and accessories. Her works are studies of modern personalities, mocking the stuffed-animal figure of the hero, an empty image of leadership, which the public demands. Her portrait of Louise Nevelson [201] rounds out her series devoted to significant 20th-century artists, addressed with respectful satire.

In his sculpture, Claes Oldenburg (b. 1929) calls attention to the character of ordinary objects by taking them out of context and changing their scale. His *Hamburger*, the symbol of American fast food, made of painted plaster-of-paris and enlarged to four times normal size, had a wide influence on the art of the 1960s. Similar painted plaster food and other products filled his *Store,* a New York establishment rented in 1961. Explaining his role as storekeeper, Oldenburg said of his pieces that galleries are "not the place for them. A store would be better." Everything he sees becomes saturated with meaning, and he has turned things inside out or upside down or changed their substance. For example, he reproduced an electric fan in soft, stuffed vinyl as a satire on our dependency on material objects [217]. Art critic Max Kozloff observes:

With Claes Oldenburg, the spectator's nose is practically rubbed into the whole pointless cajolery of our hard-sell, sign-dominated culture. Oldenburg may even be commenting on the visual indigestibility of our environment by his inedible plaster and enamel cakes and pies.

Assemblages

The refuse of our industrial culture possesses great variety and appeals to many artists as a substitute for traditional materials. They com-

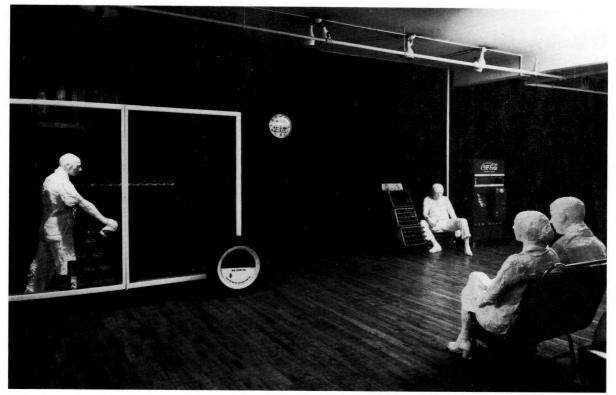

500. *George Segal. Left side:* The Gas Station. *1963–1964. Plaster, metal, glass, stone, rubber; 8 × 22 × 5' (2.44 × 6.71 × 1.53 m). National Gallery of Canada, Ottawa. Right side:* The Bus Riders, *detail. 1962. Plaster, metal, vinyl; 6'2" × 4' × 9' (1.9 × 1.2 × 2.7 m). Hirshhorn Museum and Sculpture Garden, Smithsonian Institution, Washington.*

bine debris—the rind of an orange, bits of advertisements, and found objects such as pieces of old cars—with paint to create collages and assemblages. Early examples are Cubist collages and assemblages such as the *Merzbau* of Kurt Schwitters [**435**]. Jean Dubuffet's (1901–1985) statement that "anything can come from anything" explains the attitude of artists who create assemblages. Neither painted nor sculpted in the traditional sense, and not expected to last, they are made of whatever appeals to the artist.

Joseph Cornell (1903–1972) made memorable contributions to assembled sculpture. Perhaps inspired by penny arcade fortune-telling machines, he concentrated on boxes, creating glass-fronted containers crammed with odds and ends redolent with personal associations. Occasionally they included Cubist forms and multiple images. Often containing mirrors, his assemblages suggested intimate, magical dream worlds [**501**].

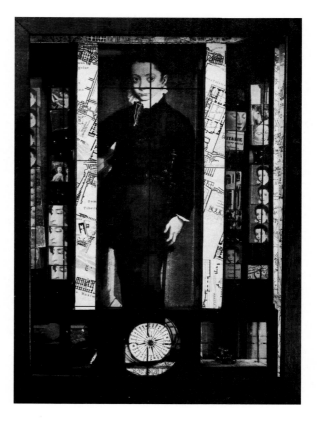

right: **501.** *Joseph Cornell.* Medici Slot Machine. *1942. Construction, 15½ × 12 × 4⅜" (39 × 30 × 11 cm). Private collection. Location unknown.*

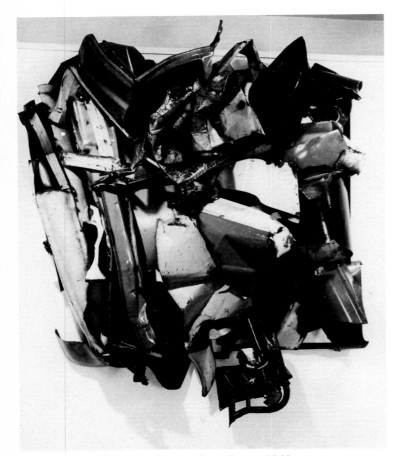

502. *John Chamberlain. Essex. 1960.*
Automobile body parts and other metal, relief;
9' × 6'8" × 3'7" (2.74 × 2.06 × 1.09 m).
Collection, Museum of Modern Art, New York
(gift of Mr. and Mrs. Robert C. Scull and purchase).

Destruction is the dominating theme of John Chamberlain's (b. 1927) assemblages. In such works as *Essex* [**502**] he builds bent and welded remnants of dead automobiles from junkyards into sculpture. These rusted, crushed, or fragmented forms have a macabre fascination for us, allowing us vicariously to experience destruction. Tinguely's self-destruction machine had a similar appeal. In many of us there seems to be an element that enjoys seeing buildings torn down, cars crashing in a movie, or a piano being torn apart, as the comedian Jimmy Durante used to do on stage nightly. We may conclude that destruction must be attractive to many people or there would not be so much of it on "stage" or in events reported by media.

Happenings

When the distinctions that separate art from reality blur, the art object may concern us less than the *making* of art. The staged happenings of the 1960s might have occurred anywhere, on the street or in the supermarket. Allen Kaprow, an assemblage sculptor who was one of the first to stage such events, believes that "the gallery has given way as a place for staging happenings to a craggy canyon, an old abandoned factory, a railroad, or the oceanside."

Happenings were performed without a real script or even a rehearsal. Participants were selected for their suitability to the plan, and props and costumes were gathered. Happenings were an art, sometimes closer to life than to theater. They were briefly a part of the American art world, perhaps because they reflected the sense of chaos many of us still observe in society.

Environmental Art

The term **Environmental Art** refers to constructions that often combine painting and sculpture in architectural settings. Built on a large scale, many surround the viewer with visual sensations, totally immersing him or her in the art experience. As such they may be called **Experiential Art.** By extension the term may include art that reworks the natural environment.

Departing from the early concept of "earthworks" that are characteristic of Environmental Art, new aspects of content emerged in the 1960s and 1970s. Alice Aycock (b. 1946) builds complex constructions like *A Simple Network of Underground Wells and Tunnels* that require a spectator to enter her sculpture to pursue its maze forms. The earth is drastically altered and enriched with archaeological associations that intrigue the participants in their pursuit of an experience laid out by Aycock, and accompanied by her philosophical notes [**503**].

In the late 1960s, while accompanying her husband Robert Smithson [**11**], Nancy Holt (b. 1938) began to design sculptures to integrate with the landscapes for which they were intended. Often planned to correlate with ancient celestial maps, these projects carry mystical associations. Keyed to the local terrain of mist-shrouded hills and the jagged coastline of the Pacific Northwest, *Stone Enclosure: Rock Rings* [**504**] consists of two concentric circles of stone walls, 10 feet (3 meters) high and 40 and 20 feet (12.2 and 6.1 meters) in diameter, hand-carved from 230-million-year-old rock. These site sculptures, like Smithson's, are always documented by drawings and photographs, and suggest in their shifting patterns of light and dark

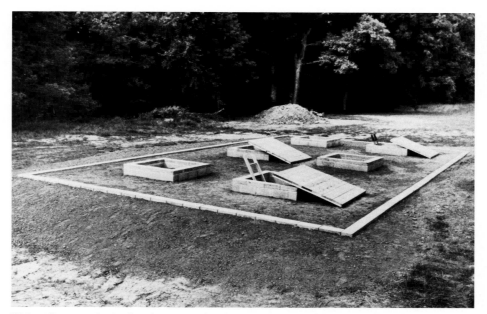

503. *Alice Aycock.* A Simple Network of Underground Wells and Tunnels. *1975. Concrete-block wells and tunnels underground, demarcated by a wall, 28 × 50' (8.54 × 15.25 m); area 20 × 40' (6.1 × 12.2 m). Temporary installation for the exhibition* Projects in Nature, *Merrieword West, Far Hills, New Jersey. Courtesy John Weber Gallery.*

ideas of sculptural stability amidst nature's fluctuations.

Alice Aycock, Nancy Holt, and others have all produced site sculptures that share salient connections of form with changing environment. In fact, as Michael Brenson, *New York Times* art critic, has said, "The flourishing of contemporary sculpture is related to the *sense of possibility* women have brought to it."

Architectural Environments

To create an architectural environment requires multiple skills. Its combination of assem-

504. *Nancy Holt.* Stone Enclosure: Rock Rings, *detail 1977–1978. Hand-quarried schism; outer diameter 40' (12.2 m); inner ring diameter 20' (6.1 m). Height of ring walls 10' (3.05 m). Western Washington University, Bellingham, Washington.*

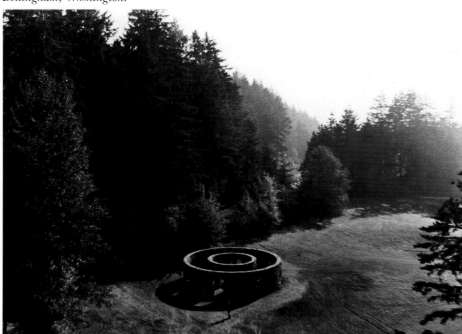

blage and other techniques is another indication of the merging of the arts after centuries of separation. Most of them permit the viewer to walk inside them, and many are rooted in the artist's response to social concerns.

In their commentaries on contemporary culture, the Pop artists Edward Kienholz (b. 1927) and George Segal seem to inherit themes of the social-protest paintings of the 1930s. Kienholz's tableaux [36] place us in the role of peeping Toms, and our own macabre fascination with what we see provides an added element of discomfort. Like Kienholz, Segal also creates groupings of people in environments [500], but instead of presenting dramatic scenes, he reveals their banality. Segal may be reporting the nondescript aspects of our lives so that we may either more fully enjoy day-to-day living or find a way to transcend its tedium.

Alexander Calder created an architectural environment in the form of a 60-foot-high (18.3 meters) direct-metal sculpture, through which automobile traffic was channeled in Spoleto, Italy. He also designed an acoustical ceiling for an auditorium in Caracas, Venezuela, in which tremendous, free-form shapes seem to float above the seats. Before Calder, architectural sculpture had been obviously attached to the building; in this work, it appeared to be a suspended element of the environment.

Working with wooden found objects and other materials, the assemblage sculptor Louise Nevelson (1899–1988) [200] is most often identified with the large environmental works discussed in Chapter 7. The art critic Cindy Nemser has said of them, "All the rubbish of Manhattan is transformed by this artist into phantom architecture." Similarly, an Italian-born tile setter named Simon Rodia designed the Watts Towers of Los Angeles. Emerging from Rodia's tiny backyard like the towers of a medieval city, the steel, mesh, and mortar spires are lovingly covered with broken tiles and other discards [7]. Rodia's environment became a living echo of himself. Here again the line between art and reality is difficult to find.

Architecture

The essence of the **International Style** (1930–1950) was its conviction that architecture could produce the millennium—a perfect society instituted by architects. The famous dicta followed in profusion: "Form follows function," "The house is a machine for living in," "Less is more," and so forth. By mid-century, Le Corbusier [505] and others had persuaded us that there could be no civilization without cities. Mies van der Rohe [242] claimed that the essence of modern build-

505. *Le Corbusier.* L'Unité d'Habitation, *Marseilles, France. 1947–1952.*
Length 550′ (167.64 m), width 79′ (24.08 m), height 184′ (56.08 m).

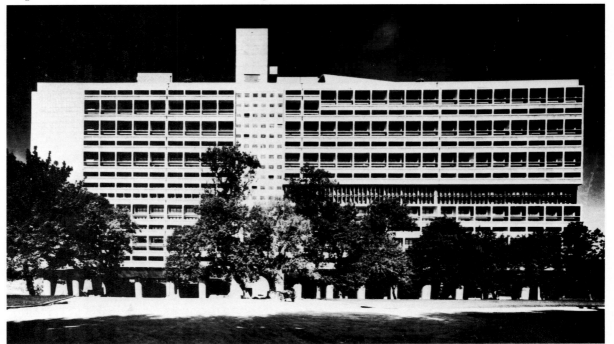

ings was "skin and bones"—the skin of glass, the bones of steel or concrete. And Walter Gropius [455] had persuaded us that the "building team" was the only effective expedient for the creation of modern construction.

If any one building sums up mid-century philosophy, it is Le Corbusier's *Unité d'Habitation* [505] in Marseilles. *Unité* is one of the most famous structures of the postwar world. It was to be the model for a series of complexes that Le Corbusier planned to build across France to house, without resorting to urban sprawl, the four million French families made homeless by the war. In its design he evolved unusual combinations of past traditions and new ideas—the pillars on which it stands taper toward the bottom, the gardens are on the roof, the streets are inside and in the air, the shopping center is on the seventh floor instead of connected to the commercial center of Marseilles.

Critics were numerous. Jane Jacobs condemned the shopping center for being too far from the center of the city. Lewis Mumford criticized the long apartment units as being too much like halls. Siegfried Giedion complained that the internal streets were all dark corridors, and journalists attacked the notion of one thousand people holed up in a vast, anonymous beehive. Nevertheless, *Unité,* efficiently constructed of precast concrete, achieved a balance of posi-tive goals: (1) twenty-three different types of apartments for all family sizes, (2) absolute privacy, (3) isolation from traffic fumes and noise, and (4) twenty-six communal facilities. Because of such work in urban architecture, Le Corbusier was asked to apply his ideas on urban design to Chandigarh, the new capital of the Punjab in India. His beliefs are still an inspiration to city planners.

Despite Le Corbusier's far-reaching goals in *Unité*, this gargantuan design has not proved to be Utopia for its inhabitants. Can it be the loss of personal identity in an autonomous living center? Or, isn't likely that the human animal depends to some degree on natural environments for survival? Certainly we may recall that Moshe Safdie *was* able to achieve in *Habitat* [279] a large communal facility, apparently so desirable that even now the supply of available apartments never equals the demand for them. And Buckminster Fuller [251] *was* able to provide efficient climate control in the U.S. Pavilion at Expo '67 and elsewhere, unlike *Unité*, which was designed before universal awareness of the ecoenvironmental balances required to accommodate efficient energy consumption.

The world of the 1990s will demand a different set of architectural priorities, as we shall soon see, and our designers will have to develop solutions to meet these needs effectively.

Exercises and Activities

Research Exercises

1. What are some of the major mid-century movements, grouped as to formalism, Expressionism, realism, and fantasy?
2. Explain how the approach of many women to art changed in the 1960s.
3. How does the art of assemblage reflect our growing concern with the wastes of our society?

Studio Activities

1. Can you think of other popular slogans as significant as the *LOVE* theme of Robert Indiana? Create a work of art in paint, sculpture, or any combination that uses Pop images or slogans.
2. Create a work of art in which motion—either natural or mechanical—is an important element.
3. Modifications of earlier geometric abstraction and nonobjective art can be seen in Op Art.

4. Environmental art can be found in painting, sculpture, and architectural design. What are the common features in all three media? What are the differences?
5. Consider a large open space in your town and try to visualize (or conceptualize) a monumental sculpture for it. What material, form, and design would express your recommendations for that space?

   Using graph paper or your own ruled squares, experiment with small units of color. Create an illusion of three dimensions by varying the sizes and colors of the units. Superimpose three-dimensional louvers made of paper or cardboard to create more exciting visual effects.
6. Create a work that recycles the materials of industry.
7. Create an artwork that deals with Feminist issues. Try to incorporate found objects in your design.

18
Our Own Time:
The 1970s and Beyond

There are more artists creating more works of art [of some sort] than ever before in our history.

Hilton Kramer, editor, *The New Criterion*

As I see it, the struggle is between those who believe art is essentially dead and make dead art to prove it, and those who don't. Either art will survive the test of time or it won't.

Eric Fischl, artist

I look for works in which I feel there are issues and feelings that need to be communicated to a larger public . . . If you write about art, you create a dialogue with artists.

Michael Brenson, critic, *New York Times*

For the young artist, it's indispensable to live in New York . . . in order to succeed, if this is the artist's ambition, he has to come to New York even from Europe . . . My advice to the young artist is to "become a genius."

Leo Castelli, dealer, New York

The arts of the 1960s were fairly easy to understand and to remember. There was Pop, and then, Op . . . Claes Oldenburg's *Giant Soft Fan* [217], Andy Warhol's cans [175], Ad Reinhardt's monochromatic paintings [485]. The 1970s showed little homogeneity. Art responds to the mood of the times and even to specific events. Our time line notes show much dissonance, and many of the arts were ephemeral. The pluralistic 1970s imagery makes rather clear how we came to where we are today: several kinds of art found room to coexist, even while contradictions abounded.

The accelerating rate of change that pervades our lives today is reflected in the art of the 1970s and 1980s. Many artists feel liberated from traditional rules and free to follow any line of exploration. Art styles constantly shift, while artists develop their styles into new forms. Categories of art become blurred. Painting, for example, often merges with sculpture in assemblage. The line between art and craft hardly exists as sculptors crochet, quilt, blow glass, or weave environments and painters use the dye techniques of crafts. New categories emerge that use light, the natural environment, or pure ideas and a polemic intensity not seen since Goya burns in the art of social conscience.

As we have traced the history of art through the centuries, we have often been rewarded with artistic expressions that affect us today as strongly as they moved observers at the time they were created. No less significant is what we may learn from history about the pattern of artistic development. Many of us might anticipate a flowering in our time of all the currents we have examined, as if art, like science, were to evolve from past experience toward a glorious new age. For others it is tempting to think that as Western society has moved in cycles in the past, today it moves faster and in wider circles. And yet we cannot be sure that either of these

THE VISUAL ARTS		HISTORICAL NOTES
		1964 *Fiddler on the Roof* opens on Broadway
		1968 *Hair* opens
		1969 Woodstock concert, N.Y.
1970 Neel, *Andy Warhol* [516]	1970	
1970 Smithson, *Spiral Jetty* [11]		
1971 Graves, *Variability* . . . [530]		**1971** *Jesus Christ Superstar* opens
1971–72 Christo, *Valley Curtain* [527]		**1971** *Grease* opens
1971–77 De Maria, *The Lightning Field* [151]		**1971** Attica prison uprising, N.Y.
1972 Kahn, Kimbell Art Museum [535]		
1973 Paik, *Charlotte Moorman* [161]		**1973** USA out of Vietnam
		1973 *All in the Family*, television show
		1973 *American Graffiti*
		1973 Supreme Court permits abortion
		1974 Energy crisis: gas lines
		1974 President Nixon resigns (Watergate)
1975 Aycock, *A Simple Network* . . . [503]	1975	**1975** *Rocky Horror Picture Show*, cult classic
1975 Bartlett, *Rhapsody* [508]		
		1976 Death of Mao Tse-tung
1977–78 Holt, *Stone Enclosure: Rock Rings* [504]		**1977** *Saturday Night Fever* and disco craze
		1977 *Star Wars*; special effects
		1978 Jim Jones: People's Temple mass suicide
1978–82 Johnson & Burgee, AT&T Building [536]		
1979 Palyka, *Picasso 2* [523]		**1979** USA: Three-Mile Island nuclear accident
1979 Chicago, *The Dinner Party* [494]		
1980 Close, *Self-Portrait/Composite* [518]	1980	
1981 Pfaff, *Dragon* [531]		**1981** Assassination attempts: Pope John, President Reagan
1982 Brown, *Wildflower* [521]		
1982 Cohen, AARON drawing [522]		
1983–85 Acconci, *Building Blocks* . . . [519]		
1984 Salle, *Midday* [525]		
1985 Singer, *Ritual Series/Syntax* [529]	1985	
		1986 USA: *Challenger* and crew explode
		1986 USSR: Chernobyl nuclear disaster

views is accurate. Without the distance that time provides, it is difficult to sift through the rich variety of today's art to distinguish the significant from the merely novel.

We may observe, beneath the surface variety that characterizes present-day art, a general continuation of the tendencies that we have already noted. The formalist trend is found in abstract paintings and sculptures into which an impulse toward expressiveness has been infused in some cases and in others a self-conscious harking back to the geometric abstraction of earlier in the century. Realism includes artists who attempt a verisimilitude perhaps comparable to the verism of late Roman sculpture (see Chapter 11). Expressionism can be found mainly in European art and young American artists for whom the real world remains an opportunity for personal emotional interpretation. Art as escape from this imperfect world through fantasy also continues, chiefly in the form of television and film. These photographic art forms, which dominate our world as never before, sometimes provide us with an imaginative existence that may explore life-styles and modes of conduct once considered taboo. The multiple image, whether film, video, or graphics, predominates, relating mechanical duplication to the repetitious electronic aspects of our world. The intellectual planning process also dominates in Conceptual art and some Environmental art, which is planned to disappear after it is made.

Formalism

Painting

In the early 1970s **Minimalism** still reigned supreme. Mathematical rigor underlies the large gridded canvases of Agnes Martin (b. 1912), grande dame of Minimalist painting [506], but the effect is of poetry and great serenity. Inspired by the sense of light and open air of New Mexico, from where Martin moved to New York,

506. *Agnes Martin.*
The Tree. *1964.*
Oil and pencil on canvas,
6 × 6′ (1.83 × 1.83 m).
Collection, Museum of
Modern Art, New York
(Larry Aldrich Foundation Fund).

the grids seem almost to float. In their tendency to induce contemplation in the viewer, Martin's paintings invoke comparisons to Buddhist philosophy.

By the middle of the 1970s, Minimalism in painting was exhausted and gave way to a reaction that embraced what the now passé movement eschewed: decoration, content, and the presence of the artist's hand. Among these early reactions to Minimalism was the movement known as "Pattern and Decoration," sometimes called P & D, a highly formal, decorative style involving the regular repetition of motifs intended to cover a surface. Abstraction during these years, until about the mid-1980s, remained in abeyance, at least according to generally accepted "official" taste. The practitioners of abstraction, such as Elizabeth Murray (b. 1940), learned to buck current trends and find their artistic identities off the center stage.

Elizabeth Murray's work is perhaps best set within the formalist painting idiom. Brilliantly inventive, her grouped canvases are shaped sometimes with curvilinear organic parts but as often rather like sharp notes in a tone poem. Each element may function independently, yet in concert creates pulsating rhythms with strong directional force **[507]**. *Art Part* is essentially the work of a giant hand with brush, palette, and cups for paint. Murray says: "I want the panels to look as if they had been thrown against the wall and that's how they stuck there." Her billowing cut-out shapes, with origins in household and other common forms, often threaten to devour one another. She brings the melodrama of daily life into a dialogue with modern art.

New Image Art   The Whitney Museum of American Art in New York presented an exhibition in 1978 called "New Image Painting"—a style prompted by Philip Guston (1913–1980) when he abandoned his beloved Abstract Expressionism in favor of new figural work in the 1970s. Maintaining a bit of his former instinctual brush strokes, he and a group of young artists of the 1970s, including Susan Rothenberg (b. 1945) **[127]** and Jennifer Bartlett, developed unique styles with some figuration reference, along with the formal clarity and systematization they had inherited from minimal art of the 1960s.

In addition, Bartlett incorporated mathematics into her first major (987-unit) work, entitled *Rhapsody,* that filled the Paula Cooper Gallery with but 6 feet (1.8 meters) to spare. She painted on 1-foot (30.5 centimeter)-square steel plates, each printed with a silkscreen grid, using a basic set of six colored enamels; the result was color-dot painting in a dazzling display of decorative abstract patterns **[508]**. Her desire to recognize reality was satisfied by including the forms of a house, tree, mountain, and ocean, reduced to

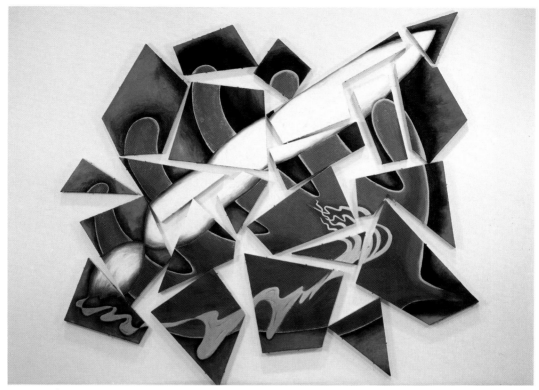

above: **507.** *Elizabeth Murray.* Art Part. *1981. Oil on 22 canvases, 9'7" × 10'4"*
(2.96 × 3.17 m). Private collection. Courtesy Paula Cooper Gallery, New York.

below: **508.** *Jennifer Bartlett.* Rhapsody. *c. 1975–1976. Enamel and baked enamel,*
silk-screen grid on steel plates; 988 plates, 12 × 12" each (30.5 × 30.5 cm);
overall 7'6" × 153'9" (2.29 × 46.89 m). Collection Sidney Singer, New York.
Courtesy Paula Cooper Gallery, New York.

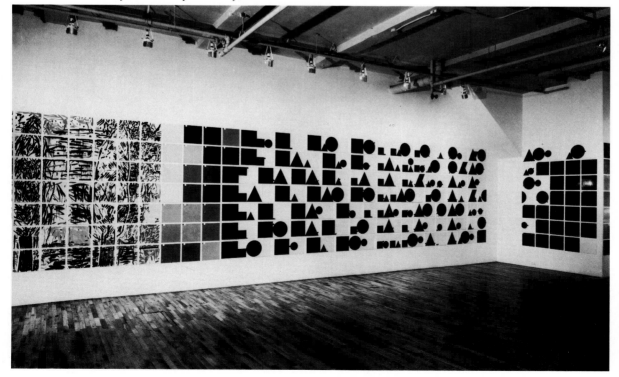

Jennifer Bartlett (b. 1941)

From kindergarten days in California, Jennifer Bartlett [509] always knew she wanted to be an artist. Even then, she worked with serial images. Her first viewing of Disney's *Cinderella* inspired her to complete about five hundred drawings, each one a different version of the dress Cinderalla wore.

At Mills College, Bartlett discovered Abstract Expressionism, but not until she was at the Yale School of Art and Architecture, under Jack Tworkov's guidance, were her creative energies fully tapped. In 1966, as Abstract Expressionism was fading for her, she produced a 9-by-18-foot (2.7-by-5.5-meter) painting with two hundred fifty 12-by-3-inch (30-by-7.6-centimeter) rectangles, each a different color. Her fascination with her need both for control in her plan and for impulse as she painted launched Bartlett into the new idiom so enthusiastically acclaimed at her first major exhibition [508]. By 1975, when *Rhapsody* was completed, however, she was $10,000 in debt for analytical therapy, paints,

and the plates so integral to her art. Each plate was painted by formula. As she states, "Freehand has to be painted standing up. By now the painting has become method."

Bartlett's ambitions were growing. She began to write more and paint less. The linear-program idea was applied to the plates, cards, and paint cups. Using a thesaurus, she wrote out all the words she could find beginning with A, then B, and so on. These dictionary words of early essays gave way to narration of packets of her experience. Her autobiographical *History of the Universe* grew into a thousand pages. *Universe* reveals less of a reaching for a transcendental universality (like *Rhapsody*) than a mind headed for self-destruction. Her voracious appetite for public exposure and her creative energies have produced a stunning array of unified complexity in which she has embraced it all—works that have "everything in it." Bartlett perhaps has led the narrative revival in painting. She sums it up, "I want to move people. Yes, I'd like to be a strong, heart-breaking artist." That seems to have happened.

509. *Jennifer Bartlett. Photograph by Ellie Thompson.*

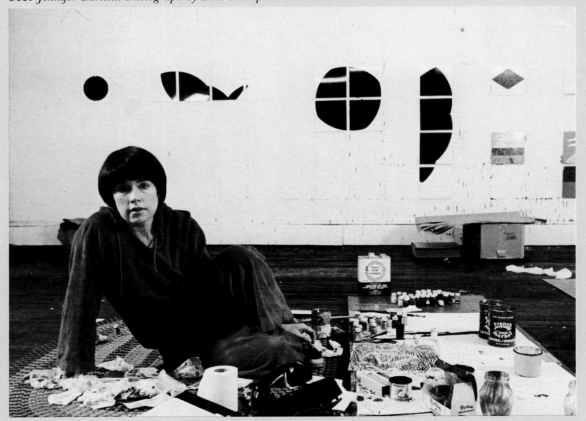

their essentials. The painting overwhelmed the first viewers; it was regarded by *New York Times* art critic John Russell as "the most ambitious single work" he had ever seen.

Sculpture

Some Minimalist sculpture concepts were difficult to execute in the late 1960s because of their large scale. Since that time a new appreciation for large-scale public art has helped make commissions possible. One of the more controversial works of public art has been *Tilted Arc* by Richard Serra (b. 1939) **[510]**, located at Federal Plaza in New York City. With a length of 120 feet (37 meters), height of 12 feet (3.7 meters), and weight of 72 tons (65 metric tons), this simple curve of steel has become the subject of much media attention. The U.S. Government's General Services Administration commissioned this piece from Serra, but complaints from government workers in neighboring buildings brought about a hearing in which Serra was asked to relocate the piece. The artist reacted by threatening to sue. The controversy highlighted questions about the relationship of the artist to the public when public funds are involved. Serra had designed the piece specifically for its site, not unmindful of potential hostility it might arouse. The dispute remains unresolved.

By placing modular repeats in a straight line, Donald Judd (b. 1928), another Minimalist sculptor, eliminates variables, or human quali-

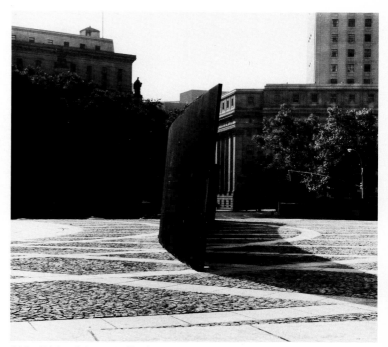

510. *Richard Serra.* Tilted Arc. *1981. Hot rolled steel, length 120' (36.6 m). Federal Plaza, New York. Photo courtesy Leo Castelli Gallery, New York.*

ties. The predictability of his sculptures, which make no reference to past traditions, reduces emotional overtones to zero. What remains is only a real construction in real space **[511]**. If we find such sculptures disturbing, it may be they remind us of manufactured environments that cannot fulfill human needs. Another sculptor

511. *Donald Judd.* Untitled. *1972. Plywood; five boxes, each 3'5" × 6' × 6' (1.04 × 1.83 × 1.83 m), spaced 1'7" (0.48 m) apart. Private collection.*

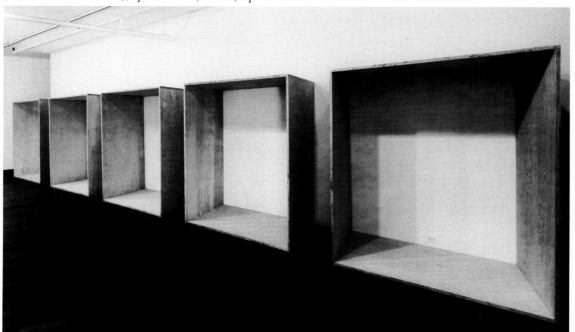

411

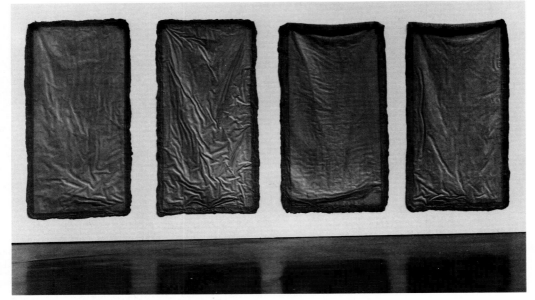

512. *Eva Hesse. Aught. c. 1968. Double sheet latex, polyethylene inside, four units, 78 × 40" (198.1 × 101.6 cm) each. University Art Museum, University of California, Berkeley (gift of Mrs. Helen Charash).*

who commented on the synthetic quality and similarity of many lives was Eva Hesse (1936–1970) [512], who arranged plastics and other synthetic materials in endless repeat patterns.

513. *Photograph of Martin Puryear with two of his sculptures.*

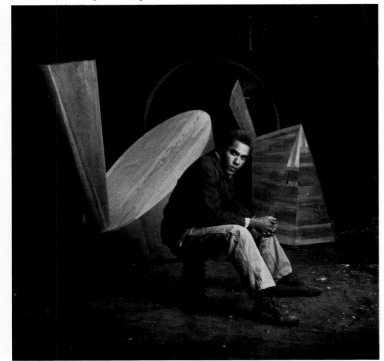

Martin Puryear's (b. 1941) sculptures of rings, arcs, and guardian-like shapes seem to pulsate and lock in soft rhythms. His feeling for public art is largely a response to his need to make art that people he grew up with can understand. His work, founded on Minimalism's economy of shape, form, and depersonalized surfaces, but unlike Minimal art, demands a relationship with the environment and firm connections with the artist. Puryear makes a clear distinction between his large-scale public work—the "amenities" he has designed, for instance, a fountain, benches, and pavilions for a garden plaza in Maryland—and sculptures made for the individual. Regarded by many as a key figure in contemporary sculpture, Puryear may be a significant bridge between the 1960s and 1980s, combining the traditions of handwork with natural materials and collaboration in site sculptures. His art is grounded in respect for craft, fierce pride in himself, and a commitment to the expressive potential of the sculptural language [513].

Light Art

Obviously, light is involved in all art. But in recent years artists have become aware of the potential of light itself as a theme [95]. Light has become a recognized medium since the late 1960s, and light artists use their material with the same skill that other artists apply to color and paint.

Thomas Wilfred (1889–1965) was one of the first artists to conceive of light as an independent aesthetic experience. His experiments in the early part of this century led to the development of the *Clavilux Lumia,* an instrument on which he performed publicly as early as 1922. From the spectator's viewpoint, the *Lumia Suite* presents a continuously changing pattern of fading and regenerating colored light, which produces a hypnotic effect similar to that of some Color-Field and Optical paintings—an effect difficult to photograph.

One of the most innovative light artists working today is West German-born Otto Piene (b. 1928), who created a light ballet that toured Europe in 1961. Piene has designed light installations of thousands of individual bulbs programmed to coordinate with activity onstage. Many light artists combine light and motion, and some have used light along with water to create moving compositions that delight the eye with artificially lighted waterfalls and fountains and gratify the ear with the sound of rushing water. Such experiences also defy photographic transcriptions. Larry Bell, whose work we have viewed, creates light environments in a world bounded by glass [222], and light artist Greek-born (Varda) Chryssa (b. 1933) combines theatrical skill with technical precision in blinking neon sculpture, enclosed in simple shapes. Her inventive work comments on today's industrialization, while at the same time it suggests the ever-expanding frontiers of science and technology. Like many of today's experimental artists, Chryssa has explored some aspects of environmental art by combining theatrical and technical elements in an aesthetically exciting spectacle. Her work is reminiscent of the glaringly lighted environment of Times Square in New York City [514] or the Strip in Las Vegas. For example, under the sponsorship of Intermedia 68 and the Museum of Modern Art, she created an electromagnetic environment in which vibrating color and light was designed to envelop the participants.

Realism

Realism has been a strong current in American art since the 18th century. Even during the great enthusiasm for Abstract Expressionism, when it was almost impossible for realistic painters to find galleries in which to exhibit their work, painters such as Andrew Wyeth (b. 1917) continued to paint recognizable people and objects, as he and others have kept on doing since then.

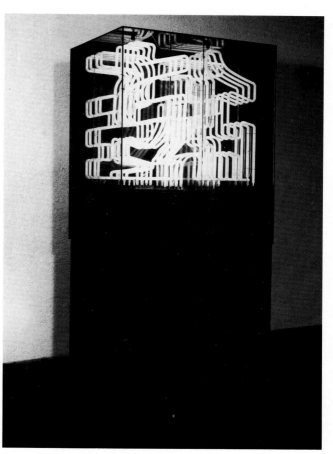

514. *Chryssa.* Fragments for the "Gates to Times Square." *1966. Neon and plexiglass, 6′9″ × 2′10½″ × 2′3½″ (2.06 × 0.88 × 0.7 m). Whitney Museum of American Art, New York (gift of Howard and Jean Lipman).*

Painting

Wyeth's approach to realism can be seen in *Christina's World* [107], a painting in which he illuminates the hardships and isolation of the handicapped. His precise tempera technique establishes a matter-of-fact world, yet he imbues his subject, a crippled girl, with pathos. However realistic the painting appears to be, Wyeth uses exaggerated perspective in the high horizon and the wide vista of the sky to increase the sense of distance between Christina and the house.

Magic Realism, or **Superrealism,** is a hyperrealistic style in which the painter exploits our camera-oriented responses but takes us beyond them. At first glance, an oil painting by Philip Pearlstein (b. 1924) may strike us as a mere copy of a photograph (an aid he never uses). His painting demonstrates in its light and shadow the harsh quality of a snapshot. But on deeper scrutiny we see that, with this kind of lighting,

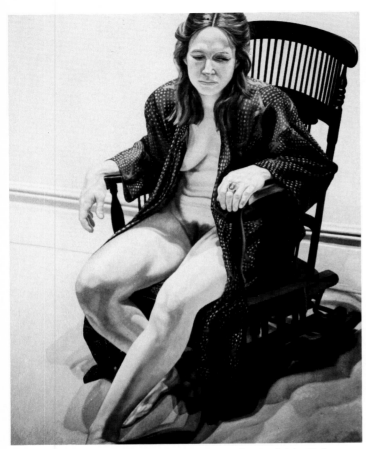

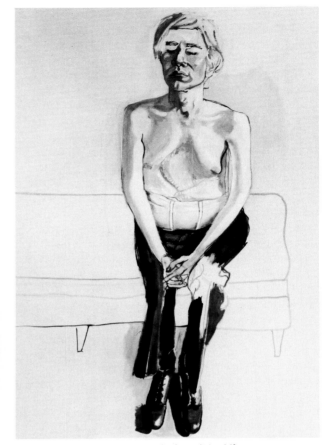

515. *Philip Pearlstein.* Female Model in Robe Seated on Platform Rocker. *1973. Oil on canvas, 6 × 5′ (1.83 × 1.52 m). San Antonio (Texas) Museum Association (purchase). Courtesy Hirschl and Adler Modern.*

516. *Alice Neel.* Andy Warhol. *1970. Oil on canvas, 60 × 40″ (152.4 × 101.6 cm). Whitney Museum of American Art, New York (gift of Timothy Collins, 1980).*

Pearlstein achieves a sharper, heightened reality, which emphasizes certain features of the model to produce a desired emotional effect, usually a rather heavy, melancholy mood, heightened by the downward glance of the eyes and the drooping hand [**515**].

Also working with traditional materials and techniques was the unconventional Alice Neel (1900–1984), an outspoken Feminist who was probably best known for her portraits. Her paintings on the theme of mother and child are incisive, sometimes shocking, transcriptions of her subjects, devoid of any sentimentality. Neel's self-portrait shows her in a rocking chair, naked but for her glasses, but her portrait of Andy Warhol [**516**] is even more revealing.

Photography, especially the Polaroid camera, has become the realist artist's ultimate research tool. Photographed sketches, often with the aid

of the airbrush, originally a tool for commercial illustration, are translated into **Photo Realist** paintings. Richard Estes' (b. 1936) camera provides detailed images of urban environments, which he then painstakingly reproduces with oils on masonite. Like Edward Hopper, he is more concerned with physical evidences of our society than with the people who created it. His particular interest in recent years has been scenes of storefronts, in which he carefully lays complex street reflections over detailed, meticulously rendered shop-window displays.

In the hands of an expert such as Audrey Flack (b. 1931), the airbrush can simulate fine (photographic) detail, making a painting almost indistinguishable from camera art. In her travels through Spain, Flack came upon a life-size Baroque terracotta and wood sculpture made in the 17th century by Luisa Roldán. Flack's oil painting of the Roldán *Macareña* is a tribute to the unrecognized genius of the Baroque sculptor as well as to her own skill [517].

A pioneer among artists who use photographs as a source of imagery, Chuck Close (b. 1940) is noted for huge, photographically precise portraits. From a distance, they seem monumentally scaled blowups of the original photographs he has used as references. At closer range, they assume alter-identities as fields of dots, brush marks, or fingerprints. Confronting his portraits is a direct experience. Of vast scale and sober countenance, they have fixed, hypnotic stares that are riveting. Recently he has turned to six-panel photographic montages produced only from Polaroid prints [518].

Sculpture

A certain amount of American sculpture, like painting, is an effort to imitate reality. Somewhat conventional forms are created with unconventional materials, such as polyester reinforced with fiberglass and wood. Surfaces are dense and opaque, and the figures are often painted and slick. Occasionally, they are placed on real props, creating a juxtaposition of art ob-

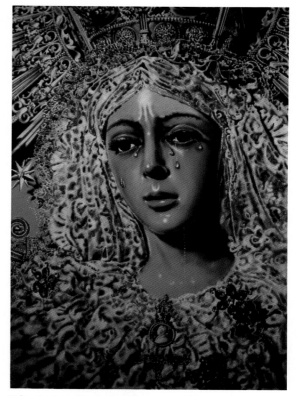

517. *Audrey Flack.* La Macarena Esperanza. *1971. Oil on canvas, 5′6″ × 3′10″ (1.68 × 1.17 m). The Oliver-Hoffmann Collection.*

518. *Chuck Close.* Self Portrait/Composite. *1980. Color Polaroid photographs; each 7′7″ × 3′8″ (2.16 × 1.13 m), assembled 14′2″ × 11′2½″ (4.32 × 3.42 m). Courtesy Pace Gallery, New York.*

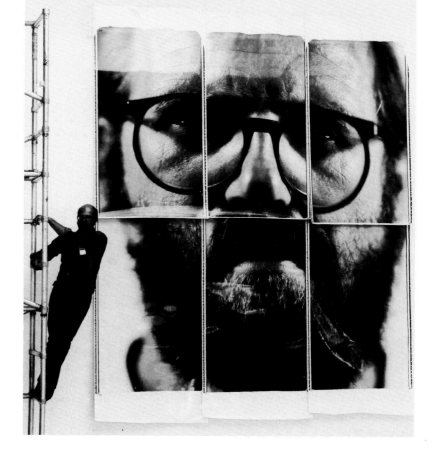

jects within real environments. Examples are George Segal's early white plaster figures of ordinary people seated in real chairs or in a gas station [500]. Others of his sculptures are painted brilliant primary colors, with powerful results.

By contrast, Duane Hanson, (b. 1925), a sculptor who feigns reality with polyresins and synthetics, cultivates the banal. His groupings are so lifelike that visitors who see them in museums are uncertain which figures in the crowd are Hanson's and which are alive. Avoiding most stereotypes of beauty, Hanson's overweight, middle-class subjects are placed in situations such as a bus stop or a fast-food restaurant [220].

Sculptors who have taken age-old traditions in ceramics and have redefined materials and processes include Peter Voulkous (b. 1924) [204], whose stoneware pots express remarkable innovation yet maintain connections to the past. In like vein, Robert Arneson (b. 1930) reaches to the past for inspiration, but with stronger affinity with Marisol [201] than with the classic commemorative sculpture he parodies. At the same time Arneson scorns tradition in pinpointing the feet of clay of our heroes or—in this case—the itchy clay shoulder of Picasso [203].

Graphics

Throughout the 1970s, the thrust of printmaking was somewhat conservative. The return to expressionism in paint was accompanied by a more personal, autographic mark in printmaking. In recent years, artists have been increasingly experimental in their approaches to printmaking, trying new methods and materials. The most notable manifestation of these changes is the growing popularity of the monotype—a unique image that utilizes a blending of inks unobtainable through direct work and also bearing a different relationship with the paper. Such works have an authority and presence similar to that of a painting.

Recent developments must be seen in the light of the great changes in the graphic arts of the last few decades. The unprecedented vitality in the production of prints can be accounted for, in part, by the growing numbers of painters (and sculptors) enthusiastically joining the ranks of printmakers in all branches of the medium. The infatuation with advertising images, first perceived by Pop artists such as Richard Hamilton [497], who carefully chose and composed the materials of his montages, persisted through the 1970s.

Changes in size and format of printed works are as extreme as changes in imagery. The advent of large sheets of paper was simultaneous with increasing concern for the quality of paper. As the craft grew, artists inevitably were introduced into the papermaking process, such as Coco Gordon [132].

Some of the major printmakers have succeeded in producing wall prints that are not unlike architectonic paintings. Vito Acconci's (b. 1940) *Building-Blocks for a Doorway*, which is almost 8 feet (2.4 meters) square, is the ultimate in the public print, a print in a public site accessible to all. One of Acconci's major concerns in all his work—concept, sculpture, and now graphics—is the interaction of people with art. It is almost impossible to consider this print without physically reacting to at least the concept of passing through it. The arch connotes a passage to a new space, perhaps metaphysical, and so the print becomes architectonic, the most public evidence of the plastic arts [519].

In addition to those noted elsewhere, the list of artists making their work more accessible through the print medium reads like a Who's Who of a substantial part of the art world: Julian Schnabel, Alex Katz, Richard Diebenkorn, Robert Kushner, Jennifer Bartlett, Chuck Close, Jim Dine, Sam Francis, Mary Frank, Nancy Graves, David Hockney, Jasper Johns, Robert Motherwell, Philip Pearlstein, Judy Pfaff, Susan Rothenberg, Richard Serra, Joel Shapiro, James Turrell, and Frank Stella. Stella [486] has progressed from single-color lithographs to giant-scale mixed media prints of dazzling complexity that have, as is the case with other artists, like Eric Fischl, fed back into his paintings. In the print *Year of the Drowned Dog,* just as in his painting, Fischl disturbingly illumines the hidden life of suburbia by escorting us through twin vistas of loneliness and pleasure so that we become witnesses and perhaps even stimulated participants. In public, we look away. In private, we stare. These prints consist of a layering that forces the viewer, at his or her own will, to connect the segments in order to interpret them. The first is a beach panorama. The second is made of three separate smaller sheets that may be affixed to the center to overlap the panorama. No matter how the viewer arranges the layers, none of the figurative groups can relate to either of the others. When assembled as shown [520], *Year of the Drowned Dog* presents an arrangement of ambivalent ideas, as may char-

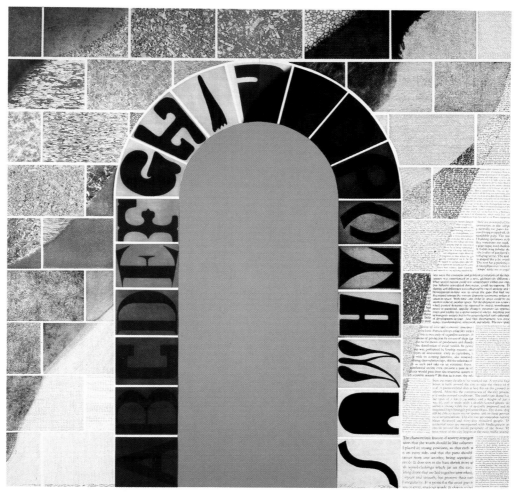

519. *Vito Acconci.* Building-Blocks for a Doorway. *1983–1985. Photo-etching, hard-ground etching, soft-ground etching, aquatint, edition of 8; 7'9⅞" × 7'10½" (2.38 × 2.40 m). © Graphicstudio, University of South Florida.*

520. *Eric Fischl.* Year of the Drowned Dog. *1983. Etching with aquatint and drypoint, six sheets of various sizes; overall 25 × 70" (63.5 × 177.8 cm). Brooklyn Museum, New York (Frank L. Babbott Fund).*

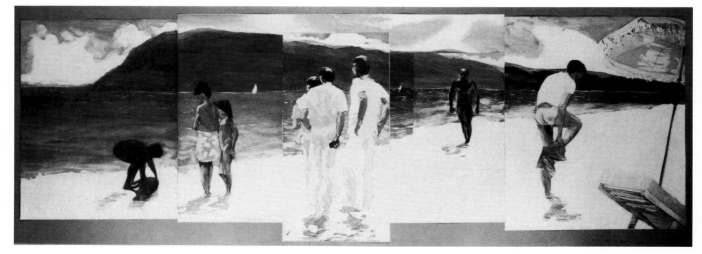

acterize all of Fischl's art. "One reason why they've become more fragmented," Fischl explains, "is that I no longer believe in the rectangular canvas, because it presents the world as holistic." The choice of segmented imagery is very much a feature of printmaking (and for that matter, painting and photography, as well) today.

While it seems a long way from the hand techniques of making fine prints to the industrial techniques of commercial reproduction, artists successfully use both. The fascination photocopying machinery holds for so many artists, perhaps beginning with Rauschenberg, has led them to investigate light-activated processes for multiplying their images. Ozalid, Cyanotype (blueprint), 3M, and the ultracomplex technology of Xerography are all being explored. Uncommonly handsome works in black and white and in color are being produced by **Xerography,** a medium that also permits the translation of solid objects into printed images. A pioneer in machine-involved art, Charlotte Brown uses a 3M color copier. Through an electrostatic technique she has developed, Brown transfers images chosen from textiles and printed papers onto hand-made paper, fabric, and clay, creating tapestry-like patterns. In her three-dimensional *Wildflower,* suspended from fabric-covered wood, she has combined floral prints onto squares, embellished with delicate clay blossoms [**521**]. Xerography offers implications for the future.

The computer, which has revolutionized so many spheres of activity, has formed a bond with art in the field of graphics. With a keyboard or electronic tablet, an artist can form a pattern on a screen, enlarging or contracting the whole design or sections of it as desired. The effect is described as drawing with electronic light on a display terminal, a possibility barely suggested by Picasso's early experiments with light [**95**].

Another way of displaying computer graphics is through a plotter on paper. By suitable programming techniques, an artist can easily draw directly all the effects created on a display unit. Artistic forms can also be developed by high-speed, computer-programmed printing and spacing of characters. Whatever method is used, the performance of the computer depends solely on the instructions of the artist. With AARON, a computer designed and programmed by Harold Cohen (b. 1928), a stylus moves up, down, and across a 22-by-30-inch (56-by-76-centimeter) sheet. Shapes appear that suggest spatial inhabitants of a future world [**522**].

Touching base with science, creative art, and Eastern philosophy is Duane Michael Palyka, computer scientist and senior artist at the Computer Graphic Laboratory of New York Institute of Technology. Palyka has explored the differences in thought processes of "the artistic state of mind" versus "the computer state of mind,"

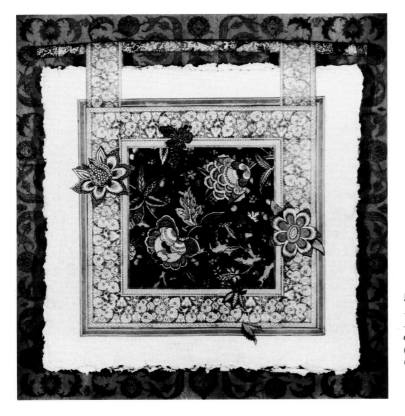

521. *Charlotte Brown.* Wildflower. *1982. Xerography; chine collé 3M process on handmade paper and wood, 41 × 45 × 5" (107 × 114 × 13 cm). Collection the artist.*

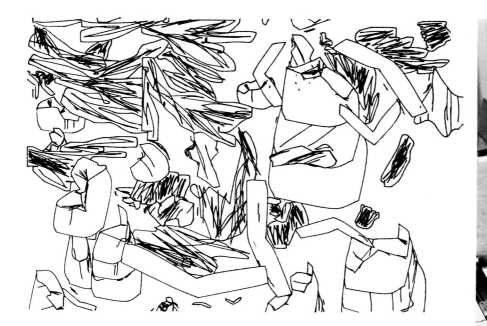

522. *Above Left: a drawing produced by AARON, a computer built by the artist Harold Cohen. 1982. Right: Harold Cohen and a computer-driven machine of his own design producing a drawing generated by his program. 1982.*

while creating computer art that can truly be considered fine art. With his own software program, requiring complex mathematics, he was able to generate female forms that with their richly colored and textured surfaces suggest a brilliant future world. The "stretched" form of the figures, a feature only possible to achieve with computers, fully utilizes (and reveals) its computer origins, qualifying *Picasso 2*, with its dynamic movement, color, line, and futuristic human forms, as a contemporary statement likely to stand the test of time [**523**].

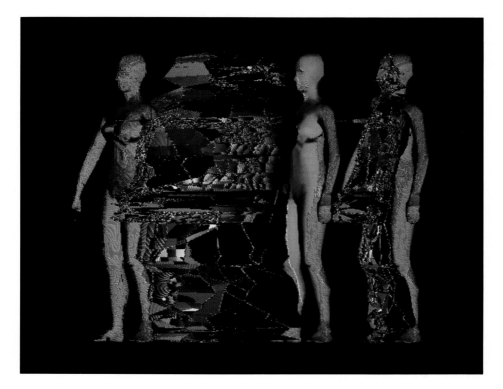

523. *Duane Palyka. Picasso 2. 1979. Computer painting. New York Institute of Technology.*

Expressionism

Neo-Expressionism

Neo-Expressionism or New Figuration is scarcely a decade old, yet seems to have achieved mature status, perhaps because the prices commanded by many of the young practitioners of art are immense. These artists rebelled against the prevailing nonfigurative, minimalist art, assuming a new intensity in gesture, color palette, and scale that the critics dubbed Neo-Expressionism—a movement that has become worldwide.

Back in 1973, the German-born Anselm Kiefer (b. 1945), then in his late twenties, as a student of Joseph Beuys at Düsseldorf Academy in the early 1970s, had already produced Expressionistic paintings that were astonishing to an art world familiar with Minimalism. The thunderous beauty of Kiefer's current works, in the opinion of many critics, marks him as the most remarkable artist to have emerged in Europe in the last quarter of this century. Apart from paint, his materials may include paper, staples, canvas, straw, oil, tar, feathers, and even

lead. And, like many artists of his generation, he has conjoined ancient myths to modern metaphors of good and evil. The tumultuous, cratered works, more than 10 feet (3 meters) high by 18 feet (5.5 meters) wide, unfold in cinematic progression. The viewer travels through them, exploring all the layers of meaning. Of *Osiris and Isis* [524] Kiefer states, "I see myths living, like the parts of Osiris gathered to make a new energy. The same process lives in nuclear fusion. I want to show something that was lost but is still here, transformed, today." He also makes books, which are marked by textured and blackened pages, soaked in oil and shellac, incorporating detailed charts painted over with acrylic and oil. The results are disturbing and haunting.

There is often a ferocious mockery of the purely aesthetic and a sense of rage in much of the work of these artists. Some of those feelings erupt in art of social conscience and others in sudden vulgarities, free re-use of historic works, contradictions, and pseudo contradictions. Among the American Neo-Expressionists, the controversial David Salle (b. 1952) embraces all the above, often expressing his feelings in the

524. *Anselm Kiefer.* Osiris and Isis. *1985–1987. Diptych, mixed media on canvas, 12'6" × 18'4" × 6⅓" (3.8 × 5.6 × .16 m). San Francisco Museum of Modern Art. Courtesy Marian Goodman Gallery.*

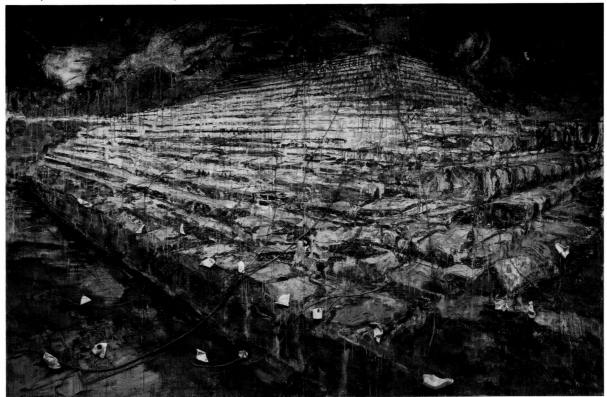

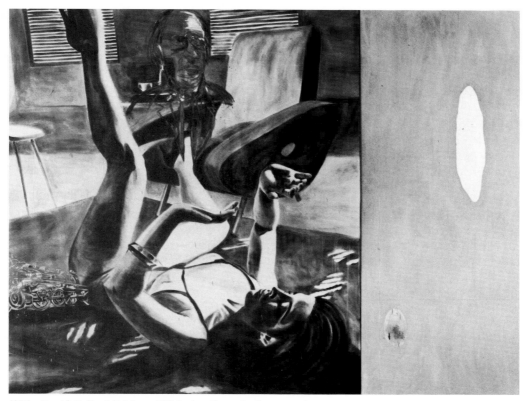

525. *David Salle.* Midday. *1984. Acrylic and oil on wood, 9'6" × 12'6" (2.9 × 3.8 m). The Saatchi Collection, London.*

segmented format that characterizes much contemporary art. Using a projector to trace his forms loosely onto the canvas, he thereby appropriates images from the past. He may also add non-art materials, such as a bra suspended from a dowel affixed to the canvas. Salle's Venus figures are clearly achieved from models posing for the artist, assuming unnatural and arduous poses, staged in quasi-pornographic set-ups designed to affront the viewer [525]. Unlike this clear reference to Caravaggio [367], many of his clues are oblique. Salle comments, "Connections that exist between things in the world, and . . . images in my pictures . . . are not random. . . . Not to perceive the difference I think could be very frustrating." Indeed, frustration is the response of many of Salle's critics, even those who acknowledge his many moments of stunning clarity and brilliance.

Protest art also exists in a humorous vein. A recent poster series was produced by the Guerrilla Girls, who claim to represent the "Conscience of the Art World." Since their formation in 1985, their black-and-white eye-catching posters have been targeted toward galleries they see as run by pricey dealers who rarely include women in their rosters. Anonymous, the women don gorilla masks in their midnight expeditions, plastering posters throughout New York City, especially lower Manhattan. Extending social awareness on the West Coast, Corita Kent's intense twenty-year crusade against war culminated in huge highway signs that exploited the media that she believed were exploiting us [13].

Photographic Arts

Like other arts, photography has been perceived as an arena for experiment, attracting painters like David Hockney [152] and sculptors like Lucas Samaras, as well as newcomers in art.

Still Photography

Photography has become accepted as an art form accorded the stature of the other fine arts by leading museums, critics, and collectors. As painters become fascinated with photography and some try to create imitation photographs on canvas, they cause an identity crisis for photographers. In reaction, some photographers tend more toward the combine paintings of Robert Rauschenberg [116] and his followers than toward the classicism of Edward Weston or Ansel Adams [143]. Many are interested in handwork on photographs. Others, however, make new use of ideas and techniques taken from the photographic past. After a quarter century of dependence on the 35-millimeter camera, many are returning to the large-format, tripod-mounted camera used by many early-20th-century photographers. Such developments may lead photography back to an era of careful preplanning, creativity, and control of scientific photographic techniques.

We have already observed Cindy Sherman's capacity for self-exploitation in images that seem to be taken from films of the 1950s but which actually express our fears in the 1980s [153]. We have seen the fragmentation of David Hockney's (b. 1937) vision, made whole in his mural-sized photo-mosaics [152]. The Starn brothers, like David Hockney, split and stretch their images to increase their impact [154], while others montage several views to form the segmented image we see in much art of the 1980s.

Film and Television

America dominates the cinema. Perhaps most important is the element of fantasy that films provide. Audiences can escape the everyday world through the fantasy of the classic romance or of science fiction, as in Stanley Kubrick's (b. 1928) *Dr. Strangelove* (1964), an omniscient reference to hypocrisy in high places, and his ground-breaking *2001: A Space Odyssey* (1968). Anticipation builds from the start of the title sequences, linked by designers to the film that follows. The brilliant sequences designed by Saul Bass for *Quest* [183] are a case in point. Bass in his own 1970s film *Why Man Creates*, a compendium of unusual animation and live photography, illumines the process of creativity, fundamental to all the arts and indeed to life itself. Designers like Bass and Steven Spielberg (b. 1947), with their technical wizardry, are changing the face of the films we see.

Tron (1982), which followed by more than a decade the revolutionary *2001*, is an electronic odyssey into tomorrow by Disney Studios, exploring special effects hitherto never seen by camera or eye [163]. More than half the film's 93 minutes of running time was generated by computers that simulate the impossible. Objects pass through one another, metamorphose from one thing to another, and appear to move with the speed of light, while live photography is daringly overlaid with electronic animation created without pen, pencil, or brush. The dramatic effects of machine-made worlds with limitless landscapes, sunsets, and moons offer a glimpse of what the computerized future holds in the arts.

Most conventional American films continue to provide escape through action and adventure. Although the American cinema is the freest in the world, and the vast sums involved in production have resulted in more specialized films by smaller film companies, the sky-rocketing costs of film-making allow less opportunity for experiment and risk today than in the film industry's infancy. The effect on cinema of television has already been felt. What changes cable television and cassette and disc recordings of motion pictures will make remain to be seen.

American film directors, however, have worked with originality and distinction. Alfred Hitchcock (1899–1980), creator of suspense films, earned increasing respect for achieving deeper intensity and increased control. Francis Ford Coppola (b. 1939) in *The Godfather* (1972) and its successors may be pointing out the all-too-frequent gulf between what we say and what we do in our sometime moral society. Other directors of the 1970s, such as Arthur Penn (b. 1922) of *Bonnie and Clyde*, Robert Altman (b. 1925) of *Butch Cassidy and the Sundance Kid* and *M*A*S*H*, Martin Scorsese (b. 1942) of *Taxi Driver*, and Michael Cimino (b. 1943) of *The Deer Hunter*, have made important statements about the value systems inherent in the periods explored in their films. The future of film, despite fewer pictures and smaller audiences, may lie with present-day directors who can survive the uncertainties of the art to create serious works that question our lives.

Television continues to play a large part in many people's lives. Over-the-air television generally serves a mass market, as we have noted. The increasing popularity of cable television makes possible a wider variety of programs and greater specialization.

Video

The incorporation of video into many other arts, such as sculpture, performance—to be discussed shortly—and earth installation projects, has been an important part of video art's history. Nam June Paik's extensive contribution to that history is a matter of record [161]. The connection and interface of video with computer art are logical in that both are electronic media and share in the manipulation of content and the formal joining of images through image processing and electronic editing. The relationship is even stronger with regard to animation, both two- and three-dimensional: arts that will surely expand as the century closes.

Many artists have both implicitly and explicitly rejected commercial television in videotapes that express a socio-cultural ideology. Martha Rosler's *If It's Too Bad to Be True, It Could Be DISINFORMATION* (1985) [526] uses the strategy of interfering electronically with network news reports recorded directly from television. Rosler's breakup of the images is her metaphor for the disinformation she believes intrudes through the media telecasts that are presented as objective reporting. Her videotape is a vivid testament to the impact and influence of the mass media, as Marshall McLuhan forewarned twenty years ago (Chapter 5).

Other video artists embrace the techniques of commercial television. Noting the impact of the choreographed multi-million-dollar Pepsi-Cola commercial made by Michael Jackson, it comes as no surprise that choreographed rock video has become one of the strongest emerging art forms, embodying surrealistic effects along with a variety of other special effects inherent only in the electronic media.

Holography

Holography, the most convincing method yet invented for creating three-dimensional photographic imagery, is little more than twenty years old, yet already scores of artists have produced a significant body of works. The principles underlying the art depend on the laser beam, a highly controllable source of coherent light. The holographic image, or hologram, is a three-dimensional picture that can be stored on glass plates, awaiting the proper light source to bring it out. The resulting image captures not only frontal views but several others, producing a volumetric result that is uncanny. While the technology dominates this art in which scale and coloration are unreal, holography forces the viewer to rethink reality and perception. Op artist Agam, well known for his relief constructions that reconfigure as the viewer passes by [487], is al-

526. *Martha Rosler,* If It's Too Bad to Be True, It Could Be DISINFORMATION. *1985. Videotape. Courtesy the artist.*

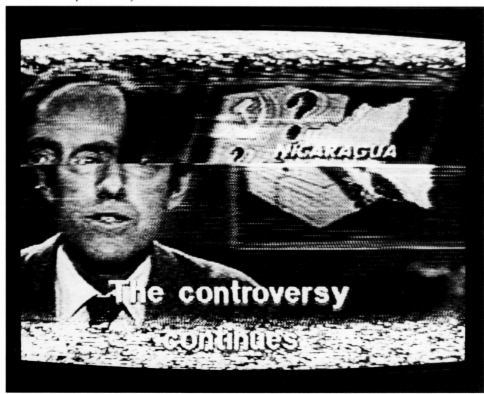

ready producing holograms that work well within his pre-established art aesthetic.

Conceptual and Performance Art

Conceptual Art

Over the last hundred years, struggling Western artists have gradually won release from many restraints society imposed on creativity. Impressionism in the 19th century and nonobjective art in the early 20th century were steps in this struggle. In the 1960s **Conceptual Art,** based on the premise that art may exist as ideas rather than as objects to be permanently displayed and evaluated, took a further step toward freeing the artist from any restrictions. Similar to a theatrical or musical performance, which leaves no art object after it is over, Conceptual Art may involve a process, but it rarely leaves material art objects. The idea itself or the process is sufficient reason for its being.

Vito Acconci, whose public print [519] relates to Conceptual Art by emphasizing the process, in this case, of passing through *Building-Blocks for a Doorway,* early in his career was inspired by a documentary television series on an American family. Creating a three-week series called *Following Pieces,* he chose a figure in the art world at random and followed the artist for a day. His written report of his findings, which he mailed to art critics, was the only record of his activity. In another event he persuaded a woman in a nearby room, through an electronic intercom, to wrap 50 yards (45.7 meters) of rope around her body until she was fully imprisoned. His goal through the years seems to have remained an interaction between subject and observer that focuses often on the process of making art.

Many Conceptual artists, influenced by views of the world provided by planes, spaceships, and satellites, create works that can be seen or photographed only from spatial vantage points. *The Lightning Field* [151] by Walter de Maria represents a work that seems to be best documented from a distant vantage point, perhaps at some elevation, during a lightning storm. Placing a label of Conceptual Art or Earth Art on the work is almost a matter of personal choice, as in his earlier huge drawing in the sand of the Mojave Desert, California. This work was eroded by winds within a month of its completion. The only record of the drawing is a photograph taken from a plane. De Maria's work echoes Indian sand paintings, which are destroyed at the end of the ceremony for which they were cre-ated. In our world of paper, plastics, and tapes, future archaeologists may find few evidences of permanence to illuminate our culture.

Endowed with a sense of the theatrical, the Bulgarian-born artist Christo (Christo Javacheff, b. 1935) selected an arena where art could happen within a specific time period of his own choosing. After twenty-eight months of planning and obtaining approvals and actual construction, on August 10, 1972, in Rifle, Colorado, at 11 A.M., a 200,000-square-foot (18,587-square-meter) curtain of woven nylon fabric of international orange was suspended across a 1250-foot (381-meter) valley between two mountains. This giant *Valley Curtain* [527] was hung from steel cables supported from concrete foundations deep within the mountains. The work confronts us with a paradox, as do so many Conceptual works and earthworks. It seemed to be functional but in fact served no practical purpose because it was translucent, allowing light to come through, and was hung to allow space for traffic to pass. More important, instead of acting like a theatrical curtain that unveiled or concealed a spectacle, Christo's curtain *was* the spectacle. In the same spirit, he wrapped 1 million square feet (92,937 square meters) of fabric and ropes around cliffs in Little Bay, Australia, and surrounded eleven islands of Florida with 6.5 million square feet (604,089 square meters) of floating pink fabric, as well as constructing a 24.5-mile (39-kilometer) cloth fence in California. Instead of making containers for works of art, he has made the packaging become art, while bringing attention to the site and the very process of making art.

Other forms of Conceptual Art are thinkworks and nihilworks. **Thinkworks** yield only information: The medium thus becomes the message. Joseph Kossuth (b. 1945), for example, imparts ideas by transferring a negative photostat of words such as *water* or *nothing* to canvas. He has said that "what is seen is the presentation of the information. The idea exists only as an invisible ethereal entity."

Nihilworks destroy themselves, like Tinguely's self-destructing machine [492]. At Alfred University, Robert Smithson [11] investigated accounts of the legendary lost continent of Atlantis and from his research roughly determined its imagined silhouette. He had students collect large, smooth, round rocks, which were positioned on a quicksand bed in the approximate shape of the continent. Slowly they sank out of sight. This type of art raises questions about permanence. Was the event still authentic art after

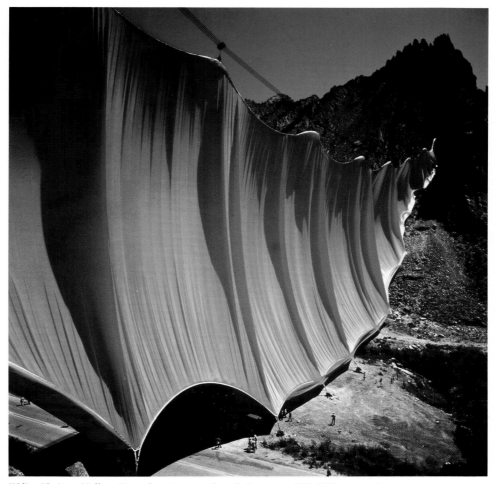

527. *Christo.* Valley Curtain: International Orange. *200,000 square feet; 110,000 pounds of cables; width 1250–1365' (381.25–416.32 m); height 185–365' (56.43–111.33 m).*

the stones were no longer visible? Can a work of art be justified if someone only remembers it? For example, did the possessions of an Egyptian pharaoh lose their value when they were buried in his tomb, to be concealed forever? Much of what has been going on in the art world in recent years raises such questions as these.

Performance Art

Many artists have found the written word as documentation of Conceptual art too confining and have broken free from all static forms, creating pieces in the temporal medium of Performance Art, with the artist himself or herself as subject. No one was more effective in this new process than Joseph Beuys (1921–1986). Shot down during World War II, he survived in blizzard-swept Crimea by having been wrapped in packings of animal grease to insulate him from

the cold. This experience was to permeate his work. His concerns were the continuity between art and life and the ever-changing nature of things. He never appeared in public without hat, ammunition jacket, jeans, and hunter's boots; he once lived in a tableau in the René Block Gallery in New York for three days with a live coyote and daily deliveries of the *Wall Street Journal.* That show was commemorated at the Hirshhorn Museum in Washington, including a yellowing stack of *Journals* and the artist's overcoat. There is no record of the coyote.

Environments

Earthworks

Art forms that involve some significant, often enduring, change in the natural environment are called **earthworks,** a term that may refer to alterations to the sea and sky as well. They are related to Conceptual Art, which is essentially an idea rather than an object, but are often more permanent.

Throughout history, artists have interacted with their environment; today the interest in large-scale art has reached a climax in earthworks. Artists such as Michael Heizer (b. 1944) and Robert Smithson (1938–1973) use the natural world itself as a medium. Like engineers, architects, or farmers, they want to change the face of the earth. They may dig trenches in a dry lake, redirect streams of water, pile up embankments of earth, or merely photograph natural geological sites. They seem to be protesting against artistic traditions and also human tampering with fragile ecosystems. Like happenings, many earthworks are too vast or too transient to be experienced permanently by many people, and they are limited by the economic resources needed to support them.

Smithson, a major innovator of earthworks, was interested in spirals, which he saw as moving from a path as close to us as our own cells out to the vastness of a spiraling nebula in space. In *Spiral Jetty* [11] he fused the concept of the spiral with his dedication to nature:

My works have been based on a dialogue between the outdoors and the indoors. . . . I'm not interested in reducing art to a set of ideas. I prefer making something physical, and the world is a part of the process. . . . Art will become less isolated and deal more in relationships with the outside world, out of the white room of the gallery into spaces that are natural.

An example of a more ephemeral earthwork, and thus one closer to Conceptual Art, is *Annual Rings,* executed by Dennis Oppenheim (b. 1938). It consisted of concentric rings the width of a snow shovel cleared on a section of the frozen St. John River at Fort Kent, Maine. Of course, this drawing in the snow could last only until the spring thaw.

Sculpture/Environments

In the 1970s and 1980s many artists have struggled to create alternate environments to the world produced by our mechanized civilization; in some ways, they have succeeded.

We might consider Walter de Maria's *The Lightning Field* [151] as an environment designed to celebrate both the awesome natural forces of atmospheric electricity and the human capacity for tapping that experience within limitless vistas, encircled by distant hills. Nancy Holt's *Stone Enclosure* [504], similarly, is a permanent outdoor installation that evokes Stonehenge [281]. The work appears to have always been there, poetically addressing the ephemeral: its lights and shadows gradually change with the movement of the earth in relationship to the sun. We are affected in a similar way by the work of James Turrell [192] and Alice Aycock [503].

Sculptor Charles Simonds (b. 1945) has constructed hundreds of tiny clay "dwellings" on such unexpected sites as an urban street corner or a vacant lot. Perhaps, in crafting these small clay structures that loosely resemble Pueblo Indian architecture [528], Simonds evolves in his

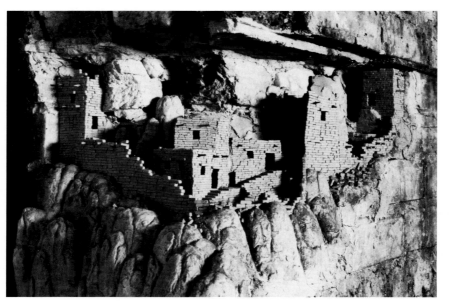

528. *Charles Simonds. Detail of* Dwelling, Chicago. *Clay, entire work 8 × 44' (2.44 × 13.41 m). Museum of Contemporary Art, Chicago (gift of Douglas and Carol Cohen).*

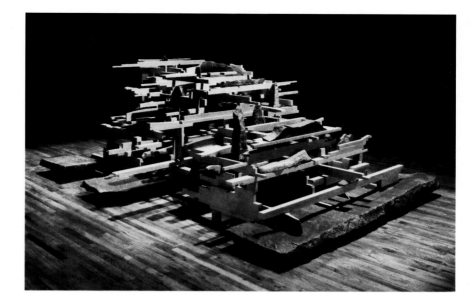

529. *Michael Singer.* Ritual Series/Syntax 1985. *c. 1985. Granite and fieldstones, 12' × 8'6" × 5'6" (3.66 × 2.59 × 1.68 m). Collection the artist.*

mind a mythical story of civilization on which we can focus, which we can contrast with the beginnings of today's society. Though his primal earthwork structures are very personal, Simonds reflects a style of primitivism common to many artists today.

Like other post-Minimalist sculptors, Michael Singer (b. 1945) began his career in the manner of earth artists within the shifting conditions of the oudoors. Relying on materials to dictate his abstract forms, Singer has assembled stones and wood beams of various lengths to form serene

structures. Yet, so fragile is their balance that the sculptures project mystery. Their mythic and symbolic importance appears inescapable, even reflecting the aura of a sacred shrine [529]. There are further ties to primal ritual as the viewer silently moves around the works, barefoot or wearing the filmy paper slippers prescribed by the artist.

In a related way, Nancy Graves (b. 1940) evokes early non-Western cultures with the sculptures and environments she creates [530], most of which embody natural and synthetic ele-

530. *Nancy Graves.* Variability and Repetition of Variable Forms. *1971. Steel, wax, marble dust, acrylic, plaster, gauze, latex, oil, 38 units; 9 × 15 × 35' (2.74 × 4.57 × 10.66 m). National Gallery of Canada, Ottawa.*

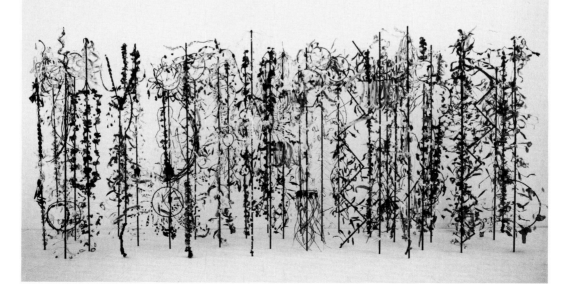

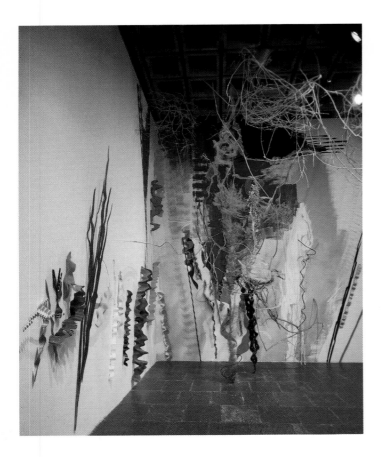

ments. As she mates organic shapes with a painter's vision in a trial-and-error approach, dominated by wit and sophistication, her work seems to compare the anxiety of modern times with primeval fears of the unknown.

Following a different road toward environments is Judy Pfaff (b. 1946), who creates on-site installations that democratically combine art and non-art junkyard and hardware store materials. London-born and American-trained, Pfaff works from a base of Abstract Expressionism, related to the work of her teacher, Al Held, at Yale. Entering a Pfaff installation is like entering a giant, gestural painting. Day-Glo-painted constructions appear to leap off the walls. In this controlled chaos, the effect is exuberant and even sensual [531].

Washington-based Sam Gilliam (b. 1933) develops works somewhat in the manner devised by Jackson Pollock. Having found Minimalism a sterile process, Gilliam became fascinated with the interrelationship of painting and sculpture and fused the two processes. He flings liquified acrylics onto stretched canvases that he later suspends (off their stretchers) from the ceiling [532]. Draped and swagged, these painted environments suggest variable landscapes.

531. *Judy Pfaff.* Dragons. *1981. Mixed media. Installation at Whitney Biennial.*

532. *Sam Gilliam.* Carousel Form II. *1969. Acrylic on canvas, 10 × 75′ (3.05 × 22.87 m). Installation view, Corcoran Gallery of Art, Washington. Courtesy the artist.*

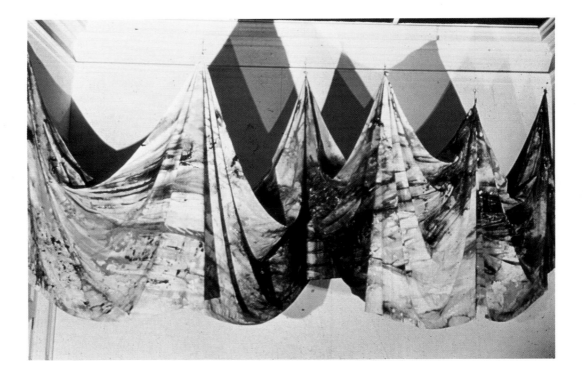

Red Grooms (b. 1937), whose print of Gertrude Stein [133] we have seen, fills entire rooms with cut-out figures and objects painted in brilliant, dissonant colors through which the visitor must pass. These "cities of the mind," as they have been described, are fun to play with. His energetic visions of Chicago or New York are of teeming places, alive with people, buildings, bridges, and even subways—all the razzmatazz of 42nd Street. His art is endearing and yet also a pointed comment on urban architecture.

Architecture

Central to the **International Style** that dominated the architecture of the middle 20th century was the belief that the architect could bring us Utopia, that properly designed buildings could influence social change. That principle pervaded the art of the Russian Revolution and of the Bauhaus designers both in Europe and later in the United States. It was fundamental to the city planning done by Le Corbusier, in Paris in 1920 and Chandigarh in the 1950s.

The principle has not, however, worked out as planned. The unadorned grid structure with curtain walls, first advanced in its newness and purity by Mies van der Rohe [242], was repeated all over the world during the building boom of the 1950s and 1960s. In the process it was debased into rubber-stamp construction, impersonal and lifeless. As Wright once said, "Doctors bury their mistakes, but architects can't." The architect Peter Blake (b. 1920) described the American scene in his book *Form Follows Fiasco* (1977):

All around the environment we have built over the past century or so, with supreme confidence, is literally collapsing: the walls of our buildings are crumbling . . . literally; the finest public housing projects to be found anywhere in the world, and designed according to the noblest precepts, are turning into enclaves of murder, rape, mugging, and dope addiction . . . literally. Something or somebody isn't quite up to snuff somewhere in the exalted regions of our architectural establishment.

Certainly the master builders of the 20th century whom we have studied so far—Gropius, Mies, Le Corbusier, Wright, Fuller, Saarinen, and Breuer—have made great contributions to their field. Others have also created outstanding works—Philip Johnson (b. 1906), mentioned in Chapter 9. I. M. Pei (b. 1917), Alvar Aalto (1898–1976), and Louis Kahn (1901–1974).

Pei, formerly a partner of Johnson, built such varied structures as the towering John Hancock Building in Boston [533] and the triangular East Wing of the National Gallery of Art in Washington. He has also designed a controversial addition to the Louvre museum in Paris—a pyramid-shaped, glass entrance structure located in the central courtyard.

Alvar Aalto, a Finnish architect, has been particularly esteemed because he evolved a rich, expressive style of understated humanism as opposed to the prevailing extremes of sterile, glass-box rationalism and curvilinear flamboyance. Each of his designs appears new, yet all share a spatial flow, are warmed by textural modifications, especially through the use of wood and brick, and are scaled to their human occupants. The concert hall of a cultural center in Helsinki, his last major work (1967–1971), is an irregularly shaped structure of white marble. The classically simple form of Finlandia Hall is an appropriate climax for a revolutionary archi-

533. *I. M. Pei and Partners. John Hancock Building, Boston. 1974.*

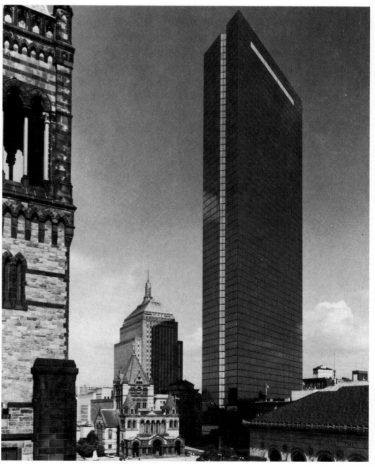

tect who was dedicated to humanizing the architecture of the 20th century [534].

Both the monuments of classical antiquity and the buildings of Le Corbusier were influences on Louis Kahn, who created some of the most fresh, most imaginative, yet timeless buildings of his era. The complex problems involved in designing an art museum—circulation, proper lighting, sufficient work and storage space, rooms for other events—were solved in a most effective way in Kahn's Kimbell Art Museum in Fort Worth, Texas [535]. In this celebrated building Kahn turned his attention to integrating the exterior into the environment and to creating a light-filled interior, at once monumental yet sensitive to the art it was built to house.

Post-Modernism

Post-Modernism refers primarily to post-Bauhaus architecture, although the term has sometimes been broadened to include painting and sculpture also. Its major exponent is Robert Venturi (b. 1925), whose *Complexities and Contradictions in Architecuture* of 1966, a witty but scholarly tract, attacked mainstream Modernism for the weaknesses we have cited. To Mies van der Rohe's comment, "less is more," Venturi retorted, "less is a bore."

Venturi's reactions to the 1950s "Glass Box" put the accent on decoration—much of it. With his wife Denise Scott Brown, a specialist in popular culture, Venturi wrote a second, even more critical, book entitled *Learning from Las Vegas*. The architect critic of the *New York Times*, Ada Louise Huxtable, joined others of the Modernist school in almost wholesale condemnation of Venturi, whom she termed the "guru of chaos," perhaps because of his free use of classical motifs in unclassical structures.

Philip Johnson, long considered the dean of American architects, praised Venturi, however, as a new voice and "leading theoretician of this country, if not the world." Johnson's own immense prestige persuaded conservative AT&T to invest more than 200 million dollars in a Post-Modern design that has become a symbol of revolt against mainstream Modernism, the company's headquarters in New York [536]. The dazzling compositional effects that Johnson and John Burgee planned were made possible by an internal structural "bridge" between the 80-foot (24-meter)-tall entry arch and the 647-foot (197-meter) tower, using architectural engineering principles that have become common in the last half-century. The colonnade of the entrance plaza, intended by Johnson to recall the epic grandeur of the Hypostyle Hall at Karnak [87], is considerably less successful because the site is very confined. No doubt the controversy over the unusual pedimented roof configuration will

534. *Alvar Aalto. Finlandia Hall, Helsinki, Finland. 1967–1971.*

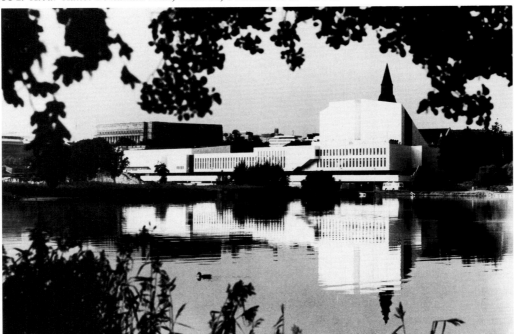

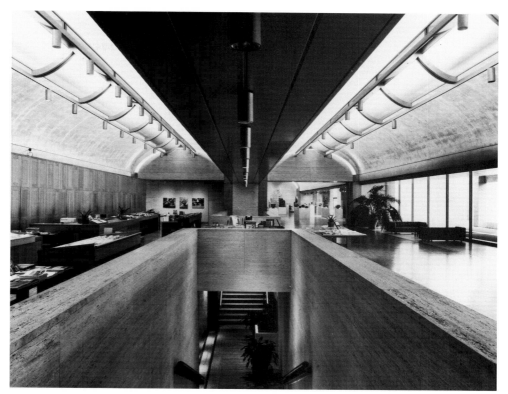

535. *Louis I. Kahn. Kimbell Art Museum, Fort Worth, Texas. 1972.*

subside as New York is refurbished with other structures, especially later Johnson and Burgee designs. Though its major critics have described the AT&T building as a "Chippendale highboy," it has also been praised for its pink granite surfaces and the three "oculi," or circular openings, that pierce the lateral walls of the plazas. Its design may portend the future.

Looking to the Future

Today it is more than ever apparent that avant-garde artists have lost their traditional power to shock even die-hard conservatives. In the last few decades such new trends as Optical Art, combine paintings, kinetic and light sculpture, Environmental Art, and Conceptual Art have exploded accepted ideas of what art should be. It is the very nature of the current scene that no single style or point of view predominates. If the categories of art, styles, and artists we have just surveyed seem overwhelming, perhaps it is because we live in a world of multiplicity, which the world of art often illumines.

We may observe certain trends. The popular taste for photographic verisimilitude is unparalleled in the modern period. Museums, galleries,

536. *Philip Johnson and John Burgee. AT&T Headquarters, New York. 1983–1984.*

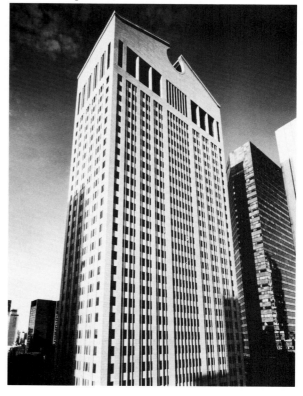

Exploring Art Through Technology

The Computer Bridge to the 21st Century

We live in a spectacular age of vast contrasts, with technology our surprising link to the distant past. Our tools have freed men and women from many of the humdrum details of survival. But the costs in our time have been staggering: the prospect of changing the face of our culture beyond recognition is sobering—dwindling resources and burgeoning wastes. Yet the cause of these problems may offer the promise of solutions. High technology may provide the best chance to strike a balance between nature and our ability to control its resources.

Tools have always been a bridge between humanity and nature, often serving as the clearest barometer of an age. The computer, like the telescope and the microscope in earlier eras, expands the range of our senses and our vision of the universe. Now, satellite communication enables us to see weather formations and patterns with unprecedented clarity. The nightly news provides us weather maps as easily as the sports scores.

Sensors scan many different regions of the electromagnetic spectrum to relay data back to earth, which artists convert to images. It may come as a surprise that computer visuals represent much of today's world, and though most of this reality-simulated art takes longer than a direct photograph to produce, computer efficiency will increase. Such images as *Picasso 2*, programmed over many months at the New York Institute of Technology by Duane Palyka, may one day be ranked with art masterpieces of all time [523].

In fact, computer graphics for fine art may be described as electronic painting! Many of these pictures are produced through the computer's reworking of images of artwork that already exist. By a process called scanning (or digitizing) that is similar to taking a picture of a picture, the colors or gradations of tones in a painting or a photograph are converted into a series of electronic signals by a camera connected to the computer. The resultant image appears on the computer's screen, but unlike the original art is now composed of thousands (or even millions) of tiny square elements known as pixels. Each pixel (picture element) is encoded into the computer's circuitry, and the whole computerized image is given a name by which it is filed into the "memory" storage of the computer, to be recalled on demand. The same digitizing camera can even work with a 3-dimensional subject, such as a human being staring into the lens, by mathematically converting the different tones of the forms into, as always, electronic signals.

Most computerized images are entirely created by a kind of electronic painting, either by personally programming a computer to shape the forms desired by an artist [523], using the procedures and language already built into the computer, or by making use of any of the hundreds of graphic "assists" provided by compatible pre-programmed software that can expand the capacity of the computer used [522]. Other graphics may evolve from combinations of scanned (digitized) images further enhanced by the electronic alterations and additions that the computer makes possible.

We may conclude that while the computer is characterized by sustained autonomous action, it is designed to extend the human brain and not to eliminate the human hand. When the computer removes human contact from the surrounding world, it violates an obvious, healthy division of labor. Let the computer continue to perform what it does well, that is, the processing of large amounts of information quickly, in the capacity of a logic machine. As artificial intelligence, the computer may aid travel to outer space, utilizing the computer's greatest potential, problem-solving, at phenomenal speeds. For the visual artist, let us begin as children to exploit the computer as a tool, then, as mature adults, continue to expand its potential. "The machine's automatism becomes the foundation for the greatest imaginative freedom of its operators."[1] Throughout the spectrum of human endeavor, the computer offers a contribution that can be directed to improve the quality of human life. In all the arts, but especially the visual arts, computers are tools that multiply our hands!

[1]J. David Bolter, *Turing's Man: Western Culture in the Computer Age* (Chapel Hill: University of North Carolina Press, 1984), p. 236.

and critics have begun to accept minority artists as professionals. In the 1980s, however, most artists have been creating as individuals, rather than as members of groups.

There was once a time when art was an important element of everyone's life, not just the artist's personal preoccupation. Today we realize that art can again become a part of everyday life, enhancing the buildings in which we live and work and even the highways on which we live and work and even the highways on which we drive. To bring art into our daily lives involves choice, commitment, and support—not only from the dedicated artists but also from citizens who care—those of us who appreciate the art in our world.

Coda

In summation, we have come to find that the artist is a creative being, with more than a small element of inspiration. We would wish the artist to be a model of free action, yet we often question those freedoms when the artist makes works that go beyond our comprehension. Perhaps, as Picasso once urged us, we need to accept art as it is and appreciate it "like the song of a bird."

The world is changing. With every passing day and increasing technology, we become more conscious of our need to live with nature as well. But, in one respect at least, art goes beyond nature to spring from ashes (death) like the mythical Phoenix (bird). The arts can reconstitute with a unity in new growth that is somehow compatible with the old.

Art springs from the human mind and spirit. It inevitably will be the human mind and its basic consciousness of high values and not high technology alone that will offer the final most promising solutions to our problems. The art in our world must stem from our basic human spirit.

Exercises and Activities

Research Exercises

1. Some artists use their art as the vehicle of social protest, while others are concerned only with form and style. Select examples of these two approaches from the artists discussed in this book, giving reasons for your choices. Is one approach more valid than the other?
2. Today the pace of change in every area of life has accelerated. How does art reflect that acceleration?
3. Light art, Conceptual Art, earthworks—all have their followings. Realistic painting also exists in the style of Magic Realism. Discuss two of these movements. What were their predecessors in earlier styles, if any? List prominent artists and their works.
4. The public usually has resisted the most pioneering artistic efforts. How do you account for the public mistrust and lack of interest in the works of experimental artists? In view of the general resistance to innovative art, how do you account for the popularity and acceptance of other new media, such as cinema, radio, and television?
5. The major architectural achievements of every civilization identify its primary concerns. Evaluate today's world on the basis of its major structures. How does our architecture suggest the directions in which we might continue to grow?

Studio Activities

1. Plan and outline a Conceptual artwork.
2. Many individual and regional styles exist in art today. No one style is dominant. Create an artwork in any medium, either based on a familiar style or in your own personal style.
3. Working within a segmented format, create a work that expresses an aspect of social concern that interests you.
4. Plan a configuration that echoes Jennifer Bartlett's *Rhapsody*, while dealing with a theme you favor, perhaps an illustrated calendar of your school's sports events.
5. Create a work that embodies written communication along with the visual imagery.

Glossary

abacus The slab that forms the upper part of the *capital* of a column.

ABC sculpture See *Minimal art.*

abstract art Art not primarily concerned with representation of nature; the artist selects and exaggerates certain aspects of reality in order to provide the essential qualities of a subject by means of *line, color, form, etc.* Inappropriately sometimes applied to nonrepresentational art.

Abstract Expressionism A painting style, also called the *New York School*, developed after World War II, combining spontaneous personal expression with abstracted or nonobjective shapes painted on large areas of canvas. The action of the artist in flinging, brushing, and dribbling the paint, using the large muscles of the body, led to the term *Action painting*. Jackson Pollock was an early Action painter.

Academy Derived from the Greek *Akademeia*, a grove where Plato lectured. The official school of art in France in the 18th century, which set forth rules dictating the style in which artists should work, controlling art by refusing to exhibit any work that did not follow these rules. The term "academic art" is now used to describe conservative art, adhering to traditional rules.

acropolis A Greek word meaning "hill town" or "fortified hill," applied to the upper section of a Greek city that usually contained the temples. The Acropolis at Athens is the best-known example.

acrylic paint A synthetic resin paint which, along with *polymer* paint, is frequently used by artists today in place of traditional *oil paint*. Quick-drying and durable, it can be used on a great variety of surfaces. Helen Frankenthaler and Morris Louis are painters who use acrylic paints.

Action painting See *Abstract Expressionism.*

additive primary colors Red (magenta), blue (cyan), and green—colors that produce white when projected onto a single area.

additive process Building up objects from plaster, clay, wood, or metal fragments, joined mechanically or by adhesives. See also *assemblage.*

adobe The clay used to make a kind of sun-dried brick of the same name; a building made of such brick.

aerial perspective See *atmospheric perspective.*

aesthetic Having to do with beauty or heightened sensory perception as opposed to usefulness or moral or emotional content.

afterimage The illusion of an *image* persisting after the original visual stimulus is removed.

airbrush A small precision spray gun, used to produce soft lines and fine graduations of paint.

aisle The portion of a church flanking the *nave*, separated from it by a row of columns or piers.

altarpiece A screen, a series of painted panels, or a sculpture placed on or behind the altar in a church. Usually decorated with religious subjects.

ambulatory The *apse* aisle of a church, such as the gallery aisle behind the altar.

analogous colors *Hues* that are close to each other on the *color wheel*, such as blue violet, blue, and blue-green.

Analytical Cubism See *Cubism.*

aperture In photography, the opening that admits light into the camera. The size of the aperture controls the amount of light that reaches the film.

apse The semicircular or polygonal area at the end of a building. First used in Roman *basilicas*, later copied by Christian church builders. The apse of a Gothic cathedral was roofed with complex *vaults* and often had small chapels opening off it.

aquatint A *print*, or an area in a print, which is textured by coating the metal plate, from which the print is made, with rosin dust. The plate is then heated and etched with acid, producing an allover textured tone. See *mezzotint.*

arabesque "Arabian-like." A flowing intricate pattern derived from stylized organic motifs, usually floral, often arranged in symmetrical designs; generally an Islamic decorative motif.

arcade A series of arches supported by *columns*, standing free or attached to a wall for decoration. First used by the Romans, later incorporated into Christian churches and *Renaissance* buildings.

arch A curved structural member that spans an opening; generally composed of wedge-shaped blocks (*voussoirs*) that transmit the downward pressures laterally. See *arcade, barrel vault.*

archaic The earliest period of Greek art from the 8th to the 6th centuries B.C. Also used to describe the beginning stages of art in any civilization.

architecture The art of building with solid materials, enclosing space in a useful and pleasing way.

architrave The lowest division of an *entablature*.

armature An internal metal or wood support for clay, plaster, or wax to be modeled into sculpture.

artist's proof The first *print* to be *pulled* that satisfies the artist's criteria.

Art Nouveau A style with decorative linear qualities that evolved from a 19th-century craft movement yet rejected all historical art connections in favor of new materials and technologies in building and decoration.

Ash Can school Early 20th-century American artists who produced realistic art concerned with unpretentious subject content.

assemblage A work of art composed of materials, objects, or parts originally intended for other purposes. See also *additive process*.

atelier A workshop or studio.

atmospheric perspective Also called *aerial perspective*. A method of creating an illusion of three-dimensional depth on a two-dimensional surface, using *color, light,* and *shade.* Objects painted in intense, warm colors with strong contrasts of dark and light appear close to the viewer. Light, cool colors with less contrast make objects appear farther away.

atrium The court of a Roman house, past the entrance and partly open to the sky.

avant garde Artists whose works incorporate the latest art trends, or may, indeed, inspire changes in the prevailing art styles.

balance The visual balancing of *colors,* shapes, or masses to create a sense of equilibrium.

baldacchino A canopy on columns frequently built over an altar.

balloon framing A lightweight wooden frame of milled lumber nailed together to support the walls, floors, and roof of a building. Developed during the 19th century and still used today.

baptistery A building used for baptism in the Christian church, usually circular or polygonal in shape. The baptistery in Florence, Italy, is a famous example.

Baroque A style of art in Europe during the 17th and early 18th centuries known for its dramatic light and shade, violent composition, and exaggerated emotion. Caravaggio was a Baroque painter.

barrel vault A roof over a square or rectangular area consisting of a continuous round arch of stone or brick that spans the space between the walls. Widely used in Romanesque churches.

base In architecture, the lowest part of a *column.* Made of stone in ancient temples, it protected the wood from the moist ground.

basilica A rectangular Roman assembly hall containing rows of *columns* that divided it into aisles, usually with a raised platform and semicircular area at one end. Early Christian churches were based on the basilica.

bas relevé See *relief sculpture.*

batik A method of producing a design or image on cloth. Wax is painted on the cloth, and the material is immersed in dye. When the wax is removed, the areas that had been covered by it retain the original color of the material.

battered Sloped, as in *battered* walls.

Bauhaus School of Design Founded in Germany by Walter Gropius, fostering learning by working with professional artisans, painters, designers, and architects.

bay A subdivision of interior space.

bearing wall The wall that supports a superstructure, such as a roof or an *entablature.*

beehive tomb A beehive-shaped type of underground tomb, constructed as a *corbelled vault.*

binder The material used in paint that causes *pigment* to adhere to the surface.

bisque Ceramics that have been fired at a low temperature, usually in preparation for receiving a *glaze.*

Boddhisattva In Buddhism, a being who is a potential Buddha.

bon à tirer The first print *pulled* that suits the artist for use as the standard for the rest of the *edition.*

bottega A shop; the studio shop of an Italian artist or craftsperson.

broken-color Application of pure tube colors onto a painting surface, intending the eye to mix the colors. See *Impressionism.*

Buddha Supreme enlightened being of Buddhism, an embodiment of divine wisdom and virtue.

buon fresco See *fresco.*

burin A pointed steel tool for engraving or incising.

buttress A solid *masonry* support, usually square, built against a wall to counteract the outward thrust of the wall and roof. Used extensively in *Romanesque* and *Gothic* churches, See also *flying buttress.*

Byzantine art Styles of painting, *design,* and *architecture* evolving from Byzantium, now Istanbul, involving round arches, massive *domes, mosaics,* stylized elongated figures, and rich use of color, especially gold.

cage construction Self-supporting steel frame used for skyscrapers and other many-storied structures. A system used by pioneer architect Louis Sullivan. See *steel cage.*

calligraphy The art of writing, or controlled, flowing *line* used in a decorative manner. Oriental characters that are written with a brush.

camera obscura A device developed during the *Renaissance* to project an image through a small hole onto a surface from which it could be traced. Forerunner of the modern camera.

campanile A bell tower, usually free-standing.

cancellation proof The proof of a *print* that is *pulled* after the block has been intentionally defaced by the artist, to verify the end of the *edition.*

cantilever A structural method in which beams or sections of a structure project beyond their support and are held in place by weight on the attached end.

capital The top part of a *column,* usually wider than the upright section, often carved. Different civilizations used a variety of decoration on capitals. See also *Greek orders.*

Carolingian style The era of Charlemagne, 8th–10th centuries. Devoted to restoration of Classical culture.

cartoon A drawing that is used as a guide for a large artwork, usually drawn the same size as the finished work. Also a humorous or satirical drawing.

carving A sculptural method in which the image is formed by removing material from a block, using sharpened tools. The opposite additive method builds up or adds material to create the sculpture.

caryatids Whole female sculptured figures supporting the roof of a building. The most famous are in the porch of the Erechtheum in Athens.

casting The process of pouring a liquid material into a *mold*, causing it to take the shape of the mold when it hardens. Used for metals, clay, and synthetic materials. An important method in metal sculpture.

catacombs A series of subterranean tunnels used for burial. Those in and around Rome were used by the early Christians for worship; they contain many paintings.

cella The main room in an ancient Greek temple, containing the ritual image of a god or goddess.

centering The method of supporting an arch in construction. Once the *keystone* is in place and the arch becomes self-supporting, the centering is removed.

ceramics Any object formed of clay, hardened by baking. Ceramic sculpture, pottery, tiles, and building materials may be built up by hand, formed on a *potter's wheel*, or in *molds*.

champlevé A style of *enamel* decoration in which areas to contain colors are dug away and bounded by ridges.

charcoal A drawing material made from charred wood. Used since prehistoric times for drawing on a variety of surfaces.

chasing A technique for decorating metal by engraving or gouging it.

chiaroscuro (kee-a-roh-skoo-roh) An Italian word meaning "light and dark." In painting and drawing, the use of gradations of light and dark areas to create the illusion of light and shade.

chine collé Printmaker's technique that includes collage elements upon which the etching is printed.

chinoiserie Chinese motifs used as decoration for furnishing, mainly during 18th-century Rococo.

choir That part of the church separated from the *nave* and altar, often designated for the singers and/or musicians during a religious service.

cinematography The art of expressing emotion or communicating meaning through moving images made with a motion-picture camera.

cire perdue See *lost wax* process.

Classical In general, the art of ancient Greece and Rome. In particular, the art of Greece of the 5th century B.C. It can also mean any art that is based on a carefully organized arrangement of parts, with special emphasis on balance and proportion. See *Neoclassicism*.

clerestory That part of a building that rises clear of adjoining roofs, and whose walls contain windows to light the central area below.

cloisonné An enameling technique in which color or design areas are separated by wire strands fused to the metal base.

cloister A court, usually with covered walks.

close-up Camera shot of subject at close range, framed tightly; E.C.U. if extreme close-up; M.C.U. if medium close-up.

codex Separate pages of vellum or parchment bound together at one side, having a cover.

coffer A sunken panel in a ceiling, often ornamented.

collage Generally two-dimensional works made of pasted paper pieces, cloth, or other materials.

collography A method of printing from a flat surface onto which a variety of materials has been attached. When damp paper is pressed against the surface, a print with indented areas is produced.

color What we perceive when our eyes sense the waves of visible light reflected from a surface. As the light hits the object, our eyes absorb certain colored rays, while others are reflected. These reflected rays cause us to see the hue of that wave, such as red, yellow, or blue. Color is also formed by coating a surface with a *pigment* that reflects certain rays. See also *spectrum, hue, value,* and *intensity.*

Color-Field painting A style of painting of the 1960s and 1970s, using large areas, or fields, of color to surround the viewer with a visual experience of color.

color wheel An arrangement of the *hues* of the *spectrum*, usually twelve. They are placed in a circular pattern, with *complementary* colors, such as yellow and violet, opposite each other.

column An upright, usually cylindrical, support for a roof or upper portion of a building. In *Classical* architecture it was made up of a *base,* a *shaft,* and a *capital,* and generally was made of stone. Today a column may be made of wood-reinforced concrete or metal.

combine art A combination of media, usually painting and diverse objects, such as an electric fan in *Pantomime* by Robert Rauschenberg. See also *assemblage.*

complementary colors The *hues* that appear opposite each other on the *color wheel,* such as orange and blue, red and green, yellow and violet. When mixed in equal amounts, these hues form neutral grays or browns.

composition The ordered grouping of *line, color, shape,* or *mass* in the visual arts. Composition implies an effort on the part of the artist to organize the parts into a whole, whether the result appears carefully organized or free and spontaneous.

computer graphics Images produced with computer assistance.

Conceptual Art A work of art or an event conceived in the mind of the artist, sometimes produced in visible form, but often merely presented as a concept.

Constructivism An art movement, overlapping *Cubism* and *De Stijl,* based on the use of nonobjective, often technological, shapes and new materials. In sculpture the artwork was constructed rather than being cast or modeled. Naum Gabo and Antoine Pevsner were the best known of the constructivist group.

content The theme, meaning, or story of a work of art communicated by its form.

contour The edge of a form or group of forms in painting or sculpture.

contrapposto The counter position of the upper and lower parts of the body, as when the weight is unevenly distributed in an active pose. The hips and shoulders are counterbalanced in nonparallel directions.

corbelled arch A method of spanning an opening by placing each stone or brick so that it projects slightly beyond the one below it.

Corinthian One of the Greek orders of temple architecture, which used slender columns topped by elaborate *capitals* decorated with carved leaves. Copied extensively in Roman and *Renaissance* times.

cornice The horizontal section crowning a *façade* or a roof.

crayon A stick of white or colored chalk with wax impregnated with a *binder*.

cross-hatching A system of lines drawn in close parallel order, crossed at an angle by other lines, which produce changes in tonality. Shading or volumes so indicated can be reproduced as *line art*, or a *linecut*.

cross vault See *groined vault*.

crossing The point of intersection where one passage crosses another, as when the transept crosses the *nave* of a church.

crypt A vaulted space, in *medieval* churches under the floor of an *apse*.

Cubism A style of painting developed in 1908 by Picasso and Braque, who built up *still lifes* and figures with cubelike shapes. Joined by other artists, the Cubists later depicted objects with flat, often transparent areas, frequently showing several views of the subject in one composition.

cuneiform A form of writing with wedge-shaped characters carved in stone or pressed into clay tablets. Used in ancient Assyria, Babylonia, and Persia.

curtain wall A non-load-bearing wall, also called a *screen* or *skin* wall.

cut-away Exterior view with one or more outside section(s) removed to expose internal structure.

Dada An early 20th-century anti-art movement ridiculing contemporary culture and conventional art. Many of its adherents later became *Surrealist* artists.

daguerreotype An early photograph in which the photographic image is fixed on a base (plate) of metal.

decorative arts See *functional art*.

De Stijl ("The Style") An art movement started in Holland during World War I, using nonobjective geometric shapes. Piet Mondrian introduced this style with Theo van Doesburg.

design The organization, structure, or *composition* of a work of art or object of use. *Industrial* or commercial *design* refers to the activity of planning and designing objects for factory production and commercial or individual use; *graphic design* applies to design for printing. Also used to describe the decoration applied to objects.

diptych A double-paneled altarpiece.

direct-metal sculpture Art constructed in metal, as contrasted with sculpture cast in metal or modeled in stone.

direct painting A painting method in which undiluted paint is applied directly to the canvas instead of being built up in layers of transparent *glazes*.

direct process In sculpture, the creation of the final work by removing wood or stone from the original block. See also *subtractive process*.

dissolve Cinematographic and television transition that permits one scene to be gradually replaced by another.

Divisionism See *Pointillism*.

dolmen An upright boulder.

dome A hemispherical roof supported on *columns* or walls. The Pantheon in Rome and the Church of Santa Sophia in Constantinople are famous domes.

Doric The oldest Greek order of temple building, in which the column has no *base*, is heavy, and is topped with a simple flat *capital*. The Parthenon in Athens is the best-known Doric temple.

drypoint A type of *printmaking* in which a sharp needle is used to cut a groove into the metal plate. The rough edge of the groove catches the ink, giving the printed line a soft edge.

dugento (duecento) The 1200s (13th century) of Italian art.

earth colors Paint *colors* derived from colored earth. Usually browns, reds, and yellows.

earthenware A type of rough *ceramic*, used for pottery and some sculpture, fired at a low temperature.

earthwork Sculpture involving the moving of earth in large amounts to shape it into an image or *composition*.

easel painting Any painting that is small enough to be painted on an artist's easel, as opposed to a large wall painting.

echinus In architecture, the convex element of a *capital* directly below the abacus.

eclectic A style of art, particularly of *architecture*, in which parts are chosen from earlier styles and combined into a new whole.

edition In *printmaking*, the number of prints taken from one block or plate, usually numbered consecutively.

elevation In drawing and architecture, a geometric projection of a building on a plane perpendicular to the horizon: a vertical projection.

embossing See *repoussé*.

emulsion A suspension, usually in a viscous vehicle—such as photographic silver salts in gelatin—coating plates, films, and so on.

enamel The method of applying ground glass to metal, fusing it with heat into a shiny, colored surface.

encaustic A method of painting with *pigments* in hot wax. Used by the Romans for funeral portraits in Fayum, Egypt, in the 2nd century A.D.

engaged column A column-like, nonfunctional form, projecting from a wall and articulating it visually.

engraving The process of making grooves in a material either to decorate it or to create an image from which prints can be made. Also the *print* that is made by pressing paper onto an inked wood or metal engraving.

entablature In *Classical* architecture, the horizontal section between the *columns* and the roof.

entasis In Greek architecture, the slight swelling of a column *shaft* to counteract the optical illusion that makes a series of vertical columns appear to curve inward.

Environmental Art Art that forms or represents a total visual environment, usually large, and frequently combining light and sound with paint and sculpture.

etching An *intaglio* printmaking process. An *image* (or area) applied to a metal plate that has been coated with a resist, thus removes the resist from those sections, allowing them to be exposed to acid. The resultant grooves can be inked and printed. The finished print is also called an *etching*.

Experiential Art Works that require audience participation.

Expressionism A style of art that developed at the beginning of the 20th century, dominated by German artists and emphasizing an artist's expression of personal emotion. Also applied to art of any period that is particularly concerned with the expression of group or individual emotion.

façade The front exterior of a building, usually containing the main entrance.

fade in, fade out Cinematographic and television procedure that defines the beginning and end of a screen event by gradually illuminating the scene from empty black screen up to full image and then back down to black screen.

fantasy Art that is irrational, mystic, or "make-believe."

Fauves See *Fauvism*.

Fauvism A style of painting in the early 20th century characterized by the use of large areas of brilliant, strong color, often with violent, distorted shapes. The name comes from the French word for "wild beasts." Henri Matisse and Georges Rouault were well-known Fauvist painters.

ferroconcrete A building material consisting of concrete with metal rods or mesh embedded in it. Also known as *reinforced concrete*.

fetish Art believed to have magical powers.

Field painting See *Color-Field painting*.

fin de siècle Characteristic of the ideas and customs of the last years of the 19th century.

fine arts Arts whose primary concern is *aesthetic*.

fisheye lens A lens used in photography to achieve a distorted image in which the central portion of a circular image is magnified.

flamboyant Flame-like as applied to aspects of Late Gothic Style, especially architectural tracery.

fluting Grooving, as in the shaft of a *column*.

flying buttress A *masonry* arch, or segment of an arch, used on *Gothic* churches to counteract the outward thrust of the *vault* of the *nave* by carrying the force to a vertical support away from the building, down to the ground.

focus A point of convergence or center of attention. In photography, the degree of sharpness of an image.

foreshortening A method of representing an object on a two-dimensional surface so that it appears to be projecting toward the viewer. Developed by *Renaissance* painters.

form In two-dimensional art, any defined area on a picture surface, flat or creating the illusion of solid, three-dimensional mass. In three-dimensional art, any solid part of the composition, or the overall shape of the composition.

formalism Art prescribed by rules of color, design, or other specific intent.

forum In the Roman world, the marketplace or public place of a city, the center of judicial business.

frame construction *Cage construction* in which all parts of a design support one another, as in a *skeleton* and *balloon frame*.

fresco A painting technique in which pigments are brushed onto wet plaster, drying to become part of the surface of the wall. Also called *buon fresco*.

fresco secco Fresco painting in which *pigments* mixed with a *binder* are applied to dried plaster. The result is less durable and brilliant than *buon fresco*.

frieze In *Classical* art, that portion of the *entablature* between the *architrave* and the *cornice*, usually decorated. Any horizontal area of decoration.

full round Sculpture in full and completely rounded form (not in relief).

functional art Any art that fills a utilitarian need and is aesthetically satisfying. Also called *decorative* and *minor arts*.

Futurism A style of painting and sculpture in the early 20th century that represented and interpreted modern machines, particularly those that moved. An attempt to represent movement and speed with nonmoving materials.

gable See *pediment*.

gallery The second story of an *ambulatory* or *aisle*.

gargoyle In architecture, a waterspout (usually carved), often in the form of a grotesque animal.

gates Vents or channels allowing air to escape in metal casting.

genre art The casual representation of everyday life and surroundings.

geodesic A structural system based on tetrahedrons; developed by Buckminster Fuller as an alternative to, and improvement on, cube structure. Used to create *domes*.

gesso A mixture of glue and chalk painted on panels or canvas as a base for *tempera* and other paints. It may be pure white or tinted.

glaze In painting, a thin, transparent coat of pigment. Traditionally used in *oil painting* since the 1500s; now possible with synthetic paints. In *ceramics*, a mixture of minerals painted onto clay that fuses into a glasslike substance when fired in a kiln.

Golden Section A ratio for determining pleasing proportions in art; the size of the smaller part relates to the size of the larger part as the larger part relates to the whole (a:b = b:a + b). Originally used by the Greeks, it was employed by *Renaissance* and later artists.

Gothic A style of architecture that spread throughout most of Europe between the 12th and 16th centuries. Characterized by an interlocking system of stone *arches*, *vaults*, and *buttresses* that carried the weight and thrust of the building, enabling buildings to reach great heights. Gothic cathedrals were constructed by communal efforts and expressed the religious faith of the time.

gouache (goo-ahsh) A form of watercolor paint in which the *pigments* are made opaque by binding with gum or glue, in contrast to pure *watercolor* paint, which is transparent.

graffiti Decoration produced by fine lines over a surface. Also, painted or drawn markings illegally applied to surfaces of public places. See also *sgraffito*.

graphic Descriptive of art involving line or flat tones. "Graphic art" usually refers to printed art, such as advertising, packaging, and editorial art.

graver A cutting tool used by engravers and sculptors.

gravure A form of commercial printing from an *etched* plate. The ink is transferred to the paper from the depressed areas of the plate, as opposed to *letterpress* printing, in which the raised areas of a plate transfer the ink to the paper.

Greek cross A cross in which all four arms are the same length.

Greek orders Three types of architectural structure developed by the Greeks: the Doric, Ionic, and Corinthian. Although the orders varied in proportion and decoration, they all consisted of a vertical *column*, *capitals*, and a horizontal *entablature* between the columns and the roof. Copied and changed by later architects, they have been used in various forms throughout Western *architecture*. See *Doric, Ionic,* and *Corinthian*.

greenware Clay objects that have been air dried and are ready for the first, low-temperature firing in a *kiln*.

grisaille A monochrome painting done mainly in neutral grays to simulate stone sculpture.

groin(ed) vault A structural method of roofing a square area. Two *barrel vaults* of the same dimensions intersect at right angles, producing edges called "groins." Introduced by the Romans and used by Romanesque church builders.

ground A preliminary base applied to a support in preparation for drawing or painting. *Gesso* is the usual prime. Also the preliminary coating—a waxy, acid-resistant substance—applied to a plate before *etching*.

halftone A metal plate used for reproducing illustrations in commercial printing. The image is photographed through a grid that breaks down the areas of tone into various-sized dots. The plate is *etched*, leaving the dots raised. When inked and run through a press, the plate transfers the *image* to paper with all the gradations of tone of the original image. Also refers to a reproduction printed from such a plate.

happening An event, generally unrehearsed and without predetermined script, produced by artists. It may include light, sound, props, and costumes and may involve audience participation.

Hard-Edge painting A mid-20th-century art style depicting geometric form, meticulously rendered.

Harlem Renaissance Black movement involving jazz, literature, and art which flourished in Harlem in New York City around 1930, and featured the black cultural heritage.

hatching A technique used in drawing, engraving, etc., in which almost parallel lines are drawn closer or further apart to achieve an effect of shading from dark to light.

haunch The part of an *arch* between the *springing* and the crown at which the lateral thrust is strongest.

haute couture Unique or limited editions of highly styled fashions designed for the trend-setters of society.

Hiberno-Saxon style Medieval style in which profuse geometric and animal forms are decoratively interlaced.

hieroglyphic System of writing using non-phonetic symbols or pictures, such as Egyptian written communication.

high key Area consisting primarily of pale or light *values*.

highlight The lightest area of an artwork. Usually refers to the spot where the brightest light is reflected from an object or figure.

holography The production of images using laser beams to record on a photographic plate a diffraction pattern from which a three-dimensional image can be seen or projected.

horizon line In *linear perspective*, the imaginary level toward which all the parallel lines receding into the picture seem to converge. Along the horizon line there may be several *vanishing points*.

horror vacui Fear of empty space; crowded design.

Hudson River School Romantic art movement initiated by Thomas Cole that concentrated its theme on regional landscape painting, often in the Hudson River area north of New York City.

hue An identifiable color on the *color wheel* or *spectrum*. Also, the element of a particular color that separates it from others.

humanities Branches of culture, especially the classics, as contrasted with science or religion.

icon An *image* of symbolic significance, often sacred.

iconography Visual *images*, conventions, and *symbols* used by a culture or religion.

idealization The representation in painting or sculpture of objects or figures in a simplified, perfected style, particularly characteristic of Greek sculpture of the 5th century B.C.

illuminated manuscript Any decorated manuscript, particularly those of the *medieval* period, in which religious scenes, daily life, animals, flowers, and humans were favorite subjects.

image A visual representation of an object, figure, or event in painting, sculpture, photography, or any visual art.

impasto Thickly applied paint.

impost Top section of a wall, serving as support for an *arch*.

Impressionism A style of painting developed in France in the last half of the 19th century that tried to capture the quality of light as it plays across landscapes and figures. Its followers used small strokes of contrasting color placed next to each other to create the illusion of vibrating light.

incising Cutting into a surface with a sharp instrument, especially on metal and pottery.

industrial design See *design*.

inlay Any material set into another material, particularly wood or metal set into the surface of an object to decorate it.

in situ In place, in original position.

intaglio A *printmaking* technique in which lines and areas to be printed are recessed below the plate surface. See *etching*.

intensity The degree of purity or brilliance of a *hue*. Also called *saturation*.

International Style Geometric architectural style, developed in Europe between 1910 and 1925 and relating to *De Stijl*; structural system emphasizing massive horizontals, based on functional design, devoid of ornament.

investiture The outer, fire-resistant *mold* used in the process of metal casting in sculpture.

Ionic One of the Greek styles of temple architecture; characterized by slender, fluted column shafts and capitals decorated with carved spiral shapes.

keystone The central wedge-shaped stone in an arch, the last one to be put in place. When the keystone is inserted, the temporary supports holding up the arch may be removed, and the pressure of the wedge-shaped stones against each other will hold the arch in place.

kiln An oven in which clay objects are baked to harden them. Simple outdoor kilns are fired with wood, while complex gas and electric kilns are capable of reaching extremely high temperatures under closely controlled conditions. Some large and complex Japanese kilns have traditionally been fired with wood.

kinetic Art that incorporates movement, usually motor-driven.

kinetic sculpture Sculpture that includes movement as part of the composition, whether provided by air, motors, or human muscles.

kiva A ceremonial American Indian structure, mainly subterranean.

kore Greek for "maiden." An archaic sculpture of a standing female, usually fully clothed.

kouros Greek for "youth." An archaic sculpture of a standing nude male.

krater (crater) Greek wide-mouthed bowl for mixing wine and water.

kylex (cylix) Greek drinking cup, shallow and having two handles and a stem.

lacquer A clear, hard-finish resin used to coat wood or metal. May also be mixed with *pigment* to give brilliant colors. Oriental artists used coats of lacquer over wood in furniture and sculpture as well as iron dishes.

laid paper Distinctly patterned paper made on a mold composed of intersecting wires of different weight. See also *wove paper*.

lantern In architecture, a small, often decorative structure, with openings to admit light, that crowns a *dome* or roof.

Latin cross A cross in which the vertical member is longer than the horizontal member.

lens The part of the camera that gathers and concentrates the light to produce an inverted image on light-sensitive film.

letterpress A method of printing in which the ink is transferred to the paper from raised type or from a raised image etched on a plate, as opposed to *gravure*, which uses grooves to hold and transfer the ink.

line A mark made by a moving point, pencil, brush, or pen. Also, the edge between two forms, or the silhouette edge of a form.

line art *Images* created by lines or dots.

linear perspective A method of determining or representing the size of objects as they recede in space. Imaginary parallel lines drawn at right angles to the viewer appear to converge at a *vanishing point* on the *horizontal line*. Widely used by painters during and after the *Renaissance* to create the illusion of space on a two-dimensional surface. Oriental art and much contemporary art may not be concerned with linear perspective.

linecut In printing, a metal plate used to reproduce images that consist only of lines or flat areas such as drawings, woodcuts, or architectural plans.

Linotype A machine that casts type for printing in the form of slugs of one-piece lines, already spaced for printing.

lintel A structure member that spans a rectangular opening between two posts, *columns*, or walls.

lithography A method of *printmaking* based on the antipathy of grease toward water. The image is drawn with a greasy crayon on a grainy plate or stone, which then is chemically treated so that it will accept the printing ink only where the crayon has

been used. The image is transferred under pressure from the stone to damp paper.

local color The natural color of the subject of an *image*.

logo (logotype) A design of two or more letters symbolizing a product, company, or an institution.

long shot Camera shot of distant subject, framed loosely; E.L.S. if very distant (extreme).

lost wax A method of casting in which wax is used to form the sculpture. Heat-resistant material is built up around the wax to form a *mold*. When this mold is baked, the wax runs out, leaving a hollow space that may be filled with molten metal to reproduce the original. Also called *cire perdue*.

low key Areas consisting primarily of dark values, as occur in night scenes.

Lung-Ch'uan ware (Longquan in Pinyin) A fine *porcelain* from southern China.

macramé A fiber technique, achieving form by knotting strands into patterns.

Magic Realism See *Photorealism*.

Mannerist A style of art in Western Europe in the 16th century that rejected the classic balance and moderation of *Renaissance* art and was characterized by exaggerated, distorted, and highly emotional images.

marquetry Complex designs of contrasting woods in furniture and floors. See also *parquetry*.

masonry Stone or brickwork used in building.

mass A three-dimensional form that has actual physical bulk. Also, the illusion of weight and bulk created on a two-dimensional surface.

mastaba Arabic term for "bench"; applied to earliest Egyptian burial monuments, from which the design of the great pyramids evolved.

matte (mat) In painting, pottery, photography, and other arts, dull finish.

mausoleum A large and elaborate tomb, usually for a person of great importance.

mechanical A pasted-down assembly of the parts of an advertisement or other pieces of art, ready for photographying to make a printing plate.

medieval Characteristic of the Middle Ages in Europe, between the 4th and late 15th centuries A.D.

medium The material, method, or techniques used by an artist to create a work of art. Also, the material used to dilute paint, such as water or turpentine.

medium shot The medium-range equivalent of a cinematographic *long shot*.

megalith A huge stone.

menhir A single large stone, usually set with others in formation.

Mesoamerica *Pre-Columbian* cultural region of Middle America, south of northern border of Mexico through Central America.

metope Square slab, often decorated with carving, alternating with triglyphs in a Doric *frieze*.

mezzotint A variant of *etching* and *engraving* in which large areas of the image are roughened to produce flat tones.

mihrab In the wall of a *mosque*, the niche that indicates the direction of Mecca.

minaret A tower outside a *mosque* from which Moslems are called to prayer.

Minimal art Painting and sculpture of the simplest contours, surfaces, and colors. The precision of

machining may dominate. *Primary, ABC, Systemic,* or *Minimal* sculptures are largely comprised of depersonalized geometric forms.

mixed media The use of several different materials, methods, or techniques in one work of art.

mobile A sculptural construction incorporating motion. The parts of the construction are moved by currents of air or by motors. See also *stabile*.

modeling In painting or drawing, the apparent shaping of a three-dimensional form by means of the gradations of light and shade reflected from its surface.

Modernism Early 20th-century American movement that rejected traditional art values in favor of radical new European styles.

module A unit that is standard in size and can be fitted into another, similar unit to form a larger composition. Used in building and in furniture.

mold The hollow form or cavity in which a liquid or pliable material is shaped or cast to create sculpture, jewelry, or *ceramics*. Also, the sieve through which the mash of fibers is poured in papermaking.

monochromatic A color scheme that uses only one hue in varying degrees of light and dark.

montage An arrangement of pictures, or parts of pictures, previously drawn, painted, or photographed. In cinematography, the splicing of several segments of film to expand or dramatize a single event.

mosaic A surface decoration made of small pieces of glass, tile, or stone set in plaster or mortar. Used widely throughout history for decorative floors and as wall decoration.

mosque A Moslem religious building, usually incorporating towers, pools, and fountains, as well as a central hall.

mural A wall painting, usually large, which may be painted with any kind of paint. Often confused with *fresco*, which refers only to a painting done on a wet plaster ground.

narthex Porch or vestibule of a church, generally colonnaded or arcaded and preceding the *nave*.

nave The central hall of a church. In *Gothic* cathedrals, the nave was much higher than the side aisles. Amiens cathedral has a well-known example of a Gothic nave.

negative space The background in a work of art; the space surrounding the main defined areas or *shapes*.

Neoclassical A style of art in the 18th century that revived much of the *Classical* art of Greece and Rome in painting, sculpture, and *architecture*. Many government buildings in Washington, such as the Lincoln Memorial, are Neoclassical.

New York School Artists in the New York area who shared a common center of artistic concern during the 1940s and 1950s.

niche A recess in a wall, usually containing a piece of sculpture.

nonobjectivism A style of art in which no object is represented. It became an important force in art in the early 20th century and continues to be so today. Piet Mondrian, Jackson Pollock, and Ad Reinhardt represent different types of nonobjective painters.

nonrepresentational art See *nonobjectivism*.

obelisk A tall, four-sided monument, sometimes covered with carved inscriptions.

objet d'art Object, figurine, etc., of aesthetic art value.

oculus Round central opening (eye) in a dome such as the Pantheon.

oeuvre The whole of an artist's output, the artist's work.

offset A method of printing in *lithography*. The image is transferred from a printing plate curved around a roller to another roller and then offset to paper. The printing plate is usually made by a photographic-chemical process.

oil painting A method of painting developed in the Renaissance in which *pigment* is combined with one of a number of oil mixtures. Applied to a surface, it dries to form a continuous film. Oil paint is still widely used today.

one-point perspective *Perspective* viewed from directly in front of a subject. Only one *vanishing point* is apparent.

Optical art Also called *Op art*. A style of art in the late 1960s and 1970s characterized by flat shapes of contrasting colors or values, placed next to each other to cause vibrations in the eye.

order See *Greek orders*.

Organic Architecture Building system developed by Frank Lloyd Wright, which satisfies in design the needs of the occupants in relationship to the site. Such constructions "grow" like living organisms.

pagoda Buddhist tower with many winged eaves, derived from Indian *stupas* and Chinese watch towers.

palette A range of colors; the surface on which an artist mixes paint.

palette knife Knife with a small, flexible wedge-shaped blade, used to mix colors on the palette; sometimes used to apply paint to an art work.

panning Moving the cinematographic camera horizontally to capture sequential views. See also *tilting*.

papyrus Plant native to Egypt used to make a paper-like writing surface.

parquetry Geometric designs of contrasting woods in furniture and floors. See also *marquetry*.

pastels Sticks of pure *pigment* with a minimum of gum *binder*. A favorite *medium* of the *Impressionists*, because of its freshness and brilliance.

patina The finish applied to a metal sculpture. Also the finish applied to wood sculpture and furniture.

pediment The triangular space forming a gable of a double-pitched roof.

pendentive A triangular construction serving to transfer weight from a *dome* to a *pier*.

perspective See *linear perspective* and *atmospheric perspective*.

photogram A photographic technique in which an object is placed on light-sensitive material and exposed.

photo montage Composite image made by assembling parts of two or more photographs.

Photo Realism An art style of the mid-20th century in which objects or people are depicted with hyper-photographic precision that invites comparison and contrast with reality.

pictograph Picture, usually stylized, that represents an idea.

pier A heavy *masonry* support, usually square.

Pietà Work of art depicting the Virgin Mary mourning over the body of Christ.

pigment A dry coloring material, made from a variety of organic or chemical substances, which is mixed with some form of liquid and a binding material to form paint, ink, crayons, or pastels.

pilaster A decorative, usually flat, non-weight-bearing column attached to a wall.

pile weave A form of weaving in which loops are left on the surface and are cut to form a soft texture. Often used in rugs and velvets.

pillar Weight-bearing member.

plain weave The simplest form of *weaving*, in which the *weft* passes over one *warp* thread and under the next. Broadcloth and burlap are examples.

plan In *architecture*, a view of the layout of space in a building, drawn as if looking down on it.

plane Any flat or level surface.

plastic Synthetic materials with varying qualities that are used in the *functional arts* as well as in painting and sculpture. Also used as a general term to describe any of the visual arts. Also, any material that has the characteristic of being easily formed or manipulated, such as clay.

Pointillism A technique of applying tiny dots of color to painting; especially referring to the work of Georges Seurat.

polymer See *acrylic paint.*

polyptych A multipaneled altar painting usually employing *tempera* on wood.

Pop Art A style of painting and sculpture in the 1950s and 1960s that used popular and commercial symbols and images as subject matter.

porcelain A form of thin, delicate *ceramic,* created from fine clays and baked at an extremely high temperature. The potters of the Orient have produced porcelain for centuries.

portico Entrance porch with roof supported by columns.

post and beam See *post and lintel.*

post and lintel A type of *frame construction* using two upright posts and one horizontal beam to span a space. Also called *post and beam.*

Post-Impressionists A group of artists active in the late 1800s who painted in varying personal styles that were outgrowths of *Impressionism.* Some, such as Van Gogh and Gauguin, were most interested in personal expression, whereas others, such as Cézanne, were more concerned with composition and structure.

Postpainterly Abstraction Art style developed in the mid-20th century in reaction against *Abstract Expressionism,* in which forms are meticulously depicted and separated; also known as "hard-edge painting." See also *Color-Field painting.*

potsherds (shards) Fragments of broken pottery that settle into geological strata, providing archaeological chronologies.

potter's wheel A circular metal, wood, or stone disk that revolves by foot or motor action on which a potter shapes wet clay into a vessel.

pottery The art of making utensils and vessels of clay. See *ceramics.*

Pre-Columbian art Art produced in North and South America before the European invasions of the 16th century.

prehistoric art Art created before written history: the only record of many early cultures. Cave paintings and rock paintings in Europe and Africa,

carved implements, and statuettes are examples of prehistoric art.

primary colors The *hues* that can be mixed to produce all other hues. In painting, the primary colors are red, yellow, and blue.

Primary sculpture See *Minimal art.*

print A multiple impression made from a wood block, a *lithographic* stone, or by *etching* a plate, screen, or other type of plate. Usually signed by the artist or under his or her direction.

printer's proofs Sample *prints* that guide the printing of a finished edition.

printing A method of producing *images*—verbal or pictorial—by transferring the ink on a master surface to another surface.

printmaking The process of making *prints,* generally done by the artist or under his or her careful supervision. Also called "graphics."

proportion The relationship of one part of a work of art to another and of each part to the whole. See *Golden Section.*

propylaea Gateway building leading to an open court.

psalter Book containing psalms.

pull To remove a *print* from the printing plate.

pylon Monumental pier, or entrance to an Egyptian temple.

quilted fabric A puffed fabric, in which ornamental stitching holds a stuffing in patterned shapes.

raku ware Rough, dark glazed ware, low-fired, as in Japanese raku ware.

raising Hammering a flat shape of metal into a hollow vessel.

rayograph See *photogram.*

ready-made *Dada* works that combined several manufactured objects into one construction. A method of working developed by Marcel Duchamp.

realism Mid-19th-century art style, developed by Gustave Courbet in opposition to contrived *Academic art.* Art style depicting subject matter, true to its appearance.

reinforced concrete See *ferroconcrete.*

relief sculpture Sculpture in which the three-dimensional forms are raised from a flat background, as contrasted to free-standing sculpture. The relief may be low, called bas-relevé, or high (haut-relevé), in which the forms are raised far above the background.

reliquary A small box, casket, or sculptural object that contains a religious relic.

Renaissance The period in Europe between the 14th and the 16th centuries; characterized by a rebirth of interest in *Classical* art and philosophy. A scientific attitude dominated, and art expressed balance, harmony, and the importance of individual humans.

repoussé A process, raising a *relief image,* usually metal, by pushing out areas from the back surface to the front. Also called *embossing.*

representational art Art that reproduces reality with little or no change or distortion.

rhythm Developing from the repetition, either regular or varied, of visual elements, such as *lines, shapes,* or *colors.* As in music, visual rhythm is an expressive tool, important in the creation of an aesthetically pleasing work of art. The repeated *pilasters* on the Colosseum in Rome are an example of rhythm in *architecture,* while the figures in Michelangelo's *Creation of Adam* show the use of a more subtle rhythm in painting.

rib vault A groin construction that follows the line of the arches and joints of the *vault.*

Rococo A style of art, popular during the 18th century, in which delicate colors, curving shapes, and sinuous lines created ornate decoration on interior surfaces, silverware, and furnishings. Paintings of the period were elegant and pleasant, reflecting the life of the aristocracy.

Romanesque A style of *architecture* and its art prevalent in Europe between the Roman and *Gothic* periods. Characterized by the round *arch,* heavy walls, and small windows, such as in Sant'Ambrogio.

Romantic movement A style of art lasting from the mid-1700s into the 19th century, emphasizing individual emotions expressed in a dramatic manner. Exotic subject matter and scenes of distant places were common. The movement rebelled against the established neoclassic art of the times.

rose or **wheel window** Large, circular window decorated with tracery that holds stained glass used in Gothic façades.

sacra conversazione Holy conversation, a group of holy figures seemingly engaged in conversation.

Salon Government-sponsored exhibition of artworks, held biennially, later annually, in Paris.

sans serif A letter, especially in printing, that has no cross strokes at top or bottom.

satin weave Weave in which the *weft* passes over several *warp* threads at a time, producing a lustrous surface.

saturation See *intensity.*

scale The size, or apparent size, of an object relative to other objects, people, or its environment. In architectural drawings, the ratio of the dimensions to the full-size building: for example, "one inch equals one foot."

scriptoria The rooms in *medieval* monasteries where manuscripts were copied and decorated.

secondary colors Three *hues* on the *color wheel* formed by mixing the *primary colors* to produce green, violet, and orange.

serif A fine line or cross stroke at the top or bottom of a letter.

serigraphy See *silkscreen.*

sfumato The hazy blending of light and dark tones in a painting, creating soft and indefinite edges.

sgraffito Decoration produced by scratching a surface of metal or plaster, often revealing a different colored ground.

shade A color that is low on the value scale; a dark color.

shaft In *architecture,* the upright portion of a *column,* usually cylindrical.

shape Any area defined by *line, color,* tones, or the edges of forms.

shards See *potsherds.*

silkscreen Also called *serigraphy.* A process of *printmaking* in which *stencils* are applied to silk that is firmly stretched across a frame. Paint is forced through the unblocked portions of the screen onto the paper or cloth beneath.

silverpoint A drawing technique in which a fine-pointed silver tool inscribes lines on paper coated with white or tinted *pigment.*

simultaneous contrast The contrast formed when *complementary colors* are placed side by side.

sinopia or *sinopie* Reddish-brown earth color; also the cartoon or underpainting for a fresco.

Siva (Shiva) Hindu god of creation and destruction.

skeleton frame See *frame construction.*

slip A creamlike mixture of clay and water, mainly used in *mold casting.*

soft sculpture Sculpture made with fabric forms or woven free-standing or hanging shapes. A technique used by *Pop artists* such as Claes Oldenburg.

solarization The reversal of gradations in a photographic image by intense or continued exposure to light.

spectrum A continuous sequence or range of colors, from the shortest (red) to the longest (violet) wavelengths.

springing The point at which the curve of an arch or a vault leaves the upright.

stabile Sculpture of flat (painted) construction, attached to the ground. Technique developed by Alexander Calder. See also *mobile.*

state Each reworking of a printing plate constitutes a new state or stage of development of a particular print.

steel cage Also called steel frame. A structural method in which steel supports, placed in a *post-and-lintel system,* are connected to produce a strong self-supporting framework. Nonsupporting walls, floors, and roof are attached to the frame. Used extensively in contemporary construction. See *cage construction.*

stele A free-standing upright stone or pillar, usually bearing an inscription or relief decoration. (Plural: stelae.)

stencil An image or design cut out of a stiff material. Paint is forced through the holes in the stencil to reproduce the cut image. Used for hand printing on cloth, paper, or walls, and in *silkscreen* printing.

still life A painting of ordinary objects such as bottles, flowers, or fruit. Also the arrangement from which such a painting or drawing is made.

stoneware A type of coarse *ceramics* fired at a high temperature.

storyboard A series of sketches (or photographs) of the key visualization points of an event that also include audio cues of sound, voice, and music, along with video cues of camera actions.

stupa The earliest type of Buddhist religious building, probably derived from the Indian funeral mound. Erected in places made sacred by a visit from the Buddha.

style The characteristic approach an artist takes to his or her theme. Also, those characteristics that identify a period, movement, or society.

subtractive primary colors Cyan (blue), magenta (red), and yellow, colors that produce black when white light is projected through them.

subtractive process Process through which form is created by removing, cutting away, or carving out unwanted materials. See also *direct process.*

successive contrast The appearance of a *complementary color* in neutral gray when the gray is placed next to a *primary color.*

Superrealism See *Photo Realism.*

Suprematism Geometric, nonrepresentational art style derived from *Cubism* by Kasimir Malevich in

1913 and defined by him as "the supremacy of pure feeling in creative art."

Surrealism A style of painting that developed in the early 20th century; based on subject matter from dreams, fantasy, and the subconscious. Its images often appear unrelated and startling. Max Ernst was a Surrealist painter. Many artists incorporate some Surrealist qualities into other styles.

symbol An image or sign that stands for something else, or the visible sign of something invisible.

symmetry Aesthetic balance achieved by distributing forms, shapes, colors, textures, etc., equally on both sides of a configuration.

Synthetic Cubism See *Cubism.*

Synthetism Gaugin's theory of art that involves broad areas of strident color and symbolic or primitive subject matter.

Systematic art Art based on a mathematical system of unit repeats that might be infinitely expanded. See *Minimal art.*

tapestry Tightly woven hangings, carrying patterns and *images.*

tapestry weave A weave in which the *weft* makes patterns only in specific design areas.

tempera A *medium,* binding *pigments* with egg yolk, gum, or casein. Egg tempera is usually applied to wood first coated with a *ground* of *gesso.*

terra cotta Hard-baked clay.

texture The tactile quality of a surface.

three-point perspective An extension of *linear perspective* in which three different *vanishing points,* widely separated, provide the effect of great depth.

thrust Outward force.

tie dye Process of hand-dyeing fabrics with ties and knots to create resist areas that will not absorb dyes.

tilting Moving the cinematographic camera vertically. See also *panning.*

Ting ware (Ding in Pinyin) Delicate creamy white *porcelain* from northern China. The *glaze* is transparent and almost colorless.

tint A light *hue,* or a *color* with a large amount of white mixed in it.

totem A symbolic *image,* usually defining blood lineage.

tracery Decorative stone openwork in the head of a Gothic window.

transept The space (axis) of a building that crosses another (usually the main axis) at right angles. Generally refers to a church or cathedral.

trecento The 1300s (14th century) of Italian art.

triglyph See *metope.*

trompe l'oeil The illusion of form, light, space, and texture, contrived so that the observer confuses the image for reality.

truss A framework of beams, bars, or rods arranged in triangles. Used to span the space between post or walls, supporting floors, or roofs. Triangular construction is more rigid than that using only right angles.

tusche A greasy black liquid used to paint images on a *lithographic* stone or plate in preparation for printing.

twill weave Weave in which *warp* and *weft* yarns are interlaced in broken diagonal patterns, as in gabardine and denim.

two-point perspective *Perspective* viewed when an object is observed from an angle. There are two *vanishing points.*

tympanum A recessed space, arched or triangular, spanning an arch or above a *lintel,* often decorated with sculpture.

typography The art of composing printed characters; a variety of typefaces of wood or metal have been designed since early Roman times.

unity The arrangement of a work in which all parts seem interrelated.

vacuum forming A method of shaping sheet plastic into sculpture. The plastic is heated and softened, then pulled against a mold by a vacuum machine, which causes the plastic to take the shape of the mold as it cools. An industrial technique adapted to art.

value The measure of lightness or darkness of a color or of tones.

vanishing point The point on the *horizon line* at which parallel lines appear to converge.

vantage point The position from which a viewer regards an object.

vault An arched covering spanning two walls, constructed of a series of continuous arches.

vehicle A liquid or emulsion used as a carrier of pigments in a paint; used interchangeably with the term *medium.*

verism Art style that includes the displeasing truth as well as the beauty of a subject.

video The visual aspect of the television medium; *videotape,* a prerecorded television presentation.

vignette Decorative elements that have no definite boundaries or frame.

visual arts Arts appealing to the optical sense— painting, drawing, *printmaking,* photography, sculpture, *architecture.*

volute Spiral or scroll-like form, as in an *Ionic capital.*

votive statue A statue dedicated to a god or goddess in fulfillment of a vow or promise. Many Greek statues were originally votive statues.

voussoir Wedge-shape block used in construction of a true arch.

warp The lengthwise threads in a loom—a machine for *weaving.* See also *weft.*

wash A thin, transparent layer of paint or ink. Wash drawings combine wash and *line.*

watercolor Any paint that uses water as a vehicle. Generally applied to paint formed of *pigments* mixed with a gum *binder* and diluted with water to form a transparent film, as opposed to *gouache,* which is opaque.

weaving The forming of fabrics by interlacing lengthwise threads (the *warp*) with crosswise threads (the *weft*).

weft The crosswise threads in a loom—a machine for *weaving.* Also called *woof* or *filling.* See also *warp.*

woodcut A *print* made from an image cut into a block of wood. The ink is transferred from the raised surfaces onto the paper.

woof See *weft.*

wove paper Smooth, virtually patternless paper made on a mold composed of fine, smoothly woven wires of even weight.

Xerography Late 20th-century art medium, utilizing a photocopy technique, in black, white, and color, derived from a process developed by the Xerox Corporation.

yakshi Female earth deity in Hindu and Buddhist pantheon.

zen Buddhist sect emphasizing enlightenment.

ziggurat Mesopotamian mountain dedicated to a god. Brick-surfaced pyramidal-shaped mound of rubble.

Bibliography and Suggested Readings

CHAPTER 1:
CREATION AND RESPONSE

Berenson, Bernard. *Aesthetics and History in the Visual Arts.* St. Clair Shores, MI: Scholarly Press, 1979.

Ehrenzweig, Anton. *The Hidden Order of Art.* Berkeley and Los Angeles: University of California Press, 1976. Interesting insights into the creative process and the psychology of the artist.

Elsen, Albert. *Purposes of Art,* 4th ed. New York: Holt, Rinehart and Winston, 1981. An engaging, personalized viewpoint, introducing art history in terms of the universal themes of the artist.

Fuller, Buckminster. *Ideas and Integrities.* Englewood Cliffs, NJ: Prentice-Hall, 1963. A leading and innovative architect of the last quarter-century shares his philosophy in easy-to-read terms.

Gombrich, E. H. *Art and Illusion,* 12th ed. London: Phaidon, 1972. Fascinating configurations that illustrate ambiguities in human perception.

Hauser, Arnold. *The Social History of Art.* 4 vols. New York: Vintage, 1957–1958. An important sociological approach to art history.

Samuels, Mike, and Nancy Samuels. *Seeing with the Mind's Eye: The History, Techniques and Uses of Visualization.* New York and Berkeley: Random House, Inc., and The Bookworks, 1975. Fresh approach to age-old beliefs.

CHAPTER 2:
EXPLORING THE ARTIST'S LANGUAGE

Albers, Josef. *Interaction of Color.* New Haven, CT: Yale University Press, 1975. A lifetime of devotion to color experiments discussed by the Bauhaus authority on color.

Bevlin, Marjorie Elliot. *Design Through Discovery,* 4th ed. New York: Holt, Rinehart and Winston, 1984. Excellent survey of design, with many fresh perspectives.

Birren, Faber. *Color and Human Response.* New York: Reinhold, 1974.

Itten, Johannes. *The Art of Color.* Trans. by Ernest Van Haagen. New York: Reinhold, 1973.

Judd, Deanne B., and Guner Wyscewski. *Color in Business, Science, and Industry,* 2d ed. New York: Wiley, 1975.

Kepes, Gyorgy. *Light Graphics.* New York: International Center of Photography, 1984. Pioneer Bauhaus artist presents his view of design.

CHAPTER 3:
DRAWING, PAINTING, AND MIXED MEDIA
Periodicals

Art in American

Art News

Arts Magazine

Chaet, Bernard. *An Artist's Notebook.* New York: Holt, Rinehart and Winston, 1979. Survey of drawing and painting techniques—traditional to contemporary.

Goldstein, Nathan. *Painting: Visual and Technical Fundamentals.* Englewood Cliffs, NJ: Prentice-Hall, 1979. Emphasis on traditional materials and techniques.

Mayer, Ralph. *The Artist's Handbook of Materials and Techniques,* 3d ed. New York: Viking, 1981. Complete survey of materials and techniques.

Mendelowitz, Daniel M. *A Guide to Drawing,* 4th ed. New York: Holt, Rinehart and Winston, 1988. Comprehensive yet compact drawing analyses with excellent illustrations—traditional to contemporary.

Read, Herbert. *A Concise History of Modern Painting.* New York: Praeger, 1985. Selective survey.

CHAPTER 4:
PRINTMAKING

Artist's Proof: The Annual of Prints and Printmaking. New York: Pratt Graphics Center and Barre Publishers. Annual review.

The Complete Woodcuts of Albrecht Dürer. New York: Dover, 1963. Works by one of the greatest printmakers of all time.

Heller, Jules. *Papermaking.* New York: Watson-Guptill, 1978.

Mayer, A. Hyatt. *Prints and People.* New York: Metropolitan Museum of Art (Dist. New York Graphic), 1980. Excellent analysis and survey.

Narazake, Munishige. *Japanese Printmaker: Essence and Evolution.* Palo Alto, CA: California Kodansha International, 1969. Works by major Oriental artists influencing the East.

Peterdi, Gabor. *Printing Methods Old and New.* New York: Macmillan, 1980. A pivotal 20th-century printmaker defines the art of prints.

Ross, John, and Clare Romano. *The Complete Printmaker.* New York: Free Press (Macmillan), 1972. One of the most up-to-date texts, incorporating all printmaking processes.

CHAPTER 5:
ART OF THE LENS

Feininger, Andreas. *The Complete Photographer.* Englewood Cliffs, NJ: Prentice-Hall, 1984. Successful teacher-photographer's text on know-how for the student.

Gernsheim, Helmut. *A Concise History of Photography.* New York: Dover, 1986. Full account of photographic history to the mid-20th century.

Halas, John. *Masters of Animation.* New York: Salem Press, 1987. Clear and well-organized text.

Karsh, Yousuf. *Karsh Portraits.* Toronto: University of Toronto Press, 1976. Gallery of famous subjects by the well-known photographer; biographical summary with each portrait.

Lyons, Nathan. *Photographers on Photography.* Englewood Cliffs, NJ: Prentice-Hall, 1966. Many of the major 20th-century photographers share their views.

MacDonnell, Kevin. *Eadweard Muybridge.* Boston: Little, Brown, 1972. Still views and multiple photographs.

McKowen, Clark, and Mel Byars. *It's Only a Movie.* Englewood Cliffs, NJ: Prentice-Hall, 1970.

Ross, R. J. *Television Film Engineering.* New York: Wiley, 1966. Lucid and well-organized text.

Souto, H. M. R. *Technique of the Motion Picture Camera.* New York: Hastings, 1967. Like the others of the series, this text is clear and complete.

Steichen, Edward. *A Life in Photography.* Garden City, NY: Doubleday, 1963. Magnificent illustrations include portraits of famous personalities, with Steichen's notes on each.

Swedlund, Charles. *Photography: A Handbook of History, Materials, and Processes,* 2nd ed. New York: Holt, Rinehart and Winston, 1981. Comprehensive text covering all aspects of photography, including 35 mm and other formats, developing, printing, special processes.

Wooley, A. E. *Photographic Lighting,* 2d ed. New York: Amphoto, 1971.

CHAPTER 6:
DESIGN IN PRINT
Periodicals

Advertising Age. Weekly newspaper for the trade.

Design Quarterly. Highlights of fine design.

Art Directors' Annual. New York: Watson-Guptill. The annual of advertising, editorial, television art and design, chosen by the Art Directors' Club of New York as the best work of the year.

Baker, Stephen. *Systematic Approaches to Creativity.* New York: McGraw-Hill, 1983. Excellent survey of the advertising art field.

Backus, William. *Advertising Graphics.* New York: Collier-Macmillan, 1986.

Cardamone, Tom. *Advertising Agency and Studio Skills,* 3rd ed. rev. and updated. New York: Watson-

Guptill, 1981. Guide to the preparation of art and mechanicals for reproduction by well-known illustrator.

Kleppner, Otto. *Advertising Procedure.* Englewood Cliffs, NJ: Garland, 1985. Leading reference for many years; voluminous survey of advertising.

Lister, Ron. *Designing Greeting Cards and Paper Products.* Englewood Cliffs, NJ: Prentice-Hall, 1984. A complete guide to cards, gift wraps, wallpaper.

Meilach, Donna Z. *Contemporary Batik and Tie-Dye.* New York: Crown, 1973.

CHAPTER 7:
THE SCULPTURAL ARTS

Itten, Johannes. *Design and Form.* New York: Reinhold, 1975. The foundation course of the Bauhaus school.

Kenny, John B. *Complete Book of Pottery Making.* New York: Chilton, 1976. Clear, comprehensive; leading text for decades.

Kepes, Gyorgy, ed. *The Nature and Art of Motion.* New York: Braziller, 1965.

Nelson, Glenn C. *Ceramics: A Potter's Handbook,* 5th ed. New York: Holt, Rinehart and Winston, 1984.

Read, Herbert. *A Concise History of Modern Sculpture.* New York: Praeger, 1964. A selected presentation in readable style.

Rottger, Ernest. *Creative Wood Design.* New York: Reinhold, 1961.

Seitz, William C. *The Art of Assemblage.* New York: Museum of Modern Art, 1961. The museum curator defines a popular medium at mid-century.

Wittkower, Rudolph. *Sculpture: Processes and Principles.* London: Allen Lane, 1977.

CHAPTER 8:
DESIGN FOR LIVING
Periodicals

Craft Horizons. Monthly periodical dealing with craft design.

Design Quarterly. Highlights of fine design.

Interiors. Furniture and interior design.

Vogue. Fashion magazine leader for decades.

Women's Wear Daily. A must for the fashion trade.

Bevlin, Marjorie. *Design Through Discovery,* 4th ed. New York: Holt, Rinehart and Winston, 1984.

Faulkner, Ray, Luann Nissen, and Sarah Faulkner. *Inside Today's Home,* 5th ed. New York: Holt, Rinehart and Winston, 1986.

Faulkner, Ray, Howard Smagula, and Edwin Ziegfeld. *Art Today,* 6th ed. New York: Holt, Rinehart and Winston, 1987.

Frings, Virginia. *Fashion: From Concept to Consumer.* Englewood Cliffs, NJ: Prentice-Hall, 1982.

Held, Shirley E. *Weaving: A Handbook for Fiber Craftsmen,* 2nd ed. New York: Holt, Rinehart and Winston, 1978.

Jackman, Dianne R., and Mary K. Dixon. *The Guide to Textiles for Interior Designers.* Winnipeg: Pequis Publications, 1984.

Joseph, Marjory L. *Essentials of Textiles,* 3rd ed. New York: Holt, Rinehart and Winston, 1984.

Murphy, Dennis Grant. *The Materials of Interior Design.* Burbank, CA: Stratford House Publishing Company, 1978.

Payne, Blanche. *History of Costume.* New York: Harper

& Row, 1965. A complete history from ancient times to the 20th century.

Quant, Mary. *Color by Quant.* New York: McGraw-Hill, 1985. Readable book by the British designer.

Rottger, Ernest. *Creative Wood Design.* New York: Reinhold, 1961.

Schiaparelli, Elsa. *Schiaparelli.* New York: Dutton, 1954. Autobiography by the grande dame of the fashion world.

Von Neuman, Robert. *Design and Creation of Jewelry.* Philadelphia: Chilton, 1962.

Zelanski, Paul, and Mary Pat Fisher. *Shaping Space.* New York: Holt, Rinehart and Winston, 1986. Fine text dealing with dynamics of three-dimensional design.

CHAPTER 9:
ARCHITECTURE AND ENVIRONMENTAL DESIGN
Periodicals
Arts and Architecture
Architectural Record
Progressive Architecture

Blake, Peter. *The Master Builders.* New York: Norton, 1976.

Conrads, Ulrich, ed. *Programs and Manifestoes on 20th-Century Architecture.* Cambridge, MA: M.I.T. Press, 1971.

Giedion, Siegfried. *Space, Time and Architecture,* 5th ed. Cambridge, MA: Harvard University Press, 1967.

Gropius, Walter. *The New Architecture and the Bauhaus.* Boston: Branford, 1965. Classic study by the founder of the Bauhaus.

Hamlin, Talbot. *Architecture Through the Ages.* New York: Putnam, 1953. Classic survey of architecture.

Halprin, Lawrence. *Citites.* New York: Reinhold, 1972.

Jacobs, Jane. *The Death and Life of American Cities.* New York: Random House, 1961. A controversial view of city planning.

Le Corbusier. *Towards a New Architecture.* New York: Dover, 1986. Leading 20th-century architect explores his philosophy.

————. *The Modular and Modulor.* Cambridge, MA: M.I.T. Press, 1980. An approach to architecture, based on a universal human scale.

Mumford, Lewis. *The City in History.* New York: Harcourt, 1968. Comprehensive survey of cities throughout history.

Neutra, Richard. *Survival Through Design.* New York: Oxford University Press, 1969.

Rudofsky, Bernard. *Prodigious Builders.* New York: Harcourt, 1979.

Wright, Frank Lloyd. *The Natural House.* New York: Horizon, 1958. Pioneer architect defines the organic system.

CHAPTER 10:
MAGIC AND RITUAL: PREHISTORY AND THE ANCIENT WORLD

Aldred, Cyril. *Egyptian Art.* New York: Thames & Hudson, 1985.

Childe, V. Gordon. *New Light on the Most Ancient East,* 4th ed. New York: Norton, 1969.

Frankfort, Henri. *Art and Architecture of the Ancient Orient.* Baltimore: Pelican-Penguin, 1977.

Guindoni, E. *Primitive Architecture.* New York: Abrams, 1978.

Laude, Jean. *The Arts of Black Africa.* Berkeley: University of California Press, 1971.

Lee, Sherman E. *A History of Far Eastern Art.* New York: Abrams, 1982. Comprehensive introductory survey of the scope of Oriental art.

Leroi-Gourhan, André. *Treasures of Prehistoric Art.* New York: Abrams, 1980.

Leuzinger, Elsy. *The Art of Black Africa.* New York: Rizzoli, 1979.

Rowland, Benjamin. *Art and Architecture of India.* Baltimore: Pelican-Penguin, 1971.

Sickman, Laurence, and Alexander Soper. *Art and Architecture of China.* Baltimore: Pelican-Penguin, 1971.

CHAPTER 11:
GODS AND HEROES: THE CLASSICAL WORLD; THE AMERICAS

Andreas, G. *The Art of Rome.* New York: Abrams, 1978.

Beazley, J. D. *Attic Red-Figured Vase Painters.* New York: Hacker, 1985.

Dinsmoor, W. B. *Architecture of Ancient Greece.* London: Batsford, 1973. The standard work on the subject brought up to date.

Lawrence, Arnold. *Greek Architecture.* Baltimore: Pelican-Penguin, 1954. A basic text.

Richter, Gisela. *Archaic Greek Art.* New York: Oxford University Press, 1949. Lucid, well-orgniazed, and illustrated. These texts and all others by Richter have remained valuable aids since publication of the first in 1929.

————. *A Handbook of Greek Art,* rev. ed. London: Phaidon, 1960.

————. *Sculpture and Sculptors of the Greeks.* New Haven, CT: Yale Universtiy Press, 1970.

Robertson, D. S. *A Handbook of Greek and Roman Architecture.* New York: Cambridge University Press, 1954.

CHAPTER 12:
FAITH: THE MIDDLE AGES

Beckwith, John. *Early Medieval Art.* New York: Thames & Hudson, 1985.

Boas, Franz. *Primitive Art.* New York: Peter Smith, 1962. Classic study of non-Western art; reissued and translated into English.

Dockstader, Frederick H. *Indian Art of the Americas.* New York: Museum of the American Indian, 1973. Comprehensive approach to American Indian art.

Graber, André. *Christian Iconography.* Princeton, NJ: Princeton University Press, 1980.

Panofsky, Erwin. *Abbot Suger on the Abbey Church of St. Denis and Its Art Treasures.* Princeton, NJ: Princeton University Press, 1946.

————. *Gothic Architecture and Scholasticism.* New York: Meridian, 1957.

Rice, David Talbot. *Art of the Byzantine Era.* New York: Praeger, 1963.

Swift, Emerson. *Hagia Sophia.* New York: Columbia University Press, 1940.

Wingert, Paul S. *Primitive Art.* New York: Oxford University Press, 1965. Pioneer scholar in African art surveys the field of African, American Indian, and Oceanic art.

Zarneki, George. *Art of the Medieval World.* New York: Abrams, 1976.

CHAPTER 13:
CROSSROADS: RENAISSANCE, BAROQUE, ROCOCO

Bazin, Germain. *Baroque and Rococo Art.* New York: Thames & Hudson, 1985. Good general text.

Berenson, Bernard. *Italian Painters of the Renaissance.* 2 vols. London: Phaidon, 1982. The long-established text on Italian painting (first published in 1952).

Kitson, Michael. *Rembrandt.* New York: Salem House, 1983.

Marle, Raimond van. *The Development of the Italian Schools of Painting.* 19 vols. New York: Hacker, 1971. Comprehensive treatment of the subject.

Milton, Henry. *Baroque and Rococo Architecture.* New York: Braziller, 1961. Clear introduction to the subject.

Pope-Hennessy, John. *The Study and Criticism of Italian Sculpture.* New York: Metropolitan Museum of Art, 1984. Good complete survey of sculpture of the Renaissance.

Portoghesi, Paolo. *The Rome of the Renaissance.* London: Phaidon, 1972. Brilliant study.

Rosenberg, Jakob, Seymour Silve, and E. H. Kuile. *Dutch Art and Architecture.* Baltimore: Penguin, 1972. Excellent regional study.

Rykwert, Joseph, ed. *Alberti's "De re Aedificatoris."* Ten Books on Architecture. London: Tiranti, 1955. Invaluable source book of the time.

Thompson, Daniel. *Cennino Cennini.* New York: Dover, 1954. Translation of Cennini's handbook for the craftsman-artist. Original document of the period.

Vasari, Giorgio. *The Lives of the Painters, Sculptors, and Architects.* New York: Biblio. Dist., 1980. Fascinating chronicle and source book.

Wittkower, Rudolph. *Architectural Principles in the Age of Humanism.* New York: Norton, 1971. Intriguing, scholarly exploration of harmonic ratios in music and architecture.

————. *Art and Architecture in Italy.* Baltimore: Penguin, 1958.

————. *Gian Lorenzo Bernini.* London: Phaidon, 1955. Penetrating specialized study of the exponent of Baroque sculpture and his age.

Wolfflin, Heinrich. *Principles of Art History.* 1932. Reprint. New York: Dover, n.d. Classic comparison of the Renaissance and the Baroque.

CHAPTER 14:
REVOLUTION AND THE MODERN WORLD: 1776–1900

Boime, A. *The Academy and French Painting in the 19th Century.* New York: Phaidon, 1970.

Canaday, John. *Mainstreams of Modern Art,* 2nd ed. New York: Holt, Rinehart and Winston, 1981. Fascinating personalized chronicle of the Romantic period through the 1920s.

Daval, J. L. *Photography: History of Art.* New York: Skira/Rizzoli, 1982.

Douglas, Frederick H., and René D'Harnoncourt. *Indian Art of the United States.* New York: Museum of Modern Art, 1970. Introduction to Indian Art.

Drucker, Philip. *Cultures of the North Pacific Coast.* New York: Harper & Row, 1965. Interesting presentation of Indian art with historical background.

Linton, Ralph, and Paul S. Wingert. *Arts of the South Seas.* 1946. Reprint. New York: Museum of Modern Art, 1972.

Rewald, John. *The History of Impressionism.* New York: Graphic Society, 1980.

————. *Post-Impressionism.* New York: Museum of Modern Art, 1977. Fundamental survey.

Reynolds, Sir Joshua. *Discourses on Art.* Ed. by Robert Wark. San Marino, CA: Huntington Library, 1959. Founder of the British Academy discusses his philosophy of art in 15 addresses delivered between November 2, 1769, and December 10, 1790.

CHAPTER 15:
TRADITION AND INNOVATION: 1900–1935

Arnason, H. H. *History of Modern Art.* Englewood Cliffs, NJ: Prentice-Hall, 1986. Comprehensive survey to the present.

Barr, Alfred, Jr. *Fantastic Art.* New York: Museum of Modern Art, 1970. Museum of Modern Art curator covers the art of dreams and the irrational world.

Bayer, Herbert, Walter Gropius and I. Gropius. *Bauhaus, 1919–1928.* New York: Avert Company, 1972. Written by founders of the Bauhaus; based on the Museum of Modern Art exhibition in 1938.

Canaday, John. *Mainstreams of Modern Art,* 2nd ed. New York: Holt, Rinehart and Winston, 1981. The *New York Times* art critic presents a fascinating account of art from the late 18th century through the early 19th century.

Hamilton, George H. *Painting and Sculpture in Europe, 1880–1940.* Baltimore: Penguin, 1981. Covers Western modern art to World War II.

Inverarity, Robert B. *Art of the Northwest Coast Indians,* 2nd ed. Berkeley and Los Angeles: University of California Press, 1967. Thorough treatment of the subject.

Kandinsky, Wassily. *Concerning the Spiritual in Art.* New York: Dover, 1977. Pioneer abstractionist explores his philosophy.

Motherwell, Robert. *The Dada Painters and Poets.* New York: Wittenborn, 1951. Insights into the non-art movement and philosophy; essays and poetry.

Raymond, Marcel. *From Baudelaire to Surrealism.* London: Methuen, 1970. Commentary on the literature of the period.

Rickey, George. *Constructivism: Origins and Evolution.* New York: Braziller, 1967. Innovator in kinetic art traces the development of the style.

Rubin, William. *Dada, Surrealism and Their Heritage.* New York: Museum of Modern Art, 1968.

Selz, Peter. *German Expressionist Painting.* Berkeley and Los Angeles: University of California Press, 1959.

————, and M. Constantine. *Art Nouveau and Design at the Turn of the Century.* New York: Museum of Modern Art, 1987. Surveys of the movements.

CHAPTER 16:
AMERICA ASCENDING: 1900–1945

Alloway, Lawrence. *Roy Lichtenstein.* New York: Abbeville, 1983.

Arnason, H. H. *American Abstract Expressionists and Imagists.* New York: Solomon Guggenheim Museum. 1961.

Brown, Milton. *American Painting from the Armory Show to the Depression.* Princeton, NJ: Princeton University Press, 1970. Survey of realistic art.

Fine, Elsa Honig. *The Afro-American Artist: A Search for Identity.* New York: Hacker, 1982.

Geldzahler, Henry. *American Painting in the Twentieth Century.* New York: Museum of Modern Art, 1965. Interesting survey of American painting.

Greenberg, Clement. *Post-Painterly Abstractions.* Los Angeles: Los Angeles County Museum, 1964.

Hobbs, Robert C., and Gail Levin. *Abstract Expressionism: The Formative Years.* Ithaca, NY: Cornell University Press, 1981.

Janis, Sidney. *Abstract and Surrealist Art in America.* New York: Arno Press, 1944. Traces the abstract movement in the United States. Reprint Ayer & Co.

———. *They Taught Themselves.* Reprint. New York. Discusses black self-taught artists. Well illustrated.

Locke, Alain. *The New Negro.* New York: Arno Press, 1968. Anthology of the period with illustrations by Aaron Douglas.

Rose, Barbara. *American Art Since 1900.* New York: Praeger, 1967.

Sandler, Irving. *The Triumph of American Painting.* New York: Harper & Row, 1976. Good accounts of individual movements.

CHAPTER 17:
THE MID-CENTURY WORLD: 1945–1970

Gardner, Helen. *Art Through the Ages,* 6th ed. New York: Harcourt, 1986. This text remains a favorite for students of art appreciation and art history.

Greer, Germaine. *The Obstacle Race.* New York: Farrar Straus Giroux, 1979. Subjective survey of women painters and their work.

Janson, Horst W. *History of Art,* 3rd ed. New York: Abrams, 1986. The definitive text for art history students and an excellent foundation for the beginning student in art.

Knobler, Nathan. *The Visual Dialogue,* 3rd ed. New York: Holt, Rinehart and Winston, 1980.

Kozloff, Max. *Renderings: Critical Essays on a Century of Modern Art.* New York: Simon & Schuster, Clarion, 1969. Inclusive essays on art and artists.

Munro, Eleanor. *Women Artists, Originals.* New York; Petersen and Wilson, 1976. Succinct summary of the achievements of women in art.

Scully, Vincent. *Modern Architecture,* rev. ed. New York: Braziller, 1974.

Withers, J. *Julio Gonzalez: Sculpture in Iron.* New York: New York University Press, 1978.

CHAPTER 18:
OUR OWN TIME: THE 1970s AND BEYOND

Ades, Dawn. *Photo-Montage.* New York: Thames & Hudson, 1986.

Arnason, H. H. *History of Modern Art, Painting, Sculpture, Architecture,* 3rd ed. New York: Abrams, 1986. All-inclusive text on the subject.

Beardsley, John. *Earthworks and Beyond: Contemporary Art in the Landscape.* New York. 1984.

Branzi, André. *The Hot House: Italian New Wave Design.* Cambridge, MA: M.I.T. Press, 1984.

Cole, Doris. *From Tipi to Skyscraper: A History of Women in Architecture.* Cambridge, MA: M.I.T. Press, 1978.

Ellis, Jack C. *A History of Film.* Englewood Cliffs, NJ: Prentice-Hall, 1985. Early film discoveries, good treatment of regional European and Hollywood productions, third-world cinema, re-emergence of American films.

Greenberg, Clement. *Art and Culture: Critical Essays.* Boston: Beacon, 1961. Fascinating philosophy of a leading contemporary art critic.

Jencks, Charles. *Modern Movements in Architecture.* New York: Penguin, 1987. Compact analyses.

Langer, Susanne K. *Problems of Art.* New York: Scribners, 1977. Fine subjective work.

Lippard, Lucy R., ed. *Six Years: The Dematerialization of the Art Object from 1966–1972.* New York: 1975.

Lucie-Smith, Edward. *Art in the Seventies.* Ithaca, NY: Phaidon, Cornell University Press, 1980. Nonchronological analysis of modern movements.

Lynton, Norbert. *The Story of Modern Art.* New York: Dover, 1980.

Read, Herbert. *Art and Alienation.* New York: Viking, 1969. The role of the artist in society.

Rose, Bernice. *Drawing Now.* New York: Museum of Modern Art, 1976. Illuminating unexpected works.

Rosenberg, Harold. *Art on the Edge: Creators and Situations.* Chicago: University of Chicago Press, 1983. Critical essays by authority on mid-20th-century art.

Rubin, William. *Primitivism in Twentieth Century Art.* New York: Museum of Modern Art, 1984.

Russell, John. *The Meanings of Modern Art.* New York: Harper & Row, 1981. Engaging account explaining modern art.

Smagula, H. *Currents: Contemporary Directions in the Visual Arts.* Englewood Cliffs, NJ: Prentice-Hall, 1983.

Wallis, B., ed. *Art After Modernism: Rethinking Representation.* New York. 1984.

Wilson, Stephen. *Using Computers to Create Art.* Englewood Cliffs, NJ: Prentice-Hall, 1986. Clear text that blends science with aesthetic considerations.

Index

PHOTOGRAPHIC CREDITS

The author and publishers wish to thank the custodians of
the works of art for supplying photographs and granting
permission to use them. Photographers and sources for photographs other than those listed in captions are given below:

A/AR: Alinari/Art Resource, New York
AR: Art Resource, New York
BPK: Bildarchiv Preussicher Kulturbesitz, West Berlin
GC: Geoffrey Clements, Staten Island, New York
G/AR: Giraudon/Art Resource, New York
H: Hirmer Photoarchiv, Munich
LCG: Leo Castelli Gallery, New York
MAS: MAS, Barcelona
PR: Photo Researchers, New York
RMN: © Cliche Musees Nationaux/Service de
Documentation Photographique de la Réunion des
Musees Nationaux, Paris
S/AR: Scale/Art Resource, New York
SPR: Stella Pandell Russell

References are to figure numbers.

Chapter 1 1: S/AR. **2:** AR. **4:** Courtesy Mayfield Pub.
Co. **5, 6:** SPR. **7:** © Seymour Rosen, Los Angeles. **8:**
Tseng Kwong Chi, New York. **9:** Courtesy Ukrainian Gift
Shop, Minneapolis. **11:** © Gianfranco Gorgone/Woodfin
Camp & Associates. **13:** Courtesy Images Gallery, Toledo,
Ohio/PSR-Corita Billboard Project, San Luis Obispo,
Calif. **15:** Photo Georg Mayer, Vienna/Courtesy Galerie
Welz, Salzburg. **16:** RMN. **20:** S/AR. **21:** A/AR. **23:**
A/AR. **24:** Georg Jensen Silversmiths—Denmark, New
York. **26:** Courtesy Department of Library Services,
American Museum of Natural History. **27:** SPR. **31:** RMN

Chapter 2 34, 35: All Rights Reserved. © Prado
Museum, Madrid. **40:** Fritz Henle/PR. **44, 45:** Photo,
Philadelphia Museum of Art. **50:** A. Russo. **52:** © 1980
Kolomputer Design. **53:** MAS. **55:** Egyptian Tourist
Authority, New York. **60:** Loomis Dean, LIFE Magazine,
© Time, Inc. **65:** Museum of Modern Art, New York. **76:**
A/AR. **80:** S/AR. **81:** A/AR. **82, 83:** Rockefeller Center,